Corporate Social Responsibility in the 21st Century

Debates, Models and Practices Across Government, Law and Business

Bryan Horrigan

BA, LLB (Qld), DPhil (Oxon)
Louis Waller Chair of Law and Associate Dean (Research),
Faculty of Law, Monash University, Australia

Edward Elgar
Cheltenham, UK • Northampton, MA, USA

Published by
Edward Elgar Publishing Limited
The Lypiatts
15 Lansdown Road
Cheltenham
Glos GL50 2JA
UK

Edward Elgar Publishing, Inc.
William Pratt House
9 Dewey Court
Northampton
Massachusetts 01060
USA

A catalogue record for this book
is available from the British Library

Library of Congress Control Number: 2009933361

Mixed Sources
Product group from well-managed
forests and other controlled sources
www.fsc.org Cert no. SA-COC-1565
© 1996 Forest Stewardship Council
FSC

ISBN 978 1 84542 956 0 (cased)
        978 1 84720 835 4 (paperback)

Printed and bound by MPG Books Group, UK

Contents

Foreword*

During my career of 37 years in government service followed by 10 years as a non-executive director of two international companies, I have seen the separate strands of corporate social responsibility grow and weave themselves into the wide-ranging concept which we have today. My time in government saw the ever-growing emphasis on individual rights, reflected not only in the human rights movement but in the attention given to equal opportunity for people of different genders, social classes and ethnic origins; to protection of consumers and stakeholders; to provision for the handicapped and disabled; and to care for the environment.

It is, however, only recently that these behavioural norms, as they affect corporate behaviour, have welded together in the concept of corporate social responsibility. If a businessperson had been asked only 20 years ago what was his or her concept of corporate social responsibility, the answer would probably have been no more than the obligation to act ethically, to obey the law and to devote some of the company's surplus wealth to charitable causes. Now these obligations and much more have come together in the concept of corporate social responsibility.

Why has this happened? One reason is no doubt the growth of mega-corporations and their importance in citizens' lives. Another is the increasing internationalisation of these corporations so that it is beyond the power of any single country to control them (except, to some extent, the United States through the power of its extra-territorial legislation on companies which have activities within its borders). A third is the media and the world-wide effect which they can have on corporate reputation, and hence on the success of the company.

It was only six years ago, in 2003, that the Board of one of the world-wide companies on which I served set up a bespoke Corporate Social Responsibility Committee for the first time, and I was asked to chair it. In the ensuing years I felt at times like the famous classical statue of Laocoön in the coils of the sea serpents. It became clear that the responsibility of the Committee to the Board covered not just the charitable activities of the company but the way it treated all classes and conditions of its customers; all classes and conditions of its employees; all the governments and social conditions of the countries in which it operated; and all its impact on its environment wherever it was located in the world. Not only this, but it had also to be concerned about the operations of other companies with which it did business, whether as customers or suppliers, so as to ensure that it was not sustaining others who were acting as bad world citizens in one way or another.

---

* Written by The Right Honourable Lord Butler of Brockwell KG, GCB, CVO, who was Secretary of the United Kingdom Cabinet and Head of the Home Civil Service from 1988 to 1998. From 1998 to 2008 he was Master of University College Oxford and a Non-Executive Director of ICI plc and of HSBC Holdings, where he was also Chairman of the Board's Corporate Social Responsibility Committee. In 2004 he chaired the United Kingdom's Review of Intelligence on Weapons of Mass Destruction following the war in Iraq.

Fortunately, the company for which I had to take on these responsibilities was one which already had deeply-ingrained traditions of good corporate behaviour. From its origins, it had believed that ethical and considerate behaviour was important, not only because it was in the long-term interests of the company but because it was right. For that reason it had always shown punctilious regard for the traditions of the countries in which it operated. It had tried to treat its employees with fairness and consideration; and there were potentially profitable opportunities for business which it had eschewed on ethical grounds.

Fortunately, also, it took the view that this type of good neighbourly behaviour was in the interests of its shareholders and there was never any indication that shareholders took a different view. It is true that there were some instances where the company robustly took a different view from pressure groups which sought to force it to give up certain types of legal business on the basis of their own ethical or political views; but, when these pressures were resisted, it was always on the ground that the company's position was not only commercially but also ethically justifiable.

Moreover, the position which the company took was not only a defensive one. It felt that it had a moral obligation to reach out to help in addressing some of the social and environmental problems in the countries in which it operated. As regards the interest of shareholders, it took the view that the cost in terms of shareholders' assets was offset by the benefit from sustenance of corporate reputation. So good behaviour and self-interest came together in a happy, mutually-reinforcing combination. But, in case shareholders took a different view, the company took care to be entirely transparent through an annual report to shareholders.

The concept continues to change and develop. Even during the time in which I served as Chairman of this company's Board Committee, this was reflected in two changes in name, first to Corporate Responsibility (reflecting the thought that the company's responsibilities went wider than what the word 'social' embraced) and then to Sustainability Committee (reflecting the thought that this area of the company's activities was necessary to sustain not only the company itself but also the environment in which it operated). But I suspect that the term 'Corporate Social Responsibility' (CSR) has become sufficiently embedded in public consciousness and it will be difficult to eradicate.

While companies have been showing increasing awareness of these obligations, and giving increasing attention to them, governments, NGOs and international organizations have also become increasingly involved. As some companies have notoriously defaulted on these obligations, citizens and the media have put pressure on governments to impose them. The result has been a huge increase in corporate legislation and regulation. Anyone who wants evidence of this needs only to compare the size and weight of companies' annual reports today with what they were only a decade or so ago. Yet as in all forms of human misbehaviour there are still loopholes as miscreants find it increasingly easy in today's world to move between one jurisdiction and another. Hence derives the need for governments and international organizations to achieve greater cooperation and coordination in dealing with these issues.

Like the man who suddenly discovered he had been talking prose all his life, companies have always been under the obligations of social responsibility as well as (or, some might say, as part of) their obligations to their shareholders. Yet, as I said at the beginning of this Foreword, the various strands have been brought together in a comprehensive concept only recently. In this book Professor Horrigan brings together the many facets of, and perspectives on, the concept, whether on the part of governments, lawmakers and regulators, international organizations or companies and their stakeholders; and he places them in the context of the development of thought in the crossover from the 20th to the 21st century. There are still many unresolved controversies in relation to the subject, which the book describes. I doubt whether such an ambitious and comprehensive account of the concept has been previously attempted. There is no doubt that it is a hugely important subject in today's world; and one which will not go away. I believe that the book will be valuable to all who need to deal with this issue, whether as government officials, regulators, businessmen, lawyers, academics, media commentators or concerned citizens. I wish it success.

Preface

CORPORATE SOCIAL RESPONSIBILITY IN THE 21ST CENTURY

Corporate social responsibility (CSR) is one of the greatest global challenges of the 21st century. Our ancestors have bequeathed to us ways of conceiving, running and regulating corporations the core elements of which are tested more in 21st century conditions than ever before. They need revisiting and even recasting for the sake of our generation, our descendants, and the planet's future. CSR is the lynchpin of that 21st century enterprise.

CSR can be studied, regulated and practised from many different angles. This book focuses upon governmental, legal and business frameworks for CSR, to accommodate corporate responsiveness to systems of governance, regulation and responsibility in the 21st century business environment. In doing so, it considers CSR from the standpoint of multiple CSR actors across public, private and community sectors, in a select range of jurisdictions across the globe. As a cross-disciplinary work anchored firmly in legal, policy and regulatory perspectives, this book contributes to building bridges, enhancing dialogue and suggesting action on CSR across major disciplinary, jurisdictional and sectoral boundaries.

The early 21st century has already witnessed an explosion of CSR standard-setting initiatives on international, regional and national fronts, embracing the G8 and G20, OECD, UN, EU, UK, and a range of other countries engaged in reforming (or at least reviewing) the CSR-sensitivity of their corporate regulatory regimes and business practices. Even one of the bastions of the traditional Anglo-American model of corporate responsibility and governance (i.e. the UK) has reorientated its system of corporate law for the 21st century around the policy of 'enlightened shareholder value'. This reform formally makes the law of directors' duties and corporate reporting ostensibly more stakeholder-inclusive, but still firmly roots it within a largely shareholder-centred model.

A similar expansion is under way in the CSR literature on multiple disciplinary fronts worldwide. CSR scholarship in the 21st century engages new debates and themes, while also making the transition from 20th century and sometimes even residual 18th and 19th century thinking and practices surrounding corporations. The true multi-disciplinary character of CSR, the reality that great societal and global problems are addressed by CSR, and new insights into CSR's deep complexity are all increasingly reflected in scholarly works devoted to the wide range of academic and work-related standpoints from which CSR must be assessed in its analysis and practice worldwide. Prestigious publishing houses are producing major works that try to do justice to CSR's multi-dimensional and cross-disciplinary complexity,[1] with some devoting even an entire series of books to CSR in its own right,[2] as an object of law and regulation,[3] or as part of a broader thematic study of corporate responsibility, governance and sustainability.

In 2002, fortieth anniversary editions appeared of the late Milton Friedman's classic polemic against the social responsibility of business, *Capitalism and Freedom*. Professor Joel Bakan's famous critique of corporations and its accompanying documentary of the same name, *The Corporation*, has raised 21st century public consciousness of corporate social irresponsibility to new levels. Along with other critiques of corporate capitalism in the post-Enron era,[4] which subject the whole system of regulating corporate responsibility and governance to fresh scrutiny, this body of work represents a new front in challenging corporate orthodoxy across a number of major national economies. By 2008, even *The Economist* finally conceded the battle to CSR in the marketplace of ideas.[5] At the same time, CSR is under fresh attack in the USA for clouding the dividing lines between political and business responsibilities, and producing an impoverished democracy in thrall to the false hope of socially responsible business, with former Clinton Administration member, Professor Robert Reich, leading the charge towards CSR scepticism with his account of 'supercapitalism'.[6] We need new rules of engagement for studying, regulating and practising CSR in the 21st century.

THIS BOOK'S MAIN AUDIENCES

This book is written with multiple audiences in mind, spread across different disciplines, countries and occupations. In particular, it focuses upon CSR lessons and prospects internationally and in the EU, UK, North America and Anglo-Commonwealth countries. Its *academic audience* comprises scholars and students from different disciplines and countries who study the theory and practice of corporate responsibility, governance and regulation in a variety of academic fields. In particular, this includes academics and students from law, business and management, as well as from other parts of the humanities and social sciences, who research and study corporations in political, legal and social theory (Chapters 1–3 and 10), social and global governance (Chapters 1–5, 9 and 10), corporate law and regulation (Chapters 3–7 and 10), corporate governance (Chapters 1–3, 5–8 and 10), and corporations in society (most chapters). It also includes scholars and students from different disciplines and geographical regions who research and study corporations horizontally from international and comparative perspectives (most chapters), or else vertically in drilling down into particular topics concerning corporations, such as corporations and human rights (Chapter 9), governmental roles and approaches towards CSR (Chapters 4–7 and 9–10), corporate risk management and reporting (most chapters), and business frameworks and models for implementing CSR (Chapters 8 and 9).

This book's *governmental and regulatory audiences* include those national, intergovernmental and international institutions and actors whose areas of work relate to CSR in lawmaking, law reform, policymaking and official regulation (Chapters 4–7 and 9–10), and increasingly in multi-stakeholder networks and standard-setting initiatives centred around CSR concerns (Chapters 1–2 and 8–9). In particular, it maps and explores governmental frameworks and models for legal and regulatory CSR reform (Chapters 4–7 and 10), as well as public sector engagement with CSR (Chapters 4 and 9–10). It also analyses and critiques the CSR-related aspects of the UK's 21st century experiment with 'enlightened shareholder value' in its new corporate law (Chapter 7), especially in terms of the strengths and weaknesses of this new corporate legislative model, its likely issues for future professional advice and 'test case' litigation, and its comparative lessons for

CSR-related legal and policy reform in other European, Anglo-American and Anglo-Commonwealth countries.

The *business and professional audiences* for this book include anyone interested in CSR who leads or manages corporations, works or invests in corporations, advises or partners corporations, or otherwise deals with corporations in the marketplace and the wider community. These audiences include company insiders such as company directors and managers, company secretaries, corporate counsel, corporate employees and corporate shareholders. Importantly, they also include company outsiders such as corporate consumers, corporate advisers (from legal, accounting and other professional services firms), banks and financial institutions, corporate and investment advisory bodies, investment managers and advisers, corporate and institutional representative bodies (e.g. shareholder representative bodies), share traders and analysts, independent corporate watchdogs and ratings bodies, and national and global members of corporate supply and distribution chains. All of these business and professional audiences share work-related interests in various CSR topics covered in this book, including new developments in thought leadership about CSR (Chapters 1–3 and 8–10), international and comparative trends in corporate regulation and practice affecting CSR (most chapters), business frameworks and steps for implementing CSR (Chapters 7–9), the regulation and reform of corporate governance in response to CSR (most chapters), and CSR-related laws and regulation in major commercial jurisdictions where vast numbers of transnational corporations (TNCs), transnational corporate groups, and members of their supply and distribution chains conduct business (Chapters 1–2, 5–7, and 9–10).

The other *global, community and civil society audiences* for this book engage with CSR as NGOs working with responsible companies and against irresponsible ones, members of communities affected directly by corporations as home or host sites of business operations, and citizens of particular countries and the world concerned about the use and abuse of corporate power. Given the multiple layers and orders of corporate regulation in the 21st century which involve non-governmental actors as well as governmental officials, this book's audiences therefore embrace a broader range of corporate regulators across the public, private and community sectors than simply the officially designated corporate and financial regulators in particular corporate regulatory systems. All of these audiences share interests in understanding, developing and assessing arguments about the pros and cons of CSR (Chapters 1–3), showing how and why corporations relate to wider issues of democratic theory and governance (Chapters 1–4 and 9–10), exploring rationales and mechanisms for opening up corporate governance regulation and organizational arrangements to stakeholder influences (Chapters 2–3, 5–8 and 10), and looking ahead to improvements in business–society relations in important areas such as business concern for human rights (Chapter 9).

THIS BOOK'S MAIN AIMS

No book on CSR can ever be all things to all people. Nor is everything worthwhile discussing about CSR reducible to a do-it-yourself CSR manual or checklist. Some books do a worthy job of highlighting and illustrating steps by which corporations can become more socially and environmentally responsible. However, they often take the case in favour of CSR for granted, and hence do little to convince those who oppose it or alternatively have to deal with its desirability, workability, and other implications as corporate law-makers, policy-makers and regulators, for example. At the other extreme, many books wrestle valiantly with CSR's theoretical debates and conceptual conundrums. However, they often do so from a perspective grounded solely or mainly in one discipline or alternatively one country or region, and often without sufficient integration of CSR theory, regulation and practice.

Accordingly, this book's *first aim* is to illuminate and illustrate the insights to be gained from examining CSR from more than one disciplinary standpoint (e.g. law, business and management), level of analysis (e.g. regulatory theory, standards and practice), occupational role (e.g. lawmakers, corporate regulators and company directors), and jurisdictional perspective (e.g. European and Anglo-American standpoints), as an exercise in the scholarship of integration, synthesis and application. As a *second aim*, this book offers a scholarly defence of an aspirational account of CSR. In doing so, it positions CSR within mainstream corporate responsibility and governance, but also takes a forward-looking approach to CSR's emerging manifestations in the 21st century and what affects their development and application into the future. Chiefly, it calls attention to the necessary transformation from unduly compliance-orientated, duty-focused and otherwise legalistic accounts of CSR's relation to corporate responsibility and governance, to a richer account of corporations as both subjects and objects of governance, regulation and responsibility at organizational, societal and global levels. This transformation focuses upon corporate responsiveness to what are described here as 'trans-modal governance', 'multi-order regulation' and 'inter-related responsibility' (Chapter 2).

A *third aim* of this book is to show how and why CSR necessarily engages a variety of actors across the public, private and community sectors, both nationally and internationally. This means grappling with the ideas and concepts of CSR with which academics, corporate executives, public officials and concerned citizens also grapple, in pursuit of CSR's connections to wider aspects of democratic and corporate governance, regulation and responsibility in the era of the TNC and the 'disaggregated state'.[7] CSR is something which requires effective descriptive and normative study (and hence is a concern for political, business and community thought leaders), governmental involvement (and hence is a concern for public policy-makers), legal and regulatory frameworks (and hence is a concern for national legislators, law reformers, courts and corporate regulators, as well as multilateral institutions and actors), and market and industry input (and hence is a concern for individual and institutional shareholders, corporate and investor representative bodies, investment analysts and decision-makers, industry and stakeholder bodies, public advocacy groups and NGOs, and lobbyists). CSR is also a vital matter of concern for effective corporate decision-making and action (and hence is a concern for company directors, managers and other corporate actors), professional advice and guidance (and hence is a concern for corporate counsel, other in-house corporate advisers and external professional advisers), and standard-setting and monitoring (and hence is a concern for industry and independent standard-setters, media organizations, ratings agencies and other corporate monitors).

A *fourth aim* is to make a contribution to moving towards a common framework for debating, regulating and practising CSR nationally and internationally. This goes beyond simply cataloguing common CSR meanings, forms and standards. It also includes but extends beyond mapping various features of the CSR landscape. It includes a legitimizing account of CSR from a variety of standpoints, as well as the articulation of frameworks capturing CSR's key manifestations, especially in its vital links to the social order, the business of government and corporate practice. It also provides arguments and options for modelling CSR in lawmaking, regulatory practice and business activity from one jurisdiction to another.

A *fifth and final aim* is to illuminate ways in which corporate law, corporate governance and resultant business practice can move ahead in their engagement with CSR in the 21st century. Internationally, we are yet to develop a comprehensive international law of CSR, although a nascent but patchy body of comparative CSR law and regulation is emerging across various countries and regions. All jurisdictions remain trapped to one degree or another in old ways of thinking, which locate CSR along linear spectra that are framed around distinctions such as those between shareholder and non-shareholder interests, corporate and other areas of law, public and private interests, mandatory and voluntary obligations, and national and global concerns. Accordingly, CSR still has a long way yet to go in 21st century corporate law, regulation and practice.

INTERNATIONAL, REGIONAL, AND NATIONAL JURISDICTIONS COVERED IN THIS BOOK

In terms of jurisdictional coverage, this book concentrates mainly upon international perspectives and a select range of comparative positions too, especially European, North American and Anglo-Commonwealth (particularly UK and Australian) corporate regulatory systems. Why focus upon these ones? The success of CSR in the 21st century probably stands or falls on the development of effective international architecture for corporate responsibility, governance and sustainability (Chapters 5 and 10). While the EU has aspirations of making Europe a global CSR leader (Chapters 1, 5, 6 and 10), strong national differences still remain to be overcome, especially in approaches to corporate regulation, governance and practice.

As a corporate regulatory system within the EU, the UK lies increasingly exposed to the influence of EU law generally (as in the modern responsiveness of UK law to European human rights jurisprudence) and EU corporate law and regulation in particular (as in various EU directives and other standard-setting initiatives affecting EU business enterprises). The arguably dominant shareholder primacy model is strongly associated with Anglo-American corporate law and governance, which also links the UK and North America, whatever cracks might otherwise be appearing in that monolithic characterization. In addition, the historical influence of UK corporate law upon the wider British Commonwealth means that this approach to corporate law and governance greatly informs the approach to corporate regulation in other Commonwealth countries, including Australia and New Zealand. At the very least, especially in light of the UK's important model of 21st century CSR-related corporate law reform in its landmark new Companies Act (Chapter 7), UK corporate law and governance is a common anchoring point in this group of jurisdictions.

Australia has special historical, regulatory and economic claims to join this select list of countries and regions for CSR study, beyond being the jurisdiction of most familiarity to the author as his home jurisdiction. Australia has undertaken major national CSR regulatory inquiries already in the 21st century (Chapter 4). Its system of corporate law and regulation offers important comparisons and contrasts with CSR-related developments in UK corporate law and regulation in the 21st century. As a member of the G20 and one of the largest economies in the Asia-Pacific region, Australia also has one of the world's largest markets for managed investment funds, which enhances its value as a CSR laboratory for responsible and sustainable investment.[8] Along with the EU, North America and other Anglo-Commonwealth countries, Australia forms part of a broader network of countries which are engaged in developing a distinctive comparative body of CSR-related law and regulation (Chapter 5).

A BRIEF WORD ON TERMINOLOGY AND OTHER FEATURES FOR READERS

This book often refers collectively to corporate responsibility, governance and regulation to emphasize the importance of these three different aspects for socio-ethically responsible corporate behaviour. References to only one or two of these aspects in other parts of the book simply highlight whichever of them seem most prominent in the context under discussion. Clearly, however, a strong underlying connection is usually present between all three aspects of corporate responsibility, corporate governance and corporate regulation. Occasionally, contrasts are drawn between conventional corporate responsibility and governance and emerging developments in corporate responsibility and sustainability.

This book also tries as much as possible to bring together in one analysis for readers the great debates (Chapter 3), model laws (Chapter 5–7) and influential standards of CSR in the terms in which their authors or drafters put them, in a balance of exposition, synthesis and analysis for the purposes of understanding, modelling and critique, given the different needs of the different CSR audiences for this book. Policy-makers, legislative drafters and law reformers looking to investigate and perhaps adopt policies and laws in their own jurisdiction in a way which is informed by what happens elsewhere hopefully can benefit from this approach of positioning important landmarks in CSR thinking and practice alongside critiques and applications of them. Company directors and other corporate actors also need an understanding of the primary laws and other forms of regulation which govern them, especially in light of the rapid evolution of CSR ideas, regulation and practices even in the short period since the start of the 21st century. However, as this is a book about CSR for those who study or practise it from different disciplinary standpoints and work perspectives, and not simply a book about comparative corporate law, references to specific laws and cases from different jurisdictions are mainly for illustrative and contextual purposes.

Suitable CSR case studies of sufficient longevity and transposability across national, sectoral and organizational boundaries remain elusive, especially in light of the quickly evolving CSR environment. None of this means that such case studies are impossible or irrelevant. They make CSR come alive and serve useful modelling purposes. Yet, case studies operate at many different levels, beyond simply examples of individual corporations in particular industries or regions which do CSR well. Given the range of CSR actors and their occupational viewpoints, CSR case studies can also embrace policy, regulatory and business frameworks too. Examples and case studies at these different levels are woven throughout this book. Given the expanding multiplicity of frameworks, models and other standard-setting tools now on offer for CSR actors, primary emphasis is given here to some overarching frameworks for CSR as a whole from governmental, regulatory and organizational perspectives, with ancillary reference to frameworks and examples covering discrete strands of CSR, such as CSR-sensitive corporate decision-making, risk management and reporting.

ACKNOWLEDGEMENTS

This book is part of a grander research programme exploring contemporary public and corporate governance from a range of disciplinary, jurisdictional and analytical perspectives. It is informed by the work on other publicly funded research projects supported by the Australian Research Council, on projects relating to democratic and judicial governance within international systems of state and non-state governance and regulation (ARC Discovery Project, 'The High Court of Australia's International Impact and Engagement – Enhancing Judicial Accountability and Australia's Place in International Law' (DP0666665), 2006–2010) as well as comparative public and corporate governance (ARC Linkage Project, 'Corporate Governance in the Public Sector: An Evaluation of its Tensions, Gaps, and Potential' (LP0348470), 2003–2007). I am fortunate to have been supported in this work by the ARC and, through the ARC, the Australian Government and Australian taxpayers.

Various people at Edward Elgar Publishing associated with the commissioning and editing of this book have been incredibly supportive of the project and tolerant in accepting how long it has taken to incorporate everything in it, especially late-breaking developments in a field as dynamic and fluid as CSR. In particular, I gratefully acknowledge the encouragement, enthusiasm and guidance of Catherine Elgar, Laura Elgar, Edward Elgar, Alexandra O'Connell, Nep Elverd, Kate Pearce, Emma Gribbon and Laura Seward.

The early stages of work on this book commenced during my research sabbatical at the Wharton Business School in Philadelphia, attached to the Zicklin Centre for Business Ethics as a Visiting Scholar in the Legal Studies and Business Ethics Department. I benefited greatly from discussions there with my academic colleagues, Centre members, and accompanying PhD students, especially Professor Bill Laufer, Professor Eric Orts, Associate Professor Nien-He Hsieh, and the late Professor Tom Dunfee. In addition, I have benefited from my work and discussions on corporate responsibility and governance with my colleagues in Allens Arthur Robinson's practice groups devoted to these areas of legal practice. This includes the opportunity to work in the team providing advice on business human rights due diligence for Harvard University's Professor John Ruggie, in pursuit of his mandate as the UN Secretary-General's Special Representative on Business and Human Rights (UNSRSG).

Finally, my heartfelt thanks also go to the research assistants who assisted me variously at different stages of this project and during their own busy student careers with research, citations, editing, referencing and indexing (i.e. Stuart Dullard, Kate McLoughlin, Tom O'Brien, Rowan Platt, Ryan Harvey, Toby Collis, Michael Adams, Nadia Giovannucci,

Natalia Antolak-Saper and Michael Beaconsfield), and to the administrative assistants who helped with the manuscript (i.e. Liz Sanelli, Wendy Calvert, Annette Hondros, Bridget Sadler, Tamana Daqiq and Sadiq Ansari) and accompanying figures (i.e. Liz Sanelli and Annette Hondros). Of course, all responsibility for what appears here remains mine.

NOTES

1. E.g. Tully, 2005; Banerjee, 2007; and May et al, 2007.
2. E.g. Edward Elgar Publishing's recent thematic collection of CSR books (including Tully, 2005; Banerjee, 2007; Boeger et al, 2008; and this book), Oxford University Press' recent CSR books (including May et al, 2007; and Crane et al, 2008), and Ashgate's Corporate Social Responsibility Series (including Crowther and Rayman-Bacchus, 2004; Cooper, 2004; Daianu and Vranceanu, 2005; Cradden, 2005; and den Hond et al, 2007).
3. E.g. McBarnet et al, 2008; and Kerr et al, 2009.
4. E.g. Mitchell, 2001; and Greenfield, 2006.
5. *The Economist*, 2008.
6. E.g. Reich, 2007.
7. Slaughter, 2005.
8. On these Australian statistics see the Australian Government's September 2007 financial markets update from the Department of Innovation, Industry, Science and Research.

Abbreviations

AICD	Australian Institute of Company Directors
ALI	American Law Institute
ASB	Accounting Standards Board (UK)
ASIC	Australian Securities and Investments Commission
ASX	Australian Securities Exchange
ATCA	Alien Tort Claims Act (USA)
BIAC	Business and Industry Advisory Committee to the OECD
BITC	Business in the Community (UK)
BITF	Business Impact Task Force of BITC
BLIHR	Business Leaders Initiative on Human Rights
BPM	business performance management
CAMAC	Corporations and Markets Advisory Committee (Australia)
CCI	corporate community investment
CDP	Carbon Disclosure Project
CEO	chief executive officer
CFO	chief financial officer
CHaSPI	Corporate Health and Safety Performance Index (UK)
CICs	community interest companies
CIGs	corporate interest groups
CLR	Company Law Review (UK)
CPWGRB	Conservative Party Working Group on Responsible Business (UK)
CR/CORE	corporate responsibility/Corporate Responsibility
CSR	corporate social responsibility
DTI	Department of Trade and Industry (UK)
EISs	environmental impact statements
EITI	Extractive Industries Transparency Initiative
ESG	environmental, social and governance
ESV	enlightened shareholder value
EU	European Union
FDI	foreign direct investment
FG500	*Fortune* Global 500
FSB	Financial Stability Board
FSF	Financial Stability Forum
G8	Group of Eight
G20	Group of 20
G100	Group of 100 (Australia)
GFC	global financial crisis
GRI	Global Reporting Initiative
HRIAs	human rights impact assessments

HSBC	The Hongkong and Shanghai Banking Corporation Limited
ICC	International Chamber of Commerce
ICCPR	International Covenant on Civil and Political Rights
IFC	International Finance Corporation
ILO	International Labour Organization
IMF	International Monetary Fund
IOE	International Organization of Employers
ISCT	integrative social contracts theory
ISO	International Organization for Standardization
KPIs	key performance indicators
MBA	Master of Business Administration
MD&A	Management's Discussion and Analysis of Financial Condition and Results of Operations (USA)
MNC	multinational corporation
NCPs	National Contact Points
NGO	non-government organization
OECD	Organisation for Economic Co-Operation and Development
OFR	Operating and Financial Review (UK)
PJCCFS	Parliamentary Joint Committee on Corporations and Financial Services (Australia)
PR	public relations
PVIs	public voluntary initiatives
R & D	research and development
SME	small-to-medium enterprise
SRI	socially responsible investing or investment
SSCLCA	Senate Standing Committee on Legal and Constitutional Affairs
TBL	triple bottom line
TCS	transnational civil society
TNC	transnational corporation
TRIPS	(Agreement on) Trade-Related Aspects of Intellectual Property Rights
UDHR	Universal Declaration of Human Rights
UK	United Kingdom
UN	United Nations
UNCITRAL	UN Commission on International Trade Law
UN Norms	UN Norms on the Responsibilities of Transnational Corporations and Other Business Enterprises with Regard to Human Rights
UN PRI	United Nations Principles for Responsible Investment
UNSRSG	United Nations Secretary General's Special Representative on Business and Human Rights
VCCs	voluntary codes of conduct
WTO	World Trade Organization

Table of authorities

CASES

LEGISLATION

Australia

Canada

United Kingdom

TREATIES, CONVENTIONS AND OTHER INTERNATIONAL INSTRUMENTS

PART 1

CORPORATE SOCIAL RESPONSIBILITY'S
CONTEMPORARY CONTROVERSIES AND
ARCHITECTURE

1. Corporate social responsibility's contemporary global context

CORPORATE SOCIAL RESPONSIBILITY IN THE 21ST CENTURY

We are All Corporate Social Responsibility Actors Now

> 'Globalisation' is giving rise to a new political struggle, not between states and multinationals or, necessarily, between North and South, but between 'people and corporations'.
>
> – Corporate social responsibility lawyer and consultant, Dr Jennifer Zerk[1]
>
> 'In a globalised market economy, CSR is part of modern business.'
>
> – Wharton Business School's Professor Tom Donaldson[2]

Corporate social responsibility (CSR) is one of the most important issues and developments of the 21st century. This is because the world of the 21st century faces problems for which CSR is part of the answer. So, it is not surprising to see CSR achieving dominance as a global issue, alongside other shared governance and regulatory challenges such as climate change, sustainable development, human rights universalization, poverty eradication and socio-economic prosperity. As developments as ostensibly diverse as climate change, global economic crises, borderless trade and humanitarian disasters starkly demonstrate, we live in a world of interdependent economies, populations and ecosystems, where what corporations do matters to their shareholders, society and the world at large.

The world's response to CSR at these early stages of the 21st century will play a significant part in determining the shape and fate of the world for generations to come. Is CSR a passing social fad, an idea whose time has come, a threat to market capitalism, an intrinsic element of corporate responsibility, or even a key to humanity's long-term survival in properly managing shared global challenges? The story of CSR in the 21st century has many chapters. It is a story of the emergence of a distinctive CSR movement worldwide.[3] More broadly, the 21st century is witnessing the emergence and convergence of different movements in a global corporate responsibility and sustainability movement, drawing upon and reorienting the constituencies and lessons of the anti-corporate and anti-globalization movements, the human rights movement, the women's movement, the socially responsible investing movement, and other movements too, including earlier incarnations of the CSR movement itself, given the change in its manifestations and orientations over time.[4]

CSR actors are engaging with phenomena such as CSR threats posed by 'supercapitalism',[5] the rise of a mass shareholding class of 'citizen investors',[6] the emergence of 'enlightened shareholder value' and other CSR-related imperatives in corporate law and regulation, and the move to 'co-created value' in new cross-sectoral alliances in developing countries.[7] In this way, CSR's 21st century story is also a story of progressive business sensitization to systems of governance beyond government, regulation beyond law, and responsiveness beyond formal responsibility. CSR literacy is quickly becoming a primary imperative for a variety of actors in a multiplicity of roles across governmental, business and community sectors, both nationally and internationally.

Twenty-first century policy and legal innovations on CSR can be found across the world's continents (e.g. in the UK, Denmark, Norway, South Africa, and Australia).[8] Despite the absence of a comprehensive international law of corporate governance and responsibility, or any other accepted global framework for CSR, a significant part of this evolving CSR landscape involves the ongoing sensitization of corporate governance law, regulation and practice to CSR influences. This development spans the European, North American and Anglo-Commonwealth jurisdictions which are the primary focus of this book. At the same time, it is informed by an emerging global CSR project which is progressively unfolding at geopolitical levels (e.g. G8 and G20 commitment to CSR), regional levels (e.g. institutional CSR dialogue between the European Parliament and the European Commission), multilateral institutional levels (e.g. the culmination of the work on business and human rights undertaken by the UN Secretary-General's Special Representative on Business and Human Rights (UNSRSG)), cross-sectoral levels (e.g. multi-stakeholder CSR initiatives across national and industry boundaries), and national levels (e.g. 21st century CSR-related legal and regulatory reform initiatives in the UK and Australia).

None of this is just a matter of concern for corporations that either resist or embrace CSR, and those from academia, the mass media and civil society groups who urge corporations in either direction. It is a vital matter of concern for other CSR actors too. In government, this is a major area of concern for policy advisers, law-makers, official corporate regulators, courts, and all others who confront questions of law and policy concerning CSR in the administration of government and the legal system. In the corporate community, CSR is a major feature of the 21st century business environment. For better or worse, it affects the work of corporate insiders (e.g. corporate shareholders, boards, managers, and employees), corporate advisers (e.g. company secretaries, in-house counsel and external legal and business advisers), corporate outsiders (e.g. corporate customers, clients, creditors and financiers), and all of the communities in which corporations operate (e.g. local business sites, transnational consumer markets and global supply chains). Everyone in the world therefore belongs in one CSR camp or another, whether you support CSR, tolerate it or condemn it.

The Great Corporate Questions

The rise of the modern corporation provokes starkly opposing views of corporations and what they do. In the context of the Great Depression of the early 20th century, one of that century's leading US judges warned of the dangers of 'removing all limitations

> (C)orporate responsibility [is] rising sharply in global executives' priorities . . .
> None of this means that CSR has suddenly become a great idea. This news-
> paper has argued that it is often misguided, or worse. But in practice few big
> companies can now afford to ignore it.
>
> – Daniel Franklin, in the leading article for *The Economist*'s 2008 special
> report on CSR[9]

upon the size and activities of business corporations and of vesting in their managers vast powers once exercised by stockholders', calling corporations 'the Frankenstein monster which states have created by their corporation laws'.[10] 'The corporate goal of stockholder wealth-maximisation not only destroys the corporation [but] also destroys our social fabric', writes George Washington University's Professor Lawrence Mitchell in *Corporate Irresponsibility*.[11] According to *The Report of the Citizen Works Corporate Reform Commission*, 'shareholder primacy is a major design flaw in the corporation and, left unmitigated, means that virtually all large publicly traded corporations present an inherent danger to society because as profit-making machines they know no limits and boundaries: they will continue to grow and expand until they have destroyed everything in their paths'.[12]

Similarly, in his 2004 best-seller, *The Corporation*, Professor Joel Bakan describes the corporation vividly as a 'psychopathic creature' with 'predatory instincts' that 'valorize self-interest', so that it 'can neither recognize nor act upon moral reasons to refrain from harming others'.[13] In an interview for the same book, leading American corporate governance thinker and adviser, Robert Monks, describes the corporation as 'an externalizing machine, in the same way that a shark is a killing machine', and one that is 'potentially very, very damaging to society'.[14] According to one of the great contemporary Anglo-American legal theorists, Professor William Twining, 'is not the perspective of a large bureaucratic corporation whose sole or primary aim is the maximization of profit very close to that of the bad man – amoral, rational, calculating, purposeful, pursuing its own agenda?'.[15]

Yet, as CSR scholar Professor Peter Madsen notes, the standpoint from which 'corporations deserve blame for many social ills and are taken as creators of evil in the world' is an incomplete one, because 'there is much about corporate institutions, especially the large multinational corporations (MNCs) that have become the backbone of our current global web of institutions that is deserving of praise'.[16] In their painstaking historical analysis of corporations, *The Economist*'s John Micklethwait and Adrian Wooldridge not only describe the corporation as 'the most important organization in the world', but also call it 'the basis of the prosperity of the West and the best hope for the future of the rest of the world'.[17] 'The limited liability corporation is one of the greatest inventions of all time', echo law firm partner Andrew Lumsden and corporate law academic Saul Fridman, given that 'the capacity of the limited liability corporation to facilitate large-scale enterprise has contributed greatly (some would say more than any other device) to the rapid improvement in the human condition (at least materially) in the last two centuries'.[18]

How can corporations and their activities generate such widely divergent reactions?

Part of the answer for a 21st century audience lies in the duality of 'corporations being both good and evil, making them appear to be both responsible and irresponsible actors', in Professor Madsen's words.[19] Another part of the answer also lies in the emergence of corporations as transnational actors in global governance and regulation, resulting in 'new expectations regarding the global social responsibility of private enterprise, initiated by the dynamic interplay between civil society organizations and transnational corporations', against the background of traditional dominance by sovereign nation-states in defining the global public interest and setting rules for achieving it.[20] The cry for greater global social responsibility by corporations comes from transnational civil society organizations in particular, which call attention to the gap between corporate rights and corporate obligations in the global legal order, the lack of adequate accountability for corporate irresponsibility worldwide, and the potential reach of corporate capacity-building for the benefit of society and the world.[21]

In the end, the burning questions of corporate responsibility, governance and regulation at the close of the 21st century are likely to be the same timeless questions about corporations that occupied the world at the beginning of this century, just as they have occupied the world since the rise of the modern corporation more than two centuries ago. What is a corporation's role in society? How is a corporation best governed to that end? Accordingly, whose interests does a corporation serve? To whom is a corporation therefore accountable? How is all of this best regulated?

These deep questions lurk below the surface of all 21st century questions of corporate responsibility, governance and sustainability. 'Is the company essentially a private association, subject to the laws of the state but with no greater obligation than making money, or a public one which is supposed to act in the public interest?' ask Micklethwait and Wooldridge in *The Company*.[22] 'How do we design the parameters for a profitable, internationally competitive corporation for the 21st century that remains accountable to its shareholders while acting responsibly towards citizens affected by its actions, in Canada and elsewhere?', asks the Canadian Democracy and Corporate Accountability Commission.[23] These basic questions remain constant, but the 21st century business environment fundamentally affects their surrounding contexts and answers.

Starting Points for Consensus

Before the end of the 21st century's first decade, one of the traditional bastions of opposition to CSR, *The Economist*, begrudgingly conceded defeat to CSR's pervasiveness

> One way of looking at CSR is that it is part of what businesses need to do to keep up with (or, if possible, stay slightly ahead of) society's fast-changing expectations. It is an aspect of taking care of a company's reputation, managing its risks and gaining a competitive edge [by] being 'embedded' in the business, influencing decisions on everything from sourcing to strategy . . . In time it will simply be the way business is done in the 21st century.
>
> – *The Economist*'s 2008 special report on CSR[24]

worldwide. Salvaging its long-standing support for shareholder value as the overriding corporate directive by concluding that, whatever is wrong with CSR, what is right about it amounts to little more than 'just good business', *The Economist* otherwise conceded the unstoppable momentum behind CSR:[25]

> Three years ago a special report in *The Economist* acknowledged, with regret, that the CSR movement had won the battle of ideas. In the survey by the Economist Intelligence Unit for this report, only 4% of respondents thought that CSR was 'a waste of time and money'. Clearly CSR has arrived.

Deep divisions amongst CSR advocates and critics, combined with multiple competing theories and models of corporate responsibility and governance, sometimes distract attention away from the remarkable degree of common ground that exists on most sides of the CSR debate. We begin the 21st century with consensus across academic disciplines, geographical borders and sectoral concerns on at least some basic points. A high level of support exists for the place and worth of socially responsible corporations in society, whatever disagreement might also exist about what it means to be a socially responsible corporation and how far that responsibility extends. There is also widespread recognition that corporations and corporate actors operate within societal contexts that traverse at least legal, economic and moral domains, with significant points of both intersection and demarcation. Put another way, there is a significant consensus that, because of these systemic interdependencies, corporate profit-making is not absolute but rather bounded, although much disagreement remains about the range of limitations on corporate profit-making beyond legal compliance, market forces and business ethics, as well as the ultimate sources and justifications of any limitations.

In countries that embrace some version of capitalism, the profit-making imperative for business is accepted, whatever else is associated with it (e.g. private property rights), whatever the limits of its legitimate pursuit (e.g. irresponsible socio-environmental harm), and whatever different ends it might serve (e.g. individual wealth-creation, functioning market economies and societal welfare). Nobody seriously questions the undoubted capacity of nation-states to regulate corporations within their jurisdictional control, however much disagreement might exist about the need for additional corporate regulation, the amenability of corporations to non-state regulation, and the extent to which any country or even the international community has a justified interest in regulating corporate irresponsibility in other countries. To the extent that corporate responsibility and governance focuses upon shareholder wealth-generation, there is now widespread acceptance that this must be considered from the long-term perspective of the company as a sustainable business enterprise in society over the long run. This dovetails with a growing awareness of the benefits for corporations in strategically aligning their business models, competitive positioning, and marketplace activity with management of their business-society relations and risks.

Finally, there is much consensus about the need for corporations and corporate actors to take account in some way of both shareholder and other stakeholder interests, together with much acceptance of the interdependence of those sets of interests. This is despite widespread confusion about what is actually involved in taking these interests into account in corporate activity, as well as widespread disagreement about how corporate shareholding and other stakeholding interests actually relate to one another. At a deeper level lies an emerging, cross-sectoral and cross-jurisdictional consensus that sustainable corporate success ultimately rests upon a number of sources of business value-creation, creates company-specific risks and benefits for both shareholders and non-shareholders, and engages companies in mutually advantageous and socially necessary relations of various kinds.[26] 'A business able to make all these factors integral components of its operations, rather than add-on features of its marketing strategy, stands a better chance of satisfying the expectations of its diverse stakeholders and delivering on its business goals', argues social enterprise advocate Nic Frances, referring to corporate measures of financial performance, environmental sustainability, workplace equity, good governance and societal impact.[27]

21st Century Global Environment for Corporate Social Responsibility

> The business of global governance is set to become one of the key international policy issues of the twenty-first century. The governance of global business is one of the most difficult action points in this agenda. New issues are still emerging, not least among them a discussion on whether there is a need for tougher transnational regulation of multinational corporations.
>
> – Halina Ward, The Royal Institute of International Affairs[28]

Despite widespread consensus on some things, global CSR debate also remains overwhelmingly stuck in bi-polar arguments and sweeping dichotomies (e.g. market capitalism versus civil society, economic efficiency versus social justice, mandatory obligations versus voluntary commitments, public interests versus private concerns, and shareholders versus other corporate stakeholders). All of this transpires within the limits of the law's historical unwillingness to embrace aspirational corporate responsibility and sustainability beyond the duty-focused concerns of minimalist legal compliance, as well as the limits of an allegedly dominant legal and economic paradigm based upon the presumed societal efficiency of corporate and regulatory models based upon shareholder value.

Theories and models of corporations are a product of their historical times and contexts, as are corporate practices and regulatory regimes. In the early stages of the 21st century, we are entering a new phase in assessing the extent to which classical corporate theories and models match the internal and external environments for corporations today, as explored further in Chapters 2 and 3. 'The multinational corporation of the 21st century bears little resemblance to its forebears', notes one cross-disciplinary group of management scholars, in light of dramatic changes such as global competition, cross-border corporate takeovers and mergers, transnational markets, multi-sector institutional investors, and international business value chains.[29]

At the very least, this raises the possibility that ideas and practices surrounding corporations and their responsibility, governance and regulation that are formulated to meet the needs of one time and place might not be fully transposable to another. For example, the value-judgments about the balance between shareholder, stakeholder and other societal interests that might be suitable in the eras of industrial capitalism and managerial capitalism do not automatically suit the needs of information capitalism and global transparency capitalism.[30] 'The directors of large corporate enterprises are in need of a more substantial doctrine than legal and economic theory has provided as a rationale for the powers they must exercise', notes one expert, adding that the various social, economic and other forces operating upon corporations 'cannot be measured by the old instruments or accounted for alone by old theories inherited from eighteenth- and nineteenth-century legal and economic theory'.[31] Our ideas and practices surrounding corporations must adapt accordingly. The strategic integration of CSR and business concerns is one of the hallmarks of CSR already in the 21st century. Markets for CSR products and services (e.g. eco-innovative technology, sustainable buildings, socio-environmentally friendly investment, and independent CSR auditing and ranking) bring CSR concerns closer to the forefront of business engagement with market forces. The insertion of CSR elements into business models, business strategies and business value chains mainstreams CSR, in ways the business and societal effects of which are not all simply characterizable as private pursuit of private interests for socially sanctioned private ends.

The 21st century is also witnessing the cycle of an explosion, fragmentation and rationalization of CSR standards in a variety of areas. In the transition through phases of 'non-state market driven governance' of standard-initiation, standard-enhancement and standard-legitimization, there occurs much proliferation, divergence and consolidation of standards, ultimately resulting in the mass acceptance and practical adoption of leading standards that outlast the rest.[32] In authoritative sources of CSR consideration as diverse as G8 and G20 Summit declarations, European Parliament resolutions, European Commission communications, UNSRSG reports, and even national governmental CSR and corporate law reform inquiries, some CSR standards and other norms are emerging from the fragmented pack of CSR initiatives with favoured status. Overwhelmingly, they include supra-national and intergovernmental initiatives such as UN initiatives,[33] OECD and World Bank initiatives,[34] ILO initiatives[35] and G8 and G20 initiatives,[36] as well as other multi-stakeholder initiatives (e.g. Extractive Industries Transparency Initiative (EITI)), and principle-based standards (e.g. Equator Principles). Other initiatives receiving endorsement from one or more of these sources include ground-breaking CSR frameworks such as the GRI's G3 sustainability framework, with additional support in some of these sources for the further development of an ISO guidance standard on social responsibility, and the creation of business CSR networks modelled on the UK's Business in the Community network, the European Multistakeholder Forum on CSR, and the European Alliance for CSR. The push for harmonization and even universalization of standard-setting flows on to data-gathering, and disclosure and verification too, with flow-on problems of corporate survey fatigue and non-harmonized corporate reporting standards, given that 'companies' approaches to social reporting are as varied as their approaches to corporate social responsibility', according to the European Commission's 2001 Green Paper on a European CSR framework.[37]

Enhanced CSR-sensitive disclosure requirements are now part of 21st century corporate regulatory regimes for investment decisions, corporate reporting, or stock exchange listing conditions in countries as diverse as the UK, France, Sweden, South Africa, Malaysia and Australia, with mechanisms as equally diverse as delisting companies for breaches of internationally accepted human rights and ethical norms (Sweden), making listed companies describe their CSR involvement or lack thereof (Malaysia), factoring socially and environmentally relevant criteria into investment decisions and practices (the UK, France and Australia), obliging companies to incorporate CSR-related information in their annual reports (the UK, France and Malaysia), and requiring companies to report on their employment, procurement and investment efforts to promote a post-apartheid economy (South Africa).[38]

CSR has become a 21st century policy priority in the European Union (EU), notwithstanding considerable ongoing debate within the institutions and member countries of the EU about the appropriate forms, limits and regulatory reach of CSR. Corporate law reform debates in the UK and Australia in the first decade of the 21st century revolve around the desirability of making the law of directors' duties, business risk management and corporate reporting more sensitive to CSR. The presumed supremacy of Anglo-American shareholder primacy models is challenged by accounts of UK corporate responsibility and governance that do not view it as a system monolithically devoted to shareholder primacy in perpetuity, but rather as a system presently 'in a state of flux', with some elements (e.g. board structures, directors' duties and takeovers) more orientated towards shareholder primacy than others (e.g. intersections between insolvency and employment law).[39] The structural features of co-determination and other European models of corporate responsibility and governance that sit apart from Anglo-American shareholder primacy also point to alternative models of corporate design and practice, even as globalizing investment markets and the spread of Anglo-American corporate regulatory values place such regulatory models under increasing shareholder-orientated pressure.[40]

Although much of the post-Enron debate about corporate responsibility and governance in the USA has concentrated heavily upon remedial measures for corporate governance, disclosure and auditing requirements, this still forms part of a larger and ongoing public project on corporate responsibility and governance in the USA, with implications for CSR too. This project at least encompasses reviewing the balance of corporate governance control and influence of shareholders,[41] and achieving the appropriate mix of corporate 'gatekeepers' against corporate abuse and excess in the post-Enron era from the potential pool of official regulators, corporate lawyers, auditors and other professions.[42] It also embraces reform of corporate law in ways that work within or even outside current corporate legal orthodoxy,[43] and renewed questioning of the viability of looking to corporations rather than governments as the ultimate champions and regulators of the social responsibility of business.[44]

Corporate law's conception of corporate responsibility and governance is also facing 21st century pressures (from within and without) to refashion itself, in ways that extend beyond simply perfecting the alignment between company, board and shareholder interests. In conventional corporate theory, a strong connection exists between corporate responsibility and governance according to law (as distinct from corporate amenability to other societal norms), the sets of interests regulated by corporate law (as distinct from other laws), and the social benefits of private interests using capital for private purposes (as distinct from the social benefits served by pursuit of social goals). In other words, a common thread runs through the orthodox divide between public and private interests, corporate law and non-corporate law, and corporate and social responsibility. Given its overall grounding in underlying strands of political legitimacy, social efficiency and governance workability, this thread points towards *a* (if not *the*) major contemporary normative objection to CSR, which is that corporate pursuit of social goals is better justified by a mandate from the body politic through law than by a self-adopted and 'open-ended internal social welfare instruction' for boards and other corporate actors.[45]

Conventional legal, economic and contractarian accounts of the corporation all converge in treating it as a collectivity of mutually agreed and beneficial relations amongst private interests regulated by private law, organized around the efficient deployment of their combined financial capital to optimal wealth-generating effect, with innate limits upon the company's capacity for genuine social responsibility and necessary constraints upon state-based regulation of business affairs.[46] Yet, in the 21st century business environment, 'we see a conflict between the old-fashioned view of "corporate governance" which sought to create mechanisms for aligning the governance of the company with shareholders' interest in profit maximisation, and the vision . . . which seeks, by regulation, to make sure that companies have proper systems in place to ensure their compliance with the requirements of society generally', according to corporate law scholar, Professor Janet Dine.[47] Even in the early stages of the 21st century, ideas and influences with revitalizing and even reformatory potential from both inside and outside corporate law pave the way for a reconfiguration of corporate governance, responsibility and sustainability, and hence of corporate law and regulation as well.

Twenty-first century corporations come in different shapes and sizes too. The motivations, forms and practicalities surrounding CSR for transnational corporations (TNCs) and their global business chains are not fully transposable to small and medium-sized business enterprises (SMEs).[48] In addition, many problems related to CSR for individual countries and the world as a whole must increasingly be considered from a systemic perspective.[49] The world's socio-ethical, politico-legal and economic orders combine to produce national, transnational and international systems of governance, regulation and responsibility. These systems of global society as a whole consist of social sub-systems – e.g. electorates, markets, business enterprises and human interactions with the natural environment – that intersect and interact with one another, generating the need for rules of engagement within and between systems and sub-systems.[50] Some of these rules of engagement are still a work in progress, especially in the realm of CSR.

On a global scale, corporate capitalism's worthwhile contributions to individual wealth-creation, mass socio-economic opportunities and human progress must be reconciled with the lack of humanity and socio-ethical concern evident in its darker side, where the unbridled pursuit of corporate self-interest, shareholder profit-maximization and market-based competition risks coming at the expense of other people and values. At the same time that debates rage worldwide about the degree of global convergence on the Anglo-American model of corporate responsibility and governance, the developing world is examining the extent to which regulatory and business models developed for the developed world are truly transposable to developing economies. In the wake of collective governmental, business and community responses to 21st century transnational disasters in the form of Southeast Asian tsunamis, North American hurricanes and the African HIV–AIDS epidemic, and with climate change risks looming on the horizon, there is a dawning realization that at least some major global challenges cannot be met successfully without acknowledging and acting upon the shared interests of governments, businesses and communities in tackling them.

Corporate Social Responsibility and the Global Financial and Credit Crisis

The international financial and credit crisis of 2008 offers a timely reminder of the need for vigilance in ensuring that systems and practices of corporate responsibility and governance serve the right balance of societal interests and in the right ways. As an immediate response to one of the greatest economic challenges since the 20th century Great Depression, national governments introduced multi-billion dollar emergency measures to stabilize their economies and restore market confidence, investment capability and capital availability. In the absence of a central regulatory framework worldwide, these governmental rescue packages were initially criticized for responding to a truly global economic crisis in nationally self-interested, parochial and counter-productive ways,[51] as well as for rewarding errant financial institutions, flawed corporate reward systems and unworthy corporate executives, by rescuing through the socialization of losses those responsible for the crisis who had already benefited from the privatization of profits.[52]

Other critics pointed variously to the impact of the global economic crisis upon conventional ideas of the appropriate balance between free-market capitalism and governmental market intervention, and the ongoing viability of 20th century-style market capitalism, at least in forms that allowed what Australian Prime Minister Kevin Rudd called the 'political and economic ideology of extreme capitalism' to demonstrate 'a fundamental failure of values'.[53] In the absence of a serious global push to dismantle the system of market capitalism, each economic cycle of boom and bust simply ushers in new waves of debate about the appropriate degree of governmental intervention in markets through deregulation or re-regulation. Writing before the 2008 crisis, but in terms that broadly framed the response of his administration to it, US President Barack Obama acknowledged the insight of famous American political leaders 'that the resources and power of the national government can facilitate, rather than supplant, a vibrant free market', reinforced by the reality that, 'in each and every period of great economic upheaval and transition we've depended on government action to open up opportunity, encourage competition, and make the market work better'.[54] At some point in the 21st century, the specific concerns about corporate governance and responsibility stemming from high-profile corporate collapses (e.g. Enron) and mass systemic breakdowns (e.g. the 2008 global economic crisis) must be brought together with ongoing CSR concerns in a more holistic account of corporate governance, responsibility and sustainability.

The 2008 international financial and credit crisis also has discrete CSR implications. Focusing upon the multi-billion dollar financial rescue packages offered by governments to ailing financial institutions across the globe, economist and former Australian political leader Dr John Hewson suggested that 'the broader community, including the business community and our banks, has a clear social responsibility to contribute as well', especially in terms of banks and financial institutions owning their share of societal responsibility for overcoming the global crisis, in their own approaches to new loans, defaulting customers and interest rate reductions.[55] 'Might some sort of broad social compact, agreement, or at least understanding, which clearly attempts to recognise broader social responsibilities, as well as economically rational/business imperatives, be worthy of consideration?', asks Hewson.[56] Whatever the merits and practicalities of such ideas, they tap into deeper concerns about social contracts as the basis of business–society relations, optimal value-creating market behaviour, interdependent conditions of socio-economic justice, and shared but differentiated responsibilities for governance and regulatory challenges affecting everyone. This is also part of the 21st century's grand CSR project that is unfolding worldwide.

Even as the world was still coming to grips with the global economic crisis, high-level governmental representatives reinforced the value of CSR as being more rather than less important in economically tough times. Australia's Minister for Superannuation and Corporate Law (Senator Nick Sherry) highlighted CSR's significance as follows:[57]

> The sub-prime examples reflects a fundamental failure of values and provides a clear example of the business and social case for CSR. The world financial crisis is not just a corporate issue; the economy is not a private product but a critical piece of social infrastructure . . . While some commentators have speculated that the financial crisis will put a stop to CSR programs – I believe this not to be the case. Such views are driven by a misunderstanding of what CSR is all about. If anything the current crisis should accelerate its adoption. Companies may need to refocus their efforts, and concentrate on the shared values between them and the wider community in which they operate. I believe the current circumstances highlight the realties of CSR as an important means of companies to manage non-financial risk and maximise their long-term value.

Describing businesses that take a long-term and innovative approach to managing staff and service delivery in weathering the GFC storm as 'the face of modern CSR during a global financial crisis', thus setting themselves up to exploit post-GFC growth opportunities, Minister Sherry reiterates the 'strong nexus between corporate social responsibility, sound corporate governance and sustainable business development'.[58] Urging the global business community not to abandon CSR in the wake of the GFC, Minister Sherry links corporate governance, ESG and SRI investment considerations, enduring business and market sustainability, and CSR as follows: 'Responsible business practice is an integral part of sound Corporate Governance practices and . . .the integration of environmental, social and governance issues into investment decisions is critical to valuing long-term investments'.[59]

Such sentiments dovetail neatly with the post-GFC views of optimistic CSR commentators who see public demands for enhanced corporate responsibility on multiple fronts as one amongst a number of factors that could drive business away from the kinds of irresponsible corporate and financial behaviour exposed by the GFC. Professor Peter Shergold aptly dissects the GFC's exposure of the gulf between public CSR commitments and real adherence to CSR values in all aspects of a business enterprise, the opportunity this creates for CSR's own reformation, and the implications for the public, private, and not-for-profit sectors, as follows:[60]

> At least before the global financial crisis it was believed that governments, and the media who influence them, may be persuaded by CSR that business is well-motivated, socially responsible and best left to regulate itself . . . The roots of collapse were the antithesis of the values that underpin CSR (to which, it should be noted, many of the financial institutions subscribed) . . . There are two key messages to take from this. First, that the aspirational goals of CSR have yet to be fully incorporated into the strategic planning of many businesses . . . The second message is that 'corporate responsibility' is too often located in a conceptual silo, separated from 'business ethics' and 'ethical investment'. The outward-looking and internally-focused aspects of CSR need to be brought into alignment and complement each other . . . The challenge to corporate responsibility brought by financial crisis and economic downturn may – by putting CSR activities under the spotlight – revitalise the concept . . . A publicly accountable CSR, built into

the business of the business, and negotiated with the 'third sector' may yet evolve into a more powerful vehicle for building and sustaining a truly civil society.

Yet, such confidence in the enduring value of CSR is not shared by other GFC commentators, who ask whether CSR will be one of the major casualties of the GFC.[61] To the extent that the GFC's impact exposes corporate hypocrisy, 'fair weather' business commitment, non-alignment of stated values and actual behaviours, and reversion to corporate marginalization concerning CSR, it signals a shake-out of the CSR industry, in ways that would clarify the divide between CSR's true believers and others in the business sector, reveal the differences between CSR as an integrated part of doing business and CSR as a luxury extra, and stimulate CSR to refashion itself in the wake of the GFC, as Professor Shergold's analysis suggests. Moreover, the post-GFC world is not one in which 'business as usual' simply means a return to core business unrelated to CSR concerns, as the pre-existing national and transnational rules of the game for business are themselves open to question and reformation in the aftermath of the GFC, as the G20 response itself demonstrates.

At the very least, we might expect in this starkly revealed era of global economic interdependence a more holistic and systemic approach to corporate responsibility and its governance and regulation, signalled by heightened discussions amongst political, business, and community leaders about responsible market and lending behaviour, fair business regulation, enhanced business ethics, and other features of truly sustainable businesses and economies. Put another way, the inward-looking and outward-looking dimensions of sustainable corporate success are inextricably connected to sustainable societal well-being, in company-specific ways that both reflect and shape the interdependence between business enterprises and the societal systems in which they operate. In terms of the connection between business and human rights, this is also the theme emphasized and justified by the UNSRSG in his 2009 report to the UN Human Rights Council, as follows:[62]

> It is often mused that in every crisis there are opportunities. In operationalising the 'protect, respect and remedy' framework, the Special Representative aims to identify such opportunities in the business and human rights domain and demonstrate how they can be grasped and acted upon . . . In the face of what may be the worst worldwide economic downturn in a century, however, some may be inclined to ask: with so many unprecedented challenges, is this the appropriate time to be addressing business and human rights? This report answers with a resounding 'yes'. It does so based on three grounds.
> First, human rights are most at risk in times of crisis, and economic crises pose a particular risk to economic and social rights . . . Second, . . . the same types of governance gaps and failures that produced the current economic crisis also constitute what the Special Representative has called the permissive environment for corporate wrongdoing in relation to human rights . . . Third, the 'protect, respect and remedy' framework identifies specific ways to achieve these objectives.

So, whatever else it teaches the world, the 2008 global economic crisis throws into sharp relief some systemic features of market capitalism in civil societies that have much resonance for anyone who takes CSR seriously. Our global systems of governance, regulation and responsibility are interdependent, including national economies. The world's economic systems exist ultimately to serve the interests of peoples across the globe, including mass numbers of employees, shareholders and others whose livelihoods and prosperity are inextricably linked to the flourishing of market capitalism. Market forces have their strengths as well as their weaknesses, with governmental intervention remaining justified when exercised in the public interest, as in appropriate governmental rescue packages for economic systems in crisis. Appropriate official regulatory oversight and standard-setting supports market functioning and corrects market gaps and excesses, as revealed by inadequacies in regulating the valuation and sale of mortgage-based securities.

The true conditions for efficient and effective markets reject rather than embrace irresponsible corporate, financial and accounting practices, whether of the kinds exposed in Enron-like corporate misbehaviour, the false value-creation associated with the sale of inaccurately rated mortgage-based securities from the US sub-prime market, or the short-term and illusory advantages (if any) of exploitative corporate self-interest by any individual business enterprises that undermines the system of free enterprise and its societal preconditions. The proper alignment of executive performance and compensation measures with sustainable business value-creation is essential, as revealed by the instances of misalignment between executive rewards, prudent risk-taking and long-term business performance in the financial and investment sectors. All of these systemic features (and more) sharpen our sensitivity to the enterprise of devising and then implementing an adequate account of corporate responsibility, governance and sustainability for the conditions and needs of this century, whatever might have been the origins and contexts from which the contemporary corporate form emerged in previous centuries.

G8 and G20 Geopolitics and Corporate Social Responsibility

Even in these early stages of the 21st century, CSR has already achieved a new focus and prominence at the highest political levels worldwide. At the G8 Summit of major world leaders in 2007, CSR clearly emerged from the shadows as a secondary global concern, entering the spotlight as a primary international policy issue of the same order as climate change, international security, sustainable development, and free trade and investment. Outlining the G8 Agenda for enhancing cross-border investment and global economic development in their 2007 Summit Declaration, the world's G8 leaders committed their countries to 'promoting and strengthening corporate and other forms of social responsibility' as one of four priority areas for action, through 'internationally agreed corporate social responsibility and labour standards'.[63] The G8 leaders also committed their countries to high level dialogue with the governments of major emerging economies such as China, India, and South Africa on key global issues, including the strengthening of CSR worldwide, under the auspices of an OECD platform for global dialogue.[64]

In addition, the G8 leaders directly addressed the need for CSR and its accompanying standards in a new way that went beyond the conventional mantra of simply emphasizing the desirability of voluntary CSR initiatives.[65] Speaking directly to companies and those responsible for them, the G8 leaders targeted CSR disclosure and corporate engagement with particular CSR standards, saying that '(w)e call on private corporations and business organizations to adhere to the principles in the OECD Guidelines for Multinational Enterprises', and '(w)e invite corporations from the G8 countries, emerging nations and developing countries to participate actively in the Global Compact and to support the worldwide dissemination of this initiative'. The G8 leaders also urged public listed companies and national stock exchanges to incorporate CSR in normal corporate report-ing requirements, saying that '(w)e invite the companies listed on our Stock Markets to assess, in their annual reports, the way they comply with CSR standards and principles'.[66] The G8 leaders affirmed this commitment to CSR in their 2008 G8 Summit Declaration, in terms that recognize the CSR value of 'good corporate governance practices', 'socially responsible investments' and 'voluntary' corporate adherence to relevant international norms.[67]

These ostensible commitments of the G8 to CSR as a major geopolitical concern must now also be read together with the formal response of the G20 to the global financial crisis (GFC), and it remains to be seen whether or not both sets of initiatives become mutually reinforcing priorities in action. At the G20 Summit in London in April 2009, world leaders agreed on a post-GFC recovery and reform plan that at least acknowledges the place of CSR as a component within that overall plan, although with ostensibly less emphasis than that afforded to other remedial measures. The Leaders Statement from this summit commits the G20 to supporting CSR in business and finance, as part of an ongoing action plan, within the context of collective G20 agreement 'to establish a new Financial Stability Board (FSB) with a strengthened mandate, as a successor to the Financial Stability Forum (FSF)', and 'to endorse and implement the FSF's tough new principles on pay and compensation and to support sustainable compensation schemes *and the Corporate Social Responsibility of all firms*'.[68]

Still, taken at face value, these G8 and G20 commitments extend beyond generic rhetor-ical support for CSR as an idea, and position it anew within contemporary international policy priorities. In short, the G8 Summit aspirations for CSR now place it in the top tier of international policy concerns, and signal clear roles for the private sector in address-ing such shared geopolitical problems as climate change, developing economies, poverty reduction and sustainable development.[69] This also sets the scene for the next stages of global CSR dialogue, framework-building and standard-setting. A similar stage has been reached in business engagement with human rights worldwide.[70] Responding to these calls is one of the key global CSR challenges for the first decades of the 21st century.

Global Investment Stakes, Reporting Trends, and Implications for Corporate Practice

By the end of the 20th century, for the first time in history, a majority of the world's largest single economic entities were business corporations instead of nation-states. According to a 2000 study of the biggest 100 economies in the world, corporations filled 51 rankings and countries only 49 of them.[71] Whatever else might be said about this commonly cited claim, clearly the size, power and resources of the largest MNCs (or transnational cor-porations (TNCs) challenge all but the largest and most influential nations.[72] By mid-way through the first decade of the 21st century, more than 75,000 TNCs existed worldwide, with 10 times that number of corporate subsidiaries and affiliates, along with millions of associated entities in global supply and distribution chains.[73] TNCs are responsible for 80 per cent of the investment from developed nations in developing nations.[74] In the 1999 Millennium Poll on Corporate Social Responsibility, which polled more than 25,000 people in 23 countries across six continents, half of the populations of those countries took notice of socially responsible business behaviour and linked their impressions of a company's reputation to its corporate citizenship.[75]

Competing priorities are the biggest impediment. Shareholder demands for strong short-term financial performance, for example, compete with environmental, social, and governance investments that are longer term by nature. The absence of clear and consistent metrics that could relate such investments to (or correlate them with) investor returns exacerbates this conflict . . . As the CEO of a financial institution noted, the standards that do exist have 'yet to become benchmarks to look up in the *Wall Street Journal*, where we can see, alongside stock prices, that a company's ESG [environmental, social, and governance] impact rating went from 2 to 12, and this somehow becomes a factor in how we value it'.

– McKinsey Consultants Debby Bielak and Sheila Bonini, and Director Jeremy Oppenheim[76]

Current reporting is dominated by measures of financial outcomes but increasing societal expectations around environmental, social and governance (ESG) responsibilities are applying pressure on businesses to report clearer information on a wider range of business activities . . . In addition to these ESG reporting pressures, recent events on Wall Street have demonstrated the risks of a reliance on backward looking financial reporting . . . BBBR [Broad Based Business Reporting] responds to these pressures, encouraging reporting of ESG as well as strategic, operational and financial matters.

– The Institute of Chartered Accountants in Australia[77]

Just as the world is seeing more major companies making the transition in corporate reporting from environmental reporting to more expansive sustainability reporting, under a combination of regulatory initiatives,[78] so too the investment domain is witnessing a trend towards the incorporation of socially responsible investing (SRI) and environmental, social and governance (ESG) considerations in investment decision-making, although this trend is yet to become embedded universally in mainstream investment practice.[79] 'There is a growing realisation within the industry that [a] range of environmental, social and governance (ESG) issues pose core investment risks with the potential to impact heavily on the long term viability of investments [and] (t)hese value drivers extend well beyond those captured in traditional financial reporting, but are nevertheless fundamentally linked to shareholder returns', according to the Australian Minister for Superannuation and Corporate Law, with the consequence that consideration of ESG factors 'should be incorporated into the investment decision making process of superannuation trustees'.[80] Highlighting evidence of the link between ESG considerations and financial performance in assessing investment value, a report for the United Nations Environment Programme Finance Initiative surveyed a number of European, North American and Anglo-Commonwealth countries in 2005. It concluded that 'integrating ESG considerations into an investment analysis so as to more readily predict financial performance is clearly permissible *and is arguably required* in all jurisdictions'.[81]

At the turn of the century, more than US$1 trillion worth of assets worldwide were held in ethical investment funds and managed under investment portfolios of socially and environmentally responsible investments.[82] In early 2007, a group of almost 300 global institutional investors managing funds worth US$41 trillion asked 2,400 of the world's largest companies by market capitalization to disclose how they managed business risks and opportunities stemming from climate change, as an investment-related consideration of growing importance.[83] Within only a couple of years of their promulgation, more than 200 signatories worldwide with investment portfolios worth in excess of US$10 trillion committed to the UN Principles for Responsible Investment (UN PRI), supporting enhanced incorporation and disclosure of ESG issues for investment portfolio decision-making.[84] As with many official corporate governance codes, the framework consists of a broad but limited set of principles, supplemented by more numerous detailed recommendations for action, as illustrated by the UN PRI's foundational principle and associated actions, as follows:

1. We will incorporate ESG issues into investment analysis and decision-making processes.

    Possible actions:
    ● Address ESG issues in investment policy statements
    ● Support development of ESG-related tools, metrics, and analyses
    ● Assess the capabilities of internal investment managers to incorporate ESG issues
    ● Assess the capabilities of external investment managers to incorporate ESG issues
    ● Ask investment service providers (such as financial analysts, consultants, brokers, research firms, or rating companies) to integrate ESG factors into evolving research and analysis
    ● Encourage academic and other research on this theme
    ● Advocate ESG training for investment professionals

Corporate responsibility and sustainability reporting is increasingly integrating financial and non-financial information as well as performance indicators that all link ESG, SRI and CSR concerns to company-specific business drivers and risks. New corporate regulatory initiatives in Europe, the UK, Australia and elsewhere reinforce this trend. According to a recent Deloitte global business survey on non-financial business information, almost 90 per cent of CEOs and senior executives globally believe that their capacity to track the financial performance of their companies is good or excellent, although slightly less than 30 per cent of them could say the same about their tracking of non-financial performance, notwithstanding that more than half of them concede that companies are under more pressure than ever before to measure their non-financial performance, with more than 80 per cent of these senior corporate executives admitting that this kind of performance information is increasingly emphasized by financial markets, investment fund managers and others.[85] This 2007 global business survey highlights in stark terms the transitional CSR-related phase in which the corporate directors, other senior executives, and internal and external advisers of the world's companies find themselves.

Other global business surveys reflect similar results. According to a recent McKinsey survey of company CEOs and more than 200 organizations with corporate headquarters located in Europe, North and South America, Asia, Africa, the Middle East and Australasia, 'more than 90 percent of them are doing more than they did five years ago to incorporate environmental, social, and governance issues into their core strategies', motivated by a combination of external pressures from employees, customers and other stakeholders, as well as perceived opportunities to confront global challenges while also securing competitive advantages.[86] Such CSR drivers have evolved over time, to the point where they are increasingly integrated within generic business elements – for example, as simply another key aspect of business strategy, stakeholder engagement, business chain value and public disclosure.

However, this trend remains a volatile one. The availability of good measurement tools for capturing and using non-financial information remains at a relatively early stage of development. In turn, this inhibits the capacity of corporate boards and senior managers to assess corporate performance and impact fully. Obstacles to be cleared away include unsophisticated non-financial performance measurement tools, organizational scepticism about the value and utility of such tools, lack of clarity about the relation between corporate success and non-financial drivers, internal accountability gaps in responsibility and rewards for non-financial performance, time and cost constraints associated with proper development and use of non-financial metrics, and concerns about counter-productive disclosure of information to market competitors.[87]

Still, the gap between the rhetoric and the reality of CSR is closing in a number of ways. In addition, the cumulative effect of integrating CSR, ESG and SRI risk and performance factors within standard business models, whether in response to regulatory innovations or not, also places new business drivers and risks on the corporate radar screen, with correlative implications for changes in boardroom focus, expertise and decision-making.

FRAMING HOW WE NOW THINK OF CORPORATE SOCIAL RESPONSIBILITY

> The relation between a country's democratic political system and its non-democratic economic system has presented a formidable and persistent challenge to democratic goals and practices throughout the twentieth century. That challenge will surely continue in the twenty-first century.
>
> – Democratic theorist, Robert Dahl[88]

Basic Schools of Thought About Corporate Social Responsibility

Our foundational perspectives in approaching corporate responsibility and governance fundamentally reflect and shape the legitimizing theories under which we either accept or reject CSR. Some debates about the respective soundness and implications of shareholder-based and stakeholder-sensitive models, for example, need to be understood against a wider background of socio-ethical and politico-regulatory debate about the desirability and workability of corporations moving from an ethos of 'acquisitive individualism' to one of collective, or at least shared, interests and trajectories for corporations and other societal organs, all playing their respective parts in addressing common global, regional and national challenges, especially in light of border-straddling capital flows, mass consumer markets, transnational supply and distribution chains, and global consequences of corporate activity.[89] In turn, this transformation of ethos itself needs to be understood against an even wider background conception of social efficiency, prosperity and justice in a civil society, in which corporations are located along with other societal actors in a shared societal inheritance of interdependent destinies in pursuit of some conception of the public interest or common good.[90] Such conceptions of social well-being must accommodate balances of public and private interests, shareholder and stakeholder interests, and economic and social justice.

On orthodox legal and economic models, a business corporation's worth lies in maximizing the 'expected net present value of [future] profit'.[91] Corporate orthodoxy in Anglo-American and Anglo-Commonwealth systems makes corporate profit-making for shareholder wealth-generation the prime directive for corporations, those who run them, and governments that regulate them. As rival schools of thought, shareholder primacy and corporate managerialism both frame the central corporate imperative in terms of corporate wealth-maximization, but disagree over the best means to that end, not least in terms of the amenability of managerial judgments to shareholder direction, and these two schools differ again from CSR, with its inclusion of a social welfare component and responsibility for corporate externalities in the standard corporate model.[92]

One of the most likely explanations for the ready equation of a corporation's interests with its shareholders' interests is the coincidence between those two sets of interests across many (some would say all) important corporate decisions and actions. Moreover, as three leading corporate scholars conclude, 'any distinction between the interests of the company and the interests of shareholders may be viewed as negligible because . . . generally what is good for the survival and growth of the company-as-entity will be good for the shareholders'.[93] Still, even if the prime directive of corporate directors is to enhance shareholder value, that still begs the question of what constitutes shareholder value, what is necessary to achieve it, and what frames and limits its pursuit.

Most debates about the legitimacy of CSR fit within one or more of the following schools of thought.[94] As with most analytical models, these schools of thought are abstractions that sometimes sacrifice the complexity of reality for the sake of analytical simplicity and clarity in throwing different schools of thought into sharp relief. Still, many academic, policy and business views on this topic start from one or more positions on CSR that broadly correspond to one or more of these basic schools of thought.

One school of thought separates CSR from mainstream corporate responsibility and governance, marginalizing CSR as a voluntary, minor and financially non-threatening addition to 'normal' corporate business activity. Another school of thought goes one step further, and accepts the legitimacy of some forms of CSR, at least to the extent that their inclusion within corporate responsibility and governance enhances shareholder gain. Here, some conceptions of shareholder self-interest simply include concern for others merely in an instrumental sense, so that the value of stakeholders to corporations is totally defined by the extent to which their interests satisfy shareholder interests. This is reflected in accounts of shareholder primacy in which the interests of non-shareholders (such as employees, customers and creditors) and broader societal consequences (such as any business impact upon the environment, economy and community) are relevant only to the extent that accommodating them serves the interests of the company and its shareholders as a whole. 'The shareholder primacy norm, if fully incorporated into the legal regime, would still require that stakeholder interests be considered when doing so has a foreseeable impact upon shareholder wealth', notes Wharton Business School's Professor Tom Dunfee.[95] This results in the common claim that taking care of all corporate stakeholders is good for business.

Under this vision of CSR, a company's socially responsible activities actually enhance its market value and profitability, and hence meet the wealth-maximizing interests of those holding equity in the company. In this way, sophisticated forms of shareholder primacy avoid the pitfall of simplistic reductionism, where the company's interests are simply equated with whatever maximizes share prices or other short-term returns for existing shareholders, regardless of any other corporate or even community concerns. Other possible conceptions of self-interest in the make-up of shareholders include a component that goes beyond instrumentalism, by making sympathetic concern for others a constituent part of one's own well-being, while others conceive of self-interest in ways that rationally justify sacrifices or compromises of self-interest for higher-order interests (e.g. justice), or otherwise set limits on its legitimate pursuit.[96] Still, some commentators are troubled by the idea that anything that ultimately results in shareholder wealth-generation is still worthy of being associated with CSR in any meaningful sense.

A different school of thought focuses upon the multi-faceted interests of 21st century shareholders, and the possibility that they might have interests in addition to profit-maximization, or at least in conditioning how profit is pursued. Some commentators argue that 'shareholder value' is a misnomer and that we should be talking about 'shareholder *values*' instead, on the basis that shareholders value a range of things, including (but not limited to) financial self-interest.[97] This recognition accepts the legitimacy of certain shareholder-focused elements of corporate responsibility and governance, but maintains that a company today is 'very much more complex than a shareholder-driven profit maximisation machine'.[98] Some contemporary theories even invite us to transform our conception of shareholders, from one solely built around shareholders as investors of corporate financial capital to one that embraces their place as members in a collective business enterprise, with distinctive membership roles of participation, decision-making and responsibility.[99] This sits within a wider trend of academic argument that extends our conception of a shareholder, beyond the paradigmatic financially self-interested wealth-maximizer, driven by a win-at-all-costs mentality on shareholder returns,[100] to a vision of shareholders as members who, while retaining that quality, also bring another order of motivations to their role as participants in a collective business enterprise, who have socio-ethical commitments and other concerns about the ways in which corporate profit-maximization should be pursued, and who hence have a pivotal role in the deliberative processes of corporations.[101]

Except at the extremes of the corporate responsibility debate, nobody seriously suggests that corporations and those who manage them do and should conform to a completely single-minded and self-focused corporate purpose without any limits at all, whatever the costs to anyone other than shareholders, even if that purpose is conceived as corporate profit-maximization and shareholder wealth-maximization. 'Rational people do not advocate the position that corporations have an unconstrained obligation to do whatever it takes to increase shareholder wealth (for example, hiring a hitman to murder a key witness against the firm in a major product liability case)', notes Professor Dunfee.[102]

'Nor do rational people expect publicly held corporations to be operated in furtherance of social or altruistic objectives with little or no concern for the interests of investors', he adds.[103] Similarly, even the late Milton Friedman's famous advocacy of shareholder wealth-maximization as the overriding imperative for business recognizes in-built limits upon corporate profit-generation, based upon 'the rules of the game' for business.[104]

Shareholder interests retain major significance even in theories and models that otherwise reject the shareholder primacy norm as a complete account of corporate responsibility. For example, team production scholars argue for a broader account of business value-creation, focused upon those constituent groups who make a relevant company-specific investment of some kind, and how companies are managed for their collective benefit.[105] Here, CSR's option is to broaden the notion of who contributes something of value to a company and its success, so that the contributions of shareholders *and* other stakeholders are sufficiently recognized and rewarded.

Stakeholder-centred approaches conventionally accommodate shareholder concerns too. Some stakeholder-focused commentators connect this interplay between shareholder and other stakeholder interests to ways in which the overriding fiduciary duty of directors to act in the company's interests might be reformulated. 'A duty to act in the interests of the enterprise could . . . be understood as a duty to protect the business for the benefit of those groups, in addition to the shareholders, whose interests are likely to be affected by its success', argues corporate law scholar, Professor John Parkinson.[106] Sophisticated forms of stakeholder pluralism avoid the pitfall of transforming this claim automatically into a legally enforceable duty owed by corporate decision-makers to non-shareholders to benefit their interests, resulting in an impossible demand for corporate decision-makers to balance truly irreconcilable obligations to multiple parties.

Moreover, even though complete congruence between all shareholder and other stakeholder concerns in mutually satisfactory win-win outcomes is impossible,[107] much apparent dissonance between these two sets of corporate constituent interests can be dissolved by further connecting how each constituent group relates to the company as a successful, sustainable and responsible profit-seeking enterprise. The closer debates about 'shareholder primacy versus stakeholder pluralism' come to connecting corporate success in pursuit of shareholder value to successful engagement with non-shareholder interests, as part of a complete account of how companies approach their business–society relations, the more it is that they reach the same end, albeit by different routes.[108] In other words, the gulf between these two poles reduces considerably if we view the corporation as an enterprise whose success must be sustainable now and into the future, with full regard to all of a company's internal and external relations, and link the corporation's interest in achieving that to how the interests of the corporation's shareholding and non-shareholding sub-constituencies relate to each other, the corporation and society in attaining that outcome.[109]

An immediate counter-response is that the more such non-shareholder dynamics are brought into the corporate equation, by reference to their connection in the long run to a company's success, the more likely it is that somebody could identify at least some kind of contingent and indirect benefit for the company and its shareholders down the track that is connected in part to such dynamics, thus effectively rendering meaningless the whole idea of connecting corporate shareholding and non-shareholding interests, at least at the extremes. After all, as Professor Einer Elhauge notes, 'courts are extraordinarily willing to sustain decisions that apparently sacrifice profits (at least in the short term) on the ground that they may conceivably maximize profits (at least in the long run)', on the basis that 'just about any decision to sacrifice profits has a conceivable link to long-term profits'.[110] 'Indeed, it is hard to see what socially responsible conduct could not plausibly be justified under the commonly accepted rationalization that it helps forestall possible adverse reactions from consumers, employees, the neighbourhood, other businesses, or government regulators', he adds – a standard which sets a low bar for connections between a company's interests and consideration of non-shareholder interests and third party effects, even beyond those regulated in some way contractually, legislatively or judicially.[111] Conversely, given possible reaction to the dilution of shareholder primacy, such counter-responses might simply evidence the limits of a mono-dimensional focus upon shareholder interests in corporate decision-making, directing attention instead to other ways of explaining the true complexity of corporate responsibility.

In this way, corporate responsibility and governance debates grapple with the complexity of CSR's elements, especially the tensions inherent between shareholder-focused and stakeholder-focused accounts of it, or what are variously described in the literature, for example, as shareholder primacy and stakeholder pluralism, monotonic and pluralistic views,[112] 'elaborated shareholder benefit' and 'pluralist' approaches,[113] contractarian and communitarian perspectives,[114] and contractual and managerialist accounts of corporations.[115] While all CSR-related theories and models do not necessarily orientate themselves so closely along a shareholder–stakeholder continuum, it is clear that concerns about shareholder interests, stakeholder interests, and their relation to each other, the corporation and society at large clearly dominate much of the debate about corporate responsibility and governance generally, and CSR in particular.

CSR's alternative tack is to show how and why corporations must accommodate interests beyond even those of these contributing shareholders and other stakeholders, even if that comes at the expense of profit-generation in their collective interest, because of higher-order societal values in play which affect business–society relations. In some forms, this school of thought highlights the contingent rather than inevitable emergence of shareholder-focused corporate regulatory regimes, which trade upon political, economic and other power relations that marginalize socio-ethical concerns and the interests of society's and the world's most vulnerable people.[116] After all, democratic institutions designed to make laws that promote the general welfare and public interest are still human institutions whose decision-making can instead result in advantages for sectional interests, whether considered from the standpoint of public choice theory's focus upon influential interest groups in legislative voting, a Marxist perspective of systemic rules designed to benefit a dominant (financial and political) class, or the power relations of capitalism and the coalition of governmental, business and lobby groups serving the interests of capital.[117]

Yet another school of thought assimilates corporate responsibility, corporate governance and CSR, and the respective values and interests associated with each of them, so that shareholder and other stakeholder interests, on one hand, and private and public interests, on the other, are all implicated in corporate responsibility, governance and sustainability, in terms of normative design as well as operational practice. This balances the corporate, market and societal imperatives associated with living in a market economy, new regulatory state and civil society.

A final and more radical school of thought refuses to give the idea of CSR any credence at all. Again, this can be for any number of claimed reasons, including the difficulty or even impossibility of giving effective meaning to the idea of CSR, the rhetorical use of CSR as a cloak for an anti-business political agenda by activist advocacy groups, and the potential for at least some forms of CSR to undermine the essential profit-making mandate of business. Either way, all roads lead to a fuller account of corporate responsibility, governance and sustainability for the 21st century.

Baselines for Thinking About Corporate Responsibility and Governance

Imagine that, in the wake of a globally significant natural disaster or other event requiring humanitarian emergency assistance on a mass scale, the board of a TNC proposes to make a significant donation of money, equipment and supplies to assist in the disaster relief effort. Indeed, this is exactly the kind of situation in which many companies found themselves in the wake of some natural disasters this century, such as Hurricane Katrina in the USA and the Southeast Asian tsunami in late 2004. Such corporate displays of philanthropy and humanitarianism raise deeper questions too. Profit-sacrificing for social ends (if that is a correct characterization), is contrary to a company's chief mandate, according to *The Economist*'s outline of major CSR criticisms in its 2008 report on CSR:[118]

> The most fundamental criticism of CSR is that what executives spend on it is other people's – ie, shareholders' – money. They may mean well, and it may give them satisfaction to write a cheque for hurricane victims or disadvantaged youth, but that is not what they were hired to do. Their job is to make money for shareholders. It is irresponsible for them to sacrifice profits in the (sometimes vain) pursuit of goodness.

Suppose that a group of shareholders objects to the proposed course of action by directors, as some shareholders and shareholder representative bodies did in those cases.[119] They might argue that, considerations of humanity and morality aside, it is not in the interests of the corporation and those investing something in it (whether as shareholders or not) to make such a large discretionary sacrifice of corporate profits, unless it can be aligned with a meaningful strategic or other competitive advantage. They might then buttress their case with various subsidiary lines of argument. They might say, for example, that such a significant donation is not warranted for geographical regions in which the corporation has no present or likely future markets for its labour, products or investments. They might add that the size of the proposed donation cannot be reconciled even with any long-term potential benefits to be gained for the corporation, in terms of its reputation in the region and at home. They might even claim that this action would be contrary to the primary obligation of directors under the laws of the corporation's governing jurisdiction to act with due care and diligence in the interests of the corporation and its members.[120]

All of these different claims might be advanced by their proponents as arguments grounded in a proper view of corporate responsibility. None of them can be dismissed by their opponents as being productive of corporate irresponsibility, at least not without first establishing a justified account of what distinguishes corporate responsibility from corporate irresponsibility. Moreover, the different standpoints and levels of argument of these various claims – the needs of national and transnational governance, considerations of humanity and morality, boundaries of regulation and law, successful business motivations and practices, and intersections between all of these things – suggest that any good account of corporate responsibility is likely to require multiple rather than singular dimensions and levels of analysis.

At the same time, any good account of corporate responsibility also must be capable of comprehension and application in the real world, by real actors performing real roles in overlapping national and transnational systems of corporate responsibility, governance and regulation. Deciding whether or not it would be better for society if sometimes companies could choose 'profit-sacrificing social responsibility' instead of rigid adherence to 'the formula of profit maximisation within the law' has important flow-on implications for systems of corporate regulation and the amenability of corporate executives to pursuing 'corporate responsiveness to the interests of non-shareholder groups'.[121] Accordingly, all corporate actors engaged in the work of corporate responsibility from various standpoints – including corporate law-makers and regulators as well as corporate directors and managers – need a working account of corporate responsibility that transcends abstract theories and models. To one degree or another, they must engage with the difficult issues of justification, interpretation and application that permeate responsible corporate decisions and actions in the real world, not least in contributing to public debate about corporate regulatory reform.

Unfortunately, there is no universally accepted starting point from which all questions about corporate responsibility can be asked. All accounts of corporate responsibility start from particular points on the landscape that frame not only their chosen approaches and preconditions but also their questions and answers. The argument that CSR should be voluntary rather than mandatory presupposes a background view of the nature, appropriateness and limits of business regulation. The argument that legal obligations protecting non-shareholder interests should be part of environmental, employment and other laws but not corporate law presupposes background conceptions of both law generally and corporate law in particular. Finally, attempts to locate a corporation's 'real' responsibility within the domain of legal responsibility alone still need to justify their relegation of social, moral and other dimensions of corporate responsibility to the margins of corporate concerns.

The Limits of Legal Responsibility as the Benchmark of Corporate Responsibility

Corporate responsibility involves more than minimum corporate legal responsibility

While CSR deserves study from multiple disciplinary perspectives, it is also fundamentally affected by how law and other forms of regulation treat it. So, a baseline of legal and regulatory perspectives informs answers to questions about corporate responsibility. Many people argue that, whatever the moral responsibility (if any) of business corporations towards society, their primary legal responsibility is confined to meeting the minimum requirements imposed upon them by law. They are usually quick to add that a company might *voluntarily* do more than this if there is a competitive advantage in doing so, but that a company's 'true' responsibility does not properly travel beyond this point, at least in terms of what society has a right to expect from companies. This distinction between mandatory and voluntary obligations is reflected in law's own distinction between 'hard' and 'soft' law, with the latter being characterized as voluntary (and hence non-binding), in the strict legal sense of direct sanctionability and enforcement under the law.

In other words, a company's responsibility is here defined first and foremost in terms of what can be legally compelled. After all, the rights of stakeholders recognized in significant instruments such as the OECD Principles of Corporate Governance are those stakeholder rights 'that are established by law or through mutual agreements', which primarily confines corporate responsibility towards stakeholders to their interests as enshrined in law and its mechanisms (e.g. contractual agreement and unilateral consent).[122] Moreover, across Anglo-American and Anglo-Commonwealth jurisdictions, but less so in Europe (at least before the onset of contemporary pressures upon stakeholder-focused approaches, due to the globalization of investment markets and their common emphasis upon shareholder value[123]), corporate law orthodoxy has kept its focus as a body of law primarily anchored in regulating the relationships between companies, boards and shareholders, with all of the duty-focused and compliance-based notions conventionally associated with law.

However, any simple equation of corporate responsibility with doing the minimum required of corporations under the law is problematic on a number of levels. Fundamentally, it frames the notion of corporate legal responsibility selectively in terms of only some of its dimensions.[124] Legal responsibility certainly includes what is legally prescribed or alternatively prohibited, but it also includes what is legally permissible. So, legal responsibility is not limited to that strand of responsibility in which legal compulsion and sanctions apply to regulate legal outcomes.[125] The law's interaction with CSR can embrace a minimum position of legal compliance and harm-avoidance where the law is lacking, a mid-way position of facilitating corporate contributions to sustainable development and other forms of community investment where the business case warrants it, and a more expansive position of 'active *alignment* of internal business goals with externally set societal goals (those that support sustainable development)'.[126]

In short, corporate responsibility therefore entails more than just corporate legal responsibility and, in turn, corporate legal responsibility has more than just compliance-based and sanction-focused elements.

Moreover, the simple equation of corporate responsibility with corporate legal compliance also promotes a legalistic account of corporate compliance that 'connotes a reactive conception of the corporation as a recipient of rules, rather than an actively responsible citizen . . . engaged with its legal, social, environmental and ethical responsibilities'.[127] In other words, an overly compliance-based and sanction-focused account of corporate responsibility overemphasizes law and its authoritative enforceability of norms as the dominant regulatory mechanism. At the same time, it underemphasizes other forms of regulation, including regulation that does not rely upon enforcement by governmental regulators and other public officials, such as reflexive self-regulation, 'best practice' industry standards, peer-accepted norms of business conduct, and even community influences upon corporate reputations and conduct.

Too narrow a view of corporate responsibility also brings costly side-effects for individual companies, regulated markets and society at large. For example, one clear pattern evident in the business crises and investor panics from even before the 1929 Wall Street crash to the present post-Enron era of the latest global economic crisis, and in the public and governmental reactions to each of them, is the increased likelihood of additional legislative regulation as a result of the build-up of political, media and investor pressures, 'rendering ineffective industry lobbying that in normal times moderates the demands of pro-regulation interest groups'.[128] So, seeking refuge in the minimum of legality and using enforceable obligations as a blunt proxy for an exhaustive account of overall corporate responsibility can be counter-productive for individual businesses and the market as a whole, especially when popular sentiment turns against perceived business excesses and harms.

Finally, responsibility for good corporate outcomes is just as integral to corporate responsibility as responsibility for bad corporate outcomes, whether that responsibility is viewed in terms of shareholder outcomes, societal outcomes or something else, because law is as much concerned with encouraging responsible behaviour as it is with sanctioning irresponsible behaviour.[129] In that sense, systems of legal, economic and moral sanctions work together in conditioning a corporation's responsiveness to its surrounding systemic environments.[130] On this view, while prosecution of a company's directors by official corporate regulators for corporate illegality involves different dimensions and standards of corporate responsibility from those triggered by widespread social condemnation of lawful but morally dubious corporate activity, both do so within the same broader framework of corporate responsibility.

Indeed, corporate choices often operate in the gap between the floor offered by a race to the bottom in meeting bare minimum conditions required by law, and the ceiling offered by a race to the top in setting aspirational standards for business–society engagement. Making the transformation in mindset from the floor to the ceiling of corporate legal responsibility involves a shift in both the orientation and the content of this form of responsibility. It resonates with similar contrasts elsewhere in legal and regulatory orders that embody notions of reflexivity, receptivity and responsiveness to externalities beyond those orders. 'In a responsive legal order, the reintegration of law and government is a way of enlarging the meaning and reach of legal values from a set of minimal restrictions to a source of affirmative responsibilities', argue responsive law scholars.[131]

Framed in this way, law fully underpins aspirational corporate responsibility. An understanding of law's place in the new regulatory state reveals 'the limits of law's regulatory reach', as well as law's own amenability to regulatory pluralism of a kind that stimulates law's continuous self-assessment of its delivery of social justice.[132] Indeed, one transcendent aspect of the interplay between different rules, principles and other norms, at least in legal systems, is the exposure of the legal order to the necessity of coping with social change.[133] Law can also promote CSR by pushing companies towards becoming institutions of continuous internal inquiry and debate about how well their responsibility-inducing processes and outcomes inculcate an 'ethic of responsibility' and a 'corporate conscience', within a legal framework that is sensitized by CSR-friendly public policies and interests, as well as providing organs of government with the stimulus and material to become vehicles of public dialogue and action orientated around shaping laws and policies to reflect both of these institutional goals.[134]

An impoverished account of corporate responsibility fails to account for the business and social need for companies and their advisers to look beyond legal compliance as an exhaustive source of corporate obligations, and to embrace continuous improvement in public transparency, reporting, and other forms of accountability as a desirable regulatory and business objective, for example.[135] Leading scholars on global business regulation point to 'continuous improvement' as a prominent principle across a number of regulated business sectors worldwide, as well as to the specific contest and interplay between continuous improvement and rule compliance in different regulatory situations.[136] This principle of continuous improvement is embraced as a desirable feature in CSR management systems and reporting.[137] The Australian Standard on Corporate Social Responsibility (AS 8003) produced by Standards Australia endorses continuous improvement as one of the core structural elements of a company's CSR programme.[138] Similarly, the international standard for social accountability for companies, Social Accountability 8000 (SA8000), proposes a management system for socially responsible corporate activity that is committed to a policy of 'continual improvement'.[139] It is embedded specifically in some steps within authoritative guidelines for implementing socially responsible corporate behaviour, such as the looped cycle of continuous improvement in management steps for practising CSR endorsed by Business in the Community's Business Impact Task Force.[140] Checklists for directors looking to implement sustainability practices within their business operations also incorporate reference to continuous improvement.[141] Business practice worldwide is therefore moving towards continuous improvement and other aspects of a culture of aspirational corporate responsibility.[142]

Accordingly, a purely prescriptive and proscriptive account of compliance-based corporate legal responsibility is neither a complete nor an adequate account of corporate *legal* responsibility or even corporate *regulatory* responsibility, let alone corporate responsibility at large. Instead, a 21st century perspective of corporate responsibility must reach beyond the floor of *minimum* corporate legal responsibility, and even beyond the boundaries of corporate *legal* responsibility itself, to embrace a richer conception of corporate responsibility, grounded in corporate responsiveness to what this book describes as 'trans-modal governance', 'multi-order regulation' and 'inter-related responsibility', as outlined in Chapter 2. By analogy, if corporate commitments that look voluntary from law's floor of minimalist compliance can seem something more from law's ceiling of aspirational responsibility,[143] might non-shareholder interests that seem instrumental, marginal or even hostile to orthodox conceptions of corporate profit-maximization assume a different character from the standpoint of either alternative conceptions of the profit-making imperative or else the societal infrastructure that supports and engages it?

The limits of law

Law interacts with CSR in various ways: (i) the corporate and non-corporate laws of many countries reflect at least some CSR concerns; (ii) law controls what business can and cannot do; (iii) law provides mechanisms to incorporate CSR standards (e.g. contractual adoption of codes); (iv) law provides the frame for CSR 'boundary' disputes about accountability for corporate irresponsibility (e.g. multinational corporate group liability for corporate harm); (v) 'soft law' standards influence the evolution of CSR (and vice versa); (vi) law informs whole-of-organization CSR approaches (e.g. corporate inculcation of internationally recognized human rights standards); (vii) international and regional agreements on trade, investment and the environment influence CSR actors towards CSR public policy goals; and (viii) even technically non-binding CSR standards can have a normative effect on corporate activity and influence the development of legal doctrines affecting corporations too.[144] Yet, despite the potential offered by law's multiple points of interface with CSR, the failures of CSR to this point are also arguably attributable to the existing legal frameworks and models for corporations, both nationally and internationally.[145]

Law has its intrinsic limits in curbing corporate irresponsibility and stimulating corporate responsibility. The conditions under which freedom of contract thrives as an efficient means of regulating agreements are often absent, given asymmetries of information, bargaining power and governmental regulatory influence between business and other contracting parties.[146] The harmful effects of corporate decisions and actions need to extend beyond what one company does in one small locality to attract legislative attention, if the priorities and politics of legislative reform even allow room for it.[147] Problems of collective action by citizens to enforce legislative change also intrude, as does the inevitable time-lag between the build-up of mass market problems or harmful corporate effects and the correlative opportunities for legislative correction.[148] Many of the difficulties of legislating morality apply to legislating CSR too. The most effective laws still fail to cover some undesired conduct because their underinclusion cannot be avoided, except at the expense of correlative overdeterring of acceptable conduct.[149] What some commentators view as gaps or inefficiencies in the law's protection of corporate and shareholder interests, such as the leeways of discretion allowed to company directors in making business judgments, are seen by others as inherently worthwhile, or at least tolerable given the costs and other problems involved in greater monitoring and review of boardroom decisions by courts.[150]

Considered from global and systemic perspectives, governance and regulatory 'gaps' in protection of human rights worldwide reinforce the limits of law as an instrument of regulation.[151] The limits of law for CSR also relate to regulation beyond law. While corporate law until the recent past might conventionally be seen as 'a one-dimensional body of law concerned with regulating the interests of investors, managers, and directors', the evolution of wider corporate regulation promises to 'transform this body of law into an emerging law of corporate governance, which seeks to integrate the policies and concerns of broad areas of regulation into corporate law', and which also 'involves using law to reconfigure the space within which directors and managers make decisions for their corporations', according to some corporate regulatory scholars today.[152] Largely, this realization is still to percolate through corporate law and its reform across many countries. This too is part of a grand global CSR project for the 21st century, in ways explored throughout this book.

In addition to accepting legally mandated corporate obligations, market influences and business ethics as important constraints on corporate behaviour in their own right, we need to see them also as paradigmatic manifestations of wider regulatory, economic and socio-ethical systemic influences that work in combination to produce socially responsible business orientations and behaviour. As the UNSRSG reminds us in the human rights context, for example, the task of setting the respective responsibilities of nation-states and corporations for human rights also requires an awareness that 'companies are constrained not only by legal standards but also by social norms and moral considerations' (i.e. 'what companies must do, what their internal and external stakeholders expect of them and what is desirable'), and that each of these sources of standards to which business responds 'has a very different basis in the fabric of society, exhibits distinct operating modes and is responsive to different incentive and disincentive mechanisms'.[153]

Just as corporate responsibility must be accepted and internalized organizationally

beyond merely rule-compliance, and not treated simply as a matter for external imposition through regulatory or market control, so too must the goals of corporate and
shareholder wealth-generation be positioned within a wider justification of corporate
purposes. 'It is certainly legitimate to wish to protect the integrity of goal-oriented corporate activity in the sphere of productive and economic wealth-creation', according to
corporate regulatory theorist Dr Christine Parker's analysis of 'the open corporation'
in the new regulatory state, '(b)ut the inevitable interaction of any organization with its
environment (human, social, physical and political) also makes it legitimate to ask how
the corporation can be made responsible for those interactions in the sphere of human,
social, environmental and political justice'.[154]

CONCLUDING REMARKS – THIS BOOK IN A NUTSHELL

Accordingly, we need a framework for understanding and perhaps even recasting the
nature and place of CSR in the 21st century, the concepts and elements of CSR, the
contemporary architecture and trends surrounding CSR, and the relation of CSR to
the standpoints and outcomes of different theories and models of corporate responsibility and governance. This theoretical and conceptual foundation occupies the chapters in
the first part of this book. It is necessary groundwork for the rich variety of CSR actors
engaged in the work of exploring the justifications, mechanisms and impact of CSR.

Assisted by this foundation, we can then map the key ways in which the institutions
and mechanisms of government and law interact with CSR, the main options for making
corporate law and corporate regulatory systems more CSR-sensitive, and the implications of the CSR-related changes in UK corporate law as a landmark 21st century experi-
mental model of CSR-sensitive regulation. This work occupies the chapters in the second
part of this book.

Finally, in light of that foundation, we can explore more fully some of the toughest
contemporary challenges of CSR for various CSR actors, informed by the latest analyses
and developments worldwide. Complementing the mapping of governmental, regulatory
and legal interactions with CSR, the work in the last part of this book commences with a
map of key frameworks for business engagement with CSR. Attention then focuses upon
business and human rights as one of the greatest present and future areas of global CSR
attention, especially in light of the ground-breaking work by the UNSRSG in the wake
of the draft UN Norms on the Responsibilities of Transnational Corporations and Other
Business Enterprises with Regard to Human Rights (UN Norms). Finally, in light of the
crucial impact of corporate law and regulation upon what corporate actors can do in
pursuing CSR's potential, the last chapter of this book explores incremental and design-
level reforms to sensitize corporate law, regulation and practice more fully to CSR's 21st
century concerns, and crystallizes a future research agenda for CSR.

NOTES

1. Zerk, 2006: 23.
2. Donaldson, 2005: 3.

3. On the evolution of the CSR movement see: Zerk, 2006: 15–29; and Campbell, 2007: 536–537.
4. For more on mass movements in this and related contexts see Braithwaite and Drahos, 2000.
5. Reich, 2007.
6. Davis et al, 2006.
7. Brugmann and Prahalad, 2007.
8. Ruggie, 2009: [3] and [25].
9. Franklin, 2008: 3.
10. *Louis K. Liggett Co v Lee*, 288 US 517 (1933), 564–565, 567.
11. Mitchell, 2001: 94.
12. Drutman and Cray, 2004: 131.
13. Bakan, 2005: 28, 60.
14. Ibid.: 70.
15. Twining, 2000: 124.
16. Madsen, 2008: 841–842.
17. Mickelthwait and Wooldridge, 2005: xv.
18. Lumsden and Fridman, 2007: 148.
19. Madsen, 2008: 842.
20. Ruggie, 2004: 500.
21. Ibid.: 511–514.
22. Mickelthwait and Wooldridge, 2005: 54.
23. CDCAC, 2002: 3.
24. *The Economist*, 2008: 22.
25. Ibid.: 6 and 8.
26. Blair, 2004: 184.
27. Frances, 2008: 98.
28. Ward, 2001: 1.
29. Whitman et al, 2008.
30. On these different forms of capitalism see Braithwaite and Drahos, 2000.
31. Eells, 1962: 11; quoted in Bottomley, 1997.
32. Bernstein and Cashore, 2007: 355–362.
33. E.g. the UN Global Compact, UN Millennium Development Goals, UN Principles for SRI, UN Environmental Programme Finance Initiative, and reports of the UN Special Representative on Human Rights and TNCs and Other Business Enterprises.
34. E.g. the OECD Guidelines for MNEs, OECD Risk Awareness Tool for MNEs in Weak Governance Zones, OECD Policy Framework for Investment, OECD Declaration on International Investment and MNEs, OECD Principles of Corporate Governance, and OECD/World Bank Regional Corporate Governance Roundtables.
35. E.g. ILO Tripartite Declaration of Principles Concerning MNEs and Social Policy.
36. E.g. the G8-initiated Dialogue between G8 member countries and major emerging economies on CSR principles and related international economic and investment challenges.
37. At 18 and 21.
38. Lydenberg and Grace, 2008.
39. Armour et al, 2003: 531.
40. Hansmann, 2005.
41. E.g. Bebchuk, 2005; cf Stout, 2007.
42. E.g. Coffee, 2006.
43. E.g. Greenfield, 2006; and Mitchell, 2001.
44. E.g. Reich, 2007.
45. Bratton and Wachter, 2007: 58–60.
46. Dine, 2000: 3–4.
47. Dine, 2005: 268.
48. Allen Consulting Group, 2008.
49. The author gratefully acknowledges discussions with Bob Hinkley about systemic perspectives on corporate responsibility and governance.
50. On the notion of business enterprises as social sub-systems which reflexively engage with other social sub-systems see Parker, 2002: 297.
51. Guy, 2008: 19.
52. Rudd, 2008: 8.
53. Ibid.: 8.
54. Obama, 2006: 150, 152.
55. Hewson, 2008: 66.

56. Ibid.: 66.
57. Sherry, 2008.
58. Sherry, 2009a.
59. Ibid.
60. Shergold, 2009: 10, 13–15, and 17.
61. E.g. Caulkin, 2009; and Porritt, 2009.
62. Ruggie, 2009: [11] and [117]-[120].
63. G8 Summit, 2007: 4, 7.
64. Ibid.: 36–37.
65. Hohnen, 2007a.
66. G8 Summit Declaration, 2007: 7–8.
67. G8, 2008: [9].
68. G20, 2009: [14]; emphasis added.
69. E.g. Ward, 2008: 15.
70. See Ch 8.
71. Bielak et al, 2007.
72. ICAA, 2008: 7.
73. Anderson and Cavanagh, 1996, cited in Freehills, 2005.
74. Orts, 2002: 556–557.
75. Ruggie, 2007: 6; and Ward, 2001: 1.
76. These statistics are cited in Canadian Democracy and Corporate Accountability Commission, 2002: 2.
77. BITF, 2000: 5.
78. KPMG, 2005.
79. UNEP FI AMWG, 2005: 23–27.
80. Sherry, 2008.
81. UNEP FI AMWG, 2005: 13; emphasis added.
82. Hopkins, 2004: 4.
83. Ridehalgh and Petersen, 2007: 63.
84. Sherry, 2008.
85. Deloitte, 2007, as reported in 'Many Firm Boards are in the Dark: Survey', *The Age*, 23 May 2007, and 'Soft Measure Predict Corporate Health', *The Australian Financial Review*, 25 May 2007.
86. Bielak et al, 2007.
87. Deloitte, 2007.
88. Dahl, 2000: 179.
89. Wheeler, 2002: 164.
90. Ibid.: 153.
91. Bottomley, 1997: 6.
92. Bratton and Wachter, 2007: 53–54.
93. Mitchell et al, 2005: 15–16.
94. For related discussion of different schools of thought on CSR see Zerk, 2006: 16–17.
95. Dunfee, 1999: 135.
96. Sen, 2000: 270.
97. Sampford and Berry, 2004.
98. Dine, 2005: 269.
99. Bottomley, 2007: 13.
100. Sampford and Berry, 2004.
101. Bottomley, 2007: 176; and Lee, 2006: 586.
102. Dunfee, 1999: 132.
103. Ibid.: 132.
104. Friedman, 2002: 133.
105. Blair, 2004: 184.
106. Parkinson, 1993: 79; quoted in CAMAC, 2006: 54.
107. Dunfee, 1999: 138.
108. Wallman, 1991: 170; and Blair, 2004: 179; both cited and quoted in Clarke, 2004: 7–8.
109. Clarke, 2005: 7–8.
110. Elhauge, 2005: 771.
111. Ibid.: 772.
112. Dunfee, 1999: 130.
113. CAMAC, 2006: 97.
114. Bottomley, 1997.
115. Austin et al, 2005: [1.41].

116. E.g. Zerk, 2006: 16; and Dine, 2005: Ch 2.
117. Parkinson, 1993: 323; and Carrigan, 2002: 215 and 220–226.
118. *The Economist*, 2008: 8–9.
119. 'Tsunami: The Backlash', *The Age*, 12 February 2005.
120. Similar legal arguments are used against political donations by corporations: see Ramsay et al, 2001.
121. Parkinson, 1993: 304.
122. OECD, 2004: Part Two, IV(A).
123. Hansmann, 2005.
124. Cane, 2003: 30.
125. Ibid.
126. Ward et al, 2007: 1; original emphasis.
127. Parker, 2002: 27.
128. Ribstein, 2005: 369.
129. Cane, 2003: 30.
130. On legal, economic, and moral sanctions operating upon corporate actors see Elhauge, 2005.
131. Nonet and Selznick, 1978: 117. For a related account of reflexive corporate self-regulation, see Parker, 2002.
132. Parker, 2007: 213.
133. Nonet and Selznick, 1978: 80–81.
134. Parker, 2002: 298; and Parker, 2007: 213–214, quoting Selznick, 2002: 101–102.
135. Braithwaite and Drahos, 2000: 168–169.
136. On these points and examples about continuous improvement and rule compliance see Braithwaite and Drahos, 2000: 521–522.
137. For further discussion of principle-based CSR framework and regulations see Ch 2.
138. AS 8003, section 2.6.
139. SA8000: [9.1].
140. BITF, 2000: 7.
141. E.g. AICD, 2003: 17.
142. See, for example, the connection between corporate responsibility and continuous improvement highlighted in Ruggie, 2008a: [63].
143. Scott, 2008: 181–182.
144. Ward, 2008: 18–19.
145. Villiers, 2008: 93.
146. Mitchell, 2001: 59–60.
147. Ibid.: 59-60; and Parkinson, 1993: 323–324.
148. Parkinson, 1993: 321, 323–325.
149. Elhauge, 2005: 740.
150. Ibid.; and Lee, 2006.
151. Ruggie, 2008a: [3], [11]–[16].
152. Corbett and Bottomley, 2004: 81.
153. E/CN.4/2006/97, [70].
154. Parker, 2002: 6.

2. Concepts and elements of corporate social responsibility

DEFINING AND ANALYSING CORPORATE SOCIAL RESPONSIBILITY

> The debate around the role of corporations in the community versus their role in maximising shareholder profits seems to fire up again and again. What surprises me is that a debate exists at all. The business case for corporate social responsibility is clear . . . (C)orporate social responsibility isn't a case of a stockholder versus stakeholder argument, but is a critical part of maximising shareholder returns. Simply, corporate social responsibility is in the best interests of our shareholders and is fundamental to profit creation and sustainability.
>
> – BHP Billiton CEO, Chip Goodyear[1]

The Meaning of 'Corporate Social Responsibility'

The house of CSR has many rooms in the 21st century. The task of defining CSR is made more difficult by mass confusion and disagreement worldwide about what counts as CSR, what responsibilities it embraces, what justifications exist for CSR, and whether the idea of corporations having any kind of societal responsibility at all even makes sense.[2] CSR has many different definitions, grounded in many different standpoints from which it can be approached. No consensus yet exists worldwide about an appropriate taxonomy for CSR, let alone its main forms and ends. 'Given the diversity of terms deployed to cover the various ethical issues relating to business, it is impossible to find a meaning that will accommodate even the majority of actual uses of the term, "CSR", let alone its increasingly popular surrogate "corporate sustainability"', suggests legal philosopher and CSR scholar, Professor Tom Campbell.[3] CSR is drenched in alternate notions of 'meeting societal preconditions for business', 'building essential social infrastructure', 'giving back to host communities', 'managing business drivers and risks', 'creating business value', 'holding business accountable' and 'sharing collective responsibility'. *The Economist*'s 2008 report on CSR, for example, says that it is 'made up of three broad layers, one on top of the other', devoted respectively to CSR as 'traditional corporate philanthropy', CSR as 'a branch of risk management', and CSR as an opportunity-based enhancement of business value and competitive advantage.[4]

Classical attempts to define CSR are packed with notions of voluntarism, social altruism and profit-sacrificing, as in its use 'to denote the obligations and inclinations, if any, of corporations organized for profit, voluntarily to pursue social ends that conflict with the presumptive shareholder desire to maximize profit'.[5] Yet, this risks making CSR marginal to core corporate concerns, and framing it in opposition to corporate profit-making and shareholder wealth-generation. Alternative formulations embrace the full gamut of CSR's profit-enhancing and profit-sacrificing forms. For example, Professor Campbell views CSR as encompassing 'those obligations (social or legal) which concern the major actual and possible social impact of the activities of the corporation in question, whether or not these activities are intended or do in fact promote the profitability of the particular corporation', in a way that distinguishes between 'corporate philanthropy' (i.e. corporate humanitarianism that is not central to core business), 'corporate business responsibility' towards shareholders and free-market competition, and 'corporate social responsibility' (i.e. obligations arising from the consequences of business activity).[6]

This account of CSR includes the two limbs of 'instrumental CSR' (which is pursued for business profitability) and 'intrinsic CSR' (which is pursued regardless of its connection to business profitability).[7] Such definitional nuances are the gateway to important questions in delineating corporate responsibilities towards groups and communities beyond shareholders, justifying corporate profitability by reference to its underlying socio-ethical utility, and recognizing the limits of a conception of CSR grounded solely in the norms and values of open market competition.[8]

Debates about the meaning of CSR therefore have significance beyond the obvious benefit of definitional clarity. Fuzzy or unsophisticated thinking about CSR's characteristics and worth simply legitimizes 'a very limited form of CSR that amounts to little more than intelligent business practice that enhances long-term rather than short-term profitability, to the virtual exclusion of responsibilities that are not justifiable in terms of the economic interests of the corporation in question', according to Professor Campbell.[9] The consequential misgrounding of CSR 'threatens the credibility of CSR programmes and impedes the articulation and implementation of CSR policies within business, government and civil society', argues Campbell.[10] Nor is this the only emasculation that CSR faces. 'Rather than developing a truly value-driven corporate culture, which would include leadership, innovation and staff happiness as well as profits, business has coopted the language of corporate social responsibility to allow it to continue to concentrate almost single-mindedly on the goal of maximising profits', argues social enterprise advocate, Nic Frances.[11] In turn, the misalignment between corporate PR and CSR rhetoric, on one hand, and substantive CSR outcomes and meaningful CSR inculcation, on the other, has societal as well as organizational ramifications. In short, the result is that no legislator, policy-maker, law reformer, official regulator, corporate executive, business adviser or community partner who is confronted with CSR issues at work can completely escape the need to engage with their normative justifications as well as their instrumental implementation.

The different descriptions of different aspects of CSR have their own linguistic nuances, focal points and boundaries of concern. In some contexts, 'corporate social responsibility' is used interchangeably with terms like 'corporate citizenship', 'responsible business', 'corporate sustainability', 'corporate social responsiveness', 'corporate social initiatives', 'corporate community investment' and 'triple bottom line' (TBL) responsibility.[12] The Corporate Social Responsibility Initiative at the John F Kennedy School of Government at Harvard University highlights the common thread running through all such terms of a contemporary enhancement of the societal roles and engagements expected of business, and defines 'corporate social responsibility' accordingly.[13] Most recently, terms like 'responsible business' are also appropriated for party-political purposes, as in the use of that term by the UK Conservative Party Working Group on Responsible Business to describe 'the process through which companies seek to maximise their positive impact on society and minimise their negative impact'.[14]

In the 21st century, CSR and its related terms all reflect not just a broadening of criteria for business success to embrace social and environmental factors as well as economic ones, but also an attempt to relate all of these factors to how businesses individually and collectively can best develop business models and business value propositions in market economies to both business and societal advantage.[15] In an effort to reorient traditional thinking about the financial bottom line for business, sustainability expert John Elkington famously describes a 'triple bottom line' for business in which considerations of 'economic prosperity', 'environmental quality' and 'social justice' combine and filter their way into the overall calculus for business.[16] Elkington's classic description of the interfaces between social, environmental and economic bottom lines in business 'shear zones' illustrates, for example, how social and economic factors affect business consideration of the social impact of a proposed economic investment, with issues concerning business ethics, human rights and stakeholder engagement arising in the 'shear zone' between those social and economic bottom lines.[17]

As CSR is neither a one-dimensional notion nor a monolithically uniform one, some commentators characterize CSR's different dimensions in terms of 'value-driven CSR', 'stakeholder-driven CSR' and 'performance-driven CSR'.[18] Some avoid the trap of one-dimensional CSR analysis by refusing to treat social, environmental and other factors as factors in opposition to financial and economic considerations, focusing instead on the interactions between the different factors in making corporate decisions. Others argue that non-economic factors like social and environmental considerations can be measured and accommodated within economic analysis itself, given that a broader use of economic analysis incorporates all relevant interests that affect business decision-making, rather than requiring a choice between a narrowly conceived single bottom line of economic concerns, on one hand, and a triple bottom line of economic, social and environmental concerns, on the other.[19]

Some scholars and commentators contrast two or more CSR-related concepts, in terms that view 'corporate citizenship', for example, as something different from basic CSR, in its holistic approach to integrating societal and stakeholder engagement within standard business operations.[20] 'Corporate citizenship means understanding and managing a company's influence on society and all its stakeholders [and] integrates social, ethical, environmental, economic and philanthropic values in the core decision-making processes of a business', according to one researcher of CSR policy.[21] In this wider sense, corporate citizenship amounts to 'business taking greater account of its social, environmental and financial footprints', in the words of one author.[22] 'Corporate citizenship, as a progression from CSR, is therefore seen as a fuller understanding of the role of business in society', in the words of others.[23] Australian-based US law firm partner and originator of a well-known code for corporate citizenship, Robert Hinkley, carefully contrasts corporate citizenship and CSR in terms that are anchored in minimizing lawful but still socially harmful corporate activity:[24]

Citizenship is different from corporate social responsibility. CSR occurs when, in an effort to protect the public interest, a company does more than the law requires. As a company becomes more socially responsible, its behaviour approaches corporate citizenship . . . The extent to which a company externalizes costs that damage the public interest can be described as a company's citizenship gap. When operating in the citizenship gap, companies act legally (and maybe even socially responsibly), but they are not being good citizens. The consequences of the citizenship gap can be seen wherever legal behaviour results in significant damage to the public interest, including global warming, Third World sweatshops and millions of people succumbing prematurely every year from tobacco.

Using CSR as a monolithic description for different forms of business–society engagement is a confusing 'oversimplification' for what should be recognized as a discrete series of related concepts, according to the Executive Chair of the World Economic Forum, Klaus Schwab.[25] 'Five core concepts – corporate governance, corporate philanthropy, corporate social responsibility, corporate social entrepreneurship, and global corporate citizenship – define the different types of business engagement', argues Schwab.[26] In short, 21st century CSR and its related concepts are packed with multiple elements and layers of meaning.

Corporate Social Responsibility's Elements, Distinctions and Criticisms

> Corporate social responsibility is a con job [and] largely all talk . . . Call yourself a stakeholder and corporate social responsibility says you get a foot in the boardroom door, to be treated no differently from a shareholder. While some activists push it for altruistic reasons, sincerely believing it's the role of business to engineer a better society, it's also a neat trick used by other NGOs as old-fashioned blackmail, the idea being that if a corporation fails to embrace social responsibility by taking up their particular agenda, then, by default, that company must be a socially irresponsible corporate citizen . . . The fundamental flaw with corporate social responsibility, and why it is a backward step, is the underlying premise that capitalism and companies have something to be embarrassed about, that they must justify their existence by going in search of some higher moral purpose.
>
> – Journalist and columnist, Janet Albrechtsen, *The Australian*[27]

Based on the analysis so far, it is clear that the meaning of CSR is standpoint-dependent, context-sensitive and multi-textured. Definitions of CSR can also be jurisdiction-orientated. What CSR means in the context of developed economies differs from its primary focus for developing economies, just as its rationale from a business perspective often differs from how governments and communities view CSR.[28]

Some critics denounce CSR fundamentally on the definitional basis that it has no fixed substantive meaning, but rather serves as a meaningless catch-cry. 'Corporate social responsibility is a political ideology that wants private interest to be subsumed by public interests, narrowly defined', according to former politician and contemporary CSR commentator Gary Johns, who adds that 'CSR is a construct of non-owner, non-contract and non-government interests to regulate corporations' and that 'CSR provides no guide as to how to achieve the right balance [and] at worst it provides a biased guide'.[29] This dovetails with criticisms of CSR as a cloak for an underlying and usually anti-business social reform agenda, in which business is pressured to take on social responsibilities beyond a core of economic, legal and contractual relations between corporations and their managers and investors.

Some people challenge the suitability of each element of the compound phrase, 'corporate social responsibility'.[30] Why should this form of responsibility be limited to *corporate* entities and not other public and private entities, why should it be limited to *social* responsibility and not other responsibilities too, and why should it be confined to corporate *responsibility* instead of wider notions of corporate citizenship and responsiveness to societal conditions?, they ask. Similarly, these compound elements have their own layers of meaning. 'Corporate *social* responsibility', for example, can direct us towards debates about society as the ultimate beneficiary of corporate responsibility, contrasts between legally mandated and voluntary socio-ethical responsibilities of corporations, and substantive differences in the orientation and content of corporate obligations owed to shareholders and other stakeholders.[31] Conversely, in Professor Friedrich Hayek's eyes, the term 'social' is unacceptably open-ended as a designator of true corporate responsibilities. 'The range of such purposes which might come to be regarded as legitimate objects of corporation expenditure is very wide: political, charitable, educational, and in fact everything which can be brought under the vague and almost meaningless term social', he says.[32]

Corporate social responsibility clearly relates to social responsibility as a whole too. Social responsibility, accountability and responsiveness are different strands of an overall system of intertwined organizational, societal and even global relations. Hence, on one view, 'social responsibility' is pregnant with notions of voluntary individualized obligations of a social kind; 'social accountability' suggests a more formal notion of responsibility, in which someone is held answerable to someone else in some way for their actions; and 'social responsiveness' takes a more functional and systemic approach of securing responsiveness to changing societal dynamics, without necessarily pre-determining a fixed set of desirable societal outcomes for such responsiveness.[33] As we shall see, these different strands are evident, for example, in CSR's tensions between mandatory and voluntary CSR standards, on one hand, and between legally enforceable responsibility and wider forms of corporate responsiveness, on the other.

As discussed in Chapter 1, CSR is sometimes contrasted with the minimum requirements of corporate responsibility mandated by law. 'A mechanism for entities to *voluntarily* integrate social and environmental concerns into their operations and their interaction with their stakeholders, which are over and above the entity's *legal* responsibilities' is how Standards Australia defines CSR in the relevant Australian Standard on this topic, for example.[34] Similarly, according to the European Commission, 'CSR is a concept whereby companies integrate social and environmental concerns in their business operations and in their interaction with their stakeholders on a *voluntary* basis . . . as they are increasingly aware that responsible behaviour leads to sustainable business success'.[35]

The presumed distinction between a core of corporate responsibility (CR) and the add-on penumbra of corporate responsibility associated with CSR is another feature in the definitional debates surrounding CSR. In a Working Paper on CSR infrastructure for Harvard University's John F. Kennedy School of Government, Sandra Waddock distinguishes 'the impacts that a company's strategies and operating practices have on its stakeholders and the natural environment' (i.e. CR) from 'those activities that companies undertake to directly benefit society' (i.e. CSR).[36]

Another grand distinction in CSR thinking concerns the difference between making business accountable through CSR processes and making business responsible for CSR outcomes. Introducing CSR-related elements into the *processes* of corporate life can be done in ways that serve to condition corporate power, without necessarily bogging down in controversies about substantive CSR public policy goals and outcomes.[37] Still, while some definitions of CSR are more process-orientated than outcome-focused or value-based, connections exist between these elements too. For example, a major study of public sector roles in CSR for the World Bank defines CSR as follows:[38]

> Corporate social responsibility is at heart a process of managing the costs and benefits of business activity to both internal (workers, shareholders, investors) and external (institutions of public governance, community members, civil society groups, other enterprises) stakeholders. Setting the boundaries for how those costs and benefits are managed is partly a question of business policy and strategy and partly a question of public governance.

Connecting the value-based outcomes of public governance concerned with corporate responsibility and sustainability to the corporate governance of individual companies also forms a large part of contemporary CSR meta-regulation.[39] Building upon this discussion of CSR-related definitions as well as the structure of regulatory scholar Professor Julia Black's tabular representation of the equally amorphous concept of 'regulation',[40] we can crystallize some of CSR's possible meanings, actors, manifestations, and tools in the form outlined in Table 2.1.

Towards Definitional Common Ground

In the end, the absence of a universally agreed meaning for CSR and the multiplicity of contexts and applications for CSR simply highlight the futility of resting upon preferred definitions of CSR in the abstract, except for their analytical use in conceptually identifying, demarcating or connecting important elements associated with CSR. Indeed, the open-endedness of CSR's meanings is both a strength and a weakness, depending upon the user's standpoint and the particular need at stake. 'There are so many different groups with different agendas and concepts claiming to speak in the name of "Corporate Social Responsibility" that the only common denominator is a warm cuddly glow', warns former Australian National Companies and Securities Commission chairman, Henry Bosch AO, in his major criticism of CSR.[41] 'The Enron statement on Corporate Social Responsibility was one of the best published by any company but it turned out to have little connection with reality', he adds.[42]

Yet, in the eyes of others, this rich field of optional CSR meanings and applications is an important organizational and boardroom mind-focusing feature in setting corporate strategy about each company's particular way of engaging in business–society relations. 'It is precisely because social responsibility is a woolly term, that it is important for boards to decide what social policies their companies should follow – and companies

Table 2.1 Corporate social responsibility matrix

(1) Meanings: What is corporate social responsibility?	(2) Actors: Who regulates, practices, or engages in it?	(3) Areas: To what areas of activity does it relate?	(4) Forms: What forms does it take?	(5) Standards: What standards (if any) apply to it?	(6) Outcomes: Who or what is affected by it?	(7) Tools: What tools (if any) are necessary and available for it?
An uncertain or meaningless concept A notion embracing or relating to 'corporate citizenship', 'responsible business', 'corporate sustainability', 'sustainable development', and 'triple bottom line' accountability An anti-business ideological position A company's voluntary socio-ethical, economic, and environmental contributions	Global institutions and organs of governance Supra-national & transnational governance networks Governments & official regulators Multi-stakeholder CSR networks and other standard-setting initiatives Non-government organizations (NGOs) & actors	Governance needs (e.g. social prosperity, peace & security, responsible power-wielding) Governance problems (e.g. disaster assistance, peace & security, poverty reduction, climate change, sustainable development) Official regulation & other forms of regulation (e.g. self-regulation, co-regulation, risk–based regulation,	Governmental and supra-governmental CSR policy frameworks CSR employee programmes: Employees' pro bono work, paid volunteering, & community secondments Corporate community investment: – Philanthropy – Charity – Sponsorship – Advocacy Social Alliances/ Partnerships: – Public– private commercial partnerships	Corporate laws: – Corporate obligations/ liabilities – Directors' duties/ defences – Business judgment rule – Business disclosure/ reporting – Management of business drivers and risks – Stakeholder protection (e.g. employees, creditors) – Third party effects (e.g. human rights, environmental protection, climate change) – Investment considerations (e.g. SRI disclosure)	Global, transnational, regional, national and sub–national governance Systems of government Systems of law & regulation (e.g. corporate regulatory systems) Official regulators (e.g. official corporate regulators) Social, economic and environmental systems Business organizations Corporate spheres of influence and operations (e.g. business impact on home and host	Policy and regulatory justifications for CSR (e.g. CSR–related theories and models) Codes of responsibility and governance: – E.g. Global Compact – E.g. OECD Guidelines/ principles (ie international) – E.g. revised ASX CGC principles (ie national) Enforcement Mechanisms – 'Hard' and 'soft' regulatory incentives/ sanctions – Others Reporting frameworks & guidelines: – E.g. Global Reporting Initiative (GRI) Sustainability Reporting Guidelines (G3) Governmental and business CSR frameworks and tools (e.g. whole–of–government CSR policies) Accounting/auditing, rating, certification, & verification tools

A cost of 'doing business' to enhance shareholder gain

An emerging element in business strategizing, risk assessment, and reporting

A core component of mainstream corporate responsibility (CR)

A key component of interconnected systems of governance, regulation, and responsibility

Others

Business & industry groups & organizations

Global CSR movement and related mass movements

Markets

Communities and societies

Others

meta–regulation)

Business–society relations

Corporate governance arrangements

Others

– Cross–sectoral partnerships for public benefit

Multi–stakeholder CSR initiatives

Others

– Corporate governance requirements
– Others

Non–corporate laws:
– Employment, insolvency, workplace, environmental, and other laws

Other official regulation:
– Official corporate governance codes
– Stock exchange listing rules (e.g. stakeholder engagement, risk management, reporting)
– Corporate regulatory rulings & guidelines (eg investment product SRI disclosure guidelines)

Multi–stakeholder CSR standard–setting

Others

communities of operation)

NGOs, mass movements, civil society

Others

– Management and certification systems (e.g. SA8000, AA1000)
– Rating indices (e.g. Dow Jones Sustainability Index, FTSE4 Good Index series, and Good Reputation Index (Australia))
– Investment decision–making guidelines (e.g. SRI and ESG guidelines)

International agreements & instruments
– E.g. human rights conditions and international trade agreements

Professional business standards
– E.g. accounting, auditing, valuation, and other CSR–related standards

Planning documentation
– CSR plans and policies
– Human rights impact and management plans
Others

have social policies, whether or not they are thought through deliberately', counters experienced corporate chairman, board member and corporate governance leader, Sir Adrian Cadbury.[43] 'Companies are called upon to address hundreds of social issues, but only a few represent opportunities to make a real difference to society or to confer a competitive advantage', add Michael Porter and Mark Kramer in their award-winning *Harvard Business Review* article on CSR.[44]

In the end, despite the nuanced differences in multiple definitions of CSR – all from their own angle, and with their own purpose and surrounding context – some common elements emerge. The European Commission attempts to capture them in its landmark 2002 Communication on CSR, linking CSR to notions of business voluntariness, sustainability, and corporate governance:[45]

> Despite the wide spectrum of approaches to CSR, there is large consensus on its main features:
> – CSR is behavior by businesses over and above legal requirements, voluntarily adopted because businesses deem it to be in their long-term interest;
> – CSR is intrinsically linked to the concept of sustainable development: businesses need to integrate the economic, social and environmental impact in their operations;
> – CSR is not an optional 'add-on' to business core activities – but about the way in which businesses are managed.

Of course, each of these CSR elements still generates its own arguments and has its own limits. For example, 'adding the criterion of voluntariness to our definition of "CSR" does not provide a workable basis for addressing questions about how well the different modes of regulation promote the goals of CSR for normative purposes', argues Professor Campbell.[46] Tying CSR's core nature to its essential voluntariness rests upon a limited conception of corporate legal responsibility (as discussed in Chapter 1) and exposes it to flaws in the dichotomy of mandatory–voluntary standards. Making CSR mainstream rather than marginal for business management still leaves questions about the orientation of that management towards shareholder-based and other societal functions. In short, even a consensus about CSR built around the core elements of voluntariness, sustainable development and business integration serves as only a starting point for further exploration of CSR for the 21st century.

Corporate Shareholders, Stakeholders and Other Constituencies

Shareholders versus other stakeholders
Debates about CSR inevitably require stances one way or another on how and why the interests of corporate shareholders and other corporate stakeholders matter. The question of defining a corporation's stakeholders is integrally connected to the great corporate questions of whose interests a corporation serves, and to whom it is accountable in some way. Professor Hayek starkly outlined the possibilities in 1960: '(t)here are four groups on whose behalf it might be claimed that the corporations ought to be run in their interest: management, labor, stockholders, and "the public" at large'.[47] The push for political intervention and civic engagement in corporate regulation and activity is 'manifested increasingly through the growing debate on the "shareholder/stakeholder" balance in corporate governance', which is further evidence that 'stakeholders will have greater powers

Rather than continuing to stress the virtues of stakeholder responsibility as an end itself, what needs to be made clear is that recognising and taking into account various stakeholder interests is actually a means to an end – that end being long-term sustainable growth for the company.

By changing our perspective slightly to focus on what stakeholders can do for the corporation, rather than adopting a narrow approach of considering how corporations are or can be made responsible to stakeholders, what we arrive at is a meeting of the minds between those who emphasise the virtues of stakeholder dialogue and those who emphasise the rights of shareholders and the importance of concentrating on the company's bottom line.

– Corporate law and governance scholar and Principal of The Corporate Research Group, James McConvill[48]

over corporate direction-giving in the twenty-first century', predicts Bob Garratt in his best-selling work on corporate governance.[49]

So, one of the great conundrums of corporate responsibility and governance thinking is who counts as a corporation's key 'stakeholders'. The relative priority of those interests, their relation to each other, and their connection to a company's success in society all generate their own debates. Indeed, the wider the net of potential corporate stakeholders is cast, the more remote the connection between a company and its outlying stakeholders becomes, thereby limiting the usefulness of stakeholder-related notions in settling questions of corporate responsibility and governance. Still, identifying a company's stakeholders is an important starting point.

Corporate stakeholders are at least defined by their legitimate interest in the process and substance of corporate decisions and actions affecting them, as well as by their contribution to a company's success, however that success is defined in terms of a company's role in society.[50] The tension between these two facets is evident in McConvill's contrast above between making stakeholder interests serve corporate interests and alternatively making corporations responsible to stakeholders. Some corporate stakeholder definitions extend beyond the groups who might be regarded as contributing in some way to a particular company's success to include potential victims of corporate irresponsibility and others who might not necessarily make any kind of company-specific investment in a corporation. To use the description of Wharton's Professor Dunfee, an expansive concept of stakeholders 'emphasizes broader constituencies or stakeholders of the corporation – variously, bond holders, suppliers, distributors, creditors, local communities, consumers, users, state and federal governments, special interest groups, etc – and has even been extended by some to include a general obligation to act consistently with the general needs of society'.[51]

According to Professor Campbell, '(t)he stakeholder approach thus incorporates the full gamut of distributive claims from bare ownership rights to full welfare considerations'.[52] 'A corporate stakeholder can be defined as any person, group or organization that can place a claim on a company's attention, resources or output', argue Booz Allen Hamilton consultant Beth Kytle and Harvard University's Professor John Ruggie, writing from the perspective of social risks for corporations – a point of intersection between CSR and conventional risk management.[53] So, in general terms, 'stakeholders' are those persons or groups who are concerned or implicated in a company's affairs and impacts, including a company's shareholders as well as other corporate stakeholders.

This broad notion of corporate stakeholders is reflected in authoritative codes and guidelines. The Australian Standard, *Corporate Social Responsibility* (AS 8003), defines a company's 'stakeholders' as follows:[54]

> Stakeholders may include anyone who has more than a passing interest in the entity's activities. Typically, they would include:
>
> (a) Employees.
> (b) Outsourced workers.
> (c) Suppliers.
> (d) Shareholders (including institutional investors).
> (e) Communities within which the firm and its suppliers operate.
> (f) Customers.
> (g) Non-government agencies.
> (h) Governments (multiple levels).
> (i) Media.
> (j) Creditors.
> (k) Major donors.
> (l) Joint venture partners.

Similarly, as defined by a major Australian Government report on CSR in late 2006, the notion of stakeholders 'has no precise or commonly agreed meaning', and includes:[55]

- shareholders, who, unlike other stakeholders, have a direct equity interest in the company
- other persons with a financial interest in the company (financiers, suppliers and other creditors), or those in some other commercial legal relationship with the company (for instance, business partners)
- persons who are involved in some manner in the company's wealth creation (employees and consumers)
- anyone otherwise directly affected by a company's conduct (for instance, communities adjacent to a company's operations)
- pressure groups or NGOs, usually characterised as public interest bodies that espouse social goals relevant to the activities of companies.

Stakeholder groups are often associated with the community sector, in contrast with the governmental and business sectors. Described in 21st century CSR literature from a global perspective as 'transnational civil society organisations', these stakeholder organizations encompass 'self-organized advocacy groups that undertake voluntary collective action across state borders in pursuit of what they deem the wider public interest', with membership including 'transnational social movements, coalitions, and activist campaigns as well as formal non-government organizations'.[56] Their force as CSR actors stems alternatively from their technical expertise, moral authority and political legitimacy.[57] As explored later in this chapter, transnational civil society (TCS) plays a pivotal CSR role through participation in multi-stakeholder alliances and standard-setting initiatives, as part of the web of global CSR governance, regulation and responsibility in the 21st century.

In short, at least five different groups of basic stakeholders might be postulated, predicated upon major differences in the basis of their relations with the company: (a) the company's shareholders as a whole (including founding members, assignee shareholders, shareholding employees and directors, and perhaps even future shareholders); (b) other corporate insiders beyond shareholders who invest something of value in a corporation (e.g. non-shareholding corporate directors, managers and employees); (c) corporate outsiders whose relations with the company are based mainly or solely on contractual and other transactional arrangements (e.g. customers, creditors, financiers, advisers, supply and distribution chain members, etc); (d) stakeholders whose relations with the company are not governed to the same extent or at all by contractual and transactional arrangements, but who each play some part in societal regulation of business (e.g. local communities in which businesses operate, governmental regulators, non-governmental organizations (NGOs), and wider civil society); and (e) stakeholders who are affected in good or bad ways by corporate activity (e.g. victims of corporate irresponsibility), but who lack meaningful capacities or opportunities to regulate their relations with corporations.

The Evolving Significance of Corporate, Societal and Global 'Sustainability'

A sustainable company develops by taking into consideration the economic, social, and environmental dimensions of its activities. In this sense, economic and competitive success, as well as social legitimacy and an efficient use of natural resources are integrated into a broader company final objective. A sustainable company is therefore a responsible company, where *responsible* refers to the ability of firms to interact with and integrate the needs and requests of its social context.

– European CSR scholars Francesco Perrini, Stefano Pogutz, and Antonio Tencati[58]

Many companies worldwide now have what is variously described as a whole-of-organization CSR policy, corporate social charter, or corporate responsibility and sustainability policy. This development immediately raises questions about the connections between CSR and sustainability. The CSR reorientation of many businesses towards corporate responsibility and sustainability is due in no small part to 'a growing perception among enterprises that sustainable business success and shareholder value cannot be achieved solely through maximising short-term profits, but instead through market-oriented yet responsible behavior', according to the European Commission.[59]

The term 'sustainability' has more than one meaning. 'Sustainable development is development that meets the needs of the present without compromising the ability of future generations to meet their own needs', in the famous words of the Brundtland Commission.[60] In this era of climate change, 'sustainability' is often associated with the preconditions for sustainable communities, sustainable development and a sustainable planet. 'The new masters of the universe will devote a portion of their leadership energy and entrepreneurial zeal to social innovation, developing new solutions to the challenge of building an inclusive and sustainable [society]', argues former Secretary of the Department of Prime Minister and Cabinet in Australia, Professor Peter Shergold.[61]

However, 'sustainability' was associated initially with environmental and ecological sustainability, before being adapted or hijacked by business (depending on your perspective) in explaining what makes successful companies sustainable over time.[62] At the very least, it emphasizes the balance of financial and non-financial factors in corporate success. As stated by David Blood, former head of Goldman Sachs Asset Management and co-partner in an investment management firm orientated around sustainability investing with former US Vice-President and Nobel Peace Prize co-winner, Al Gore, 'leading CEOs are the ones who explicitly recognize that sustainability factors drive business strategy [and] understand the drivers of their business – both financial and non-financial',[63] thereby making the connection between long-term corporate value and sustainability investing.

In their work on transforming companies into 'triple bottom line businesses', Andrew Savitz and Karl Weber favour sustainability as a core concept over what they see as more confined concepts like 'business ethics' and even 'CSR', because of sustainability's capacity to embrace 'a wide array of business concerns about the natural environment, workers' rights, consumer protection, and corporate governance, as well as the impact of business behavior on broader social issues, such as hunger, poverty, education, healthcare, and human rights – and the relationship of all these to profit'.[64] On their definition of sustainability as applied to business, 'a sustainable corporation is one that creates profit for its shareholders while protecting the environment and improving the lives of those with whom it interacts [and] operates so that its business interests and the interests of the environment and society intersect'.[65] Such approaches give impetus to a holistic view of corporate responsibility and sustainability, from a combination of organizational and societal perspectives.

Corporate sustainability can also be counter-productive if it is misdirected. 'If a corporation sustains itself by extracting net wealth from society and transferring it to its shareholders or managers or others, then its operation should be stopped [because] some companies *should* fail', argues Boston College Law School's Professor Kent Greenfield.[66] In Greenfield's eyes, this is because the principle that 'a corporation that creates wealth for society must sustain itself over time in order to maximize its value to the society it serves' is itself predicated on the corporation actually enhancing societal well-being.[67] Where profit-driven shareholder wealth-maximization derives from rises in share market prices that depend to a significant degree upon externalization of business costs upon society, '(b)ecause information about the true extent of these costs is limited, the present market value of firms is not sufficiently discounted to reflect the long-term risks which corporate strategies create'.[68] Citing sustainable development's implications for business and society as one of the 21st century's greatest challenges, the Global Reporting Initiative's (GRI's) G3 Sustainability and Reporting Guidelines proceed to marry sustainability's business and societal dimensions in recognising that '(t)he urgency and magnitude of the risks and threats to our collective sustainability, alongside increasing choice and opportunities, will make transparency about economic, environmental, and social impacts a fundamental component in effective stakeholder relations, investment decisions, and other market relations'. All of this has implications for measuring, reporting and otherwise regulating the true and complete costs and benefits of corporate activity.

In 21st century CSR, the concerns of corporate, societal and global sustainability also reflect contemporary regulatory values and principles, including principles of transparency and precaution, amongst others.[69] 'Transparency is emerging as the triumphant principle in the globalization of companies and securities regulation', conclude Professors John Braithwaite and Peter Drahos in their ground-breaking global analysis of business regulation, given that '(t)he decisive regulatory idea is transparency, demanded of US securities markets by the SEC [and] transmitted by the New York Stock Exchange and US accounting firms as a global regulatory ideal when investment globalizes'.[70] At the same time, transparency is sometimes attacked as not being a neutral value in the era of neoliberal market regulatory politics.[71]

Historically, the link between transparency and accountability is apparent in exposure of corporate wrongdoing in CSR campaigns of the 1960s and 1970s against corporate production of napalm for wartime use, investment in apartheid South Africa, and harmful distribution of infant milk formula in developing countries.[72] In a famous example from their ground-breaking text, *The Economic Structure of Corporate Law*, Judge Frank Easterbrook and Professor Daniel Fischel argue from a 'corporate contracts'-based perspective that the *New York Times* could be justified in abandoning profit-making and embracing altruistic and community interests through newspaper publishing, if it disclosed that to its equity investors and other stockholders and secured their agreement.[73] Similarly, in a 21st century public debate with Milton Friedman about CSR, Whole Foods founder-CEO John Mackey denied that his company's commitment in its mission statement to donating 5 per cent of net profits to philanthropic causes, as unanimously approved by the original owners and known and accepted by subsequent investors, amounted to philanthropic 'theft' from the company's investors.[74] All of this is also explainable in terms of the principle of transparency. Of course, the consent of shareholders in a particular company to a given course of action is not necessarily a complete normative panacea, if this is contrary to the needs of an overall system based upon the social efficiency or utility of all companies in the market remaining true to the core imperative of optimizing corporate profitability.[75]

If corporations are a means to the end of overall societal well-being, even on shareholder-based accounts of ultimate corporate legitimacy, full and transparent assessment of corporate activity's costs as well as its benefits must be part of the equation. 'A company cannot be considered a success if the total social value it creates is less than the costs it forces society to bear', argues Professor Greenfield.[76] In highlighting 'the need for shareholders and other stakeholders to make better informed judgments on non-financial aspects of corporate performance', for example, Professor Simon Deakin foreshadows that '(o)ne way forward is to assist the creation of a market in information on how firms manage the creation of *stakeholder* value'.[77] This is simply one way in which different aspects of what might be characterized as an emerging market for corporate responsibility and sustainability cuts across traditional markets for corporate control, management expertise, business investment, workforce knowledge and labour, and products and services.

If practising business in socially and environmentally responsible ways is coming to be regarded as an important item of information that factors into investment decisions, for example, transparency demands that companies report meaningfully on this aspect of their business operations and strategy, just as it demands that published business claims about their corporate responsibility and sustainability should be verifiable. Combining the rise and dominance of transparency as one of the foundational regulatory values for corporate regulatory systems worldwide with the neo-classical economic call for rational decision-making based fully upon all relevant information,[78] we might look forward to a time when non-financial corporate performance drivers, socio-environmental costs of production, non-market conditions for economic prosperity, and other CSR-related 'inputs' and 'outputs' of corporate production are valued, measured and disclosed as completely as the financial dimensions of corporate planning, budgeting and accounting.

Like other foundational principles, the principle of precaution has multiple manifestations and levels of application. It assumes particular significance in the environmental domain, and also has special application to intergenerational equity, which requires stewardship of the world's resources and ecosystems so that their use and enjoyment today does not unduly prejudice future generations. In his call to arms on climate change, noted scientist and conservationist Professor Tim Flannery endorses a precautionary approach to dealing with climate change risks sooner rather than later. 'If humans pursue a business-as-usual course for the first half of this century, I believe the collapse of civilization due to climate change becomes inevitable', he warns.[79]

The precautionary principle even manifests itself in fundamental approaches to decision-making by corporate executives. US President Bill Clinton's former national economic adviser, Gene Sperling, describes this in terms of a 'discretionary principle' of responsibility, embodying a '"last resort" ethic':[80]

> We should expect our CEOs to follow an ethic of corporate responsibility, including what I would call the 'discretionary principle', meaning that when CEOs choose among a range of options or achieving efficiency and competitiveness, they should exercise every reasonable option that minimizes job loss and community devastation. Exercising the discretionary principle is not about whether a company chooses its workers over its share holders, or social responsibility over profit. It is about expecting business management faced with 'gray' choices and discretion among economically viable options to strive for the path that minimizes harm to workers and their communities.

Private equity transactions illustrate concerns about sustainable business value that have connections to principles of transparency and precaution too. Sometimes seen as 'the ugly new face of capitalism',[81] private equity buy-outs of publicly listed companies often fuel a public perception that 'private equity is all about buying undervalued companies, slashing costs, firing workers, spinning off divisions and then listing the company at an absurd profit before anyone realises that the company is not a sustainable long-term investment proposition'.[82] At the same time, such caricatures of private equity arguably ignore 'the longer term sustainability drivers of value across the economic, environmental and social dimensions', which mean that it is counter-productive for private equity owners to jeopardize the potential yield for their institutional investors 'by destroying the company because to gain a good price with a refloat they need a company that can maximize long term value'.[83] CSR concerns here include the transparency of corporate management and operations, value-enhancement of corporate debt and credit arrangements, treatment of a company's human capital, management of stakeholder relationships, maintenance of corporate employee and community investment programmes, and structuring of taxation and regulatory relief (e.g. tax deductibility of servicing business debt), especially in view of a typical medium-term window before a public company refloat.[84]

SYSTEMIC RELATIONS BETWEEN 'GOVERNANCE', 'REGULATION' AND 'RESPONSIBILITY'

'Trans-modal Governance'

Levels and meanings of governance

> Even as our world increases in complexity and interconnectedness, govern-ments in many regions are in retreat – practically, philosophically, and politi-cally – from some of their traditional social responsibilities. This is a natural outgrowth of the triumph of laissez-faire capitalism and the collapse of social-ism that occurred throughout Europe, Asia, and much of the developing world . . . Eager to provide an attractive climate for business, many countries are deregulating industries, privatizing businesses that were once government controlled, reducing trade restrictions, opening their borders, adopting regional or global rather than local or national standards, and shifting from the traditional command-and-control model of regulation to free-market mechanisms or jointly negotiated settlements between the public and private sectors . . . The shift in power from the public to the private sector means that societies at large will be looking to business to help solve social, environmental, and economic prob-lems that were once considered solely the province of government. These new pressures will be felt in every sector of the business world.
>
> – Sustainability experts Andrew Savitz and Karl Weber[85]

Having identified some key definitional debates surrounding CSR in its own right, we can begin to define the wider relation between CSR and its surrounding landscape. One major CSR-related meta-trend of 21st century relevance is the increasing interconnected-ness of systems of governance, responsibility and regulation. What is 'governance', and how does it relate to corporations and CSR? In particular, where does 'governance' fit within a framework of corporate responsiveness to systems of trans-modal governance, multi-order regulation and inter-related responsibility? At its most basic level, the notion of governance embraces how systems are constituted and operated. In this sense, govern-ance in the abstract is concerned broadly with 'the management of the course of events in a social system', from small groups, organizations and communities to global regulatory regimes and the world as a whole.[86]

'Governance, at whatever level of social organization it may take place, refers to con-ducting the public's business – to the constellation of authoritative rules, institutions, and practices by means of which any collectivity manages its affairs', at least in the context of global governance and international relations, according to Harvard's Professor John

Ruggie.[87] At both global and societal levels, it focuses upon 'the mechanisms (institutions, social norms, social practices)' through which social goods like 'democracy, honest and efficient government, political stability and the rule of law' are 'instantiated' in such systems.[88] Various governance systems containing 'a plurality of actors' interact with one another in a series of 'interconnected governance networks', employing multiple mechanisms for distributing, wielding and rendering accountable the exercise of power in society.[89] In this way, different sectoral entities and societal actors engage in the contests of authority and values directed towards social purposes and expectations in the public domain.[90]

Many global governance concerns are now best addressed through mechanisms of engagement between nation-states, business corporations and other organs of societal governance. Topping many people's lists of the world's greatest governance challenges of this kind are subjects like global warming and climate change, global sustainable development, worldwide eradication of poverty, universal safeguarding of human rights, and transnational pandemics and health threats (e.g. HIV/AIDS). Warning the world in 2009 of the escalating fallout from food, fuel and financial crises, World Bank Group president, Robert Zoellick, recommends new levels of international cooperation under a multilateral approach to such interconnected global governance challenges, with important roles for both state and non-state actors:[91]

> Looking beyond the Group of Seven system, we need a 21st-century approach to multilateralism through the dynamism of a flexible network, not new hierarchies of a fixed or static system. The new multilateralism must maximize the strengths of interdependent and overlapping actors and institutions, private and public. It should reach beyond the traditional focus on finance and trade, to include other pressing economic and political issues: development, energy, climate change, and stabilizing fragile and post-conflict states. It needs to draw together existing international institutions, with their expertise and resources, to reform them when necessary, and to encourage effective co-operation and common action.

Deep-seated human constructs in the form of social contracts and societal hypernorms which govern business–society relations are further indicators of systemic responsibility-inducing influences upon corporations in their engagement with society and the world.[92] Moreover, concern about the specific ways in which corporations can themselves become the source of governance problems, through corporate complicity in governmental corruption, military human rights abuses, undue political interference, environmental harm, and social overconsumption, for example, leads to enlarged expectations of responsible corporate initiatives that 'implicitly or explicitly recognize the important role that businesses actually play in building healthy societies' – a role that extends beyond mere production of profit-driven goods and services.[93]

Governance therefore has multiple modes, levels and actors. In particular, both distinctions and connections must be drawn between governance at large, global governance, democratic governance, public governance, public sector governance and corporate governance. CSR is concerned in part with how and why issues of corporate governance relate to these other aspects of governance too. This extends beyond simply relating CSR to both corporate governance and a broader vision of corporate responsibility and sustainability. We are in the early stages of 'a fundamental reconstitution of the global public domain' in the realization of 'global public goods', for example – an instance of which is the recasting of 'the global public role of private enterprise' brought about through '(t)he dynamic interplay between civil society organizations and transnational firms in the area of corporate social responsibility', according to Professor Ruggie.[94] In other words, CSR both reflects and shapes the dynamics of global public governance too.

Connections between governance and corporate social responsibility

[We need] to engender a new dialogue: a dialogue about creating the conditions under which business, government, the welfare sector and individuals can address the problems of poverty, inequality and environmental sustainability . . . The way to do this, I believe, is to embrace what I have come to call value-centred market economics . . . We need to make a shift to a new paradigm of social and economic policy. We already have the language, but we have only tentatively begun to put into practice the concepts behind it. *Joined-up government*, *whole-of-government approach*, *social enterprise*, *corporate social responsibility*, *triple bottom line* and *sustainability* are some of the phrases that express this new agenda.

– Nic Frances, Schwab Foundation social entrepreneur and former CEO of The Brotherhood of St Laurence[95]

Considered from one standpoint in the governance landscape, governance on the world stage can be viewed as a transformation from reliance solely upon national governments, all interacting with one another through formal mechanisms of international institutions and law, to additional reliance upon cross-cutting networks, interactions and coalitions of interests.[96] An emerging theme is the reconfiguration of governance and regulatory relations that results from the greater 'leverage' of both business and civil society over government through globalization.[97] Indeed, TCS is at least an equal player with state-based entities and structurally entrenched capitalism in the power plays of global politics.[98] In this 'reconfiguring of state-society relations' the focus is upon understanding how and why TCS influences shape global political outcomes, rather than upon the simplistic replacement of nation-states by other actors in global politics.[99] As part of 'an emerging global public domain' of contests between governmental and non-governmental actors over 'global public goods', argue some global governance scholars, global governance and regulation increasingly accommodate 'non-state market driven governance systems', which involve 'deliberative and adaptive governance institutions designed to embed social and environmental norms in the global marketplace that derive authority directly from interested audiences, including those they seek to regulate, not from sovereign states'.[100]

Considered from another viewpoint, 'a new world order' of 'global governance' is emerging in the 21st century in which a 'disaggregated' conception of nation-states and their constituent governmental parts underpins the recognition of both 'vertical' and 'horizontal' sets of 'government networks' worldwide, joined by a range of non-governmental bodies and actors in addressing common areas of governance and regulatory concern.[101] On this view of the new world order, these government networks operate as 'global governance mechanisms' that are the hubs of a series of interconnected and transnational networks involving governmental, business and community actors, all engaged 'in the pursuit of a larger conception of the global public interest' and thereby constituting 'a kind of disaggregated global democracy based on individual and group self-governance'.[102]

Governance gaps in the global architecture for ensuring protection of human rights from encroachment by business-initiated and state-supported development activity, especially in developing countries, is one of the major global governance problems of the 21st century, as identified in reports by the UNSRSG.[103] Some 'governance gaps' threatening long-term market sustainability stem from failures or limitations of particular governments.[104] In addition, many countries are hampered by the problem of collective action if they try to increase responsible business regulation on their own, as they are susceptible to the threat of capital flight by TNCs from unwelcome business regulation. 'If one country pursues a governance regime that is less friendly to shareholders than that of other countries, then they risk losing the ability to attract the very investment from world capital markets needed to sustain employment and a growth in living standards', note corporate management experts Jay Conger, Edward Lawler and David Finegold.[105] 'Competition among developing countries to attract investment can result in a race to the bottom, as companies seek a home with the weakest labor and environmental laws', reiterates Nobel Prize-winning economist Joseph Stiglitz.[106]

The beneficial ratcheting-up of standards in developing countries by TNCs along their business supply and distribution chains gives local standards an upward lift too, while the transnational spread of good practice standards by TNCs safeguards them against the kind of 'race to the bottom' worldwide that might threaten economic competitiveness, opportunity and prosperity in developed countries.[107] The rise of multi-stakeholder coalitions and other collective standard-setting initiatives exposes such races to the bottom to greater international scrutiny and pressure. Of course, much of this assumes transnational business agreement and perhaps even universal acceptance of relevant standards, as well as host country receptivity in developing economies to such standards, matched against their own investment and developmental needs.[108]

Network governance is another important form of governance for CSR. It operates on at least two different levels. As explored later in this chapter, multi-stakeholder CSR networks and standard-setting initiatives have reached such a critical mass already in the 21st century that they constitute a distinct layer of regulatory influence in their own right, informing corporate self-regulation according to meta-regulatory standards, as well as easing CSR standards-development along the path from public and business acceptance to regulatory enshrinement and practice.[109] At the same time, the network-based nature of many 21st century global corporate groups and TNCs adds impetus to devolved authority and relationship-focused management of organizational entities, enhanced management of 'global value chains' (i.e. 'the full range of activities required to bring a product or service from its conception to end use'), regulatory challenges in making TNCs and corporate groups amenable to effective global regulation, and opportunities to access 'available entry points through which civil society actors can seek to leverage a company's brand and resources' to influence corporate activity.[110]

In the context of CSR in general, and the business value chains of MNCs in particular, network governance therefore provides points of connection between developed and developing countries, on one hand, and between the public, private, and not-for-profit sectors, on the other. In the aftermath of the 2008–2009 global economic crisis, Professor Peter Shergold articulated these points of connection in the following terms:[111]

> Responsibility for the integrity of the supply chain acts as a global link between developed and developing countries, creating a nascent CSR network . . . The experiences of values-based, mission-driven, socially-focused enterprises may well hold the keys to CSR success. Indeed the increasingly porous barriers between non-for-profit and for-profit ventures may offer opportunities for new forms of social and environmental responsibility, designed through collaboration and delivered by hybrid organisations and private-community partnerships.

A 21st century understanding of CSR's connection to multiple governance concerns therefore requires a truly global perspective on CSR. 'We propose an updated notion of corporate social responsibility – global corporate social responsibility – that reflects the fact that people hold firms responsible for actions far beyond their boundaries, including the actions of suppliers, distributors, alliance partners, and even sovereign nations', suggests one cross-disciplinary group of management scholars.[112] Elevating global corporate citizenship beyond the concerns of everyday corporate governance, corporate philanthropy, CSR and corporate social entrepreneurialism, Schwab casts business–society engagement in terms of the stake that business has in wider global governance concerns:[113]

> Above all, a new imperative for business, best described as 'global corporate citizenship', must be recognized. It expresses the conviction that companies not only must be engaged with their stakeholders but are themselves stakeholders alongside governments and civil society. International business leaders must fully commit to sustainable development and address paramount global challenges, including climate change, the provision of public health care, energy conservation, and the management of resources, particularly water. Because these global issues increasingly impact business, not to engage with them can hurt the bottom line. Because global citizenship is in a corporation's enlightened self-interest, it is sustainable. Addressing global issues can be good both for the corporation and for society at a time of increasing globalization and diminishing state influence.

'Trans-modal governance' therefore is an all-embracing term, with four main focal points. It signifies that the modern terrain of governance nationally and internationally has a number of modes, including: (a) international (e.g. UN), regional (e.g. EU), and transnational governance; (b) democratic, social, and community governance within sovereign states; (c) sectoral governance (e.g. public/private sector governance, and industry competition/co-operation); and (d) organizational governance (e.g. corporate governance of corporations in the private and public sectors). It positions corporations of all kinds, along with other entities, as organs of organizational, societal and even global governance, with individual and collective interests in addressing governance problems and challenges of various kinds. Like other contemporary analyses of the global political order and the new regulatory state, trans-modal governance recognizes the enduring significance of nations, governments and supra-national institutions as organs of national and international governance, whatever other changes have occurred in their roles and our understanding of them, as well as the limits of these entities on their own to address all governance dimensions and problems today.

The rise of multi-stakeholder coalitions and other standard-setting initiatives

> Global corporate citizenship refers to a company's role in addressing issues that have a dramatic impact on the future of the globe, such as climate change . . . The primary responsibility for meeting these global challenges still rests with governments and international organizations. But companies can contribute in an appropriately balanced partnership with the public sector and relevant civil-society groups . . . Global corporate citizenship is a logical extension of corporations' search for a consistent and sustainable framework for global engagement – and one that adds value for both companies and the global space in which they engage . . . And in relying on a multi-stakeholder approach to tackling global problems, it can point out the way to new models of effective global governance that integrate business as a key stakeholder.
>
> – Klaus Schwab, Executive Chair of the World Economic Forum[114]

The components of the 21st century's 'relatively extensive emerging institutional infra-structure around corporate responsibility' include public–private partnerships and cross-sectoral networks, social alliances and multi-stakeholder initiatives, intergovernmental and supra-national institutional standard-setting, balances of 'hard' and 'soft' law meas-ures, and a variety of other relations between governmental, business and community bodies.[115] In particular, the rise of cross-sectoral and transnational alliances of multi-stakeholder groups is one of the most significant CSR developments in the late 20th and early 21st centuries. They are described variously in the CSR literature and accompany-ing standard-setting guides as 'multi-stakeholder initiatives', 'multi-party partnerships', 'new social partnerships', 'tri-sector partnerships', 'social alliances' and 'multi-sectoral alliances'.[116]

These coalitions of groups and interests can emerge in response to a variety of stimuli, ranging from a shared need for collective lobbying for or against new regulation, to a common interest in addressing a particular problem or need for guidance across sectoral, industry and national boundaries. They can also hasten the development and acceptance of eco-innovative products and technologies, bolster community enterprises through business engagement and investment, provide additional layers and forms of network-based regulation, and meet shared responsibility in addressing particular global govern-ance challenges.[117] This shows their connection to wider governance concerns. In short, 'fragments of collaborative governance are emerging in a variety of sectors, specifically tailored for the characteristic dilemma situations in each', with significant 'spillover effects into other areas'.[118]

The international human rights arena offers some major examples of collaborative initiatives by social coalitions of companies and other social actors, as part of the 'emerg-ing architecture' of systemic and institutional arrangements for promoting CSR through human rights protection.[119] The UNSRSG highlights the importance of 'a multi-stakeholder form that engages corporations directly, along with states and civil society organizations, in addressing sources of corporate-related human rights abuses'.[120] Key collaborations mentioned by the UNSRSG include the UN Global Compact (with thousands of participating organizations worldwide), the OECD Guidelines for Multinational Enterprises, the ILO's standard-setting and country-based initiatives (including its Tripartite Declaration of Principles Concerning Multinational Enterprises), the Fair Labor Association (with supply chain value-enhancing and governance capacity-building in developing economies), and a group of collaborative initiatives in the extractive industries sector (e.g. the EITI, Kimberley Process Certification Scheme (Kimberley Process) and the Voluntary Principles on Security and Human Rights (Voluntary Principles).[121] The finance and investment domain is also witnessing high-level coalition-building and standard-setting, through financial institutions and banks subscribing to the Equator Principles (on responsible financing of project infrastructure and development to minimize social and environmental risks), the leverage gained through the adoption of some of the Equator Principles' elements in loan performance standards for the extractive sector set by the International Finance Corporation, and the promotion of SRI by investment funds more generally through landmark initiatives such as the UNPRI.[122]

Multi-stakeholder CSR networks and initiatives are therefore at the vanguard of 21st century CSR. They contribute to agenda-setting, relationship-building, knowledge-sharing, capacity-building, standard-setting, network development, and even wider aspects of societal governance and regulation.[123] Their existence and prominence are a testament to the new reality that 'civil society organizations have managed to implant elements of public accountability into the private transactional spaces of transnational firms'.[124] Their contemporary growth and significance are acknowledged in *The Economist*'s 2008 report on CSR, referring to leading 'multi-stakeholder initiatives' such as the EITI, Kimberley Process, Voluntary Principles, Ethical Trading Initiative and Business Leaders Initiative on Human Rights (BLIHR):[125]

> (R)isk management can be a lonely business . . . The answer, many have decided, is to spread the risk. Groups of them are getting together to agree on codes of conduct – usually within a particular industry, but also across industries and in consultation with governments, UN agencies and NGOs. This has become one of the most striking recent trends in CSR . . . Such 'multi-stakeholder initiatives' tend to involve companies that have elevated CSR to a strategic level.

However much multi-stakeholder initiatives might be at the vanguard of new forms of CSR, they do not attract unanimous support from CSR commentators. One of the most widely embraced multi-stakeholder initiatives – the UN Global Compact – is criticized by former OECD chief economist David Henderson in these terms:[126]

> Prominent businesses which have adhered to CSR have lent their support to dubious corporatist notions of 'global governance', in which businesses join hands with governments, international agencies and leading NGOs to raise standards across frontiers. A recent leading instance of this tendency is the so-called Global Compact, initiated by the Secretary-General of the United Nations. Besides carrying with them the danger of over-regulating the world economy, such collaborative ventures confer on organisations which are not politically accountable – both businesses and NGOs – powers and responsibilities that do not rightly belong to them.

The UK Conservative Party Working Group on Responsible Business (CPWGRB) delineates the basic features of multi-stakeholder initiatives as follows:[127]

Although very varied in focus, process and genesis, and all facing significant challenges, these initiatives have positive attributes in common. All of them:

- have been designed to tackle a very specific issue;
- include participation from business, government and civil society;
- presume that corporate responsibility for the issue in question provides only part of the solution, and that others need also to take responsibility for other parts of the equation; and
- proceed on the presumption that addressing an issue requires action by all parties.

As this attempt to encapsulate its essence shows, coalition-building of this kind often has some defining features. These features can be modelled in developing similar coalitions of groups and interests in the future. Taken together, a start-up menu of features for selection and modelling such coalition-building is outlined below.

First, some of these coalitions of groups and interests develop gradually in their own right, or else emerge from other associations and networks, but some also come into being as a more direct and immediate response triggered by a new governance or regulatory need in common. They often represent a consensus on a discrete set of principles for addressing their common concerns, thereby reinforcing at a deeper level the value of principle-based regulatory approaches, usually as part of a wider framework for action.

Secondly, this connection between principle-based standard-setting and multi-stakeholder initiatives is a recurring theme. The field of corporate responsibility and governance is already replete with principle-based frameworks and standards in the 21st century, from overarching principles with supra-national institutional endorsement[128] to principle-based corporate governance codes. Principle-based regulation now informs global responsible investment decision-making frameworks, 'a principles-based conceptual and policy framework' proposed by the UNSRSG for business and human rights worldwide,[129] and corporate governance regulation in the EU, UK and Australia.

Moreover, principle-based approaches and standards are woven into corporate governance regulation in the UK and Australia in ways that relate to CSR. For example, both the current UK Combined Code and its predecessor contain a main principle of dialogue with institutional shareholders, with a supporting principle that endorses and incorporates reference to principles developed by institutional shareholder representatives. Amongst other reasons for intervention, those principles provide guidelines for intervention in corporate affairs by institutional investors, on behalf of those whose investments they hold, when they or their agents have legitimate concerns about 'the company's approach to corporate social responsibility'. Similarly, in Australia, both the parliamentary explanatory material accompanying Australia's introduction of 21st century corporate reporting requirements and the national stock exchange guidelines on its implementation incorporate reference to guidelines developed by the Group of 100 based on both financial and non-financial corporate performance indicators.[130]

In their landmark study of business regulation worldwide, regulatory theorists Braithwaite and Drahos conceptualize 'the globalization of business regulation as a two-tiered process' in which '(a)t the first tier the process occurs at the level of rules and at the second tier at the level of principles',[131] not least because of the enhanced capacity of principle-based frameworks to achieve consensus amidst the pragmatic realities of geopolitics. In addition to their regulatory role as a basis for corporate standard-setting and ordering, principle-based approaches can also assist in garnering support for a cause and forming coalitions who agree on basic principles for an area of governance or regulation, as illustrated by Braithwaite and Drahos in international regulations of finance and intellectual property.[132] Hence, there is a strong connection between principle-based regulation and multi-stakeholder standard-setting.

A third distinguishing feature of these coalitions is their development as non-hierarchical networks and nodes of influence, both within and across wider webs of regulatory influence.[133] They fill regulatory gaps and promote continuous improvement of standards, thereby narrowing the gap between the floor and ceiling of corporate responsibility, with a complex array of shared responsibilities, multi-stakeholder relations and mutual accountability mechanisms, the status and credibility of which derive from their transparent participatory governance arrangements, internal and external monitoring, and operational and modelling effectiveness.[134] In particular, their accountability mechanisms 'begin to blur the lines between the strictly voluntary and mandatory spheres for participants'.[135] These multi-stakeholder initiatives have their own incentives and costs of exit to keep members involved, for example, such as the adverse economic consequences for companies and countries that are suspended or expelled from the Kimberley Process to limit sale in conflict diamonds.[136] The new CSR architecture includes 'an emerging voluntary responsibility assurance system', the strands of which comprise corporate impact accountability, transparency of corporate practices, internal accountability for corporate responsibility and sustainability, and meaningful engagement of stakeholders, with crucial elements that include internal corporate responsibility management systems and controls, internal and external codes of conduct (and other forms of standard-setting), internal and external reporting systems, and monitored and certified corporate responsibility assurance systems and performance.[137]

The fourth feature of these coalitions is that they transcend conventional public–private partnerships, which are structured mainly within a market-based approach of contractual performance measures and commercial gain for the non-government partners.[138] Instead, these coalitions are based upon the common ground between business, community and governmental partners that bridges commercial gain and the public interest, with the business partners becoming involved 'with an explicit interest in achieving social and environmental aims that goes beyond short-term fee-for-service or goods-for-sale strategies', and with correlative benefits for the ongoing legitimization of business within society.[139] In terms of transnational civil society organizations and their roles in such coalitions, at least in terms of shaping global public policy, common themes emerge of '(1) agenda setting – identifying a problem of international concern and producing information; (2) developing solutions – creating norms or recommending policy change; (3) building networks and coalitions of allies; and (4) implementing solutions – employing tactics of persuasion and pressure to change practices and/or encourage compliance with norms'.[140]

The fifth feature of these coalitions concerns their membership profile. Characteristically, they represent a coalition of authoritative and respected entities or groups, often across geographical, sectoral and industry boundaries, and with or without formal governmental facilitation or involvement. This membership profile itself assists in the legitimization of these coalitions and their concerns. In addition, membership offers reputational and other competitive advantages to individual corporate members associated with the network. Governmental bodies and officials might still have a coordinating and facilitative role in their development, become involved in their membership, and even retain exclusive power over some regulatory initiatives that emerge from them, but they are not amenable overall to centralized, state-controlled and bureaucratic management by public officials. This reflects a new order of 21st century regulation, with governmental CSR roles of the kinds outlined in Chapter 4.

The sixth feature of these coalitions is that they contribute to dialogue and pressure about accepting a form of corporate responsibility that is broader than simply complying with what is legally sanctioned and enforced, thereby further breaking down traditional divides between public/mandatory obligations and private/voluntary obligations, as well as contributing other layers of regulation to the system of regulatory influences operating upon corporations. At the same time as they open up the notion of corporate responsibility to the possibilities of wider corporate responsiveness, they also place boundaries on what corporate responsiveness can do on its own. The very need for a coalition itself points to the inability of any of government, business or civil society alone to address some pressing governance and regulatory needs for society and the world.

The seventh feature of these coalitions lies in the quality of their attributes and relations. They foster trust and understanding, thereby establishing conditions for long-term cooperation, ongoing policy input, refinement of standards, politico-regulatory credibility, and internal and external relationship-building. They trade on exchanges of respective knowledge, expertise and resources, although recent surveys of companies involved in such alliances with NGOs and UN-associated bodies suggest that obtaining assistance in successfully implementing CSR programmes within companies and building trust with stakeholders are more important motivations for partnering from the corporate perspective than using it to advance core business objectives or to gain insight from non-corporate partner know-how.[141] Other reported motivations in this context include stakeholder expectations of corporate citizenship, interdependence of business and societal dynamics, building employee morale, business risk and relationship management, and enhancing corporate reputations.[142]

Still, such coalitions spark new channels of information, communication and guidance which also feed into their contributing role in standard-setting. They also mark a transformation in the ways in which the group members relate to one another. In line with a more strategic and business-like approach to CSR, the business trend is away from ad hoc and unsynchronized approaches to corporate philanthropy and community engagement, and towards more selective and integrated agreement-based partnerships with quality-screened non-profit organizations, backed by a strategic business case related to core business operations, with mutual benefits for all partners.[143] Applied to the relations between NGOs and business in creating new markets in developing economies as well as niche markets in developed economies, they are part of the evolution from what Brugmann and Prahalad label the 'be-responsible stage' to the 'get-into-business stage' and finally the 'cocreate-business' stage.[144]

The final feature of these social coalitions lies in their strategic deployment by companies in synchronizing their business models with their broader business–society relations, in ways further explored in Chapter 8. 'An increasing number of companies also use community investment initiatives to build relationships with key stakeholders, including corporate critics', according to a major government-commissioned report on the attitudes and practices of more than 100 of Australia's top companies. This evidences a strong trend towards business developing 'fewer and deeper partnerships with non-profit organisations and to a lesser extent with government agencies', with these partnerships being constructed with 'clear agreements or contracts that ensure mutual benefits, clarity in roles and relationships, and specify exit arrangements'.[145]

As with other CSR aspects of the 21st century business environment, the evolution of CSR-orientated coalitions and standard-setting initiatives still has a long way to go. At the same time, they contribute only part of the solution to corporate irresponsibility worldwide. In the context of business and human rights, for example, there is high-level support for the view that even 'novel multi-stakeholder initiatives, public-private hybrids combining mandatory with voluntary measures, and industry and company self-regulation', in tandem with other global rights-enhancing mechanisms, collectively still suffer from these weaknesses: 'there are too few of them, none has reached a scale commensurate with the challenges at hand, there is little cross-learning, and they do not cohere as parts of a more systemic response with cumulative effects'.[146] Similarly, as acknowledged in an assessment of corporate partnering with NGOs and UN-associated bodies, considerable impediments to the formation of CSR-orientated partnerships also need to be overcome, including the establishment of goodwill and trust, the difficulty of identifying suitable partners and models, the conflict of profit and not-for-profit missions, and the absence of effective guidance on developing suitable partnering qualities.[147]

'Multi-order Regulation'

A broader understanding of regulation

The next step in developing a conceptual framework for corporate responsiveness to interactive systems of governance, regulation and responsibility focuses upon regulation. What is 'regulation', and how does it relate to corporations and CSR? In particular, where does 'regulation' fit within that framework? 'Nowhere is there complete adherence to the theory that companies ought to be permitted to function free of all regulation: all states operate a "mixed" system of market freedom and regulatory control', notes the University of London's Professor Janet Dine.[148] 'However, traditional discussions of corporate governance give little weight to the web of regulation which surrounds every corporate operation', she adds. This is changing.

In terms of regulation, the modern era is witnessing what prominent regulatory theorists describe as the new regulatory state, accompanied by the 'decentring' of regulation into many more strands than simply self-regulation, on one hand, and government-mandated 'command and control' regulation in the form of 'regulation by the state through the use of legal rules backed by (often criminal) sanctions', on the other.[149] As no single entity or system either nationally or internationally has a monopoly on all of the different forms of regulation affecting corporations in the 21st century, we are witnessing 'the rise of multiple sources of power and a world in which institutions with regulatory authority must compete'.[150] 'Regulatory power appears to be flowing *up* from states to international bodies and *out* from states to non-public actors like international corporations and elements of global civil society', according to Professor Larry Cata Backer.[151]

Considered from some angles, regulation is a concept that includes law, but is not limited to law. 'On this basis "regulation" is a broader social phenomenon than "law" in that regulation does not need to emanate from the state, and "law" can thus be seen as one form of regulation, ie a particular set of ordering', as leading regulatory scholar Professor Julia Black suggests.[152] Regulation and regulatory theorists are concerned with 'how law interacts with other forms of normative ordering', especially in thinking about 'the relationship of law and society or law and economy in terms of various layers of regulation each doing their own regulating', so that 'each layer regulates the regulation of each other in various combinations of horizontal and vertical influence' – a phenomenon now known as 'meta-regulation'.[153]

Regulation thus takes many forms. It can be governmental or non-governmental in origin and nature. It can be jurisdiction-specific, transnational, or even global in reach. While there is a relationship between governance and regulation, they can be distinguished for present purposes in the following way. Governance concerns how and why an entity or system structures and conducts its affairs. Juxtaposed with governance, regulation concerns how and why behaviour relating to its conduct of affairs is directed, steered and otherwise guided. Regulation therefore can be conceived broadly as 'the intentional activity of attempting to control, order, or influence the behaviour of others'.[154]

'Multi-order regulation' is therefore used here to embrace all forms of regulation in the new regulatory state and world order, including law and other forms of regulation such as government-imposed regulation, corporate self-regulation, co-regulation, risk-based regulation and meta-regulation. In this context, 'meta-regulation' encapsulates the forms of regulation by which official regulators and others exert regulatory influence upon corporations and other organizations through layers of regulation impacting upon one another, including organizations regulating themselves by reference to accepted external standards of regulation.[155] 'Multi-order regulation' is also used in juxtaposition with 'meta-regulation', given that regulatory options for corporate responsibility and governance might extend beyond meta-regulation. The point of multi-order regulation is to highlight an amalgam of corporate regulatory forces which transcends what is captured by state-backed legal compulsion and voluntarily adopted corporate commitments alone.

Meta-regulation, the new regulatory state and corporate social responsibility
In many ways, the world of CSR is now a meta-regulatory world. This world is characterized by the amenability of corporate self-regulation to external regulatory influences, the interplay between 'hard' and 'soft' regulation, the emergence of multi-stakeholder standard-setting initiatives, and the surge of principle-based, risk-based and other forms of regulation. In the enterprise of embedding CSR within corporations, the range of meta-regulatory standard-setting influences includes 'international networks of governance, more traditional state-based regulatory enforcement activity, and traditional law that authorizes, empowers, co-opts or recognises the regulatory influence of industry, professional or civil bodies to set and enforce standards for CSR processes and outcomes', according to Dr Parker.[156] Her analysis of CSR-related meta-regulation offers a useful example of how the focus of CSR-related law and regulation is shifting in the 21st century. It also fits within the broader framework of trans-modal governance, multi-order regulation, and inter-related responsibility outlined in this chapter.

At both national and international levels, meta-regulatory regimes thus create conditions for a form of corporate responsiveness to regulation that is not simply voluntary or optional, and yet is not entirely mandated by 'traditional, hierarchical legal regulation promulgated by nation states'.[157] Considered from a CSR standpoint, meta-regulation

The stance of meta-regulating law is to recognise that the main goals of a company are not merely to make sure it acts socially responsibly, but also to meet its main goals of producing particular goods and/or services, providing a return to its investors, and/or providing paid employment to its workers and managers. Meta-regulating law should allow space for the company itself to take responsibility for working out how to meet its main goals within the framework of values set down by regulation, provided its main goals can be carried on consistently with social responsibility values. Meta-regulating law should be careful to leave space, to the greatest extent possible, to allow the companies it regulates to decide for themselves how to institutionalise responsibility. This means meta-regulating law does not assume command-and-control is the only appropriate technique for regulating social responsibility. It is willing to experiment with more indirect or facilitative techniques for engendering responsibility, including through requiring or capacitating non-state agencies (such as auditors, NGOs or the public at large) to help regulate corporate behaviour (for example through audit requirements, provision of information about corporate performance to the public, and so on). It is also willing to treat firms that show different levels of inner commitment to responsibility in different ways.

– Meta-regulatory scholar, Dr Christine Parker[158]

therefore represents 'an approach to legal regulation in which the *internal* "corporate conscience" is *externally* regulated', creating a framework within which 'legal accountability for CSR must be aimed at making business enterprises put themselves through a CSR process aimed at CSR outcomes'.[159] Corporate decisions and actions are meaningfully directed towards those outcomes in applying their constituent values to specific corporate contexts, assisted by a process that 'opens up management to external values, stakeholders and regulatory influences'.[160] In effect, corporations are viewed as systems in which a range of legal, economic, socio-ethical, and other norms and values interact in specific but different ways, through the focus of internal and regulatory forces that both affect and shape one another.

Accordingly, meta-regulating law's overall CSR focus lies in generating regulatory forces to which corporations respond, 'to put in place internal governance structures, management practices and corporate cultures aimed at achieving responsible outcomes'.[161] On this view of CSR-related meta-regulation, as articulated by Dr Parker, the responsiveness of corporations to multiple interwoven regulatory forces steers them towards organizational adoption of responsibility-inducing values and processes, and hence towards self-regulation in accordance with those values and processes, all within an externally developed framework of law and regulation that embraces multiple stakeholder inputs and standard-setting influences.

In short, for CSR to be fully effective the notion of 'responsibility' associated with CSR must be embraced as an idealistic rather than formalistic one. (This reflects the notion of aspirational corporate responsibility explored in Chapter 1.) It envisages a self-aware organization which commits to an 'ethic of responsibility', which infuses its own organizational commitments and its engagement with the world beyond the company's walls, as distinct from mechanistic legal compliance that is simply directed towards deflecting any threat of external legal sanctions.[162] Organizationally, the various mechanisms for doing this include high-level organizational policy commitments to 'corporate responsibility processes and their goals', attentiveness to internal and external relations, alignment of organizational accountability and performance measures with responsibility-inducing processes and outcomes, suitable organizational communication and training, meaningful organizational analysis and reporting of responsibility-related activity, and realistic internal and external monitoring and accountability mechanisms.[163] In this way, CSR-inducing organizational values, processes and outcomes become synchronized with CSR-related public policy goals and regulatory standard-setting to which a variety of state and non-state actors might contribute.[164]

As part of their self-regulatory approach within a framework of meta-regulation, adds Parker, 'leading companies should take responsibility for deliberation with stakeholders about emerging values and responsibilities that are not yet the subject of law and regulation', and form self-regulatory responses to them, given that key stakeholders such as institutional investors and NGOs 'all have a responsibility for sustaining democracy by engaging in the dialogue about corporate social responsibility and forcing companies to take new responsibilities into account', given the evolutionary trajectory of much soft law in becoming hard law.[165] This parallels wider developments in TCS influences upon public policy, multi-stakeholder standard-setting, and democratic accountability of corporations, of the kinds discussed in the first part of this book.

The values and interests engaged in a corporation's inner and outer governance are both public and private in nature, with flow-on implications for a corporation's engagement with internal and external stakeholders in meeting its commitment to responsibility, as well as more broadly for the multi-faceted democratic role of corporations in society.[166] 'The open corporation is the good corporate citizen in deliberative democracy', says Parker.[167] More broadly, this fits within a pattern of giving a voice and other avenues of engagement and redress to those stakeholders who are significantly involved in, or otherwise affected by, corporate activity (as in corporate democracy).[168] In turn, this connects to broader visions of corporations as sites implicating a range of public and private interests (as in corporate constitutionalism), corporate self-regulation within a wider system of meta-regulation (as in corporate meta-regulation generally), and corporate responsiveness to trans-modal governance, multi-order regulation and inter-related responsibility (as canvassed throughout this book).

Of course, the idea of legal meta-regulation making 'business organisations accountable for putting in place corporate conscience processes that are aimed at substantive social values' might well be an idea that has 'little to do with most current business and government "corporate social responsibility" initiatives', as Parker argues, not least in terms of how the law presently regulates and prioritizes the interests of shareholders and non-shareholders.[169] The continuing domination of orthodox corporate law and governance by hard law and official regulation whose structures and standards still remain insufficiently conditioned by CSR meta-regulatory influences impedes the mainstreaming of CSR in business advice and practice. Such insights are important in evaluating the CSR effectiveness of existing corporate regulatory systems and models for their reform, of the kinds further explored in Chapters 5 to 7.

Unsurprisingly, given its challenge to the exclusiveness of state-mandated regulation, its reformatory impact upon corporate orthodoxy, and its general status as a form of meta-regulation, CSR meta-regulation provokes strong opposition too. In Parker's eyes, the characteristic objections to meta-regulation as a pluralistic form of regulation point to its displacement of the primacy of state-based regulation, its usurpation of conventional legal regulation in establishing benchmarks for lawful resolution of conflicts between societal and individual values, the democratic illegitimacy and non-accountability of its stakeholder power-wielding, the lack of consensus about its structural values and techniques, and the susceptibility of its regulatory outcomes to capture by its regulatory processes.[170] Some of these objections simply reinforce how different meta-regulation is from conventional state law-making, or ascribe to meta-regulation a quality that is not automatically integral to it. A genuine 'substance-oriented process' that is true to meta-regulatory values and techniques is distinguishable from one that goes off the rails as an instance of 'process driving substance', for example, and there is no inevitability about such a meta-regulatory failure.[171] Moreover, what CSR meta-regulatory analysis throws into sharp relief is that even hard law bearing upon corporations is not as demarcated from other societal influences in its design, content, and application as some corporate orthodoxy suggests, both in its own right and as part of a system of interwoven regulatory influences.

The difference between characterizing CSR meta-regulation in terms such as Parker's notion of 'the open corporation' as an organizationally 'reflexive' self-learning and self-regulating system that is open and 'permeable' to external regulatory forces of multiple kinds, on one hand, and alternatively characterizing it as something that unduly burdens business and takes it beyond its central focus, on the other,[172] ultimately rests upon politically, economically and morally based normative considerations about the nature and role of corporations in society. Although some people accept such mechanisms as part of what is needed for corporate responsibility and governance in the 21st century business environment, others view them as evidence of the increased costs and misdirections of CSR, in submission to a global governance agenda that undermines the imperatives of business.[173] In making this normative judgment, the true comparison is not simply between how business has operated until now and the supposed extra costs of doing business differently. Rather, the full cost-benefit analysis must also factor in the socio-ethical costs of continuing business as usual, the social and corporate benefits of doing business differently, and the needs of 21st century governance, regulation and responsibility.

Blurring the boundary between mandatory and voluntary regulation
The debate about CSR often revolves around the two poles of a mandated, state-regulated and legally enforced core of corporate responsibility at one extreme, and an additional, voluntary and non-enforceable set of penumbral aspects of CSR at the other. As Halina Ward highlights, 'one of the basic dividing lines of the CSR agenda in Europe, North America and Australia [is] a line between people who argue that CSR should be limited to consideration of "voluntary" business activities "beyond compliance" with legal baselines, and those who argue for a broader starting point based on an understanding of the total impacts of business in society'.[174] 'Because CSR is fundamentally about voluntary business behaviour, an approach involving additional obligations and administrative

(T)he concept of CSR calls for the strong involvement of appropriate stakehold-ers, based on open dialogue among involved parts, and, above all, is intended as *a voluntary approach beyond legal requirements*. It is in this sense that CSR and legal setting become reciprocally complementary, not different alternatives between which firms can choose their own best way.

– European CSR scholars Francesco Perrini , Stefano Pogutz and Antonio Tencati[175]

The United States remains committed to promoting *voluntary* corporate social responsibility initiatives in a variety of sectors throughout the world. We believe that these voluntary initiatives are a positive complement to rule of law and can also help foster human dignity and improved working conditions, environmental safeguards, and good governance.

– US Government's formal response to the 2007 Report of the Special Representative of the UN Secretary-General for Business and Human Rights (emphasis added)

requirements for business risks being counter-productive and would be contrary to the principles of better regulation', argues the European Commission.[176]

However, as the new directions of CSR debate and regulation in the 21st century reveal, corporate responsibility and governance are being reframed in ways which render the distinction between mandatory and voluntary standard-setting increasingly unsound. In particular, CSR debate about mandatory corporate obligations and voluntary corporate undertakings has shifted to the interplay between state and non-state regulatory meas-ures, the task of developing adequate reporting and verification tools for even voluntary CSR commitments, and creating state and non-state incentives for such commitments.[177] CSR meta-regulation is clearly in play here too.

The strict dichotomy between mandatory legal enforcement of corporate responsibil-ity and voluntary corporate assumption of responsibility is an unsatisfactory one on many levels. As argued in Chapter 1, aspirational corporate responsibility is not limited to the lowest common denominator of a company's enforceable legal responsibility. Locating CSR within the realm of voluntary business actions beyond compliance with the law undervalues 'the dynamic linkages between voluntary approaches and regulation, and the potential for voluntary initiatives of various kinds to crystallize, over time, into mandatory minimum standards'.[178] Similarly, starting with this dichotomy as a universal guide to CSR's limits 'does not make sense in the context of developing country econo-mies where tools to encourage compliance with minimum legislation can be understood as a significant element of the CSR agenda'.[179]

In addition, 'the legal baseline for CSR is itself changing' on a number of levels all at once.[180] On one level, especially given the rise of standard-setting outcomes of multi-stakeholder and intergovernmental initiatives, such voluntary initiatives either comple-ment mandatory standards, in the sense that 'voluntary approaches are designed to raise the bar whereas the starting position for mandatory approaches is the legally enforceable minimum',[181] or alternatively blur the line between voluntary and mandatory standards, because of their own in-built accountability mechanisms and consequences of withdrawal. Further blurring of the lines between 'voluntary' and 'mandatory' standards can occur as corporate and industry codes of conduct inform standards of care and other elements of legal actions (e.g. negligence), become linked to officially regulated reporting requirements and accountability mechanisms for multi-stakeholder coalitions, and achieve legally binding contractual status (e.g. incorporation of labelling or certification schemes in supply chain contracts).[182]

In her work on TNCs and CSR under international law, Dr Jennifer Zerk criticizes the 'misguided' nature of the purported distinction between mandatory and voluntary CSR requirements on a number of grounds, as follows.[183] Some corporate regulatory systems already incorporate aspects of CSR regulation. Only 'an overly simplistic view of what law is, and how it guides human behaviour' focuses just upon mandated legal compliance, and leaves aside what the law permits but does not necessarily mandate in terms of ethical corporate behaviour, non-exploitative corporate litigation tactics and inevitable corporate choices in whether and how corporations exercise their strict legal rights. Moreover, mandatory legal regulation is neither the only nor necessarily the best means of ensuring 'higher standards of corporate behaviour and transparency', given the multiple forms of regulatory influence upon modern corporations.

In short, 'the "voluntary versus mandatory" debate is based on the mistaken impression that CSR and the law are somehow separate, whereas in reality they are intertwined', which means that '(t)he crucial question is not whether CSR should be "voluntary" or "mandatory", but in light of a particular problem, what is the best regulatory response?', says Zerk.[184] Put another way, the distinction between voluntary and mandatory regulation remains most apt in distinguishing what is legally sanctionable or enforceable from what is not. However, it is least apt to capture the nuances of contemporary corporate responsiveness to multiple systems of governance, regulation and responsibility.

Whatever the impact of the voluntary–mandatory distinction for the range of public and private interests implicated in corporate and non-corporate areas of law, the presumed voluntariness of much CSR presents problems in its own right. Despite being justified on the basis of self-chosen corporate commitment to good practice, continuous improvement and endurable business sustainability, 'CSR has hardly moved beyond the starting point', on an evidence-based assessment of its impact by some influential NGOs.[185] The illusion of voluntary CSR is evident in the pressures from threatened state regulation, community activism and competitive peers which often precipitate the corporate adoption of a voluntary measure, while the limits of voluntary CSR are revealed in its facilitation of weak and inconsistent self-regulation, as well as its potential to deflect attention from necessary legal enforcement measures.[186]

Even where business commitments to major CSR standards appear voluntary and serve reputational purposes in the market, this result often occurs in a setting shaped by operative regulatory regimes, strong community advocacy and resultant public pressures for change, as in the case of banks and financial institutions 'freely' committing to elevated scrutiny of adverse social and environmental consequences of financed projects beyond minimum legal requirements, under the Equator Principles.[187] Similarly, in the wake of heightened public and official scrutiny of the financial sector after the 2008 global financial and credit crisis, and building upon national momentum towards fairer consumer contracts, an industry review of Australia's Code of Banking Practice recommended an additional commitment by subscribing banks to 'responsible lending'.

If, as *The Economist* notes in its special 2008 report on CSR, 'private equity itself is having to respond to public pressure by agreeing to voluntary codes of transparency', we need a way of fully accounting for corporate amenability to a mix of 'external pressures' of legal, economic, social and other kinds – in other words, an account that accommodates actions that are more than optional and less than compelled.[188] Similar ground is covered by the UN High Commissioner for Human Rights, Louise Arbour, in her call for 'voluntary-plus' business engagement with human right concerns, as part of the next steps in 'moving the debate from the logjam of the two rigid positions, on the one hand those advocating the development of binding norms . . . and on the other the corporate sector and others advocating just more voluntary compliance [that is] purely voluntary with absolutely no downside risk, no monitoring, no exposure'.[189] In short, the voluntary–mandatory dichotomy is of limited use, even in accounting for how business responds to multi-order regulation, let alone understanding the 21st century environment for CSR.

'Inter-related Responsibility'

> We are witnessing the development of a responsive corporation, which – if it is in fact learning – should be increasingly capable of handling new issues whether they be 'business' or 'social' . . . It is safe to say that no new rationale has been developed to take the place of the classical one, and what remains of the classical rationale clearly is being challenged frontally. If there is anything unambiguous about today's criticism of business, it is that its existence is not deemed to be justified by its ability to provide and sell goods and services at a profit . . . [The company] is being held responsible for its social impact, but at present there are no guidelines which we can evoke with confidence to say what the limits of those responsibilities are or how they may be reached.
>
> – Harvard Business School's Robert Ackerman and Raymond Bauer[190]

The dimensions of 21st century corporate responsibility

As a counterpoint to the forces of economic globalization, state-mandated regulation and socially irresponsible corporate profit-maximization, 'a whole new architecture of corporate responsibility has begun to evolve', characterized by 'the rapid evolution of movements, institutions, and organizations like the social investment movement, corporate accountability and reporting initiatives, and the rapid emergence of global standards', all of which make corporations receptive to new forms of CSR.[191] Considered from a systemic perspective, organizations (such as corporations) and institutions therefore can be conceived as organic systems the internalities and externalities of which are attuned to each other. 'A responsive institution retains a grasp on what is essential to its integrity while taking account of new forces in its environment [and] *perceives social pressures as sources of knowledge and opportunities for self-correction*', for example, at least in the context of a responsible legal order.[192] In the wake of this, how does 'responsibility' relate to corporations and CSR? In particular, where does 'responsibility' fit within a framework of corporate responsiveness to systems of trans-modal governance, multi-order regulation and inter-related responsibility?

In this context, 'inter-related responsibility' is a term that operates on a number of levels. It covers those dimensions of corporate responsibility that commonly gain a critical mass of acceptance in bodies of thinking, regulation and practice concerning corporate responsibility. However controversial the social responsibility of corporations might be as a candidate dimension of corporate responsibility, and whatever the extent to which it is enshrined (if at all) in any laws or other regulation, a considerable mass of community, regulatory, academic and even business thinking now clearly accepts social responsibility as being as much a dimension of corporate responsibility as are more conventionally accepted dimensions of corporate responsibility, such as a corporation's financial and legal responsibility. Other potential dimensions of corporate responsibility are also in play as candidates for acceptance within a complete contemporary account of corporate responsibility, including environmental responsibility, regulatory responsibility, ethical responsibility and even governance responsibility.

These distinct but inter-related dimensions of corporate responsibility have a number of features in common. Whatever arguments might be made about their suitability or enforcement potential, they capture the main candidates for dimensions of corporate responsibility reflected in corporate scholarship and practice. They embody at least the concerns of corporate responsibility increasingly reflected in corporate performance ratings based upon TBL, SRI and ESG considerations. They transcend the particular design and content of corporate regulation in any corporate jurisdiction. They each have a twin 'inside out' and 'outside in' focus. For example, governance responsibility relates not only to a company's good governance according to accepted standards of corporate governance (i.e. an 'outside in' focus), but also to a company's involvement in networks of governance as an organ of societal governance, in a wider sense of governance (i.e. an 'inside out' focus). Moreover, they all coincide at the point of decision-making for directors in taking personal responsibility for how they choose to pursue the company's interests.[193] Most importantly, their recognition reflects what is increasingly apparent in business practice, as companies develop holistic management and compliance systems that incorporate reference to some or all of these dimensions of responsibility in an integrated way.

The fact that corporate responsibility might have multi-level dimensions does not automatically mean that corporate officials have directly enforceable duties or obligations to all of the shareholder and stakeholder interests associated with those dimensions. Otherwise, this would conflate the narrower issue of legally enforceable duties, obligations and rights with the wider issue of mapping and justifying dimensions of corporate responsibility for the purposes of public debate, policy-making, regulatory reform, and business regulation and practice too. Rather, it points to the multiple dimensions of corporate responsibility with which corporations must now engage, whatever ultimate model or theory of corporate responsibility might prevail within or across corporate regulatory systems. All of this resonates with the shift from a narrow, compulsion-based and obligation-focused notion of corporate *responsibility* to a broader notion of corporate *responsiveness* to trans-modal governance, multi-order regulation and inter-related responsibility.

Beyond embracing more than a monodimensional view of corporate responsibility as the minimum required by law, the notion of 'inter-dependent responsibility' also encompasses multi-pronged notions of corporate receptivity, reflexivity and responsiveness to systems of governance, regulation and responsibility. In other words, here the notion of inter-related responsibility includes corporate receptivity to various forces in a company's internal and external environments, in shaping suitably reflexive corporate responses to those environments as an exercise of corporate responsibility.[194] In doing so, the different dimensions of individual corporate responsibility – legal responsibility, financial responsibility, environmental responsibility, socio-ethical responsibility, and so on – clearly intersect and interact with one another.

Just as corporate reflexion 'internalises the corporation's external effects and puts the responsibility on the corporation to integrate itself with other sub-systems and the society as a whole',[195] so too corporate amenability to inter-related systems of governance, regulation and responsibility shapes corporate responsiveness to them in ways that define, for each corporation, its particular trajectory of corporate governance, responsibility and sustainability. Finally, whatever the scope of any corporation's responsibility as an individual company, the notion of 'inter-related responsibility' also embraces a corporation's shared and collective responsibilities along with others, including its cross-cutting responsibilities within wider systems of regulation and governance. To this extent, the notions of trans-modal governance, multi-order regulation and inter-related responsibility are relational notions too.

Corporate Responsiveness to Systems of Governance, Regulation and Responsibility

The overall point of corporate responsiveness to trans-modal governance, multi-order regulation and inter-related responsibility is to capture the multi-faceted nature of how and why societies and companies themselves orient corporate activity in response to a wide variety of systemic conditions and dynamics. The central underlying idea is that we need a framework for exploring existing models, new challenges and changing expectations of corporations in society and the world at large, as both subjects and objects of governance, regulation and responsibility in the 21st century. Such a framework points to reasons for organizational compliance, reflexive learning, continuous improvement, and other forms of responsiveness by corporations whose force is not solely legal in character, whose conformity with CSR norms goes beyond strict legal requirements, and whose push towards CSR is facilitated but not always mandated by law.[196]

What do the various CSR actors gain from viewing CSR through the prism of corporate responsiveness to systems of governance, regulation and responsibility? First, it provides a starting point for conceptualizing and operationalizing CSR that is transportable across corporate regulatory systems worldwide. Secondly, it relates 21st century corporate responsibility, governance and sustainability from a CSR perspective to the contemporary realities of 'a new world order',[197] the new regulatory state, and the place of corporations in a global civil society. Thirdly, it is a starting point that breaks the cycle of being forced to choose between locating CSR in the domain of mandatory/public obligations under state-based regulation, and alternatively positioning it within the realm of voluntary/private commitments of uncontrolled self-regulation.

Fourthly, it places the onus squarely upon the company and those deciding or defending its actions to do so by reference to a coherent account of corporate governance, responsibility and sustainability, as applied to the unique circumstances facing each company, by reference to the important features of its internal and external business environments. Whether or not corporations and those who manage and invest in them ever consciously develop and articulate an overarching justificatory interpretation of corporate success in society, their actions amount to a stance on corporate governance, responsibility and sustainability that follows and reinforces one such interpretation or another. Fifthly, it requires corporations to view themselves as both subjects and objects of governance, regulation, and responsibility, and hence to see and act upon the organizational and systemic connections between them, in ways that mediate between the baseline of minimalist corporate compliance and the heights of aspirational corporate success. Finally, it provides a way for CSR policy-making, law reform and regulatory innovation to move beyond a framework built primarily around shareholder-focused or alternatively stakeholder-focused orientations, by repositioning the relations between corporations and the systems of which they form part in a way that transcends any purely linear relation between the extremes of shareholder primacy and stakeholder pluralism. Such deeper questions of corporating theorizing are the subject matter of Chapter 3.

NOTES

1. Goodyear, 2006.
2. Madsen, 2008: 836–837.
3. Campbell, 2007: 532–533.
4. Franklin, 2008: 4.
5. Engel, 1979: 5–6.
6. Campbell, 2007: 532–533, 541–542.
7. Ibid.
8. Ibid.: 538–539.
9. Ibid.: 530.
10. Ibid.
11. Frances, 2008: 99.
12. E.g. Perrini et al, 2006: 31; Donaldson, 2005: 3; and CCPA and BCA, 2007: vii–ix.
13. 'Defining Corporate Social Responsibility', *Corporate Social Responsibility Initiative* website, John F Kennedy School of Government, Harvard University (accessible via www.ksg.harvard.edu).
14. CPWGRB, 2007: 4.
15. Frances, 2008: 98.
16. Elkington, 1999: 2.
17. Ibid.: 84, 92.
18. Magnan and Ralston, 2002.
19. McAuley, 2001.
20. Zappala, 2003.
21. Ibid.: 1.
22. Zadek, 2001b: 7.
23. McIntosh et al, 2003: 16.
24. Hinkley, 2007: 63.
25. Schwab, 2008: 107.
26. Ibid.: 110. Using this framework of related concepts, corporate governance covers how a company is run and how it behaves (Ibid.: 110–111). Corporate philanthropy embraces 'cash contributions; grants; donations, including salary-sacrifice programs and the giving of products; services; and investments', including 'social investing' as a 'special form of corporate philanthropy' (Ibid.: 112). CSR is confined to 'addressing the wider financial, environmental, and social impact of all that a company does', but extended 'along the whole chain of value creation' (Ibid.: 113). Corporate social entrepreneurship involves 'the transformation of socially and environmentally responsible ideas into products or services' (Ibid.: 114). Global corporate citizenship transcends all of these concepts, concentrating upon

'engagement at the macro level on issues of importance to the world: it contributes to enhancing the sustainability of the global marketplace' (Ibid.: 114).

27. Albrechtsen, 2006: 12.
28. Ward, 2008: 12.
29. Johns, 2005: 1.
30. On this point and the following arguments see Cheney et al, 2007: 8–9.
31. Campbell, 2007: 534, 539–540.
32. Hayek, 1960: 105–106.
33. Krause, 1985: 96–97.
34. AS 8003–2003; emphasis added.
35. COM(2002)347, 3–5; emphasis added.
36. Waddock, 2006: 5.
37. See, for example: Parkinson, 1993; Bottomley, 2007; and Parker, 2007.
38. Fox et al, 2002: 1.
39. E.g. Parker, 2002; and Parker, 2007.
40. Black, 2002:12.
41. Bosch, 2006: 4.
42. Ibid.: 4.
43. Cadbury, 2002: 156.
44. Porter and Kramer, 2006: 91.
45. COM(2002)347, 5.
46. Campbell, 2007: 540.
47. Hayek, 1960: 102.
48. McConvill, 2005: 90.
49. Garratt, 2003: 245.
50. Donaldson and Preston, 1995: 67.
51. Dunfee, 1999: 131.
52. Campbell, 2007: 549.
53. Kytle and Ruggie, 2005; 3.
54. AS 8003-2003: 14.
55. CAMAC, 2006: 54–55.
56. Price, 2003: 580; and Ruggie, 2004: 522.
57. Price, 2003: 587–592.
58. Perrini et al, 2006: 30; original emphasis.
59. COM(2002)347, 5.
60. Brundtland Commission, 1990: 87.
61. Quoted in 'Capitalism: What Now?', *The Deal, The Australian* Business Magazine, November 2008 (Vol 1, No 2), p 34.
62. Waddock, 2006: 9; and Ward, 2008: 15.
63. Mendonca and Oppenheim, 2007.
64. Savitz and Weber, 2006: xii.
65. Ibid.: x.
66. Greenfield, 2006: 130.
67. Ibid.: 130.
68. Deakin, 2005: 16.
69. Braithwaite and Drahos, 2000: 526.
70. Ibid: 162, 173.
71. Higgins, 2006.
72. Wedderburn, 1985: 14–15, 43–44.
73. Easterbrook and Fischel, 1991: 36.
74. Mackey, 2005: 31.
75. Campbell, 2007: 544–545.
76. Greenfield, 2006:128.
77. Deakin, 2005: 16.
78. Braithwaite and Drahos, 2000: 162, 173; and Dine, 2005: 247.
79. Flannery, 2005: 209.
80. Sperling, 2005: 88.
81. Black, 2007: 2.
82. Tonuri, 2007: 2; see also Welsh, 2007: 4.
83. Welsh, 2007: 5.
84. Black, 2007: 3; and Tate, 2007: 1, 3.

85.   Savitz and Weber, 2006: 55–56.
86.   Burris et al, 2005: 30.
87.   Ruggie, 2004: 504.
88.   Burris et al, 2005: 30–31.
89.   Ibid.
90.   Ruggie, 2004: 504.
91.   Zoellick, 2009: 47.
92.   E.g. Donaldson and Dunfee, 1999.
93.   Waddock, 2006: 7.
94.   Ruggie, 2004: 519.
95.   Frances, 2008: 1, 5; original emphasis.
96.   Orts, 2002: 558.
97.   Price, 2003: 580.
98.   Ibid.: 581.
99.   Ibid.: 591–592.
100.   Bernstein and Cashore, 2007: 348.
101.   Slaughter, 2004: 12, 15 and 19–20.
102.   Slaughter, 2004: 240.
103.   E.g. Ruggie, 2008a.
104.   A/HRC/4/35, [82].
105.   Conger et al, 2001: 153.
106.   Stiglitz, 2006: 196.
107.   Ruggie, 2004: 516.
108.   Zerk, 2006: 305–308.
109.   See Ch 2.
110.   Ruggie, 2007a: 7.
111.   Shergold, 2009: 4 and 16.
112.   Whitman et al, 2008.
113.   Schwab, 2008: 108.
114.   Ibid.: 114, 115 and 118.
115.   Waddock, 2006: 7.
116.   *The Economist*, 2008: 12; CPWGRB, 2007: 18; and Zadek, 2001a: 16–17, 21.
117.   *The Economist*, 2008: 21.
118.   E/CN.4/2006/97, [52].
119.   E/CN.4/2006/97, [39].
120.   Ruggie, 2007a: 22.
121.   E/CN.4/2006/97, [40]–[51].
122.   E/CN.4/2006/97, [52].
123.   Price, 2003: 584.
124.   Ruggie, 2004: 514.
125.   *The Economist*, 2008: 12.
126.   Henderson, 2001b: 31.
127.   CPWGRB, 2007: 18.
128.   E.g. OECD Principles of Corporate Governance, UN Millennium Goals, UN Global Compact and UN Principles for Responsible Investment.
129.   Ruggie, 2008: [1].
130.   See Ch 4.
131.   Braithwaite and Drahos, 2000: 19.
132.   Ibid.: 530.
133.   On networks and nodes of governance generally see Burris et al, 2005.
134.   A/HRC/4/35, [53], [56]–[60].
135.   A/HRC/4/35, [61].
136.   A/HRC/4/35, [57], [61].
137.   Waddock, 2006: 5, 8.
138.   Zadek, 2001a: 16–17.
139.   Ibid.: 17.
140.   Price, 2003: 584.
141.   UN GC and Dalberg, 2007: 8.
142.   Ibid.: 4, 8.
143.   Allen, 2007: 63; and CCPA and BCA, 2007: vii–ix.
144.   Brugmann and Prahalad, 2007: 85–89.

145. CCPA and BCA, 2007: viii, x.
146. Ruggie, 2008: [105]–[106].
147. UN GC and Dalberg, 2007: 5.
148. Dine, 2005: 264.
149. Black, 2002: 2.
150. Cata Backer, 2005: 107.
151. Ibid.; original emphasis.
152. Black, 2004: 34.
153. Parker et al, 2004: 6.
154. Black, 2004: 34. Black's concept of regulation is also broadly accepted by other regulatory scholars, e.g. Parker et al, 2004: 1.
155. Parker et al, 2004: 6; and Parker, 2002.
156. Parker, 2007: 213, 237.
157. Ibid.: 237.
158. Ibid.: 217.
159. Ibid.: 237.
160. Ibid.: 237.
161. Ibid.: 208.
162. Ibid.: 213–214, quoting Selznick, 2002: 101.
163. Parker, 2007: 216, 218.
164. Parker, 2002: 298; and Parker, 2007: 209.
165. Parker, 2002: 298–299.
166. Parker, 2002: 297–299; and Parker, 2007: 237.
167. Parker, 2002: 293.
168. See Ch 3.
169. Parker, 2007: 4.
170. Ibid.: 214–229.
171. Ibid.: 230.
172. E.g. the critique of the WBCSD's self-assessment questionnaire for business (WBCSD, 2000: 24–25) in Henderson, 2001a: 27.
173. WBCSD, 2000: 24–25; cf Henderson, 2001a: 27.
174. Ward, 2003: iii.
175. Perrini et al, 2006: 16; emphasis added.
176. COM(2006)136, 2.
177. MacLeod, 2005: 550–551.
178. Fox et al, 2002: 1.
179. Ibid.
180. Ward, 2003: iii.
181. BLIHR, 2006: 4.
182. Ward, 2003: 5–6; and Kinley and Tadaki, 2004: 956–957.
183. On this and following arguments see Zerk, 2006: 34–36.
184. Ibid.: 35–36.
185. Villiers, 2008: 97.
186. Ibid.: 96–100.
187. Scott, 2008: 181.
188. *The Economist*, 2008: 4.
189. Arbour, 2008.
190. Ackerman and Bauer, 1976: 13–14.
191. Waddock, 2006: 5.
192. Nonet and Selznick, 1978: 77; original emphasis.
193. Compare this particular claim of corporate responsibility with the wider claim of moral decision-making responsibility in Finnis, 2003: 109–110.
194. This builds upon previous corporate responsiveness studies and meta-regulatory ideas of corporate reflexivity to internal and external business environments (e.g. Parker et al, 2004). They contrast a form of corporate responsibility limited to legally mandated and enforceable aspects of corporate responsibility with a multi-pronged form of corporate receptivity to such influences, corporate reflexivity in accommodating them, and resultant corporate responsiveness within a broader account of corporate responsibility.
195. Parker, 2002: 297.
196. Scott, 2008: 181–182.
197. Slaughter, 2004.

3.   Classic and new debates about corporate social responsibility

THE NEXUS BETWEEN CORPORATE THEORIZING AND CORPORATE REGULATORY PRACTICE

> The steadily evolving debate over CSR can no longer be dismissed as fad-dishness [and] is developing simultaneously with a radical rethinking of corporate theory. The progressive strategic integration of social and environmental concerns into the business operations and interactions with firms' stakeholder networks has been contributing to promoting a new model of economic success . . . in which CSR is integrated across all the corporate functions.
>
> – European CSR scholars Francesco Perrini, Stefano Pogutz and Antonio Tencati[1]

Theorizing properly about CSR is serious business for a wide range of CSR actors. A coherent approach to policy-making, regulation and business practice concerning CSR presupposes an underlying conceptual framework for corporate responsibility, govern-ance and sustainability. Such a framework requires attention to the status and legitimacy of corporations, and their relationship to all parts of society, from a range of legal, eco-nomic and other standpoints. Conceivably, it might take a distinct and cross-disciplinary body of theory about the place of corporations in global civil society to address more fully the deep questions of good corporate responsibility, governance and regulation at stake.[2] Indeed, given the importance for corporations of interactions between political systems (i.e. government), economic systems (i.e. markets), legal systems (i.e. adminis-tration of justice), regulatory systems (i.e. state and non-state regulation), and social systems (i.e. social ethics and cultures), the ultimate answers might well lie in the cross-disciplinary intersections between power theory, efficiency theory, justice theory and moral theory, from both national and international perspectives.[3]

Legislators, law reformers, policy-makers and others looking for comparative models in shaping and measuring how their own systems of corporate law and regulation advance good corporate responsibility and governance must grapple not only with dif-ferent CSR-related regulatory mechanisms, but also with the underlying ideological rationales, policy positions and socio-historical dynamics that give birth to them. On one view, for example, the UK's 21st century embrace of 'enlightened shareholder value' is a supposed 'Third Way' alternative to the extremes of shareholder primacy and stakeholder pluralism.[4] 'Third Way ideals as a response to the political and social events of recent years require corporations to relegitimize themselves' in a grand 'relegitimisation project' which requires a modified structure of virtue ethics for corporations, shared social agendas between corporations and other societal entities, and pursuit of governance and partnership opportunities, according to the University of London's Professor Sally Wheeler.[5] Similarly, contemporary CSR inquiries by executive governments and legislative committees must ultimately side explicitly or implicitly with one overall theoretical model of corporate responsibility and governance or another, chosen from amongst the *smorgasbord* of theories and models on offer.[6] Theoretical and conceptual intersections between corporate responsibility, on one hand, and international law and governance, on the other, are unavoidable in major institutional mapping and standard-setting initiatives on business and human rights.[7]

In the vast literature on corporate responsibility, governance and regulation, different thought leaders emerge in different times and places to set and reset the fundamental terms of debate. Their ideas become the poles around which different arguments and responses gravitate. More than 20 years ago, Lord Wedderburn crystallized how the classic debates among such famous protagonists are signposts on the path towards a coherent and comprehensive account of the interaction between corporate and societal interests, represented in national and global regulation of TNCs today:[8]

> Supranationality gives to corporate enterprises a new freedom from responsibility . . . The interests of multinational capital intersect with other constituencies, among them parent and host governments, each with its own system of national law. Complexity is, therefore, inevitable in any system of legal or quasi-legal regulation. Moreover, in a world in which the 'private' transnational enterprise deals not only in traditional commercial commodities and services but in goods which may affect the very future of life and of the planet itself (from oil and armaments to nuclear waste and biological preparations) – not to speak of the information revolution – the international 'public' interest must inevitably lean towards obligations that are both complex and high in the scale of fiduciary responsibility . . . Milton Friedman's question on who is to decide: 'what the social interest is?', is now raised to a power of international perplexity. If the corporation which Berle and Means rightly predicted would come to 'compete on equal terms with the modern state' can be reconstructed to meet new social demands only with difficulty, it is a doubly difficult task to constrain the multinational giant . . . What *is* a 'good *international citizen*' in (transnational) business, in the context (say) of the North-South debate?

This chapter tries to capture the important CSR-related ideas of some important 20th century and early 21st century thought leaders across a range of disciplines, and to bring their arguments and critiques of them to a wider audience of CSR actors. It also seeks to connect some classic CSR debates to emerging 21st century CSR concerns.

CORPORATE SOCIAL RESPONSIBILITY'S CONNECTION TO DEEP DEBATES

First Deep Debate – One Best Theory of Corporations in Society?

One deep debate concerns the possibility of accounting for everything connected with corporations and their place in the world according to one universal theory. Given the multi-dimensional complexity of corporate responsibility, governance and regulation

Is it justified for corporations to promote stakeholder and public good objectives even when these conflict with the interests of shareholders? If so, it follows that they should be legally permitted to do so. But should CSR be legally required, and if so, to what extent? And, whether or not it is legally permitted, there are further legitimation questions about the sort of participation to which non-shareholder stakeholders are entitled, and what sort of activities are acceptable on the part of other groups in the process of pressuring corporations to adopt and fulfil their legal and social obligations. Should shareholders act on the basis of their non-economic interests? What rights should non-governmental organisations (NGOs) have to put pressure on corporations to change their CR [corporate responsibility] objectives? Should consumers have duties as well as rights with respect to their marketplace decisions?

We do not have a comprehensive theory that enables us to address these questions in any systematic way.

– Legal philosopher, and human rights and CSR scholar, Professor Tom Campbell[9]

and the multiple cross-disciplinary standpoints from which these multi-faceted aspects can be examined, it is probable that no single theory or model is ever likely to achieve universal acceptance.[10] 'The policies underlying corporate law cannot (and presumably should not) be reduced to a unidimensional value, such as the economic objective of "maximizing shareholders' wealth"', explains the Wharton Business School's Professor Eric Orts.[11] 'Competing, mutually exclusive visions exist concerning the ultimate purpose and true nature of the corporation', adds his Wharton colleague, Professor Tom Dunfee.[12]

'The long-standing controversy over the rights of corporate shareholders in relation to nonshareholders involved in or affected by corporate activity is no closer to resolution today than it ever has been', concludes David Millon in his assessment of corporate law and governance at the outset of this century.[13] 'The corporate world is too complex and too variable for any single theory or discipline to be able to supply all of the answers to all of the problems of corporate governance', writes Australian corporate law and regulation scholar, Professor Stephen Bottomley.[14] Chancellor William Allen of the Delaware Court of Chancery suggests that the law of corporations is inherently 'contentious and controversial' because of the timeless way in which 'efficiency concerns, ideology, and interest group politics will commingle with history (including our semi-autonomous corporation law) to produce an answer that will hold for here and now, only to be torn by some future stress and to be reformulated once more'.[15]

Even the theory with ostensibly the greatest claim to mass political, business and academic support by the end of the 20th century in corporate regulatory systems following the Anglo-American corporate tradition – namely, shareholder primacy – must still compete for acceptance as the best corporate model for the unfolding conditions of the 21st century. Some ostensibly opposing theories might simply offer partial glimpses, or emphasize different aspects, of the full complexity of business–society relations. As in other areas of theory-building, we must be mindful of whether debates about alternative theories and models of corporate–society relations are really debates that occupy the same frames of reference, or rather go to different frames of reference. In doing so, we avoid the pitfall of 'forcing alternative theoretical approaches to play on the terrain of dominant theories', when the point of alternative theorizing and modelling is 'to point out that there are different questions being addressed for which different methods and standards of evaluation are required'.[16]

At this point, some readers might interject that, whatever the relevance of philosophising about corporate responsibility, governance and sustainability for the purpose of public and scholarly debate in an open market of ideas, this has less relevance once particular models of corporate responsibility and governance are adopted and then applied by participants within each corporate regulatory system. In other words, what use is corporate theorizing, especially in practising corporate responsibility, governance and sustainability as corporate actors, or even setting rules and guidelines for corporations as corporate lawmakers, policy-makers and regulators?

One part of the answer is that all practice requires interpretation, whether it is social practice, political practice, legal practice or business practice.[17] Another part of the answer lies in the public understanding and justification of particular systems and practices. For example, public discussion papers reviewing sanctions in corporate law cannot avoid dealing with tensions between competing regulatory approaches, such as the contrasts between 'deterrence' models of regulation, 'accommodative' models, 'responsive regulation' and risk-based regulation.[18] So, we might extrapolate from particular instances of a practice to a grand theory of it, try to make sense of features of a practice as we encounter it, or argue from a large-scale theory to its normative implications for a particular system. In doing so, we might understand theories as 'searchlights that illuminate particular judgments and show them for what they really are', given that 'theories are simply the (humanly constructed) means by which people make sense of the judgments that constitute their ethical and political worlds', rather than ideal answer guides that our practical judgments and actions in government, business and life must either meet or fail.[19]

Moreover, corporate theorizing is the bedrock of the normative justifications that inform corporate lawmaking, law reform and practice. Under the conditions of deliberative democracy, for example, there is at least some need for corporations to engage in organizational deliberation and public justification of the impact they have upon those members of society whose lives their business activity affects.[20] 'What has yet to emerge, however, is an agreed normative grounding that provides a convincing and generally accepted moral basis for the practice of CSR and for the legitimation of the pressures that are deployed to encourage its development', according to Professor Campbell.[21] In short, even if everyone agrees on the importance of corporations being socially responsible, we might still disagree over the components and boundaries of that responsibility. In doing so, we would be engaged in matters of argument and justification that pay tribute to at least some background theories of corporate responsibility and governance. Accordingly, all legal, regulatory and business reform to enhance corporate responsibility, governance and sustainability must proceed from some background conception of the relationship between corporations, their constituencies and the world around them.

Second Deep Debate – Multi-level Interconnectivity Between Corporate, Societal and Global Interests

> Where do we go from here? We go back to where we have come from, and re-examine the dynamics that came to shape us historically, so that we can rework our assumptions about state and society, enterprise and business, personal and social responsibility, and reconfigure some of these elements with the benefit of historical insight.
>
> – Vern Hughes, Executive Director of *Social Enterprise Partnerships*[22]

A second deep debate focuses upon the multi-jurisdictional and multi-sectoral systemic concerns of governance, regulation and responsibility that relate to CSR in the 21st century. In this debate, the modern company is viewed as both a subject and an object of governance, regulation and responsibility, with interactions between a micro-level organizational perspective, a meso-level jurisdictional perspective (of a national polity or economy, social democracy or corporate regulatory regime), and a macro-level global perspective of the business environment.[23] The conventional compartmentalization of governmental, business and community domains is increasingly subject to inter-penetration, with correlative implications for inter-connectedness and sharing of responsibilities. '(I)ncreasingly, we will have to work out how to bridge the gap between the public, private and civil society sectors', notes SustainAbility founder, John Elkington.[24]

Since the historical, political and economic battles seem to have been won by democracy and capitalism respectively, the question is how 21st century global society applies these forces to business within the wider systems of governance, regulation and responsibility in which business operates, or with which it otherwise interacts. A glimpse of this development appears, for example, in embryonic moves towards connecting 'value-centred market economics' to CSR, through 'a more complex approach to defining value and making that value central to government policy, business practice and the choices we as individuals make about what we buy and how we live', so that the business value proposition for corporations is conceived and practised in terms of 'a broader definition of value that includes the environmental and social impact of the decisions and actions of individuals, businesspeople, non-government organisations, corporations, politicians and policy makers'.[25]

Another part of this debate focuses upon the extent to which a neo-liberal coalition of interests across the economic and political spheres has captured the social sphere, and the flow-on implications of this for corporate responsibility, governance and regulation.[26] As Nobel Prize-winning economist Joseph Stiglitz bluntly puts it, 'politics and economics are intricately interwoven: corporations have used their financial muscle to protect themselves from bearing the full social consequences of their actions'.[27] Within this realm of debate, some people perceive a wrongful 'equation of democracy with the free operation of the market', which forms 'part of a struggle by a new transnational class associated with transnational corporations and institutions to subvert real democracy and undermine real freedom in order to extend their power'.[28] They do not perceive a natural order for corporations grounded in shareholder wealth-maximization, but rather view the contemporary corporate model and its correlative support within corporate law as contingencies reflecting 'an ordering of principles around dominant interests, at the expense of the most vulnerable'.[29]

Many critics of globalization, capitalism and corporatism sit in this camp. Critics of the phenomenon of 'corporatism', such as John Ralston Saul, point to the transnational threat it poses as the rival of representative government, creating conditions under which individual citizens become secondary rather than primary democratic participants in governance, in the sense that real power in conducting the business of government is more directed towards mediating between the interests of elite professional, expert and ownership groups than towards genuine attempts to achieve the common good.[30] Others view such talk as understating and even undermining the full benefits of corporations, capitalism and markets for society as a whole.

In attempts to connect corporate law and governance to wider aspects of societal governance and regulation, some corporate theorists maintain that the legitimacy of corporations, and hence how they are responsibly governed, must serve a wider conception of the public interest. Included within this group are advocates of social contract models, social concession and 'licence to operate' models, and social enterprise models of the corporation, as well as other advocates of socially responsible corporate profit-making. According to noted democratic theorist, Robert Dahl, for example, 'every large corporation should be thought of as a *social enterprise*; that is, as an entity whose existence and decisions can be justified only insofar as they serve public or social purposes'.[31] Some eminent corporate law scholars agree. 'To describe companies as social enterprises is thus to make a claim about the grounds of their legitimacy, and . . . (s)ince the public interest is the foundation of the legitimacy of companies, it follows that society is entitled to ensure that corporate power is exercised in a way that is consistent with that interest', adds former UK Company law Review Steering Group member, the late Professor John Parkinson.[32]

Other ideological positions lie along the spectrum between unwavering adherence to corporate orthodoxy, on one hand, and wholesale rejection of that orthodoxy and the theoretical architecture underpinning it, on the other. Even within shareholder-orientated systems of corporate regulation and practice, for example, some commentators call for reform of governmental policy, corporate law and business practice in directions that more explicitly facilitate corporate participation, harm-minimization and benefits for other stakeholders. Alternatively, corporate regulatory justifications might be grounded in recognition of the interplay between public and private interests in corporate governance and decision-making, beyond simply any private ordering of financial interests between companies and those who govern and invest in them. More broadly, such justifications might be grounded in the full conditions of liberal democratic rule, including the treatment of governed peoples as the supreme source of all politico-legal authority, and hence fully participating subjects in their own governance (and not simply objects of limitless state commands).[33] This has flow-on implications for systems of corporate governance and regulation within wider systems of societal governance and regulation.[34] Grand ideas of corporate democracy and popular sovereignty also underpin such views, as we shall see.[35]

Third Deep Debate – Market Capitalism versus Civil Society

Societal infrastructure for market capitalism

> The market economy is based on the unplanned, uncontrolled response of individual producers and of corporations, small or large, to the will and the purchasing power of the consumer at home and abroad . . . A central question, as we all know, is how much this economic entity, this machine, functions independently and how much it requires support for, and restraint on, the purchasing power – the effective demand – that empowers the system. Additionally and urgently there is the question of what guidance and control this machine must have so that it will serve and not impair the public interest; specifically, what government regulation is needed. This last ranks as one of the most contentious social and political issues of the time.
>
> – John Kenneth Galbraith[36]

A third deep debate concerns CSR's capacity to mediate between the needs of market capitalism and civil society in the 21st century. Capitalism as constructed, regulated and practised to this point arguably has inherent weaknesses and limits in meeting at least some 21st century conditions and needs. Those pressure points are most exposed in the extent to which market capitalism privileges financial wealth-generation ahead of other societal values, promotes financial capital at the expense of other forms of human capital, privatizes profits while externalizing costs, entrenches prosperity gaps between corporate insiders and corporate outsiders, and disavows ownership of collective problems of societal governance, regulation and responsibility. Of course, some distinctions can also be drawn between the normative conditions that constitute the 'internal market morality' that underpins market-based economies and business models, on one hand, and the normative conditions for other public goods, even those potentially affected by business activity, on the other.[37]

'Social democrats embrace the discipline of markets tempered by the demands of human decency' argue those politicians who embrace the Third Way's straddling of the old left and right wings of politics, striving for a vision of civil society that 'harnesses the dynamism of markets but one that never loses sight of the fact that markets are made for human beings, rather than human beings for markets'.[38] Former UK Editor of the *Financial Times*, Sir Geoffrey Owen, envisages Western capitalism's evolution since World War II in terms of moving from a phase of 'managerial capitalism' to one of 'investor capitalism', and wonders whether the 21st century is ushering in a third phase of 'socially responsible capitalism'.[39] If J.K. Galbraith's observation is correct that '(c)apitalism in its original eighteenth- and nineteenth-century design was a cruel system, which would not have survived the social tension and the revolutionary attitudes it inspired had there not been a softening, ameliorating response from the state',[40] then the mediation of the state between market capitalism and Galbraith's 'good society' is integral. Moreover, in the 21st century, this mediation is not confined to what government sets in place through the instrument of law, but rather embraces a richer mix of state and non-state contributions to societal and global governance, regulation and responsibility.

In J.K. Galbraith's vision of 'the good society', the classic contest between those who favour little or no state intervention in market economies and the rewards they reap from it, on one hand, and those who advocate such intervention 'to arrest socially damaging or deeply self-destructive tendencies', on the other, underlies debate about state intervention in markets for at least the major purposes of protecting the planet, safeguarding employees and other vulnerable groups from 'the adverse effects of the economic machine', ensuring minimum standards for goods and services, and curing the economic system's inherent inhibitions on its effectiveness.[41] Similarly, Harvard University's Professor John Ruggie (who is also the UNSRSG) introduces the notion of 'embedded liberalism' to explain 'how the capitalist countries learned to reconcile the efficiency of markets with the values of social community that markets themselves require in order to survive and thrive', as part of 'a grand social bargain' in which society's disparate groups are taken to agree to open markets only on the basis that the social adjustment costs of open markets are contained and shared.[42] Ruggie describes this as 'the essence of the embedded liberalism compromise: economic liberalization was embedded in social community'.[43]

Reporting in his capacity as UNSRSG to the UN Human Rights Council in 2008, Professor Ruggie identifies the point at which the world has arrived in the 21st century in the evolving relation between markets, business and human rights, as follows:[44]

> Business is the major source of investment and job creation, and markets can be highly efficient means for allocating scarce resources. They constitute powerful forces capable of generating economic growth, reducing poverty, and increasing demand for the rule of law, thereby contributing to the realization of a broad spectrum of human rights. But markets work optimally only if they are embedded within rules, customs and institutions. Markets themselves require these to survive and thrive, while society needs them to manage the adverse effects of market dynamics and produce the public goods that markets undersupply. Indeed, history, teaches us that markets pose the greatest risks – to society and business itself – when their scope and power far exceed the reach of the institutional underpinnings that allow them to function smoothly and ensure their political sustainability. This is such a time and escalating charges of corporate-related human rights abuses are the canary in the coal mine, signalling that all is not well.

On a broader scale, managing the tension between free-market capitalism, true corporate value-creation and global social welfare is a long-running theme in many critiques of capitalism's worst extremes, especially critiques informed by 21st century concerns of planetary sustainability, interdependent national economies and resultant transnational socio-economic prosperity. Sustainable development advocate and Chairman of the UK Sustainable Development Commission, Jonathon Porritt, reframes capitalism around the sustainable deployment of both financial and non-financial forms of capital in this way: 'At its heart, therefore, sustainable development comes down to one all-important challenge: is it possible to conceptualize and then operationalize an alternative model of capitalism – one that allows for the sustainable management of the different capital assets upon which we rely so that the yield from those different assets sustains us *now*, as well as in the future?'.[45]

According to Porritt, 'the idea of capitalism as if the world matters [is] that sustainable development provides the only intellectually coherent basis upon which to transform contemporary capitalism [since] the bipolar challenges of, on the one hand, the biophysical limits to growth and, on the other, of the terrible damage being done to the human spirit through the pursuit of unbridled materialism, will compel a profound transformation of contemporary capitalism'.[46] Similarly, in the words of the Chair of the Copenhagen Climate Council and author of *The Weather Makers*, Professor Tim Flannery, the most striking challenge confronting 21st century civilization is one of sustainable planetary existence:[47]

> This twenty-first century of ours will be faced with appalling social injustices, with conflict and pestilence. But these will not be its defining challenges. Instead, our task is a far more difficult one: to bring sustainability to a species that has not known it since it manufactured its first tool . . . If we are successful in forging a sustainable way of living in the twenty-first century, then perhaps the principles we develop will become the guiding principles of a truly sustainable global civilisation. Whatever the case, increasing awareness of our unique position and role on planet Earth will necessarily drive political, economic and social agendas long after current preoccupations have faded.

'At every step along the growth path – from subsistence to commerce to emerging markets to high-tech – both the public and private sectors have responsibilities', notes Professor Jeffery Sachs, adding that '(a)t all stages of development, the government must also ensure that the basic conditions of a functioning market-based economy are in place [in] various dimensions of social order and the rule of law'.[48] Whatever the limits on capitalism's self-contained capacity to stimulate non-market-influenced social co-operation and to redress socio-economic inequality, capitalism relies upon ethics, trust and other mechanisms within its own domain to make market dynamics work.[49] In the words of Nobel Prize-winning economist, Amartya Sen, '(s)uccessful markets operate the way they do not just on the basis of exchanges being "allowed", but also on the solid foundation of institutions (such as effective legal structures that support the rights ensuing from contracts) and behavioral ethics (which makes the negotiated contracts viable without the need for constant litigation to achieve compliance)'.[50]

However, there is a dawning realization that the preconditions that enable efficient and sustainable markets to meet the common needs of civil society, governments and business include much more than just protection for freedom of contract, property rights, open competition and informed commercial agreement and investment.[51] These market preconditions also encompass 'curtailing individual and social harms imposed by markets', including 'corporate-related human rights abuses', especially since the history of globalization initiatives in earlier eras points to the societal unsustainability of global markets and economies without systemic architecture for handling their costs as well as producing their benefits.[52]

Social theorists and activists might express this in terms of what economic prosperity requires as preconditions for its fulfillment, based upon pre-existing social trust and other elements of a civil society, instead of economic prosperity being seen as itself the precondition for social prosperity and well-being.[53] Pointing to the 'balanced interaction' between civic, governmental and economic activities in a healthy civil society, some thought leaders nominate preconditions for an effective market economy that include factors like fair competition, moral capital, public goods, full-cost pricing, just distribution and ecological sustainability.[54] Economic scholars point to societal preconditions for sustained business prosperity such as good corporate governance standards, transparent corporate operations, effective stock exchanges and financial regulatory systems, stable legal and dispute settlement frameworks, competitive markets and independent financial media scrutiny.[55] 'At the core of most successful business relationships are foundational values such as trustworthiness and promise keeping', according to two leading business ethics scholars, so that 'some ethical framework is a necessary condition for business'.[56]

Adopting a systemic perspective of global business regulation, Professors John Braithwaite and Peter Drahos point to different features of the societal superstructure enabling capitalism to flourish:[57]

> Capitalism has not flourished best when it has been centrally planned by the state, nor when it has been unregulated. Plural good governance of capitalism by states, international organizations, business self-regulation, professions and NGOs is needed for secure, egalitarian and efficient capitalism.

All corporations in society trade and rely upon these preconditions for business to flourish, even if they are sub-optimally supported or even taken for granted. In other words, there are crucial connections between the system of efficient corporate production and delivery, on one hand, and both the societal preconditions underpinning that system and the societal needs serviced by that system, on the other. This is the set of connections that a richer, multi-focal account of corporate governance, responsibility and sustainability embraces.

Market dynamics alone are no guarantee of good socio-ethical outcomes. The alignment between business advantage and societal concerns has its limits, not least because 'it is implausible to think that *all* socially beneficial corporate conduct conveniently happens to be profit-maximizing'.[58] While free-market advocates and critics alike accept that some misalignments occur in a completely unfettered market economy between the private incentives and costs of market forces, on one hand, and their social costs and benefits, on the other, they commonly disagree about the best solution.[59] Moreover, strict profit-maximization can produce inefficient outcomes, and hence detract from aggregate social wealth, because imperfect markets inevitably allow externalities and, hence, 'behaviour which is privately profitable will not be wealth-maximising overall where an actor can ignore the costs that its activities impose on others'.[60] The single-value metric of self-interested profit-maximization gives due recognition to the social value of efficient wealth-creation, but without necessarily giving correlative recognition and weight to other social interests and values that ought not to be compromised or sacrificed in its pursuit.[61]

Market dynamics also have their own limitations, including the consequences of market failure, the need for supervening governmental regulatory support and intervention, problems of incommensurability inherent in utilitarian ideas of maximizing overall welfare, identification of societal interests beyond economic efficiency, and even demonstrating the connection between economic efficiency and societal well-being. 'Corporations may be good at making money, but they are not as capable at providing things that take a long time to produce, things that cannot be easily reduced to a monetary value, things with benefits that are widely shared, or things that are valued by people with no money', notes Professor Greenfield, adding that 'the market cannot be trusted to produce and deliver many things that people truly desire'.[62] In this way, the ultimate sustainability of systems devoted to enhancing social well-being through economic prosperity is threatened by the 'fundamental institutional misalignment . . . between the scope and impact of economic forces and actors, on one hand, and the capacity of societies to manage their adverse consequences, on the other'.[63]

One classic argument says that increases in shareholder wealth through market prosperity have a 'trickle down' effect through the rest of society, so that overall social welfare increases proportionately too. An accurate empirical assessment of this argument would need to take account of multiple forms of prosperity-related benefits, and not just increased individual wealth for shareholders. Its horizon would also need to extend across developed and developing economies over time. Any 'trickle down' of wealth from the richest countries to the poorest ones by means other than foreign aid is undermined by the fact that, as leading Princeton ethicist Professor Peter Singer notes starkly, 'the rich in industrialized nations buy virtually nothing made by the very poor'.[64] While investor-driven economic development clearly can be a gateway to economic prosperity for some, the uneven spread of economic prosperity within and across countries, along with the adverse social consequences of development for some communities, together raise questions about the scope and acceptability of the associated costs to the social fabric.[65] As US President Barack Obama notes, 'today's winner-take-all economy' is one 'in which a rising tide doesn't necessarily lift all boats'.[66]

Similarly, as identified by Robert Dahl, the record in all democratic countries (and in many non-democratic countries too) shows that the social harms and costs of unregulated market economies are ameliorated by governmental regulatory interventions that are necessary not only to provide the institutional architecture for market-capitalism itself, but also to remedy the unacceptably unequal distributions of political resources (e.g. money, wealth, position and influence) that result from pure market forces.[67] In short, no matter how the defining tension between market-driven social wealth-generation and the civil society dimension of social well-being is approached and ultimately resolved, all roads eventually arrive at this same grand destination of managing this tension – a tension that is also integral to the place of corporations in society and what that means for corporate responsibility, governance and regulation.

Many supporters of the shareholder primacy model agree that corporate law and governance must serve the interests of society, especially in achieving overall social efficiency.[68] Indeed, both supporters and critics of CSR can agree that the normative justifications and limits of business activity are grounded in underlying notions of social utility.[69] In terms of efficiency, unfettered market economies that permit unbridled profit-maximization are systems in which private financial self-interest and the costs of pursuing it will not always be efficiently aligned with social costs and benefits, in which case 'the pursuit of self-interest will not result in the well-being of society'.[70] Some advocates of efficiency-based models claim that there are 'several roads to efficiency' which are not limited to an essentially shareholder-based system of corporate responsibility and governance.[71] Of course, the elements constituting social efficiency or utility are themselves subject to much debate, as is the relation of market-orientated efficiency to other aspects of societal well-being.

Similarly, the unifying economic interest that all shareholders have in corporate profit-making and shareholder wealth-generation still leaves room for debate about responsible constraints upon unfettered profit-maximization and cost-externalization by corporations,[72] values and interests of shareholders beyond their financial stake in corporations,[73] and differences between treating shareholders as investors of financial capital and treating them as members actively involved in corporate governance.[74] All of this has implications for a full account of the market value and social worth of a business enterprise.

For example, the discipline that markets for investment, labour, corporate control and products and services keep exerting in different ways upon corporate management obviously rests upon the nature of those markets, the information and terms on which market transactions occur, and the costs and benefits for market participants in those transactions, all within a wider set of governance and regulatory conditions.[75] Even working within these structures and the models underpinning them, 21st century changes in the business environment – such as decreased public, political and regulatory tolerance of externalizing costs of production in socio-environmentally damaging ways, and increased sophistication in the tools for measuring and reporting social, environmental and other consequences of business activity – all serve to produce changes in how we approach, use and reform these pre-existing structures and models.

Whatever the advantages of 'free' and 'open' markets, they therefore need regulating for different governmental, business and social reasons, and through a variety of means too. For example, fears of political instability, social disharmony and economic ruin prompted capitalist societies to create social safety nets and welfare systems in the wake of the Great Depression, not least to enhance market support and to compensate those harmed economically by market failures.[76] In the wake of the global financial and credit crisis of 2008, governmental intervention and re-regulation to stabilize the world's interdependent economies and financial systems underscored the limits of market capitalism or at least weaknesses in its regulatory infrastructure. In the eyes of former UN Secretary-General Kofi Annan, the future of the global economy and multilateral trade regime rests on reciprocal guarantees of universal human rights, employment standards and environmental protection, in a new system of global governance in which governments, business and others all have a part to play, in light of the global economy's vulnerability 'to backlash from all the "isms" of our post-Cold War world: protectionism; populism; nationalism; ethnic chauvinism; fanaticism; and terrorism'.[77]

Fourth Deep Debate – Corporate Democratization

A fourth deep debate concerns the democratization of corporate structures, powers and voices. Corporate democracy's internal concerns include the balance of authority between shareholders and managers as well as the 'participation of people in the governing of firms', while its external concerns include the formal subjection of corporate power to the rule of law as well as other forms of democratic accountability for corporations.[78] An example of corporate democracy's narrower concerns lies in contemporary debates in the USA about increasing shareholder power to bring about changes in corporate governance arrangements within large publicly listed companies with dispersed shareholdings.[79]

Yet, the desirability and mechanisms of making corporate executives more accountable to shareholders form only one key strand of this corporate democratization agenda. Its wider version extends beyond a corporation's inner relations between

(W)hy are passive shareholders (many of whom don't even vote their proxies) more important than the employees who make the corporation function, the communities where the corporation operates, the consumers who buy the corporation's products, the pensioners who used to work at the company, and the environment that supports all living systems? All of these enable the corporation to operate and are affected by its operations. Why does maximizing profit for shareholders matter most? Why is it only shareholders who have a vote in corporate elections? Why is it only shareholders who are supposed to be represented by the board of directors? And why is it only shareholders who can hold the board of directors legally accountable? . . . (I)f we want corporations to operate with a broader public purpose, they cannot be ruthlessly focused on maximizing profits for shareholders. Put simply, sometimes serving a broader public purpose is going to come at the expense of maximizing profits for shareholders.

– Lee Drutman and Charlie Cray, *The Peoples Business: Controlling Corporations and Restoring Democracy,* The Report of the Citizen Works Corporate Reform Commission[80]

shareholders and management. If, according to classical democratic theory, democracy provides a model for all of society's organizational forms, 'the collective values that underlie markets and enable the social choice of consent by the governed' might be expected to track closely the evolution of democracy's methods of establishing fairness-based social consensus.[81] Accordingly, it is not surprising to find scholars arguing that 'its decision-making processes are a legitimate subject of democratic theory (which is focused on improving the social, economic and environmental justice of decision-making)', or that access to corporate and public justice mechanisms for stakeholders with legitimate corporate expectations, grievances and claims is 'an essential part of citizenship in a contemporary democracy'.[82] In turn, corporate governance's progressive incorporation of 'the fundamental democratic procedures of enfranchisement, separation of powers and representation' creates connections between systems of corporate, political and social governance, as coherent and coordinated mechanisms by which the consent of people to the various systems governing and regulating their lives is secured and legitimized.[83] In these and other ways, corporate governance intersects with corporate democracy.

In terms of political theory, 'the concentration of power in private hands' as facilitated by corporate law's structures (e.g. limited liability) provides the platform for state and perhaps non-state involvement in setting 'the conditions subject to which that power may be exercised: a theory contending that power may be legitimately held only for the purpose of furthering the public good', according to Professor Parkinson.[84] Democracy's primary directive that all citizens are political equals with equal votes must mean, 'in relation to corporations, that every citizen has an equal say about how these powerful entities must behave', according to Professor Joel Bakan.[85] Even if governments wrongfully act on any occasion in the service of discrete corporate interests over more diffuse public interests, the pivotal democratic point is that governments retain their regulatory and law-making power, and therefore can be influenced to wield that power one way or the other.[86]

According to some theories that cut across the state and non-state domains, democratic ideas and values inform the justification, structure and processes of much contemporary corporate responsibility, governance and sustainability. In theories as diverse as deliberative democracy, corporate constitutionalism and CSR meta-regulation, for example, important mutual themes emerge of creating conditions for the implication of public and private interests in institutional power-wielding, rendering institutional exercises of power accountable to those affected by them, and providing mechanisms that give a voice to those affected in this way. The theme of enhanced deliberation across public and corporate domains as societal locations for the mutual promotion of deliberative democracy is picked up in the work of contemporary democratic theorists Amy Gutmann and Dennis Thompson, as follows:[87]

> Corporations are another, quite different, example of an institution that should be subject to more deliberation. For citizens to have influence over institutions that affect their basic liberties and opportunities, they need forums within which they can propose and debate issues concerning the basic economic structure of society, over which corporations exert a kind of control that is properly considered political, not only economic.

Considered from a meta-regulatory perspective, becoming a socially responsible company requires a company's meaningful internalization of self-regulation that is responsive to external regulatory forces of various kinds.[88] This requires institutional embedding of legal and social responsibility through various means. These include public policy goals directed towards corporate responsibility and sustainability values and processes, meaningful management commitment to an ethic of corporate responsibility and sustainability within the regulatory framework underpinning those goals, effective establishment of self-regulatory organizational functions and behaviours to that end, effective organizational integration of these corporate responsibility and sustainability goals, and evaluation of this internal system in response to regular internal reviews and external dynamics.[89] Meta-regulatory scholars such as Dr Christine Parker view the resulting corporate openness and responsiveness to this 'strategic stakeholder environment' for companies primarily through the prism of three principles of 'social responsibility self-regulation' – namely, principles of 'disclosure', 'consultation' and 'contestation'.[90]

Corporate constitutionalists respond to some of the same dynamics of internal and external corporate environments in propounding core framework principles of 'accountability', 'deliberation' and 'contestability' for corporate decision-making.[91] Considered from both legal and regulatory perspectives, this means that shareholders have societal roles as corporate members that include, but also extend beyond, their roles as suppliers of investment capital or participants in a share trading market for establishing corporate value.[92] Under this 'corporate constitutionalist framework', the three principles of 'accountability' (going to the separation of decision-making powers between managers and shareholders), 'deliberation' (going to the corporation's processes of decision-making) and 'contestability' (going to corporations as sites for contests between shareholder and non-shareholder interests within those decision-making processes) constitute 'a normative framework with which we can assess the legitimacy of corporate decision-making'.[93]

Final Deep Debate – Convergence and Divergence of Corporate Regulatory Regimes

A final deep area of debate concerns the global convergence and divergence of corporate thinking, regulation and practice. The debate about the extent of convergence worldwide on the Anglo-American model of corporate responsibility, governance and regulation lies at the heart of the famous debate in corporate legal literature ignited by claims by Professors Hansmann and Kraakman about 'the end of history for corporate law', as discussed next in this chapter.[94] Crucial developments in the balance between shareholder-regarding doctrines and stakeholder-regarding doctrines are also emerging from the intermingling of corporate regulatory doctrines and practices across jurisdictions. This leads some Anglo-American corporate law scholars to conclude that 'shareholder capitalism in the UK is beginning to diverge from its American counterpart and develop its third way: a long-term enlightened shareholder value perspective with strong elements of European stakeholder thinking'.[95]

One aspect of this debate covers the impact of different politico-legal, historical and socio-cultural influences upon the development of particular markets and corporate regulatory regimes in particular countries. Convergence across the globe upon a shareholder-based model as the most socio-economically efficient organizational model, with the accompanying rise of a mass shareholding class as a political force reinforcing this model, is traditionally contrasted with the divergence in models that accompanies different historical, institutional and cultural dynamics in each corporate regulatory system or group of systems worldwide.[96] This is manifested in varying national circumstances such as a prevailing social democratic ideology favouring employees over investors, public and political mistrust of financial power being concentrated in a few institutional hands, and the particular 'path-dependent' dynamics producing particular corporate regulatory regimes that vary from country to country.[97]

Beyond its significance for a country's corporate regulatory regime, 'a country's social, cultural and political context' also has 'considerable influence on the development of national public policies on CSR'.[98] Wharton's Professor Tom Donaldson contrasts European and US approaches to CSR in these broad terms:[99]

> In Europe, CSR is weighted more towards serving – or at least not conflicting with – broader social aims, such as environmental sustainability and human rights. Bluntly stated, when it comes to CSR, Europeans view US companies as too narrow, legalistic and compliance oriented, while Americans see their European friends as naïve and idealistic.

Beyond the Western world, India's marrying of traditional philanthropy from family firms with contemporary pressures to humanize working conditions, China's emerging engagement with CSR and climate change for its globalizing economy, African attraction of infrastructure investors from countries with non-Western CSR sensibilities, and emerging markets at 'the bottom of the pyramid' all differ in important ways from Europe's pursuit of becoming a world-class region of CSR leadership and other Western approaches to CSR.[100] 'For global companies this means that a one-size-fits-all approach to corporate responsibility may not work', concludes *The Economist* in its 2008 report on CSR.[101] Issues of convergence and divergence also arise in the emergence of a body of comparative CSR-related law and regulation across jurisdictions, as outlined in Chapter 5, with modelling implications for CSR-sensitive reform from one country to another.

CLASSIC DEBATES AND THE EVOLUTION OF ANGLO-AMERICAN AND ANGLO-COMMONWEALTH CSR-RELATED THINKING

> Competing, mutually exclusive visions exist concerning the ultimate purpose and true nature of the corporation. Variously described as communitarian versus contractarian, the *Berle v. Dodd* debate, the shareholder paradox, or the separation [of ownership and control] thesis, these differing visions reflect conflicting political and moral preferences concerning the nature of corporations. Most famously, the debate is reflected in the sharply conflicting views of Milton Friedman and his many critics. Ultimately, the basis of the disagreement boils down to a monotonic versus a pluralistic view of corporate objectives.
>
> – Wharton Business School's Professor Tom Dunfee[102]

The Classic Berle–Dodd Debate

In light of these deep debates, we can more clearly analyse now the CSR implications of some landmark contributions to thinking about corporations and their responsibility, governance and regulation. The famous Berle–Dodd *Harvard Law Review* debate from the 1930s is the reference point for much debate since then, across law and other disciplines. The Berle–Dodd debate turns upon Adolf Berle's classic thesis that 'all powers granted to a corporation or to the management of a corporation . . . are necessarily and at all times exercisable only for the rateable benefit of all the shareholders'.[103] Writing in the same shadow of publicly exposed corporate abuses and managerial excesses,[104] and agreeing with the need for safeguards against self-interested directors diverting profits to themselves instead of shareholders, Harvard's Professor E. Merrick Dodd nevertheless repudiated Berle's central thesis in his celebrated 1932 article. Emphasizing the law's treatment of boards as fiduciaries owing fidelity to the company as an institution rather than directly to the body of shareholders, Dodd exposed the fault lines in the common translation of this position into 'single-minded devotion to stockholder profit'.[105] Accordingly, 'the view that business corporations exist for the sole purpose of making profits for their stockholders' is apt to give way to a theoretically defensible and law-informing 'view of the business corporation as an economic institution which has a social service as well as a profit-making function', he argued.[106]

Berle's response to Dodd that '(y)ou cannot abandon emphasis on "the view that business corporations exist for the sole purpose of making profits for their [stockholders]" until such time as you are prepared to offer a clear and reasonably enforceable scheme of responsibilities to someone else'[107] is not simply part of a long-finished historical debate. '(C)orporate law in Delaware, like corporate law elsewhere, generally allows directors to redirect wealth from shareholders to other stakeholders', sometimes under cover of judicial rhetoric 'suggesting that actions that appear to reduce current shareholder wealth might nevertheless offer some hope of a long-run shareholder benefit', according to Professor Lynn Stout, concluding that 'Delaware courts seem to have come down rather firmly on Dodd's side of the Berle–Dodd debate'.[108] 'Directors are, and will always be, forced to choose between different interests and the only realistic criterion on which they can base their decisions is the long term survival and prosperity of the company', according to former Australian National Companies and Securities Commission chairman, Henry Bosch AO, relying directly upon Berle's identification of the need for directors to have 'a clear and reasonably enforceable scheme of responsibilities' for proper boardroom decision-making.[109]

Nevertheless, the simple equation today of Berle's position with shareholder primacy and Dodd's position with CSR misreads both the point and context of the Berle–Dodd debate of the 1930s, and the positions of both protagonists changed over time in any case, with Berle in hindsight famously conceding the outcome of the debate to Dodd at one point.[110] However, even that concession must not be taken out of context for, as Berle's later reflections reveal, he regarded his concession to Dodd as a concession to the unfolding reality of modern American corporate life, as distinct from a correct normative position about the role of corporate managers as socio-economic statesmen. '(M)odern directors are not limited to running business enterprise for maximum profit, but are in fact and recognized in law as administrators of a community system', acknowledged Berle in the mid-1960s, in characterizing capitalism's 'revolution' between 1930 and 1960 as introducing 'a measure of social ethics and human morality into the business system'.[111]

In the lead-up to the Roosevelt Administration's New Deal, public disquiet about the capitalist system's contribution to the Great Depression, and the limits of an economy grounded in corporate profit-maximization alone, mingled with public uncertainty about how governments would manage the economy and what societal role corporations might play in that enterprise.[112] Over the next quarter-century, the societal context shifted dramatically again. State power prevailed over business power in managing and stabilizing the economy, backed by a supportive socio-political consensus 'justifying government intervention for distributional purposes as well as for production efficiency'.[113] Economic power resided in mass consumer markets serviced by manufacturing and distribution corporations, with links between profitable mass production, income distribution and purchasing power.[114] Interdependence increased between a national economy, corporate power and a variety of community and corporate constituent interests.[115] Business organization became progressively more sensitized to successive state regulatory interventions in promoting allocation of resources as demanded by the community's areas of need, especially beyond the limits of what the profit motive alone might deliver.[116] Most importantly, the growth of dispersed shareholdings separated corporate ownership and control, with deep implications for corporate responsibility, governance and regulation.

Berle and Means, and the Separation of Ownership and Control

The global rise of a new mass shareholding class, institutional investors and universal owners in the late 20th and early 21st centuries adds new impetus to classic corporate debates, from the Berle–Dodds debate and the work of Berle and Means on corporate ownership and control in the 1930s to Friedmanite rejection of CSR in the 1960s and 1970s. The parameters of these debates keep shifting, as corporate governance and investment experts Stephen Davis, Jon Lukomnik and David Pitt-Watson make clear in their 21st century analysis of the rise of 'citizen investors':[117]

In the 1930s, management gurus Adolf Berle and Gardiner Means depicted a world where corporate economic power was enormous and unaccountable. To maintain public goodwill, they encouraged chief executives to behave voluntarily as if the goal of their companies was to benefit society at large. In the twenty-first century, we argue that listed companies' shareholders reflect the demands of society at large. What we are arguing is consistent both with the view of Milton Friedman – that the interests of a company are those of its shareowners – and with the view of those who argue that companies should be more socially responsible. Society and shareowners are becoming one and the same.

As Professor Parkinson noted towards the end of the last century, such classic 20th century corporate debates have a direct connection to CSR and its legal dimensions:[118]

> Whether decision-making in public companies should be guided purely by considerations of profit or should take account of the interests of third parties and social welfare more generally has been debated at least since Berle and Means raised the issue in 1932. In recent years there has been a resurgence of interest in this and related questions, manifested, for example, in a growing literature on corporate social responsibility . . .

> Identifying appropriate modes of control over management demands that we first decide what the objectives of companies should be. These questions of means and ends form part of the subject-matter of many disciplines, including moral and political philosophy, economics, and management studies. They are also part of the subject-matter of law. Whether one emphasizes the role of the state or of contract in corporate existence, companies are creations of law, their objectives are defined by law, and the law is a major source of the practical constraints on management behaviour.

In their classic work on corporations, Berle and Means identified a 'corporate revolution', evidenced by trends of 'increasing concentration [of corporate economic power], increasing dispersion of stock ownership, and increasing separation of ownership and control'.[119] Berle and Means therefore set the scene for much subsequent academic and regulatory debate, essentially revolving around the agency costs of different ways of increasing shareholder control and influence over directors, while decreasing the scope for self-interested and other forms of managerial discretion that are not in the interests of shareholders as a whole.[120]

Their great contribution lies not only in identifying the features of this corporate revolution for the times in which they wrote, but also in highlighting the unsatisfactoriness of both a 'strict property rights' account of corporations, under which corporations must be run 'for the *sole* benefit of the security owners despite the fact that the latter have ceased to have power over or to accept responsibility for the *active* property in which they have an interest', and alternatively an account of corporations based upon absolute and unfettered managerial discretion, 'giving to the groups in control powers which are absolute and not limited by any implied obligation with respect to their use'.[121] Berle and Means also foresaw the modern corporation and its economic power as a rival for the state in a competition to become the pre-eminent societal institution, with implications for the function and content of both corporate law and business practice.[122]

All of this provides the context for their important conclusion about the need for a new understanding of corporations and a 'third alternative' to the extremes of 'strict property rights' and unfettered managerial discretion:[123]

> This third alternative offers a wholly new concept of corporate activity. Neither the claims of ownership nor those of control can stand against the paramount interests of the community . . .

When a convincing system of community obligations is worked out and is generally accepted, in that moment the passive property right of today must yield before the larger interests of society. Should the corporate leaders, for example, set forth a program comprising fair wages, security to employees, reasonable service to their public, and stabilization of business, all of which would divert a portion of the profits from the owners of passive property, and should the community generally accept such a scheme as a logical and human solution of industrial difficulties, the interests of passive property owners would have to give way. Courts would almost of necessity be forced to recognize the result, justifying it by whatever of the many legal theories they might choose. It is conceivable – indeed it is almost essential if the corporate system is to survive – that the 'control' of the great corporations should develop into a purely neutral technocracy, balancing a variety of claims by various groups in the community and assigning to each a portion of the income stream on the basis of public policy rather than private cupidity.

Still, much about the actualization of this 'third alternative' remains problematic. We cannot expect 'a convincing system of community obligations' to be worked out within corporate law alone, at least as it is presently configured. Nor is that reordering likely to emerge just from the protection of non-shareholder and third party interests that increasingly occurs in departments of law devoted to human rights, environmental protection and safe workplaces, for example. This arguably takes us further into the realm of political, moral and economic drivers of this reordering as well as legal ones, as part of corporate responsiveness to the dynamics associated with developing 'a convincing system of community obligations' for the 21st century corporation. In addition, corporate wealth-sharing 'on the basis of public policy rather than private cupidity' raises challenging questions about the relations between governmental and business interests. Nevertheless, their analysis poses a challenge for defenders and critics of shareholder primacy alike, given that adequate boardroom decision-making frameworks and corporate performance criteria addressing the inherent tensions in the 'third alternative' remained elusive many decades after this initial study, as they still do today.[124]

Milton Friedman on the Business of Business

Friedman's corporate social responsibility views in context
Nobel prize-winning economist Milton Friedman's famous pronouncement on CSR is the pole around which much Anglo-American and Anglo-Commonwealth CSR debate has gravitated since the latter part of the 20th century. 'Few trends could so thoroughly undermine the very foundation of our free society as the acceptance by corporate officials of a social responsibility other than to make as much money for their stockholders as possible', argued Friedman half a century ago in his landmark book, *Capitalism and Freedom*.[125] Even considered on their own terms, Friedman's famous words are not a self-evident code of conduct or decision-making formula for corporate management. The injunction 'to make as much money for . . . stockholders as possible' begs various questions. What is the appropriate time-scale in the corporation's life-cycle over which that is assessed? Is the obligation to pursue profit qualified or limited in any way and, if so, by what? Who are the 'stockholders' in question – are they current, potential or future investors? Is there one economically focused shareholder value or are there multiple economic and non-economic shareholder values? Is the assumed separation between business and societal concerns absolute or are they interdependent and, if so, how? In what sense do 'corporate officials' owe duties to 'their stockholders', as distinct from the corporation itself?[126]

This famous statement by Friedman is preceded by a revealing comment that 'there is one and only one social responsibility of business – to use its resources and engage in activities designed to increase its profits so long as it stays within the rules of the game, which is to say, engages in open and free competition, without deception or fraud'.[127] As these qualifications reveal, nothing in Friedman's famous statement means that corporations and their directors can pursue profit-making with absolute freedom, unhindered by any legal, ethical or other constraints. Admittedly, Friedman originally conceived of the necessary boundaries on profit-making narrowly rather than broadly, in terms of how a corporation 'stays within the rules of the game concerning competition, legality, and business ethics',[128] and not in terms of broader stakeholder-focused concerns grounded in the place of corporations in civil society. Moreover, Friedman's belief in business compliance with the law was never open-ended, in the sense of tolerating whatever might be embodied in law through stakeholder pressures and lobbying, as he clearly disapproved of legal enshrinement of business obligations of social responsibility that were inimical to core business profitability for shareholders.[129]

Friedman's later formulation of his grand claim in his landmark 1970 *New York Times Magazine* article on CSR expressly contemplates constraints upon business grounded both in law and business ethics, in terms of a corporate executive's responsibility to the corporation's investors 'to make as much money as possible while conforming to the basic rules of the society, both those embodied in law and those embodied in ethical custom'.[130] That article's title neatly encapsulates Friedman's whole argument: 'The Social Responsibility of Business is to Increase its Profits'. Yet, by these various concessions on the limiting effect and conditioning influences upon corporate profit-making and shareholder gain of imperatives grounded in legal norms, market forces and business ethics, Friedman's own analysis at least opens the way to deeper questions about the source and nature of such constraints, and how we identify them. In other words, without a legitimizing account of corporate responsibility, governance and regulation, we cannot properly set and reset these boundaries in light of changing societal and global conditions.

The debate in this era preceded modern shareholder value's mass acceptance of corporate profit-generation for shareholder wealth-creation as the primary corporate mandate, undiluted by pursuit of social goals except as mandated by the state under its laws. Friedman's famous fellow travellers, such as Professor Friedrich Hayek, argued against corporations using their resources 'for specific ends other than those of a long-run maximization of the return on the capital placed under their control', warning that 'the fashionable doctrine that their policy should be guided by "social considerations" is likely to produce most undesirable results'.[131] Like Friedman, Hayek drew an important distinction between the central goal of business and the framework within which that goal is pursued and even restrained by 'general legal *and* moral rules', so that 'generally accepted rules of decency and, perhaps, even charitableness should probably be regarded as no less binding on corporations than the strict rules of law'.[132] This returns us to the central problem of an overarching normative basis for subjecting corporations to a range of societal norms that include, but are not limited to, legal norms.

Responding in 2005 to Whole Foods founder-CEO, John Mackey, in one of his last published contributions to the CSR debate, Milton Friedman argued that his own classic statement that 'the social responsibility of business is to increase its profits' is equivalent to Mackey's conclusion that 'the enlightened corporation should try to create value for *all* of its constituencies'.[133] Of course, what Friedman meant by this equivalence is that serving shareholder value is the best way of ensuring a company's success for the sake of all of its constituencies. This echoes the long-standing argument that acting in the interests of shareholders is the best path to overall social well-being. Still, even on a Friedmanite view, accounts of corporate responsibility and governance must explain and justify the interplay between shareholder and non-shareholder relationships with corporations, one another and wider society.

All claims about the social responsibility of corporations must be assessed according to their time, context and place of origin. Importantly, as even Friedman concedes, his claims were originally made against the background of two major battles in the post-World War II period. One was the battle for supremacy between democracy and socialism in the Cold War era. Importantly, Friedman was originally writing in the midst of the Cold War's perceived threats to democracy, capitalism and freedom from totalitarian and Marxist alternatives. As reflected in his famous 1970 article in the *New York Times*, one of his underlying concerns lay in the advantages of a market-based system of free enterprise over 'a centrally controlled system', thus fuelling his belief that 'the doctrine of "social responsibility" involves the acceptance of the socialist view that political mechanisms, not market mechanisms, are the appropriate way to determine the allocation of scarce resources to alternative uses'.[134]

The other was the battle over the appropriateness and degree of governmental intervention in matters of individual and business freedom, in an era of debate about the welfare state, government spending and regulated markets. Viewed against such a background, calls to resist the socialization of the fruits of corporate success resonate most forcefully. On this view, legitimizing the redirection of resources from shareholders to enable social engineering by directors (if that is a correct characterization) undermines free enterprise and obliterates the dividing line between business and politics. In addition, Friedman wrote at a time when some corporate giants had considerably more leeway in practising CSR, in terms of their dominant positions in the market.[135]

Underlying Friedman's criticism of CSR is a belief in the superiority of what he called 'the current largely free-market private-property world' in delivering economic and civic freedom in the most efficient way, and the incompatibility of this with 'exercising a social responsibility unrelated to the bottom line'.[136] On this view, a company's strategic alignment of its business and societal relations to its best competitive advantage simply reinforces the shareholder primacy model, whether such alignment is worth characterizing as CSR or not. However, the background political dynamics influencing Friedman's conception of 'social responsibility' and its connection to a correlative political–business divide do not match all circumstances or manifestations of CSR today. Nor does this view capture, for example, the different interactions between government, business and society in the 21st century business environment that make business responsive to new governance, regulatory and responsibility-inducing dynamics in CSR-enhancing ways.

Other responses to Friedman's view of corporate social responsibility

Friedman also makes a series of zero-sum arguments about business and social interests, with these striking examples:[137]

What does it mean to say that the corporate executive has a 'social responsibility' in his capacity as businessman? If this statement is not pure rhetoric, it must mean that he is to act in some way that is not in the interest of his employers. For example, that he is to refrain from increasing the price of the product in order to contribute to the social objective of preventing inflation, even though a price increase would be in the best interests of the corporation. Or that he is to make expenditures on reducing pollution beyond the amount that is in the best interests of the corporation or that is required by law in order to contribute to the social objective of improving the environment. Or that, at the expense of corporate profits, he is to hire 'hard-core' unemployed instead of better qualified available workmen to contribute to the social objective of reducing poverty.

Ultimately, these arguments misfire or are at least misdirected. First, shareholder and stakeholder interests are not always bound together in zero-sum terms. A bank that develops new low-cost housing and small business finance packages that give it entry to new sections of the housing and business market, which in turn enables local political leaders to attract families and investment in rebuilding a run-down urban community, expands its business competitiveness and profitability in a way that benefits both its shareholders and local community stakeholders.[138] Another bank that develops a policy of supporting a new and socially beneficial sector might discover that its loan officers become more knowledgeable about that sector and more sure about the bank's position on it, leading to better internal guidelines and more confident lending in that sector.

Similarly, as C.K. Prahalad argues in his ground-breaking book on eradicating poverty in the developing world, *The Fortune at the Bottom of the Pyramid*, tackling the poverty of millions of people worldwide presents new market opportunities that can be structured in ways that meet the needs of profitability and human dignity alike.[139] Of course, Friedman's response to all of this would be that such counter-examples simply reinforce the proposition that businesses should focus upon whatever will enhance their sustainable profitability. Yet, such a counter-response does not go to the primary criticism here, which is that Friedman's examples set up a zero-sum relation between what corporate executives might do if they practise 'social responsibility' and what they should be doing as business people.

Secondly, Friedman's examples are all examples of corporate executives behaving like social engineers and policy-makers, at the direct expense of the economic interests of a company and its shareholders. Moreover, they all take the conclusion reached on business grounds and set it aside on non-business grounds. This is at the extreme and impermissible end of business decision-making. Corporations and their executives do not have to commit business suicide in order to act responsibly. How and why they accommodate shareholder and non-shareholder interests in their decision-making matters, but the claim that corporate power must be exercised responsibly is not a claim that inevitably casts corporate executives as governmental policy-makers or social engineers.[140] Of course, some of CSR's extreme forms and advocates might suggest such roles, but that simply points to the need for clarity about which type of CSR is under discussion. Moreover, the role and reasoning adopted by business executives in managing their company's business–society relations differs fundamentally from the role and reasoning of public sector officials in considering societal interests.

Thirdly, and most importantly, not all business leaders see things Friedman's way. Some reject the Friedmanite sacrifice of other responsibilities at the altar of shareholder primacy, as well as the equalizing of responsibility towards shareholders and non-shareholders alike under stakeholder pluralism. Steering a middle path instead between these two extremes is one of the UK's most experienced board chairmen and contributors to corporate governance thinking and reform, Sir Adrian Cadbury, who chaired the UK Committee on the Financial Aspects of Corporate Governance, whose recommendations are enshrined in what has become known as the Cadbury Code. Writing in the wake of the landmark overhaul of corporate law by the UK Company Law Review Steering Group and its assessment of the kind of corporate law needed in the 21st century business environment, he noted the choice in 'recognising the social dimension in business decisions' between efficient business pursuit of profit with proportionate devotion of some profits to social causes by the company or its shareholders, and alternatively viewing social and business aims as interdependent, with the vast majority of companies taking the middle path of 'not keeping the social dimension completely at arm's length, but seeking ways of usefully combining their commercial and social goals'.[141]

In his 21st century reflections on corporate governance and responsibility Cadbury makes three important objections to the Friedmanite view of business. First, Friedman's concern for preserving the distinct domains of economic and political freedom results in companies pursuing economic freedom and 'leaving the interaction between business and society to the political process', which is an overly simplistic dichotomy in practice, given that 'the economic elements of business decisions' cannot be compartmentalized away 'from their social consequences, because companies are part of the social system'.[142] Secondly, taking a necessary long-term business perspective begins to blur any dividing line between purely financial concerns and wider social ones. 'Investing in people and in the standing of the company involves social as well as commercial judgments', Cadbury argues. 'The further a company looks ahead, the more difficult it becomes, in holding that balance, to maintain a simple separation between economic and social goals', he concludes.

Finally, the Friedmanite assumption that all shareholders have a common objective in maximizing corporate wealth-generation denies the practical reality that 'shareholders have different views on how companies should make their money and on how they should distribute it, in ways that do not focus simply upon disagreement about distributing the best surplus profits within an otherwise efficient economic role for companies'.[143] In light of the interdependence between societal, governmental and business interests, 'companies cannot be neatly detached from the communities of which they are a part, as Professor Friedman's approach to social responsibility would require', Cadbury concludes.[144] All of this has implications not only for corporate risk management approaches and systems, but also for frameworks for corporate governance and its regulation.[145]

LATE 20TH AND EARLY 21ST CENTURY PERSPECTIVES ON THE SHAREHOLDER PRIMACY MODEL

Hansmann and Kraakman on Standard Shareholder-based Models

'The End of History' according to Hansmann and Kraakman
The classic arguments in favour of shareholder primacy include its productive and social efficiency, the link between shareholder wealth-generation and overall social

> Although there remained considerable room for variation in governance prac-
> tices and in the fine structure of corporate law throughout the twentieth century,
> the pressures for further convergence are now rapidly growing. Chief among
> these pressures is the recent dominance of a shareholder-centred ideology of
> corporate law among the business, government, and legal elites in key com-
> mercial jurisdictions. There is no longer any serious competitor to the view that
> corporate law should principally strive to increase long-term shareholder value.
> This emergent consensus has already profoundly affected corporate govern-
> ance practices throughout the world. It is only a matter of time before its influ-
> ence is felt in the reform of corporate law as well.
>
> – Professors Henry Hansmann and Reinier Kraakman, 'The End of History for
> Corporate Law'[146]

welfare, managerial deference on social policy issues, the problems of multi-fiduciary
responsibilities for directors, the capacity for non-shareholding interests to secure
protection through contractual or other legal means, the moral rights of shareholders
as corporate owners or beneficiaries, and the unsuitability of corporations being amenable to other-regarding regulation from outside rather than inside corporate law.[147]
In their landmark assessment of the modern status of corporate law Yale University's
Professor Henry Hansmann and Harvard University's Professor Reinier Kraakman
state that the end of the 20th century sees 'the recent dominance of a shareholder-
centred ideology of corporate law among the business, government, and legal elites
in key commercial jurisdictions', to the point where '(t)here is no longer any serious
competitor to the view that corporate law should principally strive to increase long-
term shareholder value'.[148]

In their famous essay, 'The End of History for Corporate Law', Hansmann and
Kraakman commence their argument with the claim that business corporations in every
major commercial jurisdiction worldwide today exhibit at least five basic features. Those
features are: (i) full and separate legal personality; (ii) limited liability for shareholders
and managers; (iii) shared corporate 'ownership' by capital investors; (iv) centralized and
delegated management (under a board structure); and (v) shareholding transferability.[149]
Having identified common corporate features across major jurisdictions, Hansmann and
Kraakman then articulate what they claim is a descriptive and normative consensus in
favour of the 'standard shareholder-oriented model' of corporations, comprising these
elements:[150]

> The principal elements of this consensus are that ultimate control over the corporation should
> be in the hands of the shareholder class; that the managers of the corporation should be
> charged with the obligation to manage the corporation in the interests of its shareholders; that
> other corporate constituencies, such as creditors, employees, suppliers, and customers should
> have their interests protected by contractual and regulatory means rather than through partici-
> pation in corporate governance; that noncontrolling shareholders should receive strong protec-
> tion from exploitation at the hands of controlling shareholders; and that the principal measure
> of the interests of the publicly traded corporation's shareholders is the market value of their
> shares in the firm.

Although hotly contested by others, their core claim is about the advantages of the 'standard shareholder-oriented model' over state-oriented, stakeholder-oriented and manager-oriented models.[151] As they later explain elsewhere, the desirability of the 'standard shareholder-oriented model' does not translate simplistically and one-dimensionally into calls simply to serve the best interests of shareholders alone by, for example, maximizing market share prices and financial returns for shareholders at all costs.[152] Rather, this shareholder-focused model provides the best orientation for those managing a company to follow if they are to help the corporation to achieve its mission and thereby contribute to society. In other words, this shareholder-based model takes the three-fold position that, firstly, 'shareholders alone are the parties to whom corporate managers should be accountable'; secondly, 'social welfare is best served by encouraging corporate managers to pursue shareholder interests'; and, thirdly, non-shareholder protection is important but not primarily the province of corporate law.[153]

In that sense, corporate law is just like other branches of law in having ultimate social ends that justify and condition it. In their eyes, this means that 'the appropriate goal of corporate law is to advance the aggregate welfare of a firm's shareholders, employees, suppliers, and customers without undue sacrifice – and, if possible, with benefit – to third parties such as local communities and beneficiaries of the natural environment', all in 'the pursuit of overall social efficiency'.[154] As a result, the corporation and its shareholders mutually have 'a direct pecuniary interest in making sure that corporate transactions are beneficial, not just to the shareholders, but to all parties who deal with the firm'.[155] Making a focus upon these interdependent benefits for shareholders the primary imperative of corporations and their managers therefore becomes the best way of ensuring that corporate law and business practice 'serve the broader goal of advancing overall social welfare'.[156]

Importantly, all of this informs the true meaning of the widely used notion of 'shareholder value'.[157] On this view, any 'non-efficiency-oriented' dilutions of shareholder-focused corporate laws or other detractions from shareholder value in particular corporate regulatory systems are explainable as either tolerable minor inefficiencies or else products of sub-optimal legislative compromises.[158] Alternative explanations for regulatory divergences from shareholder primacy arguably include socio-historical influences upon the development of corporate regulatory systems, ideological undercurrents in each system, pressures from powerful interest groups, and the pragmatics of what is possible in non-major corporate jurisdictions.[159]

In the world-view of these shareholder primacy scholars, corporations and societies subscribing to the shareholder-based approach seem to outperform others, on multiple levels. As neither governments nor non-shareholding stakeholder groups seem able to compete with markets in aggregating all stakeholder (including shareholder) interests, and as shareholders as a whole have a uniquely homogenous financial stake in the corporations in which they invest and hold shares, participatory governance and voting rights are best left in the hands of shareholders, they argue. Corporate directors and managers cannot satisfactorily meet simultaneous duties to protect and advance the interests of both shareholders and non-shareholders, given the significant ways in which those interests can compete at various points throughout a corporation's life-cycle.[160] Overly entrenched management is at risk of engaging in self-seeking behaviour or other forms of mismanagement or misinvestment, to the detriment of shareholders and non-shareholders alike. Finally, state control and interference in corporate affairs bring with them goals beyond, and even unrelated to, the central corporate role of efficient production.[161] 'Since nothing in the foreseeable future seems likely to change these constraints on the organizational forms that are productively efficient, the principal competitors to the standard shareholder-oriented model will remain badly handicapped', concludes Professor Hansmann.

Other evidence and arguments also seem to point in the same direction. For example, there is some evidence in the present structure, content and priorities of corporate law for the conclusions that 'the core of corporate law remains fairly explicitly preoccupied with the rights of shareholders' and that 'interests of non-shareholder stakeholders do not figure prominently'.[162] Even recent governmental moves to embrace the concept of 'enlightened shareholder value' in the UK are strongly rooted in the primacy of shareholder interests and the subservient relationship of other stakeholder interests to shareholder interests. Shareholders have some ultimate control rights over directors and corporations, numerous participatory rights in corporate governance, and specific rights to some corporate benefits, while other stakeholders have none or little of these. Yet, there remains a distinction, at least for analytical purposes, between this doctrinal preoccupation with shareholder-focused inputs and outcomes, on one hand, and its capacity to explain and guide all facets of corporate regulation and conduct, even in achieving those outcomes.

Reactions and counter-responses to the 'standard shareholder-based model'

Historical cracks in the model
Does the history of the modern corporation truly bring us in the 21st century to the peak of corporate evolution, or simply to a point in the corporate evolutionary timeline in which the historical, theoretical and other cracks in corporate orthodoxy in light of the past are increasingly exposed as we confront the challenges of the future? Midway through the 20th century, even Adolf Berle questioned the relevance and place of shareholders in the modern corporation, in a way which challenges classical rationales for shareholder primacy:[163]

> (O)ne effect of the corporate system has been to set up a parallel, circulating 'property-wealth' system, in which the wealth flows from passive wealth-holder to passive wealth-holder, without significantly furthering the functions of capital formation, capital application, capital use or risk bearing. Yet these functions were the heart of the nineteenth-century 'capitalist' system . . . Now, clearly, this wealth cannot be justified by the old economic maxims, despite passionate and sentimental arguments of neo-classic economists who would have us believe the old system has not changed.

Similarly, the 2004 Report of the Citizen Works Corporate Reform Commission queries whether the historical bases for shareholder primacy can carry the work of justifying it today:[164]

> Today, most investors contribute very little, if anything, to the corporation. Most stockholders today own shares that they did not originally purchase from the company in exchange for investment capital. Rather, they purchased them from another investor, who purchased them from another investor, until, somewhere down the line, somebody made a direct investment in the company and got a stock certificate in exchange.

The simple fact is that the stock market of today is not actually a significant source of invest-ment capital for corporations . . . So, if today's shareholders contribute virtually nothing to the corporate enterprise, why do their interests factor so dominantly in the calculus of corporate decision making?

The centuries-old factory-based model for corporations is a recurring point of refer-ence in the literature on corporations. 'Economists persist in arguing that shareholders own a company in which they are investors as a way of interpreting 21st century capital-ism as a simple extension of the 19th century Manchester model, in which the owner of a mill managed it', argues finance scholar, John Legge.[165] Other corporate governance experts echo this realization that corporate evolution over time has outstripped the modern corporation's origins:[166]

This corporate governance model may have been a relatively good fit for corporations of the Industrial Age, where the owners of a company contracted with workers and suppliers for the raw materials and the low-skilled labor that they used to produce finished goods. In other words, this was a world in which contracts for mostly generic inputs were easy to specify, physical capital was the scarce commodity, and the owners of this capital bore the risk.

This same model, however, appears to be an increasingly poor fit for many of today's corporations . . . For such network-based, knowledge-intensive organizations, it is clearly no longer accurate to claim that the equity holders, whose shareholdings are often part of a diversified portfolio, bear all the risks associated with operating a corporation. Rather it is all those groups who make personal and resource investments that are firm-specific who should be considered the stake-holders, or shared owners, of the enterprise.

Unshackling the company at one point in its historical evolution from having its exist-ence and purpose tied to state patronage and needs, such as assisting imperial expansion and control in colonial outposts or establishing essential socio-economic infrastructure (e.g. building railways between cities), frees the company in the next phases of its societal evolution from some of the constraints and conditions on its reason for being in earlier stages of that evolution.[167] The fallacy of allowing the historical contexts and rationales for corporations to drive their governance and regulation for evermore, even in the face of very different societal and global conditions in the 21st century, is starkly exposed in Professor Blair's rejection of such accounts of shareholder value and corporate governance:[168]

The primitive model of corporations in which shareholders are seen as earning all of the returns and bearing all the risk is a throwback to an earlier time when the typical corporation owned and operated a canal, a railroad, or a big manufacturing plant. Entrepreneurial investors put up the financial capital, which was used to build or buy the railroad, canal, or factory and to make initial payments to hired managers. The managers, in turn, arranged to buy raw materials and energy, hire labor, oversee production or manage the operations, and (in the case of the factory) ship the goods to market. The proceeds from the sale of those goods was used to meet payroll (including the manager's salary), pay taxes, buy more raw materials, keep the machinery in working order and pay off any loans, and all of these inputs were acquired at the going market rate. Anything left over after that was 'profit', and it seemed reasonable and appropriate that the profits belonged to the initial investors (shareholders), who were the only parties with significant assets tied up and at risk in the enterprise.

. . . For firms that look like this, corporate governance arrangements that provide for them to be run for shareholders and that accordingly give as much control to shareholders as possible, serve to encourage wealth creation by fostering and protecting investments in physical capital and entrepreneurial efforts [but] fewer and fewer publicly traded corporations actually look like the factory model. Much of the wealth-generating capacity of most modern firms is based on the skills and knowledge of the employees and the ability of the organization as a whole to put those skills to work for customers and clients . . . Moreover, the idea that the wealth of a corporation is in its people has important implications for corporate governance arrangements.

In short, the original *context* in which shareholder-based ideas and practices develop is not necessarily a complete or even apt frame of reference for the *content* of corporate law and regulation today. The counter-response of shareholder primacy advocates might be that, even if the particular contexts and rationales that originally emphasized shareholder interests have changed, the operative contexts and rationales today still favour shareholder primacy. For example, although shareholders are neither the only nor the most important suppliers of financial capital today for corporations, it is the existence of stock markets, stock exchanges and listed companies that enables original investors to reap the benefit of their investment in selling their shares to others and also allows the market value of shares to be set. In addition, shareholders play particular roles in corporate governance that no other stakeholders play, whether their roles are justified alternatively by ownership, efficiency or trusteeship for society.

However, since the last quarter of the 20th century, some measures of shareholder value have arguably distorted it towards short-termism in ways that have needed formal correction already in the 21st century, through mechanisms as diverse as the enshrinement of long-term considerations in legislative statements of directors' duties in the UK, heightened institutional shareholder pressure for executive remuneration packages to match sustained corporate performance, and heightened attention to ESG factors as measures of lasting business value. By at least the last quarter of the 20th century, corporate governance began to frame the legal role of the board more forcefully in terms of monitoring management and its performance.[169] At this point, systemic dynamics as varied as the fixation of investment industry metrics upon quarterly and annual returns, the development of the junk bond market, the use of stock options in management remuneration, and a wave of takeover activity all arguably coalesced around short-term shareholder gain as a manifestation of shareholder value, thereby testing the limits of taking a long-term view of profit-maximization, shareholder wealth-generation and the company's interests.[170] The contingent rather than inevitable nature of that course in corporate evolution is succinctly summarized by Cambridge University's Professor Simon Deakin in these terms:[171]

> The current focus on shareholder value is therefore the consequence not of the basic company law model, but of those institutional changes which have occurred in capital markets and securities law with increasing rapidity, in particular since the early 1980s, namely the rise of the hostile takeover bid, and the increasing use of share options and shareholder value metrics. Thus the contemporary 'norm' or reference point of shareholder primacy is the result of a complex mix of institutional changes, the emergence of new forms of self-regulation and soft law, and shifts in corporate culture.

Such lines of thinking inform Deakin's claim that prevailing notions of shareholder value are shifting to accommodate 'the idea that shareholders exercise their powers not as the representatives of the market, but as agents of society as a whole', not in any narrow sense of non-shareholder interests trumping shareholder interests to the detriment of profit-driven shareholder gain, but through a different account of shareholders as society's gatekeepers in holding corporate management to account. This perspective informs his prediction that '(t)he corporate governance of the future will be centrally concerned with how this idea is worked out in practice'.[172] As Professor Bottomley explains, conventional shareholder primacy still 'permits attention to be given to shareholders' non-financial concerns (such as concerns for the social or environmental impact of their corporation's activities) and, through the medium of the shareholders, the model can also take account of the interests of non-shareholders'.[173] All of this has clear implications for how we reorient traditional ways of thinking about shareholder and non-shareholder interests, their interplay in corporate governance arrangements, and their integration within 'enlightened shareholder value' in service to their assigned societal roles.

Theoretical cracks in the model
The standard shareholder-based model favoured by Hansmann and Kraakman remains the subject of sustained attack by scholarly critics of corporate, regulatory and market orthodoxy today. 'The superior efficiency, at least in theory, of a corporate governance rule that allows directors to take account of the interests of all of the corporation's constituents is increasingly acknowledged both in corporate scholarship and in corporate case law', argues team production scholar, Professor Lynn Stout.[174] 'The plain truth is that the most prominent alternative to the stakeholder theory (i.e. the "management serving the shareowners" theory) is morally untenable', argue business ethics and management scholars, Tom Donaldson and Lee Preston.[175]

One of the most sustained attacks on shareholder-based models at the turn of the century comes from 'team production' corporate theory. Considered from a team production standpoint, corporations are not managed exclusively for shareholder wealth-maximization. 'The appropriate normative goal for a board of directors is to build and protect the wealth-creating potential of the entire corporate team – "wealth" that is reflected not only in dividends and share appreciation for shareholders, but also in reduced risk for creditors, better health benefits for employees, promotional opportunities and perks for executives, better product support for customers, and good "corporate citizenship" in the community', according to the two chief contemporary advocates of corporate team production thinking, Professors Margaret Blair and Lynn Stout.[176] 'The essence of team production is that the whole can be made bigger than the sum of its parts', they suggest.[177]

On this view, 'the public corporation can be viewed most usefully not as a nexus of implicit and explicit contracts, but as a nexus of firm-specific investments made by many and varied individuals who give up control over those resources to a decision-making process in hopes of sharing in the benefits that can flow from team production . . . in a fashion that maximizes the *joint welfare of the team as a whole*'.[178] 'The implication of team production and stewardship theories for corporate social responsibility is that management systems should be (a) easily permeable to stakeholder concerns and interests . . . and (b) roles, responsibilities and decision-making powers in relation to social and legal responsibility are well defined and accepted', according to Dr Parker.[179]

As the team members in team production theory voluntarily submit to the 'mediating hierarchy' of the corporation itself, with the board at its apex as an efficiency-driven means of pursuing their own self-interests, team production theory sits within the nexus of contracts tradition.[180] Professor Blair delineates the team production approach's key points of divergence from shareholder primacy as follows:[181]

> In short, it is possible to reject the simplistic finance model or property conception of the corporation to the extent that it implies that directors' only duty is to maximize value for shareholders, and still retain the compelling logic that private control of private property leads to the most efficient use of society's resources. I argue that the view of corporations as wealth-creating machines, with a social purpose of maximizing wealth, provides a clear basis for thinking about how control rights to that machine should be allocated [but] I make a much more general assumption about what the source of value creation is, and who it is that bears the risk and receives the gains in most corporations today.

Two of the postulated strengths of team production theory are that it provides an account of corporate value beyond what is explainable by shareholder value and avoids extreme forms of both shareholder primacy and stakeholder pluralism. Team production theory also attracts strong criticisms. Given that it places most emphasis upon the contributions that team members make to the collective business enterprise and its success, the interests of stakeholders who do not meet that benchmark figure in the equation only to the extent that they bear upon the dynamics affecting team members. Leading advocates of shareholder-focused models dismiss it as an offshoot of stakeholder-based theory, with all of the weaknesses of that body of theory.[182] 'The caveat with the team production approach is the same caveat that applies to other stakeholder approaches: how to effectively mediate between different claims on the corporation', echo other commentators on team production theory, who argue that 'given the pressures of the stock market and the powers (albeit quite limited) of shareholders, it is not clear how we could get from shareholder primacy to a team production approach without either changing the ownership composition or else establishing an external prod (such as holding directors responsible for violating the rights of various constituencies . . .)'.[183]

Team production theory's counter-response to this particular criticism is that it mischaracterizes the team production model, which keeps boards free from undue control by shareholders and other stakeholders alike, 'because if either shareholders or stakeholders were given greater leverage over boards, they might use that leverage to pressure boards to opportunistically threaten the interests of other members of the corporate "team"'.[184] In the team production model, the emphasis is upon the benefit to both shareholders and other stakeholders of having corporate boards that are not unduly accountable to either group, 'because board governance, while worsening agency costs, also promotes efficient and informed decisionmaking; discourages intershareholder opportunism; and encourages valuable specific investment in corporate team production' by both shareholders and stakeholders alike.[185] Accordingly, the apparent rise and dominance of the shareholder primacy norm reflect nothing more than the relatively greater economic, political and legal bargaining power of shareholders over others under prevailing conditions that are nevertheless subject to change, as the product of 'underlying economic and political factors [that] may well shift back again'.[186]

One criticism of the team production approach questions its capacity to displace the presumed dominance of shareholder primacy in much corporate regulation and practice.[187] Another criticism doubts the behavioural evidence for a team production approach, as well as its grasp of the problem of CEO-dominated companies in the

USA.[188] Other critics doubt the applicability of team production theory to the corporate history and regulatory cultures in countries beyond the USA, given differences in different countries in the balance of corporate power between directors and shareholders, as well as differences in the leeways afforded to directors in resisting takeovers and other changes of corporate control.[189] Yet another set of critics rejects the dominance of the 'efficiency framework' and 'nexus of contracts' traditions within which both shareholder primacy and team production theory are positioned, and points to the limitations of substituting questions of efficiency and profitability for questions of morality, justice and other values that are implicated in corporate conduct.[190]

Other critics of shareholder primacy do not necessarily deny the current dominance of some kind of shareholder-based model as a systemic pillar of corporate governance and regulation in at least some countries, or that reforms to current thinking, regulation and practice surrounding corporations should best start with that model in light of its pre-eminence.[191] Still, even if the prevailing Anglo-American and Anglo-Commonwealth systems of corporate regulation at the end of the 20th century can be characterized in terms of this 'standard shareholder-based model' to any degree, follow-up questions intrude about the comprehensiveness of this characterization in accounting for the full complexities of business–society relations, the extent of deviance from this model that can be allowed before its integrity is compromised, its capacity to accommodate the rapid expansion of CSR initiatives and mechanisms occurring worldwide, and its transportability to emerging markets and developing economies.

Despite the helpful concession by Hansmann and Kraakman that 'corporate enterprise should be organized and operated to serve the interests of society as a whole', given that 'the interests of shareholders deserve no greater weight in this social calculus than do the interests of any other members of society',[192] in the eyes of Professor Greenfield they make too many unjustified slides from what is good for corporations, as they are currently structured and regulated, to what is good for society as a whole.[193] On his analysis, the Hansmann and Kraakman account of shareholder primacy equates what is good for society and the economy with what is self-interestedly best for corporations and their shareholders, and cites justifications for that equation – such as global business competition, transnational capital markets and organizationally effective investment of financial capital – that relate more to the corporation's ability to optimize shareholder wealth than to promotion of the economy or even society at large. 'The structure of the argument is tautological: the shareholder-oriented model is superior because it is better at maximizing shareholder welfare [and] Hansmann and Kraakman's argument thus shows only that shareholder-oriented firms will beat out other firms if the measuring stick for the competition is shareholder advantage', argues Greenfield.[194] Hence, the model's claimed superiority over alternative state-orientated, labour-orientated, manager-orientated and other (stakeholder) models rests upon the yardstick being shareholder advantage.[195]

Moreover, factoring in non-shareholder interests neither means adopting a completely different system (e.g. state-owned and state-directed business enterprise)[196] nor necessarily accepts the weaknesses and inefficiencies associated by Hansmann and Kraakman with consideration and participation of employees and other stakeholding groups in corporate law and governance.[197] Enhancing 'aggregate social welfare' and the 'one-value metric' of maximizing shareholder wealth also raise all of the problems of incomparability and incommensurability of multiple interests that plague utilitarian views, given the impossibility of fitting all competing individual interests within a higher-order collective interest that 'balances' them all.[198] As Greenfield puts it, noting that 'current corporate law contains within it the same principles as traditional utilitarianism', the critique 'that utilitarianism is irrational insofar as it requires a dependence on commensurability and maximization, is as powerful a response to contemporary corporate law as it was to nineteenth-century economic theory', with the consequence that 'current corporate law doctrine is simply irrational, requiring corporate managers to make decisions in an impoverished way'.[199]

Justifications for shareholder primacy grounded in notions of shareholder ownership of corporations, agency costs for shareholders, shareholder property and dividend entitlements, residual risk-bearing by shareholders, and overall societal efficiency are attacked in contemporary corporate legal scholarship as being inadequate or limited justifications for shareholder primacy.[200] To the extent that any of these underlying justifications have any force, some of them also apply to stakeholders other than shareholders, including employees who face their own problems as corporate stakeholders in bearing the agency costs of monitoring the company's management of their employment relationship, investing a valuable form of capital in the company, retaining residual and contingent interests that fluctuate according to the company's fortunes, and navigating investment in employment relationships the aspects of which are not all easily protected through corporate agreements and employment contracts.[201] Beyond considerations of efficiency, shareholder primacy is sometimes considered problematic on other moral grounds, as it 'substitutes questions of profitability for all questions of justice that may arise in the conduct of the business'.[202]

Much of the conventional economic, contract-based and business thinking in support of shareholder primacy is predicated on the idea that those who invest in a company are its true 'owners', on whose behalf and in whose interests alone corporations are managed. This idea suits the factory-owning industrial company well, at least for owner-managers who invest most or all of the financial capital in a local company's factory and hold all of the shares. Of course, everything hinges on what 'ownership' means in this context. If the fundamental rationale offered is to promote accountability to those who are said to 'own' the corporation in some sense, it needs to be shown, firstly, why this selective isolation of one set of contributors to the corporation's success is justified and, secondly, why 'ownership' is the correct characterization of a shareholder's stake in a corporation.[203] On the first aspect, isolating those corporate actors who contribute in some meaningful way to a company's success focuses upon the notion of who can be taken to 'invest' something of value in a company, including but not limited to shareholders as investors of financial capital. On some formulations, it might even embrace contributors of other kinds of capital too, such as labour, intellectual capital, and even social capital, including community forebearance in imposing additional business regulation by law.

On the second aspect, the very notion of shareholders as the 'owners' of a corporation at least trades upon some notions of property, even though shareholders do not actually 'own' the company in any strict legal sense, but rather own shares in a company on specified contract-based terms.[204] Hence, one response to the shareholder ownership view of corporations points to the law's clear recognition of the company as a distinct entity that is not 'owned' in strict legal terms by its shareholders at all, whatever control, participatory rights and contingent expectations of benefits they have. Lord Macnaghten summarised the basic Anglo-American legal position in the famous UK *Salomon* case more than a century ago, stating that '(t)he company is at law a different person altogether from the subscribers [and] though it may be that after incorporation the business is precisely the same as it was before, and the same persons are managers, and the same hands receive the profits, the company is not in law the agent of the subscribers or trustee for them'.[205]

Another response is that ownership consists of a bundle of different rights of possession, control and other attributes, not all of which remain vested in shareholders in the modern corporation, given the separation of ownership and control famously articulated by Berle and Means. The standard counter-response to these responses is that, such legal niceties aside, there is still a meaningful sense of 'ownership' in which the shareholders collectively hold sway over the company in ways that markedly differ from the involvement of other corporate stakeholders.

Even if 'ownership' applies, goes another response, this still begs the question whether ownership carries with it any responsibilities, in the same way that use of power must inherently be exercised responsibly to avoid becoming abuse of power. Meeting that response takes us into the realm of deciding whether ownership (in whatever sense is relevant) has inherent or ascribed value, and the socio-ethical basis upon which any such value is afforded to shareholding ownership. On one view, for example, even conventional agency theory does not automatically ascribe management control rights to shareholders as the real corporate owners, but rather rests on a justificatory claim that is at least one step removed from the company itself and inherently socio-political in nature. 'Even if shareholders do not own the company, ownership of shares confers upon them the right, exclusively of all the stakeholder groups, to hold directors and managers accountable', notes Professor Deakin, adding that 'agency theory tells us that company law grants shareholders the right to call managers to account not because of an *a priori* ownership claim, but essentially because it is in society's interests that they should perform this task'.[206]

If different bundles of rights are comprised in notions of property, *and* if property rights describe relations between different interests, *and* if the value that society places upon those relations is a conditional rather than absolute value, *and* if all rights and interests have at least some limitations, it is not surprising to find alternative bodies of thinking that locate the value of property rights in coherent underlying accounts of social, distributive and other forms of justice. Noting that 'the traditional view has been that a focus on property rights justifies the dominance of shareowners' interests', Donaldson and Preston highlight the ironic situation that 'the fact that property rights are the critical base for conventional shareowner-dominance views makes it all the more significant that the current trend of thinking with respect to the philosophy of property runs in the opposite direction'.[207] On their view, a number of considerations all combine to point towards a theory of corporate responsibility and governance that 'does not support the popular claim that the responsibility of managers is to act solely as agents for the share-owners'.[208] Those considerations include the location of property rights in human rights, the inherent restrictions on harmful uses of property rights that are built into notions of responsible ownership, the absence of any theoretical justification for unlimited ownership rights, the break-up of property rights into distinct bundles of rights, and the integral relation between property rights and stakeholder interests under notions of distributive justice.

Hence, on their view, the principles of distributive justice that focus on considerations 'such as need, ability, effort, and mutual agreement' in deciding how societal resources are distributed and used and the basis on which those keeping and using those resources do so also relate to the societal value to be allocated to all corporate stakeholders, based upon the different 'stakes' they have in corporate activity, according to the particular element or combination of elements of distributive justice in play. This forms the basis for their conclusion that 'the normative principles that underlie the contemporary pluralistic theory of property rights also provide the foundation for the stakeholder theory as well'.[209] In other words, at a deep level of socio-ethical justification the source for the legitimacy of property rights conventionally associated with shareholding interests also becomes the source for the recognition and justification of other interests in the corporate enterprise – and hence for what must occupy corporate structures, governance arrangements and decision-making mechanisms.[210]

The argument that the supporting notions of societal justice and fairness which justify assigning value to shareholdings and other forms of property ownership also legitimize the incorporation of other stakeholder interests in corporate decision-making has wider parallels. It has some connections to political concerns about the collective values of justice and fairness that both legitimize and provide the context for the consent of the governed to markets and their place in corporate governance, especially the democratic features of procedural fairness built into processes that respect enfranchisement (e.g. equal treatment and voice in decision-making, separation of decision-making powers and representation in decision-making).[211] In turn, this has connections to wider concerns about corporate democracy, as well as to the representation, deliberation and contestability of various corporate interests in 21st century corporate theories such as corporate constitutionalism.[212]

Empirical cracks in the model

As Hansmann and Kraakman admit, demonstrating that pursuit of shareholder value actually advances social welfare is a larger empirical matter that requires evidence and provokes much disagreement.[213] So, shareholder primacy's empirical claim is best understood as a descriptive claim about the common shareholder-orientated features of Anglo-American corporate regulatory systems, rather than a fully tested claim about the actual achievement of social efficiency, including what effect corporate pursuit of shareholder wealth-maximization has upon other aspects of social welfare, such as social cohesion, justice and governance. To that extent, shareholder wealth-maximization acts as a proxy for social efficiency, and social efficiency in turn acts as a proxy for overall social well-being.

In other words, it is one thing to treat the public goods secured by efficient deployment of private capital as a policy justification for a market-based system of interactions between private goods (e.g. private property, capital and contracts), without those public goods intruding into that private domain as anything other than ultimate social ends for the system promoting those private goods. It is another thing to test and prove empirically that a market-based system actually produces this result, and does so better than any alternatives, all the time cautioning that '(w)hether, in fact, the pursuit of shareholder value is generally an effective means of advancing social welfare is an empirical question on which reasonable minds can differ'.[214] Complete evidence and proof of that kind still lies beyond our existing knowledge and tools of measurement.

Even these leading contemporary proponents of the standard shareholder-based model accept the possibility of a contrary argument, still awaiting definitive proof, that this model's claim to efficiency 'involves too steep a trade-off between material prosperity and social order'.[215] Indeed, even any convergence worldwide towards shareholder-focused corporate regulatory regimes, with their priority for transparent market disclosure, shareholder accountability mechanisms and preservation of competitive markets could be threatened by threats to capital markets and the global economic order from transnational wars, global terrorism, climate change or other catastrophes.[216]

Jurisdictional cracks in the model

Pressures for convergence towards the Anglo-American model of corporate responsibility and governance embodied in the shareholder primacy norm are said to stem from factors such as globally responsive economies, international capital markets, shareholder-focused institutional investment dynamics, expansion of free trade, modelling of shareholder-orientated reforms, and the unparalleled success of capitalism as a system of productive efficiency.[217] At the same time, this characterization of Anglo-American corporate law as conforming to the standard shareholder-orientated model remains controversial as an account of corporations and corporate law across all Anglo-American corporate regulatory regimes.[218] Convergence sceptics point to the equally important path-dependent ways in which different models or hybrids in different jurisdictions respond to differences of economic environment, regulatory orientation and historical corporate ownership patterns, thereby making complete convergence worldwide unlikely.[219] Hansmann and Kraakman's strong account of a transcontinental shareholder-orientated focus in corporate law can also be juxtaposed with an emerging body of comparative law and regulation in this first part of the 21st century that is more responsive to, and conditioned by, concerns of CSR than its immediate predecessors.[220]

Doubts about the ongoing viability of locating the EU-influenced UK corporate regulatory regime wholly within a shareholder-centred Anglo-American model arise from the evolution of institutional investment strategies away from short-termism, as well as from the development of bodies of insolvency, employment and related areas of law towards greater accommodation of non-shareholding stakeholder concerns.[221] This suggests that 'the [UK] system, rather than stabilising around a norm of shareholder primacy, is currently in a state of flux', even though the core strands of corporate law's coverage of directors' duties, takeovers and mergers, board structures, and shareholder rights and remedies otherwise remain firmly shareholder-centric in their orientation.[222]

Equally, some American corporate scholars point to a number of features in US corporate law and the surrounding politico-regulatory environment that ostensibly seem to undermine shareholder primacy's claim to complete dominance.[223] The law is either unwilling or unable to impose and police an absolute duty of maximizing profit for shareholder gain, with major commercial jurisdictions habitually being reluctant to cast directors' duties in such overriding and unqualified terms.[224] The prevalence of state statutes authorizing unprofitable donations and contributions for charitable, educational and other public purposes is another feature ostensibly advantaging non-shareholder interests. Judicial moulding of business judgment jurisprudence to allow limited profit-sacrificing exercises of discretion by directors also arguably points in this direction, without sacrificing overall systemic integrity or efficiency as a result.[225] Similarly, US-style corporate constituency laws allow non-shareholder constituencies and third party effects to be considered by directors, either generally or else in takeovers and other battles for corporate control.

Even case law from the US jurisdiction commonly regarded as the most amenable to shareholder value (i.e. Delaware) is at odds with simplistic accounts of shareholder primacy. Delaware's corporate case law permits a zone of directorial discretion that 'seems inconsistent (to put it mildly) with shareholder wealth maximization, at least if we are focusing on the wealth of the shareholders who own stock in that particular firm at that particular time'.[226] Examples of this discretion cited by Professor Stout include the following: 'directors can use earnings to raise employees' wages rather than to declare a dividend; they can "reprice" executive stock options even when share prices are falling; they can retroactively increase retirees' pension benefits; and they can donate corporate funds to charity'.[227] One possible counter-response is that all of this is still consistent with the principle, acknowledged in Delaware corporate jurisprudence and elsewhere, that accommodating non-shareholder interests must have some connection with benefits for the company and its shareholders as a whole over the long run. If so, we are still far beyond crude stakeholder-marginalizing and short-term profit-maximizing accounts of corporate and shareholder value.

Finally, even if shareholder primacy reigns supreme, its sensitization to other stakeholder considerations might occur in ways that do not all threaten the model's integrity or otherwise fulfil the worst fears of dilution of overall corporate and social efficiency. At least some forms of this sensitization are not properly characterized as giving rise to 'a shift in the American model of the primacy of shareholder value', but rather as stimulating a responsive internal reconfiguration of this model, so that 'shareholders are being given the opportunity to define *shareholder* value to include *stakeholder* concerns', either because of the intrinsic economic significance for the company of those stakeholder concerns or else because shareholder (and stakeholder) empowerment in corporate governance embraces these other ends.[228] In other words, the two-way connection between shareholder concerns and stakeholder interests is increasingly reflexive in nature. To the extent that these trends concerning institutional investors apply across jurisdictions, the result is 'some increased pressures on American corporate managers to converge on the European model of thinking about stakeholders without any fundamental restructuring of the American governance model'.[229]

Demographic cracks in the model

In addition to the rise in the last few decades of a 'shareholder class' of a wide cross-section of society's demographic groups in many developed countries,[230] who hold shares directly or indirectly (e.g. through institutional investment funds and superannuation schemes), the latter half of the 20th century witnessed the emergence of a new class of institutional investors as 'universal owners'. They hold investments in a 'broad cross-section of the listed company sector' and hence 'have interests in the economy as a whole'.[231] In other words, we are witnessing the rise of a mass shareholding movement with a financial stake in how the economy serves society, and not just in the fortunes of individual companies.

Of course, nobody can yet claim that the incentives and interests of citizen investors as a new mass shareholding class completely coincide with everything that is needed to achieve social equity and justice in a civil society. However, at the very least, given their interest in long-term investments across industry sectors and even whole economies, their focus extends beyond short-term fluctuations in share prices, premium-induced takeovers that change corporate control without lasting value, and other ebbs and flows in the fortunes of particular companies, at least as considered from a whole-of-economy and 'diversified portfolio' perspective.[232] This has correlative implications for official and other regulatory mechanisms relating to corporate consideration of relevant socio-ethical and environmental concerns, corporate incorporation of such concerns in risk management controls, corporate disclosure of such non-financial drivers of corporate financial performance, corporate dialogue and engagement with universal owners and other institutional investors about socially responsible corporate performance, and individual corporate engagement with shared market and societal concerns.[233]

In the words of the influential Hermes Principles, for example:[234]

> The primary goal of a company should be to maximise shareholder value. In financial terms this is best measured by the present value of the cash flows from investment, discounted at an appropriate cost of capital . . . Business, of course, has to work in a competitive environment. This can create the conditions where there is a high incentive for businesses to 'externalise' costs – ie to make a profit for the company while high costs are incurred by society at large . . . However, most investors are widely diversified; it makes little sense for them to support activity by one company which is damaging to overall economic activity. The ultimate beneficiaries of most investment activity include the greater part of the adult population who depend on private pensions and life insurance. It makes little sense for pension funds to support commercial activity which creates an equal or greater cost to society by robbing Peter to pay Paul. Where companies are aware that such conditions exist, it is appropriate for them to support measures to align shareholder interests with those of society at large.

In this new institutional investment environment, civil society groups are not restricted to old-style shareholder activism and public lobbying for greater corporate responsibility towards society and the environment. Instead, by focusing on the common interest that civil society groups and institutional funds share in representing the interests *en masse* of citizen-investors, they can become part of a socio-economic coalition able 'to form a consensus adequate to wield effective ownership clout' and shape the corporate agenda, in a more finely tuned alignment between shareholder value and CSR.[235] In this new 'circle of accountability', corporations and their executives focus more attentively upon the drivers and outcomes of responsible and sustainable corporate success, thus enhancing the ownership-wielding clout of their investors and the corporate agenda-influencing clout of the coalition of civil society groups, investment industry bodies and other societal actors collaborating with them.[236] Here, the civil economy meets civil society.

Cracks in the model's account of corporate law

Corporate law's constituent interests   Law reform attempts to socialize directors' duties are regularly opposed by advocates of the view that corporate law and governance is properly the domain of relations between companies, boards and shareholders. In its 1989 *Report on the Social and Fiduciary Duties and Obligations of Company Directors*, the Australian Senate Standing Committee on Legal and Constitutional Affairs endorsed shareholder primacy as follows:[237]

It is the shareholders' investment that creates the company. Directors' fiduciary duties are premised on this fact and are designed to protect that investment. If company law were to impose new and, at times, contradictory duties (such as looking after interests which may be directly opposed to those of the corporators), directors' fiduciary duties could be weakened, perhaps to the point where they would be essentially meaningless. In general, requirements aimed at securing responsible corporate behaviour are therefore best provided in other than company law.

Shareholder primacy also supplied the rationale for the Committee's ultimate recommendation that 'matters such as the interest of consumers, or environmental protection, be dealt with not in companies legislation but in legislation aimed specifically at those matters'.[238] The Committee's stance assumes a natural order of division between the concerns of corporate law and the concerns of other areas of law. This raises wider questions about the desirability and limits of one branch of law regulating another.[239] It also looks at the accommodation of non-shareholder interests through a duty-focused legal prism. Finally, it simply adopts a particular characterization of the financial contribution of shareholders to the modern corporation as an assumed starting point rather than a fully reasoned conclusion, albeit one that is consistent with much political, business and academic orthodoxy.

However, this long-standing orthodox view that corporate law and governance is largely or even wholly a matter of private law, and hence concerned with the ordering of interests between companies, management and shareholders, is increasingly under attack. As Harvard's Professor Einer Elhauge explains, '(i)t leaves corporate law scholars free to ignore issues about any effects the corporation may have on the external world as topics best addressed by other legal fields, and to focus on more tractable models about which corporate rules would maximize shareholder value'.[240] It also denies any place for wider public interests beyond being passive public policy rationales for the doctrines of corporate law, as distinct from actively structuring and conditioning the interpretation and application of those doctrines.[241] As Lord Wedderburn of Charleton indicated in a landmark lecture on CSR, 'the ordinary fiduciary duty . . . is imposed in private law, but with a *public* function . . . [as] the vehicle of a social purpose'.[242] Contrarian corporate scholars such as Professor Greenfield bluntly deny that corporate law must be kept cordoned off and unaffected by the wider societal concerns supposedly associated more closely with other areas of law:[243]

[T]here seems to be no good reason to insulate corporate law from the same obligations of other areas of law. All areas of law, including corporate law, should be instrumental to moving our society closer to what we want it to be. The mainstream claim that corporate law should serve only the interests of the shareholder and managerial elite is highly suspect, especially if we believe that the purpose of corporations is to serve society as a whole rather than a small, wealthy minority.

The conventional rationales for complete compartmentalization of corporate law and non-corporate law are problematic. To the extent that corporate law already prescribes or permits accommodation of non-shareholder interests – for example, in directors' duties, business judgment safeguards, corporate and board reporting, superannuation and pension fund investment criteria, security of accrued financial employment benefits, and creditor protection upon insolvency – some degree of interpenetration of both domains already occurs, in ways that cannot all be explained simply as rendering non-shareholder interests subservient to shareholder interests. So, corporate law is already evolving from within, in its accommodation of non-shareholder interests. None of this means, of course, that *all* corporate stakeholders have an equal claim upon a company in terms of legal duties and obligations, corporate governance participation, and financial and other benefits, given the need to distinguish between those stakeholders 'whose interests should be protected as part of the larger, external democratic polity' and those stakeholders deserving 'an internal voice in governance and a share in profits'.[244]

In conceptual terms, any analytical divide between corporate law's concerns and those of other areas of law becomes blurred at the point where business chooses strategies and activities that successfully align competitive business advantage with enhanced social prosperity. In terms of a meta-regulatory understanding of law, any absolute divide between corporate law and non-corporate law would deny their regulatory influence upon each other, and upon their combined impact for holistic corporate compliance and risk management. This holistic approach is consistent with the trend towards testing directors' duties by reference to how well directors manage risk in exercising oversight of corporate systems overall.[245] 'I believe that the best corporate model is one that gives due regard to the goal of realizing the preferences of shareholders but also does not deify those preferences at the expense of other stakeholders, the firm as a whole, or society in general', argues Professor Greenfield.[246]

Similarly, the assumption that corporate law should internalize shareholder interests and externalize other stakeholding interests, to be protected through other mechanisms such as contractual arrangements with companies or supervening governmental regulation in other areas of law, is also increasingly under attack. The argument that non-shareholding corporate stakeholders can and should protect themselves through contractual, legislative and other regulatory measures outside corporate law stands or falls on their realistic capacity individually or collectively to access such mechanisms, especially if those other arenas are also dominated by shareholder and market interests, given that market dynamics are supplemented and even supported by supervening governmental and regulatory measures.[247] The set of claims that shareholders can effectively obtain enough information about a company to exercise proper discipline over management, care only about making money, agree on what will produce overall wealth-maximization, actually have an effective capacity to participate collectively and meaningfully in contemporary corporate governance, and even care about the fortunes of any single company (as distinct from their overall investment portfolio) are all challengeable claims as well.[248]

Defenders of shareholder primacy as the prevailing regulatory norm will point in response to the way in which corporate law has remained largely compartmentalized and focused primarily upon the relationships between companies and their managers and investors, free of the non-shareholder protections that have progressively woven their way into other bodies of law, such as employment law, insolvency law, anti-discrimination law and environmental law. As one Cambridge law professor describes, in a famous contribution to the Anglo-Commonwealth debate about corporate regulatory reform, company law in at least the last half of the 20th century remained remarkably self-contained and immune from the inroads into corporate responsibility progressively occurring elsewhere in the law and related disciplines:[249]

> It was inevitable that the shift away from nineteenth-century self-interest to modern theories of the business enterprise and the 'responsible' corporation should lead to pressure for some

recognition within company law of the view that the providers of share capital are not the only contributors to the wealth-making process; and in particular, for explicit acknowledgement of the role of the workforce. But despite the enthusiasm with which this cause has been taken up by many influential authors, the response has been lukewarm and it has found very little expression in company law.

Although corporate law's response has perhaps been 'lukewarm' until now, at least in terms of what the realities of interest group politics, market economics and transnational flows of investment and trade have enshrined in many corporate regulatory systems, the dynamics pressing upon corporate law's self-containment are neither scant nor wholly ineffective. At the same time, the emergence of the comparative body of CSR-related law and regulation (as highlighted in Chapter 5) illustrates the developments that are taking place within 21st century corporate law too.

Penetrating the public–private divide   Corporate responsibility and governance debates, and hence CSR debates too, are awash with classic dichotomies between corporate and other areas of law, mandatory and voluntary standards, and public and private responsibilities. Having dealt with the first two dichotomies already in this book,[250] this is the appropriate place to address the third dichotomy squarely. As Professor Larry Cata Backer from Pennsylvania State University puts it, '(t)he corporate social responsibility debate is ultimately a debate about the fundamental character of corporations as principally private or public entities'.[251] This means taking a stand, one way or another, on how public and private goods relate to each other in the context of corporate responsibility, governance and sustainability. Those who seek to keep corporations, corporate law and corporate governance cordoned off from the intrusion of concerns from the public domain, except in limited and controlled points of intersection, largely through the medium of agreements, laws and market forces must argue for that position as much as those who take the contrary view. There is no default or stand-alone position.

This grand query about the interplay of public and private interests in corporations has discrete strands, and can be expressed in many different ways. One strand locates the ultimate legitimacy of any corporate regulatory regime in how well corporations and the regulatory system in which they operate serve higher-order public goals such as social efficiency, welfare and prosperity. According to Professor Bakan in *The Corporation*, for example, 'the fact that corporate law and policy rest upon a *conception* of the public good, albeit a narrow one, only confirms that the *concept* of the public good remains the ultimate measure of the corporation's institutional worth and legitimacy', and hence the only institutional purpose of the corporation is 'to serve the public interest (and not some circular conception of the public interest that equates it with the interests of business)'.[252] For Bakan, the in-built corporate structural imperatives of corporate profit-making and shareholder wealth-generation inevitably lead to mass corporate irresponsibility towards society that requires significant regulatory correction.

However, the fundamental relation between public and private goods in corporate responsibility and governance can be taken even further. Instead of being confined to an ultimate societal justification for a particular way of organizing corporate responsibility and governance, public goods could also be integrally involved, along with private goods, in all aspects of a corporation's actions and decisions. For example, theories like corporate constitutionalism focus upon the sense in which corporations are entities in which both public and private interests are intrinsically engaged. 'In short, corporate law has both an external dimension, dealing with relations between corporations and society, and an internal dimension, dealing with intra-corporate relations', argues corporate constitutionalist Professor Bottomley, so that 'the means by which corporations are governed and by which they govern should be constituted by state *and* corporate inputs'.[253]

Here, corporations are viewed as having more than a private role in collective capital investment and deployment, with a public role 'as a type of intermediary organisation, occupying a place between individual citizens and the state', as a deliberative forum for the articulation and battle of contesting views about issues relating to the corporation, including (but not limited to) 'the self-interest of the individual corporate participants'.[254] Indeed, if corporate decision-making sites such as boardroom and shareholders' meetings are truly sites of organizational deliberation in which both public and private concerns are engaged, but within a corporate (as distinct from governmental) context that shapes such deliberation and its accountability mechanisms accordingly, corporate constitutionalism points the way to how the corporate governance process of the company might be used to consider claims and interests of non-shareholders as well as shareholders.[255] This has important implications for CSR.[256]

The decentring of regulation in a system of CSR-related meta-regulation offers insights into the ongoing viability of this public–private divide too.[257] For a long time in the history of corporate responsibility and governance as regulated by law, the public–private distinction has underpinned 'resistance to the idea of *public* accountability of internal governance processes, because the assumption is that corporate governance can be reduced to property and contractual relations between *private* individuals', as Dr Parker notes.[258] Professor Julia Black's articulation of the demise of the public–private distinction lays the conceptual groundwork for a better appreciation of the emergence and significance of tri-sectoral CSR alliances and other multi-stakeholder initiatives in the contemporary CSR world, of the kind explored in Chapter 2:[259]

> In the decentred understanding of regulation, regulation happens in the absence of formal legal sanction – it is the product of interactions, not of the exercise of the formal, constitutionally recognized authority of government. The collapse of the public/private distinction as a useful tool for analyzing governance and regulation is manifested in the identification of 'hybrid' organizations or networks that combine governmental and non-governmental actors in a variety of ways . . . Added more recently are networks: the interactions of a range of actors, of which the state is only one, and which it has been argued government both does use and should use to govern. As noted above, governance and regulation are seen to be the outcome of the interactions of networks, or alternatively 'webs of influence' which operate in the absence of formal governmental or legal sanction.

Having broken through the barrier of keeping the supposedly private domain of shareholder interests and the presumed public domain of wider stakeholder interests completely separate in corporate law and regulation, we compound the previous error of strict dichotomies if we then try to make the relevance and consideration of non-stakeholder interests within internal corporate decision-making match exactly what happens in the public domain. Critics who argue that opening up boardroom decision-making to considerations beyond market-based shareholder interests necessarily confers upon corporate executives a quasi-governmental role in determining and implementing good social policy, for which they are neither elected nor suited, commit a basic error in using the areas of real distinction between governmental and business functions to carry a different order of arguments about the standpoints, interests and reasoning processes in play in performing those functions. Governmental, corporate and community spaces are all different. So, the decision-making orientations, structures and contexts are different within each space. 'Recognition of corporate culture and connection to employee values and self-identity need not mean that the "civic space" within organizations must be modelled on attempts at civic space in public politics', for example, as Dr Parker reminds us.[260]

Considered from a meta-regulatory perspective, the unsatisfactoriness of the public–private distinction has other implications in the corporate domain too, especially for deep debates about corporate democracy, conceived in terms of a company's outward engagement with society as well as society's inward engagement with companies. 'Improving the way in which the decision-making of large corporations with tens of thousands of employees, and the capacity to influence millions of lives, connects with social values and concerns ought to be as much the concern of democratic theory as is framing the power of the state', according to Dr Parker, who views the corporation as 'a participant in and a receptor for democratic deliberation'.[261] On her view, we need 'a deliberative democratic model of permeability of the corporation to responsibility to external values and stakeholders' in a form of 'corporate responsiveness to democratic social control'.[262] All of this aligns on deeper levels with corporate democracy, as well as corporate responsiveness to systems of trans-modal governance, multi-order regulation and inter-related responsibility.

A final strand within this public–private debate concerns the fundamental governance reality of the people's democratic sovereignty over the regulatory conditions under which corporations exist and operate. At its weakest, this acknowledges the undoubted capacity of sovereign jurisdictions to regulate corporations, without necessarily translating into a stronger interpretative claim in which corporations owe their status and benefits to society's regulation and forebearance from imposing extra regulation, and hence owe society something in return, as postulated by 'licence to operate' and 'concession' theories of corporate responsibility. Here, a distinction can be made between such a licence to operate as a formal precondition for conferment of corporate status and privileges by society, on one hand, and the more substantive social licence to operate that any corporation needs to foster in practice to garner support for its products, services and place in the communities in which it does business, on the other.[263]

On a wider plane, limiting citizens who are subject to the use and abuse of corporate power only to formal means of democratic control over societal power-wielding, such as periodic votes in elections, accounts for only part of the framework of societal governance, democratic accountability and corporate regulation within which companies operate today.[264] In addition, the democratic legitimacy of all exercises of power over the people allowed by the state (including the exercise of non-state power) ultimately rests with the sovereignty of the people within the state. This foundation for the legitimization of power infuses both the constitutionalization of corporate power (i.e. the notion that corporate power contains and must be exercised within limits of various kinds) and the democratization of corporate power (i.e. the idea that those people whose interests are affected by the corporate exercises of power are entitled to have their interests taken into account).[265]

21ST CENTURY ATTACKS ON CORPORATE SOCIAL RESPONSIBILITY

Henderson's 'Misguided Virtue'

> Is it really the case that what the overwhelming body of public opinion now wants and expects from companies is that they should (1) embrace the objective of sustainable development, (2) recognise explicitly that this has three dimensions, economic, environmental and social, and (3) run their affairs, in close conjunction with an array of different 'stakeholders', primarily with a view to meeting specific targets and obligations under each of these heads, even if this results in higher costs and prices for the products and services they are selling?
>
> — Former OECD chief economist, David Henderson[266]

Some CSR sceptics view CSR as proposing a new set of societal roles for business which not only extend beyond the conventional place of business in society, but also risk undermining what business can contribute to society. Former OECD chief economist, Professor David Henderson, stakes out his position in his polemic against CSR, *Misguided Virtue: False Notions of Corporate Social Responsibility*. In his eyes, CSR goes too far in creating external pressures upon business from public opinion and NGOs that undermine the basis of a market economy in their attempt to humanize capitalism and globalization. According to Henderson, 'a combination of recent changes on the world scene and pressures from public opinion now requires businesses to take on a new role, a newly-defined mission', in which companies play 'a leading part in achieving the shared objectives of public policy and making the world a better place', which he characterizes as a form of 'corporate citizenship that embraces an agenda of "global Salvationism" in giving capitalism "a human face"'.[267] On this view, CSR 'forms one element of new millennium collectivism', ushering in harmful systemic effects in profit-sacrificing and performance-hindering actions by business enterprises that push for competitors and regulation to follow suit, thereby subverting the profit-making imperative, limiting competition and weakening the overall economy.[268]

In addition, Henderson views sustainable development and its economic, social and environmental dimensions as ill-defined and far from generally accepted. In particular, he views this as involving businesses in embracing a shared goal of 'sustainable development' in ways that dilute a proper focus upon corporate profitability and shareholder value – all for the sake of producing, reporting and verifying corporate performance on sustainable development's three dimensions of economic, social and environmental performance for the supposed good of society.[269] This line of argument suggests that the presumed connection between CSR and profit-enhancement overstates the case for business responding to societal expectations because of reputational and other business concerns, and also understates the costs and negative consequences for business in taking this path. Here, Henderson identifies the main concerns about extra and unnecessary business costs of CSR as follows:[270]

The main factors here are (1) the wider range of goals and concerns that would bear on management at all levels, (2) the need to devise and maintain more elaborate accounting and reporting systems, with new cadres of expertise, and (3) the involvement of management in new time-consuming consultation, negotiation and review processes with a range of outside groups, many of them unconcerned with the commercial success of the business in question and some of them deeply hostile or suspicious.

Counter-responses to this view might embrace Henderson's illumination of the need to examine properly both the costs and benefits of CSR, but still maintain a healthy degree of scepticism about the suitability (or even plausibility) of adhering strictly to corporate profit-maximization as a total account of corporate responsibility and governance, for any of the multitude of reasons canvassed throughout this book. For example, the cost-benefit calculus of CSR for both business and society has multiple strands and levels. It cannot be conceived too narrowly, simply in terms of any disruption to 'business as usual'.

Ultimately, Henderson views the 21st century march of CSR as an adverse development for business profitability and resultant social prosperity. In short, his polemic is against the kind of CSR that tries to create 'a new world order' of societal governance that subverts the core function of business at the expense of promoting the control and agenda of civil society groups. This frames CSR in ways that depend upon fundamental preconceptions of social efficiency and prosperity. In his eyes, refashioning and humanizing corporate capitalism to make it more responsive to changing societal expectations and dynamics 'confuses ends and means':[271]

> It may well be true, or become true as the doctrine prevails, that firms must take the path of CSR in the interests of survival and profitability in an unfriendly world. But in so far as their doing so weakens enterprise performance, limits economic freedom and restricts competition, it deprives private business of its distinctive virtues and rationale.

Today, such CSR-adverse views remain prevalent in some quarters, but are also increasingly under threat from the evolution of thinking and practice elsewhere about CSR, its growing acceptance across societal and industry sectors, its integration in various ways into corporate regulatory regimes worldwide, and its connection to wider governance, regulatory and other systemic needs.

Robert Reich's 'Supercapitalism'

The elements and implications of 'supercapitalism'
Just as Milton Friedman assessed CSR and found it wanting in the context of prevailing conditions affecting political and economic freedom in the Cold War environment, so too Professor Robert Reich's *Supercapitalism* finds CSR wanting in the prevailing conditions for capitalism and democracy that confront 21st century business corporations. More broadly, *Supercapitalism* sits within a long-running debate from at least the time of the Berle–Dodd contest onwards about best sensitizing corporations to necessary public interest concerns through 'revision of the legal model of the corporation', or alternatively by governmental management and intervention in market economies in pursuit of social goals through the medium of 'outside regulation'.[272]

In his liberal critique of CSR, this former Clinton Administration Secretary of Labor

> In recent years, 'corporate social responsibility' has become the supposed answer to the paradox of democratic capitalism [but] (d)emocracy and capitalism have been turned upside down . . . The message that companies are moral beings with social responsibilities diverts public attention from the task of establishing such laws and rules in the first place [and] (m)eanwhile, the real democratic process is left to companies and industries seeking competitive advantage.
>
> The first step in turning democracy and capitalism right side up is to understand what's really happening.
>
> — Professor Robert Reich, former Secretary of Labor in the Clinton administration and author of *Supercapitalism*[273]

argues forcefully that companies are severely constrained in their capacity to practise real CSR in the era of what he calls 'supercapitalism', and that CSR activism by consumers, investors and citizens is more usefully directed towards making governments rather than businesses address social problems. As *The Economist* notes in a review of Reich's book, this includes recognizing 'that governments are responsible for setting rules that ensure that competing, profit-maximising firms do not act against the interests of society'.[274] Writing mainly in an American context in *Supercapitalism*, Reich nevertheless intends his account of the consequences of supercapitalism to have resonance in comparable countries too, especially those encountering the same dilemmas of the interplay between investor-based and consumer-based capitalism, on one hand, and citizen-focused democracy, on the other.[275]

'Supercapitalism' has the following characteristics, according to Reich. It marks the rise of the power of consumers and investors over the power of citizens.[276] At the same time that 'consumers and investors have access to more choices and better deals', not least through developments in meeting the needs of mass consumerism and institutional investment, 'the institutions that once gave voice to citizen concerns have all but disappeared', including unions, public interest agencies, and even local interest groups, against the backdrop of the growing influence of corporate lobbying, corporate campaign financing and strategic corporate litigation.[277] 'In supercapitalism, the corporation as a whole must, for competitive reasons, resist doing anything that hurts – and will place a very low priority on anything that doesn't help – the bottom line', with the consequence that '[corporations] *cannot* be socially responsible, at least not to any significant extent', argues Reich.[278]

In the past, when 'big companies tended to be oligopolies with significant power over their prices and markets', different societal conditions for CSR prevailed, and 'many companies still had sufficient discretion to be socially responsible', not least because of the different market and competitive conditions at that time.[279] More recently, increased national and global competition has seen the demise of giant corporations dominating entire markets and industries.[280] This demise in market power of individual corporations is accompanied by a redirection of corporate efforts in the governmental domain to secure political and legal outcomes that secure them advantages over their competitors.[281]

'Supercapitalism has spilled over into politics, and engulfed democracy', in Reich's assessment.[282] 'Under supercapitalism, a commitment to social virtue is no substitute for obsessive dedication to shareholder value', Reich concludes.[283]

This is only the start of a broader critique of CSR. In Reich's eyes, the misguided contemporary focus on CSR produces multiple problems. Influenced by CSR rhetoric, communities are deluded into thinking that business is a meaningful alternative to government in addressing particular social problems. 'The half-truths, mythologies, and distortions that now litter the border between the private sector and the public sector make it impossible for the public to keep straight the distinct roles of corporate executives and public officials' argues Reich, with the result that 'muddled thinking confounds efforts to prevent supercapitalism from overrunning democracy'.[284] Misplaced faith in CSR results in the public giving in to pressures (e.g. corporate lobbying) which forestall real political reform of the rules of the game for business in ways that would genuinely promote socially responsible business behaviour.

Finally, this mistaken popular investment in CSR fails to address other systemic features in contemporary democratic government that make it harder than ever before for citizens to force governments to rewrite those rules of the game. 'Instead of guarding democracy against the disturbing side effects of supercapitalism, many reformers have set their sights on changing the behavior of particular companies – extolling them for being socially virtuous or attacking them for being socially irresponsible', argues Reich, with an outcome of 'some marginal changes in corporate behaviour', but where 'the larger consequence has been to divert the public's attention from fixing democracy'.[285]

The corporate mandate's incompatibility with corporate social responsibility

> Companies are not interested in the public good. It is not their responsibility to be good. They may do good things to improve their brand image, so as to increase sales and profits. They will do profitable things that may happen to have socially beneficial side effects. But they will not do good things because they are considered to be good. To suggest that a vast, untapped reservoir of corporate benevolence is available for the asking is to seriously mislead the public – and once again divert attention from the important job of deciding what such regulations should be.
>
> – Professor Reich, *Supercapitalism*[286]

Much here turns on foundational preconceptions of what truly contributes to shareholder value, as well as the characterization of the interaction between profit-generation and social goods in oppositional or other terms. In a post-book interview for *Forbes.com*, Reich further delineates the true boundaries of CSR in his eyes, in terms which compare and contrast his views to those of Milton Friedman:[287]

In the early 1970s, Milton Friedman argued that corporations should not be socially responsible because they had no mandate to be; they existed to make money, not to be charitable institutions. But in the economy of the 21st century, corporations *cannot* be socially responsible, if social responsibility is understood to mean sacrificing profits for the sake of some perceived social good. That's because competition has become so much more intense. As to the meaning of 'corporate social responsibility', Friedman and I would agree: If a certain action improves the corporation's bottom line, there's no point in labeling it 'socially responsible'. It's just good business.

On this view, society mistakenly treats as 'socially responsible' business behaviour favouring the bottom line that is best characterized as simply good business management. So, in Reich's eyes, we cannot properly call business actions such as using cheaper but environmentally friendly packaging or providing employee insurance and health programmes to reduce staff turnover truly socially responsible ones, because '(t)o credit these corporations with being "socially responsible" is to stretch the term to mean anything a company might do to increase profits if, in doing so, it also happens to have some beneficent impact on the rest of society', which would effectively mean that 'all profitable companies are socially responsible'.[288] In short, business is seen as having no competitive capacity for profit-sacrificing CSR activity, but gains no CSR credit for social benefits that are also profit-enhancing.

The trouble with this view of CSR is that it gives CSR little room to move and no meaningful place to go in Reich's analysis, beyond an old-style form of corporate philanthropy that is unsustainable in the competitive world of 21st century capitalism, or else an alignment between social good and private profit that strips the result of any socially responsible characteristics by definition. In other words, *Supercapitalism*'s view of corporations locks them into a position in which any meaningful business contribution to society either goes against their presumed mandate or else gains them no extra socioethical legitimacy because it simply meets that mandate in other ways. In short, corporations are damned if they do and damned if they don't practise CSR.

Ultimately, there is a false dichotomy between an impoverished form of CSR which instrumentally serves an underlying business imperative and an unjustified form of CSR which is incompatible with that imperative, as there is much more in play here than just mono-dimensional characterization in terms of ultimate mandate satisfaction. We miss a wider point if we characterize a profitable outcome with socially beneficial side-effects as simply nothing more than good business management, unworthy of being captured in any meaningful sense of CSR. There are meaningful CSR elements here in what companies place on their corporate radar and what choices they make in pursuing profit, for example.

In addition, strategic emphasis on company-specific ways to build competitive advantage in socially beneficial ways feeds into other systemic layers of sustainable and responsible profit-making, as part of responsible corporate self-regulation according to the social ends of meta-regulatory values. Indeed, if corporations are spaces for the interplay of particular public and private interests, CSR has a role in the way in which business meets societal values that cannot simply be dismissed as either marginal to the profit-making mandate or else subsumed by it. Individual and shared business responsibility in the 21st century for both public goods and private gain extends beyond the norms and values associated with economically efficient market relations as the default proxy for overall social utility.[289]

Is there really nothing of CSR value worth characterizing in the differences between a profit-centred business adopting cost-effective actions that also have a socially beneficial side-effect, voluntarily aligning strategy and operations with socially orientated business drivers, making social responsibility a point of competitive differentiation, and joining with governments and non-government parties alike in tackling particular social problems in ways best suited to business? The governance and regulatory realities of a 21st century world steer corporate receptivity and responsiveness to CSR in ways that transcend what corporate oligopolies once might have undertaken as corporate philanthropy and what governments are still able to set as rules of the game for business. Business has a socially responsible role to play that must be set from both societal and company-specific standpoints, and not simply from the perspective of enlightened corporate self-interest. Moreover, it is precisely because of the practical impediments to citizens, NGOs and other CSR actors in the political process, due to factors such as corporate legislative lobbying, electoral campaign financing and business capture of official regulators, that these CSR actors look to the business sector's embrace of CSR and how they might exert pressure to that effect.[290]

Rehabilitating corporate social responsibility in the era of 'supercapitalism'

> We can, if we choose, fashion a democratic capitalism more suited to our nobler aspirations for the twenty-first century. Yet to do that, it is necessary to separate capitalism from democracy and guard the border between them.
>
> – Professor Reich, *Supercapitalism*[291]

Having evolved from a CSR believer into a CSR sceptic,[292] Reich outlines a menu of options for achieving socially responsible businesses. One set of solutions involves separating the false promises of CSR from what is truly achievable. Amongst other things, this involves abandoning CSR expectations and being sceptical about political claims that 'the public can rely on the "voluntary" cooperation of the private sector to achieve some public purpose or goal', in tandem with wariness of 'any claim by corporate executives that their company is doing something in order to advance the "public good" or to fulfil the firm's "social responsibility"'.[293] It also involves correcting the 'anthropomorphic fallacy' of extending a panoply of legal rights and duties to corporations that properly belong to human beings, as well as limiting participation in democratic governance to people and not companies.[294] In addition, the domains of public policy-making and lawmaking need serious remedial help to prevent corporations from securing competitive advantages for themselves over their rivals through manipulation of the machinery of government, including reformatory measures that strike at corporate lobbying, political contributions, non-disclosure of expenditure and relationships, and inadequate regulatory policing.[295]

Of course, Reich's main concern is that expecting too much real CSR from corporations that are now structurally and competitively unable to provide it distracts attention from democratic government as the proper forum for resolving major societal problems, including problems of market failure and mass corporate harm. Reich's antidote for the problems of supercapitalism places heavy emphasis upon solutions through legal and political means of fixing the rules of the game for business. 'It is illogical to criticize companies for playing by the current rules of the game; if we want them to play differently, we have to change the rules', Reich argues.[296] Again, all of this makes most sense in the contexts that Reich describes, such as the undoubted need to lay the appropriate political and legal groundwork for conditions of corporate compliance and responsiveness. In this vein, dynamics such as broader regulatory influences beyond governmental regulation, socio-economic trends and even moral imperatives combine with formal resetting of the rules of the game for business through legal and political means. In other words, the regulation advocated by Reich through state-directed means, important as it is, must be complemented and even shaped by a broader array of regulation too, in a 21st century world of interdependent systems of state and non-state governance, regulation and responsibility.

Supercapitalism's greatest strengths lie in exposing the false hope of expecting too much of CSR alone, and in providing a wake-up call which redirects attention to neglected areas of the politico-legal landscape in recreating conditions for business activity that better serves society. At the same time, it reinforces a bright dividing line between mandatory state-imposed obligations and voluntary business actions, on one hand, and between what is properly a matter for government and properly a matter for business, on the other. In the era of supercapitalism, business cannot and should not take on any of the social responsibilities properly falling upon government, and likewise business should not unduly intrude into the domain of government in pursuit of political and legal outcomes to their competitive advantage. Acknowledging and respecting these boundaries is part of the solution according to Reich, just as failing to acknowledge and respect them has been the source of the problems of supercapitalism:[297]

> The triumph of supercapitalism has led, indirectly and unwittingly, to the decline of democracy. But that is not inevitable. We can have a vibrant democracy as well as a vibrant capitalism. To accomplish this, the two spheres must be kept distinct. The purpose of capitalism is to get great deals for consumers and investors. The purpose of democracy is to accomplish ends we cannot achieve as individuals. The border between the two is breached when companies *appear* to take on social responsibilities or when they utilise politics to advance or maintain their competitive standing.

'In general, corporate responsibilities to the public are better addressed in the democratic process than inside corporate boardrooms', concludes Reich.[298] Yet, while these dividing lines might remain bright in the contexts that Reich describes, there are other contexts where they are bypassed or even blur, without necessarily attracting the negative consequences he fears. Multi-stakeholder networks that share information, build capacity, set standards and develop trust are CSR creations that straddle governmental, business and community domains. In addition, the conditions under which any business might engage with societal matters is very different from the conditions under which any government does so. Nor can everything about corporate self-regulation within wider systems of meta-regulation be positioned simply within these strict dividing lines. In short, this timeless debate about a divergence between the business of business and the business of government is real on some levels but misfires on others.[299]

Certainly, political and legal intervention in the rules of the game for business might be a necessary condition for outcomes that individual companies cannot or will not choose alone – namely, making companies internalise otherwise externalized costs, setting uniform rules for all business that cannot be achieved by any single company voluntarily undertaking something that its competitors can avoid, and ensuring that virtuous choices by individual consumers and investors amount to more than a personal sacrifice in the light of choices by all others, in all of the ways that Reich outlines.[300] So, in relation to environmental protection and climate change risks, Reich rightly draws attention to the limits beyond which voluntary corporate initiatives cannot travel, as well as the short-sightedness of expecting businesses to address what can only properly be addressed through governmental regulation in this field.

As in other major CSR debates, however, the choice is not a stark and simple one between looking to either governments or business alone to solve society's problems and meet its needs. Indeed, here and elsewhere, one of the greatest 21st century challenges concerning CSR is to make the transformation in business, regulatory and public mindsets from thinking in bi-polar terms about mandatory and voluntary obligations, public and private responsibilities, and governmental and business roles. Here, this means identifying 'when and where corporate responsibility strategies are effective and appropriate – and when they are not'.[301] 'A more nuanced CSR paradigm', according to the future strategy mapped out for CSR progressives by Aaron Chatterji and Siona Listokin, involves 'progressives using CSR tactics in limited cases, but most often working for government action, sometimes armed with the lobbying and financial muscle of corporate America itself'.[302]

This requires development of a credible basis for differentiating, for example, between the kinds of societal problems and needs that only governments can address (e.g. state-based regulation to cure major failures or deficiencies of markets) and those societal problems that call for pressuring the business sector for action or alternatively lobbying for greater cross-sectoral corporation between business, governments and civil society groups in tackling particular large-scale societal challenges.[303] What unites Reich's unflattering portrayal of CSR as currently conceived, regulated and practised and what a 21st century vision of CSR promises through corporate responsiveness to trans-modal governance, multi-order regulation and inter-related responsibility is a common concern for a more careful delineation of the conditions under which corporations, governments and other societal actors together take ownership of such problems. All of this reinforces the need for adequate 21st century normative architecture in addressing great questions of corporate responsibility, governance, and sustainability, and the distinctive but related roles that state and non-state actors now play in the CSR landscape.

NOTES

1. Perrini et al, 2006: 2, 4.
2. I am indebted to Eric Orts from the Wharton Business School on these points and ideas about business theory.
3. Cf Roy, 1997: 76–77.
4. CLRSG, 2001. On 'enlightened shareholder value' as a Third Way see Williams and Conley, 2005a: 510–522; and Conley and Williams, 2006: 2–4.
5. Wheeler, 2002: 170.
6. PJCCFS, 2006; and CAMAC, 2006.
7. Ruggie, 2007b.

8. Wedderburn, 1985: 40, 42–43; original emphasis.
9. Campbell, 2007: 551.
10. Orts, 1993: 1567–1574.
11. Ibid.: 1587.
12. Dunfee, 1999: 129.
13. Millon, 2001: 28; quoted in Bottomley, 2007: 7.
14. Bottomley, 2007: 12.
15. Allen, 1992: 280–281.
16. Price, 2003: 600.
17. For an account of this notion of interpretation as applied to law generally see Dworkin, 2006: Ch 1.
18. Australian Treasury, 2007: 4–10.
19. Sunstein, 1996: 52.
20. Gutmann and Thompson, 2004: 34–35.
21. Campbell, 2007: 529.
22. Hughes, 2005.
23. On this macro-level, meso-level and micro-level framework see Banerjee, 2005.
24. Quoted in Frances, 2008: 107.
25. Ibid.: 5–6.
26. Banerjee, 2005.
27. Stiglitz, 2006: 209.
28. Gare, 2006: 21.
29. Zerk, 2006: 16.
30. Saul, 1995: 74–75.
31. Dahl, 1972, quoted in Parkinson, 1993: 23; original emphasis.
32. Parkinson, 1993: 23.
33. Higgins, 2006: 16–17.
34. For a recent discussion of how corporate responsibility and governance straddle the public and private domains see: Bottomley, 2007.
35. This chapter and Ch 10.
36. Galbraith, 1996: 75–76.
37. Campbell, 2007: 539, 545–546.
38. Australian Labor MP (subsequently Prime Minister), Kevin Rudd, in Rudd, 2006: 17.
39. Foreword by Sir Geoffrey Owen, in Henderson, 2001a: 8.
40. Galbraith, 1996: 113.
41. Ibid.: 76–77.
42. Ruggie, 2002: 1.
43. Ibid.: 1.
44. Ruggie, 2008a: [2].
45. Porritt, 2007: 31; original emphasis.
46. Ibid.: 331, 347.
47. Flannery, 2008: 63–64.
48. Sachs, 2008: 211–212.
49. Sen, 2000: 263.
50. Ibid.: 262.
51. A/HRC/4/35, [1]–[2].
52. A/HRC/4/35, [1].
53. Cox, 1995.
54. Korten, 2001: 95–97, 102; citing Daly and Cobb, 1989: 49–60.
55. Farrar, 2005: 492, citing Backman, 1999: 3.
56. Donaldson and Dunfee, 1999: 25.
57. Braithwaite and Drahos, 2000: 35–36.
58. Elhauge, 2005: 745; original emphasis.
59. Stiglitz, 2006: 190, 195.
60. Parkinson, 1993: 42.
61. Ibid.: 41–42.
62. Greenfield, 2006: 19–20.
63. A/HRC/4/35, [3].
64. Singer, 2007: 20.
65. Mintzberg et al., 2002: 72–3.
66. Obama, 2006: 146, 180.
67. Dahl, 2000: 175–177.

68. Hansmann and Kraakman, 2004a: 42.
69. Campbell, 2007: 538.
70. Stiglitz, 2006: 190.
71. Gordon and Roe, 2004b: 27–28.
72. Parkinson, 1993; Stiglitz, 2006; Mitchell, 2001; Bakan, 2004; Greenfield, 2006; Lee, 2006; and Elhauge, 2005.
73. Sampford and Berry, 2004; and Deakin, 2005.
74. Bottomley, 2007.
75. Deakin, 2005: 17.
76. Annan, 1999.
77. Ibid.
78. Cf Visentini, 1998: 849.
79. E.g. Bebchuk, 2005.
80. Drutman and Cray, 2004: 116–118.
81. Gomez and Korine, 2005: 740–747.
82. Parker, 2002: 213, 227.
83. Gomez and Korine, 2005: 740–747.
84. Parkinson, 1993: 30–31.
85. Bakan, 2004: 145–146.
86. Ibid.: 154.
87. Gutmann and Thompson, 2004: 34.
88. Parker, 2002: 214.
89. Ibid.: 57–60, 214.
90. Ibid.: 215, 221; original emphasis.
91. Bottomley, 2007: 12.
92. Ibid.: 13.
93. Ibid.: 12.
94. Hansmann and Kraakman, 2004a.
95. Williams and Conley, 2005a: 499.
96. Gordon, 2004: 161–162.
97. Cheffins, 2002; Roe, 2004; and Bebchuk and Roe, 2004.
98. Albareda et al, 2007: 124.
99. Donaldson, 2005: 3.
100. *The Economist*, 2008: 17–18.
101. Ibid.: 17.
102. Dunfee, 1999: 129–130.
103. Berle, 1931: 1049.
104. Mitchell, 2001: 186.
105. Dodd, 1932: 1163.
106. Ibid.: 1148.
107. Berle, 1932: 1367, quoting Dodd, 1932: 1146.
108. Stout, 2002: 1203–1204.
109. Bosch, 2006: 2.
110. Bratton and Wachter, 2007: 3–7, 51–60.
111. Berle, 1960: 68; and Berle, 1966: xii.
112. Bratton and Wachter, 2007: 4–6.
113. Ibid.: 40, 43, 55.
114. Berle, 1960: 66–67.
115. Bratton and Wachter, 2007: 48.
116. Berle, 1960: 80–81.
117. Davis et al, 2006: 52. See also Ch 2.
118. Parkinson, 1993: vii–viii.
119. Berle and Means, 1968: xxix.
120. Austin et al, 2005: 62–63.
121. Berle and Means, 1968: 311.
122. Ibid.: 313.
123. Ibid.: 212–213.
124. Ibid.: xxv.
125. Friedman, 1962: 133.
126. Sampford and Berry, 2004: 121–123; and Cadbury, 2002: 156–158.
127. Friedman, 2002: 133.
128. Ibid.: 133.

129. Campbell, 2007: 540.
130. Friedman, 1970.
131. Hayek, 1960: 100.
132. Ibid.; emphasis added.
133. Friedman, 2005: 33.
134. Friedman, 1970.
135. Reich, 2008: 9.
136. Friedman, 2005: 32–33.
137. Friedman, 1970.
138. For discussion and authorities on a similar illustration see Horrigan, 2002.
139. Prahalad, 2005.
140. For further discussion of corporate social engineering, see Ch 4.
141. Cadbury, 2002: 157–158.
142. Ibid.: 156.
143. Ibid.: 157.
144. Ibid.: 166.
145. Ibid.: Ch 12.
146. Hansmann and Kraakman, 2004a: 33–34.
147. Parkinson, 1993: 305–309; and Greenfield, 2006: 136–142.
148. Hansmann and Kraakman, 2004a.
149. Ibid.: 34.
150. Ibid.: 35.
151. Hansmann, 2005.
152. Hansmann and Kraakman, 2004a: 18.
153. Ibid.: 42–43.
154. Ibid.: 18.
155. Ibid.: 18.
156. Ibid.: 18.
157. Ibid.: 18.
158. Ibid.: 18.
159. Elhauge, 2005: 736–738; and Greenfield, 2006: 142–143.
160. For more on game-setting, game-changing and game-ending decisions and rule-setting for corporations throughout their life cycle, and the need for greater shareholder influence in these processes at various points of that life cycle see Bebchuk, 2005.
161. On all of these claims see Hansmann, 2005.
162. Mitchell et al, 2005: 17.
163. Berle and Means, 1968: xxii–xxiii; emphasis added.
164. Drutman and Cray, 2004: 116–117.
165. Legge, 2008: 32.
166. Conger et al, 2001: 147–148; emphasis added.
167. Micklethwait and Wooldridge, 2005: xvi–xvii.
168. Blair, 2004: 184.
169. Bratton and Wachter, 2007: 52–53.
170. On this point and its accompanying discussion see Allen, 1992: 263–264, and 273–275.
171. Deakin, 2005: 14.
172. Ibid.: 16.
173. Bottomley, 2007: 175.
174. Stout, 2002: 1199.
175. Donaldson and Preston, 1995: 88.
176. Blair and Stout, 2006.
177. Blair and Stout, 1999: 766.
178. Ibid.: 767, 777; original emphasis.
179. Parker, 2002: 5.
180. Blair and Stout, 1999: 753, 756.
181. Blair, 2004: 184.
182. E.g. Hansmann and Kraakman, 2004a; and Bebchuk, 2006.
183. Drutman and Cray, 2004: 126.
184. Stout, 2007.
185. Ibid.
186. Blair and Stout, 1999: 755, 757–758, and 767; original emphasis.
187. Millon, 2000.

188. Dent, 2007.
189. Austin et al, 2005: 53–54.
190. Lee, 2006: 585.
191. Bottomley, 2007: 8–9.
192. Hansmann and Kraakman, 2004a: 42.
193. Greenfield, 2006: 22–25.
194. Ibid.: 25.
195. Ibid.: 25.
196. Ibid.: 241.
197. Ibid.: 24–25.
198. Ibid.: 224.
199. Ibid.: 224.
200. E.g. Stout, 2002; and Greenfield, 2006.
201. Greenfield, 2006: 70–71.
202. Lee, 2006: 585.
203. Wood, 2002. The following distillation of arguments and counter-arguments about 'ownership' draws upon the analysis in Blair, 2004 and Stout, 2002 in particular.
204. Blair, 2004: 181.
205. *Salomon v Salomon & Co* [1897] AC 22 at 51.
206. Deakin, 2005: 12–13.
207. Donaldson and Preston, 1995: 83.
208. Ibid.: 84.
209. Ibid.: 85.
210. Ibid.: 84–85.
211. E.g. Gomez and Korine, 2005.
212. Bottomley, 2007.
213. Hansmann and Kraakman, 2004a: 18.
214. Ibid.
215. Hansmann, 2005: 3.
216. Ibid.: 4–5.
217. Hansmann and Kraakman, 2004a; and Hansmann, 2005.
218. Armour et al, 2003; and Deakin, 2005.
219. Bebchuk and Roe, 2004; and Schmidt and Spindler, 2004.
220. See Ch 5.
221. Armour et al, 2003: 531–532.
222. Ibid.
223. On the following summary of features and arguments see Wallman, 1991; Orts, 1992; Allen, 1992; Donaldson and Preston, 1995; Eisenberg, 1998; Blair and Stout, 1999; Stout, 2002; Blair, 2003; Lee, 2005; Elhauge, 2005; and Lee, 2006.
224. Elhauge, 2005: 738–739.
225. Elhauge, 2005; and Lee, 2006.
226. Stout, 2002: 1203.
227. Ibid.: 1202–1203.
228. Williams and Conley, 2005a: 499 (original emphasis).
229. Ibid.: 530.
230. Hansmann and Kraakman, 2004a.
231. Deakin, 2005: 16; and Armour et al, 2003: 546.
232. Deakin, 2005: 16; and Armour et al, 2003: 546.
233. Deakin, 2005: 16; and Armour et al, 2003: 546–547.
234. Hermes, 2006: 8 and 18.
235. Davis et al, 2006: 200–201.
236. Ibid.: xiii–xiv.
237. SSCLCA, 1989: [6.51].
238. Ibid.: [6.56].
239. Black, 2004; 42–49: and Parker et al, 2004: 285.
240. Elhauge, 2005: 737.
241. Wedderburn, 1985: 24.
242. Ibid.
243. Greenfield, 2006: 141–142.
244. Kelly, 2001: 150.
245. Dine, 2005: 272–276.

246. Greenfield, 2006: 27.
247. Ibid.: 20–21.
248. Ibid.: 15, 26.
249. Sealy, 1987: 170.
250. Chs 2 and 3.
251. Cata Backer, 2005: Abstract.
252. Bakan, 2004: 156, 158.
253. Bottomley, 1999: 254–255; original emphasis.
254. Bottomley, 2007: 15.
255. Bottomley, 1997: 302.
256. See Ch 10.
257. Parker, 2000: 12; and Black, 2001: 111.
258. Parker, 2002: 3; original emphasis.
259. Black, 2001: 110–111.
260. Parker, 2002: 210.
261. Ibid.: 6–7.
262. Ibid.: 6–7, 31.
263. Bottomley, 1997; and Bottomley, 1999.
264. Dine, 2005: 278.
265. Such notions have deep connections to the deliberation, contestability and accountability of corporate decision-making illuminated in 21st century terms in theories such as corporate constitutionalism, on which this account of constitutionalization of corporate power also draws: see Bottomley, 2007.
266. Henderson, 2001a: 39–40.
267. Henderson, 2001b: 28, 29, and 30.
268. On all of these points see Henderson, 2001a.
269. Henderson, 2001b: 28.
270. Henderson, 2001a: 29.
271. Henderson, 2001b: 31.
272. Bratton and Wachter, 2007: 58.
273. Reich, 2008: 2, 55–56.
274. *The Economist*, 2007, 67.
275. Reich, 2007: 129 and 209.
276. Ibid.: 5.
277. Ibid.: 7, 164–165.
278. Ibid.: 169–170.
279. Ibid.: 173.
280. Ibid.: 7.
281. Ibid.: 163.
282. Ibid.: 164.
283. Ibid.: 174.
284. Ibid.: 213.
285. Ibid.: 210.
286. Ibid.: 204–205, 214.
287. 'Supercapitalism: Transforming Business', *Forbes.com*, 6 September 2007.
288. Reich, 2007: 171; *The Economist*, 2007, 67.
289. Campbell, 2007: 539.
290. *The Economist*, 2007, 67.
291. Reich, 2007: 167.
292. Ibid.: 171.
293. Ibid.: 214.
294. Ibid.: 216 and 223.
295. Ibid.: 210–211.
296. Ibid.: 214.
297. Ibid.: 224; original emphasis.
298. Ibid.: 215.
299. See Ch 4.
300. Reich, 2007: 173 and 204; original emphasis.
301. Chatterji and Listokin, 2007.
302. Ibid.
303. Ibid.

PART 2

CORPORATE SOCIAL RESPONSIBILITY'S REGULATORY MAPS AND OPTIONS

4. Mapping governmental frameworks and roles on corporate social responsibility

OVERVIEW

CSR no longer simply affects relationships between businesses and society. It has become a way of rethinking the role of companies in society, which takes governance and sustainability as its core values and changes the focus of CSR public policies.

– CSR public policy scholars Laura Albareda, Josep Lozano and Tamyko Ysa[1]

The Government understands that it has a strategic role to play in encouraging the right conditions for sustainable business practice . . . I believe the role of Government is in creating an environment that – first encourages, facilitates and promotes the integration of CSR into companies' business practices and secondly opens those practices up to accountability and transparency.

– Australia's Minister for Superannuation and Corporate Law, Senator Nick Sherry[2]

The study of CSR in the first part of this book provides a platform for mapping how its contemporary features and debates manifest themselves in particular corporate regulatory systems. Such a mapping exercise starts with governmental policy, legal and other regulatory measures directed towards CSR. Governmental CSR concerns in the 21st century are national, regional and global in focus. 'The discourse on CSR has moved away from an emphasis on the social, economic and political development of the native country to more universal concerns about environmental integrity and global welfare', notes Wharton's Professor Donaldson.[3] Despite the varying historical, social and political dynamics shaping different governmental approaches to CSR in different countries and regions, governments that want to foster CSR can usefully model policy and regulatory approaches elsewhere. 'The European strategy on CSR and sustainable development', for example, 'tries to reconcile economic growth, social cohesion and environmental protection, and could give an interesting perspective for other countries and other regions', according to three European CSR scholars.[4]

The relationship between governments and CSR must be designed, practised, and studied on multiple levels all at once. Twenty-first century evidence of this relationship's global significance is found in G8 and G20 commitments to CSR, governmental involvement in multi-stakeholder CSR networks worldwide, 21st century scholarly mapping of governmental CSR roles and functions,[5] and initiatives associated with the operation-alization of Professor John Ruggie's official 'protect, respect and remedy' framework for business and human rights, in terms of 'the State duty to protect against human rights abuses by third parties, including business, through appropriate policies, regulation, and adjudication'.[6] For example, his recommendation to the UN for 'greater policy coherence in business and human rights' is accompanied by the cooperation of the Office of the High Commissioner for Human Rights in surveying UN member states about their CSR policies generally and their incorporation of international human rights standards in particular.[7]

However, in mapping CSR from the governmental perspective, we need to recognize that governments do more than simply make policies that might affect CSR and then pass laws to implement them. Accordingly, this chapter explores the multiple connec-tions between CSR and government in ways designed to inform scholarly study, policy and regulatory reform, and interactivity between governmental, business and civil society actors. In particular, this chapter analyses governmental involvement in CSR through a multi-pronged framework that explores governmental and business responsibilities for CSR, whole-of-government approaches to CSR, public policy and CSR, CSR-orientated regulatory reform, and dimensions of CSR activity for government. Building upon existing CSR literature, regulation and practice, and within the inherent limitations of any analytical mapping or cataloguing exercise, this chapter concludes with a nine-fold categorization of governmental CSR functions and related actions.

THE BUSINESS OF BUSINESS V THE BUSINESS OF GOVERNMENT

Are corporations and business leaders who preach and practise CSR thereby trespassing upon the business of government, and hence committing illegitimate corporate social engineering? The argument that business has a role in society does not mean that busi-ness has the same societal role as government, or even that business must adopt a role neglected by government. As the UNSRSG makes clear in his 2008 report to the UN Human Rights Council:[8]

> While corporations may be considered 'organs of society', they are specialized economic organs, not democratic public interest institutions. As such, their responsibilities cannot and should not simply mirror the duties of States [and] there is no need for the slippery distinction between 'primary' and 'secondary' corporate obligations – which in any event would invite endless stra-tegic gaming of the ground about who is responsible for what.

As *The Economist*'s stance demonstrates, one of the most common and long-standing arguments against CSR is that it involves business in something that extends beyond the proper realm of business expertise and into 'the proper business of government'.[9] Similarly, the Australian Government's Corporations and Markets Advisory Committee (CAMAC) starkly puts the conventional case for a clear boundary between business and non-business responsibilities in its 21st century report on CSR:[10]

> (T)he role of companies is to carry out their business or other objectives, subject to legal and other constraints. While the community may look to companies to behave responsibly and to

contribute in ways relevant to their business, they should not be expected to bear a general fiduciary duty to solve societal problems.

What increasingly matters for corporate responsibility and governance in the 21st century, however, is not a fixed and absolute dividing line between supposed matters of public (or governmental) concern and correlative matters of private (or business) concern, but rather an understanding of the multiple levels on which business, governments and society now relate to one another. This is particularly important in light of CSR's 21st century evolution on two fronts, towards an outward-looking repositioning of corporate settings and objectives in terms of their relation to the world beyond the corporation, together with an inward-looking strategic corporate integration of CSR within standard business models by reference to that world.[11]

Whatever boundaries might exist for other purposes between state and business domains of responsibility, deliberation upon both public and private goods happens within both domains of responsibility, albeit in different contexts and under very different institutional conditions. Approaches to corporate responsibility and governance such as corporate constitutionalism recognize this. Its constitutionalist character 'suggests that there are values and ideas in our public political life that can provide useful insights when considering the legal regulation of corporate governance and decision-making', while its corporate character 'indicates that within the corporate context these values and ideas will have different formulations, applications, and consequences than in other political contexts'.[12]

It is indeed desirable to establish a clear division of duties between business and government. Governments, which are accountable to their electorates, should decide matters of public policy. Managers, who are accountable to their shareholders, should run their businesses . . . (B)usinesses should not try to do the work of governments, just as governments should not try to do the work of businesses . . . Managers, acting in their professional capacity, ought not to concern themselves with the public good: they are not competent to do it, they lack the democratic credentials for it, and their day jobs should leave them no time even to think about it. If they merely concentrate on discharging their responsibility to the owners of their firms, acting ethically as they do so, they will usually serve the public good in any case.

The proper guardians of the public interest are governments, which are accountable to all citizens. It is the job of elected politicians to set goals for regulators, to deal with externalities, to mediate among different interests, to attend to the demands of social justice, to provide public goods and collect the taxes to pay for them, to establish collective priorities where that is necessary and appropriate, and to organize resources accordingly.

The proper business of business is business. No apology required.

– *The Economist*, 'The Good Company: A Survey of Corporate Social Responsibility'[13]

Any simple demarcation of business and governmental domains also glosses over areas of shared concern across both domains, as well as points of interaction between them. On a broad scale, for example, major global challenges such as climate risk, sustainable development, human rights advancement and mass epidemic prevention are ones in which governments, businesses and communities have both a common interest and distinct roles to play. On a much narrower scale, a business in a high-risk AIDS region in a developing country that sets up an on-site medical facility to stimulate AIDS awareness and precautions for its employees and their families obtains benefits in terms of maintaining a productive, healthy and happy workforce. It might also supplement governmental and community AIDS-prevention efforts, interact with other governmental and community initiatives aimed at improving social prosperity and well-being, dovetail with wider governance needs and coordination in fighting mass epidemics nationally and globally, and otherwise contribute to a variety of societal goods. In these examples and countless others, the sharp analytical divide between business, governmental and community domains gives way to a much more complex reality of interactive and responsive corporate engagement in the real world.

For example, well-regarded corporate reporting guidelines include the political and public policy connections of business as standard sustainability reporting categories and key performance indicators (KPIs). The GRI Sustainability Reporting Guidelines (G3) contain a couple of relevant reporting categories and indicators in this context, such as the core public policy KPI, in the social performance category, of a company's political lobbying, involvement in developing public policy, and public policy stances, and the ancillary public policy KPI of monetary and in-kind contributions to political organizations.[14] These are in addition to other categories and KPIs where corporate performance can have an indirect impact upon public policy, such as the community KPI of a corporation's evaluation of its means of assessing and managing the impact of its business operations upon local communities, from entry to exit.

If a company chooses to report its performance under G3 categories like the 'nature, scope, and effectiveness of any programs that assess and manage the impacts of operations on communities, including entering, operating, and exiting', for example, how much of that is properly characterized as society-regarding and how much as business-regarding? So, companies might not make or determine public policy, in terms of the demarcated functions of business and government. Yet they can clearly influence and affect policy and regulatory developments, create consequences to which public policy and regulation must respond, align their business activity with necessary public outcomes, and engage with government on their own behalf or for others with whom they have relationships.

Some attempted criticisms misfire in their attempts to draw absolute dividing lines between governmental and corporate domains of responsibility, and to characterize some manifestations of CSR as leading directors astray into areas of societal concern that lie beyond their capability and responsibility. We might readily agree that directors have no place usurping the role of politicians in deciding what is good public policy, and yet still think that this zone of clear governmental–business demarcation does not exhaust all meaningful business–governmental interactions. Corporate engagement in public policy and regulation includes funded support for social causes related to business and political lobbying for or against extra regulation, with boundaries on what business properly does in each case. Business often uses its standing and influence with governments to lobby on business regulation, and business is also increasingly effective in influencing international agreements and standard-setting in matters affecting free trade, investment and intellectual property.[15]

Accordingly, nobody should be too surprised that 'at least partially as a result of pressure from the business lobby', the home states of TNCs commonly exhibit 'a distinct preference for extraterritorial initiatives that "facilitate" (rather than compel) better CSR standards abroad'.[16] Business and political influences are so closely intertwined that regulation of political donations and expenditure by corporations is a proper matter for regulation in modern corporate legislation.[17] Businesses that leverage their corporate power through governmental lobbying to influence business law and policy cannot then turn round to argue that business involvement in public policy concerns necessarily falls into the error of corporate social engineering.

The public policy risks and pitfalls of the capture of government and its policy, legislative and other processes by big business is a strong theme in much corporate responsibility literature, from a variety of disciplinary angles. As seen in Chapter 3, some commentators see a wider societal problem in separating democracy from capitalism if corporations are too successful in manipulating or at least influencing the political domain, to secure political and legal outcomes that offer them competitive advantages over their market rivals.[18] Other voices reinforce the narrative that the widespread political, regulatory and business preference for maximizing voluntary CSR engagement and minimizing mandatory CSR obligations not only inhibits CSR from taking hold systematically in mainstream business regulation and practice, but also results in influential 'corporate elites' exercising undue control over public policy-making, with the result that 'governmental policies often play a crucial role in cases of corporate social *ir*responsibility'.[19]

For example, considered from the perspective of 'interrelated sources of power' on political, legal, economic and other fronts, with the state mediating around and between these 'modes of power' and their strategic use and capture by various societal elites, the various controls and pressures exerted upon political and legal outcomes by the business sector generally (and particular heavyweight industries and major companies within it) produce what some commentators view as corporate hegemony.[20] On this view of corporate hegemony and the influence of corporate elites upon the governmental domain, business has a range of options and advantages in securing business-favouring outcomes from the political and legal systems, allowing business considerable choice within the 'fragmented public policy-making network' in targeting the best levels of government, public officials, policy development timeframes, and other access points for wielding corporate influence over government.[21]

In addition, corporations inevitably interact with national and supranational governmental institutions in making laws and setting standards that affect business. Corporate influencing of society's rules for conducting business is an important aspect of the legal part of a competitive business strategy.[22] Wharton Business School's Professor G. Richard Shell argues, for example, that the legal strategy for business in proposing or responding to competitive and regulatory risks includes elements relating to the legal merits of a business position, as well as its public legitimacy, strategic positioning, deployment of resources and opportunities for rule-making access and influence, thus positioning corporations to maximize their leverage in setting the rules of the game for business.[23]

In other words, business has a stake in putting its position and even becoming involved in the process of reviewing and reforming rules which govern business operations and the market, because non-involvement risks leaving those rules to be set or influenced by others, without the benefit of such input and the business experiences behind it.

As national and international norms governing corporations further develop, their impact upon business naturally results in corporations seeking both a voice and influence in the promulgation, implementation and enforcement of such norms. Community actors who call for extra business regulation to make corporations more socially and environmentally responsible must accept that business will want a seat at the rule-making table. In the words of leading international law academic and practitioner, Philippe Sands QC:[24]

> Deregulating international capital flows, promoting private investments overseas and increasing global trade have greatly extended the international role of the private and corporate sectors. Not surprisingly, these players are not content with a backseat role in the making and applying of international law. They want to influence the content of the rules and contribute to their enforcement. They do so by pressuring governments and, increasingly, participating directly in international treaty negotiations. The result is that governmental and commercial interests act together at the international level, so that international laws accommodate changing requirements and provide for an increased role for the private sectors in the design of those rules.

In the human rights domain in particular, contemporary interactions between business and human rights show that we have passed beyond the point of a clear divide between nation-state responsibility for human rights under international law and completely voluntary, regulation-free and sanction-less human rights obligations and benefits for business. This point is clear from these summary observations of the UNSRSG:[25]

> It seems clear that long-standing doctrinal arguments over whether such firms could be 'subjects' of international law are yielding to new realities on the ground. For example, firms have acquired significant rights under various types of bilateral investment treaties and host government agreements, they set international standards in several sectors, and certain corporate acts are directly prohibited in a number of civil liability conventions dealing with environmental pollution. Thus, at minimum *transnational corporations have become 'participants' in the international legal system,* . . . with the capacity to bear some rights and duties under international law.

As more businesses embrace a form of strategic CSR that seeks competitive advantage from better aligning corporate responsibility and sustainability with wider societal needs and impacts, the gap narrows between what is essential for a company as a business and what is necessary for society, even if that still leaves many social problems and areas of public policy untouched and unreachable by any particular company's self-chosen strategic CSR.[26] Moreover, the need to ground a corporation's engagement with public and private concerns in something connected with its business enterprise still leaves much work for the role of governments, multi-lateral bodies and other public governance institutions.

Finally, any 21st century reconfiguration of the relationship between business and government must also accommodate not only the evolution of a system of interdependent global governance involving relations between governments, business and communities, but also any moves towards a global form of government. 'The design and evolution of new structures of government beyond the boundaries of nation states, informed by an ethos of service and committed to the same tasks of protection, welfare, justice and truth as national states, is the greatest task of the new century, and essential to human survival', according to Geoff Mulgan, former adviser to British Prime Minister Tony Blair.[27] In a world order of increasingly interdependent governance, regulation and responsibility, 'it cannot credibly be denied that domestic governments and multinational corporations often exercise the kind of political power that calls for some greater degree of public accountability on an international level', according to leading contemporary advocates of deliberative democracy.[28]

None of this means that all demarcations between governmental and business roles fall away, or that undue business influence upon public policy-making and law-making is not a problem. None of it means that business corporations are expected to offer a panacea for all social ills or that they must take over responsibilities that properly lie with government or the community. Nor does it mean that they can be targeted for a disproportionate share of the governance and regulatory burden to be shared across government and society, or that they must be forced to do something that is inimical to their essential nature and business purpose. It simply means that these domains have common points of connection and interdependence, common points of interest and shared concern, and a common interest in the development of 'a new way to look at the relationship between business and society that does not treat corporate success and social welfare as a zero-sum game'.[29]

GOVERNMENTAL POLICY AND REGULATORY FRAMEWORKS FOR CORPORATE SOCIAL RESPONSIBILITY

Basic Connections Between Public Policy and Corporate Social Responsibility

CSR, a management tool for business, is also a powerful policy instrument of the European Union . . . More broadly, CSR is an instrument that can contribute to the objectives of EU policies, as well as to development and better global governance, by supplementing existing tools such as legislation and social dialogue.

– Francesco Perrini, Stefano Pogutz and Antonio Tencati, *Developing Corporate Social Responsibility: A European Perspective*[30]

One implication of corporate responsiveness to trans-modal governance, multi-order regulation and inter-related responsibility is that 21st century CSR is connected to societal and global concerns that extend beyond simply what companies self-adopt as CSR for business reasons and what governments develop as CSR-orientated public policy. Halina Ward identifies the links between public governance, public policy and CSR as follows:[31]

There are wider links between CSR and public governance, as distinct from public policy specifically directed at CSR. There is a strong business interest (if not a mainstream 'business case') in addressing issues of good governance overall. For responsible businesses, that interest extends well beyond the traditional 'enabling environment' for private sector activity and investment, to a recognition of the value of strong civil society, investment in the public goods necessary for human development, respect for human rights, and effective mechanisms for the collection and distribution of taxes, among other areas. These basic areas of public governance must all properly be considered integral parts of the 'enabling environment' for corporate social responsibility.

At the policy level, CSR has strong connections to a wide range of public policy goals. Corporate citizenship advocate and advisor, Dr Simon Zadek, urges governments to organize public policy favouring CSR around four core principles of 'corporate citizenship', 'competitive citizenship', 'civil accountability' and 'global accountability', for example.[32] 'To ensure that CSR both in the marketplace and in public policies contributes to sustainable development, it is essential to use benchmarks which properly reflect its components; that is, competitiveness, social cohesion and environmental protection', argue Perrini, Pogutz and Tencati.[33]

Considered from a European policy perspective, CSR contributes to public policy goals such as integrated and socially inclusive labour markets (e.g. recruitment from disadvantaged groups), competitive participation of an ageing workforce in a global knowledge economy (e.g. 'investment in skills development, life-long learning and employability'), public health improvements (e.g. responsible food and product labelling), innovative business solutions to social problems (e.g. stakeholder-receptive and innovation-conducive working environments), and resource and environmental sustainability (e.g. eco-innovation, voluntary environmental management and labelling, and reduced pollution). CSR also contributes to public policy goals such as encouragement of business entrepreneurship (e.g. developing favourable public images and reputations of entrepreneurs), enhancing human rights in developed and developing countries (e.g. business measures promoting human rights, environmental protection and labour standards), and advancing progress towards major global goals (e.g. poverty alleviation under the UN Millennium Development Goals).[34]

Public policy goals for CSR might draw upon frameworks that capture core business 'competencies' (and capabilities) of relevance for CSR, tangible and intangible business 'assets' that relate to CSR, and corporate 'spheres of influence' in governmental and non-governmental domains,[35] with correlative implications for how businesses set strategies, create business models, develop competitive advantages and otherwise respond to public policy and regulation concerning CSR. Considered from both societal and organizational perspectives, the best conditions for realization of such public policy goals occur when business regulation requires or at least encourages businesses to integrate CSR ends (e.g. corporate responsibility and sustainability outcomes) and CSR means (e.g. corporate responsibility and sustainability processes) in their internal governance and operations.[36]

This is a key part of CSR meta-regulation in the 21st century. Increasingly, this body of public policy on CSR is global in orientation and not exclusively governmental in origin, given the growing influence of the business sector and civil society upon the shape of public policy. Beyond the level on which particular public policy goals enshrine particular aspects of corporate responsibility and sustainability, there is also a broader level on which law and regulation generally, and corporate law and regulation in particular, serve the public policy ends of social efficiency, justice and well-being. At the same time, whole-of-government approaches to CSR policy and regulation remain an important anchoring point for that activity.

Whole-of-Government Approaches to Corporate Social Responsibility

The 'enabling environment' for CSR [is] a product of the drivers, the tools and the human capacities and institutions directed towards that goal [but] is far from optimal anywhere in the world . . . In short, neither the market nor the public sector is playing its role in such a way as to lead to optimal CSR outcomes.

– Halina Ward, former Director of the Business and Sustainable Development Programme, International Institute for Environment and Development[37]

An overarching CSR policy framework is a fundamental foundation for countries which take CSR seriously. 'A consistent "whole of government" approach to the development and implementation of policies and administrative arrangements that have implications for corporate conduct and practices is desirable', recommends Australia's official corporate and market advisory agency.[38] Similarly, in its 2006 official report on CSR to the Australian Parliament, the Parliamentary Joint Committee on Corporations and Financial Services (PJCCFS) 'recommends that the Australian Government's various corporate responsibility programs be coordinated through a whole-of-government approach'.[39]

Governments can commit themselves to CSR as a matter of policy, and develop an overall framework for promoting CSR outcomes across the public, private and not-for-profit sectors. Starting with a governmental CSR policy framework can stimulate CSR awareness, facilitation and coordination, and give CSR an appropriate policy priority in government, which has an important flow-through effect in galvanizing and orientating departments and agencies to support government, business and the community in this policy field. It offers important control over CSR policy direction from a whole-of-government standpoint, in setting the framework within which other reforms might happen. It is also capable of encompassing international CSR developments and standard-setting as they evolve.

A whole-of-government CSR framework can stimulate public sector commitment to making CSR work and create incentives for regulatory, business and stakeholder groups to work cooperatively in CSR standard-setting (e.g. CSR information-gathering, indicator-setting, risk-assessment, decision-making and reporting guidelines for directors). It can also allow the government to coordinate CSR expertise and guidance within government that is needed across various portfolios domestically and internationally, including material to inform national responses to ongoing CSR-related standard-setting initiatives internationally (e.g. the human rights responsibilities of TNCs). Such a policy framework might even contain desirable CSR performance benchmarks for the business community, although these are best developed in tandem with the business and civic sectors.[40] It can enable governments to set desirable CSR indicators for the national benefit, with a measured menu of both regulated and voluntary initiatives. In doing so, it combines 'top down' and 'bottom up' progress towards CSR solutions, through a blend of mandatory regulation, self-regulation and co-regulation. It also provides an opportunity for the development and testing of more comprehensive information on CSR performance and impact than is now available for evidence-based policy reform in this area.

Recent models appear in the governmental CSR policy frameworks developed in the EU and the UK. The UK Government, for example, has set priorities and associated actions for government involvement in CSR that start with '(t)aking a leading role internationally' (i.e. 'to work with all stakeholders to support the contribution business can make to achieving our sustainable development goals [and] to play an influential role in EU and international fora aimed at ensuring practical outcome based approaches to encourage wealth creation while tackling environmental challenges and inequalities and reducing poverty'), and '(r)aising awareness and creating an environment in which CSR can thrive' (i.e. by 'providing a policy and institutional environment that encourages and rewards socially and environmentally responsible behaviour [and] setting the agenda and communicating on responsible behaviour'). These UK CSR priorities and associated actions conclude with '(m)ainstreaming CSR into general business practice' (i.e. 'to support the full integration of CSR into the way we do business'), and '(r)eaching a wider audience and tackling key sectors' (i.e. 'to reach beyond those already engaged with CSR as well as targeting our approach to business sectors').[41] This multi-pronged menu of governmental initiatives includes legislation (e.g. changes to corporate law and reporting), taxation and other fiscal measures (e.g. UK Community Investment Tax Relief Scheme), funding and support for research and development (e.g. new sectoral reporting guidelines relating to impact upon poverty alleviation in developing economies), and cross-sectoral and cross-national collaboration and partnering (e.g. the UK Partners for Water Sanitation (PAWS) project involving the UK and African countries).[42]

CSR has a policy priority and overarching framework in the EU too. In its 2006 communication to the European Parliament on proposals for further embedding CSR practices within the EU, the European Commission emphasizes a menu of government-related CSR activities, comprising '(a)wareness-raising and best practice exchange', '(s)upport to multi-stakeholder initiatives', '(c)ooperation with Member States', '(c)onsumer information and transparency', '(r)esearch', '(e)ducation', 'SMEs' and their CSR practices, and '(t)he international dimension of CSR'.[43] The earlier European Green Paper on CSR identifies a 'holistic' approach to CSR which embraces '(s)ocial responsibility integrated management', '(s)ocial responsibility reporting and auditing', '(q)uality and work', '(s)ocial and eco-labels', and '(s)ocially responsible investment'.[44] In its 2007 resolution responding to the Commission, the European Parliament affirms 'that increasing social and environmental responsibility by business, linked to the principle of corporate accountability, represents an essential element of the European social model, Europe's strategy for sustainable development, and for the purposes of meeting the social challenges of economic globalisation'.[45] Other illustrative components of these whole-of-government CSR frameworks are the encouragement and development of certification and labelling schemes (e.g. the European Alliance for CSR, European Ecolabel and UK Green Claims Code and Green Claims Practical Guidance), official support for standard-setting initiatives (e.g. EITI), the adoption of corporate citizenship and sustainability policies and practices across the governmental sector, the stimulation of public CSR awareness-raising and expertise-sharing, and the facilitation of both governmental and business involvement in intergovernmental and other supranational standard-developing initiatives.[46]

In short, whole-of-government approaches to CSR offer multiple advantages. Whole-of-government frameworks for CSR can usefully identify and coordinate a wide range of different governmental activities concerning CSR within a broader policy, legal and regulatory structure. In particular, such frameworks signal the status of CSR as a policy priority for government. They also provide a coherent overarching focal point for synchronization of various governmental initiatives aimed at advancing CSR. At the same time, these frameworks must themselves be positioned within the broader governmental infrastructure for CSR, as illustrated by the nine-fold schema of governmental CSR functions outlined later in this chapter.

CSR-related Policy, Regulatory and Law Reform

My research and consultations indicate that most governments take a narrow approach to managing the business and human rights agenda. It is often segregated within its own conceptual and (typically weak) institutional box – kept apart from, or heavily discounted in, other policy domains that shape business practices, including commercial policy, investment policy, corporate law, and securities regulation. This is roughly equivalent to a company setting up a corporate social responsibility unit in splendid isolation from its core business operations. Inadequate domestic policy coherence is replicated internationally.

– UN Secretary General's Special Representative for Business and Human Rights, Professor John Ruggie[47]

Ultimately, any governmental move towards advancing CSR reform has to focus at some point upon the relation between CSR and the operative system of corporate law and regulation within any government's own jurisdiction. The orientation and scope of the terms of reference for governmental reviews and other institutional reform initiatives concerning CSR shape the avenues of inquiry and the possible outcomes of these important governmental CSR initiatives. Increasingly, any such governmental initiatives must be conducted with a view to wider international and comparative CSR developments too. This includes an appropriate policy, regulatory and legal analysis of the emerging body of comparative CSR-related corporate law and regulation across the European, Anglo-American and Anglo-Commonwealth domains outlined in the next chapter.

In particular, European and Anglo-Commonwealth corporate law reform has displayed much preoccupation at the end of the 20th century and the beginning of the 21st century with the extent to which it is possible and desirable to incorporate CSR elements within corporate law. The institutional dialogue on CSR in European Commission communications and corresponding European Parliament resolutions in the early 21st century shows signs of grappling with the same dilemma. In the UK, the terms of reference for the landmark review of corporate law straddling the 20th and 21st centuries clearly paved the way for the stakeholder-inclusive approach to 'enlightened shareholder value' ultimately embodied in the UK Companies Act in 2006. Importantly, those terms of reference included the following pivotal objective, which focuses upon relevant shareholder and non-shareholder interests as they relate to business activity:

> To consider how core company law can be modernised in order to provide a simple, efficient and cost-effective framework for carrying out business activity which:
>
> a.   permits the maximum amount of freedom and flexibility to those organising and directing the enterprise;
> b.   at the same time protects, through regulation where necessary, the interests of those involved with the enterprise, including shareholders, creditors and employees; and
> c.   is drafted in clear, concise and unambiguous language which can be readily understood by those involved in business enterprise.

The 21st century emphasis upon possible reform of directors' duties, corporate reporting and other stakeholder-sensitizing regulatory reforms in Anglo-Commonwealth corporate law and regulation is also exemplified in the terms of reference for the Australian inquiry into CSR by CAMAC. Referring to the primary corporate legislation in Australia (i.e. the Corporations Act), the Australian Government set the following terms of reference for CAMAC in 2005:[48]

> (1)   Should the Corporations Act be revised to clarify the extent to which directors may take into account the interests of specific classes of stakeholders or the broader community when making corporate decisions?
> (2)   Should the Corporations Act be revised to require directors to take into account the interests of specific classes of stakeholders or the broader community when making corporate decisions?
> (3)   Should Australian companies be encouraged to adopt socially and environmentally responsible business practices and if so, how?
> (4)   Should the Corporations Act require certain types of companies to report on the social and environmental impact of their activities?

Significantly, from a comparative and modelling perspective, the terms of reference for the parallel CSR inquiry by Australia's PJCCFS explicitly included reference to relevant lessons from comparable overseas jurisdictions:[49]

> On 23 June 2005, the Parliamentary Joint Committee on Corporations and Financial Services resolved to inquire into Corporate Responsibility and Triple-Bottom-Line reporting, for incorporated entities in Australia, with particular reference to:
>
> a)   The extent to which organisational decision-makers have an existing regard for the interests of stakeholders other than shareholders, and the broader community.
> b)   The extent to which organisational decision-makers should have regard for the interests of stakeholders other than shareholders, and the broader community.
> c)   The extent to which the current legal framework governing directors' duties encourages or discourages them from having regard for the interests stakeholders other than shareholders, and the broader community.
> d)   Whether revisions to the legal framework, particularly to the Corporations Act, are required to enable or encourage incorporated entities or directors to have regard for the interests of stakeholders other than shareholders, and the broader community. In con-

sidering this matter, the Committee will also have regard to obligations that exist in laws other than the Corporations Act.

e) Any alternative mechanisms, including voluntary measures that may enhance consideration of stakeholder interests by incorporated entities and/or their directors.

f) The appropriateness of reporting requirements associated with these issues.

g) Whether regulatory, legislative or other policy approaches in other countries could be adopted or adapted for Australia.

In inquiring into these matters, the Committee will consider both for profit and not-for-profit incorporated entities under the Corporations Act.

Given their specific attention to CSR aspects, these Australian terms of reference can serve as starting points of reference for similar inquiries in comparable jurisdictions. Each of them explicitly or implicitly envisages reference to comparative and international experiences and models. Each of them also extends beyond the common topics of directors' duties and corporate reporting to embrace business practices as well as policy, regulatory and legislative matters affecting CSR. In doing so, they broaden the focus of CSR-related policy, legal and regulatory reform beyond simply those important areas of corporate law, including exploration of governmental CSR functions. Finally, whatever criticisms might be made of their analysis and conclusions, the reports of both inquiries at least attempt to engage with developments in corporate responsibility and governance thinking, regulation and practice worldwide.

The broader legitimization of CSR as a mainstream part of corporate responsibility and governance is also evident in such reform initiatives. In its report, for example, the PJCCFS makes recommendations that establish whole-of-government CSR policy frameworks and regulatory infrastructure, create regulatory incentives and relief for socially responsible corporate changes of behaviour, and provide official recognition of the need for improvements in voluntary corporate responsibility and sustainability reporting. In addition, the PJCCFS report offers official support for the creation of new CSR-focused business partnerships and networks, supports research and development initiatives in areas of necessary CSR research, and calls for standards for greenhouse-energy performance (as part of coordinated national and global efforts to combat the effects of climate change).

Although CAMAC clearly comes down on the side of less governmental imposition of CSR and more business freedom in self-adopting CSR, CAMAC also settles upon a three-pronged 'framework within which companies can respond to issues of social responsibility', which importantly includes a governmental prong. This framework consists of: (a) sufficient flexibility for directors under existing corporate law to decide and act in socially responsible ways; (b) disclosure of relevant financial and non-financial information about corporate activity as part of effective corporate accountability and reporting arrangements; and (c) governmental encouragement of responsible business behaviour through a variety of 'light touch' rather than heavy-handed regulatory and supportive measures.[50] In the end, despite having negligible impact so far upon changes to the content of Australian corporate law, both of these official national inquiries on CSR serve to legitimize and mainstream CSR for Australian business of all kinds, including SMEs. Their articulation of multiple CSR roles for government dovetails with the nine-pronged framework outlined in this chapter.

MULTI-PRONGED GOVERNMENTAL ROLES IN ADVANCING CORPORATE SOCIAL RESPONSIBILITY

A Nine-fold Governmental Model

Is there a simple, coherent and reasonably comprehensive way of mapping the multiple avenues of governmental engagement with CSR, especially of a kind suitable for public understanding, scholarly research and multi-stakeholder (including governmental) use? The variety of governmental measures potentially in play makes this need abundantly clear. In a mapping of responsible business practices in its landmark 2006 CSR report, for example, CAMAC identifies a wide range of governmental measures promoting CSR, including:

(1)   legislative initiatives (e.g. CSR-enhancing changes to corporate duties and reporting);

(2)   governmental harmonization and rationalization of laws (e.g. agreed legislative frameworks across a national federation for industry reporting of greenhouse gas emissions and energy use);

(3)   domestic implementation of international CSR-related obligations (e.g. domestic legislation enshrining corporate obligations and liabilities under international law, and National Contact Points under the OECD Guidelines For Multinational Enterprises);

(4)   governmental agency development and promotion of responsible business practices (e.g. government-facilitated methodologies for corporations implementing the GRI reporting framework);

(5)   governmental modelling of CSR through governmental agency implementation of sustainability policies and reporting;

(6)   CSR policy development from a whole-government perspective;

(7)   governmental CSR-related certification initiatives (e.g. government-approved measures for voluntary corporate social labelling of products that meet designated socio-economic and environmental standards);

(8)   prescriptive and facilitative regulation (e.g. prescribed codes of conduct for large-scale businesses and claw-back mechanisms to recover performance-based executive compensation where financial provision and disclosure for environmental and socio-economic liabilities is inadequate); and

(9)   a menu of regulatory, fiscal and market incentives and sanctions (e.g. taxation of CSR-unfriendly activity, favourable regulatory enforcement options for good corporate citizens, tighter CSR-related preconditions for public licences for business infrastructure and development, and linkage of government grants and financial assistance (e.g. subsidies, loan guarantees, and export finance) to evidence of socially and environmentally responsible business behaviour).

Scholarly analysis provided for the World Bank offers a simple and yet all-encompassing framework of public sector roles for enhancing CSR, grounded in basic governmental functions of 'enabling', 'facilitating', 'partnering' and 'mandating' CSR.[51] Using and adapting this framework, the US Government Accountability Office allocates a range of

US Government activities on CSR to these outlined categories, such as making official speeches supporting CSR (i.e. 'endorsing'), providing information and grants on CSR (i.e. 'facilitating'), encouraging and forming public–private alliances (i.e. 'partnering') and officially regulating CSR (i.e. 'mandating').[52] Governmental CSR roles might also be mapped differently, according to the appropriate vertical level of government (i.e. from the global to the local level), horizontal level of government (from one governmental arm or institution to another), jurisdictional base of TNCs, or target CSR audience, for example.[53]

The limits of this mapping of generic governmental CSR roles are acknowledged by its creators, who realize that its analytical usefulness in identifying different roles still leaves many important questions about reasons for choosing between different roles, on one hand, and different policy and regulatory instruments attached to each role, on the other.[54] Notwithstanding criticisms of such analytical categorizations of governmental CSR activities for displaying an overly hierarchical bias towards governmental CSR interactions, nevertheless there is considerable value in a mapping of such activities that identifies the multiple ways in which government can now become involved in CSR, matched to appropriate accounts of governance and not simply treated as abstract categories.[55] The revision of these generic governmental CSR roles within a five-pronged framework of 'regulating', 'facilitating', 'partnering', 'endorsing' and 'demonstrating' CSR simply reinforces the worth of exploring different analytical ways of characterizing distinct and related CSR roles for government.[56]

Some of these governmental roles seem easier for governments to embrace than others. Even allowing for 'the thorny questions of NGO legitimacy and accountability' in public policy, the distance that many governments are yet to travel on CSR is illustrated by the unequal attention they give to business–society partnerships over public investment in consumer and civil society support for minimizing corporate harm, deploying drivers of corporate reputational risk, and providing remedial and accountability mechanisms for corporate irresponsibility.[57] Some of these categories of governmental CSR roles also break down into various sub-categories. For example, in canvassing ways in which government might facilitate and encourage socially responsible business behaviour, CAMAC suggested a range of sub-categories in its 2006 CSR report, including 'policy coherence and integration' from a whole-of-government perspective, governmental 'leadership by example' in CSR standard-setting, CSR 'promotion' through information dissemination and commissioned research, and 'encouraging participation' through corporate consultations on intergovernmental developments and support for corporate participation in non-governmental initiatives.[58]

More widely, there are other discrete ways in which governments foster CSR which build upon and extend this basic four-fold scheme of 'endorsing', 'facilitating', 'partnering' and 'mandating' CSR activity, and its extension to embrace 'demonstrating' (or modelling) CSR too. Mechanisms for regulating CSR extend beyond simply mandating and then enforcing CSR obligations. Important functional differences emerge even between 'mandating' and 'enforcing' CSR. In other words, the variety of ways in which government is involved in regulating CSR requires discrete delineation, beyond these generic descriptions.

Governments also have important roles in legitimizing, standardizing, and modelling CSR, for example, in ways that relate to the initial four-fold categorization, but which are worthy of separate identification and treatment in their own right, as recognized in the subsequent inclusion of governments' role in 'demonstrating' CSR. Governments have an important societal role in legitimizing CSR, for example, to establish conditions under which CSR might then be endorsed, facilitated or otherwise fostered in discrete ways, many of which might otherwise founder in a surrounding environment that is hostile to CSR as anything other than a marginalized or voluntary component of core business responsibility. Moreover, whatever governments might do in endorsing, facilitating, mandating and partnering CSR activity, they also have a distinct role in modelling socially responsible behaviour themselves through various institutions and arms of government, as an example to business and others in the community. In addition, even if elements such as standard-setting also relate to activities of facilitating and mandating CSR, standardization of CSR (including both standard-setting and mainstreaming qualities) is also an important and distinct governmental CSR role. So too is leveraging government's unique position to CSR's benefit.

Building upon this initial categorization, these commonalities and differences can serve as starting points for mapping the ways and means by which government fosters CSR, whatever conceptual categorization is ultimately adopted. For present purposes, the balance between analytical simplicity, discrete differentiation and practical guidance can be achieved using a nine-fold categorization, comprising key governmental functions and means of 'legitimizing', 'standardizing', 'endorsing', 'facilitating', 'partnering', 'mandating', 'enforcing', 'leveraging' and 'modelling' CSR.[59] For summary reference, Table 4.1 distils this nine-fold scheme, and its underlying policy positions and correlative governmental CSR activities, as reflected in the CSR literature.[60]

Of course, many policy, regulatory and legal initiatives might embrace more than one of these governmental CSR functions at the same time. Many of them relate to one another. However, this simply reinforces their distinct importance for analytical purposes, in identifying and understanding them from a range of angles. For example, in its policy platform for the 2007 Australian federal election, the incoming Labor Government included policy reform initiatives that cut across the roles of legitimizing, endorsing, facilitating and partnering CSR initiatives:[61]

> Recognising that business also needs support and resources to make their operations more sustainable, Labor will:
>
> - ensure business has access to the tools and best practice information to assist them manage social and environmental risks, and the recognition of opportunities as part of normal business operations;
> - partner with business to establish, as required, eminent roundtable forums to address sustainability issues of concern to business and society; and
> - consider other incentives for encouraging business to behave more responsibly.

Legitimizing

Governments and their various emanations have an important role in legitimizing public CSR debate, business acceptance of CSR, and mainstream recognition of CSR across the public, private and community sectors. Already this century, Australia's landmark official national inquiries into potential CSR law and regulatory reform, for example, play their part in bringing CSR into the mainstream, notwithstanding their ultimate

Table 4.1 Mapping CSR and the public sector

CSR Public Policy Rationales	CSR Models	CSR Thematic Focus	CSR Functions & Means	CSR Roles	Indicative CSR Activities
National competitive advantage of CSR adoption[1]	'Partnership model'[1&2]	Standard-setting & compliance[9]	Legitimizing	CSR systems & structures	'Defining the boundaries of the CSR agenda in the local/national context'[9]; 'Ensuring that business is accountable to civil society'[9]; 'Creating government departments and committees to discuss CSR'[9]; 'Frameworks for voluntary agreements'[9]; 'Reforming political financing'[9]; 'Legislation as policy setting for voluntary action'[9]; 'Engaging business in public policy processes'[9]; 'Forums for debating public policy proposals'[9]; 'Including business representatives in policy arenas'[9]; 'Endorsing specific standards, systems and approaches'[9]; 'Empowering regulatory agencies to act in stakeholders' interests'[13]; Creating CSR-orientated governmental portfolios, committees, and reference groups[6]; Transforming corporate regulatory ideology'[3]; 'Setting minimum standards for business'[9]; 'Formal and informal judging of what constitutes good practice'[9]; 'Collating and disseminating information on good practice, and encouraging replication'[9]; 'Highlighting individual companies' good practice'[9]; 'Endorsing guidelines'[9]; 'Creating and allocating official standard-setting functions and bodies'; 'Ensure innovative and adaptable core standards'[9]; 'Participating in codes of conduct (local and international)'[9] (e.g. 'Brokering voluntary agreements and codes'[9] and 'Multi-stakeholder code development'[9]; 'Promoting best practice in business'[9] (e.g. 'Issuing codes, publicizing initiatives that promote responsible practice'[9]; 'Promoting international guidelines for business'[9] (e.g. 'Promoting international standards as basis for business reporting'[9]; 'Endorsing metrics and indicators'[9]; 'Developing sectoral guidelines'[9]; 'Supporting supply chain initiatives and voluntary certification'[9]; 'Engaging in standards-setting processes'[9]; Fostering public labelling, certification, and verification standards
'New Governance' shared between states, markets, & civil society[1&10&14]	'Business in the community model'[12]	'Public policy role of business'[9]			
	'Sustainability and citizenship model'[12]	'Public policy case for corporate citizenship'[1]			
CSR-related institutional uncertainty governance[10]	Corporate constitutionalist model[3]	'Responsible investment'[9]			
Electoral popularity of CSR adoption[1]	'Market-making' model[1]	'Philanthropy and community development'[9]	Standardizing	CSR standards & practices	
	Social contract/enterprise model	'Pro-CSR production and consumption'[9]			
CSR's 'social policy complementarity'[1]	Stakeholder pluralism model	'Pro-CSR reporting and transparency'[9]			
Business engagement in deliberative democracy[11]	Co-determination model				
	'Challenge' model[1]	'Pro-CSR certification, "beyond compliance" standards, and management systems'[9]			
	'Statutory' model[1]				
Governance/policy advantages of public-private partnerships	CSR-sensitive shareholder primacy model (including the				

Table 4.1 (continued)

CSR Public Policy Rationales	CSR Models	CSR Thematic Focus	CSR Functions & Means	CSR Roles	Indicative CSR Activities
(PPPs) and social alliances[12&13]	'enlightened shareholder value' model	'Multilateral processes, guidelines and conventions'[9]	'Endorsing'/ 'Enabling'[1&9]	CSR engagement & education	'Informing and educating businesses, consumers, employees, investors, and regulators'[9]; 'Informing the international CSR debate about the local and national CSR context'[9]; 'Explaining CSR to companies and other stakeholders'[9]; 'Ensuring access to information'[7&9]; 'Facilitating understanding on minimum good practice abroad'[7&9]; 'Supporting civil society engagement'[7&9]; 'Dialogue', 'Education', 'awareness raising', and 'best practice' exchange[7&9]; Developing networks for disseminating CSR knowledge, skills, and experience to governments, MNCs, and NGOs[3]
Systemic 'enabling environment' for CSR[15]	'Agora model'[12]	'Stakeholder engagement and representation'[9]			
Complementary societal and business cases for CSR	Team production model[7]				
	State-based direction model	'Corporate governance' and regulation systems[9]		CSR promotion & advocacy	'Promoting innovation'[9]; 'Promoting concept of corporate citizenship'[9]; 'Promoting good practice: education, advocacy'[9]; 'Giving CSR a higher profile and coordinating across departments'[9]; 'Political support'[9] (e.g. 'Supporting civil society initiatives'[9]); 'Publicity and praise'[9] (e.g. 'Publicizing leading corporate givers'[9]); 'Defending key stakeholder interests in key forums'[9]
CSR's contribution to addressing global challenges (e.g. sustainable development, climate change, human rights, and poverty)	Meta-regulatory model		'Facilitating'[1&9]	CSR measurement & indicators	'Establishing targets'[9] (e.g. 'Setting targets and enforceable minimum standards'[9]; 'Promoting internalisation of costs'[9]; 'League tables to promote peer pressure'[9]; 'Global/national community prosperity and well-being indicators beyond GDP[3]; 'Socio-economic measures in "best practice" governance guides and codes'[3]
				CSR incentives & disincentives	'Creating fiscal incentives for pro-CSR activities'[9]; 'Legal and regulatory incentives'[9] (e.g. 'Tax incentives and penalties'[9] and 'Legal and fiscal penalties and rewards'[9]); 'Include CSR in procurement and export credit guarantees'[9] (e.g. 'Pro-CSR export initiatives'[9]; Including CSR criteria in public tender, audit, and procurement criteria[3&9], Socio economic tender, audit, and outsourcing performance conditions[3]; 'CSR-based government funding schemes'[3]; Alignment of regulation/funding with ethical investment and governance'[3&9]

	CSR enabling & capacity-building	'Capacity building and technical support'[9] (e.g. 'Technical assistance to companies and citizen groups'[9]); 'Initiating and supporting websites, networks, and multi-stakeholder partnerships to maximize positive impact of business'[9]; 'Contributions to compliance expertise'[9]; 'Working with multilateral agencies and civil society to build capacity'[9]; 'Business advisory services'[9]; 'Joint government-industry investment in capacity'[9]; '"Enabling" legislation'[9]; 'Research on CSR'[25]; 'Developing the technical knowledge base for pro-CSR business'[9]; 'Capacity building to help companies meet external CSR requirements'[9]
	CSR markets & constituencies	'Enabling and promoting pro-CSR consumer choice'[9]; 'Stimulating pro-CSR markets (for example through public procurement)'[9]; 'Creating framework conditions (for the market)'[9]; 'Developing markets that encourage corporate citizenship'[9] (e.g. 'product labeling, public procurement and contracting, fiscal policy (including pension fund rules)'[9]); 'Leverage as investor and purchaser'[9]; 'Stimulating markets'[9]
'Partnering'[1&9]	CSR cooperation & partnering	'Working in partnership: intergovernmentally and/or with business and civil society'[9]; 'Support to multi-stakeholder initiatives' & 'Facilitating stakeholder partnerships & voluntary initiatives'[5&9] (e.g. 'Promoting partnerships for setting standards'[9]; 'Stakeholder engagement'[9] and 'Facilitating dialogue and multi-stakeholder processes'[9]; 'Build internal capacity to participate in partnerships'[9]; 'Encouraging partnerships: in supply chains and between stakeholders'[9]; 'Cooperate with other governments' (e.g. 'Cooperation with Member States' of the EU)[5&9]; 'Public-private partnerships'[9]; 'Supporting business-to-business partnering/mentoring'[9]; 'Coordinating network for disseminating CSR knowledge and expertise across sectors'[3]
'Mandating'[1&9]	CSR policy & regulation	'Implementing international principles'[9]; 'Fiscal policy (especially taxation)'[9]; 'Negotiating and enforcing global principles and goals'[9]; 'Establish regulation'[9] (e.g. 'Command and control legislation driving pro-CSR innovation'[9] and 'Company law'[9] and 'Stock exchange

Table 4.1 (continued)

CSR Public Policy Rationales	CSR Models	CSR Thematic Focus	CSR Functions & Means	CSR Roles	Indicative CSR Activities
					regulations and codes'[9] and 'Facilitating legislation for SRI'[9]); Translation of 'soft law' standards into 'hard law'; 'Including CSR elements in other policy areas'[9], 'Guidelines for FDI'[9], 'Requirements for government loan guarantees'[9], 'Mandating corporate contributions'[9], 'Mandatory environmental management systems'[9], 'Implementing guidelines through legislation'[9], CSR conditions in international agreements[3], 'Mainstreaming CSR' in public policies and programs[8], 'Human rights conditions in international agreements'[33], 'Institutionalising community and stakeholder relationships and inputs in policy-making and law-making'[3]
			Enforcing	CSR disclosure & reporting	'Guidelines for reporting'[9], 'Mandatory reporting'[9] (e.g. 'Increase quantity and quality of company information'[9]); 'Encouraging business reporting'[9] and 'Encourage disclosure'[9] (e.g. 'Guidelines for voluntary reporting'[9]); 'Mandatory disclosure of payments to public bodies'[9], 'Labeling schemes'[9] (e.g. 'Voluntary CSR labels'); 'Commending reporters'[9]
				CSR regulators & inspectorates	'Encouraging and ensuring compliance'[9], 'Establishment of enforcers and inspectorates'[9]; 'Supporting citizen legal action'[9]; 'Naming and shaming poor performers'[9], 'Shared monitoring'[9]; 'Empowering regulatory agencies to act in stakeholders' interests'[3]
			Leveraging	CSR value-adding and outcome-maximizing	Using governmental contacts and relations with others to advantage business and civil society; Leveraging governmental status and credibility to enhance take-up of multi-stakeholder initiatives; Combining governmental, business, and community resources to greater overall CSR effect; Leveraging governmental purchasing and contracting requirements to foster CSR outcomes; Linking CSR public policy goals to legislative standards, judicial interpretation,

| Modelling/ 'Demon-strating'[15] | CSR leadership & modelling | and governmental administration concerning CSR; Leveraging CSR compliance into corporate continuous improvement, reflexive self-learning, and aspirational responsibility; 'Setting policy goals and overall strategy frameworks for private sector action'[9]; 'Defining socioeconomic priorities from which businesses can take a lead'[9]; 'Linking businesses' CSR activities to public sector expenditures'[9]; 'Setting frameworks for business participation in public policy'[9]; 'Use public funds to lever private resources'[9]; 'Promoting "joined-up" government on CSR by coordinating across departments'[9]; 'Combining resources'[9] 'Setting of vision and goals for the role of business in society'[9]; 'Leading by example, especially public procurement'[9]; 'Convenor bringing together stakeholders'[9]; 'Develop a coordinated CSR policy, provide leadership, support research'[9]; 'Clearly defining societal priorities'[9]; 'Guidelines for public investments'[9]; 'Pro-CSR management in public sector bodies'[9] |

Notes:

1 Zappala, 2003.
2 Albareda et al. 2006: 116-121 (with particular relevance to EU CSR public policy models).
3 Horrigan, 2002.
4 E.g. UK ministerial portfolio for CSR.
5 Commission of the European Communities, *Implementing the Partnership for Growth and Jobs: Making Europe a Pole of Excellence on Corporate Social Responsibility* (2006).
6 Bottomley, 2007.
7 Blair and Stout, 1999.
8 European Parliament resolution of 13 March 2007 on corporate social responsibility: a new partnership.
9 Fox et al, 2002.
10 Lepoutre et al, 2007.
11 Gutmann and Thompson, 2004.
12 Guarini and Nidasio, 2003.
13 Joseph, 2003.
14 Midttun, 2005.
15 Ward, 2008.

unwillingness to embrace significant CSR-related law reform. Despite refusing to recommend mandatory consideration of stakeholder interests in the law of directors' duties and mandatory corporate sustainability reporting, Australia's PJCCFS still concluded in its landmark public report on CSR in 2006 that '(c)orporate responsibility is emerging as an issue of critical importance in Australia's business community', adding that 'there is a need to seriously consider options to encourage greater uptake and disclosure of corporate responsibility activities'.[62] The UK's Company Law Review and the EU policy framework for CSR also elevate stakeholder-sensitivity in corporate affairs to new levels of public legitimacy.

Similarly, changes in business and regulatory cultures present challenges in legitimizing CSR that must be met before measures that facilitate or otherwise promote CSR are likely to take hold. In its policy platform for the 2007 Australian federal election, for example, the incoming Labor Government sought to legitimize corporate responsibility and what it means for changes to business approaches and practices in these terms:[63]

> Labor's emphasis on corporate responsibility is grounded in our commitment to sustainable economic growth. Labor believes sustainable, responsible businesses are integral to our future prosperity and international competitiveness . . . Many leading businesses have already embraced corporate responsibility. Labor seeks to build on this trend by encouraging greater take-up of corporate responsibility. To achieve this, Labor believes that a change in mainstream business culture will be required. Labor is committed to ensuring that business leaders understand community expectations about their role in society and will assist and encourage Australian business to build the capacity to act responsibly and sustainably.

Once in government, high-level public officials then endorsed the relationship between good corporate governance, good corporate disclosure and reporting, and good corporate responsibility and sustainability. In particular, ministerial endorsement was given for a corporate reform agenda, stimulated by 'a heightened awareness of environmental and corporate social responsibility issues'.[64] In light of the acknowledged connection between 'long-term shareholder value' and 'a broad range of social and environmental factors in [corporate] decision-making', and the correlative governmental need 'to encourage and facilitate this kind of corporate decision-making', executive government support was given for 'examining ways to strengthen disclosure regarding corporate sustainability reporting, without imposing regulatory burdens on business'.[65]

Whether as part of an overarching CSR policy framework or not, official support and even partial public funding for multi-stakeholder CSR alliances can also be an important plank in legitimizing and embedding CSR in community consciousness. For example, the UK's successful Business in the Community network, with strong business and industry leadership and involvement in developing socially responsible business practices, has been recommended as a model for adoption in Australia, with public funding for its establishment.[66] Australian governmental funding to investigate and promote CSR practices amongst SMEs is another example. Legitimization also occurs in a more particularized form when official backing of a country's businesses smooths their way in gaining access to overseas markets and is predicated upon what is characterized in one European government's landmark CSR report as 'the assumption that the companies will conduct themselves decently and comply with international guidelines for social responsibility'.[67]

Standardizing

One of CSR's greatest needs this century lies in establishing CSR standards of sufficient sophistication and acceptance to embed CSR in mainstream regulation and corporate practice. Government has both an individual and a collective role in this endeavour that is different from the roles of other CSR actors. In the domain of legal standardization of CSR norms, for example, all three democratic arms of government have distinct and related roles to play in standardizing CSR, just as government as a whole has a unique role in the translation of the 'soft law' standards that emerge often from multi-stakeholder standard-setting initiatives into the kind of 'hard law' standard-setting that is the province of government alone.

As with other basic governmental CSR roles, the role that standardization plays has connections to those other roles, but also distinct value in its own right. It is one thing for a government to support moves towards necessary CSR standards, publicly endorse particular CSR standards, give official status to preferred CSR standards, or enforce legally enshrined standards. It is another thing altogether for government as a whole to play the kind of multi-faceted role in standardizing CSR at a systemic level that only government can perform. Government can become involved at various points, and must become involved at some key points, in the evolution of CSR standardization from standard-development, standard-endorsement, standard-adoption and standard-multiplication, at one extreme, to standard-rationalization, standard-certification, standard-monitoring and standard-enforcement, at the other.

At the national level, depending on public expectations and political circumstances, government might need to take the lead in establishing policy frameworks and principles for the development of specific CSR standards, setting CSR standards itself, allocating CSR standard-setting responsibility to appropriate bodies, or otherwise putting major CSR standard-setting initiatives together. At the international level, only governments can establish the necessary intergovernmental and international legal and regulatory architecture for CSR that provides the framework and baselines for CSR standard-setting across the globe. At both of these levels, standardization of CSR also relates to aspects of universalization, harmonization and synchronization of CSR standards within and between CSR policy and regulatory regimes.

Given the 'plethora of CSR-related initiatives', the work of standardizing worthwhile CSR norms is therefore a crucial one for governments, within the wider context of the collective power and responsibility in this area shared between the public, private and community sectors, nationally and globally.[68] This is a vital part of the politico-regulatory infrastructure of what the legal and regulatory CSR literature calls the 'enabling environment' for CSR.[69] It also takes place within the context of meta-regulatory standard-setting that involves a variety of governmental and non-governmental actors in steering the corporate sector towards publicly clarified and beneficial CSR outcomes.[70]

Endorsing

Cross-overs between legitimizing, standardizing, endorsing, and even modelling CSR occur in institutional dialogue about CSR between the different arms of democratic government. This can occur in forms that set or contribute towards building a governmental vision for CSR, as part of national responses as nation-state members of the international community to major international and intergovernmental CSR initiatives. In turn, these national responses can contribute to the development of an international consensus for particular CSR frameworks and standards, in the ways canvassed in Chapter 2. In the wake of the UNSRSG's mid-2008 report on business and human rights to the UN Human Rights Council, for example, the Australian Senate passed a motion proposed by a non-government party, the passage of which was then referred to by the UNSRSG in his 2009 report to the UN Human Rights Council as part of the evidence towards transnational 'uptake' of his suggested global policy framework for business and human rights.[71] The relevant Australian Senate motion was in the following terms:[72]

> (T)he Senate –
> (a)   welcomes the Government's engagement with the United Nations (UN) and commitment to human rights . . .
> (b)   notes that:
>
>> (i)   Australian companies are increasingly active in developing countries, some of which have weak regulatory environments,
>> (ii)   the Special Representative of the UN Secretary-General on the issue of human rights and transnational corporations and other business enterprises has reported to the Human Rights Council on the responsibilities of host and home states and the corporate responsibility to respect human rights,
>> (iii)   the Special Representative emphasises that it should be an 'urgent priority of governments' to 'foster a corporate culture respectful of human rights at home and abroad', and that states must provide access to remedies, and
>> (iv)   the Special Representative advises that companies have a responsibility to respect human rights, undertake human rights impact due diligence, and institute rights-compliant grievance mechanisms; and
>
> (c)   calls on the Government to:
>
>> (i)   encourage Australian companies to respect the rights of members of the communities in which they operate and to develop rights-compliant grievance mechanisms, whether acting in Australia or overseas,
>> (ii)   consider the development of measures to prevent the involvement or complicity of Australian companies in activities that may result in the abuse of human rights, including by fostering a corporate culture that is respectful of human rights in Australia and overseas, and
>> (iii)   support development at the international level of standards and mechanisms aimed at ensuring that transnational corporations and other business enterprises respect human rights.

Having laid the groundwork of legitimizing CSR through establishing the necessary politico-regulatory infrastructure and creating conditions for business receptiveness to CSR, governments can move from their own endorsement of CSR to enlisting other influential bodies in that endeavour. In its major CSR recommendations in 2006, for example, Australia's PJCCFS 'recommends that industry associations and peak bodies actively promote corporate responsibility to their members'.[73] Governmental actions in support of CSR also include endorsement of the need for enhanced CSR-related guidance and encouragement of leading CSR standards. Here, Australia's PJCCFS recommends that official corporate regulators 'issue detailed guidelines . . . to clarify for superannuation trustees their position in relation to allocating investments to sustainable responsible investment fund managers', and urges investors to 'consider becoming signatories to the United Nations Principles for Responsible Investment' (UNPRI).[74]

Governmental support also extends to awareness-raising, educational and training activities. For example, Australia's PJCCFS calls on the Australian Government to 'develop educational material to promote the UN Global Compact and to encourage Australian companies to become signatories where it is appropriate for them'.[75] Governmental endorsement of CSR's importance can also be demonstrated through governmental funding for projects to enhance business take-up of CSR, as in the Australian Government's multi-million dollar funding for a national corporate responsibility project in conjunction with the St James Ethics Centre from 2008 onwards. 'There may be some scope for government to assist companies, investors and other interested parties to understand better the range of issues relating to corporate responsibility, through collating and disseminating information and, if necessary, commissioning relevant research or other material', suggests Australia's governmental advisory body on corporate affairs.[76]

Governmental endorsement of CSR can facilitate business take-up of favoured standards. In 2006, for example, Australia's federal parliamentary inquiry into corporate responsibility broadly endorsed the UNPRI and the UN Global Compact, and offered qualified support too for the GRI framework.[77] Governmental endorsement of CSR also flows through to incorporation of CSR-related research in officially identified national and regional research priorities. Government-sanctioned research priorities and support for university (and other publicly funded) research can play a significant role in encouraging or alternatively marginalizing future research on CSR. In 2006, the European Commission recognized the need for more cross-disciplinary CSR research as one of its priority areas for future action, centred largely upon research on 'links at the macro- and meso-levels between CSR, competitiveness and sustainable development; the effectiveness of CSR in reaching social and environmental objectives; and issues such as innovation, corporate governance, industrial relations, and the supply chain', together with research on SMEs and CSR.[78] Similarly, the Norwegian Government's 2009 report on CSR endorses further university research and educational initiatives on CSR and 'urges the Research Council of Norway to continue and strengthen its programme for the funding of CSR-related research'.[79] By contrast, Australia's officially designated national research priorities are silent on the prominence of CSR as a research policy priority.

Facilitating

Beyond legitimizing and endorsing CSR, governments can facilitate CSR in other ways that extend beyond 'command and control'-style legislation prescribing minimum legal requirements for good corporate conduct. One of the two major Australian governmental inquiries into corporate social responsibility in 2006 accepted, for example, that 'government has an important role to play in encouraging and facilitating corporate responsibility', and suggested a number of moves towards greater governmental involvement in that direction.[80] Here, the range of regulatory levers available to government includes 'self-regulation, use of incentives, awards and accreditation systems, market-based initiatives, disclosure obligations, publication of league tables, allocation of private statutory rights, statutory compensation schemes, publicity and government-sponsored information and education campaigns'.[81]

As an example, the UK Conservative Party Working Group on Responsible Business (CPWGRB) highlights a number of ways in which government can stimulate private voluntary initiatives (PVIs) towards responsible business. These measures include: setting regulatory standards for PVIs, assisting the formation of new PVIs in transnational markets through intergovernmental relations, and creating incentives for PVIs by 'using state procurement contracts, providing favoured access on trade missions to PVI participants and by putting pressure on international financial institutions to add PVI-like requirements as a condition of finance provision'.[82] All of this fits with notions of the new regulatory state, in which governmental regulation is less oriented towards mandatory prescription and control, and more oriented towards steering, monitoring and facilitating self-regulation, within a wider system of meta-regulation.[83]

Government also has a significant and different role from business in facilitating CSR. This includes meeting the CSR-related international obligations of nations, assisting companies and their investors to gauge CSR effects upon corporate and industry competitiveness, promoting ecologically sustainable development and business strategies, and developing and facilitating CSR-based taxation incentives and other regulatory incentives.[84] It also includes facilitating CSR partnerships and networks, promoting CSR outcomes within government procurement and departmental operations, and setting an overall framework, agenda and set of key indicators for CSR outcomes for the greater well-being of the community.[85]

Some governmental mechanisms to enhance facilitation of CSR are structural in nature. Ministerial portfolios for CSR embedded within business-orientated departments of state, as in the UK, together with cross-party legislative reference groups and even legislative committees with a dedicated CSR focus as one of their responsibilities can all advance CSR policy initiatives and keep them integrated with ongoing policy and law reform concerning business regulation generally. Parliamentary CSR reference groups provide structural opportunities for CSR-related information-sharing, policy dialogue and engagement within government and between legislators and the outside world, as part of a 'new world order' of government-facilitated governance and regulatory networks.[86] Legislative committees that scrutinize draft legislation for its constitutionality, consistency with other laws, and impact upon human rights can also be encouraged to add promotion of socially responsible corporate behaviour to their checklist of scrutiny criteria. In addition, laws governing the interpretation of legislation can also have built into them sensitivity towards promoting public policy goals through socially responsible business behaviour (e.g. fair competition, equitable workplaces, sustainable development, greenhouse gas reduction, etc.). These mechanisms not only facilitate CSR. At a deeper level, they also serve to legitimize it within the public domain and to embed it within the infrastructure of government.

The use of regulatory and fiscal incentives/rewards and disincentives/sanctions mixes elements of endorsing, facilitating and mandating CSR, as another example of the overlap that commonly occurs between the various governmental roles in this nine-fold scheme. In her discussion of TNCs and CSR, for example, Dr Jennifer Zerk notes a range of common regulatory strategies of this kind:[87]

As a form of regulation, incentives are usually popular with companies, for obvious reasons. Regulatory incentives are commonly associated with the tax system (which can either reward a company directly, or remove a financial *dis*incentive associated with a socially beneficial course of action). Incentives can also take the form of preferred status in public sector procurement processes, or programmes that reward good behaviour with lower administration or licensing costs, or simply with praise and public recognition, such as award schemes. Market-based initiatives, such as tradable emissions permits, are another potentially useful way of encouraging companies to invest in less polluting technologies. A good social and environmental record can also be rewarded through compulsory public compensation or insurance schemes. Not only do these schemes provide a basis for compensation, they can also encourage greater investment in environmental and health and safety improvements by linking premiums to past performance.

Governments can use a variety of mechanisms that steer corporations towards CSR adoption through regulatory incentives and disincentives. In response to new evidence of climate change's potential environmental and economic consequences, for example, some European countries have mooted proposals to impose a special tax on imported goods the production of which generates unacceptable levels of carbon emissions, thereby linking regulatory responses on carbon emissions to business chain arrangements designed to reduce harmful greenhouse gases. The penetration of corporate responsibility and sustainability reporting into mainstream business practice can be stimulated by taxation write-offs for initial sustainability reporting costs for companies in moving to this new system of reporting.[88]

Wider regulatory relief and flexibility in approaches to regulatory enforcement can be used to encourage corporations to adopt voluntarily a range of CSR-related actions.[89] In the wake of the financial and credit crisis that struck the world in 2008, governmental proposals to connect the level of governmental regulation, executive compensation and responsible lending practices constitute strong public endorsement at the official level of CSR-related implications of the global crisis.[90] National and supranational governmental institutions and intergovernmental bodies also have an important facilitative role in mediating and brokering harmonization of standards for CSR, for accommodation in corporate governance and self-regulation within a system of meta-regulating law and other regulation.[91]

A meta-regulatory approach to governmental initiatives on corporate governance, responsibility and sustainability increasingly informs 21st century reform options in the political and regulatory domains. According to the CPWGRB, for example:

> Clearly there is a greater opportunity for regulators to modernise and use the corporate social responsibility and socially responsible investment agendas to encourage better corporate self-regulation. This would need to be done carefully, with the primary accountability for regulating corporate performance resting with the relevant government authority.
>
> However, most regulators have overlooked the opportunity to use the influence of other market participants.[92]

In particular, the CPWGRB emphasizes the potential use of business performance indices, which enable a series of official regulators, investor bodies, stakeholder groups and business competitors to contribute to regulating responsible business performance. Citing pilot work in the UK on the Corporate Health and Safety Performance Index (CHaSPI), the CPWGRB identifies ways in which government can improve business uptake of such initiatives, including 'lighter-touch' regulatory inspection regimes and more lenient reporting requirements for companies with good health and safety performance according to the Index.[93] The CPWGRB also highlights the potential application of performance indices to other areas of reportable corporate responsibility performance, with environmental regulators developing environmental governance performance indices, and financial regulators developing customer fairness performance indices, for example. The cited benefits of performance indices for business include reduction of data-collection and questionnaire fatigue, generation of business benchmarking data, and production of material for corporate communication, reporting and target-setting.[94]

Partnering

Governmental involvement in CSR partnering similarly occurs on a number of levels and takes a number of forms. The spectrum extends from conventional public–private partnerships for commercial gain to multi-stakeholder and cross-sectoral networks and standard-setting initiatives worldwide.[95] Accordingly, in this context, governmental-business-community partnerships on CSR concerns might embrace everything from the diffuse sense of governments setting regulatory and policy directions that require business and community follow-up for their success to the more focused sense of specific governmental and business involvement in multi-stakeholder partnerships. 'Governments must create the right frameworks and incentives, but business leadership is needed in adopting efficiency measures, mobilising capital, creating new markets, developing new technologies, driving innovation, deepening our skills base and developing partnerships across the whole community', according to Australian Prime Minister Kevin Rudd, speaking in the context of climate change as 'the great economic, environmental and moral challenge of our time'.[96]

Australia's PJCCFS recommends appropriate governmental action to 'facilitate and coordinate the participation of Australian corporations in international corporate responsibility initiatives'.[97] In promoting the UK idea of new 'responsibility deals' to promote responsible business, with government as the catalyst for a focused partnership addressing specific societal problems of shared concern for governmental agencies, business enterprises and community groups, the CPWGRB envisages that the outcomes of these 'deals' would be meaningfully owned by the members of these partnerships, without always needing legislative back-up for their enforcement, thus opening the way to different regulatory dynamics operating upon these partnerships.[98] On another level of government-based social and global partnerships, Professor Anne-Marie Slaughter's innovative concept of the 'disaggregated' state and the role of governmental networks in global governance positions them as 'the spine' of a broader series of alliances and networks embracing a variety of governmental and non-governmental actors.[99] The rise of social enterprises which address social problems in conjunction with governmental and business partners is another manifestation of CSR partnering, and one which results in new forms of social investment and innovation, as part of what a former politician and university centre director foresees as necessary 'sectoral cultural change so that governments and corporations move from seeing themselves as "top-down providers" to "social investment partners"', with the result of 'the third sector . . . having a meaningful and equal voice in national conversations, alongside the public and the private sectors'.[100]

Mandating

As these other elements of governmental CSR engagement show, mandating CSR responsibilities through law-making and other official regulatory means forms only one part of CSR regulation overall. Still, mandating CSR remains a pivotal CSR regulatory tool, and hence is worthy of analysis in its own right. Given that mandatory regulation is mostly passed into law by elected legislators and administered by public officials appointed by governments, who represent and respond to electoral reactions and expectations surrounding the excesses of corporate behaviour, this means of controlling corporate internalization of costs and harms also operates as an important public means of democratization of corporate regulation.[101] Actively implementing CSR in the legislative domain importantly includes, but also extends beyond, the design and content of corporate law, legislative architecture for ancillary state-based regulation of corporate responsibility and governance (e.g. legislative sanctioning of non-legislative corporate standard-setting by official regulators), and legislative protection of third party and community interests implicated in corporate activity (e.g. non-discrimination in workplaces, environmentally sensitive business development, and consumer protection).

Many suggestions for government-mandated CSR-enhancing mechanisms stem from the field of stakeholder pluralism and its reaction to perceived weaknesses in the structure of shareholder primacy embodied in orthodox corporate regulation and practice.[102] Options here include mandatory reporting of the social and environmental impact of business, mandated board representation for particular groups of stakeholders (e.g. employees), mandatory appointment of specific 'public directors' to represent the public interest in boardroom deliberations, and mandatory stakeholder consultation generally or as a condition for business project approval affecting local communities.[103] Apart from their dilution of shareholder-centred control, other policy objections to such mechanisms are based largely upon their perceived interference with market forces, business entrepreneurialism and socio-economic efficiency.[104]

CSR elements can also be embedded legislatively within components of other systems of regulation too, in ways that reinforce CSR across the policy and legislative domains of government. Consider, for example, the interlocking ways in which governmental policy and legislative mechanisms in support of CSR can make socially responsible business behaviour a precondition to doing business with government. Governmental procurement, purchasing and outsourcing policies applying to businesses that hope to secure government work can set conditions of pre-qualification for eligibility or even preferred status in relation to securing such work, based upon reported and verified compliance with corporate responsibility and sustainability measures. Legislation can also build verifiable corporate responsibility and sustainability performance into the regulatory requirements for granting business licences and approvals, in much the same way as compliance with regulatory codes of conduct and satisfactory social audits, environmental impact statements (EISs), and human rights impact assessments (HRIAs) can become preconditions for licences and other governmental approvals. As companies start to align their own businesses with these public regulatory measures, organizational and state responsibility-inducing processes and outcomes become further integrated.[105]

Governments can also legislatively prescribe disclosure and transparency requirements designed to promote socially responsible corporate behaviour and curb socially irresponsible corporate behaviour. Such measures include mandatory certification and labelling requirements for products and services, 'naming and shaming' publication and legislative tabling of lists of companies with poor records of social and environmental responsibility, 'compulsory publication of pollution statistics', and mandatory greenhouse gas and carbon emission reduction targets and performance.[106] Mandatory disclosure, reporting and transparency initiatives can serve a number of public policy goals all at once. They do not necessarily have to provide a detailed set of standards and enforcement machinery, as the introduction of an obligation to disclose or report something can itself generate the need for companies to put their systems and processes in order to meet this need. This has the benefit of integrating these requirements into standard corporate data-capturing, internal reporting, and organizational decision-making mechanisms, as an integral step leading to publication of required performance information and analysis.

The taxation system offers multiple opportunities for mandating incentives for CSR, as well as disincentives for what might be characterized, at best, as corporate non-alignment with CSR-orientated public policy goals and, at worst, corporate irresponsibility towards society and the environment. Corporate taxation incentives and disincentives can be used to promote corporate research and development (R & D) on CSR, link taxation deductibility for workers' compensation employment premiums to industry averages (thus penalizing companies with poor workplace records and hence higher premiums, and rewarding companies with good workplace safety records and hence tax rebates), and provide for differential corporate taxation rates based upon demonstrated performance in environmental sustainability, greenhouse gas reduction, contribution to workplace education and training, and perhaps even other forms of corporate community investment (CCI).[107]

Here, taxation issues intermingle with socio-economic externalities, full social costing of corporate activity, and the implications of transparency as a primary regulatory value. 'To the extent that a company's operations are not sustainable its reported profits include unrequited externalities', argues John Legge, with the consequence that '(c)ompanies that profit from the work of skilled and professional staff that do not contribute to their training are profiting from externalities as effectively and immorally as firms that profit from polluting the environment', in ways that lend themselves from a public policy perspective to differential taxation treatment.[108] Where society's official regulators find that public companies and companies subjected to private equity buyouts are favouring short-term or even medium-term investment horizons over more sustainable investments in society's long-term interest, taxation and regulatory regimes can introduce differential treatment for companies on this basis, thereby affecting the financial viability of unsustainable corporate self-interest.[109] Whatever their policy merits, such initiatives again reinforce the meta-regulating connection between CSR-related processes and CSR-related outcomes.[110]

The progressive CSR-sensitization of corporate governance, management and reporting systems in practice reflects, at least in part, what governments mandate for CSR. More broadly, this feeds into a wider meta-regulatory system too. As Dr Zerk explains, for example, in relation to TNCs and CSR:[111]

> Alternatively, states and their regulatory authorities can require the publication of certain health and safety, environmental or social information. While this kind of regulation does not

lay down substantive standards regarding the operations of a company, the obligation to disclose certain information (or the threat of inclusion in a public list of poor performers) can be a powerful incentive for a company to improve its social and environmental performance. This may only be a side-effect of legislation designed primarily to ensure that the public have the information necessary to take steps to protect themselves from risks or that investors are able to make informed decisions about a company's future prospects. However, there are cases where disclosure regulation has been used expressly to put pressure on companies to be more 'socially responsible'.

Corporate disclosure of socially and environmentally responsible corporate behaviour of designated kinds can occur in a variety of mandatory, voluntary or hybrid forms. Zerk cites the 'comply or explain' approach under the Johannesburg Stock Exchange Listing Rules, under which companies must annually report on the extent of their compliance with designated corporate governance standards on an 'if not, why not' basis, as an example of corporate disclosure regulation that exerts pressure upon companies to be more socially responsible. To the extent that they encompass CSR, the prevalence of 'comply or explain' approaches to corporate disclosure and reporting in the EU, UK and Australia as well as South Africa highlights the growth and significance of this dimension of CSR-related activity within the arena of corporate governance, as part of a broader transnational body of CSR-related law and regulation.[112]

Courts engage with mandating CSR too, in multiple ways. In the common law world, for example, the judiciary's institutional roles in developing and applying judge-made rules and presumptions of statutory interpretation, interpreting and applying constitutions and legislation, creating judge-made law, and contributing to the development and legitimization of a cross-jurisdictional body of comparative law are all potentially triggered by the judiciary's engagement with CSR in adjudication. Even where the content of directors' duties is legislatively fixed and clear, the application of that content and the promulgation of standards for meeting it both engage judges in at least some assessment of community expectations of business.[113] More widely, judges across countries arguably exercise forms of international jurisdiction even in national adjudication, not least when ruling on instruments or questions that raise 'relevant universal principles of fundamental human rights observed by civilized countries', which can relate to judicial assessment of corporate liability and complicity in actionable human rights breaches.[114]

Enforcing

Governments and regulatory authorities can establish statutory frameworks that embody a variety of regulatory incentives and disincentives (i.e. regulatory 'carrots' and 'sticks') to develop and reinforce effective corporate self-regulation of CSR processes and outcomes.[115] Enforcement approaches and options must be assessed within that wider framework of a balance of CSR measures. One standard legal meta-regulatory technique, as highlighted in Dr Parker's account of CSR meta-regulation,[116] involves official regulators using 'liability incentives' for good corporate self-regulation, choosing between enforcement options and bringing enforcement proceedings to an end in ways that are sensitive to institutionalization of self-regulating corporate consciences based upon responsibility values and correlative processes. Considered from the standpoint of corporate regulatory investigation and enforcement, relevant legal meta-regulatory measures on Dr Parker's account also include 'sentencing incentives' (e.g. reduced penalties for companies with self-regulation systems that meet designated guidelines for good self-regulation), 'reactive liability' (e.g. reduced liability for timely self-correction of breaches), 'corporate probation' (e.g. enforcement outcomes requiring companies to improve their self-regulatory systems and practices in accordance with the designated self-regulation guidelines) and 'regulatory incentives' (e.g. lighter regulatory requirements, regulatory audit exemptions, regulatory certification for good corporate conduct, and easier licensing conditions for good self-regulating companies).[117]

Other connections between official regulatory enforcement and corporate self-regulation are equally important. Enforcement options within multi-stakeholder CSR initiatives involving governments have a different character from purely state-based enforcement regimes, as well as an important leveraging effect. Corporate self-regulation can be enhanced by promoting organizational inculcation of a corporate culture of meaningful regulatory compliance, making corporate executives responsible for oversight of compliance systems, and tying all of this to conditions for organizational and personal liability as well as sentencing outcomes for corporate officials. The US Sentencing Guidelines for Organizational Defendants, for example, require that US and foreign companies subject to US law develop 'an organizational culture that encourages ethical conduct and a commitment to compliance with the law', through a compliance and ethics programme as part of 'due diligence to prevent and detect criminal conduct'. Similarly, federal principles of corporate criminal responsibility in Australia explicitly recognize that a bad 'corporate culture' can result in corporate non-compliance, resulting in official regulatory investigation and enforcement.

Enforcement regimes for CSR can include both mandatory and other standards. The principle-based 'comply or explain' regime for corporate governance regulation in the EU, UK, and Australia, for example, is adaptable for CSR purposes too. Indeed, the combination of prescribing CSR reporting, certification, and other requirements with sufficient flexibility to allow corporate choice of reporting frameworks and justified corporate deviance from prescribed requirements is important in the interim period before a consensus coalesces around reliable frameworks and standards, as with the GRI. On another level, even supposedly voluntary multi-stakeholder alliances with governmental partners can develop in-built enforcement mechanisms, such as at least identifying and possibly sanctioning or expelling members who demonstrably breach publicized conditions of membership. So too can governmental regulatory regimes combine enforcement with other regulatory strategies devoted to CSR, as when legislative bills of rights that ostensibly apply only to the public sector have statutory opt-in mechanisms for businesses too.[118]

Leveraging

The central idea of leveraging CSR is that the overall CSR effort through governmental involvement is enhanced in mass, scale and effect beyond any particular initiative alone. In other words, the CSR whole is greater than the sum of its parts. Moreover, government is in a unique position to achieve this leveraging effect for its own CSR efforts, alone or in combination with those of non-state actors, as well as for the cause of CSR as a whole.

In its simplest form, for example, this kind of leverage appears in government–business partnerships on CSR that deploy resources together to greater combined effect.[119] In such instances, more can be achieved by government and business together than either can achieve alone. In public procurement and outsourcing, government can also leverage its position as a major supplier of contracts, buyer of services and gatekeeper for resources in CSR-supportive ways. Common examples include contractual incorporation of public interest elements, such as including community service obligations in governmental contracts awarded to the private sector, and enshrining state rights to regulate (on public health, safety, environmental and human rights grounds) in investment agreements between states and corporate investors.[120]

In this way, government can leverage its considerable power and resources to influence responsible business activity by incorporating CSR elements into the requirements for businesses that seek to provide services to government, receive government benefits and obtain government licences and approvals. In other words, something that might be characterized in terms of a facilitating or even mandating role also has an important leveraging role too. In accordance with a public policy CSR principle of 'civil accountability', government partnering with the business community can incorporate a significant element of CSR leverage, as 'governments may well continue to offer public contracts across the entire spectrum of the business community, but should seek to restrict "partnerships" to those relationships formed with businesses that demonstrate common cause in addressing public policy objectives', for example.[121]

At a broad governmental level, the alignment of a whole-of-government CSR policy with effective legislative, judicial and regulatory back-up reinforces the overall CSR effect, not least in presenting a unified front to business, community and global actors about the CSR priorities of any single government. In relation to climate change, for example, governments can leverage to greater effect how they approach the collective global problem of climate change by aligning that approach with a correlative whole-of-government CSR approach and associated synchronized elements for climate change policy and regulation. These elements include, for example, official regulatory oversight of enhanced corporate responsibility and sustainability reporting, promotion of ESG considerations for investment decisions and products, and differential taxation and enforcement regimes, according to participation in emission trading regimes and greenhouse gas reduction by business.

Conversely, the absence of a positive leveraging effect is apparent in legal and regulatory mechanisms that are justly criticized for fostering form over substance, thus leading to unproductive and legalistic tick-a-box approaches to legal CSR compliance, at least without meaningful legal and regulatory alignment of corporate orientations and CSR values, established through public CSR priority-setting and policy-making. This is one of the chief criticisms, for example of corporate law reforms that inadequately attend to the combined thread underlying reflexive corporate learning and governance, meaningful corporate decision-making and reporting, legal obligations of companies and their boards, and 'an appropriate "enabling environment" for responsible business practices'.[122] Simply making companies report on their social and environmental activity in ways and for purposes that are completely at large, for example, risks paying lip service to CSR.

At a legal level, the establishment of a legal framework for CSR that results in more CSR outcomes than simply what is achievable through legal compliance and enforcement alone represents another form of leverage, and one that is unique to government.

In global public policy terms, the use of state-based and international legal and regulatory mechanisms to orientate business activity around public policy goals of sustainable development, poverty alleviation, socio-economic interdependence and even climate risk management represents yet another distinct and important opportunity for leverage.[123] So too does the unique capacity of governments to create intergovernmental and international legal and regulatory architecture for CSR.

Modelling

Governmental mechanisms in support of CSR from a whole-of-government perspective can encourage organs of government to lead the way as model corporate citizens in their own right, in doing their bit for sustainable development, climate change and ethical organizational behaviour, for example. Indeed, as public sector entities of many kinds must walk the fine line between meeting public interests and being business-like and commercially focused too, the corporate sector can sometimes learn things from the public sector in addressing both public and private values.

Governments embracing whole-of-government CSR policy frameworks can insist that governmental departments, official regulatory bodies, statutory authorities, governmental business enterprises and other public bodies adopt CSR principles and practices in their own organizational structures, activities and relationships. For example, the Australian Government announced in mid-2008 'an internal government examination of the sustainability of government operations, in recognition that the Government accepts that it must demonstrate leadership in this area'.[124] Given the close correlations between elements of corporate governance in the public and private sectors, such as accountability to different sectoral audiences through public reporting, governmental entities can become models of organizational responsibility and sustainability reporting too.[125] In the words of the first CSR report of its kind by the Norwegian Government, the arms of the state must themselves become model exemplars of CSR:

> State-owned enterprises must lead the way in exercising social responsibility. The Government will seek to promote this by actively exercising ownership rights.[126]

Non-financial performance indicators and community service obligations are a common feature of the statutory and corporate charters of many state-owned companies. Corporate governance arrangements and official instructions from a whole-of-government perspective for state-owned authorities and companies can integrate such CSR-related elements into corporate and public governance. This trend is illustrated by examples as diverse as ministerial Statements of Intent for statutory authorities and corporations in the Australian federal public sector, China's official 2008 instructions about state-owned enterprises and their social and sustainability responsibilities, and sustainability reporting for state-owned Swedish companies in accordance with the GRI G3 guidelines.[127]

Other forms of governmental CSR modelling are also possible. The common policy-making and lawmaking device of ensuring that financial and regulatory impacts are specifically considered and documented in terms of financial and regulatory impact statements, as a matter of course for all new policies or proposed laws, can also be modelled for CSR as a governmental policy priority. By adopting such measures, governments can show that they are taking seriously the geopolitical significance of CSR, as endorsed by the G8 and G20. Other aspects of international, comparative and national legal and regulatory architecture for CSR remain to be explored in the next chapter.

NOTES

1. Albareda et al, 2007: 404–405.
2. Sherry, 2008.
3. Donaldson, 2005: 2.
4. Perrini et al, 2006: 184.
5. E.g. Fox et al, 2002; Albareda et al, 2006 ; Lepoutre et al, 2007 ; and Hohnen, 2007.
6. Ruggie, 2009: [2].
7. Ibid.: [22].
8. Ruggie, 2008a: [53]–[55].
9. *The Economist*, 2008: 8.
10. CAMAC, 2006: 169.
11. Perrini et al, 2006: 4, 30. For more discussion of strategic business–society engagement see Ch 8.
12. Bottomley, 2007: 12.
13. *The Economist*, 2005: 14, 16.
14. E.g. 'Public policy positions and participation in public policy development and lobbying' (SO5) and 'Total value of financial and in-kind contributions to political parties, politicians, and related institutions by country' (SO6).
15. Stiglitz, 2006: 196–197.
16. Zerk, 2006: 303.
17. E.g. Companies Act 2006 (UK), Part 14.
18. Reich, 2007: 163.
19. Conrad and Abbott, 2007: 418–419.
20. Ibid.: 423–424.
21. Ibid.: 431–432.
22. Shell, 2004; and Reich, 2007.
23. Shell, 2004.
24. Sands, 2005: 19.
25. Ruggie, 2007b: 8; emphasis added.
26. For further discussion of strategic CSR see Ch 8.
27. Mulgan, 2007: 321.
28. Gutmann and Thompson, 2004: 39.
29. Porter and Kramer, 2006: 80.
30. Perrini et al, 2006: 16, 19.
31. Ward, 2008: 22–23.
32. Zadek, 2001a: 33–41.
33. Perrini et al, 2006: 18.
34. COM(2006)136, 4.
35. Ward, 2008: 25–26.
36. Parker, 2007.
37. Ward, 2008: 11.
38. CAMAC, 2006: 169.
39. PJCCFS, 2006: xxiii.
40. E.g. level of industry-specific or overall business spending on average on charity and philanthropy, level and range of voluntarily reported mechanisms for ensuring due consideration of stakeholder interests, increases in the reported commissioning of expert socio-economic impact analyses to inform business decision-making, increases in formal and informal involvement of stakeholders in corporate governance mechanisms, co-operative development of CSR regulatory guidance, level of industry-specific or overall business reporting on average on CSR activities and outcomes etc.
41. UK government, 2004: 24–25.
42. E.g. ibid.: and CAMAC, 2006: 162.
43. COM(2006)136: 6–8.

44. COM(2001)366.
45. European Parliament resolution of 13 March 2007 on corporate social responsibility: a new partnership.
46. E.g. UK government, 2004: and CAMAC, 2006: 162.
47. Ruggie, 2008b: 4.
48. CAMAC, 2006: 3–4.
49. PJCCFS, 2006: vii.
50. CAMAC, 2006: 78–79.
51. Fox et al., 2002.
52. US GAO, 2005: 22.
53. Fox et al, 2002: 31.
54. Ward, 2008: 20.
55. Lepoutre, Dentchev and Heene, 2004: 18; and Lepoutre, Dentchev and Heene, 2007: 392.
56. Ward et al 2007: 5; and Ward, 2008: 20.
57. Ward, 2008: 12.
58. CAMAC, 2006: 9.
59. Much (if not all) of this framework of governmental CSR functions and roles is consistent with Paul Hohnen's dozen 'soft power' CSR option for government: see Hohnen, 2007b.
60. Taking the revised five-fold scheme of governmental CSR roles and associated activities by Fox et al as a key starting point, Table 4.1 positions that scheme within corresponding parts of the literature, reorientates its features in line with the nine-fold scheme of governmental functions and means outlined in this chapter, and outlines the correlation between CSR thinking and policy/regulatory design, on one hand, and CSR functions, roles, and activities, on the other.
61. ALP, 2007: Ch 5 [44].
62. PJCCFS, 2006: xiii and xvi.
63. ALP, 2007: Chapter 5 [36], [41].
64. Henry, 2008: 12.
65. Ibid.: 14.
66. PJCCFS, 2006: xvii.
67. Norwegian Ministry of Foreign Affairs, 2009: 94.
68. Villiers, 2008: 105–106.
69. Ward, 2008: 11.
70. Scott, 2008: 182.
71. Ruggie, 2009: [3]. For a European example of governmental 'uptake' of the UNSRSG's policy framework for business and human rights, see Norwegian Ministry of Foreign Affairs, 2009: 12 and 77–78, also referred to by Ruggie above.
72. Parliament of the Commonwealth of Australia, Journals of the Senate No. 18-23, June 2008, available at http://parlinfo.aph.gov.au/parlinfo/download/chamber/journals/2008-06-23/toc_pdf/jnlf_018.pdf;file Type=application%2Fpdf#search=%22(%20senate)%2042%20journals%22.
73. PJCCFS, 2006: [8.39].
74. Ibid.: [5.44] and [5.55].
75. Ibid.: [8.126].
76. CAMAC, 2006: 169–170.
77. PJCCFS, 2006, [5.55], [7.55], [8.122], and [8.126].
78. COM(2006)136, 7.
79. Norwegian Ministry of Foreign Affairs, 2009: 103.
80. PJCCFS, 2006: xvii.
81. Zerk, 2006: 37.
82. CPWGRB, 2008.
83. Zerk, 2006: 37; Braithwaite and Drahos, 2000: 28; and Parker et al, 2004: 7.
84. E.g. the UK Community Investment Tax Relief ('CITR') scheme.
85. See, e.g., *Corporate Social Responsibility: A Government Update*, UK Government (www.csr.gov.au).
86. Slaughter, 2004.
87. Zerk, 2006: 38–39.
88. PJCCFS, 2006: [8.146].
89. Ibid.: [8.151].
90. Sherry, 2008.
91. Parker, 2002: 241.
92. CPWGRB, 2008: 14.
93. Ibid.: 13.
94. Ibid.: 14.

95. See Ch 2.
96. Rudd, 2008b: 3–4.
97. PJCCFS, 2006: [8.129].
98. CPRBWG, 2007: 18–20.
99. Slaughter, 2004: 240.
100. Kernot, 2009: 36-37.
101. Bakan, 2004: 149–150.
102. Parker, 2002: 212.
103. Ibid.: 212–213.
104. Ibid.
105. Parker, 2007.
106. Zerk, 2006: 36.
107. On some of these taxation suggestions see Legge, 2008.
108. Ibid.: 36.
109. Tate, 2007: 3.
110. Parker, 2007; and Scott, 2008.
111. Zerk, 2006: 39–40.
112. See Ch 5.
113. E.g. Ramsay, 2005c.
114. *White v Director of Military Prosecutions* [2007] HCA 29 at [135].
115. Parker, 2002: 241–242; and Parker, 2006: 19–23.
116. On the following techniques and examples of legal meta-regulation of CSR see Parker, 2007: 218–221; and Parker, 2002: 241–242.
117. Parker, 2002: 241–242.
118. E.g. Human Rights Act 2004 (ACT), section 40D.
119. Ward et al, 2007: 7.
120. E.g. Mann, 2008: 18–20.
121. Zadek, 2001a: 38.
122. Parker, 2007: 232–233; Scott, 2008: 178; and Ward, 2008: 20–21.
123. Ward, 2008: 16–17, 20–21.
124. Sherry, 2008.
125. PJCCFS, 2006: [8.92].
126. Norwegian Ministry of Foreign Affairs, 2009.
127. Uhrig, 2003: 8; Ruggie, 2008a: [30] and [32]; SASAC, 2008; and Lydenberg and Grace, 2008.

5. Charting the regulation of corporate social responsibility and its reform

OVERVIEW

Any attempt at official CSR reform at governmental and intergovernmental levels must increasingly be grounded in an international and comparative assessment of CSR's legal and regulatory landscape. This is particularly important in light of the significant potential, sometime in the 21st century, for the development of an international system of CSR law and regulation, complemented and shaped by an emerging body of comparative CSR-related law and regulation across major jurisdictions, as outlined here. Consistently with the growth of modelling regulatory schemes and strategies from one domain to another in business regulation worldwide,[1] across jurisdictions there is 'a certain amount of cross-fertilisation of regulatory ideas and tactics, as different home states watch and learn from each other'.[2] These legal and regulatory aspects of the governmental mapping of CSR are the focus of this chapter.

MAPPING INTERNATIONAL AND COMPARATIVE LAW AND REGULATION OF CORPORATE SOCIAL RESPONSIBILITY

International CSR-related Law and Regulation

> Much of international law is simply social responsibility and neighbourhood writ large [and] we ought to accept that the corporation always has the social responsibility of a citizen and often has that of a government.
>
> – Corporate law professor, Suzanne Corcoran[3]

International law has much potential to regulate corporate responsibility, although it presently has limited application to TNCs directly, in the absence of a comprehensive international law of corporate responsibility and governance. International law speaks more to the obligations of nation-states than to those of non-state actors, although that balance is shifting. The orthodox framework of international law envisages direct imposition of obligations upon nation-states under international law, for their own actions as well as the actions of others for whom they are responsible within their sovereign domains, together with indirect imposition of flow-on obligations upon individuals, corporations and other actors under domestic law, in fulfilment of those state obligations.

At the same time, this system of primary and secondary rules for state responsibility under international law interacts with other rules of international law affecting corporate and non-corporate actors, as strands of an emerging international law of corporate responsibility.[4] As an international law of multinational corporate responsibility develops, transcending the 'state-centredness' of current international law, this body of law can be expected to evolve notions of sovereignty, extra-territoriality and jurisdiction that accommodate a fresh focus upon multinational corporate responsibility.[5]

Although the world remains in the early stages of developing a comprehensive global platform for corporate responsibility, governance and sustainability, the international legal community is already taking significant steps in that direction. This development is evident in the nascent development of principles of international legal responsibility and their application to TNCs, creation of nation-state supervisory obligations and other regulatory obligations over corporations, and generation of business-related norms and other standards that might yet solidify in customary or treaty-based international law, especially in select areas of law that are particularly sensitive to harmful corporate activity, such as environmental and human rights law.[6] It gains even more force through the embrace of a '"bottom up" approach to international law [that] offers a framework for understanding the relevance of other, self-regulatory and "non-binding" initiatives that would otherwise (under traditional international legal theory) be accorded only peripheral status at best', given the historical '"state-centredness" of international law'.[7]

The existing mechanisms for subjecting corporations to some level of international scrutiny are limited in nature and scope, but they lay the groundwork for the development of the next level of international CSR architecture. Attention is turning to components of the multinational business value chain, including possible avenues of multinational parent and group liability for the controllable actions of corporate subsidiaries and possibly other members of a multinational supply and distribution chain.[8] International trade and investment laws set the rules of engagement for corporations from home states of incorporation conducting business transnationally in host countries of operation. They also affect a range of agreements to which corporations are parties, including business–state agreements for infrastructure and development projects. Even in the absence of a comprehensive international law of corporate responsibility, UN treaty-reporting mechanisms are already being used to scrutinize how well countries monitor and remedy offshore corporate abuses by multinationals located within their jurisdictions,[9] with further potential for improvements under treaty-monitoring systems in state reporting obligations on CSR, direct corporate monitoring, stakeholder and NGO scrutiny, and remedial mechanisms for victims of multinational corporate abuses.[10]

At some point in the 21st century, the need will arise to bring together the patchwork of 'hard law' and 'soft law' standards covering general corporate governance and responsibility, on one hand, and CSR-related matters (including business responsibility for human rights), on the other, into a body of international law governing corporations that transcends international law's present state-centredness.[11] Equally important in this context are national and regional policy frameworks for CSR, such as those developed in the UK and the EU. Soft law norms and codes emanating from bodies like the UN, ILO, OECD, World Bank and EU are not only important in their own right, but also provide official credibility and impetus for the development of complementary multi-stakeholder CSR initiatives at industry, regional or wider levels of focus, and with membership across public, private and community sectors.[12] Moreover, the emerging body of comparative law and regulation surrounding the socio-ethical, environmental and governance responsibilities of corporations serves not only as a touchstone for corporate regulatory models and reforms in comparable national systems, but also both shapes and reflects evolving notions of multinational responsibility under 'hard' and 'soft' rules of international law.[13]

The ripple effect of these multi-stakeholder and standard-setting developments does not necessarily depend upon who has agreed to them, whether they reflect governing laws and how otherwise enforceable they are. As described by corporate legal scholars, Professors Cynthia Williams and John Conley, business executives who seek refuge in a minimalist and legalistic compliance-based view of international norms affecting business are increasingly putting their supposed delivery of shareholder value at risk:[14]

Many global companies recognize that the norms these governance regimes are creating are becoming the moral norms by which companies are increasingly being judged by consumers, communities, investors, and civil society, whether a particular company has signed onto them or not. A narrow focus by a board of directors or its subsidiary's board or officers on the substantive standards of any one country's domestic law may fail to meet the norm-based expectations of a wider swath of important stakeholders, with serious consequences to the company and its shareholders.

At the international level, 'soft law' standards can still have considerable 'regulatory value', even though they might not amount to binding and enforceable obligations upon nation-states or anyone else.[15] In her recent study of TNCs and CSR under international law, Dr Zerk identifies a range of emerging international legal principles that are capable of application to TNCs, particularly as a consequence of various international CSR-related 'soft law' standards.[16] The emerging principles reflected in such standards serve multiple purposes, 'as a way of testing attitudes, developing consensus around an issue and shaping future norms', as well as in building momentum towards formal treaties between states on CSR matters and demonstrating evidence of new CSR-related practices under customary international law.[17] She identifies a growing international consensus about: (i) basic principles of minimum health, safety and environmental standards; (ii) responsibility within multinational supply and distribution chains; (iii) sustainable development and investment, via informed consent and other obligations to consult and warn; (iv) a 'precautionary principle applicable to environmental and non-environmental areas of corporate activity'; (v) environmental risk and impact assessments; (vi) openness, transparency and other key regulatory values; and (vii) external monitoring, assurance and verification of standards.[18]

In these ways and others, according to Zerk, 'soft law instruments can be a way of galvanising support for a particular programme or policy [and] can help to focus thinking about certain issues, to clarify positions and to develop understanding between states'.[19] Professor Peter Muchlinski crystallizes how the international legal domain might yet yield meaningful CSR results, in terms that further reduce the significance of the distinction between mandatory (public) regulation and voluntary (private) regulation, as follows:[20]

At the international level, soft law can 'harden' into positive law, where it is seen as evidence of emergent new standards of international law. For these purposes the origin of the legal principle in a soft law instrument, such as a voluntary code of conduct or a non-binding resolution of an international organisation, is of little consequence if a consensus develops that the principle in question should be viewed as an obligatory standard by reason of subsequent practice . . . Therefore, to dismiss voluntary sources of international or national CSR standards as irrelevant seems to fail to appreciate how formal rules and principles of law emerge . . . The real issue is when and how will all this 'codification' turn into detailed legal standards that can act as fully binding benchmarks for the control of unacceptable lapses in corporate conduct at the international and national levels. That is, of course, an issue of ideological contest, but one which seems to be veering slowly towards an acceptance of some kind of articulated set of minimum international standards for CSR, as a trade-off for greater corporate freedom in the market.

All of this fits within a global CSR framework of corporate responsiveness to governance beyond government, regulation beyond law, and responsibility beyond sanctionability. One future possibility is that CSR-related international instruments and other initiatives might form the basis for a coherent regime of international corporate legal responsibility, with a balance of correlative obligations upon both nation-states and corporations themselves, including as a constituent part 'an international law of CSR' for companies.[21] On Dr Zerk's analysis, the elements of this future 21st century framework for CSR internationally might include:[22]

(1) a landmark overarching international convention on CSR;
(2) creation of a supra-national institution to monitor and regulate TNCs;
(3) enhancement of existing human rights monitoring mechanisms under international instruments in their application to multinational corporate activity;
(4) incorporation of social and environmental responsibilities of investors within multilateral investment and development agreements;
(5) bolstering of foreign direct investment and liability laws 'to compensate more effectively those whose lives are damaged as a result of corporate negligence or wrongdoing'; and
(6) improvement in the overall coherence and coordination of international and supra-national institutions and initiatives relating to CSR.

In short, the future progress of international and transnational architecture for CSR depends equally upon a recast view of the global governance and regulatory landscape for corporations, new legal and regulatory institutions and norms devoted to CSR, and justifications that address normative controversies of the kinds highlighted in Chapter 3. This is matched by the development of a comparative body of CSR-related law and regulation too, as explored below.

An Emerging Body of Comparative CSR-related Regulatory Developments

An emerging body of comparative CSR-related law and regulation is starting to take shape in the 21st century across a select range of comparable corporate regulatory systems. The emergence of a mass of CSR-related law and regulation across comparative jurisdictions can happen without necessarily becoming one homogenous body of norms. The degree of harmonization goes to a different debate about convergence and divergence in corporate regulation and governance. The important point for present purposes is that there are discrete categories of law and regulation in common that inherently relate or increasingly pay attention to CSR-related concerns, and which combine across juris-dictions in sufficient mass and scale overall to represent an important body of regulatory norms that frame business practice and politico-regulatory modelling on CSR.

Comparative CSR-related law and regulation also has developing points of connection with international CSR-related law and regulation. It contributes to the kind of international consensus developed through state and corporate practices that is necessary for any new customary international laws and treaties governing CSR.[23] It bears the hallmarks of the wider CSR movement's impact upon the shape and direction of corporate law and regulation as a whole.[24] It is anchored in comparative corporate law and regulation, but increasingly embraces other areas of law and other forms of regulation too, some of which intersect with the concerns of corporate law. For example, corporate compliance and due diligence systems required under corporate laws must accommodate legal obligations of corporations under other laws too. In practice, all of these disparate areas of corporate and non-corporate law and regulation must be brought together, at least from a boardroom perspective, in overarching corporate systems of management, control and compliance. Hence, corporate governance becomes a key contemporary vehicle for the inculcation and accommodation of many CSR-related concerns, especially as CSR becomes part of how a company does business.

At the same time, the emergence of a distinct body of comparative CSR-related law and regulation still leaves room for different forms of leadership, modelling and emphasis across different corporate regulatory systems. For example, social and environmental activism has traditionally manifested itself more acutely in North American use of the shareholder proposal rule than in North American corporate reporting, in contrast with more recent European and UK regulatory efforts to incorporate social and environmental considerations within corporate governance and reporting. Australia, the UK and some European countries lead the way in regulation that embeds socio-ethical and environmental considerations in institutional investment policy and investment product disclosure. 'For the future of global CSR, we suggest that corporations look to the European Union for product safety and environmental standards, to the United States for corporate governance guidelines, and to international NGOs for human and labor rights rules', according to one group of cross-disciplinary corporate governance scholars.[25]

The menu of policy, regulatory and legal options for CSR actors interested in CSR governmental reform can start conveniently with corporate law, regulation and governance, even within corporate regulatory systems that broadly subscribe to a model of shareholder value. The major topic areas with some CSR relevance include:

(1)   preconditions for incorporation and continued corporate existence (e.g. revocable corporate charters and winding-up on public interest grounds for socially and environmentally irresponsible companies[26]);
(2)   corporate objectives and powers (e.g. capacity for corporate philanthropy and corporate community investment);
(3)   directors' and officers' duties and defences (e.g. stakeholder-sensitive directors' duties and business judgments);
(4)   business risk management requirements (e.g. CSR-related business risk factors);
(5)   corporate disclosure and reporting obligations (e.g. non-financial and sustainability reporting requirements);

(6) shareholder (and stakeholder) participation in corporate decision-making and governance (e.g. socially and environmentally orientated shareholder proposals);

(7) consideration and treatment of employee, creditor and other stakeholder interests in corporate governance and decision-making (e.g. stakeholder-sensitive corporate legal and regulatory obligations);

(8) creation of incentives and removal of disincentives for socially and environmentally responsible corporate behaviour (e.g. matching government procurement, regulatory treatment and business opportunities to business regulatory compliance and corporate citizenship track records);

(9) standards for corporate governance and behaviour (e.g. corporate stakeholder engagement requirements);

(10) conferral of standard-setting authority on others (e.g. legal backing for CSR-related accounting, auditing and other standards set by corporate regulators); and

(11) prescription of the boundaries, conditions and limitations of liability for corporations in their home jurisdictions of operation for their harmful effects in host jurisdictions (e.g. corporate codes of conduct for TNCs and foreign direct liability mechanisms).

CORPORATE GOVERNANCE MECHANISMS AND CORPORATE SOCIAL RESPONSIBILITY

The Enron case demonstrates that a company can be widely respected for CSR in its environmental record, triple bottom line reporting, code of conduct respecting human rights and philanthropic contributions and yet have gross breaches of fiduciary duties by its key executives. CSR needs to be seen as part of corporate governance and not a substitute for it.

– Professor John Farrar, *Corporate Governance: Theories, Principles and Practice*[27]

The Significance of Corporate Governance Standpoints

Academic debates over corporate law and governance now break into discrete camps, some of which are cross-jurisdictional (e.g. the convergence–divergence debate), and others of which are jurisdiction-specific (e.g. reallocation of control between US shareholders and managers in the post-Enron era). The different regulatory responses in the USA, UK and Australia, for example, to the corporate scandals and collapses of the Enron era, in combination with perceived corporate governance gaps in some of those responses, serve to cast some doubt upon any shift towards 'a unified common law corporate governance model'.[28] In their wake, there is renewed attention in different jurisdictions to enhancement of shareholder participatory and control mechanisms over boards, realignment of managerial performance and shareholder value in executive earnings and bonuses, the respective merits of rule-based and principle-based regulatory regimes in restoring confidence in market regulation, and the relationship between shareholder value and CSR.[29]

In the USA, the UK, Australia and elsewhere, periodic episodes of high-profile corporate deviance or other well-publicized corporate problems often provoke legislative tightening of corporate governance regulation, concentrated upon aspects of corporate governance formalities such as independence of corporate directors and auditors, financial risk management, and business disclosure and reporting. One common criticism applicable across jurisdictions is that sometimes legislatures and politicians see newsworthy corporate collapses and mismanagement as the tip of an iceberg of corporate misconduct and react in a knee-jerk fashion, without rigorous evidence-based policy assessment of systemic problems in need of reform.[30] Certainly, the wave of legislated corporate governance reforms in the USA, the UK, Australia and other countries in the immediate aftermath of Enron's collapse might be characterized in this way, however much they might also have addressed some systemic problems.

Other aspects of comprehensive corporate governance regulatory reform are yet to take hold across jurisdictions, focused upon substantive matters of corporate responsibility and sustainability. Responding to the European Commission's 2006 CSR communication, the European Parliament's 2007 CSR resolution moves clearly in the direction of integrating good corporate governance with CSR-related concerns of corporate responsibility and sustainability:

> The European Parliament . . . (b)elieves that the CSR debate must not be separated from questions of corporate accountability, and that issues of the social and environmental impact of business, relations with stakeholders, the protection of minority shareholders' rights and the duties of company directors in this regard should be fully integrated into the Commission's Corporate Governance Action Plan [and] points out that these issues should form part of the debate on CSR . . .

Debate about corporations and the public interest is no longer confined simply to arguments over the social efficiency of corporate profit-maximization and corporate internalization of a public welfare imperative to advance social goals. It turns as well to the mix of public and private interests served through a company's corporate governance arrangements. Just as corporate responsibility is increasingly intertwined with at least some aspects of CSR, so too corporate governance is evolving to embrace both. Indeed, as the enlightened self-interest of corporations becomes enshrined officially in shareholder primacy offshoots such as 'enlightened shareholder value' under UK corporate law, with a correlative broadening of the sources of value-creation for business as well as the societal interests implicated in contemporary corporate governance, CSR is increasingly seen as the hallmark of sustainable corporate capitalism. Still, the connection between CSR and corporate governance does not meet with universal acclaim. 'The recently fashionable doctrine of "corporate social responsibility", and particularly the notion of the "triple bottom line", poses an emerging threat to good governance which, if it lasts, could be serious', according to experienced company director and corporate governance regulator, Henry Bosch.[31]

Viewed through the prism of the 'set of legal tensions and relationships that find their focus point within the company', corporate governance has a wide-angle concern 'with the overall structure, not only of corporate regulation, but also of all those other areas of law affecting corporate action and the exercise of power within the corporation'.[32] As corporate governance has both formal aspects (i.e. 'hard' governance) and less formal aspects (i.e. 'soft' governance), and also incorporates organizational attentiveness to the internal and external business environments, corporate governance increasingly has a threefold focus upon its structural, behavioural and relational dimensions.

Corporate governance has evolved beyond a 'top down' vision of how corporations are structured, managed and controlled. Its coverage also extends beyond the relations between corporate directors, managers and shareholders as corporate actors engaged in private ordering of private interests:[33]

> (C)orporate governance is more than simply the relationship between the firm and its capital providers. Corporate governance also implicates how the various constituencies that define the business enterprise serve, and are served by, the corporation. Implicit and explicit relationships between the corporation and its employees, creditors, suppliers, customers, host communities – and relationships among these constituencies themselves – fall within the ambit of a relevant definition of corporate governance. As such, the phrase calls into scrutiny not only the definition of the corporate form, but also its purposes and its accountability to each of the relevant constituencies.

The variety of standpoints from which we might conceive the *point* of corporate governance from the outset inevitably affects the approach we take to *define* what corporate governance means. In turn, this affects how we characterize the relation (if any) between corporate governance and CSR. The importance of this methodological insight for how we frame corporate governance is illustrated in how Bessler, Kaen and Sherman conceive of perspectives on corporate governance:[34]

> One perspective approaches the corporate governance debate as part of the larger question of how to organize economic activity to achieve more fundamental societal objectives related to equity, fairness, freedom and citizen responsibilities. The other perspective is more narrowly concerned with economic efficiency objectives and, at the risk of exaggeration, considers economic efficiency to be an end in itself rather than a means to non-economic societal objectives.

These grand differences in starting positions for framing an understanding of corporate governance lead naturally in different directions, as summarized by leading Australian corporate law and governance scholars Austin, Ford and Ramsay, as follows:[35]

> According to one of these perspectives, good corporate governance should have as its objective the maximisation of shareholders' wealth. The broader perspective (which might be called the stakeholder perspective of corporate governance) focuses upon companies being 'socially responsible' and often subordinating profit maximisation to other goals. It can, therefore, be seen that the corporate governance debate is intrinsically linked to the important question: For whom do directors govern? Do they govern for shareholders or for a broader range of stakeholders?

Considered from a regulatory perspective, the point of reflexive corporate governance is that the influences upon companies in relating to the world around them are much more complex than a product simply of what society makes them do by law or leaves entirely to their discretion, with commitment to CSR by individual companies forming only part of a wider system of CSR norm-generating 'regimes' involving a multiplicity of corporate, governmental and community actors.[36] The corporate governance of any single organization is a system that interacts with other systems, whatever the characterizations of such systems[37] and the frameworks for analysing them.[38] 'The thrust of the literature on reflexive governance is to suggest that governance mechanisms should be targeted at creating structures within which actors such as corporations can reflect both on how they see the world, in terms of the problems which their organization is supposed to be addressing, and their own position in that world in terms of what they might do and achieve and what the pay-offs might be', according to regulatory theorist Colin Scott, who adds:[39]

> The ideas of reflexive governance recognize the embeddedness of social processes within legal, competitive and community structures. This insight encourages us to conceive of meta-regulation as defining the reasons for action more broadly than legal compliance, and to include also the reasons for acting which derive from participation in competitive markets and in communities.

In most countries that subscribe to a model of shareholder primacy as the foundation of corporate governance, a gap still often arises in practice between the rhetoric of shareholder benefit and the reality of shareholder involvement. In their report for the Citizen Works Corporate Reform Commission, Lee Drutman and Charlie Cray describe this as a 'paradox of corporate governance', in these terms:[40]

> All this sets up a confusing dynamic. On the one hand, owners are completely disenfranchised. The corporation is run without their input, and managers are largely unaccountable to anybody. Yet, at the same time, corporations are run primarily for the financial benefit of shareholders – often with disastrous consequences and at great cost to workers, consumers, the environment, other stakeholders, and, paradoxically, sometimes even to shareholders themselves. Though it sounds contradictory, that is how corporations operate. Accordingly, attempts to use corporate governance to mitigate the harmful tendencies of large corporations essentially fall into two approaches.
>
> In one approach, socially conscious investors use the powers of ownership that are given to them (shareholder resolutions, the ability to buy and sell) to pressure corporations to alter their behaviour. Although this can yield some modest results, the truth is that the corporate governance structure makes it extremely difficult for shareholders to leverage much pressure on management . . . The second set of approaches involves trying to change the laws and incentives that drive the corporation's unrelenting focus on maximizing shareholder profit in the first place. Potential reforms under this approach include making directors and managers responsible for protecting the public good (instead of just shareholder value), changing investment incentives, increasing the influence of a wider group of stakeholders, and requiring corporations to measure and make public a broad range of performance yardsticks (instead of just their finances). Though these reforms have varying potential benefits, none appear particularly capable of significantly altering the corporation's primary purpose.

At the very least, corporate governance in the 21st century embraces more stakeholder sensitivity, business–society relationship awareness and intermingling of public and private concerns than the orthodoxy of much pre-21st century thinking on corporations. One of corporate governance's key post-GFC challenges is to work through the points of intersection and alignment between corporate governance and public governance in an era of interdependent economies, renewed state engagement and intervention in markets, and heightened global scrutiny of CSR's contribution to geopolitical policy and regulatory priorities.

Internationally and Nationally Authoritative Corporate Governance Standards

Authoritative supranational corporate governance standards such as the OECD Principles of Corporate Governance (OECD Principles) and the OECD Guidelines for Multinational Enterprises (OECD Guidelines) have important implications for CSR. Introducing the revised OECD Guidelines accepted by 33 countries in mid-2000, the Chairman of the Ministerial Council and Australian Treasurer, Peter Costello, spoke of them as 'a meaningful instrument for the international business community' as well as 'a useful reference point and tool for promoting corporate social responsibility'.[41]

The OECD Guidelines mention the range of company-specific investments by various stakeholders that contribute to a company's success. A company's interests need to be assessed over the long term, and it is in a company's long-term interests to stimulate 'wealth-creating cooperation among stakeholders'. The interests of stakeholders that deserve respect by companies are those interests 'established by law or through mutual agreements'. All of these things also relate to a company's governance arrangements. The institutional and regulatory framework supporting corporate governance must accommodate this link. Accordingly, in the words of the OECD:[42]

> Corporate governance is also concerned with finding ways to encourage the various stakeholders in the firm to undertake economically optimal levels of investment in firm-specific human and physical capital. . . . The governance framework should recognise that the interests of the corporation are served by recognising the interests of stakeholders and their contribution to the long-term success of the corporation.

Similarly, under the OECD Principles, '(t)he corporate governance framework should recognize the rights of stakeholders established by law or through mutual agreements', given corporate governance's need 'to encourage the various stakeholders in the firm to undertake economically optimal levels of investment in firm-specific human and physical capital', given that it is 'in the long-term interest of corporations to foster wealth-creating co-operation among stakeholders'.[43]

At the national level, the enhancement of corporate responsibility and governance occurs through multiple corporate governance regulatory mechanisms. These include mechanisms such as requiring compliance with authorized principles of corporate governance, developing industry and corporate codes of conduct, setting standards for corporate governance and responsibility, developing corporate and boardroom decision-making frameworks and guidelines, putting forward shareholder proposals, calling corporate meetings, engaging investors (especially institutional investors) in corporate dialogue and voting, and even initiating actions on behalf of a company.

Corporate governance principles endorsed by the New Zealand Securities Commission, for example, expressly or implicitly embody stakeholder-regarding elements going to business ethics (i.e. '(d)irectors should observe and foster high ethical standards'), risk systems (i.e. '(t)he board should regularly verify that the entity has appropriate processes that identify and manage potential and relevant risks'), and stakeholder consideration (i.e. '(t)he board should respect the interests of stakeholders within the context of the entity's ownership type and its fundamental purpose').[44] Similarly, the 10 original principles of good corporate governance formulated by the Australian Securities Exchange Corporate Governance Council (ASX CGC) in 2003 contain a number of principles with formalized or potential stakeholder-regarding elements, including Principle 3 (i.e. '(p)romote ethical and responsible decision-making'), Principle 7 (i.e. '(r)ecognise and manage risk'), Principle 8 (i.e. '(e)ncourage enhanced performance'), and Principle 10 (i.e. '(r)ecognise the legitimate interests of stakeholders').[45]

As corporate responsibility and sustainability becomes further integrated with corporate governance, other reform options are increasingly likely to arise on the political and regulatory agenda. In its 2008 recommendations on responsible business, for example, the UK Conservative Party Working Group on Responsible Business (CPWGRB) suggests political consideration of measures such as: (i) requiring corporate remuneration committees to report on senior management consideration of corporate responsibility and sustainability in setting executive bonuses and incentives; (ii) stimulating regulatory and investor pressure for non-financial risk reporting; (iii) introducing advisory (i.e. non-binding) votes on corporate responsibility and sustainability reports at company AGMs; (iv) assessing the success of pension and superannuation laws in promoting incorporation of socio-ethical and environmental considerations in investment decision-making and institutional investor policies; and (v) reviewing the UK Combined Code from the overall perspective of promoting responsible business.

'Putting a requirement for boards to seriously consider their corporate values and ethical standards – in other words, real corporate responsibility – into the Combined Code would have a beneficial effect on encouraging enlightened self-interest from business', urges the CPWGRB.[46] 'Encouragement should also be given by requiring companies to report on how human rights policies and principles are incorporated into their overall strategy, as part of their compliance with a revised Combined Code on Corporate Governance', adds the CPWGRB.[47] This suggestion marries corporate governance and business-related human rights concerns in a way that is being duplicated in other initiatives that connect corporate governance, corporate law, and human rights. For example, the UNSGSR continued his mandate through a corporate law tools project in 2009, in which leading law firms worldwide assisted him in documenting 'how the consideration of human rights by companies and their officers are addressed, explicitly or by implication, in laws and guidelines relating to incorporation, directors' duties, reporting, stakeholder engagement, and corporate governance generally'.[48] These are examples of corporate governance's transition from framing corporate governance in terms associated simply with matters concerning board–shareholder control, executive remuneration and financial audit and disclosure, and towards framing corporate governance in wider terms of corporate responsibility and sustainability. They dovetail with the wider common agenda of corporate democratization, CSR meta-regulation and corporate responsiveness to trans-modal governance, multi-order regulation and inter-related responsibility, in rendering corporations amenable to the full range of societal interests genuinely implicated in 21st century corporate responsibility, governance and sustainability.

Corporate Existence and Regulatory Status

Although not as extensive across jurisdictions as other areas of this comparative body of CSR-related law and regulation, the legal existence and regulatory status of corporations under corporate regulatory regimes are pregnant with CSR possibilities, some of which are progressively being realized. Even in the absence of corporate law reform directed towards the socialization of directors' duties and corporate reporting, some existing mechanisms within corporate law and regulation in some jurisdictions can be turned to CSR purposes. One common illustration from the CSR regulatory literature lies in the recognition of grounds for corporate incorporation and registration, criteria for preferential corporate taxation and regulatory treatment, bases for awarding public licences and business project approvals, and conditions for winding-up to include public interest elements that make protection of the community against major social and environmental corporate irresponsibility (including long-term harm to corporate victims) a primary public policy goal.

For example, where the creation and perpetual existence of a company are not automatic, corporate charter laws and related mechanisms can be used to end an irresponsible company's right to trade. Similarly, public interest grounds for liquidating a company might embrace corporate irresponsibility too. Preconditions for becoming and remaining listed on national stock exchanges can touch upon the extremes of corporate irresponsibility, given the reputational damage for companies, markets, and even stock exchanges associated with the worst corporate excesses, especially in light of the activity of some influential stock exchanges in developing CSR and SRI indices and promoting CSR-related disclosure. 'Companies that through their operations risk or commit serious or systematic violation of human rights or other ethical international norms shall be carefully investigated in conjunction with a listing on OMX Nordic Exchange', according to listing guidelines for the OMX Nordic Exchange, for example.[49]

Even differential taxation treatment of companies according to their orientation towards CSR public policy goals can have an impact upon a company's financial viability, and hence has significance beyond being simply a matter of compliance. Contemporary examples here include taxation incentives for clean energy, greenhouse gas reduction, and eco-friendly imports and exports. In terms of official enforcement approaches, being a good company or a bad company under the law matters, not least because of what might ultimately threaten the reputation, liability, and even financial viability of an irresponsible company, in serious breach of its legal compliance requirements. More particularly, flexibility in official enforcement approaches according to a company's track record of corporate compliance or non-compliance, on one hand, and responsibility or irresponsibility in meeting designated CSR public policy goals, on the other, can have a crucial impact on a company's future.

Stakeholder Engagement and Enforcement Mechanisms

In some Anglo-Commonwealth countries, existing corporate law and regulation offers discrete opportunities for a variety of corporate stakeholders to access mechanisms of engagement and even enforcement. Importantly, this includes CSR-related opportunities to engage in company dialogue or even intervene in company affairs through formal means of exercising discipline over management. The UK Combined Code contains principles for dialogue between companies and their institutional investors that cross-refer to investment industry guidelines, and which recognize the legitimacy of intervention by institutional investors in corporate affairs because of their concerns about how a company approaches CSR.[50]

Australian corporate law contains a provision with unrealized CSR potential that empowers courts, on the application of Australia's official corporate regulator (ASIC) or affected parties from inside or outside the company, to prevent corporate conduct in breach of corporate law that harms relevant shareholder interests and possibly other stakeholder interests too.[51] So, the prospect has existed for some time in Australian corporate law that parties other than shareholders might use one of corporate law's own devices to intervene in corporate affairs and obtain various remedies where their interests were unduly threatened.[52] 'The terms of [the relevant provision, ie section 1324 of the Corporations Act] are broad enough to enable a creditor, an employee or others who believe they may be at risk in the context of the relevant transaction to seek court intervention', notes one of Australia's leading corporate lawyers and commentators, adding that this potential device has been 'rather surprisingly little used in trying to make directors accountable to a broader range of persons'.[53] 'The future battleground for lawyers . . . might be based around provisions like s1324 and corporate social responsibility provisions, however cast', warn other commentators.[54]

Shareholder Proposals on Socio-ethical and Environmental Concerns

Shareholder proposal and advisory resolution mechanisms have a long history and still much unrealized potential in ventilating CSR, ESG and SRI concerns at company meetings. Many major commercial jurisdictions provide for shareholder-initiated proposals for company consideration that have at least some capacity to raise matters of social, environmental and other stakeholder concern, although there are differences across jurisdictions in their scope, exceptions, triggering requirements and interpretation by courts.[55] Such mechanisms can be viewed formally as instruments of corporate governance and dialogue between corporate management and shareholders, or more substantively as instruments of active corporate membership, decision-making and democracy, within a wider system of business meta-regulation. 'Set against the backdrop of the internationalization of corporate activities, the ability of shareholders to utilize basic corporate law building blocks to reshape the orientation of their corporations toward evolving political and cultural circumstances is essential (particularly in an era of increasing institutional ownership)', notes one North American proponent of shareholder proposal reform to enhance corporate social and human rights accountability.[56]

In recent decades, especially in North America, shareholder proposals have gone beyond a primary preoccupation with conventional corporate governance issues of corporate rules, executive remuneration, voting issues and formal meeting requirements, sometimes moving towards socio-ethical corporate activism, as in shareholder proposals to disinvest from apartheid South Africa, and sometimes becoming 'something of a hybrid, combining elements of social policy and corporate governance', as in matters of environmental protection and now climate change.[57] North American and Anglo-Commonwealth experience also suggests that shareholder activism pursued through shareholder-initiated proposals is more likely to produce results in either successful shareholder proposals or corresponding management responses when employee, environmental and community concerns reflected in those proposals are not left at large, but are aligned to corporate governance, reporting and performance concerns affecting corporate success.[58]

The modern trend towards these hybrid concerns is reinforced in the concerns of individual shareholders, institutional investors, share analysts and ratings bodies about a company's CSR, SRI and ESG performance. 'In 2005, 360 different CSR-related shareholder resolutions were filed on issues ranging from labour conditions to global warming', note Harvard's Michael Porter and Mark Kramer,[59] as part of an increasing trend of shareholder proposals calling for companies to manage and disclose business risks and opportunities arising from greenhouse gas emissions.[60] By the 2008 proxy season, shareholder proposals specifically on corporate responses to global warming and climate change almost doubled the number of shareholder proposal filings two years earlier.[61]

Directors' Duties and Business Judgments

US corporate constituency and anti-takeover laws

Directors' duties and defences go to the heart of personal liability for directors. Hence, this aspect of corporate law is crucial for the social enculturation of directors. Given their importance, legal options for reframing directors' duties and defences are canvassed in Chapter 6. Here, the emphasis is upon their place in corporate governance. The corporate law of many comparable jurisdictions now permits and sometimes even requires corporate directors to consider not only shareholder interests, but also non-shareholder interests and the third party effects of corporate decisions and actions too, as reflected in laws governing corporate charters, business takeovers and directors' duties.

For example, fuelled by calls for socially responsible corporate conduct amidst public campaigns targeting high-profile examples of corporate involvement in socially harmful activity (e.g. the *Exxon Valdez* environmental disaster, investment in apartheid-era South Africa, tobacco and asbestos illnesses, and exploitative practices in developing countries), corporate charter amendments were adopted in some US corporations in the late 1970s and early 1980s to authorize directors to consider the wider socio-economic effects of proposed acquisitions and takeovers on the target company's key constituencies.[62] In addition, corporate constituency statutes in more than 20 US states mean that directors can consider a wide range of interests in corporate decision-making, including the interests of employees, customers, creditors and local communities, either generally or in particular situations (e.g. takeovers). Their impetus lay in equivalent amendments to corporate charters by members, the long-standing debate about CSR, the rise of stakeholder theory in influential American business and management schools, and the need for legislated anti-takeover protection in the USA in the last quarter of the 20th century.[63]

EU and UK developments on boardroom obligations

In its 2007 CSR resolution, responding to the European Commission's 2006 communication on CSR, the European Parliament '(r)ecommends that the Commission extends the responsibility of directors of companies with more than 1,000 employees to encompass the duty for the directors themselves to minimise any harmful social and environmental impact of companies' activities'. Under the new statutory duty of loyalty for company directors imposed under the UK's 2006 Companies Act, directors who are looking to 'promote the success of the company for the benefit of its members as a whole' must at least take account of a range of legislatively laid down shareholder-related and other stakeholder-related considerations. These considerations include 'the likely consequences of any decision in the long term', 'the interests of the company's employees', 'the need to foster the company's business relationships with suppliers, customers, and others', 'the impact of the company's operations on the community and the environment', 'the desirability of the company maintaining a reputation for high standards of business conduct' and 'the need to act fairly as between members of the company'.[64]

Inevitably, this comprehensive legislative review of UK company law is bound to generate important questions of interpretation, application and practice for some time to come for a variety of CSR actors in the UK, as well as for those interested in such comparative developments and experiments from afar, as explored in Chapter 7. Its many untested issues and implications will progressively unfold in judicial test cases, professional corporate advice, official regulatory guidance (including corporate governance standards), and the practice of corporate decision-making, risk management and reporting in the UK. As has already happened in Australia, governmental entities such as policy-making bodies, official inquiries and law reform agencies charged with investigating and recommending alternative legal models for enhancing corporate responsibility, governance and reporting might cast a comparative eye to the law and practice surrounding the UK Companies Act 2006 as it unfolds.[65]

Australian and Canadian developments on boardroom obligations

Although Australian corporate law does not expressly deal with shareholder and non-shareholder interests in the same terms as UK law in its formulation of the duties of directors, the Australian Government's Corporations and Markets Advisory Committee (CAMAC) and the Australian Parliamentary Joint Committee on Corporations and Financial Services (PJCCFS) both concluded earlier this century that the current law implicitly affords sufficient leeway for company directors to consider both shareholder and non-shareholder interests. For example, the PJCCFS' *Corporate Responsibility* report concluded that Australia's main corporate legislation 'permits directors to have regard for the interests of stakeholders other than shareholders', thus alleviating any need for legislative amendments to this effect.[66]

'Although there may be no direct legal obligation in company law on directors to take other interests into account, it does not follow that directors cannot choose to do so', conclude three of Australia's leading corporate law and governance scholars, joining the chorus of elite thinking on this point.[67] Still, directors have no entitlement or obligation under the existing Australian law of directors' duties to consider and give effect to non-shareholder interests for their own sake. Similarly, in its landmark interpretation this century of the cognate statutory duty of loyalty imposed upon directors under Canadian corporate law, Canada's highest court accepted 'as an accurate statement of law' the legal proposition 'that in determining whether they are acting with a view to the best interests of the corporation it may be legitimate, given all the circumstances of a given case, for the board of directors to consider, inter alia, the interests of shareholders, employees, suppliers, creditors, consumers, governments and the environment'.[68]

Comparative position on directors' duties and defences

Accordingly, in a number of comparable jurisdictions, the applicable corporate law clearly requires or permits reference by corporate directors to relevant non-shareholder interests as well as shareholder interests in their decision-making. Where business judgment rules or defences apply, or other legal elements are in play that give some leeway or discretion to company directors, the corporate law in applicable jurisdictions contains an extra layer of protection for directors who do so. Still, there seems little legislative or judicial appetite across North American or Anglo-Commonwealth jurisdictions for reforming directors duties' beyond permitting or even requiring boards to consider employee, customer, creditor and other community interests to the extent needed to manage a company's business, resist unworthy takeovers and maintain corporate profitability over the long run, subject possibly to ongoing EU policy and regulatory developments in the direction of making directors' duties more socially and environmentally sensitive.

Socially Responsible Investing

The notion of a corporate duty to respect human rights is relevant to investment decision-making . . . in two key respects.

The first is the extent to which legal duties imposed on institutional investors consider or accommodate ethical considerations such as socially responsible investment (SRI) or environmental, social and governance (ESG) factors. The second is the legal requirement for vendors of financial products with an investment component to disclose SRI and ESG considerations involved in the creation, retention and realisation of that investment.

Although neither of these sets of requirements mandate consideration of human rights issues, if a vendor of financial products did declare an intention to take SRI and ESG factors into account in investment decision-making, it would need to have in place due diligence processes to ensure it was actually weighing these factors with the rigour it claimed to be exercising.

– Report by law firm Allens Arthur Robinson for the UN Special Representative of the Secretary General for Business and Human Rights[69]

A 2005 report by international law firm Freshfields Bruckhaus Deringer for the United Nations Environment Programme Finance Initiative aimed to address the following major question: 'Is the integration of environmental, social and governance issues into investment policy (including asset allocation, portfolio construction and stock-picking or bond-picking) voluntarily permitted, legally required or hampered by law and regulation; primarily as regards public and private pension funds, secondarily as regards insurance company reserves and mutual funds?'.[70] In an expansive review of the positions in France, Germany, Italy, Japan, Spain, the UK, the US, Canada and Australia, the report noted that none of these jurisdictions completely prescribes how investment decision-makers should incorporate ESG considerations in their investment decisions, before concluding that 'decision-makers are required to have regard (at some level) to ESG considerations in every decision they make . . . because there is a body of creditable evidence demonstrating that such considerations often have a role to play in the proper analysis of investment *value*'.[71]

Given the emerging evidence and increasing acceptance of the relationship between a company's financial performance and ESG considerations, 'integrating ESG considerations into an investment analysis so as to more reliably predict financial performance is clearly permissible and is arguably required in all jurisdictions', the report adds.[72] In practice, Freshfields suggests a three-step approach for institutional investors to follow when incorporating ESG considerations into their investment decisions, which cover formulating an investment strategy, gathering ESG-related investment data, and assessing the ESG implications of investments, all against the background of applicable law.[73]

Whether or not in practice we have reached the point where mainstream investment decision-making compels reference to relevant ESG, SRI and related considerations as a matter of law, both scholarly analysis and legal advice are heading in the direction of accepting that, at least for pension and superannuation funds, 'trustees can consider adopting sustainable investing practices without necessarily compromising their fiduciary duties'.[74] Under UK law governing pension trusts for employees and others, the trustees must develop and act according to a statement of investment principles that not only records their policy on how they will exercise voting and other rights concerning their investment portfolios, but must also identify 'the extent (if at all) to which social, environmental or ethical considerations are taken into account in the selection, retention and realisation of investments'.[75] Both actions are a route to enhanced CSR through institutional involvement in corporate governance.

Similarly, under Australian corporate law, product disclosure statements for share schemes, superannuation funds, and other investment products with an investment component must disclose 'the extent to which labour standards or environmental, social or ethical considerations are taken into account in the selection, retention or realisation of the investment', with the national corporate regulator (ASIC) being statutorily authorized to develop compliance guidelines for such claims.[76] Both these requirements and the guidelines on SRI developed by ASIC[77] afford considerable discretion and flexibility for those regulated by these requirements in identifying relevant labour, social, environmental and ethical standards and considerations, and in describing the methodology by which they are taken into account where relevant in investment decision-making. While some investors might be influenced by such considerations in making their own investment choices, these requirements fall well short of compulsory incorporation and disclosure of SRI and ESG standards.

Whatever the correlation between CSR and corporate financial performance, there is at least some evidence that how a company approaches CSR can be a good indicator of overall corporate health and successful management.[78] At the same time, extrapolating too much from this dimension of corporate affairs can be dangerous. 'A company's attention to environmental, social and corporate-governance issues is only one factor among others in determining its long-term success', notes *The Economist* in its assessment of CSR.[79]

Corporate Responsibility and Sustainability Reporting

The evolution of corporate disclosure and reporting
Corporate reporting worldwide seems to be heading in the same general and seemingly irreversible CSR-related direction.[80] One strong trend concerns the increase in the

number of leading companies worldwide who are reporting on CSR-related concerns, the change in the range of CSR-related matters covered by such reporting, and the variety of forms and tools for that reporting.

Mandatory corporate reporting of environmental compliance and impact is now a standard feature of many corporate regulatory regimes. Environmental compliance and impact was the topic of greatest emphasis in those company reports detailing non-financial information about corporate performance in the early 1990s.[81] Since then, corporate reporting has expanded significantly in business popularity and coverage to include 'triple bottom line' (i.e. social, economic and environmental) reporting, ESG reporting and other sustainability reporting. By 2005, reporting on business-related social, economic and environmental matters had become mainstream within the annual reporting practices of the top 250 companies of the Fortune 500, and was approaching mainstream acceptance amongst the Top 100 companies in more than 15 countries.[82]

All of this sits within wider CSR trends in the alignment of business strategy and CSR, identification and management of both financial and non-financial material risks, and disclosure and reporting of business-related elements that interact with social, environmental and other concerns.[83] The trend towards business use and disclosure of both financial and non-financial information is also part of what is commonly termed 'business performance management' (BPM), which increasingly focuses upon categories of information such as business information, corporate governance information, management information, financial performance measures and non-financial performance measures.[84]

Corporate reporting frameworks under the corporate laws of the USA, the UK and Australia either permit or require reference to financial and non-financial information about corporations, and how that information relates to the social, economic and environmental dimensions of their governance and success. EU directives are progressively expanding the range of necessary matters for corporate reporting, and the European Parliament's 2007 resolution on CSR perhaps signals a hardening of resolve on the need to move beyond voluntary social and environmental reporting by European companies, to place sustainability reporting on an equal footing with mandatory financial reporting. Corporate self-reporting, external report auditing and independent corporate ratings in the area of corporate responsibility and sustainability are becoming mainstream, although reliable socio-ethical standard-setting still lags behind relatively recent environmental standards as well as long-standing financial, auditing and accounting measures of corporate performance.

Importantly, non-financial information and yardsticks can often relate as much to the company as a wealth-creating business enterprise as they do to the company as a socially responsible entity. This is particularly true of non-financial yardsticks such as market share, employee satisfaction and efficiency, rate of corporate non-compliance and other regulatory breaches, product safety and reliability, web traffic, stakeholder engagement mechanisms, and customer loyalty and satisfaction (e.g. customer complaints and responses, delivery timeframes, and after-sales service and follow-up).[85] Many similar categories and items of information are also relevant under major CSR reporting frameworks, such as the GRI G3 guidelines. All of this underscores the rapidly expanding body of business literature and practice about the points of connection that are possible and even desirable nowadays between CSR, business models and market positioning.[86]

At the same time, tensions and differences remain between financial and non-financial reporting of various kinds.[87] This leads some commentators to differentiate conceptually between what might be termed 'non-financial reporting excluding social responsibility disclosure' and 'corporate social responsibility disclosure', as part of a call to recognize that 'corporate social responsibility disclosure' has its own regulatory rationales and audiences, and hence needs its own regulatory regime, whatever connections that regime might have with its counterpart.[88] In other words, what is material in a financial report for a target audience of existing and potential investors, investment analysts and other actors in the investment community can be very different in relevance and targeting from other reporting purposes, as demonstrated by variances in the corporate responsibility reporting approaches of different major companies globally and nationally.[89]

The connection between contemporary regulatory values and corporate reporting requirements is a major 21st century challenge for CSR-related corporate reporting. Under corporate regulatory systems which value transparency as a globally recognized corporate regulatory value,[90] the question is whether full transparency also requires corporate disclosure and reporting that is directed at wider public policy ends than current corporate regulation, not least in terms of recognizing and disclosing the full societal costs of corporate activity as well as its benefits for investors.[91] At this stage in the evolution of corporate disclosure and reporting, the primary normative approach underlying governmental regulation of non-financial reporting of all kinds, at least in the USA and the UK, and to a large extent in the EU too, is to facilitate credit and investment assessments, especially by shareholders but also by other providers of financial capital to companies, as distinct from enabling these and other stakeholders to assess a company's impact upon its host communities as well as its general contribution to societal and global well-being.[92] In other words, the orientation is still more towards current and potential investors, and the investment community more widely, as the primary focus for corporate disclosure and reporting, than towards satisfying the corporate expectations of other societal stakeholders or in demonstrating how well companies meet the public interest or otherwise serve the common good.[93] However, even in corporate regulatory regimes with this orientation, some opportunities for CSR-related disclosure and reporting arise in corporate governance requirements for managing and reporting material business risks, including business risks that stem from issues of corporate responsibility and sustainability, as recent Australian experience shows.[94]

International and comparative perspectives

Authoritative international and comparative sources of corporate reporting requirements demonstrate the recognized importance today of the interaction between business and societal sustainability, financial and non-financial business drivers, and even corporate governance and CSR reporting. 'The two main features of sustainability reporting are that, first, they attempt to deal with the three strands of social, environmental and economic dimensions in one report and, secondly, they express a commitment to involving stakeholders directly in the reporting process', notes one contemporary scholar of comparative corporate law and reporting, Bristol University's Professor Charlotte Villiers.[95] For the moment, the emphasis of officially regulated sustainability reporting remains firmly confined to sustainability reporting from the perspective of how companies relate discrete societal drivers to their material business strategies, risks and operations, as exemplified explicitly and most notably in sources as diverse as the OECD Guidelines,

OECD Principles, EU Accounts Modernisation Directive and other directives, UK business review requirements and Australian corporate reporting requirements.

The central requirement under the OECD Guidelines is for multinational business enterprises to provide disclosure 'regarding their activities, structure, financial situation and performance'.[96] This requirement extends beyond adequate financial disclosure, as they are 'also encouraged to apply high quality standards for non-financial information including environmental and social reporting where they exist'. Essential disclosures include '(m)aterial foreseeable risk factors' and '(m)aterial issues regarding employees and other stakeholders', either of which might straddle both shareholder and other stakeholder matters, on one hand, and financial and non-financial business information and drivers, on the other. In addition, businesses are 'encouraged' to disclose 'information on the social, ethical and environmental policies of the enterprise and other codes of conduct to which the company subscribes', as well as '(i)nformation on relationships with employees and other stakeholders'. Disclosure is mainly investor-centric and market-centric, as it is aimed squarely at what is needed 'to fully inform the investment decision and to avoid misleading the investor', and is further limited by considerations of business cost, administrative burden and secrecy of competitive success. In other words, the primary emphasis is upon what companies *must* disclose because it goes materially to the enterprise's financial performance in the eyes of the market, with social, environmental and non-financial dynamics and information being viewed through that prism.[97]

The OECD Principles similarly reinforce these principles of disclosure and transparency, particularly their primary focus upon investor-focused analysis of company finances and operations, even in relation to material risks, employee and stakeholder matters, and the focus of non-financial information about corporate performance.[98] Like the OECD Guidelines, the OECD Principles 'do not envision the disclosure of information in greater detail than is necessary to fully inform investors of the material and foreseeable risks of the enterprise'.[99] The emphasis in disclosing employee and stakeholder issues remains squarely upon anything that 'may materially affect the performance of the company'.[100] The OECD Principles also recommend disclosure of any stakeholder-orientated company policies and public positions covering 'business ethics, the environment, and other public policy commitments', because of the value of this information 'for investors and other users of information to better evaluate the relationship between companies and the communities in which they operate and the steps that companies have taken to implement their objectives'.[101] Framed in this way, the business–society nexus does not embrace all of the aspects of social and democratic accountability that are now part of the global CSR debate.

European corporate responsibility and sustainability reporting requirements

European initiatives match a wider trend worldwide towards inclusion of socio-ethical, environmental and governance aspects in both voluntary and officially regulated corporate reporting. For some time, policy and regulatory debate in the EU has progressively sharpened its focus upon enhancing overall corporate responsibility, governance and reporting in general, together with boardroom accountability in particular. As noted in the preamble to the June 2006 Directive of the European Parliament and of the Council, companies operating in the EU 'should be obliged to disclose an annual corporate governance statement as a specific and clearly identifiable section of the annual report', with relevant attention to business-related social and environmental concerns. In enhancing boardroom reporting accountability for a company's business, for example, EU directives accept that relevant disclosure 'should not be restricted to the financial aspects of the company's business', so that 'where appropriate, this should lead to an analysis of environmental and social aspects necessary for an understanding of the company's development, performance or position'.[102] Accordingly, 'the analysis shall include both financial and, where appropriate, non-financial key performance indicators . . . including information relating to environmental and employee matters', at least '[to] the extent necessary for an understanding of the company's development, performance, and position'.[103] Other directives further enhance collective boardroom responsibility for corporate governance and reporting, emphasize the importance of disclosing relevant corporate governance information and, in that context, note the relevance of social and environmental information for investors' understanding of the company's success and prospects.[104]

Improvements to date in the modernization and harmonization of requirements for financial accounting, business reporting and corporate governance set the scene for a further wave of policy and regulatory attention to other aspects of boardroom accountability (e.g. the scope and content of directors' duties) and corporate reporting (e.g. broader corporate sustainability reporting requirements). The European Parliament's 2007 resolution on CSR, for example, signals the future possibility of more expansive corporate responsibility and sustainability reporting requirements, 'so that social and environmental reporting is included alongside financial reporting requirements', especially in light of the inadequacies of voluntary trends in social and environmental reporting, in which 'only a minority of the reports use internationally accepted standards and principles, cover the company's full supply chain or involve independent monitoring and verification'.[105] While boardroom accountability to companies, investors and regulators for the fairness and correctness of conventional financial corporate reporting is now a standard feature in many jurisdictions, non-financial information and drivers of business success constitute a category of information with which many directors are still unfamiliar, uneasy, or both.

UK business review and reporting requirements
Under the impetus of applicable EU directives, UK law is moving further in the direction of narrative reporting, along the European path of enhanced reporting of non-financial information, collective boardroom accountability and improved corporate governance disclosure. UK corporate law now requires annual directors' reports for particular businesses to include a business review which, in the case of listed public companies, must contain relevant information and appropriate business-related performance indicators about 'the company's employees', 'social and community issues' and 'environmental matters (including the impact of the company's business on the environment)'.[106] This is explored further in Chapter 7.

Australian corporate reporting requirements and the revised ASX CGC principles
In terms of CSR-related reporting, Australia is moving gradually from a corporate reporting regime that requires environmental reporting to one that also facilitates some aspects of corporate governance, responsibility and sustainability reporting. In Australia, annual directors' reports must include 'details of the [company's] performance in rela-

tion to environmental regulation', for example. However, corporate responsibility and sustainability factors that materially affect business operations and performance fall within additional legislative reporting requirements for listed public companies.[107] Official regulatory requirements affecting corporate responsibility and sustainability reporting by companies listed on the Australian Securities Exchange (ASX) appear in ASX listing rules[108] and revised Corporate Governance Principles and Recommendations from the ASX CGC. Australia's corporate regulatory requirements ultimately remain firmly fixed upon relating any use of non-financial information and sustainability reporting to business risks and drivers for corporate strategies, finances and operations.[109] At this stage, the integration of financial and non-financial information, and any reference to social, environmental and sustainability perspectives, are all channelled tightly through that reporting focus.

Although Australia's legislative requirements for annual corporate reporting are not as detailed as UK corporate law in their coverage of business review and reporting requirements for non-financial and sustainability reporting, other regulatory and business guidelines clearly signal the arrival of this kind of reporting as part of mainstream corporate reporting in Australia. Both ASX listing rule requirements and the explanatory parliamentary material accompanying the introduction of Australia's version of the superseded UK Operating and Financial Review (OFR), for example, incorporate reference to authoritative guidance from the Group of 100 (G100) that heads in this general direction.[110] According to reporting guidelines developed by this association of senior finance and accounting executives associated with Australia's major corporations and government-owned business enterprises, the reported review of a company's operations and financial condition should contain 'a discussion and analysis of key financial and non-financial performance indicators (KPIs) used by management in their assessment of the company and its performance', with these KPIs covering 'multiple perspectives such as sustainability measures including social and environmental performance measures'.[111]

The primary legislative requirement for Australia's equivalent of the UK's reportable business review is as follows:[112]

> The directors' report for a financial year for . . . a listed public company must also contain information that members of the company would reasonably require to make an informed assessment of:
>
> (a) the operations of the entity reported on; and
> (b) the financial position of the entity; and
> (c) the entity's business strategies and its prospects for future financial years.

This broad framework for reporting on a company's operations, financial position and prospects is one within which companies might take a narrow or wide approach to reporting matters of socially orientated corporate responsibility (CR) and sustainability. 'This requirement has the potential to increase sustainability/CR reporting and other disclosure by companies', according to the ASX CGC.[113] In short, under revised ASX CGC guidelines that commenced operation in 2008, corporate responsibility and sustainability risks that constitute material risks for a business enterprise are reportable matters. 'Where a company has risks relating to sustainability or corporate social responsibility (CR) that are material to its business they should be considered in the context of the revised Recommendation 7.2', according to the ASX CGC.[114]

By the end of 2008, the Australian Government was moving towards greater official recognition and regulation of the relationship between CSR and sustainability reporting, through a self-described customized and consultative approach, as distinct from indiscriminate mandatory regulation across all business organizations and industry sectors. Noting that the level of corporate responsibility and sustainability reporting voluntarily undertaken by Australian companies lagged well behind international best practice, Australia's Minister for Superannuation and Corporate Law announced new governmental proposals 'to examine opportunities that might improve the disclosure of sustainability risks and the strategies companies have in place for managing those risks', in light of the Australian Government's belief in 'the development of socially and environmentally sustainable business practices as vital to our future prosperity and international competitiveness'.[115]

US corporate reporting requirements

US regulation of corporate reporting broadly reinforces the contemporary need for some kind of narrative from directors to the market about a company's business performance, position and prospects. As in the EU, the UK, Australia and elsewhere, environmental compliance and protection are singled out for special attention. Under US securities law, for example, Regulation S-K's Item 101 (Description of Business) requires a business narrative that is heavily financial in focus, but with particular details that go explicitly to aspects of environmental compliance and sustainable business development under the law. For example, appropriate disclosure is required of present and anticipated 'material estimated capital expenditures for environmental control facilities', as well as any material impact of environmental compliance upon a company's or group's 'capital expenditures, earnings and competitive position'.[116] Disclosure of this and other information is required '(t)o the extent material to an understanding of the [company's] business taken as a whole'.[117] Similarly, disclosure of environmental proceedings against companies is also singled out for attention amongst the kinds of legal proceedings that can materially affect a company and its prospective liabilities.[118]

More widely, in terms of the potential for using and disclosing non-financial information and wider dimensions of social, environmental and sustainability performance, Regulation S-K's Item 303 (Management's Discussion and Analysis of Financial Condition and Results of Operations) (MD&A) requires disclosure of specific matters and other information that the company believes is 'necessary to an understanding of its financial condition, changes in financial condition and results of operations'.[119] Again, the focus remains tightly upon how these matters affect a company's business, considered primarily in terms of their impact upon its financial position and prospects from an investment perspective. It is aimed at providing investors 'and other users' with meaningful information for assessing a company's 'financial condition and results of operations'.[120]

Commenting from a comparative perspective on Anglo-American developments in the field of non-financial reporting requirements, one commentator crystallizes what the UK business review and the US MD&A have in common in concluding that '(t)he UK business review is similar to the US MD&A [as] disclosures are to be made to shareholders as part of the directors' annual reporting obligation to shareholders, enhancing traditional financial disclosure, in order to facilitate assessment of investment value and facilitate shareholder discipline with respect to corporate profitability'.[121] Each of these components is important. They orientate and condition corporate responsibility and sustainability reporting in some directions (e.g. reporting what investors and markets need to know about a company's business dynamics) and not others (e.g. facilitating social accountability to all stakeholders for all corporate harm-causing or benefit-conferring actions). In the USA, as elsewhere, the question of wider social costing of corporate activity as an officially regulated reporting matter is another frontier in the 21st century rise of multinational corporate activity, climate change, and related concerns.

Climate risk and corporate disclosure

Climate risk creates new CSR-related disclosure problems. It adds new dimensions to old disclosure problems too. In the USA, the post-Enron Sarbanes–Oxley Act's overhaul of select aspects of corporate governance, disclosure and financial auditing and reporting expands the scope, timeliness and responsibility for disclosure in ways that lead to predictions that 'Sarbanes–Oxley may render CEOs and CFOs ultimately liable for the accuracy of disclosure of environmental-related liabilities in company financial filings, including climate change'.[122] Data collected for the global coalition of more than 200 signatories to the Carbon Disclosure Project (CDP) suggest that, while many leading companies in each national economy have a general awareness of climate change's potential implications for a business' future earnings, liabilities and risk profile, not all of them have a detailed knowledge of risks related to climate change or specific steps in place to address them.[123]

The potentially reportable business risks of carbon emissions, greenhouse gases and climate change fall into the following basic groups of risks. Physical risks of extreme weather events include workforce injury and illness, property damage and project delays. Social risks include demographic changes affecting business that result from climatic and ecological changes, such as consequent shifts in the migration and consumption patterns of mass populations. Technological risks include the impact of eco-innovative technology and renewable energy sources upon businesses and industries using traditional energy sources. Competitive risks include decreased consumer demand for products producing unacceptable greenhouse gas emissions, consequent loss of market share, and increased costs from being a late-mover in converting to alternative energy sources and products. Economic risks include the company-specific impact of market-led carbon pricing, capping and trading mechanisms. Regulatory risks include the business impact of the unfolding panoply of national and international laws and other official regulation designed to address climate change, partly in response to perceived inadequacies in voluntary responses to climate risks by individual countries and industry sectors. Litigation risks include everything from class actions by mass victims of corporate inaction in addressing climate change impacts to accommodation of the impact of major development and infrastructure projects in official decisions about licensing and other project approvals.[124]

Wider dimensions of corporate responsibility and sustainability reporting

The optimal conditions for social, environmental and sustainability reporting are yet to emerge across international, regional and national corporate regulatory regimes. At this stage, regulated corporate reporting requirements across major commercial jurisdictions overwhelmingly favour market-centric and investor-centric perspectives over stakeholder-centric and societally orientated perspectives, in the sense that the primary emphasis is upon how financial and even societal factors relate to corporate profitability rather than societal accountability. 'To be effective, social and environmental reporting activity requires recognition of corporate social responsibility and accountability and an acceptance of the view that the needs and interests of those affected by corporate activity are as relevant as the profit-maximisation interests of shareholders', notes Professor Villiers in her landmark analysis of corporate reporting requirements in Europe, the UK and elsewhere, adding that 'for social and environmental reporting to be fully effective in a way that ultimately improves corporate behaviour it arguably requires to be viewed as important independently and regardless of the financial performance of the company'.[125] On some levels, of course, the gap between corporate profitability and societal accountability is narrowed through a broadening of corporate vision to factor in societal conditions that might meaningfully have a ripple or bounce-back effect upon corporate profitability, without ever becoming co-extensive with everything that is needed for the common good.

Twenty-first century developments in corporate responsibility and sustainability are progressively exposing the weaknesses and limits of conventional corporate disclosure and reporting. Until relatively recently, corporate disclosure and reporting have been heavily financial in focus and methodology, more based upon financial than non-financial drivers of corporate success, more backward-looking upon historical corporate financial performance than forward-looking about corporate prospects and risks, largely orientated towards informed investors and markets as its desired audience, and heavily centred upon the kinds of financial wealth-maximizing concerns presumed to dominate the investment considerations of those investors and markets.[126] As Professor Villiers describes, this dominant approach privileges particular kinds of information, methodologies, audiences and orientations over others that might equally bear upon sustainable corporate profit-making or else serve public policy goals beyond corporate profit-maximization for shareholders. Indeed, even within its own frame of reference, the traditional approach to corporate disclosure and responsibility is increasingly being revealed as one that is also limited in its capacity to deliver its desired shareholder-centred ends.[127]

Corporate responsibility and sustainability reporting frameworks and measures are gathering acceptance worldwide, most notably through the GRI, its infusion of sustainability perspectives, its alignment with other frameworks (e.g. the Global Compact) and its high-level political endorsement.[128] Areas for improvement in future internal and external corporate reporting include: (a) greater integration between corporate responsibility and corporate governance arrangements; (b) further embedding of corporate responsibility within organizational operations and decision-making; (c) closer alignment of risk management and controls with corporate responsibility and sustainability concerns; (d) better articulation of the relation between financial and non-financial performance risks and drivers; (e) enhanced assessment of the organization-specific business case for building corporate community initiatives into business strategy and competitive positioning; (f) more information about plans, outcomes and targets for corporate responsibility matters generally and for corporate relationship-building and community investment in particular; (g) greater integration of full supply and distribution chain standard-setting, monitoring and enforcement within reporting of overall corporate responsibility and governance; (h) increased use of internationally accepted CSR-related reporting frameworks and standards; and (i) increased certification and verification of disclosed and reported matters on corporate responsibility, governance and sustainability.[129]

Still, there is much work yet to do. In her comparative study of corporate reporting regimes, Professor Villiers outlines requirements for enhancing socially responsible and reportable corporate behaviour as follows:[130]

> A clear rationale for mandatory social and environmental reporting is required [and] a critical question for policy-makers is how far disclosure of social and environmental impacts can be an effective means to improve corporate behaviour. To make it effective a number of other criteria for reporting must be met: the issues that can be reported on must match the interests of stakeholders; there must be a measure or a metric that accurately captures performance and can be applied across organisations; that measure or metric should be audited; that measure or metric should be communicated to the appropriate stakeholders; and the relevant stakeholders should respond. These points indicate that more than just transparency is required. Public response to corporate activity is also necessary, entailing a two-way discussion that leads to influence on the decision-making process and activities of the company.

As in other areas of CSR implementation, such requirements reflect the values and associated processes of consensual setting of reportable corporate performance measures, meaningful stakeholder participation in reporting-related aspects of corporate governance, publicly verified and trustworthy corporate communication, and corporate openness to public and stakeholder influences. All of this brings corporate disclosure and reporting back full circle to the interests properly served by corporate governance and the systems for regulating and practising it. The evolution of corporate governance beyond a solitary focus upon issues of corporate management and control arising between companies, boards and shareholders pushes corporate disclosure and reporting at least some way towards meaningful stakeholder-sensitive corporate responsibility and sustainability reporting. In that light, CSR raises important 21st century questions about exploring afresh the connections between the three elements of corporate governance, corporate responsibility and sustainability, and corporate disclosure and reporting. In turn, these connections are grounded in the deeper themes and mechanics of corporate democracy, constitutionalism, and meta-regulation explored in earlier chapters.

NOTES

1. Braithwaite and Drahos, 2000: 539–543.
2. Zerk, 2006: 284–297, and 303.
3. Corcoran, 1997: 65.
4. Ratner, 2001: 489–496.
5. Zerk, 2006: 299–310.
6. Ibid.: 61.
7. Ibid.: 61.
8. Zerk, 2007.
9. E.g. UN Doc. CERD/C/USA/CO/6 (February 2008).
10. Zerk, 2007: 32.
11. See Ch 10.
12. See Ch 2.
13. Zerk, 2006: 134–140; and Bantekas, 2004: 317–327.
14. Williams and Conley, 2005b: 103.

15. Zerk, 2006: 243.
16. Ibid.: 262.
17. Ibid.: 262.
18. Ibid.: 263–276.
19. Ibid.: 70–71.
20. Muchlinski, 2007: 456–458.
21. Zerk, 2006: 262.
22. Ibid.: 279–283, 303–310.
23. Ibid.: 299.
24. Ibid.: 26.
25. Whitman et al, 2008.
26. Zerk, 2007: 11–12.
27. Farrar, 2008: 502.
28. Hill, 2007: 16.
29. Ibid.: 9–13, 15–16.
30. Laufer, 2006.
31. Bosch, 2002: 290.
32. Visentini, 1998: 834–835.
33. Bradley et al, 1999a: 11.
34. Bessler et al, 1997: 3; quoted in Austin et al, 2005: 7.
35. Austin et al, 2005: 7–8.
36. Scott, 2008: 172, 182.
37. E.g. 'networks', 'webs', 'nodes' or 'regimes' of governance: see ibid.: 172.
38. E.g. steering, complying with and realigning governance behaviour under cybernetic analysis of governance controls, or the 'enabling environment' of 'drivers', 'tools' and 'human capacities and institutions' as foundations for CSR: see Scott, 2008: 172–173; and Ward, 2008: 11.
39. Scott, 2008: 178.
40. Drutman and Cray, 2004: 90–91.
41. OECD, 2000: 6.
42. OECD, 2004: 46.
43. Ibid.: 46.
44. NZSC, 2004.
45. ASX CGC, 2003.
46. CPWGRB, 2008: 12.
47. Ibid.: 16.
48. Ruggie, 2009: [27].
49. Quoted in Lydenberg and Grace, 2008: 28.
50. UK Combined Code, Section 2, E.1; and ISC, 2002: 4.
51. Corporations Act 2001 (Cth), section 1324.
52. Baxt, 2002: 163–167; and Lumsden and Fridman, 2007: 173, 177.
53. Baxt, 2002: 163–164. See also Lumsden and Fridman, 2007: 177.
54. Baxt, 2002: 163–164. See also Lumsden and Fridman, 2007: 177.
55. Dhir, 2006. For other academic discussion of the position of shareholder proposals in different countries see Bottomley and Forsyth, 2007.
56. Dhir, 2006: 407–408.
57. Monks and Minow, 2004: 162.
58. Black, 2006; and Dhir, 2006.
59. Porter and Kramer, 2006: 80.
60. Ross et al, 2007: 264–265.
61. As reported in 'Investors File 54 Global Warming-Related Shareholder Resolutions', Environmental Leader   (http://www.environmentalleader.com/2008/03/09/investors-file-54-global-warming-related-shareholder-resolutions/), 9 March 2008.
62. Hanks, 1991: 98; and Orts, 1992: 20.
63. On these points see Orts, 1992: 16–25.
64. Companies Act 2006 (UK), section 172.
65. For more detailed analysis of the CSR-related aspects of UK corporate law see Ch 7.
66. PJCCFS, 2006: [4.78].
67. Austin et al, 2005: 281. See also Heydon, 1987: 134–135.
68. *Peoples Department Stores Inc (Trustee of) v Wise* 2004 SCC 68.
69. AAR, 2008: 10. The author was involved as a consultant in the preparation of this report.
70. UNEP FI, 2005: 6.

71. Ibid.: 10–11; original emphasis.
72. Ibid.: 13.
73. Ibid.: 13–14.
74. Donald and Taylor, 2008: 57.
75. Pensions Act 1995 (UK), section 35; and Occupational Pension Schemes (Investment) Regulations 1996 (UK), regulation 11A, inserted by the Occupational Pension Schemes (Investment, and Assignment, Forfeiture, Bankruptcy etc.) Amendment Regulations 1999 (UK).
76. Corporations Act 2001 (Cth), sections 1013D(1)(l) and 1013DA.
77. ASIC, 2003.
78. *The Economist*, 2008: 22.
79. Ibid.: 9.
80. For further discussion of CSR-related aspects of corporate disclosure and reporting, see Chs 1, 3, 4, 6 and 7.
81. CCPA and BCA, 2007: 10; KPMG, 2005: 7.
82. KPMG, 2005: 4.
83. See Ch 8.
84. Chiu, 2006a.
85. On these non-financial yardsticks see ibid.
86. E.g. Porter and Kramer, 2002; Porter and Kramer, 2006; and Brugmann and Prahalad, 2007. See also Ch 8.
87. Chiu, 2006a.
88. Ibid.
89. KPMG, 2005.
90. On transparency as a regulatory value see Braithwaite and Drahos, 2000.
91. On social costing of corporate activity see Greenfield, 2004.
92. See, in particular, the Anglo-American analysis along these lines in Chiu, 2006a.
93. Villiers, 2006 authoritatively distinguishes between conventional corporate responsibility and sustainability reporting (which is grounded in a company's financial success and market accountability) and 21st century needs for corporate responsibility and sustainability reporting to service a wider range of public accountability needs. This fundamental distinction informs much of the analysis here. Much work remains to be done in transcending this distinction in theory-building, regulatory schemes, and business reporting practice, in light of emerging awareness of the dependence of sustainable corporate success upon interaction with other systems of governance, regulation, and responsibility, as canvassed here.
94. ASX CGC, 2006a; and ASX CGC, 2006b.
95. Villiers, 2006: 232.
96. On these and following requirements see OECD, 2000: 20.
97. OECD Guidelines, 2000: 45.
98. OECD Principles, 2004: 22, and 53–54.
99. Ibid.: 53.
100. Ibid.: 53.
101. Ibid.: 50–51.
102. Directive 2003/51/EC.
103. Ibid.
104. Directive 2006/46/EC.
105. European Parliament Resolution of 13 March 2007 on *Corporate Social Responsibility: A New Partnership*.
106. Companies Act 2006 (UK), sub-sections 417(5) and 417(6). UK corporate reporting requirements are discussed in more detail in Chs 6 and 7.
107. Corporations Act 2001 (Cth), sections 299(1)(f) and 299A respectively.
108. Especially, in this context: Listing Rule 4.10 (Disclosure of Corporate Governance Practices) and Listing Rule 4.10.17 (Review of Operations and Activities).
109. ASX CGC, 2007b.
110. ASX LR 4.10.3; ASX Guidance Notes 9, 9A, and 10; G100, 2003; G100 and KPMG, 2008; and Nolan, 2007.
111. G100, 2003: [8].
112. Corporations Act 2001 (Cth), section 299A(1). Disclosure exemptions apply to material which 'is likely to result in unreasonable prejudice' to the companies involved: see section 299A(3).
113. ASX CGC, 2006b: 31.
114. ASX CGC, 2007c: 2.
115. Sherry, 2008.
116. Item 101(c)(1)(xii).

117. Item 101(c)(1).
118. Item 103 (Legal Proceedings).
119. Item 303(a).
120. Item 303(a), Instructions (paragraph 2).
121. Chiu, 2006b: 295.
122. Ross et al, 2007: 266.
123. Gettler, 2006.
124. This catalogue of risks draws significantly upon Jeffery, 2007.
125. Villiers, 2006: 229–230.
126. Ibid.: 296.
127. Ibid.: 296.
128. E.g. PJCCFS, 2006; and G8 Summit, 2007.
129. KPMG, 2005: 19; CCPA and BCA, 2007: x–xi; Grant Thornton, 2008; and European Parliament resolution of 13 March 2007 on CSR.
130. Villiers, 2006: 261.

6. Sensitizing boardroom obligations to corporate social responsibility

COMPARATIVE 21ST CENTURY TRENDS IN REGULATING BOARDROOM OBLIGATIONS

> Internationally, there is a growing realization that directing enterprises with integrity must be taken seriously if we are to have effective wealth-generating, and public service delivering, organizations. The future realization of a 'civil society' depends on it. Across the world the general public and politicians are realizing that matters cannot continue as they are for boards of directors . . . There are two significant pressures for change which will bring about a trans-formation. First, the demand for more 'shareholder democracy' needs to be accommodated if boards are to answer the public's perception that boards tend to put their own interests before their shareholders' . . . The second pressure for change is political intervention in corporate affairs on behalf of the general public, which is manifested increasingly through the growing debate on the 'shareholder/stakeholder' balance in corporate governance.
>
> –Best-selling corporate governance writer Bob Garratt, *The Fish Rots From The Head (The Crisis in Our Boardrooms – Developing the Crucial Skills of the Competent Director)*[1]

CSR is progressively making its presence felt in the legal and regulatory frameworks underpinning corporate governance, boardroom decision-making and business reporting in Europe, North America and the broader Commonwealth. In this way, the develop-ment of corporate regulatory systems bears the hallmarks of the wider CSR movement's impact upon corporate law and regulation as a whole.[2]

The transnational examples of this trajectory are reaching critical mass, as illustrated in this chapter. In the ongoing 21st century roll-out of Europe's broad CSR agenda, recent institutional dialogue between the European Commission and the European Parliament about CSR includes debate about the balance of public and private interests properly covered by directors' duties and other boardroom obligations. In the USA, directors' duties and business judgments are responsive to Delaware-led corporate jurisprudence as well as to the wave of anti-takeover and corporate constituency laws progressively passed in many US states in the last quarter of the 20th century, all of which frame boardroom consideration of the relation between shareholder interests and other corporate stake-holder interests in discrete ways. At the start of the 21st century, Canada's highest court explicitly recognized that directors' duties embrace a wide range of shareholder and stakeholder interests.

Viewed through the prism of CSR, the UK Company Law Review process, begun in the death throes of the last century and brought to fruition mid-way through the first decade of this century, has produced reforms of directors' duties, business reviews and corporate reporting which explicitly factor non-shareholder interests into the new regulatory mix. By mid-way through the first decade of the 21st century, two major Australian governmental bodies reported on possible CSR-based reform of directors' duties,[3] while the country's premier standard-setting body for corporate governance overhauled its approach to regulating corporate governance in ways that put corporate responsibility risks and sustainability reporting squarely in the spotlight.[4]

In short, we are witnessing the bounded socialization of corporate obligations generally and directors' duties in particular across all of these jurisdictions, in one shape or another. This trend is one of 'socialization' because of the stakeholder-sensitivity it introduces, and yet 'bounded' because of the limits imposed upon it through various shareholder-orientated mechanisms. Still, the debate is no longer over *whether* but *how* boardroom decision-making and reporting should accommodate a company-specific balance of shareholder, non-shareholder and societal considerations, *and* to what ends. The law regulating the obligations, liabilities and reporting requirements confronting company directors is a strong driver and moderator of socially responsible corporate behaviour. As experienced corporate lawyer and corporate responsibility advocate Robert Hinkley notes,[5] what each jurisdiction puts into the content of directors' duties offers a critical point of leverage in bringing about necessary changes in both boardroom conduct and wider corporate behaviour.

At the same time, we are yet to see a paradigm shift in the orientation and content of corporate law and regulation, towards a vision of corporate governance, responsibility and sustainability, for TNCs in particular, that fully accommodates corporate, societal and global concerns *as they relate to* the corporation. In light of the pivotal importance of directors' duties to both corporate law and CSR, and their prominence already in transnational corporate law reform initiatives, this chapter focuses directly upon different legal and regulatory models for sensitizing boardroom legal obligations to CSR concerns. This includes optional models for directors' duties, associated business judgment rules, and the arguments surrounding each model, as well as the implications for corporate risk management and reporting. Such an analysis of the policy and regulatory options on offer can inform future CSR-related law reform of boardroom obligations across different corporate regulatory systems.

MAPPING POLICY, REGULATORY AND LAW REFORM OPTIONS FOR DIRECTORS' DUTIES

Overview

Directors' duties can be socialized in a variety of ways. So, law reform options on directors' duties can take a number of forms. At least on the orthodox view of corporate law, introducing heightened stakeholder-sensitivity into the law of directors' duties must be done (if at all) in a way that does not threaten the integrity and coherence of corporate law itself, as this late 20th century warning from a prominent Anglo-Commonwealth scholar of corporate law reveals:[6]

> (C)ompany law (at least as it stands, but probably in any form it could potentially take) must acknowledge that it has no mechanism to ensure the fulfilment of obligations of social responsibility . . . To extend directors' duties so as to embrace the interests of employees and similar groups (and a *fortiori* so as to include more general concerns such as the environment) is to deny any effective role for the law and the courts. The concept of 'duty' ceases to be justiciable, and company law lacks proper enforcement procedures. At best, these enlarged 'duties' can only provide directors with a defence against self-centred claims brought by shareholders.

Importantly, any changes to corporate law must also be assessed by reference to their potential knock-on effect elsewhere in the system of corporate law. As the UK Company Law Review Steering Group noted in its final report, leading to the development of what ultimately became the UK Companies Act in 2006, a change to the law of directors' duties to make it more stakeholder-sensitive generates follow-up issues about shareholder rights, stakeholder remedies and regulatory enforcement. So, any policy-making, law reform or other modelling of options for increasing the stakeholder-sensitivity of the law of directors' duties must also have an eye to these ancillary consequences for other parts of a corporate regulatory system.

The relationship between shareholder and non-shareholder interests under the law of directors' duties has a number of structural features. First, in most (if not all) jurisdictions consideration of shareholder and non-shareholder interests is not an end in itself, in terms of advancing any of those interests for their own sake, detached from their relationship to the collective business enterprise. Rather, it is a means to the end of acting in the best interests of a corporation, however that notion might be conceived, including variations that encompass corporate success within a wider societal context.

Secondly, there are important distinctions between what is proscribed, prescribed and permitted under the law of directors' duties. Being allowed to take account of a particular interest is different from being required to consider it, which differs from deciding in favour of that interest. In turn, this differs from assessing and disclosing how that interest affects a company's business drivers and risks, which in turn differs from accounting for how that interest and its consideration relates to wider societal interests. So, directors will not necessarily be in breach of their duties simply by failing to take account of something that they are entitled to consider, but are not compelled to consider, in their boardroom decision-making.[7] Even where consideration of designated corporate interests is mandated, a failure by corporate boards to consider relevant interests adequately or at all still might not amount to a breach of duty, at least not at the instance of any non-shareholders whose interests are affected, unless that failure forms part of a wider set of circumstances that lead to actionable financial loss for the company and those who legally stand in its shoes. Some of those issues await further exploration under the UK's 21st century model for directors' duties, as detailed in Chapter 7.

Thirdly, the societal purposes served by mandated or permissive inclusion of designated interests in boardroom decision-making extend beyond facilitating the self-interestedness of shareholders and non-shareholders alike. Wider societal values of inclusion, participation, transparency and accountability, for example, are also at stake in corporate deliberative processes. Finally, various elements of the corporate law relating to directors' duties can be modified or reformulated without necessarily changing the structure of directors' duties themselves, as when the notion of what constitutes a company's interests for the purposes of various directors' duties is refashioned to include particular stakeholder interests along with shareholder interests. For example, 'the duty to act in the best interests of the corporation . . . must logically include a requirement that corporate directors and officers cause a corporation to act in a socially responsible manner, both as a good citizen and as a good governor', urges corporate law professor, Suzanne Corcoran.[8]

Other corporate law doctrines that relate to boardroom obligations might be interpreted or modified to accommodate the full range of shareholding and non-shareholding interests in play, such as recasting accepted doctrines (e.g. doctrines concerning 'fraud on the company') in ways that recognize 'the enlarged constituency' of corporate interests potentially affected.[9] Of course, even radical steps to increase employee participation and empowerment in corporate governance and decision-making cannot completely replace the need for non-employee stakeholder safeguards and other official regulatory controls.[10] Here, as elsewhere, a balance of reform mechanisms is required.

Directors can also be required to engage with non-shareholding stakeholders in ways that travel beyond simply considering their interests, but which still fall short of owing any enforceable legal duties to them directly, such as obligations of consultation, disclosure and corporate governance participation in favour of such stakeholders. Long before his involvement in the UK's CLR Steering Group, the late Professor John Parkinson foresaw the considerable difficulties inherent in 'proposals to extend further the list of groups whose interests management should consider in running the company', at least 'with a view to limiting the harmful effect of corporate activities on them', with the consequence that reformation of directors' duties could travel only a limited distance in improving socially responsible corporate behaviour.[11] Hence, in reframing directors' duties, the basic choice is between empowering corporate boards to consider a wide variety of interests, incorporating a broader set of societal interests in the boardroom decision-making calculus, and giving voices to a broader set of stakeholders in corporate governance.

Business antipathy towards being forced by law to achieve particular CSR outcomes can be alleviated, at least in part, by treating CSR in procedural rather than substantive terms, at least in boardroom decision-making. Instead of turning the boardroom decision-making process towards socio-ethical controversy by making it strive for a notional best outcome based upon an ultimately unobtainable calculus of societal values, the focus is turned towards measures such as designated statutory criteria for corporate decision-making, as well as '*procedural* fiduciary duties [of] disclosure, audit, justification, consultation and organization'.[12] Treating CSR 'as a process concept thus takes responsibility to be an attribute of decision-making processes rather than as involving compliance with a set of specific standards for guiding conduct', thereby bypassing the asserted danger of corporate social engineering by businesses ill-equipped to decide controversial issues of public ethics and policy.[13] At the same time, this process-based conception of corporate responsibility works in tandem with the model of managerial discretion under prevailing legal orthodoxy, by sensitizing it to the inclusion of third-party interests.[14]

Key Boardroom Decision-making Objections

Options for remaking the law of directors' duties with CSR in mind must be framed with sensitivity to the fundamental objections that such law reform efforts generate. For example, the submission by the Australian Institute of Company Directors (AICD) to one of Australia's official national CSR inquiries in the 21st century warns against the nightmarish vision of 'a generalized "social responsibility" obligation' being additionally imposed upon directors, under which a 'vague' and largely indefinable mass of unbalanceable stakeholder interests results not only in accountability to shareholders being 'diluted', but also in directors having their essential decision-making 'compass' thrown out of kilter.

Some CSR sceptics believe, for example, that broadening the responsibilities of corporate management beyond service to the financial interests of the shareholding constituency increases the costs of decision-making, and also dilutes management's amenability to the discipline of shareholder oversight as a societally effective means of keeping corporate management in check.[15] The problems with this school of thought include understating some important things – namely, the problems of effective shareholder oversight in companies with mass shareholdings, the complexity of shareholder interests and investor motivations, the ways in which corporate directors and managers in practice already approach the task of making decisions that include various shareholder and non-shareholder interests, and the changed conditions of the 21st century global business environment.

The commonest and seemingly most threatening objection to expanding corporate law's concerns beyond orthodox corporate governance concerns, at least as a decision-making mandate for directors, is two-pronged. It rests upon the unworkability of having multi-fiduciary obligations to numerous interest-holders (i.e. the 'pluralist duty' objection), together with the unavailability of a suitable metric for ordering them (i.e. the 'decisional guidance' objection). The first prong echoes the classic criticism of Easterbrook and Fischel that 'a manager told to serve two masters (a little for the equity holders, a little for the community) has been freed of both and is answerable to neither'.[16] Similarly, in the pithy conclusion of corporate governance theorist and World Bank economist, David Ellerman, '(o)ne sometimes has the suspicion that "stakeholder" governance ideas are being floated by managers who know that, by being responsible to everyone, they will be accountable to no one'.[17] This echoes the concern about diluted corporate accountability expressed by leading Australian corporate law and governance scholar, Professor Ian Ramsay:[18]

> A powerful argument in favour of the existing law is that it does provide for an effective review of the actions of directors. If the law were changed so that directors had direct duties to a broad range of stakeholders, the irony is that this may result in directors being less accountable.

The objection's first prong can be answered in a number of ways. As corporate law already recognizes, directors' duties are characteristically owed to the company and not directly to shareholders. As a focus for directors' duties, the success of the company as a collective business enterprise can be cast in different ways. Adding more interests to the boardroom decision-making mix might mean that 'for the future it may be necessary for the law to conceptualize "the company" not as the corporate *membership* but as the corporate *enterprise*, as an aid to the formulation of new rules of directors' duties in cases where interests other than purely membership-interests are affected', argues one Anglo-Commonwealth corporate law professor.[19]

Moreover, duties to the company as a collective business enterprise are not fulfilled simply by doing what favours a majority of shareholders at a particular point in time. Legal duties concerning shareholders can accommodate non-shareholder interests too, at least where they coincide in achieving corporate success. In addition, while some shareholder and non-shareholder interests might be competing or incommensurable, others are not. Moreover, due consideration and involvement of non-shareholder interests can occur in corporate decision-making without the need for a duty-focused legal obligation to advance the interests of all stakeholders.

If the public good served by shareholders exerting discipline over corporate executives is reconceived in terms of optimizing shareholder wealth-generation within the collective bounds of legal, market and socio-ethical norms, the interaction of public and private interests served through the law of directors' duties is not reducible to short-term financial gain for present shareholders. In any case, within both corporate law and other areas of law impinging upon corporations, the priority of shareholder interests over all else is already postponed in various circumstances. Finally, framing different interests in terms of their trumping quality can be transcended by higher-order alignment of corporate and societal interests in company-specific ways, as in the public goods of giving corporate voices to a diverse corporate constituency affected by corporate activity and incorporating democratic imperatives in all of society's major institutions.

In terms of the objection's second prong, even different groups of shareholders can have competing interests and investment motivations too, notwithstanding their common interest in financial gain, which at least complicates the corporate decision-making calculus. Corporate executives already 'balance' a variety of public and private interests in making decisions that comply with all corporate and general laws. The reality that consideration and protection of a wide variety of non-shareholder interests (e.g. environmental protection, climate change mitigation, equal opportunity and diversity in the workplace, etc.) can be introduced into the calculus of boardroom decision-making through the medium of compliance with the law reinforces an important distinction. Questions about the source and legitimacy of any need to take account of non-shareholder interests must not be confused with the workability of doing so under prevailing corporate methodology. In any case, corporate practice is moving towards more sophisticated treatment of financial and non-financial factors in business strategizing, risk management and public reporting.

Making decisions about a wide spectrum of societal interests is not inherently impossible, as public officials regularly apply 'public interest' criteria. Additional objections based upon a strict dividing line between business, governmental and community areas of responsibility properly go to different points about organizational functions, decision-making contexts and reasoning processes. For example, a company that considers the specific social, environmental and other consequences of a proposed development project is engaged in an enterprise that cannot simply be characterized as an impermissible usurpation of government's responsibility for social welfare or an incomprehensible attempt to satisfy and balance a set of incommensurable societal interests. The fact that prevailing business decision-making mindsets and tools do not yet encompass all that is required of them in making companies responsive to trans-modal governance, multi-order regulation and inter-connected responsibility is not a good reason for denying this need, given the unfolding 21st century business environment worldwide.

First Option – Unconfirmed Regulatory Consensus on Permissible Stakeholder Consideration

> (T)he legal model has traditionally regarded the shareholders' interests as exclusive, in the sense that other groups may be benefited only to the extent that this furthers the interests of the members. Thus the interests of employees, customers, or the local community, for example, may be served only as a means of increasing shareholder wealth and may not be treated as ends in their own right . . . But while promoting non-shareholder interests is not a permissible management objective, the (limited) satisfaction of third party expectations is often a prerequisite of maximising profits, and hence consideration of them is not precluded by the legal model.
>
> – Professor John Parkinson, *Corporate Power and Responsibility: Issues in the Theory of Company Law*[20]

Even in jurisdictions where no corporate laws explicitly permit or alternatively require directors to consider both shareholder and non-shareholder interests as they relate to the company, the issue of stakeholder consideration by directors remains alive. This is because the governing law still must take a position on the issue, as authoritatively confirmed or else left undetermined at the highest legislative and judicial levels. Moreover, even if the prevailing official regulatory consensus in any jurisdiction is that the legal duty of directors to the company is to advance the interests of shareholders as a whole, this still leaves important questions for directors, their advisers, and those who adjudicate on such laws about the extent to which other stakeholder consideration is necessary, and to what ends.

Accordingly, the first possible model of directors' duties for a corporate regulatory system is a demonstrable but officially unconfirmed regulatory consensus about the propriety of boardroom consideration of all stakeholder interests. This is the situation that prevails in jurisdictions where the law on directors' duties is not explicit on this point, but where nevertheless there is a strong consensus among political, business and legal elites that the existing law permits appropriate reference to relevant stakeholder considerations.

The argument is commonly made by business, company lawyers and corporate scholars that current Australian law on directors' duties, for example, implicitly permits directors to consider non-shareholder interests, where doing so relates to the company's interests and benefit. As one of Australia's leading corporate law academics, Professor Ian Ramsay, concludes:[21]

> (T)he argument has been made that the existing law does not allow directors to consider the interests of stakeholders other than shareholders. I suggest this isn't correct. Directors must act in the best interests of the company and this typically means the shareholders.
>
> However, this doesn't mean that directors cannot consider the interests of other stakeholders.

One problem is immediately apparent. If directors are implicitly allowed to take account of non-shareholder interests as part of what they do in fulfilling their statutory directors' duties, but without additional legal imperatives conditioning that decision, different boards might reach different views on when and how to do so. This risks producing inconsistent results from a regulatory perspective.

The tension between legal clarity and practical certainty is particularly acute in the outcomes of Australia's most recent official national inquiries into CSR. These inquiries reject the new UK legislative approach to directors' duties, encourage Australian company directors to incorporate appropriate CSR-related concerns in their business approach, accept that this is already permitted under Australian corporate law, and reinforce the importance of voluntary business uptake of CSR, but in ways that still leave much about the operationalization of this position at large. '(T)here is fundamental tension between two parallel views expressed by the Australian government inquiries [because] the committees roundly endorsed the view that to legislate along the lines of the United Kingdom would introduce uncertainty into Australian law [but] the committees have not given sufficient weight to the reasoning of how corporate social responsibility can be implemented into a workable and practical corporate law framework', according to one critical assessment of the outcomes of these early 21st century Australian CSR inquiries.[22]

In the USA, authoritative sources such as the American Law Institute's (ALI) *Principles of Corporate Governance*, many state corporate constituency statutes, and even the corporate jurisprudence of Delaware (as the premier corporate jurisdiction) all combine to allow considerable discretion for directors, in terms of the connection (if any) required between what directors decide and what benefits the company. US case law remains mixed in its judicial comments and outcomes on this point, leading commentators to suggest that the corporate regulatory system's overall efficiency trades on this ambiguity about the sufficiency of any connection between profit-sacrificing accommodation of non-shareholder interests and a corporation's business interests.[23]

The American Law Institute's recommendations, for example, outline the basic objective of a corporation as being 'the conduct of business activities with a view to enhancing corporate profit and shareholder gain', but immediately go on to qualify that basic position in these terms:[24]

> Even if corporate profit and shareholder gain are not thereby enhanced, the corporation, in the conduct of its business:
>
> (1) Is obliged, to the same extent as a natural person, to act within the boundaries set by law;
> (2) May take into account ethical considerations that are reasonably regarded as appropriate to the responsible conduct of business; and
> (3) May devote a reasonable amount of resources to public welfare, humanitarian, educational, and philanthropic purposes.

Although these ALI Principles offer distilled wisdom and authoritative guidance mainly for American audiences, in terms that are broadly consistent with the position in

US corporate law generally, their attempt to answer deep questions about the interplay between shareholder and non-shareholder considerations in corporate law and governance has analogous relevance beyond the USA too.[25] Significantly, this fundamental statement is framed in terms of a corporation's responsibility, as distinct from the specific duties and obligations of its directors and management, although the two are obviously linked.

The structure of the ALI Principles is still positioned within an orthodoxy of shareholder primacy, notwithstanding some elements that might suggest otherwise. 'The only qualifications to shareholder primacy and profit maximisation are that these aims should be achieved within the boundaries of the law; taking into consideration ethical considerations; ensuring responsible conduct of business; and that a reasonable amount of resources should be given to public welfare, humanitarian, educational and philanthropic purposes', as described by three Anglo-Australian scholars of comparative corporate governance in their assessment of the ALI Principles.[26] The pursuit of legal, ethical, philanthropic and other authorized objectives is limited to what a corporation might do 'in the conduct of its business', and not simply at large for society's sake. Accordingly, many of the deep questions of corporate responsibility and governance are still left to be resolved within this overarching structure.

Delaware corporate jurisprudence emphasizes that 'while concern for various corporate constituencies is proper when addressing a takeover threat, that principle is limited by the requirement that there be some rationally related benefit accruing to the stockholders'.[27] As this example illustrates, the law can use various limiting devices to control managerial discretion that goes too far away from shareholder primacy, including devices grounded alternatively in reasonableness (as to the amount of profit-sacrificing involved), rational benefit (to the investors), incidental proximity to the corporate business, and even long-term indirect advantages for the corporation and the market system to which it belongs.

In contrast to US corporate law, with its arguably more permissive approach to directors considering wider societal benefits in appropriate circumstances,[28] Anglo-Australian corporate law traditionally seeks a closer nexus between a corporation's business and any benefits conferred upon non-shareholders.[29] However, this still affords considerable discretion to directors. In the words of leading Australian corporate law and governance scholars, Anglo-Australian case law confirms that 'management may implement a policy of enlightened self-interest on the part of the company but may not be generous with company resources when there is no prospect of commercial advantage to the company'.[30]

Second Option – Judicial Confirmation of Implicit Permissible Stakeholder Consideration

The second possible model for a corporate regulatory system is authoritative judicial confirmation of the legal permissibility of considering a wide variety of stakeholder interests in boardroom decisions. This is the situation which prevailed in Canada this century in the immediate aftermath of its Supreme Court's landmark decision on directors' duties in *Trustee of Peoples Department Stores Inc v Wise*.[31] The Canada Business Corporations Act imposes what the Canadian Supreme Court termed a 'statutory fiduciary duty'[32] on directors to 'act honestly and in good faith with a view to the best interests of the corporation',[33] as well as a statutory duty of care on directors to 'exercise the care, diligence and skill that a reasonably prudent person would exercise in comparable circumstances'.[34] As explained by the Court, the first duty is what is commonly recognized as a duty of loyalty to a company and its interests, while the second duty is what is commonly recognized as a duty of care and diligence in supervising and managing a company's affairs.

The Court suggested that the statutory notion here of the 'best interests of the corporation' did not equate simply with the 'best interests of the shareholders'. It decided that consideration of stakeholder interests was legally permissible in appropriate circumstances, as part of calculating a company's best interests. 'We accept as an accurate statement of law that in determining whether they are acting with a view to the best interests of the corporation it may be legitimate, given all the circumstances of a given case, for the board of directors to consider, inter alia, the interests of shareholders, employees, suppliers, creditors, consumers, governments and the environment', the Supreme Court concluded.[35]

In an authoritative Canadian judicial statement on stakeholder-sensitive directors' duties last century also endorsed in this case, the court in *Teck Corp v Millar* outlines a connection between directors' duties and stakeholders which broadly reflects the general evolution of corporate law elsewhere in the Anglo-Commonwealth world too:[36]

> A classical theory that once was unchallengeable must yield to the facts of modern life. In fact, of course, it has. If today the directors of a company were to consider the interests of its employees no one would argue that in doing so they were not acting bona fide in the interests of the company itself. Similarly, if the directors were to consider the consequences to the community of any policy that the company intended to pursue, and were deflected in their commitment to that policy as a result, it could not be said that they had not considered bona fide the interests of the shareholders.
>
> I appreciate that it would be a breach of their duty for directors to disregard entirely the interests of a company's shareholders in order to confer a benefit on its employees . . . But if they observe a decent respect for other interests lying beyond those of the company's shareholders in the strict sense, that will not, in my view, leave directors open to the charge that they have failed in their fiduciary duty to the company.

Still, this statement of position simply means that legitimate shareholder and stakeholder consideration relates back to the company's interests in some way. It neither endorses nor precludes alternative ways of framing corporate interests that differ from the orthodox correlation between shareholder and corporate interests.

Third Option – Legislative Confirmation of Permissible Stakeholder Consideration Generally

The third possible model for directors' duties is explicit legislative confirmation that directors are entitled to consider a variety of shareholder and other stakeholder interests. The best example of this model in Anglo-American law lies in the various corporate constituency laws, anti-takeover laws, and other laws defining corporate objectives in a number of US states by the end of the 20th century. For example, US-style corporate constituency laws offered one option for recent inquiries into possible CSR-related reform of directors' duties in both the UK and Australia. Despite clear modelling from one state to another as a wave of corporate constituency statutes and other anti-takeover laws progressively swept across approximately 30 US states in the last quarter of the 20th century, clear differences also emerged. These differences can be explained in part as the product of variations in the political, electoral and business dynamics from state to state.

The standard form of US-style corporate constituency laws permits directors to consider non-shareholder interests along with shareholder interests, but without forcing them to do so.[37] This feature alone now differentiates the standard US position from the prevailing UK position. The relevant non-shareholder interests commonly cited include employees, creditors, customers, suppliers and local communities affected by corporate operations. Factors in addition to designated non-shareholder groups are also added in some states, such as the resources and conduct of someone attempting a takeover, state or national economies, or other pertinent factors as decided by directors. Some laws mention both short-term and long-term corporate interests, and how those interests are served by the corporation's ongoing existence and independence. Some laws also make consideration of any non-shareholder interests contingent upon how they relate to the company's interests, the interests of shareholders, or both.

Most importantly, a few states mandate that directors are not required to give primacy to any particular set of shareholder or non-shareholder interests. One of the authoritative judicial figures in Delaware corporate jurisprudence says that this move appears 'explicitly to decouple directors' duties to the corporation from any distinctive duty to shareholders', thus severely undermining corporate law's centuries-old idea 'that the law ought to try to align directors' action with shareholder interests by imposition of fiduciary duties'.[38] While some of these US laws tie consideration of non-shareholder interests mostly to situations of possible takeovers and other major changes to the nature or control of the business, others permit such consideration at large. The absence of a corporate constituency statute in the premier corporate law jurisdiction of Delaware is ameliorated by judicial developments to similar effect in that state, which authorize directors to consider non-shareholder interests along with shareholder interests in designated circumstances.[39] As the Delaware court affirmed in *Paramount Communications v Time*, 'directors may consider, when evaluating the threat posed by a takeover bid, . . . the impact on "constituencies" other than shareholders'.[40]

Commentators accept that many of the corporate constituency statutes in American states were introduced not simply to guard against undesirable takeovers as such, but to ensure that state employment and services provided by companies for local communities would not be adversely affected by the corporate asset-stripping, business sell-offs, and employee lay-offs inevitably resulting from some takeovers. Still, one common criticism is that these laws use the rhetoric of consideration for non-shareholders and other third party effects of importance to state politicians, such as the impact on local economies and employment, simply to secure greater discretion for directors in resisting takeovers and hence securing their own ongoing control of their companies. Another criticism is that these laws simply serve to confirm in clear terms for takeover situations the wide managerial discretion generally afforded to directors already by a variety of legal means (e.g. the business judgment rule). Yet another criticism is that the superficial CSR-sensitive appeal of these stakeholder-regarding laws has never been realized, in light of how the regulatory, business and legal cultures in each state have perceived and used these laws. At the same time, the context of their original introduction and their relative lack of success so far in CSR terms does not completely preclude their applicability to CSR contexts in the future.[41]

In addition to conditioning the duties of directors to accommodate non-shareholder interests and third party consequences through the vehicle of corporate constituency laws, many US state laws expressly confer powers upon corporations to similar effect. Some even legitimize exercises of power that might not have any direct or indirect benefit for an individual company and its investors. New York's Business Corporation Law, for example, makes this explicit in conferring philanthropic power upon corporations to 'make donations, *irrespective of corporate benefit*, for the public welfare or for community fund, hospital, charitable, educational, scientific, civic or similar purposes, and in time of war or other national emergency in aid thereof'. These apparent examples of laws that detract from a profit-maximizing shareholder norm are sometimes explained away in the literature as tolerable inefficiencies, inevitable legislative compromises, or marginal inroads into shareholder wealth-generation.

Building upon the features suggested in comparable legislative models and academic discussions, the decision-making framework under this option for directors' duties might include some or all of the following factors:

(1) the immediate, near-term and long-term consequences of corporate decisions and activities;
(2) the sustainability of the company and its ongoing success;[42]
(3) the need for a fair and proper return to shareholders for their investment in the company;
(4) the need for due consideration and treatment of all interests in the corporate constituency (however defined), according to their relationship to the company's success (including the need for members to be treated 'fairly'), with or without designated priority for particular groups of interests;
(5) the establishment and nourishing of essential business, credit and employment relationships;
(6) the need to comply with corporate regulatory requirements as a necessary but not sufficient condition for achieving corporate success;
(7) the need for stakeholder-sensitive elements that are relevant to a company's success to be embedded within the company's ordinary decision-making and other frameworks, processes and procedures (e.g. risk management, operational reviews, business strategy and corporate reporting), at least for companies of particular kinds (e.g. large publicly listed corporations, as distinct from SMEs);
(8) the importance to its competitiveness and success of a company's reputation for certain values (e.g. product and service quality, business ethics, customer satisfaction, fair pricing and other CSR-related values);
(9) the desirability of minimizing or eliminating avoidable adverse effects of the company's activities and decisions upon local communities, the environment and society generally; and
(10) the appropriateness of particular kinds of corporate contributions to society's governance and prosperity, including contributions of socio-economic, environmental and 'free enterprise' benefit.[43]

Fourth Option – Legislative Mandating of Stakeholder Consideration Generally

> Many people believe directors of large corporations, including banks, insurance companies, telecommunications companies etc, should have regard to a broader set of community obligations. However, if that is the way society wants to regulate such companies (I do not agree this is the best way of dealing with the problems that may face the community, but it is an option that is favoured by some), then legislation governing the duties of the directors of such companies should be clarified . . . If directors are expected to run the activities of their companies with the interests of the community at the forefront of their obligations, then they must have adequate protection in law (and from the courts), that should shareholders feel they are not receiving the same level of dividends they had been accustomed to, the directors will not be in breach of those duties.
>
> – Professor Bob Baxt, law firm partner and former Chairman of Australia's Trade Practices Commission[44]

The fourth possibility for corporate regulatory systems is a legislatively mandated obligation upon directors to consider relevant non-shareholder interests and third party effects, along with shareholder interests, in corporate decision-making. This is not the standard situation under most US state corporate constituency statutes. However, as detailed further in Chapter 7, UK corporate law now compels directors to take meaningful account of designated shareholder and non-shareholder interests in corporate decision-making and reporting.

So, considered from the standpoint of shareholder primacy and comparative assessment of US and UK law in this area, on one level 'the UK position is even more of a concern than constituency statues for, Connecticut apart, American directors are merely permitted to consider non-shareholder interests while British directors are required to have regard to non-shareholder interests'.[45] At the same time, as explained by respected Australian corporate law scholar and judge, Justice Robert Austin, casting his comparative eye over recent debates about CSR and directors' duties in the UK and Australia, '(t)here is a world of difference between legislating to require directors to act in the interests of shareholders *having regard to* the interests of other "stakeholders", and legislating to require directors to act in the interests of shareholders *and also* in the interests of other "stakeholders"'.[46]

Fifth Option – Legislative or Judicial Confirmation of Permissible Consideration of Specific Stakeholder Groups

The fifth possibility for directors' duties is legally confirmed authority for company directors to take account of specific non-shareholder considerations in boardroom decision-making. Two groups of stakeholders are commonly mentioned in this context – namely, the company's current and former employees (including members of the management team), as well as the company's creditors. In fulfilling their statutory duty under the

Canada Business Corporations Act 'to act honestly and in good faith with a view to the best interests of the corporation', for example, Canadian company directors have judicially confirmed authority to consider employee interests amongst a wide range of shareholder and non-shareholder interests bearing upon that assessment.[47]

Treatment of employee interests

In terms of employee interests, UK corporate law has proceeded from judicially emphasizing the connection between a company's interests and any benefits conferred upon employees, through legislatively singling out employee interests as interests that directors might properly consider, to today's position of requiring employee and other stakeholder interests to be considered by directors. In this way, the absorption of employee interests within the set of legislatively mandated considerations for boardroom decision-making in the UK's Companies Act 2006 can be viewed as the culmination of UK corporate law's evolution towards broader stakeholder sensitivity, albeit still bounded by a company-shareholder nexus.

One strand of UK jurisprudence on the connection between corporate interests and any benefits conferred on particular constituencies has been decided largely in the context of corporate donations or employee benefits. In one famous 19th century case, the court had permissible benefits for employees in mind in saying that '(t)he law does not say that there are to be no cakes and ale, but there are to be no cakes and ale except such as are required for the benefit of the company'.[48] Similarly, '(t)he view that directors, in having regard to the question what is in the best interests of their company, are entitled to take into account the interests of the employees, irrespective of any consequential benefit to the company . . . is not the law', ruled the court in a 1962 case.[49] Hence, as these cases illustrate, paying for employee gratuities, past services by directors or pension arrangements for the family of a dead employee in order to encourage staff productivity might all legitimately be seen as having a sufficient connection to the company's interests as a going concern, but this connection is broken if the company is not continuing in business or the surplus on selling a business goes only to employees.[50]

This standard was later modified in two key ways in statutory UK company law. To remove any doubt in light of these cases about a company's ability to make provision for employees or ex-employees at the end or transfer of its business, UK company law allowed companies to make provision for employees and ex-employees in these circumstances.[51] Directors were also given statutory approval to consider 'the interests of the company's employees in general', along with the interests of the company's members.[52] Importantly, however, the directors' duty involving consideration of employee interests remained a duty 'owed by them to the company (and the company alone)' and was enforceable in the same way as other directors' duties.[53] Given company law's various rules about who can complain about breaches of directors' duties and who can bring actions on behalf of the company, this provision in favour of employee interests never operated as a free-standing right for employees or other third parties to hold companies to account for inadequate consideration or accommodation of employee interests. There is no reason at this stage to suspect that the latest statutory mandate to consider employee interests under statutory directors' duties in the UK's 2006 Companies Act will lead to any greater complications on this score.[54]

In light of the UK position on employee interests prevailing at that time, an Australian federal parliamentary committee with terms of reference in the late 1980s to investigate 'the social and fiduciary duties and responsibilities of company directors' recommended to the Australian Government 'that the companies legislation be amended to make it clear that the interests of a company's employees may be taken into account by directors in administering the company'.[55] This recommendation was not implemented. Support for it had waned by the time that the next major Australian governmental inquiries on company directors' social responsibilities reported in 2006, although some special protection for employee entitlements was legislated in the interim, after union and public disquiet about attempts to circumvent employee entitlements in some high-profile industrial disputes.[56] Accordingly, courts today are likely to take a less restrictive view of the relevance of employee interests in various contexts, especially in light of these legislative inroads in favour of protecting or considering particular employee interests in a number of Anglo-Commonwealth jurisdictions.

Of course, the preceding discussion about employee interests is mainly in the context of corporate transactions and decision-making, as distinct from accommodation of employee interests through governance mechanisms such as European-style employee representation on corporate boards, with a capacity to influence corporate policy and act as an informational conduit between other directors and non-shareholder groups.[57] Here, the wider legal options for advancing and protecting employee interests in a variety of contexts relating to corporate responsibility and governance, with flow-on implications for boardroom decision-making, include these safeguards:

(1) employee-inclusive corporate governance arrangements, such as boardroom representation for employee interests (i.e. structural inclusion), and factoring of employee interests into strategic and operational decisions (i.e. substantive inclusion);

(2) specific legislative devices to facilitate or require consideration of employee interests in boardroom decision-making (e.g. employee-sensitized formulations of directors' duties);

(3) legal restrictions on management arrangements and organizational restructuring to circumvent employee benefits;

(4) priority protection for employee financial benefits in situations of actual or imminent corporate insolvency;

(5) specific employee protections under employment, workplace, equal opportunity, non-discrimination and other employment-related laws; and

(6) public policy goals relating to employee interests that are enshrined in regulatory standards, to which well-governed corporations must respond (e.g. accommodation of employee interests in official corporate governance principles and codes).

Treatment of creditor interests

The extent to which corporate directors must factor the interests of the company's creditors into corporate decision-making, or might even owe some kind of legal duty to creditors, remains a problem for the law across many jurisdictions. No less an authority than the US Supreme Court pronounced in the first half of the 20th century that a director's fiduciary obligation to the company 'is designed for the protection of the entire community of interests in the corporation – creditors as well as stockholders'.[58] Yet, this broad statement of principle falls short of explicitly mandating that directors owe a direct and enforceable duty to creditors not to prejudice their interests, either generally or in the context of insolvency, although subsequent US case law suggests that directors might have some kind of fiduciary duty towards creditors as a company approaches insolvency.[59] Such a duty no doubt might undermine somewhat the conceptual integrity of the shareholder primacy norm, but no court in the common law world has upheld such a direct and enforceable duty owed to creditors by directors.[60]

Indeed, much confusion reigned in Anglo-Commonwealth law in the last quarter of the 20th century about the existence, nature and scope of any such duty owed by directors concerning creditors, even though historically no fiduciary relationship exists directly between directors and creditors under UK, Australian and New Zealand law.[61] Its ongoing controversial status is reflected in the reluctance of the UK Parliament to legislate one way or the other on this point in its statutory scheme of directors' duties in its ground-breaking Companies Act 2006.[62] According to one UK corporate law scholar closely involved in the UK Company Law Review, 'the so-called directors' duty to creditors has not altered the traditional common law formulation that directors' duties are owed to the company, but rather the position is that, as the company nears insolvency, the company should be understood as embracing not just the interests of the shareholders but also and perhaps eventually exclusively the interests of the company's creditors'.[63] Of course, there is a difference between not undertaking a course of action that might unduly prejudice creditors' interests when the company is in the vicinity of insolvency, and being forced to give creditors' interests absolute priority ahead of all other considerations – even shareholder-centred ones – at other stages in a company's life.[64]

Certainly, in hindsight, the leading Australian[65] and New Zealand cases from the 1970s and 1980s on the need for directors to take account of the interests of creditors did not go so far as to decide that directors owe a duty to creditors of a kind that creditors can directly enforce in their own right. In the Australian High Court decision, *Walker v Wimborne*, two judges agreed that 'the directors of a company in discharging their duty to the company must take account of the interest of its shareholders and its creditors', not for the purpose of advantaging creditors as such, but rather because '(a)ny failure by the directors to take into account the interests of creditors will have adverse consequences for the company as well as for them'.[66] In the New Zealand Court of Appeal decision, *Nicholson v Permakraft (N.Z.) Ltd*, one judge commented that 'duties of directors are owed to the company [and] this may require the directors to consider inter alia the interests of creditors'.[67] Later Australian judicial authority confirms that, at most, 'there is a duty of imperfect obligation owed to creditors' which cannot be enforced by creditors but only by the company itself or someone acting through it (e.g. a liquidator).[68]

Accordingly, in the words of one Australian High Court judge, 'the duty to take into account the interests of creditors is merely a restriction on the right of shareholders to ratify breaches of the duty owed to the company', given that creditors have an interest in the affairs of the company as it approaches insolvency that shareholders cannot override.[69] Subsequent case law suggests that meaningful consideration of creditors by directors is not necessarily confined to situations of technical insolvency, as 'a financial state short of actual solvency could be sufficient to trigger the obligation to take into account the interests of creditors'.[70] Beyond the hazy zone of financial troubles which still fall short of insolvency, this line of authority also leaves open some questions about the extent to which something that could affect creditors down the track could also affect a company's interests, and hence may be factored into what a company's directors decide as part of fulfilling their duties.[71] In other words, a company's obligations towards its creditors form part of a company's affairs, limit what shareholders can excuse, and do not equate to a separate and enforceable duty to creditors. This Anglo-Commonwealth line of authority has ongoing significance for the ultimate resolution of the relation between creditors' interests and directors' duties under UK corporate law.[72] The relation between creditors' interests and corporate obligations more broadly is also regulated legislatively now in many of these jurisdictions.

Sixth Option – Legislatively Mandated Consideration and Active Protection of Stakeholder Interests

Corporate code of conduct proposals in the UK, USA and Australia

The sixth possibility for corporate regulatory systems is more radical than the previous models. It combines active consideration and protection of stakeholder interests with correlative legal sanctions and remedies. Since at least the beginning of this century, attempts have been made to introduce into the laws of the UK, the USA and Australia a basic requirement for companies to exercise CSR-related responsibilities (especially for human rights) in their corporate locations at home and abroad, but through different regulatory approaches.[73]

Although largely unsuccessful to date, these proposals for corporate codes of conduct collectively offer legislative models for CSR reform that work through issues of: (i) extra-territoriality of corporate responsibility laws; (ii) effective regulation of cross-national corporate groups; (iii) threshold requirements for the attachment of corporate responsibility obligations; (iv) appropriate delineation of standards for corporate activities; (v) relationships between national and international laws on corporate responsibility; (vi) extension of corporate responsibility obligations to others within corporate supply and distribution chains; (vii) official regulatory monitoring and reporting; (viii) correlative enforcement mechanisms embracing civil and criminal sanctions; (ix) governmental procurement and aid measures; and (x) corporate decision-making and reporting requirements.[74] 'The United States Bill emphasizes access to government procurement contracts and financial assistance; the United Kingdom Bill emphasizes directors' duties and provides criminal sanctions; while the Australian Bill provides, among other remedies, for civil penalties arising from an investigation by a government agency', notes one commentator on legislative corporate codes of conduct across jurisdictions.[75]

As a point of comparison, the UK's 21st century 'enlightened shareholder value' approach to modernizing directors' duties can be compared and contrasted with an earlier attempt by NGOs and other stakeholder groups in the UK's Corporate Responsibility (CORE) Coalition to enshrine stakeholder consideration and protection in UK corporate law in the Corporate Responsibility (CORE) Parliamentary Bill earlier this century. The CSR-related policy rationales underlying the CORE Bill were crystallized by the CORE Coalition (including Amnesty International UK and Friends of the Earth, amongst others) in this way:[76]

> In recent years multinational corporations have faced criticism from consumers, community groups, non-governmental organisations and even the United Nations, for not paying sufficient

attention to the side effects of their business activities. In their pursuit of profit, companies have been accused of everything from violating labour rights, to destruction of the environment, to co-operating with oppressive regimes.

As a result, there has been increasing awareness amongst company executives and employees that, in a globalised world, decisions and actions can have unforeseen consequences in many different locations. As this awareness has grown, so has the idea that corporations must ensure that, as a minimum, their business activities do not have an adverse impact on the various 'stakeholders' they affect – including workers, consumers, local communities and the environment . . . A number of firms have taken steps to identify and address areas where their activities pose a risk to the well-being of people and the environment.

. . . Change, however, has been slow and in many cases only superficial steps have been taken. A mismatched patchwork of voluntary best-practice standards and codes of conduct has materialised, obscuring the main priorities and encouraging companies to undertake a 'pick-and-mix' approach to corporate social responsibility (CSR).

For clear and consistent practices of CSR to emerge, companies need a common set of enforceable rules. This is where the Government must play a role. The current laws governing corporate conduct, set out nearly 150 years ago, no longer equates with the way businesses conduct their affairs in an age of increased globalisation. New company law legislation is now needed to level the playing field and ensure that corporations based in Britain are not only more responsible to their wider stakeholders, but are also legally accountable for their actions both here and overseas.

The CORE Bill was promulgated during, and in response to, the UK Government's recent landmark review of company law, while the Government was still considering the ultimate form of the UK Companies Act 2006 generally and its foundational statutory statement of directors' duties in particular. The CORE Bill can be viewed as a counter-response to a dominant corporate regulatory focus upon (a) the shareholder primacy model and (b) voluntary standard-setting on CSR by the business sector, through codes of conduct and related measures. Amongst other things, its provisions required companies to: (i) comply with a variety of CSR-related standards; (ii) report on corporate policies and consequences along social, environmental and economic lines; (iii) take reasonable steps to consult relevant stakeholders, especially through environmental, social and economic impact statements; (iv) disclose and give access to corporate information; (v) accept parent company liability for both home and host country operations; and (vi) compensate materially affected stakeholders for breach of duties flowing from its enlarged benchmarks for corporate responsibility.

Under the CORE Bill, the applicable CSR-related standards for corporate activities were aligned with the operative national and international laws and policies that prevail in a company's various countries of operation, as follows:[77]

Activities of companies

A company shall carry out its activities in accordance with administrative practices and laws of the countries in which it operates, as well as international agreements, responsibilities and standards, including but not limited to, those relating to:-
   (a) the preservation of the environment;
   (b) public health and safety;
   (c) the goal of sustainable development;
   (d) employment;
   (e) human rights; and
   (f) consumer protection.

The CORE Bill focused most directly upon directors in its conception of directors' duties, directors' personal liabilities and directors' reporting obligations. It added environmental and social duties to the duties of directors, as follows:[78]

Environmental and social duties of directors

A director of a company shall, when considering any matter or taking any decisions, act in the way which in his opinion would be most likely to promote the success of the company, but in so doing it shall be the duty of the directors of any company –

    (a)   to consider –
        (i)   the environmental, social and economic impacts of their operations and any proposed operations; and
        (ii) the interests of all their stakeholders
        when making any decision in respect of those operations or proposed operations;
    (b)   to take all reasonable steps to minimise any negative environmental, social and economic impacts of any such operations or proposed operations; and
    (c)   to prepare an annual report which identifies any risks to the company as a result of the company's environmental, social and economic impacts and how any such risks would be managed.

The CORE Bill added to these additional socially and environmentally focused directors' duties by statutorily mandating personal liability for directors whose negligence or wilful misconduct caused significant stakeholder harm, as follows:[79]

Responsibilities of directors

The directors of any company to which this Act applies shall be liable for any significant adverse social, environmental or economic impacts of their operations which arise from –

    (a)   any negligence by them;
    (b)   any wilful misconduct by them in relation to the duties of any company under this Act; or
    (c)   any wilful misconduct by them relating to the disclosure of information required by this Act.

Confining personal liability of directors to negligent or wilful acts goes only some way towards ameliorating concerns of directors (and their insurers) about the potential expansion of liability under such laws. In particular, their concerns about such reforms characteristically focus upon additions to directors' duties and corporate obligations beyond the conventional limits of much corporate regulation, with untested and often open-ended standards, without correlative business judgment defences or other due diligence safeguards for directors, and also without adequate guidance for pricing insurance risk.

Similar policy imperatives and proposals to those in the CORE Bill emerged in the Corporate Code of Conduct Bill 2000 and its later versions, sponsored by the Australian Democrats in Australia's federal parliament. Aiming to establish a statutory framework for the conduct of business operations offshore by large Australian companies and their subsidiaries, the Australian Bill effectively established a code of conduct for corporations covering adherence to accepted standards of environmental protection, workplace health and safety, consumer health and safety, employment conditions, human rights, consumer protection and trade practices, and whistleblower protection.[80] The Bill sought to create personal liability for corporate executives whose behaviour produces or allows a breach of the code of conduct to occur.[81] This organizational and personal liability of corporate wrongdoers was reinforced by the Bill's provision for court proceedings to be instituted against such wrongdoers by official regulators, stakeholders suffering loss or damage because of non-compliance with the code of conduct, and public interest groups acting on behalf of the victims of corporate wrongdoing.[82]

The Bill also provided for mandatory reporting in the form of a Code of Conduct Compliance Report to Australia's corporate regulator, the Australian Securities and Investments Commission (ASIC), with a prescribed framework of factors for inclusion in the Compliance Report as well as potential for 'naming and shaming' of non-complying companies in annual ASIC reports to parliament.[83] The Corporate Code of Conduct Bill was subject to heavy criticism from the parliamentary committee charged with reporting on the Bill to the Australian Parliament. It never achieved the status of law.

Further lobbying to push the UK law of directors' duties more in this direction occurred during parliamentary deliberation of the new statutory statement of directors' duties in the Companies Act 2006. The CORE Coalition and the Trade Justice Movement, for example, called for a much more radical formulation of directors' duties in the 'enlightened shareholder value' model than the position finally legislated. Their formulation called for a duty on directors 'to take reasonable steps to minimise any significant adverse impacts on workers, local communities and the environment'.[84] Urging more extensive stakeholder-sensitive changes to directors' duties, they suggested the following statutory formulation of the duty of loyalty owed by directors to a company:

Introduction of positive duty to minimise negative impacts

In fulfilling their primary duty to promote the success of the company for the benefit of its members as a whole, directors should also be required to endeavour to:
  (a) have regard to the likely consequences of any decision in the long term,
  (b) promote the interests of the company's employees,
  (c) foster the company's business relationships with suppliers, customers, and others,
  (d) minimise any adverse impact of the company's operations on the community and the environment,
  (e) maintain a reputation for high standards of business conduct, and
  (f) act fairly as between members of the company.

Tactically, this kept the proposed changes closely tied to the structure of the UK Government's proposal to ensure that this duty is a duty to the company in advantaging its members, as well as to the identified stakeholder considerations in the Government's proposal. The notes accompanying this suggested legislative change outlined its purpose as follows:

The primary purpose of this amendment is twofold:
  1. To incentivise directors to be proactive as opposed to passive in their consideration of the impacts of their business operations on employees, communities, suppliers, and the environment; and
  2. To protect those directors who do act responsibly from being sued by shareholders who are only concerned with the short-term success of the company and are therefore happy for the company to externalise its costs by harming people and the environment in pursuit of this end.

These notes suggest that this change would help rather than hinder directors, by affording a safe harbour for directors who balance short-term shareholder gain against long-term shareholder gain and stakeholder sensitivity in the way outlined. Critics focus upon a different consequence in arguing the contrary position, highlighting the impossibility of simultaneously protecting both shareholder and stakeholder interests in all situations and the dilution of meaningful accountability that would result.

Hinkley's code of corporate citizenship

> The corporate law establishes rules for the structure and operation of corporations. The keystone of this structure is the duty of directors to preserve and enhance shareholder value – to make money. Under this structure, the objective of stockholders – making money – becomes the duty of directors which, in turn, becomes the marching orders for the corporation's officers, managers and other employees . . . Most corporate decisions are made by people who have little incentive to promote corporate citizenship or social responsibility (which in some measure requires corporate sacrifice) unless such promotion also can be shown to improve profitability . . . To the extent that there is any restraint on the duty of directors to make money, it comes in the form of government regulations.
>
> – Anglo-American law firm partner, corporate commentator, and promoter of a code of corporate responsibility for directors, Bob Hinkley[85]

Such unconventional extensions of directors' duties dovetail with former US law firm partner and Anglo-American corporate lawyer Robert Hinkley's well-publicized call for changes to directors' duties to promote a code for corporate citizenship. Hinkley starts from the basic regulatory and behavioural position that, as 'the point of highest leverage' for influencing corporate conduct is '(t)he duty of directors to make money' for the company, changes to this duty (and hence to the basis of personal duties and liabilities of directors) are necessary to achieve corporate citizenship.[86] Like Joel Bakan in *The Corporation* and others before him, Hinkley locates the source of the problem in the in-built structural dedication of corporations to shareholder value as conventionally practised. He starkly identifies the ineffectiveness of more than a century's efforts of trying to legislate corporate responsibility, as follows:[87]

> Over the past 120 years, state and federal governments have enacted volumes of laws and regulations to curb the problem of corporate abuse of the public interest. Examples include legislation to protect the environment, eliminate child labour, create equal opportunity, increase workplace safety, limit anti-competitive behavior and protect the public interest in other ways which corporations have been unwilling or unable to do voluntarily. Notwithstanding all this legislation, the damage that continues to be inflicted is more extensive than ever.

In equally striking terms, he goes on to characterize corporate abuse and its underlying cause as follows:[88]

> The cause of most corporate abuse is no secret. The thing that keeps greenhouse gases pouring out of smokestacks and tailpipes is the same thing that results in vendors of designer sneakers

paying Third World children less than a dollar an hour. It's also the same thing that keeps tobacco companies marketing their products to children, fast food companies paying less than a living wage and meat packing companies maintaining dangerous working conditions. That thing is the dedication of the corporation to the pursuit of profit.

In Hinkley's eyes, making money for shareholders thus 'becomes the marching orders for everyone who works for the corporation', thereby placing even well-intentioned people in institutional roles that compel them towards the single-minded pursuit of profit.[89] 'As long as directors, managers and employees are guided only by the doctrine of shareholder primacy, their companies will continue to do damage to the environment, human rights, the public health and safety, the dignity of employees and the welfare of their communities', he concludes.[90] His solution is a code for corporate citizenship in which standard legal formulations of directors' duties are conditioned by adding 28 qualifying words so that directors can legitimately pursue shareholder interests through corporate profit-making 'but not at the expense of the environment, human rights, the public health or safety, the communities in which the company operates or the dignity of its employees'.[91] Conversely, speaking strictly in the Australian context, corporate lawyer and former Australian competition regulator head, Professor Bob Baxt, argues that '(w)e need no further expansion of the duties of directors under the Corporations Act to give priority to interest groups that society believes need protection', and that '(t)o require directors to sacrifice their primary obligations would be to further stifle the entrepreneurial spirit that is seriously in danger of being extinguished as a result of over-regulation'.[92]

As with proposals for even less radical modifications of directors' duties, standard attacks on this proposal point to alleged uncertainties in its meaning and application, thus highlighting the difficulty for regulators in enforcing it and even for sympathetic directors in adhering to it. What is the catalogue of 'human rights' that must not be harmed, and what is the benchmark for avoidable detriment to 'the local communities in which the corporation operates', for example? For advocates of such a radical reformulation of directors' duties, these objections are matters to be addressed, if at all, at the level of follow-up regulatory detail and guidance. They are not fatal objections at the level of legislative design. That design introduces a revolutionary mindshift, in which the law no longer takes the piecemeal approach of existing responsibility-inducing legislation, which 'only addresses where and how companies should be allowed to damage the public interest, rather than eliminating the reason why they damage it',[93] instead targeting that underlying reason and fundamentally reorientating the starting point from which directors must frame their corporate role and correlative legal duties. In addition, given the potential dislocation to existing corporate investments and behaviour, Hinkley suggests a long transitional period to enable companies to put their houses in order.

Certainty is a highly sought after quality in law, especially when legal obligations and liabilities are at stake. On some levels, this advocated extension to directors' duties is no more open-ended than what now appears elsewhere in the law, such as those qualifications to human rights listed in international instruments and statutory bills of rights that 'are necessary in a democratic society in the interests of public safety' or other public concerns. Nor is existing corporate law free of broad standards, given the relatively open-ended way in which many US corporate constituency statutes and the business judgment rule permit reference by corporate directors to a wide range of non-shareholder and community concerns.[94]

Over time, courts and other regulatory bodies inside and outside government can develop guidelines for their interpretation and application, as happens in the wake of radical new corporate laws (such as Australia's 1970s introduction of corporate liability for misleading or deceptive conduct) and other landmark laws (such as the introduction of a bill of rights into the law of a jurisdiction). In short, the need for medium-term systemic adjustment to a new regulatory order is not alone a sufficient reason for rejecting an otherwise beneficial change. Of course, that threshold normative assessment of any change is the lynchpin of this option and similar ones.

Seventh Option – Business Judgments and Directors' Leeways of Discretion

The seventh option for corporate regulatory systems in this mapping of legal models for accommodating shareholder and non-shareholder interests in boardroom decision-making from a CSR perspective concerns the promotion of socially responsible business judgments. The business judgment rule occupies an important place at the heart of the interface between corporate governance, directors' duties and socially responsible business behaviour. The normative bases for the socialization of business judgment elements in corporate law include commercial morality, socio-ethical community standards, and affording 'a safe harbour for corporate managers who do take socially responsible decisions'.[95]

The business judgment rule has more than one possible manifestation in corporate law.[96] Whether mandated in corporate law in the form of what is commonly called a 'safe harbour' for directors as a protective safeguard from liability, incorporated within the elements of directors' duties to create space for commercial judgments, or simply adopted over time as a judicial approach of deference to boardroom assessments of a company's circumstances at the relevant time, the business judgment rule now has a strong presence in the USA, Australia and elsewhere.[97]

Traditionally, the business judgment rule is rationalized in terms of an efficient balance between the need to encourage entrepreneurial innovation and risk-taking by directors and the need for judicial review of unlawful commercial activity. Considered from an American perspective, '(t)he basic policy underpinning of the business judgment rule is that corporate law should encourage, and afford broad protection to, informed business judgments (whether subsequent events prove the judgments right or wrong) in order to stimulate risk taking, innovation, and other creative entrepreneurial activities . . . based on a desire to limit litigation and judicial intrusiveness with respect to private-sector business decision-making'.[98]

In orthodox terms, directors' duties and the correlative business judgment rule work together from the perspective of corporate law's contribution to economic efficiency. 'The imposition of directors' duties addresses a concern that market forces may not provide sufficient incentives for company officers to act in a manner that best promotes the interests of the company (and indirectly its members) [because] (u)nless this higher standard of conduct was required of directors and company officers, an inefficiently low level of capital would be made available to fund corporate activity', in the words of one governmental review of corporate law sanctions.[99] Conversely, too restrictive an approach to directors' duties and the consequences of breaching them in a corporate regulatory system can affect any company's capacity to attract good directors, hinder responsible risk-taking and entrepreneurialism, and produce overly cautious boardroom decisions. Views differ on the extent to which the business judgment rule promotes efficient and just business decision-making, given the latitude it affords directors to make both profit-enhancing and profit-sacrificing decisions, especially since too much judicial review of boardroom decisions would produce its own inefficiencies in terms of additional regulatory costs and the general unsuitability of having courts make commercial judgments.[100]

The UK has not formally enshrined a business judgment rule in its 21st century overhaul of directors' duties, although some business judgment elements (e.g. good faith) underpin it. By comparison, a form of business judgment defence as a so-called 'safe harbour' for directors is a relatively recent innovation in Australia. In recommending the introduction of a business judgment rule into Australian company law, the Senate Standing Committee on Legal and Constitutional Affairs concluded in 1989 that, 'so long as directors stay within the bounds of the business judgment rule, they should not be liable for the consequences of their business decisions [because] (i)n the expectation of profit, shareholders must accept the risk of the directors' business judgments, provided the business judgment is made on a competent basis'.[101]

The American version of the business judgment rule conventionally has elements that require a director who is making a business judgment in good faith to ensure that the director is personally disinterested in the matter, appropriately informed, and rationally believes that the decision is in the company's best interests. This formulation is encapsulated in the American Law Institute's *Principles of Corporate Governance*:[102]

> (a)   A director or officer has a duty to the corporation to perform the director's or officer's functions in good faith, in a manner that he or she reasonably believes to be in the best interests of the corporation, and with the care that an ordinarily prudent person would reasonably be expected to exercise in a like position under similar circumstances. This Subsection (a) is subject to the provisions of Subsection (c) (the business judgment rule) where applicable.
>
> . . .
>
> (c)   A director or officer who makes a business judgment in good faith fulfils the duty under this Section if the director or officer:
>
> > (1)   is not interested in the subject of the business judgment;
> > (2)   is informed with respect to the subject of the business judgment to the extent the director or officer reasonably believes to be appropriate under the circumstances; and
> > (3)   rationally believes that the business judgment is in the best interests of the corporation.

The degree of modelling that occurs across corporate regulatory systems in the structure and elements of business judgment provisions is evident in its Australian counterpart, whatever other modifications and terminology differences apply. Under Australian corporate law, a modified form of the business judgment rule is incorporated as a defence in the context of directors' duties, as follows:[103]

> (1)   A director or other officer of a corporation must exercise their powers and discharge their duties with the degree of care and diligence that a reasonable person would exercise if they:

(a) were a director or officer of a corporation in the corporation's circumstances; and
(b) occupied the office held by, and had the same responsibilities within the corporation as, the director or officer.

. . .

(2) A director or other officer of a corporation who makes a business judgment is taken to meet the requirements of subsection (1), and their equivalent duties at common law and in equity, in respect of the judgment if they:

(a) make the judgment in good faith for a proper purpose; and
(b) do not have a material personal interest in the subject matter of the judgment; and
(c) inform themselves about the subject matter of the judgment to the extent they reasonably believe to be appropriate; and
(d) rationally believe that the judgment is in the best interests of the corporation.

The director's or officer's belief that the judgment is in the best interests of the corporation is a rational one unless the belief is one that no reasonable person in their position would hold.

As originally enacted, the Australian business judgment rule is confined to being a formal defence for breach of only one of the key statutory directors' duties (i.e. the duty of care and diligence). A company director who commits a breach of a different duty, for example, by allowing the company to trade while insolvent, cannot invoke the business judgment defence in Australia. In ongoing reviews of corporate law, the Australian Government has publicly canvassed the possibility of both extending the reach of the business judgment rule to other directors' duties and reshaping its elements to provide a general defence for directors for all business decisions made 'in a bona fide manner', 'within the scope of the corporation's business' 'reasonably and incidentally to the corporation's business' and 'for the corporation's benefit'.[104] A proposal for a parallel ethical judgment rule, empowering directors to take account of well-founded ethical concerns (including stakeholder considerations), was considered and rejected in one of the two major Australian governmental CSR inquiries reporting in 2006, largely because of fears that 'even as a defence of last resort, the ethical judgment would be called upon by directors who had failed in their duties'.[105]

In 2005, the then chairman of Netherlands-based James Hardie Industries, Meredith Hellicar, explicitly linked business judgment reform to CSR, in the aftermath of a governmental inquiry in Australia into the underfunding of a compensation fund for the asbestos victims of building products by subsidiaries within its corporate group. In establishing James Hardie's compensation fund for asbestos victims in 2001, she stated, its directors 'believed we had achieved the goal of fulfilling our duties as directors to current and future stakeholders, both legally and in the context of corporate social responsibility, by separating our asbestos liabilities from the balance sheet to enhance our attraction to foreign capital markets to fund future international growth, and by meeting our responsibilities by providing for future asbestos claimants'.[106] Hellicar cautiously postulated the possible need for clarity in this area of law, to provide directors with a 'business judgment' safeguard against potential liability for making socially responsible decisions that accommodate the interests of other stakeholders as well as shareholders.[107]

At a wider level, this is one reason why some commentators suggest that directors might even benefit from legislative clarification of their consideration of stakeholder interests, to assist them in meeting the expectations, if not the legal claims, of disgruntled shareholders. This would be on the basis that legislative permission or even direction to consider relevant non-shareholder interests would 'shield' directors from both share-holder and regulatory action.[108] In other words, directors might take some comfort in being able to point expressly to something in the law which relates to non-shareholder interests to explain and justify their decisions if need be to investors, the market and official regulators.

Are there other legislative options for sensitizing directors to CSR concerns, akin to the business judgment rule? Other variations that incorporate leeways of discretion for directors include a directors' duty of environmental sustainability, bolstered by the 'safe harbour' of an environmentally orientated business judgment rule.[109] In corporate regula-tory regimes that have a facility for replaceable corporate rules or corporate constitutional changes, companies might adopt a tailored version of what constitutes the best interests of the company, at least as between the company and its members and management, by reference to available models that incorporate shareholder, non-shareholder, and even societal interests into the equation. Available models include the corporate objective of 'lawful, ethical and public-spirited profit seeking' enshrined in the ALI Principles of Corporate Governance and more recently the stakeholder-sensitive statutory formulation of a director's duty of loyalty to the company under UK corporate law.[110] These options need assessment too by reference to their impact upon official regulatory enforcement, shareholder complaints, non-shareholder remedies, and available defences under the general law.[111]

Empowering Non-directors and the Impact Upon Boardroom Decision-making

The final option in this set of reform options for socializing directors' duties looks to the impact of formalizing corporate governance and decision-making roles for non-directors. This more radical reform option lies in 'increasing the power of interest groups to shape corporate conduct', through either 'strengthening their ability to impose pressure on the company from the outside or by giving them some constitutional status within the organisation', with equal attention to avoiding the inequality of power relations that can result.[112] Corporate profit-sacrificing is justified under this more radical model of corporate responsibility and driver of corporate behaviour 'as the product of reformed decision-making processes, where the object of reform is not merely to encourage man-agers to take third-party interests into account, but rather to induce an organisational response through interest group empowerment'.[113]

As a structural mechanism, empowering such non-director groups sets up interac-tions with directors in corporate decision-making, which flow through to what directors consider and decide. Objections to such a reform on the presumed grounds of share-holder primacy dilution, boardroom decision-making complexity and reduced corpo-rate efficiency, for example, need to be assessed alongside the values served by it too. Arguably, for example, it might even enhance corporate governance and efficiency, on a fuller view of corporate responsibility, governance and sustainability than that which prevails in many places. It also gives effect to values of deliberation and contestation of corporate interests, in the way envisaged by corporate constitutionalism and CSR meta-regulation, and in service to the wider concerns of corporate democracy canvassed in Chapter 3.

A Matrix of Issues for CSR-related Reform of Directors' Duties

Accordingly, in light of these various options for socializing directors' duties, a working list of major issues from law reform, policy-setting and legislative drafting perspectives is as follows:

(1) whether directors' duties and business judgments are best framed directly or indirectly in terms of obligations to the company (i.e. the ongoing success of the collective business enterprise), a particular corporate constituency (e.g. shareholders), or a hybrid of the two (e.g. the company's success for the benefit of its members overall, as in the UK's 21st century recasting of directors' duties);

(2) whether directors are simply entitled or alternatively obliged to consider (and even avoid undue harm to) an exhaustive or illustrative set of designated shareholding and non-shareholding interests, with or without the benefit of the 'safe harbour' of a business judgment rule or other legal safeguards for directors;

(3) whether breach of any requirement to consider stakeholder interests can generate any actions and remedies for non-shareholders for breaching it;

(4) whether other kinds of regulatory mechanisms are needed to condition companies to develop suitable correlative decision-making and reporting frameworks (e.g. stakeholder-based participatory corporate governance arrangements, avenues for legal intervention to prevent actions harming specific shareholder or non-shareholder interests, the link between directors' duties and reportable business review requirements in the UK, and public policy goals for CSR that shape boardroom decision-making responses); and

(5) the extent to which any of these elements should be enshrined as absolute legal requirements or alternatively regulated in other ways (e.g. replaceable corporate rules, official corporate governance standards, etc.).

FROM BOARDROOM DECISION-MAKING TO CORPORATE REPORTING

A well-developed law reform or policy agenda for continuous improvement of corporate responsibility and governance in the contemporary business arena needs a menu of potential options beyond changes to directors' duties and correlative business judgment safeguards.[114] At the very least, it requires attention to correlative corporate reporting requirements, for various reasons. Asking companies and their boards to report on *how* they take both shareholder and non-shareholder interests into account presupposes a firm legal basis upon which they *can* or *must* take those interests into account. In the next chapter, we explore these dynamics through the vehicle of the UK's bold new experiment in 21st century regulation of directors' duties, business reviews, and corporate reporting.

Company reporting and disclosure of information (voluntary or mandatory) is one aspect of corporate governance which has the potential to make a significant difference to ordinary citizens' ability to make companies responsible for failures of social responsibility. The principle is simple in theory: companies should disclose high-quality (i.e. relevant and reliable) internal information about their own processes for managing legal and social responsibilities, and their performance or outcomes, to those stakeholders affected by their actions. This will put those stakeholders in a good position to hold them accountable through the markets for their securities, products and services, reputations, insurance and debt, and through accountability in the courts and other regulatory processes (if the information discloses the basis for a legal liability or sanction).

– CSR meta-regulation scholar, Dr Christine Parker[115]

NOTES

1. Garratt, 2003: 243, 245.
2. Zerk, 2006: 26.
3. PJCCFS, 2006; and CAMAC, 2006.
4. ASX CGC, 2007a; ASX CGC, 2007b; and ASX CGC, 2007c.
5. Hinkley, 2002.
6. Sealy, 1987: 176, 187.
7. Attenborough, 2007: 322.
8. Corcoran, 1997: 63.
9. Sealy, 1987: 182.
10. Parkinson, 1993: 398.
11. Ibid.: 86.
12. Ibid.: 372, quoting Teubner, 1985: 167.
13. Parkinson, 1993: 345.
14. Ibid.: 366.
15. Greenfield, 2006: 136.
16. Easterbrook and Fischel, 1991: 38.
17. Quoted in Kelly, 2001: 150.
18. Ramsay, 2005a.
19. Sealy, 1987: 174.
20. Parkinson, 1993: 81–82.
21. Ramsay, 2005a.
22. Attenborough, 2007: 321–322.
23. Elhauge, 2005: 775–776; and Lee, 2006: 557–558.
24. ALI, 2005: s.2.01.
25. E.g. Farrar, 2008: 496–497
26. du Plessis et al, 2005: 293.
27. *Revlon Inc v MacAndrews & Forbes Holdings Inc* 506 A. 2d 173, 176 (1986).
28. E.g. the needs of government, charitable and educational causes, environmental and community impact, and support for the free enterprise system.
29. Heydon, 1987: 136.
30. Austin et al, 2005: 281–282.
31. 2004 SCC 68. See also *BCE Inc v 1976 Debentureholders* 2008 SCC 69.
32. 2004 SCC 68 at [32].

33. S. 122(1)(a).
34. S. 122(1)(b).
35. *Peoples Department Stores Inc (Trustee of) v Wise* 2004 SCC 68 at [42].
36. (1972) 33 DLR (3d) 288 at 314, endorsed in *Peoples Department Stores Inc. (Trustee of) v Wise* 2004 SCC 68 at [42].
37. On this and the following summary of features of corporate constituency statutes see in particular: Hanks, 1991; Allen, 1992; Orts, 1992; and Elhauge, 2005.
38. Allen, 1992: 276.
39. Elhauge, 2005: 742.
40. 571 A.2d 1140, 1153 (Del. 1989), quoting *Unocal Corp v Mesa Petroleum Co* 493 A.2d 946, 955 (Del. 1989), cited in Hanks, 1991: 102.
41. On these and related points about US corporate constituency and anti-takeover statutes see Deakin, 2005: 11–18; and Orts, 1992.
42. While some commentators decry the hijacking of the term 'sustainability' for use in a business context (as distinct from its use in the context of environmental sustainability), this simply highlights the need in both cases to clarify the sense of sustainability under discussion.
43. This set of factors reflects, and sometimes extends beyond, factors that are listed in the UK statutory proposal on directors' duties and some US constituency statutes, as well as some factors discussed in Wood, 2002.
44. Baxt, 2002: 162.
45. Keay, 2007a: 612.
46. Austin, 2007b: 2; original emphasis.
47. *Peoples Department Stores Inc (Trustee of) v Wise* 2004 SCC 68 at [42].
48. *Hutton v West Cork Railway Co* (1883) 23 Ch. D. 654 at 673.
49. *Parke v Daily News Ltd* [1962] 2 All ER 929.
50. Heydon, 1987: 135.
51. Companies Act 1985 (UK), s. 719(1).
52. Ibid., s. 309(1).
53. Ibid., s. 309(2).
54. See Ch 7.
55. SSCLCA, 1989: [6.24].
56. Corporations Act 2001 (Cth), Part 5.8A (Employee Entitlements).
57. Hansmann and Kraakman, 2004b: 63–64.
58. *Pepper v Litton* 308 U.S. 295, 307 (1939).
59. *Crédit Lyonnais Bank Nederland v Pathé Communications Corporation* (Delaware Chancery Court 1991); Hansmann and Kraakman, 2004b: 66; and Hertig and Kanda, 2004: 89.
60. Davies, 2005: 9–10.
61. Heydon, 1987: 124; citing *Re Wincham Shipbuilding Boiler & Salt Co* (1878) 9 Ch. D. 322 at 328; *Bath v Standard Land Co Ltd* [1911] 1 Ch. 618 at 627; *Re H. Linney & Co Ltd* [1925] NZLR 907 at 922; and *Re J.H. Hurdley & Son* [1941] NZLR 686 at 726.
62. Companies Act 2006 (UK), s. 172(3).
63. Davies, 2005: 10–11.
64. Davies, 1997: 603.
65. E.g. *Kinsela v Russell Kinsela Pty Ltd* (1984) 4 ACLC 215 at 221, 223.
66. *Walker v Wimborne* (1976) 137 CLR 1 at 6–7.
67. [1985] 1 NZLR 242.
68. *Re New World Alliance Pty Ltd; Sycotex Pty Ltd v Baseler* (1994) 122 ALR 531 at 550, cited approvingly in *Spies v The Queen* [2000] HCA 43 at [94]–[95].
69. Ibid.
70. *The Bell Group Ltd v Westpac Banking Corporation (No 9)* [2008] WASC 239 at [4445].
71. *The Bell Group Ltd v Westpac Banking Corporation (No 9)* [2008] WASC 239 at [4396]–[4450].
72. Companies Act 2006 (UK), s. 172(3).
73. E.g. Corporate Code of Conduct Bill 2000 (USA); Corporate Code of Conduct Bill 2000 (Australia); the Corporate Responsibility Bill 2003 (UK).
74. McBeth, 2004; Muchlinski, 2007; and Deva, 2004.
75. McBeth, 2004: 251.
76. 'With Rights, Come Responsibilities', CORE Coalition, 2003.
77. CORE Bill, cl. 2.
78. Ibid., cl. 7.
79. Ibid., cl. 8.
80. Corporate Code of Conduct Bill 2004 (Cth), ss 7–13.

81. Ibid., s. 17(1). Note that similar preconditions to wrongdoing by corporate executives attach to non-compliance with reporting requirements: see s. 15(6).
82. Ibid., Part 4.
83. Ibid., Part 3.
84. CORE et al, 2006: 3.
85. Quoted in Baxt, 2002: 161.
86. Hinkley, 2000: 32–33
87. Hinkley, 2002.
88. Ibid.
89. Ibid.
90. Ibid.
91. Ibid., also quoted in 'Options Canvassed for Hardie Law Changes', *The Australian Financial Review*, 12 November 2004, 59.
92. Baxt, 2004: 55.
93. Hinkley, 2002.
94. Companies Act 2006 (UK), ss 172(1)(d) and 417(5).
95. Corcoran, 1997: 63.
96. Baxt, 2002; and Horrigan, 2005.
97. E.g. ALI Principles of Corporate Governance (USA); *Peoples Department Stores Inc (Trustee of) v Wise* 2004 SCC 68 (Canada); and Corporations Act 2001 (Cth), s. 180(2) (Australia).
98. ALI, 2005: [1.4], Introductory Note.
99. Australian Treasury, 2007: 7.
100. Lee, 2006; cf Elhauge, 2005.
101. SSCLCA, 1989: [3.33] and [3.35].
102. ALI, 2005: [1.4], Section 4.01.
103. Corporations Act 2001 (Cth), s. 180.
104. Australian Treasury, 2007: [3.2].
105. PJCCFS, 2006: [4.63]–[4.68].
106. Hellicar, 2005. The author is a consultant for a firm which has done legal work for the James Hardie group, including some work involving the author.
107. For the result of subsequent legal proceedings against James Hardie directors (including Hellicar), see *Australian Securities and Investments Commission v Macdonald (No 11)* [2009] NSWSC 287.
108. Beerworth, 2005.
109. McConvill and Joy, 2003.
110. E.g. Corcoran, 1997: 63–64; Langton and Trotman, 1999: 179–181; and Lumsden and Fridman, 2007: 175–178.
111. PJCCFS, 2006: [4.69]–[4.75]; and Lumsden and Fridman, 2007: 175–178.
112. Parkinson, 1993: 346.
113. Ibid.: 329.
114. Parkinson, 1993: 86.
115. Parker, 2002: 216.

PART 3

CORPORATE SOCIAL RESPONSIBILITY'S
APPLICATIONS AND FUTURES

7. Recasting UK corporate law for the 21st century

OVERVIEW

> Today, corporate social responsibility goes far beyond the old philanthropy of the past – donating money to good causes at the end of the financial year – and is instead an all year round responsibility that companies accept for the environment around them, for the best working practices, for their engagement in their local communities and for their recognition that brand names depend not only on quality, price and uniqueness but on how, cumulatively, they interact with companies' workforce, community and environment. Now we need to move towards a challenging measure of corporate responsibility, where we judge results not just by the input but by its outcomes: the difference we make to the world in which we live, and the contribution we make to poverty reduction.
>
> – Gordon Brown, as UK Chancellor of the Exchequer (subsequently Prime Minister)[1]

The most extensive overhaul of UK company law for more than a century is pregnant with potential CSR implications for CSR actors in the UK and beyond. The landmark Companies Act enacted in late 2006 embodies the UK Government's adopted policy of 'enlightened shareholder value' (ESV). It legislatively enshrines for the first time in UK corporate law a formulation of directors' duties that also offers an overarching structure and matrix of factors to guide boardroom decision-making. In particular, it makes the crucial triumvirate of directors' duties, business risk management and corporate reporting more explicitly long-term, relational and stakeholder-sensitive, while ostensibly anchoring these developments in a reorientated notion of shareholder value. It also marks another milestone in the development of UK corporate law in directions that are sensitive to wider EU standards for boardroom accountability and corporate reporting, while also providing important points of contrast with some corporate orthodoxies in other Anglo-Commonwealth countries (e.g. Australia). All of this sits within the wider context of being a constituent part of an emerging body of comparative CSR-related law and regulation worldwide for the 21st century, as discussed in Chapter 5.

In doing so, the UK Companies Act offers a dramatic 21st century example of governmental codification of norms for the contemporary global business environment facing UK companies, in ways that make the 'private' spaces of boardroom decision-making and corporate reporting responsive to wider 'public' accountability,[2] even within the shareholder-orientated tradition of UK company law. Positioned within a broader canvas of global governance and regulatory mechanisms, this UK experiment in 'enlightened shareholder value' is a 'far-reaching measure, both in stipulating heightened social expectations about the public role of private enterprise and the requirement that companies issue an annual directors' report of social and environmental information relevant to an understanding of the entire business'.[3]

Indeed, the boardroom reforms introduced under the UK Companies Act are already resonating in international debates about corporate regulatory reform. In his 2008 report for the UN Human Rights Council on a new three-pronged framework for advancing the global agenda on business and human rights, the UN Secretary-General's Special Representative on Business and Human Rights (UNSRSG) cites the new requirement under UK company law for directors to take account of such matters as a company's community and environmental impact as an example of how countries might engage in 'redefining fiduciary duties'.[4] Drawing a parallel with the position under US state constituency laws, one leading US law firm rejects any movement towards extra business regulation of this kind that might extend corporate obligations to respect human rights. 'To the extent the UK Companies Act forms one of the bases on which the UN Human Rights Council may endorse the State's duty to protect against human rights abuses, such a new legal standard would mark a dramatic expansion beyond traditional [US] constituency statutes', according to Wachtell, Lipton, Rosen and Katz.[5]

Closer to home, UK courts face new challenges in marrying a new corporate regulatory regime based explicitly upon 'enhanced shareholder value' with pre-existing doctrines of corporate law. Legal and business professionals engaged in corporate advisory and transactional work face the additional challenge of translating that evolving body of law over time into reliable practices and safeguards for corporate executives. Corporate directors, managers and employees must test and, where necessary, adapt and develop their business models and practices to accommodate this new 21st century era of 'enlightened shareholder value' in UK corporate law. In short, there are likely to be at least some test cases for advice and litigation in the roll-out of the UK's new corporate law, which might take some years to come to light.

The UK Companies Act offers a 21st century approach to legislating boardroom and corporate obligations that not only has relevance for those whose work or study embraces CSR, but also serves as one model for comparative reform of corporate law and practices for policy, legal and regulatory purposes beyond the UK, especially in terms of alternative ways of expressing directors' duties and other corporate obligations in a 21st century business environment. As evidenced by recent corporate law reforms in both the UK and Australia, any CSR-related corporate law reform in the future must engage with comparative models and regulatory measures available in other jurisdictions, as a necessary part of the policy analysis, public consultation and justification of final recommendations. In addition, courts in common law countries whose corporate law doctrines and concepts share a common Anglo-American and Anglo-Commonwealth heritage will continue to have comparative reference to how UK courts interpret and apply these reforms and the legal doctrines underpinning them.

THE ROAD TO 'ENLIGHTENED SHAREHOLDER VALUE' IN UK CORPORATE LAW

Corporate social responsibility has developed and evolved over time. The relationship between business interests and the wider world is changing all the time . . . I strongly believe that businesses perform better, and are more sustainable in the long term, when they have regard to a wider group of issues in pursuing success. That is a common-sense approach that reflects a modern view of the way in which businesses operate in their community: they interact with customers and suppliers; they make sure that employees are motivated and properly rewarded; and they think about their impact on communities and the environment. They do so at least partly because it makes good business sense.

– Margaret Hodge, UK Minister of State for Industry and the Regions[6]

The landmark overhaul of UK corporate law initiated by the UK Government's Company Law Review (CLR) in the last few years of the 20th century culminated in a comprehensive update and modernization of UK corporate law in the passage of the Companies Act 2006. The most significant changes for CSR in the UK Act concern directors' duties to consider non-shareholder interests, and the forward-looking business review and reporting requirements. The latter requirements supersede the originally proposed Operating and Financial Review (OFR). These CSR-related changes relate relevant employee, environmental and community interests to corporate operations, and integrate them to that extent within standard corporate decision-making and reporting.[7]

The UK's Companies Act 2006 and the CLR processes and recommendations built upon the work of earlier Law Commissions in the UK. The CLR Steering Group was charged with terms of reference from the UK Government which included recommending a new corporate law that 'protects, through regulation where necessary, the interests of those involved with the enterprise, including shareholders, creditors and employees'.[8] By the CLR Steering Group's own admission, its task went beyond the limits of previous reforms aimed at implementing EC directives and piecemeal legislative responses to periodic corporate collapses and scandals, instead embarking upon the largest and most comprehensive review of UK corporate law for at least 150 years.[9]

In the CLR Steering Group's own words, the corporate reform process was designed 'to turn our Victorian infrastructure into a modern framework designed for the 21st century'.[10] It gathered evidence, received submissions and conducted consultations that suggested considerable confusion and disagreement in at least some business and public quarters about the true foundations and reach of corporate responsibility. 'Companies striving to act responsibly – not only for their shareholders, but also their employees, creditors, trading partners and the wider community – are uncertain where their legal duties lie', concluded the Steering Group in its final report.[11] Accordingly, 'company law should reflect the reality of the modern corporate economy, where those who run successful companies recognise the need to develop positive relationships with a wide range of interests beyond shareholders – such as employees, suppliers and customers', it added.[12] At the same time, the CLR Steering Group also signalled that embracing the policy of ESV was intended to do little (if anything) to disturb the pre-existing fabric of corporate law. Anything more radical would have been likely to generate considerable opposition from many in the business and legal communities.

The UK Government responded to the CLR Steering Group's final report in two White Papers in 2002 and 2005, the latter containing draft clauses for public consultation and debate, including for the first time in UK corporate law a legislative statement of directors' duties. The Company Law Reform Bill emerging from this process was introduced into the UK Parliament in November 2005, emerging one year later in its final form in the Companies Act 2006.

THE MEANING AND FOCUS OF 'ENLIGHTENED SHAREHOLDER VALUE'

> There was a time when business success in the interests of shareholders was thought to be in conflict with society's aspirations for people who work in the company or in supply chain companies, for the long-term well-being of the community and for the protection of the environment. The law is now based on a new approach. Pursuing the interests of shareholders and embracing wider responsibilities are complementary purposes, not contradictory ones.
>
> – Margaret Hodge, UK Minister of State for Industry and the Regions[13]

Does the much-heralded embrace of ESV in modern UK corporate law anchor that body of law in the camp of conventional shareholder primacy, or alternatively open up its future development in other directions? The short answer is that the baseline of shareholder primacy remains firmly in place, but is reorientated towards the UK Parliament's vision of shareholder value in the 21st century business environment. In the words of the UK Minister of State for Industry and the Regions, Margaret Hodge, the new statutory formulation of directors' duties has both backward-looking and forward-looking characteristics:[14]

> There are two ways of looking at the statutory statement of directors' duties: on the one hand it simply codifies the existing common law obligations of company directors; on the other – especially in section 172: the duty to act in the interests of the company – it marks a radical departure in articulating the connection between what is good for a company and what is good for society at large.

Even from its earliest days, the CLR Steering Group recognized the dualistic nature of the corporation as a site for the interplay of both public and private interests.[15] Referring to arguments 'that wider considerations, beyond relations between members, creditors and directors ("externalities") are already properly and rightly dealt with by specialized legislation bearing equally on all businesses, companies or not (e.g. employment, health and safety, consumer protection and environmental laws, the weight of which has increased substantially in recent years)', the CLR Steering Group continued as follows:[16]

> We recognise the concern that introduction of extraneous considerations into rules governing continuing relationships within companies may prevent management from focusing on the key business of managing to generate wealth. But we also recognise that the corporate sector remains the most important component of the productive economy; the laws governing its constitution, management and accountability already recognise wider interests. Best practice often goes further. Companies can be viewed largely as contractual entities, created and controlled under agreements entered into by members and directors; but we do not accept that it follows that the law has no place in securing that they are operated so that a wider range of interests are met. It is a proper question of public policy whether company law is an appropriate vehicle to achieve this, and what constraints and conditions should be attached to corporate status and limited liability. But we believe that, in designing a legislative and broader framework to enable companies properly to respond, we should ensure wherever possible that the law enables both internal and external interests to be satisfied.

Taken at face value, this crucial contextual statement goes beyond a simple rejection of the idea that non-shareholder interests such as employee, consumer and environmental interests lie beyond the proper reach of corporate law. It also points to the limits of contract-based and market-based views of companies in capturing the balance of public and private interests properly infusing corporate law and practice. Regardless of the compromises and relatively conservative outcome reached by the Steering Group in its final recommendations, such statements arguably open up the interplay between public and private interests in corporate responsibility and governance to new possibilities.

In making its final report to the UK Government, the CLR Steering Group concluded that answering one of the most fundamental questions of corporate responsibility – namely 'in whose interests should companies be run'[17] – needs to be done 'in a way which reflects modern business needs *and* wider expectations of responsible business behaviour'.[18] The CLR Steering Group's conception of ESV aligns the company's interests with those of its members as a whole, given that 'our proposed statement of the duty of loyalty makes clear the obligation of each director to act to serve the purposes of the company as laid down in the constitution and as set for it by its members collectively: that is, it sets as the basic goal for directors the success of the company in the collective best interests of shareholders'.[19] Next comes an important gloss. 'But it also requires them to recognise, as the circumstances require, the company's need to foster relationships with its employees, customers and suppliers, its need to maintain its business reputation, and its need to consider the company's impact on the community and the working environment', adds the CLR Steering Group.[20]

Moreover, in an immediate follow-up comment, the CLR Steering Group identifies the connection between this fundamental rationale and its manifestation in both directors' duties and corporate reporting obligations. 'Just as companies should be required to provide an account of these factors in their annual reports where relevant to their business, so the need to take account of them should be reflected in the way in which directors' duties are expressed', according to the Steering Group.[21] This dual relevance of the ESV approach for directors' duties and corporate reporting obligations is also reflected in the UK Government's endorsement of the broad outcomes of the CLR in its 2005 White Paper, *Company Law Reform*:[22]

> The CLR proposed that the basic goal for directors should be the success of the company for the benefit of its members as a whole; but that, to reach this goal, directors would need to take a properly balanced view of the implications of decisions over time and foster effective relationships with employees, customers and suppliers, and in the community more widely. The Government strongly agrees that this approach, which the CLR called 'enlightened shareholder value', is most likely to drive long-term company performance and maximise overall competitiveness and wealth and welfare for all. It will therefore be reflected in the statement of directors' duties, and in new reporting arrangements for quoted companies under the Operating and Financial Review Regulations.

The CLR Steering Group explained the deficiencies in some conventional approaches to shareholder value and the superiority of the idea of ESV in the following terms:[23]

> Those who adopt an approach of this kind argue that the ultimate objective of companies as currently enshrined in law – i.e. to generate maximum value for shareholders – is in principle the best means also of securing overall prosperity and welfare. Many who take this view point out as well, however, that in practice neither maximum value for shareholders, nor overall prosperity and welfare, may be achieved. This is said to be because management may fail to recognise that the way to success is in many cases through building long term relationships dependent on trust (and that, where this is so, this is what the law requires). It is argued that exclusive focus on the short-term financial bottom line, in the erroneous belief that this equates to shareholder value, will often be incompatible with the cultivation of co-operative relationships, which are likely to involve short-term costs but to bring greater benefits in the longer term. Thus the law as currently expressed and understood fails to deliver the necessary inclusive approach.

Yet, significantly, the CLR Steering Group conceded that 'the enlightened shareholder value approach is not dependent on any change in the ultimate objective of companies, that is, shareholder wealth maximisation', and that accordingly this approach did not require a change to the fundamental fiduciary obligations of directors towards companies.[24] Rather, what was needed was a change in the 'expression' and 'focus' of the existing law, rather than a radical overhaul of the design and content of that existing law. 'The argument is that these duties, as currently expressed, and as interpreted in practice, often tend to lead to an undue focus on the short term and the narrow interest of members at the expense of what is in a broader and a longer term sense the best interest of the enterprise, and thus its value to them as ultimate controllers able to realise that value', concluded the CLR Steering Group.[25]

The connection between 'enlightened' shareholder-focused models, corporate orthodoxy and limited forms of CSR is not a new one. 'If the social responsibility of business merely means a more enlightened view as to the ultimate advantage of the stockholder-owners, then obviously corporate managers may accept such social responsibility without any departure from the traditional view that their function is to seek to obtain the maximum amount of profits for their stockholders', as Professor Dodd noted in the classic Berle–Dodd debate of the 1930s.[26] So, what difference does ESV really make, at least in CSR terms?

FEATURES OF THE DUTY OF DIRECTORS TO PROMOTE A COMPANY'S SUCCESS

> For the first time, the Bill includes a statutory statement of directors' general duties. It provides a code of conduct that sets out how directors are expected to behave. That enshrines in statute what the law review called 'enlightened shareholder value'. It recognises that directors will be more likely to achieve long term sustainable success for the benefit of their shareholders if their companies pay attention to a wider range of matters. . . . Directors will be required to promote the success of the company in the collective best interest of the shareholders, but in doing so they will have to have regard to a wider range of factors, including the interests of employees and the environment.
>
> – Alistair Darling, during parliamentary debate about the UK Companies Act[27]

Enshrining 'Enlightened Shareholder Value' in Directors' Duties

The version of the fundamental directors' duty of loyalty to the company that finally emerged from the UK Parliament in the Companies Act in November 2006 is in the following terms:[28]

Duty to promote the success of the company

(1) A director of a company must act in the way he considers, in good faith, would be most likely to promote the success of the company for the benefit of its members as a whole, and in doing so have regard (amongst other matters) to –
   (a) the likely consequences of any decision in the long term,
   (b) the interests of the company's employees,
   (c) the need to foster the company's business relationships with suppliers, customers and others,
   (d) the impact of the company's operations on the community and the environment,
   (e) the desirability of the company maintaining a reputation for high standards of business conduct, and
   (f) the need to act fairly as between members of the company.

(2) Where or to the extent that the purposes of the company consist of or include purposes other than the benefit of its members, subsection (1) has effect as if the reference to promoting the success of the company for the benefit of its members were to achieving those purposes.

(3) The duty imposed by this section has effect subject to any enactment or rule of law requiring directors, in certain circumstances, to consider or act in the interests of creditors of the company.

This legislative instruction requiring directors to consider designated shareholder and stakeholder interests was summarized in parliamentary debate on the Act in January 2006 as follows:[29]

> The duty to promote the success of the company answers one of the fundamental questions in company law: 'in whose interests should companies be run?'. In line with the recommendation

of the Company Law Review, the Bill's answer is that directors should run the company for the benefit of its members collectively. However, directors will not be successful in promoting the success of the company if they focus on only the short-term financial bottom line. Successful companies see business prosperity and responsible business behaviour as two sides of the same coin. That is why, in line with the recommendation of the Company Law Review, the Bill adopts an approach known as 'enlightened shareholder value', under which a director must, in promoting the success of the company, have regard to factors such as the long-term consequences of business decisions and the impact of the company's activities on employees, the community and the environment.

Elements and Critiques of the Duty to Promote Corporate Success

(T)here is little guidance as to how directors are to act in practice. The provision sets out a menu of non-shareholder interests to which directors are to have regard, but fails to give any guidance as to the form this 'regard' should take and as a consequence gives no indication for directors as to what they must do in order to comply with the provision.

– University of Leeds' Professor of Corporate and Commercial Law, Professor Andrew Keay[30]

In both structure and content, this statutory duty of loyalty bears a similarity to at least some corporate constituency laws in the USA. It grafts some elements of stakeholder-regarding constituency statutes onto a shareholder-centred account of directors' duties. Its main list of decision-making factors contains the most important framework-setting considerations for directors, but is not exhaustive. Its mandatory nature extends only to an obligation to take account of particular interests, as distinct from an obligation to give effect to them. So, there is no obligation to advantage employees or any other non-shareholder interests at all, and certainly not ahead of shareholder interests.

This legislated directors' duty does not offer any guidance to directors on how to follow its mandate. That is left for the courts or other forms of regulatory guidance. In other words, it presumes but makes no contribution itself towards measures for assessing, weighing and deciding between different shareholder and non-shareholder interests. As the duty is formulated as a duty owed to the company, there is no direct conflict of legal duties owed to different parties, however difficult it might be to resolve competitions of interests at a secondary level in fulfilling that overriding duty. In addition, directors will still need to exercise independent judgment, use care and diligence, and otherwise comply with other directors' duties in the exercise of identifying and considering relevant decision-making factors contemplated by the duty of loyalty to the company.[31] Whatever their justification, some of these features are problematic in practice.[32]

As noted by other Anglo-Commonwealth commentators on these UK developments, the UK formulation of a directors' duty of loyalty to the company remains focused on the duty of directors to pursue the company's success for the collective benefit of its shareholders, with their obligation to consider relevant interests of employees, customers and others in the community being structured within that overriding duty.[33] What frames the mandatory obligation to have regard to a range of shareholder-related and other stakeholder-related interests is the director's good faith judgment that a particular decision or course of action 'would be most likely to promote the success of the company for the benefit of its members as a whole'.[34] In short, it seeks to tie its stakeholder-inclusive elements to that overriding norm, thereby circumventing any concern about possible erosion of boardroom accountability to shareholders, due to the explicit introduction of non-shareholder considerations in boardroom decision-making. However, what remains unclear is the extent to which the orientation of that shareholder-based focus is itself conditioned by the follow-up legislative list of designated decision-making considerations, especially in framing what truly contributes to corporate success in the 21st century UK business environment.

The clear link between corporate success and shareholders' interests in this legislative formulation of directors' duties limits its capacity to travel too far beyond enlightened corporate self-interest. Nevertheless, citing concerns expressed by legal professional bodies during parliamentary consideration of the Companies Bill, corporate governance scholars foresee other potential problems with its interpretation and application:[35]

> A director cannot discharge the duty without having regard to the factors listed . . . The introduction of a list of factors which the directors are obliged to consider makes it more likely that the courts will intervene in matters previously left to business judgment.

> It is unclear how extensive are the inquiries which the directors are required to make in order to obtain information relevant to the matters which are listed. It is also unclear what weight the directors are expected to attribute to the competing factors. Although the basic duty is clarified by reference to the directors' good faith, the obligation to have regard to the factors listed is absolute. The Law Society regards this as a significant change from the current law and thought that it would make it more difficult for directors to manage.

Still, whatever criticisms might be made of the statutory duty to promote a company's success, it responds to acknowledged features of the 21st century business environment. First, it amounts to clear and unequivocal official rejection of short-termism, and endorsement of the need for a long-term business vision that is also inclusive of key business relationships. At the same time, the limits of short-termism must not be overstated. 'The concern for short-term corporate performance is dominant in the Anglo-American corporate model, as most shareholders are institutional shareholders whose primary concern (rightly or otherwise) is the short-term financial gain on capital', notes one commentator.[36] Making long-term corporate value the primary or sole benchmark for corporate value compels all shareholders 'to keep their capital in the company for a long time until rewards can be seen'.[37] Yet, different kinds of shareholders have different but equally valid investment objectives and time-frames, so that a short-term investment horizon is not inherently worse than a long-term one, at least from their standpoint, if not from the company's standpoint. They exercise different forms of market discipline over companies accordingly, such as the threat of exit by those most upset about short-term drops in share prices, and the use of voice at company meetings by those most concerned about the socio-ethical impact of a company's choice of profit-making options.[38]

Secondly, it establishes a common framework for boardroom decision-making that is consistent with pre-existing UK corporate law, but which more explicitly and comprehensively relates that framework and body of law to the UK Parliament's perception of the

21st century business environment. At the very least, the structure of the decision-making framework and the additional mandatory obligation to consider designated interests in a proper way together combine to shift the focus away from any free-market fundamentalist and reductionist shareholder-centric view of the company and what is necessary for its success. One of the architects of the CLR Steering Group's final report to the UK Government makes this clear:[39]

> As far as directors' duties are concerned, this is the heart of the ESV approach. The aim is to make it clear that although shareholder interests are predominant (promotion of the success of the company for the benefit of its members), the promotion of shareholder interests does not require riding roughshod over the interests of other groups upon whose activities the business of the company is dependent for its success. In fact, the promotion of the interests of the shareholders will normally require the interests of other groups of people to be fostered. The interests of non-shareholder groups thus need to be considered by the directors, but, of course, in this shareholder-centred approach, only to the extent that the protection of those other interests promotes the interests of the shareholders.

Thirdly, it has a mix of elements of different qualities that broadly reflect the dynamics affecting directors in practice. These different elements include explicit shareholder-sensitive elements (e.g. 'act in the way [which] would be most likely to promote the success of the company for the benefit of its members as a whole') and explicit stakeholder-sensitive elements (e.g. 'the interests of the company's employees'). They also include intra-constituency decision-making factors (e.g. 'the need to act fairly as between members of the company') and general decision-making factors (e.g. 'the likely consequences of any decision in the long term').

Fourthly, it recognizes the need for a comprehensive informational base for internal and external corporate reporting purposes that is integrated with boardroom decision-making, with a cohesive blend of financial and non-financial considerations. This is reinforced in the explicit connection now drawn in the UK Companies Act 2006 between the information provided to investors under a company's business review and how well the directors are meeting their obligation to promote the company's success. Finally, it is capable of accommodating greater interaction of corporate and societal interests within the mechanisms of corporate governance, decision-making and reporting.

At the same time, there remains considerable doubt about the extent to which ESV represents a real departure from shareholder primacy or the pre-existing law. Some commentators view ESV as striking a middle path between the two polar extremes of shareholder primacy and stakeholder pluralism,[40] while others view it as embodying the rhetoric of CSR but remaining firmly grounded substantively in the structures and outcomes of conventional shareholder primacy. Arguably, a government fully embracing a public policy of corporate citizenship, which recognizes that 'the purpose of business is more than just to make a financial profit, and that business is therefore more broadly accountable to society than its responsibilities to shareholders', would extend corporate law reform beyond even ESV.[41]

'The Company Law Review, for example, whilst extensive and in many ways progressive, has failed to set the stage for . . . a broadening of business purpose', according to corporate sustainability advocate, Dr Simon Zadek, 'in that it argues that the responsibility of companies to their broader stakeholder community should be limited to where it serves the interests of their shareholders', notwithstanding that 'the European policy debate emerging following the publication of the EU Green Paper on Corporate Social Responsibility offers an important route for promoting a broadening of the purpose of business'.[42] This tension between the terms in which UK corporate law now encapsulates such CSR concerns and the ongoing evolution of broader CSR policy and regulatory debate within the EU is more likely to increase rather than decrease as the interpretation and application of the new UK corporate law unfolds, with correlative implications in each domain for their respective CSR-related reforms. 'Arguably, the only enlightened element seems to be found in the recognition that directors may take into account material interests, namely those enumerated in section 172(1), if they wish and not be sued for doing so, but this is only provided that the action that they take promotes the success of the company for the benefit of the members as a whole [and] the overall effect of section 172(1) is that ESV can be classified as a "shareholders first interpretation"', argues Professor Andrew Keay.[43] However, even such critics of the real value of ESV accept the possibility 'that ESV will legitimise what is already occurring in the UK, Australia, and even the US, namely far-sighted managers considering the interests of non-shareholder stakeholders so far as it fosters corporate profits'.[44] In short, the ESV approach to directors' duties offers neither complete maintenance of the status quo nor a complete clean slate. There is still much legal work of interpretation and application to be done, and possibly some surprises yet to unfold.

The Composite Merger of Corporate and Shareholder Interests

> (T)he main purpose in codifying the general duties of directors is to make what is expected of directors clearer and to make the law more accessible to them and to others.
>
> – Lord Goldsmith, during parliamentary debate about the UK Companies Act[45]

One of the key structural features of the new statutory directors' duty of loyalty is its unequivocal mandate to directors to govern the company with a view to its success for the collective benefit of its shareholders. Under this statutory formulation, the company's success and the interests of the members are integrally linked. Both conceptually and operationally, how satisfactory is this co-identification of company and shareholder interests, and its correlative treatment of other stakeholders? In linking 'the success of the company' with 'the benefit of its members as a whole', the legislated duty conflates those two things to the exclusion of other aspects of the relationship between a corporation and the various shareholding and stakeholding elements of its corporate constituency. The idea of the members as a whole is an abstraction that does not automatically correspond to the interests of an existing mass of shareholders at any actual point in time. The question of interpretation under UK corporate law now is how this notion relates to the company's success and to the designated statutory criteria that relate to that success.

UK corporate law has not always spoken with one voice about the relation between a company's interests and its overall corporate constituency, especially in the nuances of the case law surrounding proper corporate purposes and the interests of the company in a variety of contexts.[46] Directly connecting the company's interests to the interests of shareholders as a whole works best for those doctrinal areas of corporate law where the two are co-extensive, especially in relation to directors' duties. 'Under the traditional rules of company law, directors' duties are regarded as being owed to the company and to the company alone; and for this purpose the company's interests are equated with the interests of the members collectively', as one Anglo-Commonwealth scholar described the general position under corporate law, decades before the 2006 Companies Act.[47] However, the composite merger of corporate and shareholder interests arguably creates some infelicities of fit for other doctrines which depend more firmly upon distinctions between the company as a distinct legal entity, the discrete interests of different groups of shareholders beyond their collective corporate role and other corporate stakeholder interests.[48]

To this point, it is evident that the explicit linkage of a company's interests and the benefit of its shareholders in the new UK legislative duty of loyalty still leaves open the question of exactly what is required to achieve the success of the company for that purpose. In particular, this still leaves some questions about how the interests of other constituencies relate to this particular formulation of corporate success, especially in light of the decision-making framework and list of factors also relating to this statutory duty of loyalty. 'It will take a number of cases to determine whether success is the same as maximising wealth', warns Australian corporate commentator, Dr Bill Beerworth, noting a possible slide in emphasis here from the law's traditional conception of shareholder wealth-maximization to perhaps a broader conception of corporate success.[49] Similarly, one of the two Australian governmental bodies reporting in 2006 on possible CSR reform reported concerns that the UK provision, if adopted in Australia, 'could result in a radical change from traditional company law . . . as some form of general departure from the current obligation of directors . . . to act in the best interests of the shareholders generally'.[50] Moreover, if concepts like 'the interests of the company' and its 'success' can be aligned by judicial interpretation over time with changing community expectations of companies and their directors, there is already an in-built capacity to integrate corporate and community interests, at least to some degree.[51]

Assessing what constitutes 'the success of the company for the benefit of its members as a whole' cannot be disentangled from the fact that the duty is one owed to the company itself and not to any particular corporate constituency.[52] This does not mean that the interest of the company is to be considered as an end in itself. The member-orientated formulation of the statutory duty of loyalty works against this. So too does the irrationality of imbuing a non-human entity with purposeful existence beyond serving as a vehicle for fulfillment of human interests, as recognized by the body of Anglo-Commonwealth case law identifying the corporation's shareholding constituency as the relevant body for this purpose.[53] 'The duty of management can accordingly be stated as a duty to promote the success of the business venture, *in order to* benefit the members', concluded CLR Steering Group member, the late Professor John Parkinson, reflecting on the law's orthodox position on this point, more than 10 years before the UK's enactment of the new statutory duty of loyalty of directors.[54] However, this still leaves considerable avenues of judicial interpretation in identifying what is necessary to foster the success of a company *as an enterprise*, as now conditioned in new legislative ways.

Likewise, the companion component of 'the benefit of its members as a whole' is likely to be shaped heavily by pre-existing law in various contexts on what constitutes the collective interest of shareholders. The conclusion in UK and Australian law at least is that, in the context of directors' duties, the interests of the company's shareholding constituency include the interests of both existing and future shareholders.[55] This does not mean that directors who act in the short-term interests of existing shareholders necessarily breach their duty to the company's shareholders as a whole.[56] Rather, the inclusion of future shareholders here signifies that the interests of shareholders in the company is 'a continuing one', and that the time horizon over which the interests of the members as a group properly fall to be assessed is longer than simply an immediate takeover threat, this year's opportunity for dividends, or the next quarterly movement in share prices.[57] 'The directors are accordingly not obliged to maximise current profits in order to satisfy short-term demands for dividends at the expense of a growth in profitability over a longer period', as Professor Parkinson concludes.[58] Once again, the new statutory formulation of a director's duty of loyalty reinforces rather than detracts from this position.

What is significant for the future is that the composite concept, 'the success of the company for the benefit of its members as a whole', *as conditioned by* the designated list of mandated boardroom decision-making factors, does not have the kind of baseline of pre-existing law that surrounds more discrete notions such as 'the interests of the company' and 'the shareholders as a whole' under existing doctrines of corporate law.[59] The general corporate law from which this statutory formulation of duty emerges has evolved and adapted to different corporate and societal conditions over time. The statutory formulation can be expected to do the same, although its present structure will prevent any court from ever interpreting it to produce a situation where company directors directly owe duties or provide remedies to multiple stakeholders. Still, the question for the future is how much judges might be able to use this controlling composite concept to shape interpretation of the elements of the statutory statement of duty in ways that extend beyond current law.

Future Possibilities in Argument About Directors' Duties

The full potential of the UK duty of loyalty for directors can only be appreciated and realized against the background of a deeper conception of corporate responsibility. On one model of responsibility potentially in play here, as described by Professor Parkinson, directors transparently and fully take non-shareholder interests and third-party effects into account, still within the incentive structures and other constraints of markets and legal regulation.[60] In this holistic view of corporate responsibility, the organization and its executives behave responsibly through decision-making processes analogous to those of human beings as moral agents, with considerations of rationality, other-regarding respect, and moral evaluation of likely consequences.[61] The 'process' of CSR associated with the first model therefore is one in which the company's decision-making procedures are 'moralised', so that directors properly consider and appropriately weigh the interests of those affected.[62] As Professor Parkinson describes:[63]

> The aim is not to institutionalise any specific moral code, nor to produce any particular morally approved outcomes. What is envisaged instead is that by factoring an awareness of third-party interests into the decision-making process, and requiring decision makers to reflect on the

consequences of corporate actions, a better balancing of company and external interests is likely to result.

On a different model described by Parkinson, enhanced responsibility is achieved by reforming managerial decision-making processes to 'induce an organisational response through interest group empowerment'.[64] This view perceives socially responsible corporate behaviour as 'the product of decision-making processes that are open to influence by the parties affected by corporate activity'.[65] The 'process' of CSR associated with the second model is to enhance corporate responsiveness to the interests of affected parties, by increasing their power to influence and shape corporate behaviour.[66] This can be done by affording them internal constitutional status for corporate governance purposes, increasing their ability to put external pressure upon the company, or other strengthened means of calling the company to account in some way.[67] The ultimate aim is to enhance 'the rationality of the interest-weighing process', while also navigating the traps of interest group power-wielding,[68] in conditioning business decision-making to the true mix of corporate and public interests in play.

In practice, the two models complement each other in Parkinson's eyes, with reform initiatives often relying upon a combination of these models.[69] Both models also rely upon a form of 'social responsibility as a process concept', thereby avoiding the political and moral controversies conventionally associated with theorizing about 'substantive corporate social responsibility'.[70] Both models view that form of responsibility 'as a characteristic of decision-making processes rather than as involving compliance with a particular set of substantive behavioural norms',[71] about which there is endless philosophical and ideological debate. In other words, CSR is viewed in terms of qualities of the corporate decision-making process, instead of substantive outcomes to be achieved.[72] At the same time, nothing in the notion of CSR as a 'process' concept prevents meta-regulatory alignment between responsibility-inducing organizational systems (including boardroom decision-making processes) and designated public policy goals for CSR that enhance this institutional inculcation of responsibility.[73] This is part of the new order of corporate governance in the 21st century, which itself forms part of wider systems of governance, regulation, and responsibility, in ways explored throughout this book.

The present UK position on the directors' duty of loyalty is closer to the first model than the second model outlined above, although its internalization of business externalities is conditioned by its firm anchoring in ESV. Writing long before the new UK Companies Act was even in contemplation, and with real-life models such as the American Law Institute's *Principles of Corporate Governance* in mind, Professor Parkinson highlighted the normative implications of directors being obliged to consider particular interests, in terms that have some resonance with the new orientation of UK directors' duties, as follows:[74]

> (B)roadening directors' discretion to permit them to depart from the requirements of profit maximisation would be a necessary adjustment to create an appropriate legal setting for the changes in management behaviour that are the intended consequence of other methods of inducing responsibility. *A reformed fiduciary duty might accordingly stipulate that the directors are under an obligation to conduct the business for profit, but that in so doing they must take account of affected interests (which might be specified)* . . . To the extent that the objection is simply that directors would be free to act in ways that are not designed to maximise shareholder wealth, that is, of course, the point of the change.

In other words, corporate success might be predicted upon responsible corporate profit-making that achieves realistic shareholder wealth-generation but not shareholder wealth-maximization at all costs, with built-in checks and balances that condition the corporation's responsible pursuit of profit by requiring corporate executives to focus upon who the company affects, how those effects relate back to the company's success, and what a morally responsible director would do. Still, in the absence of clear legislative intent in the 2006 Companies Act to effect a radically reformed notion of UK directors' duties, reinforced by pre-existing case law heavily built around notions of shareholder primacy and value, UK courts are unlikely to use the Act's conception of corporate success for the members to travel too far in the opposite direction, except perhaps in conditioning directors' duties through new interpretations of the interplay between elements in the legislated duties. In other words, there are considerable in-built safeguards against overly enthusiastic judicial innovation in this area.

However, even if the new statutory formulation of a director's duty of loyalty is largely held to reflect the pre-existing UK corporate law on directors' duties, it still offers a number of potential benefits from a CSR perspective. An express and official declaration of the importance of both shareholder and non-shareholder interests in boardroom decision-making, and the explicit inclusion of factors going to both kinds of considerations in the new legislative framework, has considerable public value. At the very least, it is no longer plausible for company directors, professional corporate advisers, regulatory officials or anyone else to make the easy intellectual slide from the interests of the company to the interests of the shareholders as a group, and from there to short-term shareholder advantage by whatever means necessary as a proxy for both notions. Breaking these false connections is of considerable substantive benefit in its own right. At the same time, the statutory duty of loyalty does more than simply list non-shareholder interests and third party effects to be taken into account merely in an instrumental way. It also positions them within a broader boardroom decision-making framework, concentrating upon what truly makes a business enterprise successful in the 21st century business environment. To that extent, it opens up space for a wider exposition of the elements that truly constitute corporate success, as affected by its relationship with other societal dynamics.

In particular, this new frame for directors' duties could place more intangible, long-range, non-financial matters on the corporate radar as elements going to corporate risk and the drivers of corporate success. If so, it might not be as revolutionary as currently thought in some quarters for a court, acting with the benefit of hindsight and in the wake of crystallized financial losses for companies, to link these losses to a failure by directors to satisfy the requirements of their statutory duty of loyalty to the company. This might be done in terms that broaden the boardroom horizon beyond conventional boundaries, at least by reference to the range of interests, information bases and timescales for assessment, given the mandated considerations now enshrined in UK corporate law as matters relating to corporate success. In other words, is it really so fanciful to imagine that a court might try to give some meaning to a board's collective failure to have due regard for 'the impact of the company's operations on the community and the environment', for example, in a situation of corporate financial loss resulting from a board's failure to respond early enough or at all to a richer, more complex and more interactive set of corporate drivers and risks than conventionally imagined by some boards in the business community under prevailing business practice?[75]

All of this has wider implications for a system of corporate meta-regulation too. In other words, it makes a difference in regulatory approach whether something like the statutory duty of loyalty is viewed simply as a self-contained, state-mandated framework for boardroom decision-making, capable of being approached on a minimalist compliance basis, or alternatively an exercise in 'meta-regulation of the corporate conscience' that is grounded in law, but also focused upon opening up corporate processes to more dynamic interest assessment as an exercise of corporate self-learning, as one of a number of mutually reinforcing regulatory measures.[76] Assessed from this perspective, the ultimate success or failure of the UK's new legislative regime for directors' duties will depend as much upon other regulatory and behavioural responses as upon its legal content as interpreted and applied by UK courts.

Other Corporate Purposes?

In the UK statutory formulation of the duty of loyalty, the duty to promote the company's success for its members' collective benefit is predicated upon that being the company's purpose. Other purposes are accommodated by making the statutory decision-making framework and correlative list of designated decision-making factors apply to them too, 'as if the reference to promoting the success of the company for the benefit of its members were to achieving those purposes'.[77] This provision has been criticized for not providing meaningful guidance for courts or anyone else on when these other purposes might apply and what they might be,[78] but this criticism is misdirected. As explanatory material accompanying the original Company Law Reform Bill indicates, this provision is aimed at companies of a different kind such as community interest companies (CICs).[79] It is not designed to open up the possibility that small business enterprises, publicly listed companies or other profit-orientated corporations might have purposes that diverge too far or at all from the primary purpose of advancing the company's success for its members.

Decision-making Framework for Company Directors

Much confusion and scepticism in some quarters still surround the function and operation of the boardroom decision-making framework and correlative list of key decision-making factors outlined in the directors' statutory duty of loyalty. Although the official Guidance on Key Clauses accompanying the Company Law Reform Bill's introduction into the UK Parliament indicated that directors must not simply pay lip service to the provision's requirements, at the same time it could prove difficult evidentially to prove that they have duly considered the stipulated factors.[80] One common criticism, but of limited effect, is that this formulation of the directors' duty of loyalty is too uncertain, in that it offers no meaningful guidance on how directors must consider and weigh the designated factors within the framework. For example, the Australian Parliamentary Joint Committee on Corporations and Financial Services (PJCCFS) criticized the UK model of the duty of loyalty as one that 'requires directors to have regard to a menu of non-shareholder interests, but gives no guidance as to what form this "regard" should take, and therefore gives no guidance to directors on what they must do in order to comply'.[81] The PJCCFS also concluded that such 'directive' laws risk breeding a 'compliance-driven, box-ticking' culture.[82]

> The Government believe that our enlightened shareholder value approach will be mutually beneficial to business and society . . . Consideration of the factors will be an integral part of the duty to promote the success of the company for the benefit of its members as a whole. The clause makes it clear that a director is to have regard to the factors in fulfilling that duty. The decisions taken by a director and the weight given to the factors will continue to be a matter for his good faith judgment.
>
> The words 'have regard to' mean 'think about'; they are absolutely not about just ticking boxes. If 'thinking about' leads to the conclusion, as we believe it will in many cases, that the proper course is to act positively to achieve the objectives in the clause, that will be what the director's duty is. In other words 'have regard to' means 'give proper consideration to' . . .
>
> – Margaret Hodge, UK Minister of State for Industry and the Regions, during parliamentary debate about the UK Companies Act[83]

The later Corporations and Markets Advisory Committee (CAMAC) Report on CSR took a similar line, agreeing that Australian corporate law is already 'sufficiently broad to enable corporate decision-makers to take into account the environmental and social impacts of their decisions, including changes in societal expectations about the role of companies and how they should conduct their affairs'.[84] Contrary to the CLR Steering Group's conclusions and the UK Government's agreement in enacting the 2006 Companies Act, CAMAC foresaw no meaningful improvement in the clarity and application of the law or the quality of boardroom decision-making from prescribing designated decision-making factors by law:[85]

> The Committee is not persuaded that the elaboration of interests that, where relevant, can already be taken into account would improve the quality of corporate decision-making in any practical way. A non-exhaustive catalogue of interests to be taken into account serves little useful purpose for directors and affords them no guidance on how various interests are to be weighed, prioritised or reconciled.
>
> Also, the courts, through their interpretation of the law, including the requirement . . . for directors and others to act in the 'best interests of the company', can assist in aligning corporate behaviour with changing community expectations. Given this, it is unnecessary to amend [the law] along the lines of section 172 of the UK Companies Act and no worthwhile benefit is to be gained.

CAMAC went further, characterizing any new law that required or permitted directors to consider particular decision-making factors or stakeholder interests as one that could be 'counter-productive' as it might 'blur rather than clarify the purpose that directors are expected to serve', with the possible result of decreased accountability of directors to shareholders, but without any correlative enhancement in stakeholder protection.[86]

Even allowing for the ideological positions that underlie pre-existing corporate law in both countries, such criticisms seek from this kind of law more certainty and decision-making guidance than legislation generally can offer,[87] or even than the general law already supplies in many areas, including the amount of practical guidance capable of being extracted from current case law and legislation on directors' duties. At the very least, this kind of law explicitly and clearly denounces any connection between true corporate interests and the kind of damaging short-termism that fixates on short-range share price fluctuations and shareholder wealth-maximization at all costs, at a time when business short-termism is an acknowledged and pervasive problem. It poses no threat to the legitimate circumstances in which CAMAC considered that directors might rightly consider both short-term and long-term consequences in reaching proper decisions about corporate best interests.[88]

It also sets a common framework for boardroom decision-making as a matter of regulatory consistency for companies of different sizes and in different sectors. Such a framework inevitably requires complementary regulatory guidance, from official corporate regulators, the business and legal sectors, and others. Hence, a more potent source of criticism might focus upon the legislated duty's lack of support from other policy and regulatory goals enhancing corporate responsibility and governance outcomes,[89] on one hand, and other state and non-state regulatory sources of boardroom decision-making guidance, on the other.

Whatever those skilled in law might know about the law of directors' duties beyond what is laid down in legislation, such legislative statements of duties make apparent for directors and others a legal framework for decision-making (and a correlative range of decision-making factors) that is otherwise fully discernible only from legal textbooks, court judgments and professional advice. Its enshrinement in legislation avoids inconsistencies in how different boards might discern what the law of directors' duties requires or permits when it comes to considering a wide range of stakeholder interests. The impact of such a law is more structural, generic and process-orientated than substantive, context-specific and outcome-orientated. In short, it is not designed to delineate specific ways in which various decision-making factors should be weighed and prioritized in reaching particular conclusions in specific circumstances about what lies in a corporation's best interests.

LEGISLATIVE RULES FOR INTERPRETING UK DIRECTORS' DUTIES

Although the duties in relation to directors have developed in a distinctive way, they are often manifestations of more general principles . . . [It] is intended to enable the courts to continue to have regard to development in the common law rules and equitable principles applying to these other types of fiduciary relationships. The advantage of that is it will enable the statutory duties to develop in line with relevant developments in the law as it applies elsewhere.

– Lord Goldsmith, Lords Grand Committee, during parliamentary consideration of the UK Companies Act[90]

The statutory statement of directors' duties for the UK outlines a comprehensive range of duties, with counterparts in other Anglo-Commonwealth corporate regulatory regimes.[91] However, UK corporate law now does more than simply codify the existing common law position on directors' duties, thereafter leaving the development, interpretation and priority of the legislative formulations of the duties to the normal rules of statutory interpretation in common law systems. In the UK, the transformation of directors' duties into legislative form is accompanied by these legislative guides to their interpretation and effect:

170 Scope and nature of general duties

    (1)   The general duties . . . are owed by a director of a company to the company.

. . .

    (3)   The general duties are based on certain common law rules and equitable principles as they apply in relation to directors and have effect in place of those rules and principles as regards the duties owed to a company by a director.

    (4)   The general duties shall be interpreted and applied in the same way as common law rules or equitable principles, and regard shall be had to the corresponding common law rules and equitable principles in interpreting and applying the general duties.

In short, this means that UK directors' duties are grounded in a firm baseline of pre-existing law and legal techniques for interpreting that body of law, but are also open to further development within the boundaries of the legislated duties, by reference to corresponding developments in the legal doctrines underlying these duties, such as corresponding doctrines of tortious and fiduciary obligations. So, future developments in the underlying doctrines that support the body of law on directors' duties will have ongoing relevance, together with judicial exposition of the meaning and application of the legislative statements of directors' duties as test cases on these provisions wind their way through the courts.

Commenting on the statutory instructions in section 170, leading Australian corporate law scholar and judge, Justice Robert Austin, predicts that these legislative guides for interpreting UK directors' duties 'may be the progenitors of a new judicial technique'.[92] Similarly, Lady Justice Mary Arden from the Court of Appeal of England and Wales, who was a member of the CLR Steering Group, notes this 'novel' statutory instruction on interpretation and its judicial potential, and places it against the wider background of other European inroads into modern UK judicial interpretation of legislation, such as the primacy of applicable EU law over inconsistent UK law, as well as the need to interpret UK legislation in conformity with European human rights jurisprudence.[93]

Accordingly, UK courts must do more than simply use the pre-existing body of case law on directors' duties to inform their equivalent codifications, all the time giving primacy to the statutory words over pre-existing formulations of the equivalent duties under the general law. Rather, the pre-existing law goes on to shape and condition interpretation of the codified forms, even if that produces 'a strained interpretation' of the legislation.[94] This could raise additional questions of interpretation, for example, about the extent to which the type and content of relevant background legal principles are amenable to further development in their application to directors' duties, informed by the law's evolution in both corporate and non-corporate areas of UK law and perhaps even wider Anglo-Commonwealth law relating to directors' duties.[95] This reinforces the ongoing need for comparative judicial, policy and law reform assessments in this area of law.

PRACTICAL IMPLICATIONS FOR DIRECTORS OF UK COMPANIES

Impact Upon Standard Boardroom Documentation and Procedures

> The clause does not impose a requirement on directors to keep records, as some people have suggested, in any circumstances in which they would not have to do so now.
>
> – Margaret Hodge, Minister of State for Industry and the Regions, during parliamentary consideration of the UK Companies Act[96]

Having canvassed some of the questions of legal interpretation that might be raised in future advice and test cases on the UK Companies Act 2006, we can turn our attention to the equally important area of practical implications for UK company directors. Will the new era of statutory directors' duties in UK corporate law mean extra vigilance and safeguards for company directors, at least in the settling-in phase of the new law? Is it now easier or harder for shareholders or someone else to challenge what directors do? Can any new or interim uncertainty be exploited tactically by activist shareholders or corporate outsiders in raising arguments in court proceedings that cannot easily be dismissed out of hand?[97] If the legal liability or correlative practical work for directors increases as a result, will that have the flow-on effect of making it harder for companies to recruit good directors?[98]

Some commentators predict that the new statutory statements of directors' duties in the UK will make little (if any) practical difference to boardroom practice or advice. In particular, the mandatory requirement for directors to consider designated stakeholder interests under their duty of loyalty to the company is thought, on one view, to allow directors 'to pay lip service' too easily to the designated factors, with the consequence that even such a mandatory requirement of consideration 'will make very little difference to how boards make decisions'.[99] Other commentators see some potential for at least some impact upon boardroom practices and advice. Both Lady Justice Arden and Justice Austin forecast that the embodiment of the ESV approach to directors' duties in the UK will probably raise the bar in practice for directors, especially in terms of practical safeguards to ensure that they can satisfy investors and regulators that they are meeting the right standard. Commenting on the UK reforms to directors' duties in the 2006 Companies Act, especially the pivotal duty of loyalty, Justice Austin says:[100]

> It seems likely that the reform will have an effect on boardroom process. Directors will have to be sure that their consideration of the effect of their decisions on the six matters listed in [section

172] is duly and adequately minuted. It remains to be seen whether corporate decision-making will be affected in any substantive way.

Lady Justice Arden also foreshadows the impact of the statutory directors' duties upon corporate law and boardroom practice, with particular emphasis upon the overriding directors' duty of loyalty to the company. Firstly, she identifies what the legal parameters of the duty of loyalty mean for how directors approach their decision-making role:[101]

> Section 172 states that a director must 'have regard' to relevant matters. This does not mean that a director must act with the aim of furthering those matters, for example the interests of the company's employees. They must give these matters appropriate weight . . . The weight to be given to particular matters will remain a matter for the judgment of the directors. It seems unlikely that the courts are to be required to substitute their views on such matters for those of the directors . . . However, lip service is unlikely to constitute appropriate consideration. A director must genuinely take the relevant matters into account, but his decision need not be dictated by them if that is not, in his good faith opinion, appropriate for the purpose of promoting the success of the company as a whole . . . In identifying the relevant considerations, the directors will be expected to act with reasonable skill and care in accordance with the further duty [of care, skill, and diligence].

Next, Lady Justice Arden applies this framing of directors' duties to standard boardroom documentation. Turning to how the necessary decision-making considerations might need to be brought to the attention of directors and recorded in a suitable form to meet any later challenge to their decisions, she suggests:[102]

> The relevant matters are often set out in the papers presented to the board of directors, and directors will generally be able to rely on such papers having been properly prepared. Board minutes are always important, and it would be sensible for directors to ensure that the minutes identify the relevant considerations for the purpose of section 172(2). However, where there are board papers, the minutes can often do this by reference to the board papers.

Some UK-based legal practitioners share these two judges' belief that this brave new world for company directors of evidencing how they comply with the framework of decision-making under section 172, especially its balancing of different specified factors, will inevitably increase the need for vigilance and documentary safeguards for directors, at least until UK courts develop clear signposts for due process in boardroom decision-making. Citing early fears of a 'compliance-driven approach to the exercise of directors' duties rather than one based on making good faith judgments', lawyer Alex Kay foresees the possibility of 'greater pressure on directors and, at the least, a bigger procedural burden, leading to lengthier board minutes that seek to evidence that the board has indeed taken the various factors into account'.[103]

Directors might take some comfort from the observation that the intention behind the legislative statement of directors' duties is not to second-guess the commercial judgments of directors, and yet remain sceptical about how far that margin of appreciation will extend before judicial intervention occurs, especially in the absence of a formal business judgment defence for directors. Developing case law will determine whether courts interpret this new statutory framework for a form of due process in boardroom decision-making in procedural or more substantive ways. Indeed, this inherent ambiguity in how section 172 in particular should be approached might well have assisted its ultimate parliamentary passage in this form.[104]

The Fall-back Safeguard of Shareholder Ratification

Unlike directors in other Anglo-American jurisdictions, directors who are subject to directors' duties under UK corporate law have no explicit business judgment rule or defence as a fall-back 'safe harbour' for their commercial decisions. This does not necessarily leave directors high and dry. 'The UK [Companies Act] does not provide any analogy to the business judgment rule, but it directs the attention of those who may seek to protect directors to the prospect of shareholder ratification', notes Justice Austin.[105] Thus, an alternative safeguard for directors lies in the use of shareholder ratification to cure what might otherwise amount to a breach of duty or other legal defect by directors, subject to the inherent limits of shareholder ratification.

Doubts remain in Australia about the extent to which all kinds of breaches of directors' duties encapsulated in legislative form can be excused by shareholders.[106] Principally, this is because the elevation of directors' duties to the level of publicly legislated standards of behaviour for directors takes the context beyond a simple matter of agreement between a company's directors and shareholders as a 'private' matter for the company and those connected with it, and elevates it to a 'public' matter of legislated standards for directors. Importantly, the UK Companies Act goes one step beyond current Australian law in legitimizing shareholder ratification of what might otherwise amount to a breach of a legislated duty. Legislative authorization is given for 'the ratification by a company of conduct by a director amounting to negligence, default, breach of duty or breach of trust in relation to the company', achieved through a resolution passed by a majority of shareholders who have no connection to the directors whose conduct is being ratified.[107]

Relationship Between the Directors' Duty to Promote the Company's Success and Other Obligations

Are there important connections between the duty of directors under section 172 and other directors' duties that, in practice, raise the standard even higher for boardroom decision-making? Section 179 of the UK Companies Act says:

> Except as otherwise provided, more than one of the general duties may apply in any given case.

One practical effect of this provision for directors is that their duty of loyalty to the company can interact with other directors' duties, with a correlative impact upon what they must do in practice to meet their legal obligations. In addition to the important duty of loyalty, for example, directors are also under the equally important duty of care and diligence, which is expressed in these terms in section 174 of the Act:

Duty to exercise reasonable care, skill and diligence

(1) A director of a company must exercise reasonable care, skill and diligence.
(2) This means the care, skill and diligence that would be exercised by a reasonably diligent person with –
  (a) the general knowledge, skill and experience that may reasonably be expected of a person carrying out the functions carried out by the director in relation to the company, and
  (b) the general knowledge, skill and experience that the director has.

So, combining this duty of care and diligence with the duty of loyalty, as section 179 allows, means that directors must also exercise care and diligence in their consideration of relevant shareholder and non-shareholder interests under their duty of loyalty.[108] In other words, they must properly consider those interests, whatever benchmark the courts apply to that requirement and whatever legal consequences attach to breaching it. This does not automatically mean that directors must generate any more of a paper trail to demonstrate fulfilment of both duties than would otherwise be required for each duty alone, but it highlights the reinforcing effect of the duty of loyalty in tandem with other directors' duties.

This interactive effect applies to connections between directors' duties and other corporate obligations too. Under section 417 of the UK Companies Act, the annual directors' report must include a 'business review', which must contain 'a fair review of the company's business' and 'a description of the principal risks and uncertainties facing the company'. The stated statutory rationale for this 'business review' links it directly to the duty of loyalty owed by directors and the use that the company's shareholders might make of the 'business review' in assessing how well the company's directors are performing that duty, as follows:[109]

> The purpose of the business review is to inform members of the company and help them assess how the directors have performed their duty under section 172 (duty to promote the success of the company).

Can Judges Second-guess Boardroom Decisions on Due Process Grounds?

> One proposition [is] that the result of this codification will be increased litigation. That is not how we see it . . . As in existing law, the general duties are owed by the director to the company. It follows that, as now, only the company can enforce them. Directors are liable to the company for loss to the company, and not more widely . . . [On] the provision of new duties, we do not see why that should lead to increased litigation either. For example . . . the need to have regard to the interests of employees as part of the main duty to promote the success of the company . . . was part of case law before becoming statute . . . We have no reason to expect that there will be a greater degree of litigation on those duties than there is now.
>
> – Lord Goldsmith, during parliamentary debate on the UK Companies Act[110]

In the abstract, numerous hurdles prevent the mandatory consideration of relevant non-shareholder interests by directors from becoming a litigation minefield for corporations and a corresponding litigation windfall for external stakeholders. The first hurdle is whether a failure by directors to consider relevant interests adequately (or at all) is a failure of due process that is justiciable in the courts. The second hurdle concerns the appropriate standard for due consideration of relevant stakeholder interests. Even if the matter is justiciable, UK judges immersed in regulatory and legal cultures that recognize some leeways of commercial judgment for directors are unlikely to set the bar too high for what constitutes due consideration in this context.

The third hurdle concerns who has standing to make a complaint about a failure of due consideration. Importantly, as the duty of loyalty is framed as a duty owed to the company, only the company and those who act through it (including shareholders who bring derivative actions in the company's name) are legitimate claimants. The fourth hurdle covers the onus of proof. Anyone with adequate standing to bring an action and who alleges a failure of due consideration of relevant interests by directors bears the usual onus of proof in making good that claim. The fifth and final hurdle concerns the appropriate remedy for an established failure of due consideration of relevant interests.

The twin concerns here are legal and practical. Legally, concern about the scope and likelihood of such challenges will remain, at least until the courts either reject the possibility of judicially reviewing boardroom decisions on grounds related to a failure of due process, or else establish clear boundaries for judicial intervention (if any) on process grounds. Even if these fears go unrealized, there remains the potential for expanding or at least recasting directors' duties in their current legislated form in ways that differ from the position that prevailed before their enactment. Practically, the concern is that the immediate post-enactment period of legal uncertainty about how courts will interpret and apply the new UK law on directors' duties will lead to an overly cautious and 'compliance-driven' emphasis upon the form and documentation of boardroom decisions, and a dampening of legitimate entrepreneurial decision-making.[111] 'It is likely that at least when the [Companies] Act is first brought into force there will be a number of challenges to decisions made by boards of companies in circumstances where such challenges would not previously have lain', predicted Lady Justice Arden soon after enactment of the UK Companies Act in late 2006.[112] At the same time, she tempered this prediction with the reality-check that 'it is unlikely that the courts will become involved in disputes about the process of corporate decision-making unless it results in a breach of duty which causes damage or loss to the company'.[113]

Although the potential exists for 'due process' claims based on inadequate consideration of stakeholder interests, others closely associated with the UK Company Law Review process hold little fears about this possibility:[114]

> It is true that the new requirement to take into account stakeholder interests in deciding what will promote the company's success is formulated partly in an objective way: where relevant such matters must be taken into account, subject to a reasonably practicable defence. In theory, therefore, there is opened up a new avenue of attack on directors' decisions, i.e. that although the decision was taken in subjective good faith, the directors did not take account of all relevant considerations. My guess, however, is that British judges will not use this opportunity to develop public-law like controls on the exercise by directors of their discretion and certainly the CLR's strategy did not depend upon their so doing – or even wish to encourage them to do so. Rather the enforcement message which the CLR envisaged as likely to have main impact in practice was disclosure via the OFR, plus action taken on the basis of that disclosure.

Continuing in this vein, Lady Justice Arden emphasizes the considerable obstacles that any litigant now faces in convincing UK judges to review boardroom decisions on due process grounds associated with the directors' duty of loyalty and its requirement to consider the listed interests.[115] While the UK has no formal business judgment rule or defence, in substance the weight to be given to different business considerations remains a matter for the commercial judgment of directors and not for second-guessing on their merits by the judgments of courts in hindsight.[116] In addition, there is a high threshold if the onus of proof is on the party alleging a failure by directors to consider something significant (and some harm arising from that). Furthermore, parties to contracts with a company will not be able to walk away from those contracts simply because of some failure by directors to consider a relevant interest connected to something listed in section 172, as any breach of duty would ordinarily be a breach of a duty owed to the company and not to the other contracting party.[117] Most significantly, due consideration of the official list of decision-framing factors in section 172 is not an end in itself, and so due process failures on their own are a necessary but not sufficient criterion for a breach of duty.

New Opportunities for Shareholder Actions Against Directors?

As the codified directors' duties are expressed as duties owed to the company itself, and not directly to anyone else for enforcement purposes, this codification 'does not open up the prospect of the duties being enforced by persons other than the company, or members acting on its behalf via the new derivative action procedure or by a liquidator in the event of winding up'.[118] In practice, this means that companies are unlikely to bring actions against their directors, even if they have been negligent in their consideration of relevant interests, unless there has been a significant change of corporate circumstances, such as a change of corporate management or the onset of corporate insolvency, in combination with a clear loss to the company demonstrably resulting from the directors' failure. 'Accordingly, where what has occurred is merely a failure in the process of decision-making by directors required by section 172, with no adverse financial effect on the company, it is difficult to see that any court would give permission for a derivative action to be brought', concludes Lady Justice Arden. Liquidators need the commercial incentive of reasonable prospects of success to make it worthwhile to bring proceedings to enlarge the pool of funds available to corporate creditors, and the statutory rules for derivative actions by shareholders in the company's name are 'heavily circumscribed'.[119]

Nevertheless, the structure and elements of the new UK legislative regime for directors' duties present novel opportunities for how actions against directors are cast. Shareholders might seek to frame their complaints against directors within the structure of the decision-making framework outlined in section 172. For example: long-term investors might complain that the directors are inhibiting real long-term returns by their short-term focus or failing to secure the right long-term relationships needed to ensure the company's success over the long run; employee-shareholders might complain of the directors' treatment of employee interests; members who live or have business dealings in a local community in which the company operates might complain about the impact of the directors' decisions upon their community; or shareholders with a social conscience or activist bent might seek to give effect to that motivation by calling attention to something grounded in a breach of section 172's requirements.[120] 'It is likely . . . that the only situation that will require directors to be accountable is where shareholders, who are allied to groups covered by s 172(1), are ready to take proceedings against directors', notes Professor Keay.[121] At the same time, the structure of section 172 affords opportunities for directors facing any derivative action by shareholders to argue that they have considered the relevant factors but simply decided in good faith on a different outcome.[122]

Future Connections Between Corporate Losses and Boardroom Failures to Consider All Stakeholder Interests Properly

A less obvious and yet far more dangerous potential stalking horse for directors lurks in the shadows of the statutory duties of loyalty and care. Although non-shareholders who are harmed by corporate actions face considerable obstacles of the kinds outlined above in seeking to engage courts in sanctioning directors on due process grounds, circumstances can arise in which the statutory framework of decision-making factors points in a direction that bolsters claims by shareholders, liquidators or the company itself against directors. The framework makes explicit the possibility of corporate loss caused by a breach of duty being attributable to failures by directors to act earlier rather than later in addressing significant risks, to place and assess properly all designated matters on the corporate risk radar, to manage and consider all relevant information and drivers relating to corporate success, and to exercise due care and diligence in doing so. Viewed in that light, seemingly abstract and routine legislative considerations such as 'the likely consequences of any decision in the long term' and 'the impact of the company's operations on the community and the environment' can have a more focused and potent impact upon liability in the crystallized circumstances of corporate financial loss.

Most importantly in this context, some of the legislatively mandated considerations are themselves framed in ways that focus upon how the connections between shareholder-related and other stakeholder-related considerations bear upon corporate success as a business enterprise, raising the potential for financial loss to the company from failures to accommodate and manage the interplay between those factors. For example, both 'the need to foster the company's business relationships with suppliers, customers and others' and 'the impact of the company's operations on the community and the environment' are matters the mismanagement of which can result in corporate loss. In addition, mandated considerations such as 'the desirability of the company maintaining a reputation for high standards of business conduct', when combined with similarly mandated considerations such as 'the likely consequences of any decision in the long term', point the way to a reconceptualization and perhaps even broadening of the matters which need to be on the corporate radar in terms of forward-looking identification, assessment and management of the financial and non-financial drivers of corporate financial success.

For example, a company's slowness in addressing potential pollution or other environmental problems, because of the directors' concerns about the immediate costs and effects of a shut-down of operations to remedy the problem, might not only put the directors in breach of applicable environmental laws but also enhance the chances of shareholders (or a subsequently appointed liquidator) successfully arguing later that, by delaying, the short-termism of directors has caused a greater and more costly problem for the company over the long run.[123] Similarly, in balancing the sustainability of the business, shareholder interests and other stakeholder interests, the directors might face a choice that involves other short-term increases in costs assessed against intangible, contingent, long-term gains. Consider, in this light, Justice Austin's example and its implications for directors faced with a new order of decision-making factors, such as those now enshrined in UK corporate law on directors' duties:[124]

On many occasions in practice, company directors are forced to choose between taking action likely to improve or protect the share price, and action reflecting the company's responsibility to other 'constituencies'. Acutely difficult issues arise in the practical application of the law – especially, in discerning where the objective boundary line is drawn. For example, the directors of a company might abandon its plan to construct a waste disposal plant near a local community because of resolute opposition within the community, pursuing a decidedly more expensive waste disposal option and justifying their decision by emphasising the importance of the company's image and its 'green' credentials. Is the decision open to challenge?

At the extremes, even a failure by directors to foresee and properly address in a timely fashion the need for early steps towards a long-term change in a company's energy use or production, perhaps in advance of likely inroads into a company's competitive position by significant regulatory regime changes in the era of climate risk, might lead to accusations down the track that a failure to accept short-term business disruption and cost, and to broaden the range of business drivers and risks appropriately, has produced a larger problem and cost for the company in the long run, contrary to what the framework of boardroom decision-making outlined in section 172 envisages. Might the same be said of a failure by directors to consider a wide range of interests relevant to a company's reputational risk, including social risk factors beyond what conventional financial risk management might identify?

This prospect is enhanced by the legitimacy afforded now to non-financial drivers of business success and the different factors that they place on the corporate risk radar, as accepted by the UK Parliament in framing business review and reporting requirements. In other words, directors might face the twin possibilities that section 172 not only imposes a new order of informational and risk assessment for directors, but also makes it easier rather than harder for boardroom failures in complying with the legislatively mandated considerations to be connected in retrospect to a company's financial losses. At the very least, the combined effect of legislatively designating particular factors relating to business success, and then mandating their consideration in boardroom decision-making, affords those who are looking to sue directors with new pegs on which to hang their arguments.

Boardroom Consideration and Treatment of Employees' Interests

The problem is: what happens if directors do just pay lip service to the factors? If 'X', a member of one of those constituents that are referred to in s 172(1) (a)–(f), is of the view that directors have breached the provision in that the directors failed to have regard to the interests of X's constituency, is X able to take any legal action against the directors? The plain answer appears to be 'no', certainly under the Act (or any other corporate law provision). This has been one of the problems with s 309 of the 1985 legislation . . .

– University of Leeds' Professor of Corporate and Commercial Law, Professor Andrew Keay[125]

The specific inclusion of employee interests within the boardroom decision-making framework in section 172 replaces the previous provision in UK corporate law for consideration of employee interests in corporate decisions. Previously, under section 309(1) of a predecessor UK Companies Act, '(t)he matters to which the directors of the company are to have regard in the performance of their functions include the interests of the company's employees in general, as well as the interests of its members'.

On one view, this superseded provision changed corporate orthodoxy by reconstituting a company's interests in terms that embraced employee interests as well as shareholder interests, without any predisposed ordering of shareholder interests ahead of other interests.[126] If true, such a change in the law would also have had a flow-on impact upon other areas of corporate law, including consequences for the capacity of shareholders to approve or ratify actions by directors and the ability of directors to resist takeovers, at least where employee interests were also at stake.[127] Yet, even if such a shareholder-decentring view was ever tenable, it was unachievable at the instigation of employees in practice, given the framing of the duty as one owed to the company and not to any part of its constituency, as well as the legal realities of mechanisms for enforcing duties owed to the company by its directors.[128]

Turning his attention to the likely judicial approach to the requirement to consider employee interests amongst others, in light of the emphasis upon employee interests under section 309 of the predecessor Companies Act, Justice Austin notes:[129]

> Experience under section 309 of the 1985 Act has generated a measure of scepticism. The existing section has not been properly tested in litigation. What, it might be asked, will a court do if it finds that the directors have given insufficient regard to the interests of employees? The directors can be ordered to reconsider their decision but the outcome may not be of any assistance to the employees. The directors may simply make their decision again, but this time have fuller 'regard' for the employees' interests. For reasons such as these, Professor Sealy described section 309 as 'either one of the most incompetent or one of the most cynical pieces of drafting on record'.

In its full form, Professor Sealy's famous condemnation of section 309 two decades earlier also has some resonance today for how courts might approach requests for due process remedies against directors, based upon the framework for decision-making established under the new statutory director's duty of loyalty in UK corporate law:[130]

> A supposed legal duty which is not matched by a remedy is a nonsense. If, as most would accept, there is no room within the established framework of company law for a direct remedy against directors to be sought by (say) a group of employees or creditors, we have to think of a remedy enforced through the company . . . In the case of employees, what could a court be asked to *do* for them, supposing that it is established that insufficient regard has been had to their interests? At best, it might be possible to think of some woolly form of declaratory or injunctive relief which obliged the directors to reconsider their decision. (We are almost into the realms of administrative law! Even so, there could be no question of requiring the directors to give the employees' case a hearing, since shareholders have no similar right.) The emptiness of the UK's section 309 is thus exposed. It is either one of the most incompetent or one of the most cynical pieces of drafting on record.

This echoes other criticisms of section 309's emasculation. Surveying the history of section 309's use and overall impact, Professor Keay labels it as 'something of a lame duck, and next to useless'.[131] Speaking of the need for a company's internal control and enforcement systems to meet the needs of proper employee protection, Professor Janet Dine bases her call for reform in this direction partly on the poor amount of employee protection actually afforded by section 309:[132]

> No longer should the risks run by employees be seen as imposing an external cost – 'red tape' for companies – their risks should be managed by internal systems with an integral enforcement mechanism. The dangers of not pursuing this route may be illustrated by the ineffective section 309 of the Companies Act 1985 which infamously requires directors to take account of the interests of employees and provides that the enforcement mechanisms are to be the same as for any other duty of directors, i.e. exclusively in the hands of shareholders, with the result that it has been entirely ineffective.

Elsewhere in the UK's new Companies Act, the broad legislative provision of benefits is maintained for present or former employees when a business ends or changes hands. It is framed in these terms:[133]

> The powers of the directors of a company include . . . power to make provision for the benefit of persons employed or formerly employed by the company, or any of its subsidiaries, in connection with the cessation or the transfer to any person of the whole or part of the undertaking of the company or that subsidiary.

This power of directors to provide for employees takes precedence over the duty of directors to promote the success of the company.[134] Its exercise requires appropriate authorization by a company or board resolution.[135]

UK BUSINESS REVIEW AND REPORTING REQUIREMENTS

> The enhanced business review, which for quoted companies must now include information on environmental, employee, social and community issues, is another key example that builds on the growing consensus that it is good business sense for companies to embrace wider social responsibilities.
>
> – Margaret Hodge, Minister of State for Industry and the Regions[136]

EU and UK Policy Background on Corporate Responsibility and Sustainability Reporting

The UK's provision for a business review in its 2006 Companies Act takes UK law further in the direction of narrative reporting, under the influence of EU directives and related requirements that lead to enhanced reporting of non-financial information, greater collective boardroom accountability, and increased corporate governance disclosure. Commentaries by those closely involved with the CLR Steering Group suggest that, in their internal policy debate, the *quid pro quo* for maintaining a shareholder-centred view of directors' duties was the bolstering of socially and environmentally responsible reporting elements in the now discarded OFR, which was the predecessor of the business review. [137] One of the members of the CLR Steering Group, Professor Paul Davies, crystallizes the overall balanced package of measures as follows:[138]

> (W)e endorsed the traditional shareholder-centred philosophy of British company law, but advocated a modernised version of it, which we dubbed 'enlightened shareholder value'. Second, the ESV approach showed itself not only, or, in my view, even most prominently, in the formulation of directors' duties, but also in the additional mandatory reporting requirement contained in the OFR. It's not an exaggeration to say that the OFR was, in the eyes of many people, the other side of the bargain in which a relatively traditional formulation of directors' duties was adopted . . . Thus, there is no doubt that the CLR's formulation of the basic objective of directors' duties is towards the shareholder, rather than the stakeholder, end of the spectrum.

In the end, a compromise position was reached in which the minimal scope of changes to directors' duties was offset against requirements for enhanced disclosure of social, environmental and other non-financial matters going to a company's success. The pushback from that position in the UK's sudden rejection of the OFR on the eve of its implementation arguably upsets the balance of measures in the total UK reform package, except to the extent that OFR-like requirements reappear in the business review and correlative reporting provisions. The strong connection between these two elements of the corporate reform package remains, as explicitly confirmed by the statutory indication in the Companies Act for shareholders to use the business review in assessing the performance of directors' duties to the company.

Legislative Requirements for a Business Review in the Annual Directors' Report

As summarized by the UK Department of Trade and Industry (DTI) on the passage of the UK Companies Act into law, the business review requirements are as follows:[139]

> The Act promotes forward looking narrative reporting by companies covering risks as well as opportunities, together with explicit requirements for quoted companies to report, as part of their business review and to the extent necessary for an understanding of the business, information on
>
> (i)   environmental matters,
> (ii)   employees and
> (iii) social and community issues,
>
> including information on any policies relating to these matters and their effectiveness, plus contractual and other relationships essential to the business.

The full requirements for a business review in annual reporting by directors appear in section 417 of the UK Companies Act 2006 in these terms:[140]

417 Contents of directors' report: business review

(1)   Unless the company is subject to the small companies' regime, the directors' report must contain a business review.

(2)   The purpose of the business review is to inform members of the company and help them assess how the directors have performed their duty under section 172 (duty to promote the success of the company).

(3)   The business review must contain –

    (a)   a fair review of the company's business, and
    (b)   a description of the principal risks and uncertainties facing the company.

(4)   The review required is a balanced and comprehensive analysis of –
    (a)   the development and performance of the company's business during the financial year, and
    (b)   the position of the company's business at the end of that year,
    consistent with the size and complexity of the business.

(5)   In the case of a quoted company the business review must, to the extent necessary for an understanding of the development, performance or position of the company's business, include –
    (a)   the main trends and factors likely to affect the future development, performance and position of the company's business; and
    (b)   information about –
        (i)   environmental matters (including the impact of the company's business on the environment),
        (ii)   the company's employees, and
        (iii) social and community issues,
    including information about any policies of the company in relation to those matters and the effectiveness of those policies; and
    (c)   subject to subsection (11), information about persons with whom the company has contractual or other arrangements which are essential to the business of the company.
If the review does not contain information of each kind mentioned in paragraphs (b)(i), (ii) and (iii) and (c), it must state which of those kinds of information it does not contain.

(6)   The review must, to the extent necessary for an understanding of the development, performance or position of the company's business, include –
    (a)   analysis using financial key performance indicators, and
    (b)   where appropriate, analysis using other key performance indicators, including information relating to environmental matters and employee matters.
'Key performance indicators' means factors by reference to which the development, performance or position of the company's business can be measured effectively.

(7)   Where a company qualifies as medium-sized in relation to a financial year (see sections 465 to 467), the directors' report for the year need not comply with the requirements of subsection (6) so far as they relate to non-financial information.

. . .

(10) Nothing in this section requires the disclosure of information about impending developments or matters in the course of negotiation if the disclosure would, in the opinion of the directors, be seriously prejudicial to the interests of the company.

(11) Nothing in subsection (5)(c) requires the disclosure of information about a person if the disclosure would, in the opinion of the directors, be seriously prejudicial to that person and contrary to the public interest.

These business review requirements have significant limitations and exceptions. As discussed in more detail below, everything is structured in terms of assessing the company's business from an investment perspective, as distinct from a socio-ethical impact assessment, for example. Relevant information about a company's supply and distribution chain corresponds to 'information about persons with whom the company has contractual or other arrangements which are essential to the business of the company', subject to considerations of privacy, confidentiality, competitiveness and other countervailing interests precluding the disclosure of such information.

Given the different scale and cost of complying with these requirements for small, medium and large business enterprises, important exemptions from some or all of these requirements apply to different kinds of companies. Small businesses are exempted from needing to do a business review at all; medium-sized enterprises are excused from reporting non-financial information in their business reviews; and companies that are not publicly listed escape some business review requirements.[141] These exceptions provoked immediate criticism from some NGOs, who argued that some large enterprises that are not publicly listed companies would escape the net of enhanced business review elements for listed companies, and that non-financial information is relevant for both medium and large enterprises, as well as their investors.[142]

Analysing the Elements of the Business Review

The primary audience for the business review envisaged by the legislation is the company's shareholders, although the information and analysis in the business review will also be of interest and relevance to the company's other stakeholders. The final Reporting Statement on the OFR from the UK Accounting Standards Board accepts that, while aimed primarily at investors, this kind of reporting is relevant for 'users other than members, for example other investors, potential investors, creditors, customers, suppliers, employees and society more widely', with the consequence that boards 'should consider the extent to which they should report on issues relevant to those other users where, because of those issues' influence on the performance of the business and its value, they are also of significance to members'.[143]

The business review has both backward-looking and forward-looking elements. The financial and non-financial indicators of a company's business activity provide the evidence-based platform for the business review's analysis. The requirement imposed upon particular kinds of companies to include reference in the business review to information going to employment, environmental and social concerns, as well as other non-financial information, is not an absolute requirement. Rather, the inclusion of such material in a company's business review is contingent upon its precise relationship to 'an understanding of the development, performance or position of the company's business'.

This limitation of social and environmental reporting to what affects the company's business, as distinct from society at large, tends more towards shareholder primacy than stakeholder pluralism.[144] As is the case elsewhere in European, Anglo-American and Anglo-Commonwealth domains, the emphasis is upon reporting how the company's internal and external affairs affect the company and its prospects (i.e. 'narrow' corporate sustainability), as distinct from reporting on how the company and its affairs affect and otherwise relate to the societal landscape around them (i.e. 'wide' corporate sustainability). In other words, this condition keeps these aspects of the business review tightly focused upon how they relate to the company's business, as distinct from the performance and impact of companies in connection with wider public interests of sustainable development, stakeholder harm-minimization and other CSR-orientated public policy goals from a societal perspective.[145]

Corporate responsibility and sustainability reporting that serves some public ends (such as informational needs of investors and markets) does not necessarily serve other public ends as well (such as corporate democracy and sustainable business development). 'There is an urgent need to . . . bring closure in agreeing a basic framework for social, environmental and overall sustainability accounting, auditing and reporting that will underpin tomorrow's Generally Accepted Accounting Principles for Sustainability (GAAPS)', so that a common baseline standard is in place in the form of 'an effective GAAPS [that] must fulfil the needs emerging as a result of new statutory legislation, such as the social and environmental elements of the . . . revision to UK Company Law', notes Dr Zadek.[146]

The discretion afforded to directors in deciding whether something is publicly reportable because of its connection to 'an understanding of the development, performance or position of the company's business' has both advantages and disadvantages. Its advantages include greater flexibility for directors and location of judgment about these matters primarily with directors rather than external regulators. Its disadvantages include inconsistencies and anomalies in how different boards treat the reportability of similar matters in similar circumstances, at least in the absence of supplementary regulatory guidance, especially in light of the possibility that some identified interests (e.g. employee relations) are so integral to corporate performance that their reporting deserves legislatively mandated status.[147] On the other hand, a potential criticism of these detailed reporting requirements and equivalent law reform proposals in other countries, from the practising corporate director's perspective, is that they cross the fine line between asking directors to report on how they run the company and telling directors how to run the company.[148]

Practical Implications of Business Review Requirements for Corporate Boards and their Advisers

The explicit connection drawn in the legislation between directors' duties and business reviews has both legal and practical implications. The kinds of matters legislatively required to be canvassed in the business review go to the long-term and relationship-focused elements of a successful business, upon which the proper performance of directors' duties turns.[149] Operationally, boards also face the pressing tasks of relating the business review requirements to internal corporate governance and reporting, as well as meeting the expectations of investors and the market about what boards publicly report.[150]

A number of features in the UK Companies Act 2006 combine to reinforce the practical imperative for directors to remain tightly focused upon the interests and reactions of shareholders, notwithstanding the explicit and amplified treatment of stakeholder interests under both directors' duties and business review reporting requirements. First, the duty of loyalty to the company is clearly structured in the legislation to focus upon the interests of the company and its shareholders.[151] Secondly, the business review requirements are also structured to inform investors of how well the directors perform that duty.[152] Thirdly, in appropriate circumstances, shareholders are legislatively empowered to ratify breaches of duty by directors.[153] Fourthly, the provision for a derivative action by shareholders provides an avenue for action against directors in the name of the company.[154] Finally, directors are liable to compensate the company for any loss to the company due to 'untrue or misleading' statements in relevant directors' reports.[155] All of these features in particular combine to focus the minds of directors upon the consequences of their decisions for shareholder financial gain, whatever other obligations they might have to consider and report on their treatment of other interests too, at least as they relate to the company's business.[156]

Connecting business reviews with investor oversight of directors' duties[157] also has a number of flow-on implications. It provides more information and evidence to enable investors, aided by others in the investment industry, to hold directors accountable. For example, it supplies material to assist corporate dialogue with institutional investors and analysts, provide the basis for active participation by institutional investors through corporate governance mechanisms, stimulate questioning of directors at annual general meetings and inform actions against directors for breaching their duties. As directors' duties evolve within Anglo-Commonwealth law in particular to encompass some level of responsibility for systems of risk assessment and control,[158] in addition to conventional financial accountability and legal compliance, narrative reporting and business reviews add an additional element to the corporate governance mix. At the same time, tensions and demarcations are increasingly likely between management responsibility for implementing systems of risk assessment and control, and board oversight responsibility for the effectiveness of those systems.[159]

Considered from the strategic boardroom perspective of developing overall systems of reporting management and control, there is a high level of interplay between what must be done for a business review and what must be done to meet various duties of directors. For example, the business review contains items for information-gathering, evaluation and reporting that have a correlation with some of the designated considerations for boardroom decision-making under the legislated duty to promote the company's success. Requirements concerning the company's employees, environmental impact, social affairs and essential business relationships are relevant for both purposes. To that extent at least, the business review and reporting processes that companies put in place can also feed into the informational bases and other supporting processes for boardroom decision-making, in fulfilment of the duty of directors to pursue the company's success, including due consideration of a wide range of shareholder and non-shareholder interests in doing so.

The fact that narrative reporting and business reviews can present challenges that are quite different for directors from what they might be accustomed to in annual reporting is reflected in the UK Accounting Standards Board's first review of narrative reporting in early 2007. It found that companies were much better at describing their markets, strategies and performance than disclosing forward-looking information, identifying sources of business risk, and explaining their approach to managing those risks.[160] Considered from both strategic and operational perspectives, the UK ASB's analysis also raises important practical questions about what non-financial information boards need to do their jobs properly, how stakeholders are best engaged in reportable corporate matters, and where business review reporting needs to be aligned with other corporate needs. These are ongoing CSR reporting challenges in the UK and elsewhere.

CONCLUSION

The bounded socialization of boardroom duties, business management systems, corporate disclosure and reporting requirements, and other features of the 21st century CSR landscape is exemplified in the UK Companies Act 2006. After initial consternation and uncertainty about these changes to UK corporate law, some quarters of the legal and business communities have settled into an initial 'business as usual' mindset upon commencement of this new UK corporate law for the 21st century. Yet the CLR Steering Group and the UK Government clearly intended these changes to have some regulatory and practical effect, albeit within the framework of pre-existing corporate law. As this chapter shows, there are crucial issues of legal interpretation and practical application that await development. Moreover, test cases on some of these changes – both privately in professional advice and practice, and publicly in the courts and other official regulatory action – are likely to be years in the making.

The success of the UK's 21st century reformulation of important aspects of corporate law and governance will stand or fall on more than simply the bare legislative framework for boardroom decision-making and reporting contained in the UK Companies Act. Additional regulatory back-up measures might become necessary, depending upon how companies and regulatory bodies approach the legal requirements, especially if parliamentary expectations of directors' duties under the prevailing ESV philosophy are not met, or a 'form over substance' and 'tick-a-box' response to ESV takes hold in the business community, facilitated by professional advice that is limited in its vision of ESV's full potential in 21st century conditions.

'Mechanisms for nudging companies towards CSR indirectly (for example, tax incentives or government procurement policies aimed at encouraging CSR) or in a way that is aimed at CSR generically without setting specific substantive standards or goals (such as the UK's repealed OFR requirement) are likely to fail badly unless they are adequately buttressed by specific regulatory regimes which specify social policy goals, and identify and give rights to stakeholders to participate in or contest corporate decisions', warns Dr Parker.[161] In other words, regulatory measures that ostensibly favour CSR by introducing CSR-orientated processes but without adequate linking of those processes to substantive regulatory CSR outcomes are unlikely on their own to produce internalization of a corporate conscience or organizational ethic of responsibility.[162]

All of this is unlikely to remain the last word on CSR-related reform of corporate law and regulation in Anglo-Commonwealth corporate law.[163] For example, the UK Companies Act 2006 momentarily submerges some deeper issues of corporate responsibility, governance and sustainability that remain to be addressed in the ongoing evolution of relations between market capitalism and civil society. This is reflected in the following assessment of the Act's key deficiency by the London School of Economics' Emeritus Professor of Commercial Law, Lord Wedderburn of Charlton:[164]

> A radical enactment would perhaps have spoken about regulating the new relationships born of the marriage of private equity and the derivatives market, in which are accommodated both the new social inequalities in Britain and the economic power of multinational capital. A decade from now the next 'company law review' will need to explain this odd result of our recent company law debates.

Indeed, future corporate law reform efforts in the UK and elsewhere will need to grapple more forcefully with the national dimensions of multinational corporate activity. Building upon her foundational analysis of the contemporary international legal and regulatory context for TNCs and CSR, Dr Jennifer Zerk proposes further reform of UK law and regulation to cure multinational corporate abuses. More broadly, her reform suggestions offer models for other countries, in reforming the corporate law of a TNC's home country to hold it accountable for activities in the TNC's host countries of operation, as follows:[165]

(1) reforming UK company law on directors' duties, corporate reporting and winding-up on public interest grounds for corporate irresponsibility;[166]
(2) clarifying UK criminal law's regulation of offshore multinational corporate abuses;[167]
(3) enhancing private and public rights of action against parent companies and groups for corporate irresponsibility of their subsidiaries, suppliers/distributors and contractors;[168]
(4) creating taxation and market-based incentives for offshore corporate performance, according to designated social, environmental and human rights standards;[169]
(5) extending trade practices laws regulating product marketing of unsafe and unhealthy products, as well as false and misleading CSR-based claims of corporate performance for both onshore and offshore operations; and
(6) improving corporate transparency through 'right to know' legislation covering companies performing public functions and services, together with statutory disclosure obligations of parent companies concerning information about relevant health, safety and environmental risks posed by their corporate subsidiaries offshore.

Whatever might become the new baseline for minimum legal compliance with UK legislative requirements for directors' duties, business reviews and corporate reporting, that floor of legal responsibility still does not approach the ceiling of aspirational corporate responsibility, in the sense discussed in Chapter 1. It does not necessarily reach the heights of success targeted by companies who seek continuous improvement, strategically align their business interests with societal interests, or otherwise reorient their business model around this new legislative architecture in ways that transcend mere legal compliance. Nor does it necessarily extend towards everything that society might want companies to disclose publicly for the common good, whatever connection such disclosure might have to the company's success as a business enterprise. Still, the success or failure of this early 21st century legislative model for directors' duties, business reviews and corporate reporting will have a significant impact upon other CSR-related legal and policy reforms in comparable countries for some time to come.

NOTES

1. Quoted in UK Government, 2004: 2.
2. Ruggie, 2004: 513–514.
3. Ibid.
4. Ruggie, 2008a: [30].
5. Wachtell et al, 2008: 4; cf Weil et al, 2008: 1–2.
6. DTI, 2007: 2–3.
7. These latter business review components relate to another corporate law mechanism for CSR, considered further below.
8. CLRSG, 1999: 4.
9. CLRSG, 2001: ix.

10. Ibid.: xi.
11. Ibid.: x.
12. Ibid.: xi.
13. DTI, 2007: 2.
14. Ibid.: 1.
15. For a theoretical account of this interplay see Bottomley, 2007.
16. CLRSG, 1999: 9–10.
17. The other being 'what is a corporation?'.
18. CLRSG, 2001: [3.7]; emphasis added.
19. Ibid.: [3.8].
20. Ibid.: [3.8].
21. Ibid.: [3.8]. This connection between directors' duties and corporate reporting obligations is explicitly drawn in the Companies Act's stipulation that the business review in annual directors' reports is linked to reviewing how well directors have performed in meeting this duty of loyalty to the company: see Companies Act 2006 (UK), s. 417(2).
22. White Paper, 2005: 20.
23. CLRSG, 1999: 37.
24. Ibid.: 39.
25. Ibid.: 39.
26. Dodd, 1932: 1156.
27. DTI, 2007: 7.
28. Companies Act 2006 (UK), s. 172.
29. HL Debs, vol. 677, col. 184, 11 January 2006.
30. Keay, 2007c: 597.
31. Arden, 2007: 167–169.
32. On some of these criticisms also see Ramsay, 2005c; and Mallesons Stephen Jacques, 2005.
33. Ramsay, 2005a; and Ramsay, 2005b.
34. Companies Act 2006 (UK), s. 172(1).
35. Farrar, 2008: 496.
36. Chiu, 2006a: 259–260.
37. Ibid.: 293.
38. Ibid.: 267–268.
39. Davies, 2005: 5.
40. Williams and Conley, 2005a: 515.
41. Zadek, 2001a: 33–34.
42. Zadek, 2001a or b: 34–35.
43. Keay, 2007c: 592.
44. Ibid.: 600.
45. DTI, 2007: 5.
46. Keay, 2007a: 106.
47. Sealy, 1987: 187.
48. Lumsden and Fridman, 2007: 176.
49. Beerworth, 2007a: 41.
50. CAMAC, 2006: 106.
51. Ramsay, 2005a; and Ramsay, 2005c.
52. Companies Act 2006 (UK), s. 170(1).
53. Parkinson, 1993: 76–77.
54. Ibid.: 77; original emphasis.
55. Ibid.: 80–81; Keay, 2007a: 109; and Austin, 2007c: 8.
56. Austin, 2007c: 8.
57. Parkinson, 1993: 81.
58. Ibid.
59. Lumsden and Fridman, 2007: 176.
60. Parkinson, 1993: 329.
61. Ibid.: 364–365.
62. Ibid.: 345.
63. Ibid.: 346.
64. Ibid.: 329.
65. Ibid.: 365.
66. Ibid.: 346.
67. Ibid.

68. Ibid.: 372, quoting Teubner, 1985: 167.
69. Ibid.: 366.
70. Ibid.: 344.
71. Ibid.: 364.
72. Ibid.: 345.
73. E.g. Parker, 2007.
74. Parkinson, 1993: 371; emphasis added.
75. See the discussion and commentaries on this prospect later in this chapter.
76. Parker, 2007: 233.
77. Companies Act 2006 (UK), s. 172(2).
78. PJCCFS, 2006: [4.46].
79. Arden, 2007: 170.
80. Keay, 2007a: 108.
81. PJCCFS, 2006: [4.46].
82. Ibid.: [4.48].
83. DTI, 2007: 9.
84. CAMAC, 2006: [3.12].
85. Ibid.: [3.12].
86. Ibid.: [3.12].
87. Arden, 2007: 170.
88. CAMAC, 2006: [3.12].
89. E.g. Parker, 2007.
90. DTI, 2007: 5.
91. Austin, 2007c: 6.
92. Ibid.
93. Arden, 2007: 166.
94. Ibid.: 167.
95. Ibid.
96. DTI, 2007: 8.
97. Kay, 2006: 53.
98. Ibid.: 51.
99. Attenborough, 2007: 318.
100. Austin, 2007c: 9.
101. Arden, 2007: 167–168.
102. Ibid.: 168.
103. Kay, 2006: 51.
104. Comments by Professor John Coffee on the tension between procedural and substantive regard to the relevant interests in s. 172, on the occasion of the launch of Austin, 2007a.
105. Austin, 2007c: 17.
106. *Angas Law Services Pty Ltd (In liquidation) v Carabelas* [2005] HCA 23 at [32].
107. S. 239 (1), (2), (3), (4).
108. Arden, 2007: 168.
109. Companies Act 2006 (UK), s. 417(2).
110. DTI, 2007: 6.
111. On both concerns see Arden, 2007: 171.
112. Ibid.: 171.
113. Ibid.: 170.
114. Davies, 2005.
115. On these due process hurdles see Arden, 2007: 171.
116. Ibid.: 167.
117. However, in those jurisdictions where an outsider contracting with a company can rely upon particular legal assumptions about the propriety of the company's own internal management in committing the company to the transaction, including assumptions about proper compliance with all relevant legal duties under what is conventionally known as the 'indoor management' rule, the outsider's actual or constructive knowledge of a breach of duty by directors can disentitle the outsider from having an effective contract with the company: see, for example, ss 128–129 of Australia's Corporations Act 2001.
118. Arden, 2007: 166.
119. Ibid.: 171.
120. Keay, 2007a: 110.
121. Keay, 2007c: 606.

122. Keay, 2007a: 110.
123. This scenario was suggested by Professor John Coffee on the occasion of the launch of Austin, 2007, as an illustration of the real, shareholder-focused context of concern for directors arising from s. 172.
124. Austin, 2007c: 8–9.
125. Keay, 2007c: 606–607.
126. Parkinson, 1993: 83.
127. Ibid.: 86.
128. Ibid.: 83.
129. Austin, 2007c: 9.
130. Sealy, 1987: 177; original emphasis.
131. Keay, 2007a: 109.
132. Dine, 2005: 277.
133. S. 247(1).
134. S. 247(2).
135. S. 247(4).
136. DTI, 2007: 3.
137. Davies, 2005.
138. Ibid.
139. 'Bill to Save Business Millions Receives Royal Assent', Media Release, UK Department of Trade and Industry, 8 November 2006.
140. Minor follow-up adaptations to s. 417 also appear in the Companies Act 2006 (Commencement No. 3, Consequential Amendments, Transitional Provisions and Savings) Order 2007 (SI 2007/2194), in ways which do not detract from the substantive discussion here.
141. S. 417(1) and 417(7) respectively.
142. CORE et al, 2006: 4.
143. ASB, 2006: 9.
144. Keay, 2007c: 604.
145. Villiers, 2006: 239 and 296–297.
146. Zadek, 2001a: 39.
147. Villiers, 2006: 216–217.
148. Cf 'ASX Corporate Governance Principles: Make Your Opinion Count", *Company Director*, Vol 23, No 1, February 2007, at 30–31.
149. Villiers, 2006: 216.
150. White Paper, 2002: [4.33]: and Villiers, 2006: 219–221.
151. Companies Act 2006 (UK), s. 172(1).
152. Ibid.
153. Ibid.
154. Ibid.
155. Ibid.
156. Attenborough, 2007: 317–318.
157. S. 417(2).
158. Dine, 2005: 273–277; citing *Re Barings plc and Others (No 5)* [1999] 1 BCLC 433.
159. 'ASX Corporate Governance Principles: Make Your Opinion Count", *Company Director*, Vol 23, No 1, February 2007, at 30–31.
160. *Review of Narrative Reporting by UK Listed Companies in 2006*, Financial Reporting Council, 2007.
161. Parker, 2007: 237.
162. Ibid.: 233–237.
163. Beerworth, 2007b.
164. Quoted in Legislative Comment, 'Companies Bill 2006 Receives Royal Assent' (2007) 28(2) *Company Lawyer* 46 at 46.
165. Zerk, 2007: 9–32.
166. E.g. mandatory corporate reporting on social, environmental and human rights impacts, as well as positive obligations upon directors to accommodate employee, environmental and other community impacts and to monitor corporate subsidiary and supply chain activity as part of that responsibility.
167. E.g. offences for 'aiding and abetting' violations of core labour, human and environmental rights in offshore operations that are attributable to systemic management failures or the fault of individual directors, as well as new criminal sanctions for multinational corporate failures concerning the health and welfare of employees, consumers and local communities in offshore business operations.
168. E.g. instituting new regulatory complaints mechanisms for offshore corporate abuses; bolstering private rights of action in tort against parent companies for the actions of their domestic and foreign subsidiaries and business chain members; and creating public rights of action by regulatory bodies, public

advocacy groups and victims under statutory duties concerning the welfare of employees, consumers and communities affected by corporate subsidiaries and business chain members.

169.   E.g. preferential dividend taxation rates for well-performing foreign subsidiaries, CSR-based conditions on tax credits for foreign corporate income, import bans on products failing CSR standards for production and manufacture, and mandatory socio-ethical and eco-labelling schemes.

8. Putting corporate social responsibility into practice for business

BACK TO BASICS

> Every company, like it or not, has a CSR policy. The first issue is whether they recognise the fact, and the second is how far they are alert to changes in what society expects of them in this field.
>
> — Sir Adrian Cadbury, architect of the UK Cadbury Report on corporate governance reforms[1]
>
> (E)ven if ... companies first discovered CSR the hard way, by suffering a knock to their reputation, many now see it as more than just a tool of risk management; they are convinced that it can be a competitive advantage and a source of growth in its own right.
>
> — *The Economist*'s 2008 special report on corporate social responsibility[2]
>
> It is impossible for managers to sidestep corporate social responsibility (CSR).
>
> — Wharton Business School's Professor Tom Donaldson[3]

Putting CSR into practice for business is much more complex than following a 'one size fits all' CSR instruction manual on business–society engagement. The 'how' of CSR is integrally connected to the 'why' of CSR. The conventional normative justification of what is commonly called 'the business case for CSR' is now matched by increasingly sophisticated guidance on how to align CSR to a company's unique business model, competitive positioning and marketplace advantage, with suitable corporate governance arrangements to match.[4]

Moreover, companies must at least develop and articulate a comprehensible normative account of their company-specific commitment to CSR. At the very least, they must do so for the purposes of engaging in dialogue with investors and other stakeholders about CSR issues, establishing CSR credibility with stakeholders and industry peers, participating in public debate about corporate irresponsibility, and entering the governmental arena to lobby and otherwise exert influence upon CSR public policy development. For example, as a recent McKinsey business survey on CSR reveals:[5]

> Business leaders must become involved in socio-political debate not only because their companies have so much to add but also because they have a strategic interest in doing so. Social

and political forces, after all, can alter an industry's strategic landscape fundamentally; they can torpedo the reputations of businesses that have been caught unawares and are seen as being culpable; and they can create valuable market opportunities by highlighting unmet social needs and new consumer preferences.

So, where and how should a CSR-minded company, board or individual director start? The short answer is that CSR's operationalization has to be attacked on a number of fronts all at once. A glimpse of this reality appears in *The Economist*'s assessment of the standard characteristics of CSR leaders, as follows:[6]

> Like most industries, the corporate-responsibility business has a handful of leaders, a large number of followers and many laggards . . . The leaders typically have a committed CEO who champions the policy, a chief officer for corporate responsibility – or sustainability or whatever – who reports to the boss, and a cross-functional board committee to ensure that strategy is co-ordinated throughout the company. Non-financial measures of progress often play an important part in the overall assessment of the company's performance. These are companies, in short, that are seeking to 'embed' CSR in the business [on] everything from sourcing to strategy. These may also be the places where talented people will most want to work.

Contemporary CSR literature points to some common prerequisites for inculcating CSR within a company. High-level organizational commitment, communication and resourcing is fundamental, including both structural and behavioural ways of embedding CSR responsibility within line management and boardroom roles.[7] 'If optimising financial performance in the long run requires at least some attention to CSR, then the debate shifts partly to how managers should think', notes Wharton's Professor Donaldson.[8]

Having committed to CSR, a company needs starting frameworks for developing and implementing CSR policies, strategies and measures. A meaningful whole-of-organization approach and holistic organizational plan for CSR are both essential, with mutually reinforcing effects. All other business strategies, operations and performances are best aligned with them throughout the organization, at both institutional and personal levels. In other words, the framework of CSR policies, implementation measures and monitoring systems must be sufficiently clear and customized to secure real understanding and commitment to the central CSR cause up, down, and across the organization. It also must be useful enough for sub-organizational units and their people in relating all CSR options to their own work responsibilities, choosing between different CSR initiatives, and deploying CSR-sensitive business modelling and other tools in core business activities.

Corporate responsibility and sustainability information must feed into internal and external reporting mechanisms. Corporate systems and practices must be synchronized with organizational values that make CSR integral and, in turn, those values and correlative systems and practices must meaningfully reflect and accommodate public policy outcomes focused upon CSR. All of this must be managed holistically by a system of management and control that takes an overarching view of the company's performance in managing its legal obligations, organizational risks and business drivers.

In practice, companies that commit to CSR should undertake preliminary internal due diligence before going public on CSR. At the bare minimum, they should conduct an organizational CSR health-check against suitable external CSR standards, not least to avoid reputational damage and potential liability from premature or otherwise ill-conceived CSR claims. This also has the advantage of helping companies to make advance preparation for the kind of external CSR scrutiny to which they might be subject, for example, as participants in published CSR rankings or screened members of someone else's business services chain.

To guide companies and their boards, especially in the initial post-commitment stages, suitable implementation and advisory vehicles include board-level CSR committees, organization-wide CSR steering groups, and external professional and stakeholder advisory bodies. Suitable generic terms of reference for these organizational vehicles include:

(1) coordinating CSR implementation and monitoring advice for the board;
(2) suggesting world-class CSR reporting and certification standards;
(3) auditing existing organizational CSR systems and procedures;
(4) vetting standard organizational contracts and practices from a CSR standpoint;
(5) developing CSR policies and training material;
(6) liaising with external stakeholders on organizational CSR matters;
(7) screening external CSR communication and reporting; and
(8) providing CSR implementation guidance and support to other organizational units.

At the same time, the journey towards CSR is not something that individual companies achieve simply by self-reflection, voluntary commitment and then self-regulation alone. They are located within networks of public, private and community actors, with 'mechanisms for steering behaviour associated with each (markets for firms, law for government, and community for NGOs)', including processes of enculturation and norm-setting that include 'dialogue between firms, between firms and NGOs, between firms and governmental actors and between NGOs and governmental actors' – all facilitated within an underlying framework of law and wider regulation but not completely predetermined and dictated by it.[9] Moreover, as Professor Charlotte Villiers concludes, there are limits to what might be expected of companies alone in the realm of CSR:[10]

> *CSR should not be left in the hands of companies.* An enabling environment is necessary which allows companies to act responsibly. This requires the creation of enforceable regulations that will ensure that CSR is not just an aspirational term. States, international institutions and civil society together have power and responsibility to create the right regulatory environment [and] there is a shared political responsibility among all parties to create the structural processes necessary to ensure legally and socially responsible behaviour by corporations.

In short, the practice of 21st century CSR needs the legal and regulatory infrastructure for CSR to optimize the capacity for corporations to orientate themselves towards CSR for a mix of interconnected global, societal, and organizational reasons which are matched to each corporation's unique mission, capacity, and surrounding context. This complex and nuanced vision of corporate responsibility and sustainability is not achievable through either mandatory corporate regulation to force business to embrace CSR goals for public policy purposes nor voluntary corporate self-regulation that leaves the practice of CSR to business self-interest alone. Accordingly, the starting point for organizational CSR design and implementation must embrace the 'how' and 'why' of company-specific CSR in ways which transcend divisions between laws and other company-affecting norms, position corporate interests to respond to a blend of relevant public and private interests, and relate CSR to all or particular aspects of a company's business model and success.

This chapter focuses upon the synchronicity between these justificatory and practical dimensions of CSR in operation, within an overall framework of corporate responsiveness to systems of trans-modal governance, multi-order regulation and inter-related responsibility. In exploring the interplay between the 'how' and the 'why' of CSR, the various dimensions of the standard business case for CSR are crystallized and then accompanied by a distillation and analysis of some landmark whole-of-organization CSR frameworks. This operational platform sets up a broader discussion of innovative corporate engagement with the business–society nexus, in forms that accommodate the dynamics of both effective market competition and other public policy goals of relevance to CSR.

21ST CENTURY BUSINESS–SOCIETY ENGAGEMENT

The Business Case for CSR

Does it matter to you if:

- Your company has a poor reputation for honesty and trustworthiness?
- Your customers have a bad opinion of your impact on the environment?
- Future employees don't have the skills you need?
- It's difficult to attract and retain good people?
- The marketplace in which you sell isn't prospering?
- Your organisation is unattractive to business partners?
- The negative views of local authorities are making planning business expansion difficult?
- Ethical investment funds choose not to hold your shares?

Companies can't afford to ignore these questions. They are central to success. Socially responsible businesses have additional tools at their disposal which help them score more highly on all these fronts.

— Business in the Community's Business Impact Task Force[11]

The business case for socio-ethically responsible business activity is now commonly accepted, even amongst business leaders. 'In the past decade, "corporate social responsibility" (CSR) has become the norm in the boardrooms of companies in rich countries, and increasingly in developing economies too', according to *The Economist* in late 2007.[12] 'There is a growing recognition, too, that corporate social responsibility benefits businesses as well as the community', notes social enterprise champion, Nic Frances.[13] This alignment of business and social value is emphasized in the McKinsey Award-wining article on CSR from the 2006 *Harvard Business Review*,[14] although recent public[15] and scholarly[16] debate has reignited over the extent to which such an alignment of public and corporate interests is worthy of being called CSR at all.

While comprehensive and reliable confirmation of the correlation between good corporate governance, profitable corporate performance and socially responsible business remains elusive, glimpses of this correlation emerge from reports across countries and industry sectors about companies with better governance, social, environmental and human rights performance records who outperform their competitors economically too.[17] Similarly, a meta-study examining 25 years of other studies of corporate performance from the 1970s to the 1990s shows a positive correlation between a company's financial performance and how it practises CSR.[18] Of course, like the causal connection between good corporate governance and good corporate performance, the causal connection between CSR and corporate performance also remains the subject of much debate and conflicting evidence. Good companies that do everything well might simply practise corporate governance and responsibility well too, or at least have more resources available to deploy in these endeavours because of their overall financial success.[19] Still, such an interpretation also risks undervaluing the emerging ways in which these companies align CSR with their corporate governance and performance. Evidencing the wider trend towards a more strategic business focus upon CSR, a major government-commissioned 21st century report on corporate community investment in Australia identified that more than 90 per cent of companies required a business case for their community engagement, with approximately one quarter of them seeking a specific financial return on investment from this activity.[20]

CSR has at least 10 major benefits for business, as follows.[21] First, CSR relates to that part of socio-ethical business responsibility and shared societal infrastructure that involves business contributing to the common good, whether for altruistic or self-interested reasons (e.g. choosing to avoid corporate social irresponsibility because it is the right thing to do, as distinct from making business contributions to civil society to ensure preconditions for successful profit-making). A recent McKinsey global survey of thousands of senior business executives worldwide found that more than 80 per cent of respondents agreed that 'making broader contributions to the public good should accompany generating high returns to investors', with fewer than 20 per cent of them viewing such returns as their company's only focus.[22]

Secondly, CSR helps a business to adapt and respond to changes in its surrounding business environment. These changes embrace CSR-related business drivers and risks, such as socio-economic trends, eco-technological innovations, consumer and NGO pressures, and internet-fuelled awareness of CSR issues amongst mass populations worldwide. They also embrace broader aspects of the mushrooming CSR infrastructure surrounding business and markets, such as the rise of the CSR movement, the growth in ethical investment funds, the emergence of CSR-based corporate rating bodies and tools, and the increase in CSR-related official regulation. Thirdly, some CSR benefits for business relate directly or indirectly to improved corporate governance. For example, CSR can improve corporate governance arrangements, management structures and stakeholder engagement processes through improved business relations, communication and reporting.

As a fourth category of business benefit, CSR offers partnering, networking and coalition-building advantages for business. This includes relationship-developing, trust-enhancing and expertise-sharing business advantages through participation in cross-sectoral multi-stakeholder initiatives involving governments, NGOs and business, as canvassed in Chapter 2. Fifthly, a business might perceive correlations between CSR practices and corporate performance, such as leveraging CSR partnership advantages, exploiting new markets and otherwise generating financial returns on socially and environmentally responsible business activity. This includes ways in which CSR helps a business to maintain competitiveness, in meeting CSR-related expectations and standards set by competitive peers and official regulators, as in business-to-business and business-to-government contractual performance conditions that tie contracting, supply and distribution arrangements to CSR-related performance standards.

As a sixth category of benefit, CSR offers distinct corporate reputational advantages, especially given the 21st century significance of corporate reputations and brands as tangible assets, predicated on numerous bases of shareholder and stakeholder support. This includes improving corporate reputation and corporate brand identification through cause-related marketing, social advocacy and other CSR-related promotion. Seventhly, as corporate reputations and brands are increasingly affected by external assessments from shareholder representatives, investment institutions and analysts, corporate ratings and advisory bodies, and NGOs, another benefit for business lies in meeting CSR-related investment decision-making, project financing, corporate rating and public interest criteria.

As an eighth category of benefit, CSR can also be aimed at improving governmental, regulatory and community relations, as a means of forestalling societal demands for extra business regulation as well as securing political and legal advantages over competitors. This includes enhancing links with local communities and governments in home and host countries of operations, and building community trust and goodwill, both generally and with a view to facilitating community support for particular business activities. Ninthly, meeting employee and customer needs has multiple business benefits, such as attracting and retaining good employees and customers, developing customer brand awareness and loyalty, and broadening management and staff perspectives and expertise. Finally, in light of the growth of CSR-related law and regulation highlighted throughout this book, CSR can also relate to corporate compliance, not simply in terms of the lowest common denominator of minimum legal compliance with CSR-related law and regulation, but more fruitfully in terms of multi-dimensional corporate success achieved through aspirational corporate responsibility. In the words of others who analyse 21st century CSR through a legal lens, 'the multitude of new laws, legal decisions and quasi-regulatory initiatives which support the assertion that "corporate social responsibility" is, amongst other things, a legal concept', collectively compel us to 'cast off any lingering and misconceived ideas that CSR does not incorporate legal responsibilities and is *purely* voluntary'.[23]

Of course, many elements of the business case for CSR are themselves multi-dimensional in character. Corporate branding and reputations are relevant, for example, in being an employer of choice, a brand or company of choice for clients and consumers, an investment of choice for CSR-sensitive individual and institutional investors, a corporate neighbour of choice in local communities in which a business operates, a business partner of choice in public and private partnerships, a multi-stakeholder participant of choice in standard-setting initiatives, and a recognized responsible corporate citizen by official regulators in their approach to regulatory guidance, investigation and enforcement.[24] This multi-dimensionality of the business case for CSR is important in aligning community investment and engagement with business strategy and activity.

Strategic Company-specific Alignment of Business–Society Interests

The mainstreaming of CSR into management practice is central to maximising its contribution to business success and to greater sustainability goals. In providing a more holistic view of the business and its activities, CSR can stimulate better policies, decision making and business practice and stronger long-term profits. I am a strong believer that companies which take a broader range of social and environmental factors into account when making business decisions are more likely to grow long term shareholder value.

– Australia's Minister for Superannuation and Corporate Law, Senator Nick Sherry[25]

Too often, 'corporate social responsibility' (or corporate citizenship) has been defined almost exclusively in terms of philanthropic engagement with not-for-profit community organisations or 'green' initiatives. It is increasingly accepted that social investment helps improve the attractiveness of business to its customers and employees. However, the effect of such worthwhile activities (workplace giving, volunteering, financial support) is limited if they are not integrated into corporate strategic intent. There is a need for the value of CSR to be reflected in the ethical behaviour that drives business enterprise . . . Companies need to embrace a wider definition of business ethics and to instil a stronger sense of community responsibility in executive leadership.

– Professor Peter Shergold, chief executive of the Centre for Social Impact, and former Secretary of the Department of Prime Minister and Cabinet (Australia)[26]

Multi-level organizational and societal alignment

At the most basic level, a strategic approach to CSR aligns company-specific circumstances with societal and even global needs. 'Shareholder value should continue to be seen as the critical measure of business success', although 'it may be more accurate, more motivating – and indeed more beneficial to shareholder value over the long term – to describe business's ultimate purpose as the efficient provision of goods and services that society wants', which reflects 'the fundamental basis of the contract between business and society', and reinforces the need for business 'to build social issues into strategy in a way which reflects their actual business importance', according to McKinsey's managing director, Ian Davis.[27] As recognized in the European Union's policy framework for CSR, socially responsible business practices support a number of public policy objectives, including in the European Commission's own words:[28]

–   more integrated labour markets and higher levels of social inclusion, as enterprises actively seek to recruit more people from disadvantaged groups;
–   investment in skills development, life-long learning and employability, which are needed to remain competitive in the global knowledge economy and to cope with the ageing of the working population in Europe;

- improvements in public health, as a result of voluntary initiatives by enterprises in areas such as the marketing and labelling of food and non-toxic chemicals;
- better innovation performance, especially with regard to innovations that address societal problems, as a result of more intensive interaction with external stakeholders and the creation of working environments more conducive to innovation;
- a more rational use of natural resources and reduced levels of pollution, notably thanks to investments in eco-innovation and to the voluntary adoption of environmental management systems and labelling;
- a more positive image of business and entrepreneurs in society, potentially helping to cultivate more favourable attitudes towards entrepreneurship;
- greater respect for human rights, environmental protection and core labour standards, especially in developing countries;
- poverty reduction and progress towards the Millennium Development Goals.

At a systemic level, the synchronization of CSR public policy goals, other forms of state and non-state CSR regulation, and CSR-responsive organizational systems and processes can generate paradigm shifts in how companies and societies view and practise CSR, at least from the standpoint of CSR meta-regulation.[29] At an organizational level, effective business strategizing and risk analysis aligns CSR closely, for example, with a company's market orientation towards its corporate constituency, and with its competence orientation towards its core capabilities and skills, instead of ad hoc social investments with fewer two-way business returns.[30] Successful corporate risk management over the longer term is about guaranteeing 'our sustainability as a business' and not simply 'giving cheques to charities', insists Foster's director of government, industry and community relations, Natalie Toohey, adding that 'aligning what you do with what you say you do' translates for the brewing company into improvements like injury-proofing bottles, improving product information labelling and reducing pollution and water wastage in production.[31]

The strategic benefit for corporations in aligning their business with broader social needs is now widely acknowledged in the business and professional services sectors. Putting this into practice involves enterprise-specific steps in competitive advantage and positioning, focused upon both opportunities and risks that arise from the surrounding business environment:[32]

> The challenge is to find a way for companies to incorporate an awareness of socio-political issues more systematically into their core strategic decision-making processes. Companies must see the social and political dimensions not just as risks – areas for damage limitation – but also as opportunities. They should scan the horizon for emerging trends and integrate their responses across the organization, so that the resulting initiatives are coherent rather than piecemeal.

Moreover, the more that CSR becomes an embedded part of mainstream business models, the more endurable it becomes in the face of mixed corporate fortunes and economic downturns, when corporate activities and personnel of perceived marginal value to a company's business model and long-term success are more vulnerable. This aspect of alignment reflects how well the CSR-focused activities of corporate PR and marketing divisions, *pro bono* and charity committees, and even company-established charitable foundations relate to the competitive orientation of the rest of the business enterprise. In this way, a company's CSR focus develops beyond isolated and unrelated acts of corporate philanthropy and marginalization of CSR activity away from core business priorities. These lessons are even more important in the wake of the international financial and credit crisis of 2008.

A further critical area of alignment occurs at more detailed levels between the business enterprise and reliable indicators of its CSR-related performance. Business activities involving political lobbying and donations, cause-related marketing and sponsorship, publicized positions on government policy and regulation, and other business interactions with government officials not only cover an aspect of the business enterprise that is covered in authoritative guidelines for sustainability reporting. They also present both dangers and opportunities for a company's public reputation and influence, in terms of the degree of congruence or mismatch between a company's public positions and its own activities. The G3 guidelines on public policy positions and other participation in policy-related activity by business, for example, include an emphasis on 'the extent to which publicly-expressed positions on sustainability are consistently embedded across the organization and aligned across different units', thereby enabling both the company and outsiders (including investors and official regulators) to make 'a comparison of organisational priorities (particularly when making comparisons within the same sector)' and assess 'transparency for lobbying activities for those concerned with the integrity of the practices and potential impacts on stakeholders'.[33]

Distinguishing between strategic and non-strategic corporate social responsibility

Several significant characteristics of community investment reflect the shift from the periphery to a deeply strategic approach. There is typically a deep alignment between the needs and specific competencies of companies and the activities they pursue. So banks are engaged in financial literacy, mining companies in environmental and indigenous affairs, and pharmaceutical companies in public health.

Deeper engagement leads to fewer, better leveraged and more sustainable partnerships, negotiated with a focus on greater mutual accountability and obligation. The alignment between social engagement and business strategy puts paid to the Friedmanite injunction that companies should not so engage in the interests of shareholders.

– Geoff Allen, Chairman of the Centre for Corporate Public Affairs[34]

The points of intersection between social responsibility and corporate competitiveness therefore define what has come to be known as 'strategic CSR'. Savitz and Weber contend, for example, that 'any company that can find and operate within the sustainability sweet spot – the area of vital overlap between business and social interests – will ultimately make more profit, outcompeting and outlasting its less savvy competitors'.[35] This notion of a 'sweet spot' is also evident in *The Economist*'s endorsement of strategic CSR approaches in its 2008 report on CSR:[36]

The simple solution is that businesses should concentrate on the sweet spot where initiatives are good for both profits and social welfare. This is the sort of 'win-win' situation that executives love to talk about: the smart thing to do as well as the right thing to do. Green policies currently offer lots of opportunities for win-wins, which is why so many firms are eagerly embracing them:

cut fuel costs and you help both the planet and the bottom line; expand your range of organic food and increase your market share. The same logic should lead senior management, faced with a bewildering spectrum of socially worthy activities, to select those that are most relevant to their business.

Others view strategic alignment of business–society interests in similar terms. 'With corporate community investment becoming an increasingly strategic and core business activity', notes a major government-commissioned Australian report on corporate–community interactions in 2007, there is a need for 'all large companies to develop cohesive rationales for corporate community investment activities, based on clear business drivers'.[37] What makes a responsible business profitable from a company's perspective, however, is not necessarily the same as what society or the world wants from business to sustain a civil society for the common good. The gap between these two dimensions is one of the major limits of strategic CSR and an ongoing 21st century CSR challenge.

Strategic CSR does not encompass all forms of CSR. At its most basic level, strategic CSR is characterized by socially beneficial corporate activities that are integral to the business. This can be expressed in different ways and takes different forms. One set of commentators defines strategic CSR in terms of 'the set of actions that promotes long-term profit for the firm given its competition, consumers, suppliers, and market environment', in a way that aligns making money with doing good.[38] Environmentally friendly production technology might benefit society by reducing greenhouse gases, for example, while also benefiting a company by reducing costs, just as corporate philanthropy might aid society's charitable needs while also solidifying a corporation's reputation, customer loyalty and community goodwill towards its business endeavours.[39] Conversely, these commentators view non-strategic CSR as being 'business behavior that is at direct odds with short- and (reasonably) long-term profit maximization'.[40] For these authors, 'a patchwork of confusing codes, voluntary standards, and weak or nonexistent monitoring', partly in response to the growth of non-strategic CSR demands by civil society upon corporations, obscures the need to look to governmental rather than business solutions to address large market failures, and to use '(a) more nuanced CSR paradigm' of working with business selectively in genuine areas of common ground.[41]

Their view is challenged by another set of commentators,[42] who allow room for business flexibility and choice in accommodating 'the growing importance of a wide spectrum of stakeholders to a company's bottom line', with a resultant obliteration of the distinction between strategic and non-strategic CSR, because '*all* responsible CSR is in fact "strategic CSR"'. So, instead of seeing a hotchpotch of ineffective measures, due partly to the explosion of non-strategic CSR demands and resulting fragmentation of CSR standard-setting, they see the emergence of authoritative consensus for a critical mass of CSR commonality, as reflected in industry and organizational corporate codes of conduct and other standards from institutions such as the ILO, UN and OECD.[43] Here and elsewhere, CSR reality is in the eye of the beholder.

Another group of commentators do not simply divide CSR into strategic and non-strategic camps, but distinguish between different forms of CSR in ways that still have relevance for the distinction between strategic and non-strategic CSR. Attorneys Dan Feldman and Sarah Altschuller mark out different phases of CSR development by labelling the development and refinement of industry and organizational codes as 'CSR 1.0', elevation to 'robust monitoring, benchmarking, and communication strategies' associated with organizational and multi-stakeholder standard-setting initiatives as 'CSR 2.0', and exploration of the boundaries of business–society relations through the linkages between company operations and wider societal issues as 'CSR 3.0', with CSR 3.0 in particular providing fertile ground for differentiation between strategic and non-strategic forms of CSR.[44]

The late Professor Parkinson distinguished between 'relational responsibility' and 'social activism' in a way that parallels the distinction between strategic and non-strategic CSR.[45] Here, 'relational responsibility' goes to the welfare of groups affected by the company's business activity (e.g. employees, customers and neighbouring residents and businesses), with emphasis upon harm-minimization and fair treatment concerning these groups.[46] 'Social activism' covers business activity that might be beneficial to particular groups or society as a whole, but which lies beyond what is integral to the company's business.[47] This distinction also has implications for the relation between corporate responsibility and social responsibility, since 'relational responsibility involves an attempt to achieve an improved accommodation of the various interests affected by corporate activity, but does not envisage a wider social role for the company', whereas social activism 'constitutes an effort by companies to address social issues that arise independently of the way the company conducts its business and thus represents an extension of corporate activity into essentially non-commercial spheres'.[48]

This has flow-on consequences for the legal duties of corporate executives too. 'It is undoubtedly an exercise of non-strategic, profit-sacrificing social responsibility that is most likely to be in breach of corporate law duties', notes corporate law academic Therese Wilson, adding that '(s)trategic CSR will be tolerated by corporate law in the sense that its ultimate goal remains profit maximisation for shareholders'.[49]

Porter and Kramer on step-by-step approaches to strategic corporate social responsibility

Steps in developing a company's strategic framework for corporate social responsibility
Strategic CSR is the lynchpin of the CSR approach recommended by Michael Porter and Mark Kramer in their award-winning 21st century *Harvard Business Review* article on CSR. In their eyes, strategic CSR offers a business and societal justification of CSR that is lacking in what they characterize as the four main alternative justifications in favour of CSR – namely 'moral obligation, sustainability, licence to operate, and reputation'.[50] They reject all four alternative CSR justifications for their weaknesses in common. In their eyes, these purported justifications for CSR offer generic rather than company-specific rationales for action. They direct attention to the tension between business and societal interests instead of their interdependence. They offer no real organizational framework or tool 'to help a company identify, prioritise, and address the social issues that matter most on which it can make the biggest impact', resulting in fragmented and uncoordinated CSR activities 'that neither make any meaningful social impact nor strengthen the firm's long-term competitiveness', and which are therefore vulnerable to 'a change of management or a swing in the business cycle'.[51]

According to Porter and Kramer, a number of steps are involved in developing a truly strategic CSR framework. The first step is to concentrate upon 'points of intersection' between business and society, which in practice means that 'a company must integrate a social perspective into the core frameworks it already uses to understand competition

CSR should not be only about what businesses have done that is wrong – important as that is. Nor should it be only about making philanthropic contributions to local charities, lending a hand in time of disaster, or providing relief to society's needy – worthy though these contributions may be. Efforts to find shared value in operating practices and in the social dimensions of competitive context have the potential not only to foster economic and social development but to change the way companies and society think about each other. NGOs, governments, and companies must stop thinking in terms of 'corporate social responsibility' and start thinking in terms of 'corporate social integration'.

. . . The fact is, the prevailing approaches to CSR are so fragmented and so disconnected from business and strategy as to obscure many of the greatest opportunities for companies to benefit society. If corporations were to analyse their prospects for social responsibility using the same frameworks that guide their core business choices, they would discover that CSR can be much more than a cost, a constraint, or a charitable deed – it can be a source of opportunity, innovation, and competitive advantage.

– Harvard Business School's Michael Porter and Harvard University's John F Kennedy School of Government senior fellow Mark Kramer[52]

and guide its business strategy'.[53] The second step is to build this interdependence into the framework through the twin prongs of 'inside out linkages' and 'outside in linkages'.[54] The former concentrate upon the positive and negative ways in which corporate activity affects society, while the latter focus upon how the external environment affects a company in terms of both risk-based and opportunity-based business drivers. In this way, the relationship and alignment between a 'company's value chain' and its societal linkages, and a company's 'competitive context' and its societal linkages, are both brought into sharp relief.[55]

The next step lies in understanding the different features and uses of these twin linkages. 'When a company uses the value chain to chart all the social consequences of its activities, it has, in effect, created an inventory of problems and opportunities – mostly operational issues – that need to be investigated, prioritised, and addressed' in attempting to 'clear away as many negative value-chain social impacts as possible'.[56] Company supply, distribution, and production activities have societal consequences in terms of transportation impacts, greenhouse gas emissions, resource usage and pollutions and hazards, for example.[57]

By contrast, the tool of 'outside in linkages' in a company's 'competitive context' focuses directly upon how the company responds in its own unique way to social influences in marking out its own unique competitive positioning and advantage. It builds upon Porter's earlier work in developing a four-fold diamond framework for analysing competitive advantage in societal and organizational system-specific ways.[58] This framework comprises 'factor (input) conditions' (i.e. business inputs), 'local demand conditions' (i.e. business outputs and markets), 'related and supporting industries' (i.e. local business infrastructure support) and 'context for firm strategy and rivalry' (i.e. business competitive context). Collectively, these 'social dimensions of the company's competitive context' constitute its 'outside in linkages' affecting its competitive strategizing, positioning and productivity.[59] So, for example, the preconditions of a well-functioning economy, fair competition, respect for property rights (including intellectual property), freedom of contract and the rule of law all form part of the business competitive context in each locality where a company does business. Similarly, the availability of high-quality local suppliers and distributors forms part of a company's local business infrastructure support.

In this way, identifying the external societal influences upon a company's competitiveness enables the company to identify, prioritize and choose strategic CSR options in each of the four areas of the diamond framework that enhance its competitiveness while simultaneously benefiting society, through a relation that pinpoints precisely how one affects the other. Again, the underlying imperative of mutuality is paramount. 'The essential test that should guide CSR is not whether a cause is worthy but whether it presents an opportunity to create *shared* value – that is, a meaningful benefit for society that is also valuable to the business', argue these advocates of strategic CSR.[60] Such a view of business–society relations takes us deep into the territory of debate about whether or not profitable business activity counts as CSR in any meaningful sense.

These two tools produce a total set of prioritized and company-specific social issues for strategic CSR. This includes working out the differences between generic community engagement that is part of their background business context but does not greatly affect their long-term competitiveness (e.g. community arts sponsorship by a professional services firm), social trends that affect a company's underlying business (e.g. an energy and resources company's need to confront mass consumer take-up of clean energy technologies and products), social factors that impinge upon business operations (e.g. the impact of AIDs and mass pandemics on local workforces), and social dynamics that align with competitive advantage and market positioning (e.g. the reputational advantages for a bank being known for financing only environmentally sustainable projects).[61]

Categorizing, prioritizing and choosing between social issues on the basis of their connection to a company's value chain and competitive context therefore enables a company to move to the stage of developing a cohesive and comprehensive 'corporate social agenda'.[62] This stage lies at the heart of a company's differentiation of strategic CSR from non-strategic CSR. Here, 'strategic CSR' moves beyond non-strategic good corporate citizenship and mitigation of harmful corporate value chain impacts that characterize responsive CSR, focusing instead on a small and highly selective range of business initiatives that produce the highest leverage of 'both inside-out and outside-in dimensions working in tandem'.[63] Although there are wider levels on which commentators point to the convergence of corporate responsibility and CSR, here we have a particularized integration of value chain practices and competitive context investments in which 'CSR becomes hard to distinguish from the day-to-day business of the company'.[64]

The final step in how Porter and Kramer envisage implementation of strategic CSR focuses upon developing the necessary business organizational mindset and framework for embedding a strategically focused social dimension within the company's distinctive business model:[65]

> Operating managers must understand the importance of the outside-in influence of competitive context, while people with responsibility for CSR initiatives must have a granular understanding

of every activity in the value chain. Value chain and competitive-context investments in CSR need to be incorporated into the performance measures of managers with P & L responsibility . . . The short-term performance pressures companies face rule out indiscriminate investments in social value creation. They suggest, instead, that creating shared value should be viewed like research and development, as a long-term investment in a company's future competitiveness.

For example, a commercial property developer and manager looking to build a reputation for sustainability might develop an organization-specific matrix of criteria for selecting responsible partnering organizations, choosing environmentally sound properties for development, and meeting sustainability expectations of investors in those projects. Here, strategic trade-offs, cost-benefit assessments, endurable success indicators, and other standard business methodologies inform a company's CSR judgments, from a whole-of-organization perspective. For example, a recommendation from a company's PR department to increase the company's 'green' credentials by replacing all existing lighting in the company's portfolio of managed commercial buildings with more energy-efficient lighting might not be as economically, environmentally and strategically feasible as placing higher priority on the longer-term aim of making all new commercial property holdings meet higher sustainability standards across the board.

As one corporate executive of such a sustainability-orientated business put it to the author, 'We're future-proofing our business'. In further discussion, it became clear that this meant fine-tuning their business model through the prism of sustainability, with improved methods of costing, pricing and modelling to match. As another executive of the same sustainability-related business put it to the author, he needed their organization's integrated approach to sustainability to flow into sophisticated business modelling tools, enabling him to put a menu of pricing options to prospective tenant clients for sustainable buildings, with a sales pitch along these lines: 'Look, you'll pay more annual rent up front to be in this sustainable building than in our competitor's building down the road, but you'll also pay less in outgoings over time, plus you'll have the corporate PR advantage of being "green"'.

Critique and lessons

The alignment between business advantage and societal concerns has its limits, not least because 'it is implausible to think that *all* socially beneficial corporate conduct conveniently happens to be profit-maximizing'.[66] In other words, no-one needs to be an anti-capitalist to argue that the strategic fit between a company's business activity and wider societal concerns does not match everything that humanity needs. Conversely, any strategic fit between a company's business and societal needs to the company's profit-making advantage risks being characterized simply as smart business and not CSR at all, as discussed in Chapter 3.

The response to such criticisms from the advocates of strategic CSR is multi-pronged. The alignment between corporate self-interest and societal needs comes in *shared* value-creation. Every company can do no more than what it is uniquely equipped to do. The social welfare gap this leaves must be addressed in other ways, by other companies or societal actors. Strategic CSR unquestionably produces socially beneficial outcomes, in ways that transcend the strict public–private and mandatory–voluntary divides. It therefore distils and evidences a meaningful and possibly best form of CSR.

At the same time, this version of strategic CSR has its weaknesses and limitations too.

The rejected justifications of CSR (e.g. 'licence to operate' justifications) are selective characterizations, belying the considerable support and complex rationales for them in the CSR literature. In addition, corporate justifications for CSR are often multi-factorial. For example, pharmaceutical companies making low-cost life-saving HIV/AIDS and other medication available in regions with mass victims of illness and disease might do so for combined motives of humanitarianism, community goodwill, business relationship-building, corporate PR and negotiation leverage with national governments over intellectual property rights.

Viewed out of context, this account of strategic CSR also risks being used to bolster arguments which assign CSR largely to voluntary corporate action as a matter of self-interested self-regulation, disengaged from the mutual business-society relation that its authors intend and the interwoven forms of regulation which affect that relation. At the very least, strategic CSR cannot address or discourage forms of corporate irresponsibility for which the best solution on national and international fronts lies in the legal domain.

The steps in the argument sometimes submerge the gulf between shared win-win outcomes of business–society engagement and zero-sum competitions between public and private interests, as in the endorsement of the otherwise worthy principle of 'shared value'.[67] 'If either a business or a society pursues policies that benefit its interests at the expense of the other, it will find itself on a dangerous path [because] temporary gain to one will undermine the long-term prosperity of both', for example.[68] What companies undertake as strategic CSR forms only part of a wider CSR equation, involving CSR actions of governments and civil society organizations too. Moreover, the way in which the relation between business and society is conceived through strategic CSR puts business rather than society very much in the driver's seat of determining appropriate boundaries for CSR, at the risk of marginalizing the equal importance of CSR as a form of corporate responsiveness to wider forces of governance, regulation and responsibility too.

Considered from this perspective, the strategic alignment of business and societal interests is not one-way traffic from the completely self-chosen and self-interested standpoint of an individual corporation, but rather involves transparent synchronicity between public policy goals and regulation in support of CSR, on the one hand, and the discrete and strategic ways in which any individual corporation aligns its business model with that wider CSR-embracing societal orientation, on the other. In other words, strategic corporate management of business–society relations is responsive to more in the external business environment than just a voluntary community-minded motivation or instrumental use of CSR to secure competitive advantage. It must be responsive to a wide range of meta-regulatory influences too.

PRACTICAL CSR FRAMEWORKS AND TEMPLATES FOR CORPORATE DIRECTORS, MANAGERS AND ADVISERS

Practical Guidelines for Company-specific CSR Policies and Programmes

One school of thought in the CSR literature suggests twin transformations in how business leaders now conceive and practise CSR, firstly in terms of assertively looking for

There is no one-size-fits-all approach and model for performing corporate social responsibility. The key is to incorporate CSR considerations into the company's mission, vision, strategies and operating activities and to evaluate and continuously improve its behaviours against measurable criteria.

– 'Draft Guidelines on Corporate Social Responsibility Compliance by Foreign Invested Enterprises', Chinese Academy of International Trade and Economic Cooperation, 2008

Corporate social responsibility is a very broad agenda. Please give us something we can do differently on Monday morning to make things happen.

– One common business reaction to CSR in practice, according to the World Business Council for Sustainable Development[69]

business opportunities from CSR rather than simply reacting out of fear (e.g. loss of business reputation and fear of litigation), and secondly in terms of viewing CSR as a 'built-in' component of ordinary business strategy and operations rather than simply as a 'bolt-on' addition.[70] Business experts and CSR advocates, David Grayson and Adrian Hodges, view this transformation as a transformation from CSR to 'corporate social opportunity', the three dimensions of which cover new products and services (i.e. 'innovation in products and services'), new markets (i.e. 'serving unserved markets'), and new business models (i.e. 'building new business models' for designing, developing, financing, marketing or distributing products and services).[71] Broader themes of alignment and integration of corporate responsibility and CSR are present here too.

All of this results in a basic framework for 'corporate social opportunity' of seven step-by-step phases in a continuous loop, each with its own sub-steps, as follows:[72]

- 'Step 1: Identifying the triggers' (e.g. business environment/stakeholder triggers and impact assessment);
- 'Step 2: Scoping what matters' (e.g. strategizing around stakeholder, market and operational issues);
- 'Step 3: Making the business case' (e.g. strategic alignment with organizational business drivers and culture);
- 'Step 4: Committing to action' (e.g. alignment between strategic actions and organizational values, leadership and governance arrangements);
- 'Step 5: Integration and gathering resources' (e.g. alignment between resource needs/gaps, operational changes and business strategies);
- 'Step 6: Engaging stakeholders' (e.g. stakeholder impact-assessment and role-clarification in strategy implementation); and
- 'Step 7: Measuring and reporting' (e.g. identification, measurement and reporting of relevant information, within a review framework).

Triple bottom line advocates Andrew Savitz and Karl Weber offer seven key elements of a corporate 'sustainability management system', comprising: (a) 'vision' (i.e. how the company positions itself, its business and its industry in relation to its economic, social and environmental risks, opportunities and challenges); (b) 'strategy' (i.e. a plan for effecting the vision); (c) 'goals' (i.e. specific goals and targets aligned with strategy); (d) 'procedures and protocols' (i.e. well-described and well-communicated operating requirements for all organizational actors); (e) 'key performance indicators (KPIs)' (i.e. specific measures and milestones for assessing progress and success); (f) 'measurement and reporting' (i.e. measured alignment between organizational goals, strategies, operations and performance); and (g) 'stakeholder engagement' (i.e. integration of stakeholder influences throughout all steps).[73] Their correlative 'framework for assessment, design, and implementation of a sustainability management system' involves stages of corporate sustainability self-assessment, corporate sustainability strategizing, corporate sustainability programme implementation, sustainable corporate organizational resource deployment, corporate stakeholder engagement on sustainability, corporate sustainability monitoring and reporting, and sustainable corporate culture development.[74]

Standards Australia's *Corporate Social Responsibility* Standard (AS 8003) outlines a number of systematic step-by-step operational elements for a corporate CSR programme. Those basic elements are as follows:[75]

(1) identifying company-specific CSR issues concerning strategies, operations and performance;
(2) matching identified CSR issues to relevant operating procedures and organizational responsibilities;
(3) developing a detailed CSR implementation strategy and action plan;
(4) creating a feedback system to ensure continuous CSR improvement;
(5) introducing appropriate record-keeping, to support training, monitoring, reporting and other organizational needs;
(6) investigating and rectifying non-compliance with CSR procedures;
(7) developing transparent internal and external reporting on CSR;
(8) engaging stakeholders at all stages of the process of developing, implementing and continuously improving the company's CSR programme; and
(9) monitoring, supervising, training and other fostering of the company's CSR policy.

Each of these major steps has its own important sub-steps. For example, the first step of identifying company-specific CSR issues across multiple corporate areas of attention requires an organizationally focused issues map that includes issues of profit-generation (e.g. profit-making, standard competitive practices and pricing), governance (e.g. adhering to business ethics and avoiding political corruption, bribery and unfair political lobbying or tactics), workplace and employee issues (e.g. work-related basic rights, non-discrimination and legal compliance on wages and benefits), supply and distribution chain issues (e.g. community involvement, fair trading, and ethical and legal requirements), health and safety issues (e.g. workplace health and safety, personal health needs, and safe and healthy workplace environments), and sustainable development and environmental issues (e.g. community impact and environmental regulatory compliance).[76]

All of these operational elements must be aligned with structural elements for implementing CSR, including high-level board and management commitment, a company-specific CSR policy, appropriate management responsibilities for CSR, adequate CSR resourcing, and a commitment to continuous improvement in CSR at all levels of the organization.[77] Again, each of these basic elements has its own sub-elements. For example, high-level commitment to CSR:

> can manifest itself through a number of initiatives including:
> (a) Preparation of a coherent CSR plan, its goals and how these will be achieved
> (b) Designating a senior manager with responsibility for overseeing implementation of CSR within the entity
> (c) The CSR manager (i.e. a delegated representative within the entity) to be given sufficient authority to achieve CSR outcomes
> (d) CSR to feature on a regular basis on board/board committee agendas
> (e) Reports to be received from the CSR manager
> (f) Adequate resourcing of the CSR function and program
> (g) Regular dissemination of information on CSR to stakeholders.[78]

After listing seven facets of CSR (i.e. purpose and values, workforce, marketplace, environment, community, human rights and guiding principles), the Business Impact Task Force (BITF) of Business in the Community (BITC) identifies three major ways in which socially responsible business practice promotes business success. Those three ways are: (i) building the business (e.g. meeting consumer demand for socially responsible products and services); (ii) building the workforce (e.g. recruiting and retaining highly skilled employees who value and seek socially responsible businesses and workplace environments); and (iii) building trust (e.g. developing a reputation as a reputable and trustworthy business in relations with employees, suppliers, customers, investors, financiers, creditors and local licencing and regulatory authorities).[79] Adopting the Management Model of the Ashridge Centre for Business and Society, the BITF then endorses the following management steps in developing and managing a socially responsible business, in a looped cycle of continuous improvement:[80]

> 1. Secure commitment
> 2. Identify external concerns and relate to business interests
> 3. Review any current policies, processes and performance
> 4. Define strategy, plans and targets, and allocate resources
> 5. Put into practice
> 6. Measure performance
> 7. Report and communicate
> 8. Dialogue with external parties to review progress

Inherent within these steps is the core idea that the ways in which a business chooses to engage with stakeholders and wider society must be matched in an organization-specific way to a particular business model, the surrounding business environment and the wider societal content. So, identifying external concerns (Step 2) looks to 'the issues that are most relevant for your own company', and defining strategy (Step 4) 'must align with both business interest and stakeholder concerns', given that the overall aim 'is to embed social responsibility into the way your company conducts its business'.[81]

Importantly, this business-specific approach to CSR infuses the specific policy and process steps that BITF suggests for the seven core aspects of CSR at three different levels of CSR engagement, from first-time CSR adoption (i.e. Level 1) to more sophisticated CSR approaches (i.e. Level 2) and finally to public CSR leadership (i.e. Level 3).[82] So, for example, a suggested Level 1 activity in the marketplace aspect of CSR is to undertake a formal review of the positive and negative impacts upon society of the business' goods and services – an activity that inherently frames societal impact in enterprise-specific terms, matched to the particular goods and services of that business within its unique competitive setting. Similarly, the suggested Level 2 activity in the workforce aspect of developing comprehensive support programmes for employees (e.g. pension and superannuation needs, compassionate and other forms of leave beyond standard recreational and sick leave, and targeted drug and alcohol abuse programmes) is matched to the specific demographics and needs of a company's workforce.

Similarly, the suggested Level 3 activity in the environmental aspect of ensuring consideration of environmental impacts in product/service development, as well as strategic investment decision-making, links the company's particular production, service delivery and decisional activities to their correlative environmental consequences. The combined Level 2 and Level 3 human rights activities of establishing a company human rights policy and implementation plan, undertaking employee and management training in human rights awareness, setting corporate and individual performance indicators tied to a company's human rights performance, and monitoring and enforcing human rights standards in the company's contracts and supply/distribution chains all correspond to company-specific circumstances and needs, within a framework of general categories of corporate activities that each company must customize and tailor for itself, aided by whatever industry or other regulatory guidance might apply.[83] All of this reinforces the value of holistic approaches to CSR integration and alignment.

Other standard-setters also frame their guidance for corporations and their boards and management in terms which accommodate the different stages through which companies typically progress on their CSR journey. In boardroom guidance produced for the Conference Board of Canada by Strandberg consulting, a CSR 'road map' is divided into two stages – one stage for boards starting to embrace CSR and another stage for boards as they shift gears in their CSR efforts to a higher level.[84] Collectively, these stages encapsulate steps that relate CSR to a company's 'mission and values', communicated board commitment, risk and opportunity horizon, business model and strategy, committee structures, and performance reporting (i.e. Stage 1), along with rewarding CSR performance by executives, building CSR expertise into board and CEO recruitment, training directors in CSR, facilitating meaningful board access and input for stakeholders, and making CSR an essential factor in major board decisions.[85]

Industry Canada offers guidance for companies on a CSR implementation framework which is orientated around the basic conceptual phases of planning, doing, checking and improving CSR. This approach embraces the following step-by-step tasks and associated activities:[86]

(1) 'Conduct a CSR Assessment' (e.g. create CSR team, define CSR, audit organizational material and actions, and engage stakeholders);
(2) 'Develop a CSR Strategy' (e.g. build organizational support, benchmark against others, and identify company-specific CSR options and their correlative business case and associated costs/benefits);

(3) 'Develop CSR Commitments' (e.g. engage in preliminary stakeholder consultations, prepare consultation draft, and discuss with 'affected stakeholders');

(4) 'Implement CSR Commitments' (e.g. establish 'an integrated CSR decision-making structure', 'a CSR business plan', readily identifiable and measurable performance indicators, appropriate management and employee training and commitment, adequate review mechanisms, and internal/external communication, disclosure, and reporting mechanisms);

(5) 'Verify and Report on Progress' (e.g. measure CSR performance, report on CSR performance, and involve stakeholders meaningfully at all stages of this performance cycle); and

(6) 'Evaluate and Improve' (e.g. evaluate CSR performance, identify areas for improvement, commit to continuous improvement, track continuous improvement, and engage stakeholders meaningfully at all stages).

The practical CSR tool kit developed for the UK financial services sector by a coalition of governmental departments, financial services bodies and consultant stakeholders offers another leading example of integrated stages and steps, with some key features in common with equivalent tools developed elsewhere:[87]

(1) 'Stage 1: Complete a strategic review of the business case';
(2) 'Stage 2: Prepare Business Case and obtain Board approval';
(3) 'Stage 3: Design governance arrangements';
(4) 'Stage 4: Complete a detailed CSR review to identify CSR impacts/risks/opportunities';
(5) 'Stage 5: Prepare and begin implementation of stakeholder engagement plan';
(6) 'Stage 6: Draft a CSR policy and/or specific CSR issue policies and objectives';[88]
(7) 'Stage 7: Design and develop the CSR management and reporting system';
(8) 'Stage 8: Implement and operate the CSR management system';
(9) 'Stage 9: Audit the management system';
(10) 'Stage 10: Complete Board level review'; and
(11) 'Stage 11: Prepare CSR reporting (internal/external)'.

Finally, in terms of good CSR practice, Wharton's Professor Donaldson summarizes the essential early steps for companies in these terms:[89]

Many CSR specialists recommend that, as a first step, companies join one or more of the international organisations devoted to CSR, including the United Nations' Global Compact or the Global Reporting Initiative (GRI). Other recommendations from CSR specialists include:

- Engaging stakeholders (and sometimes NGOs) in a dialogue
- Establishing principles and procedures for addressing difficult issues such as labour standards for suppliers, environmental reporting and human rights
- Adjusting reward systems to reflect the company's commitment to CSR
- Collecting, maintaining and publishing data relevant to CSR
- Having the senior leadership team and members of the board of directors engage regularly in an ongoing process of CSR risk and evaluation
- Establishing anonymous reporting and whistle-blowing policies and procedures
- Educating employees and managers about CSR policies and the company's commitment to CSR

- Having the senior leadership team communicate CSR priorities and set an example through their own behaviour.

One of the most recent recommendations for best practice invokes creative philanthropy ['corporate social initiatives'] . . . linked to the company's core values in a way that leverages core competencies.

In light of this select sample, what do the best CSR frameworks have in common? They exhibit a significant degree of consensus about a number of key things at the design level – namely, the relation of CSR to corporate responsibility and governance, the alignment of CSR with business models and competitive positioning, the integration of CSR elements within standard corporate governance arrangements, and the synchronization of CSR performance, roles and rewards at all organizational levels. They also commonly emphasize basic operational elements too, such as boardroom and management CSR commitment, whole-of-organization CSR policies and procedures, meaningful stakeholder engagement, CSR-based performance indicators, and CSR-focused governance, management and reporting arrangements. They acknowledge areas of CSR that closely track and span accepted categories of expanded corporate responsibility (e.g. responsibilities towards the environment), categories of stakeholders (e.g. workforces, suppliers and local communities), and categories of major national and international regulation (e.g. labour and other human rights).

Many of the frameworks for embedding corporate social responsibility within business practice take the form of step-by-step, process-orientated frameworks, some of which gain enhanced legitimacy through endorsement by authoritative multi-stakeholder alliances. They set up multiple levels of CSR alignment with standard corporate strategic and operational elements. Even where companies have separate CSR or corporate responsibility and sustainability strategies, they are increasingly integrated and managed within an overall framework of corporate governance, as corporate governance's traditional components (e.g. strategy, accountability, performance, compliance and assurance) adapt and evolve to include elements of CSR (e.g. stakeholder-sensitive corporate governance, reporting and management of non-financial risks, and CSR performance assessment and compensation).

More broadly, practical guidelines for implementing CSR within companies focus variously upon organizational CSR integration, (e.g. collating non-financial information relating to business drivers), component-related aspects of CSR programmes and infrastructure (e.g. having organization-wide CSR managers and policies), relational CSR interactions (e.g. identifying and engaging stakeholders), systemic and structural features (e.g. whole-of-organization alignment of strategic and operational CSR-related dynamics), substantive outcomes (e.g. organizational inculcation of corporate responsibility values, optimization of organization-specific alignment of business–society relations for competitive advantage, etc.), or various combinations of these things. They commonly emphasize values such as transparency, inclusion and continuous improvement.

Professional CSR Advice and Assistance to Companies and Boards

The practical impact of CSR upon the work of professional services firms is two-pronged, covering not only what they provide to clients but also how clients perceive their professional services providers as part of their business value chain. Firstly, professional services firms are increasingly called upon to provide businesses with various forms of CSR-related advice and assistance. CSR is therefore a growth practice area for professional services firms in the 21st century. 'There exists a large CSR industry and consultants, accountants, lawyers and others will advise companies on how to direct their CSR strategies and how to present them', notes Professor Charlotte Villiers.[90] The range of professional services firms offering such work to businesses now extends beyond legal, accounting and management consulting firms, to embrace services in corporate crisis management, corporate recruitment, corporate lobbying, corporate ratings, corporate education and training, corporate investment and fund-raising, and corporate partnering.

The map of CSR-related services provided by such organizations includes the following services:

(1) providing consultancy advice on CSR start-up and gear-up initiatives, including advice and assistance for internal CSR steering groups (e.g. board CSR committees);

(2) reviewing corporate and boardroom CSR policies and codes of conduct, as well as assisting in the drafting of internal CSR-related codes, policies, compliance programmes, and educational/training resources;

(3) conducting litigation risk audits on CSR-related grounds for infrastructure and development projects;

(4) helping business and development proposals that require public approvals or licences to meet socio-economic, environmental, human rights, and other relevant considerations for public officials considering such applications;

(5) advising on compliance with national and international CSR-related regulation;

(6) keeping corporate clients informed generally of looming national and international politico-regulatory developments in CSR that affect businesses from compliance, litigation and reputational perspectives;

(7) notifying corporate clients of major reports, media mentions and commencement of litigation directly involving those corporate clients, their corporate group members, their affiliates (e.g. major supply/distribution chain members), and industry peers, given the potential implications for the corporation reputations of those involved;

(8) offering strategic legal and other advice in the immediate aftermath of corporate CSR crises (e.g. environmental disasters, media-alleged complicity in human rights abuses, etc.), which might generate possible reputational damage and potential litigation;

(9) monitoring media, stakeholder and CSR rankings and ratings of a company's performance in the public domain;

(10) monitoring adverse stakeholder, media and regulatory reporting of a company's involvement in particular projects or causes;

(11) offering in-house and on-site presentations, training and resources for company executives and staff on CSR-related company policies, practices and compliance;

(12) assisting with external policy and legal submissions and reports on CSR-related regulatory initiatives, for corporate interest groups as well as individual corporate clients; and

(13)   assisting with socio-economic impact statements, environmental impact assessments, human rights impact assessments and management plans, and formal stakeholder consultations and negotiations.

Secondly, the reorientation of corporate law and governance towards CSR puts the CSR spotlight clearly upon law firms and other professional services firms too, in terms of their own corporate governance and performance. 'Law firms, like all businesses, are under increasing pressure to be good corporate citizens [and] clients, particularly those who make a big deal around marketing themselves as being socially responsible . . . are looking at the credentials of anyone in their "supply chain"', reports Anne Susskind.[91] Beyond CSR considerations in legal services auditing by clients, the CSR reputation and performance of law firms can also be a factor in conditions for obtaining governmental work, including criteria such as *pro bono* performance, gender-neutral practices in appointing courtroom advocates, and published organizational track records in environmental responsibility and other aspects of regulatory compliance.

Award-winning CSR leaders in the legal services industry, such as international law firm Freshfields Bruckhaus Deringer, realize the importance of developing firm-wide CSR policies across local and international offices, designating leadership positions and steering groups with organizational responsibilities for CSR, integrating CSR with both business development and community activities of law firms, introducing auditable reporting measures for internal and external communication, developing CSR credibility in dialogue with governments and NGOs, and cultivating strategic relationships for law firms (and to the advantage of their client base) with key governmental, business and civil society organizations. As acknowledged in the literature on CSR and SMEs, 'existing associations and consultants (banks, accountants, lawyers) with which SMEs engage and seek advice are legitimate messengers of responsible business practices and advice'.[92]

Future consideration of CSR in the context of professional legal practice must confront 'the nexus between corporate responsibility and the wider public functions of the legal profession', in light of the accepted position that lawyers not only owe duties to their clients and the courts, but also 'owe wider duties to ensure that their practice reflects a commitment to the proper administration of justice'.[93] So, CSR for the legal profession extends beyond its instrumental guises of a new practice area, client services auditing, *pro bono* work, and marketing as an employer of choice, and potentially extends to how commercial lawyers practise, how they engage with public policy debate about law, and how they choose to act in advice and litigation for clients, with differentiation between the CSR roles of external legal advisers, in-house corporate counsel and lawyers as board members.[94]

INNOVATIONS IN BUSINESS–SOCIETY ENGAGEMENT

Social Dividends and Human Rescue

The panorama of business–society relations extends beyond serving strategic CSR for individual companies. A significant part of 21st century corporate theorizing, governmental policy and business regulation worldwide will be devoted to business engagement

Every company can add to global sustainable development. First and foremost, each company should abide by standards of corporate social responsibility, for example, by adhering to the norms and standards of the United Nations Global Compact. But more than that, each company has special technologies, organizational systems, employee skills, and corporate reputations that can contribute to meeting the Millennium Promises. We've emphasized that corporate social responsibility is not philanthropy but good business practice. Customers, suppliers, and, most important, employees themselves rally to the cause of companies that take these responsibilities seriously . . . This does not mean to turn the company upside down or into a charitable institution, but rather to identify the unique contribution the company may make as part of a broader effort to solve a major social challenge. This is the real meaning of corporate social responsibility: to operate in a manner that promotes broad social objectives, including nonmarket goals, in a way consistent with core business principles, values, and practices. It means much more than simple corporate philanthropy. It demands creativity.

– Professor Jeffrey Sachs, Director of Columbia University's Earth Institute, and author of *The End of Poverty* and *Common Wealth: Economics for a Crowded Planet*[95]

with major national, regional and global governance problems. Even corporate theories that purport to link advantages for particular corporate constituencies (e.g. shareholders) and the corporation itself (e.g. as a collective business enterprise) to optimal forms of business organization and governance from the wider standpoint of overall social efficiency do not necessarily provide an adequate platform for addressing shared governance problems of the order of climate change risks, greenhouse gas reduction, interdependent economics and sustainable development. In turn, major challenges such as global peace, conflict resolution and other stabilizing conditions for a civil society, also present governance problems that can engage business on multiple levels, ranging from the societal preconditions for business efficiency (e.g. stable political, economic and legal systems) to particular business–society interactions (e.g. avoidance of business complicity in governmental human rights abuses and political corruption). Similarly, the strong connection between business engagement and global governance needs is exemplified in business contributions to the Millennium Development Goals, as Professor Sachs highlights.[96]

Corporate philanthropy, charity and community investment are integral features of CSR, but the question is whether or not the justified social dividends of business success now extend beyond these conventional forms. It is no longer exceptional for major TNCs to pledge significant amounts to CSR activity, such as a given percentage of profits to various forms of corporate community investment and engagement. Richard Branson's commitment of his Virgin group to investing $3 billion in developing biofuels because of climate change, principally funded through Virgin's transport network, illustrates the strategic alignment between what business does and its particular societal impact.[97] Many business executives believe that they best benefit society, in addition to voluntary community contributions, through the by-products of running their businesses well, such as enhancing shareholder wealth-generation, providing jobs, developing technological innovations, providing goods and services, aiding local economies and paying taxes.[98]

A wider question is whether there is a legitimate socio-ethical expectation that requires wealthy businesses to contribute financially in socially beneficial ways, either generally or in special circumstances (e.g. disaster relief). Drawing parallels with the embedded international practice of wealthier countries donating a designated part of their wealth to developing countries, and its demonstration of 'a relatively well settled moral expectation that very rich institutions should donate part of their wealth to the more needy', one group of corporate governance scholars suggests that 'a strong argument can be made that corporations do in fact have a moral responsibility to contribute to the improvement of the communities in which they operate'.[99] The limits that they place on this socio-ethical obligation are that it 'only crystallises when a corporation is very successful in achieving its wealth generating objective', must not divert corporate actors from their normal business into sideline social pursuits beyond their expertize and function, and must be directed towards the most pressing social needs.[100] Their suggested mechanics of implementation involve a 'social dividend' payment, by companies and corporate groups making billion dollar annual profits, of 5 per cent of each profit dollar above that threshold, to be diverted primarily to basic human needs like health, shelter, and subsistence.[101]

In socio-ethical terms, people and organizations with a special capacity to affect vulnerable social groups for better or for worse arguably have an obligation to consider this potential effect upon those interests,[102] just as those with a special capacity to assist in human catastrophes arguably have an obligation to exercise that capacity in appropriate ways.[103] Recent business responses across various industry sectors and national boundaries to the human relief effort needed in the wake of tsunamis, hurricanes, the AIDS crisis, other mass pandemics, and even global poverty are a testament to this. Alternatively, is there a business obligation of some kind to assist in extreme situations of human rescue, even if there is no general business obligation to pay society any dividend based upon business success?

In terms of corporate obligations in situations calling for human rescue, Professor Dunfee posits a 'statement of minimum moral obligation' for businesses with suitable human rescue capabilities.[104] Under this obligation, and except where other genuine financial needs intervene, companies possessing 'a unique human catastrophe rescue competency' must commit to this purpose at least the larger of (a) their latest annual investment in social initiatives, (b) the industry average or their own five-year average for such investment, or (c) the average annual investment in social activities by companies in their home country of operation, with the caveat that this corporate social investment can only be diverted away from rescuing humans afflicted by catastrophe and towards other socially worthy initiatives (e.g. local community arts sponsorship) where an equally compelling case for such investment exists.[105] Framed principally with global pharmaceutical companies combating HIV/AIDS in sub-Saharan Africa in mind, this basic obligation goes way beyond the normal bounds and conditions of corporate philanthropy, instead resting upon 'devastating, overwhelming instances of human need' and 'the simple claim that possession of a unique capacity to respond to a devastating catastrophe creates a mandatory obligation of rescue consistent with the confines of the legal/socio-economic role of the organization'.[106]

This obligation to invest in corporate social rescue initiatives can be justified variously in politico-moral terms by social contract and 'licence to operate' expectations, corporate and business citizenship obligations derived from membership of a global community, and pragmatic acceptance by target corporate groups of their unique capability, relative proximity, and felt obligation to meet such extraordinary societal demands.[107] 'To the extent that MNCs are wealthy organisations, and many are phenomenally wealthy, it is arguable that this triggers obligations based on considerations of humanity to make a proportional contribution to meeting the material human rights needs where they are in a position to do so effectively', according to legal theorist and human rights scholar, Professor Tom Campbell, viewing corporate humanitarian obligations through the prism of human rights.[108]

Any such obligation dovetails with the primary regulatory value of transparency too.[109] It also feeds into corporate responsibility and sustainability reporting. In disclosing social investment rationales and activities to investors and other stakeholders, companies desirably should disclose and justify their adherence or non-adherence to such a social obligation, their performance in social rescue investment relative to the designated benchmarks of prior company-specific or sectoral practice, and any financial exigencies that mitigate or explain their investment record, with this disclosed material thereby informing how employees, consumers, investors, socially screened funds and others relate to these companies.[110]

In regulatory terms, any requirement to disclose this form of investment on a 'comply or explain' basis maintains a considerable degree of business freedom in choosing whether and how to engage in CSR, but enhances corporate democratic accountability through public justification of a company's business stance. To the extent that business views this as something that unduly raises public expectations of business to a point that few companies could resist with their reputations intact, this reflects the modern reality of corporate ratings based on matters of corporate responsibility and sustainability. Moreover, by linking performance expectations to industry and sectoral averages in equivalent performance by corporate peers, competitiveness and objectivity are maintained. As explored further below, such measures also extend beyond the extreme context of human rescue situations. They are equally applicable to corporate community investment, and philanthropic and charitable activities in general.

Recasting Corporate Responsibility and Sustainability Disclosure's Purposes and Audiences

Companies across all sectors and geographical boundaries now increasingly feel the need to make public their approach to being responsible and sustainable businesses, often extending that focus to their supply chain and partnering arrangements too. This emphasis upon responsible corporate supply and distribution chains is duplicated in new public policy priorities both within and beyond Europe.[111] Standard corporate governance reporting is moving beyond formal reporting of corporate governance structures and arrangements, to embrace wider dimensions of corporate responsibility and sustainability too. At the same time, much of this is still tightly focused in most corporate regulatory regimes upon business-related concerns rather than what matters to society at large about how a business is behaving and the social footprint that it leaves.

Innovative suggestions for additional forms of disclosure and reporting include not only the public disclosure by companies of whether or not they have a CSR policy, but also benchmarks for discrete areas of performance under such a policy, including how well companies perform in their corporate philanthropy, charity and humanitarian efforts, measured against their own historical performance, industry averages or other demonstrated responsiveness to community expectations and needs.[112] In this way, regulation of CSR-related reporting can be tied to the market norms set by businesses themselves across business groupings, industries and regions, so that individual companies have some obligation to account publicly for their socially responsible activities, relative to what is accepted and demonstrated by their corporate peers.[113] Companies that do not meet sectoral or industry rolling-year averages for voluntary social/CSR reporting and activities for companies of that size and nature could be asked to disclose and account for their relative performance, for example.[114] This would go some way towards alleviating the inequity of imposing extra obligations of claim-justification upon companies that purport to make CSR a priority while allowing those companies that make no such claims to hide under the public radar. Again, any inequities for companies of particular sizes and natures in particular sectors can be alleviated by matching any disclosure obligation to the average for companies of those kinds, so that the norm for large publicly listed companies is not necessarily the norm for everyone.[115]

Asking companies to disclose how their practice or non-practice of CSR (however defined for this purpose) matches their industry or sectoral average promotes transparency and provides information of value to investors and other stakeholders, without necessarily adding to the overall regulatory burden for business, especially if other reporting burden trade-offs are factored into the equation. Some business objections to the imposition of CSR reporting obligations, for example, can often be characterized as broader objections either to any form of extra business regulation or to the overall level of corporate reporting obligations generally. If companies choose not to make socially responsible business behaviour and other legitimate CSR outcomes a major part of their business when others of the same size and nature in the same industry sector do, that choice is theirs but it should come at the cost of disclosing and perhaps even explaining their business policy on CSR engagement. Whatever other objections might be made to these reforms, they cannot all be characterized and dismissed easily as calls for additional, burdensome and unnecessary reporting obligations for business corporations.

Alternatively, the reporting obligation could be more focused, and limited to corporations that claim to be socially responsible, in terms of requiring them to justify how they verify that claim, beyond self-publicity (e.g. demonstrated compliance with independent CSR standards, verification by independent experts or non-aligned ratings body, vetting by stakeholder advisory body, compliance with published CSR-centred guidance from official corporate regulators, and so on).[116] If companies make public claims about conducting their business in socially responsible ways, and seek to gain a competitive or reputational advantage, secure employee commitment, attract finance and investment, or solidify relations with governments or communities on that basis, those claims should be justifiable, verifiable and accountable. Simply requiring companies who make claims about being socially responsible to prove those claims is not the same as imposing an additional and general burden on all companies to engage in social/CSR reporting. Similarly, requiring companies to disclose and account for whether or not they make claims about being socially responsible is not the same as imposing an additional and general burden on all companies to make themselves socially responsible.

Instead of being viewed as additional regulation and extra costs imposed by government, such reporting initiatives can also be viewed as means by which business improves its information base and expertise for assessing the risks and responding to the opportunities stemming from the interaction of socio-economic, environmental and ethical dynamics in business matters.[117] Choosing an appropriate and well-regarded reporting framework as well as suitable assurance, auditing, verification and certification mechanisms for all forms of CSR-related disclosure and reporting is another nascent area of development in the integrity of corporate responsibility and sustainability reporting. 'The new regulatory state is yet to develop appropriate standards for corporate social responsibility reporting and for "meta-evaluating" audits, evaluations and certifications by third party monitors', as Dr Parker notes.[118]

'Responsibility Deals', Social Compacts and Other Business–Society Agreements

'Responsibility Deals' are the centrepiece of the UK Conservative Party Working Group on Responsible Business (CPWGRB) proposals for making business more socially and environmentally responsible. As envisaged by the CPWGRB, responsibility deals are a means by which governments can use market dynamics to steer business towards business–society partnerships that fulfil public policy objectives focused upon corporate responsibility and sustainability. 'Our proposal to achieve this is the introduction of the Responsibility Deal – a mechanism that enables companies to collaborate more effectively with other groups in society to address issues of common concern in a coherent and focused way', explains the CPWGRB.[119] In brief, responsibility deals are intended to operate as follows:[120]

> Responsibility Deals would be based on genuine collaboration throughout the process from beginning to end. Using this mechanism, government, business, and civil society would jointly define the issue needing attention; agree which party is best placed to do what; and move forward with defined responsibilities and agreed goals and targets.

'Such deals represent a fundamental shift in the model of government in the UK, from the current top-down, bureaucratic approach, to one that stresses collaboration and collective action', with capacity to stimulate 'business contributions to tackling obesity, problem drinking, climate change, and reducing and recycling waste', adds the CPWGRB.[121] In this way, responsibility deals also fit within wider governance and regulatory debates about the new regulatory state, new public management and democratic governance.

On a wider scale, these responsibility deals represent another 21st century development straddling the extremes of state-imposed mandatory regulation on matters of public concern, on one hand, and individual voluntary business self-regulation of business–society engagement for corporate advantage, on the other. At this level, they feed into broader ideas and practices associated with interests that governments, businesses and communities share in common. Like other forms of strictly non-enforceable agreements, such as social compacts and other cross-sectoral consensus-based frameworks, they provide a structure within which governmental, business and community actors can address shared and collective problems, with agreed rules of engagement and desired outcomes. As such, they extend beyond the minimalist forms of governmental and business engagement with other societal stakeholders that are conventionally associated with marginal community policy consultation and profit-driven stakeholder engagement.

The critical features of responsibility deals as outlined by the CPWGRB are as follows.[122] High-level government involvement is needed at ministerial level to identify suitable problems for responsibility deals, put relevant stakeholders together, and steer the process and its outcomes from the governmental side, including coordination with business and community leaders charged with heading each responsibility deal. Membership of responsibility deals could be expected to bring reputational, regulatory, influential and other attractions for members. Relevant representatives from government, business and the community would meet to establish a shared understanding of the designated problem and approach to addressing it. Respective expectations, responsibilities and outcomes would also need to be negotiated. Relevant performance indices might be used.

Meaningful dialogue and participation for members, leading to agreed outcomes deliverable by different parties, would enhance ownership of the process and its results by members of each responsibility deal. Independent expert auditing and public reporting of the outcomes of responsibility deals would increase their accountability, as well as feed into normal reporting by corporate participants on their corporate responsibility and sustainability. Any initial business reluctance to participate in responsibility deals would be mitigated by the importance of the problems addressed for business, investor and NGO pressures upon business participation, and governmental reinforcement through differential regulatory approaches towards well-performing business participants and an 'engage or explain' approach to non-participants. This would be modelled upon the principle-based 'comply or explain' approach to corporate governance regulation that now prevails in the UK, EU and elsewhere (e.g. Australia).

By providing a framework for collective action, responsibility deals minimize the risks and costs of responsible business behaviour for companies acting alone, while preserving space for companies to seek competitive advantage through such behaviour. The social, environmental and economic consequences of business can be addressed in a way that also serves the wider public policy interests of 'joined-up' government and participatory governance. Responsibility deals might also be a key vehicle for the meta-regulatory alignment of CSR public policy goals and corporate inculcation of CSR values and processes. Whatever becomes of this particular political proposal, the concept and elements of responsibility deals relate strongly to other features of the 21st century CSR landscape, including cross-sectoral CSR partnerships and multi-stakeholder initiatives of the kinds featured in Chapter 2.

Social Risk Assessment and Management as a Multi-dimensional Governance Challenge

The 21st century trend towards incorporation of both financial and non-financial factors in corporate risk management and reporting paves the way for a broader risk horizon for companies and other societal actors too. This development accommodates but also transcends strategic CSR.

At the levels of risk-awareness and risk-identification, the traditionally confined emphasis upon financial, legal and (more recently) environmental risks for companies is

Global companies face a new reality that has changed the nature of risk and risk management: networked operations and global value chains, empowered stakeholders, and the dynamic tension among sectors. The emergence of the new forms of social risk cannot be mitigated through traditional means. The new environment requires innovation by companies in both sensing and understanding these risks, and in adapting risk management systems to include new tools and network-based models of information sharing.

Risk management by global companies should be adapted to include corporate social responsibility programs. CSR provides the framework and principles for stakeholder engagement, supplies a wealth of intelligence on emerging and current social issues/groups to support the corporate risk agenda, and ultimately serves as a countermeasure for social risk.

– Booz Allen Hamilton consultant Beth Kytle and Harvard University's Professor John Ruggie[123]

giving way to an expanded set of potential risks that also includes social, governance and other risks. These additional avenues of business risk include regulatory risks (e.g. major changes to business regulation because of governmental responses to climate change or well-publicized corporate misbehaviour), and geopolitical security risks (e.g. disruption to global workforces, supply and distribution chains, and key markets through political unrest, civil disorder, terrorism and loss of governmental business support). They even embrace demographic risks (e.g. impact upon corporate operations of ageing populations, cultural employee diversity and offshore outsourcing)[124] and socio-ethical risks (e.g. reputational damage, unfavourable ratings agency and share analyst reports, increased NGO activism, loss of consumer loyalty and market share, reduced political and industry standing, and other consequences of bad corporate citizenship and other breaches of community trust). In terms of regulated corporate governance reporting, these risks are all characterizable as 'material business risks'.[125]

'Increasingly companies manage social issues in the same way as they manage any other strategic business issue and there are a growing array of tools available to assist and guide them', notes the World Business Council for Sustainable Development.[126] Booz Allen Hamilton consultant Beth Kytle and Harvard University's Professor John Ruggie (who is also the UNSRSG) view the network-focused and stakeholder-sensitive 21st century business environment for companies as one creating a series of social risks that cannot necessarily be handled in the ways in which companies conventionally approach legal, financial and other risks.[127] In terms of risk-canvassing with stakeholders, Kytle and Ruggie offer the practical suggestion that '(c)ompanies should begin the process by 1) identifying the empowered stakeholders and their key issues and 2) determining the highest level of engagement and information sharing necessary to address their concerns and reap the mutual benefits from improved accountability and better relations with stakeholders'.[128] In terms of risk-addressing, their suggested set of developmental steps includes: (a) informational requirements for early warning systems; (b) reporting protocols (e.g. reporting chain, frequency and templates); (c) risk-metrics (e.g. material risk assessment, measurement, prioritization and impact); (d) early warning protocols for action or reporting; (e) internal and external information sources on risks; and (f) reporting tools.[129]

However, the enterprise of recasting risk identification, assessment and management to include social and other risks beyond conventional financial risk analysis is not simply a company-specific activity. The need for cooperation and collective action by different organs of societal governance provides a good illustration of the alignment of company-specific and global risk concerns, as 'mitigating global risks often requires the cooperation of different groups [and] issues of how to manage collective action impact heavily on how individual and global risk mitigation priorities can be successfully aligned'.[130] This is another illustration of the meta-trend towards societal alliances and networks across the public, private and civic sectors tackling shared and collective problems of governance, regulation and responsibility.[131] Viewed through the prism of risk, human rights also fall into this category, as explored in the next chapter.

NOTES

1. Cadbury, 2003: 1.
2. *The Economist*, 2008: 13.
3. Donaldson, 2005: 2.
4. E.g. Porter and Kramer, 2006.
5. Bonini et al, 2006: 21.
6. *The Economist*, 2008: 21–22.
7. Parkinson, 1993: 395.
8. Donaldson, 2005: 3.
9. Scott, 2008: 182.
10. Villiers, 2008: 87; emphasis added.
11. BITF, 2000: 4.
12. *The Economist*, 2007: 67.
13. Frances, 2008: 6.
14. Porter and Kramer, 2006.
15. *The Economist*, 2007: 67–68.
16. Reich, 2007.
17. As cited in Canadian Democracy and Corporate Accountability Commission, 2002: 11.
18. Orlitzky et al, 2003, cited in Amnesty International Australia, 2005.
19. Chatterji and Listokin, 2007.
20. Allen, 2007: 63; and CCPA and BCA, 2007: viii.
21. This distillation of categories and examples draws mainly upon Anderson and Landau, 2006: 13; CPWGRB, 2007: 13–15; and CCPA and BCA, 2007: 38–60. For further discussion of CSR's various drivers, see: Kerr et al, 2009: Ch 2.
22. Bonini et al, 2008.
23. Kerr et al, 2009: 31; original emphasis.
24. CCPA and BCA, 2007: 46–47.
25. Sherry, 2008.
26. Quoted in Edwards, 2008: 34.
27. Davis, 2005.
28. COM(2006)136: 4.
29. E.g. Parker, 2007; and Scott, 2008.
30. Bruch and Walter, 2005.
31. Kitney and Buffini, 2006: 61.
32. Bonini et al, 2006: 21.
33. GRI, 2006: Reporting Indicator SO5.
34. Allen, 2007: 63.
35. Savitz and Weber, 2006: 243.

36. *The Economist*, 2008: 9.
37. CCPA and BCA, 2007: xi.
38. Chatterji and Listokin, 2007.
39. Ibid.
40. Ibid.
41. Ibid.
42. Feldman and Altschuller, 2007.
43. Ibid.
44. Ibid.
45. Parkinson, 1993: 267.
46. Ibid.
47. Ibid.
48. Ibid.
49. Wilson, 2005: 279.
50. Porter and Kramer, 2006: 80, 92.
51. Ibid.: 81.
52. Ibid.: 83.
53. Ibid.
54. Ibid.
55. Ibid.
56. Ibid.: 87.
57. Ibid.: 86.
58. Porter, 1990: 71–73, 127.
59. Porter and Kramer, 2006: 87.
60. Ibid.: 84; emphasis added.
61. Ibid.: 85.
62. Ibid.
63. Ibid.: 89.
64. Ibid.
65. Ibid.: 91.
66. Elhauge, 2005: 745; original emphasis.
67. Porter and Kramer, 2006: 84.
68. Ibid.
69. WBCSD, 2000: 5.
70. Grayson and Hodges, 2004: 8–9.
71. Ibid.: 11–12.
72. Ibid.: 17, 18, 54, 101, 140, 165, 205 and 244.
73. Savitz and Weber, 2006: 253–255.
74. Ibid.: 255–264.
75. AS 8003, 2003: 7–8.
76. Ibid.: 12.
77. Ibid.: 10–11.
78. Ibid.: 10.
79. BITF, 2000: 4–6.
80. Ibid.: 7.
81. Ibid.: 7, 9.
82. Ibid.: 9–11.
83. Ibid.: 10–11.
84. 'Implementing Corporate Social Responsibility', *CSR Tools*, Industry Canada Website (www.ic.gc.ca). For further discussion of this Canadian governmental CSR framework, see: Kerr et al, 2009: 15–17.
85. Strandberg, 2008: 26–27.
86. Ibid.
87. FORGE Group, 2002: 29–55.
88. The sub-steps here comprise the following: 'Define the scope of the policy' (e.g. Board-approval, stakeholder insights, and relevant organizational and sub-organizational commitments), 'Establish policy context' (e.g. integration of CSR policy with governance structures and arrangements, embedded within compliance, monitoring and review processes), 'Research the content of the CSR and/or specific CSR issue policies and objectives' (e.g. assess company CSR policies using financial and non-financial information and evidence of world-class practices, and evaluate connections with other relevant company policies and strategies), 'Draft policy content', 'Obtain Business Unit/function and Board commitment and policy sign-off', and 'Distribute the Group CSR policy and/or specific CSR issue policies'.

89.   Donaldson, 2005: 3.
90.   Villiers, 2008: 89.
91.   Susskind, 2008: 20.
92.   Allen Consulting Group, 2008: 3.
93.   Ward, 2008: 31.
94.   Ibid.: 31–33.
95.   Sachs, 2008: 321, 338.
96.   E.g. Business For Millennium Development.
97.   Branson, 2007: 128–129.
98.   Bonini et al, 2008.
99.   du Plessis et al, 2005: 360.
100. Ibid.: 360–361.
101. Ibid.
102. Wood, 2002.
103. Dunfee, 2006.
104. Ibid.: 186.
105. Ibid.
106. Ibid.: 187.
107. Ibid.: 197–198.
108. Campbell, 2006: 260.
109. On transparency see Ch 2.
110. Dunfee, 2006: 195.
111. E.g. COM(2006)136, 12 (supply chain issues as policy priorities for the European Alliance for CSR); and Companies Act 2006 (UK), s.417(5)(c) (reporting on supply chains under UK business reviews).
112. Dunfee, 2006.
113. Ibid.
114. Ibid.
115. For a similar proposal see ibid.
116. Some PJCCFS submissions call for positive assertions of CSR claims by companies to be justified, e.g. Griffith Submission to PJCCFS, 2006.
117. Some submissions to the parallel PJCCFS inquiry (e.g. Griffith Submission) make similar points about framing the positive aspects of this for business.
118. Parker, 2002: 219.
119. CPWGRB, 2008: 5.
120. Ibid.: 9.
121. Ibid.
122. On this summary of steps see ibid.: 9–11.
123. Kytle and Ruggie, 2005; 15.
124. Line, 2004.
125. E.g. ASX CGC, 2007.
126. WBCSD, 2000: 3.
127. Kytle and Ruggie, 2005; 1, 6 and 15.
128. Ibid.; 15.
129. Ibid.; 12.
130. WEF, 2007: 22.
131. For further discussion of cross-sectoral multi-stakeholder alliances see Ch 2.

9. Corporate social responsibility's emerging human rights challenges

A MULTI-DIMENSIONAL VIEW OF CORPORATIONS AND HUMAN RIGHTS

> (T)he corporation has become a global institutional form [and] the protection of human rights has become a global concern . . . (T)he relationship between corporations and human rights can be considered from four different but related perspectives – corporations as:
>
> - violators of human rights;
> - protectors or promoters of human rights;
> - beneficiaries of human rights protections; and
> - institutions in which members' rights are important.
>
> – Professor Stephen Bottomley, Director of the Centre for Commercial Law, Australian National University[1]

Corporate responsibility for human rights is one of the great CSR issues of the late 20th and early 21st centuries. The unfolding global CSR project covered throughout this book includes new developments in the relation between CSR and human rights that are broadly heading in the same rights-enhancing direction. These developments include the stimulus to debate generated by the promulgation of the draft UN Norms on the Responsibilities of Transnational Corporations and Other Business Enterprises with Regard to Human Rights (UN Norms), the subsequent search for new global frameworks for regulation and practice surrounding business and human rights, and the emerging intersections between human rights and various areas of national and international law. They also include the increasing sophistication of business tools for incorporating human rights issues in corporate operations and reporting, the incorporation of human rights elements in business supply and distribution chains, and the potential for multi-faceted corporate due diligence on human rights to mainstream human rights consideration in corporate decisions and actions.

Business is a key player in the integration of human rights and corporate concerns that forms a large part of this grand global CSR project. Strong connections exist between CSR, human rights and business ethics. These connections cover theory (e.g. theories about corporate models), education (e.g. the design and content of MBA and law courses) and regulatory practice (e.g. codes of conduct). For example, legal theorist and human rights scholar, Professor Tom Campbell, argues for meta-regulatory steering of

TNCs towards voluntary codes of conduct (VCCs) with strong human rights dimensions and deep integration in corporate structures and cultures, so that these rights-focused VCCs become 'totally binding within the organisation and used internally as the basis for the full range of management incentives and sanctions, including performance assessment, promotions, disciplinary procedures, training opportunities and dismissal'.[2]

The 21st century work of the UN Secretary-General's Special Representative on Business and Human Rights (UNSRSG), Harvard's Professor John Ruggie, sets a new platform and agenda for human rights policy, regulation and practice for government, business and civil society worldwide. The gradual emergence of a range of duty-bearers and rights-holders recognized by international law, together with the progressive unfolding of corporate rights and liabilities under some parts of international law, 'makes it more difficult to maintain that corporations should be entirely exempt from responsibility in other areas of international law', according to the UNSRSG.[3] The processes triggered by the work of the UNSRSG promise some improvements in addressing transnational governance weaknesses and gaps, especially as 'soft' law develops to incorporate what even leading international business associations recommend as a principle of equal corporate responsibility across strong and weak governance zones, in accordance with obligations under relevant international instruments, irrespective of governmental enshrinement or enforcement of such obligations under national law.[4]

At the heart of these developments, however, twin tensions remain between state and non-state responsibility for human rights, on one level, and the effective justification and operationalization of any business responsibility for human rights, on another. As the European Commission announced in its landmark 2001 Green Paper on a European framework for CSR:[5]

> Corporate social responsibility has a strong human rights dimension, particularly in relation to international operations and global supply chains . . . Companies face challenging questions, including how to identify where their areas of responsibility lie as distinct from those of governments, how to monitor whether their business partners are complying with their core values, and how to approach and operate in countries where human rights violations are widespread.

Although corporations are sometimes perceived simply as potential abusers of human rights, such a mono-dimensional view of corporations and human rights does not do justice to the multiple roles that corporations play in the global human rights arena.[6] Nor are those roles limited to the two polar extremes of corporations as destroyers or alternatively claimants of human rights. For example, Professor Bottomley describes a basic four-dimensional matrix of relations between corporations and human rights, which embraces corporations as violators of human rights, beneficiaries of human rights, venues for the ventilation of human rights issues (e.g. workplace non-discrimination) and supporters of human rights. So, corporations might become the subjects of human rights protection, as when corporations assert that they are the holders of particular human rights under national or international laws. Conversely, corporations might be the objects of a human rights regime, as when corporations use their power in rights-supporting ways or alternatively abuse their power in violating acknowledged human rights.[7]

More discrete relations might also be extrapolated from this matrix. Corporations act as multi-faceted regulators of human rights, as when they hold members of their business service chains to account for maintaining accepted human rights standards, and scrutinize potential business or multi-stakeholder partners on human rights grounds. The legitimization and modelling of good corporate performance concerning human rights is facilitated by corporate due diligence on human rights and inclusion of human rights performance in corporate disclosure and reporting. Holders of human rights also hold interests as corporate stakeholders, and any serious account of corporate responsibility must address the extent to which concern for human rights holders in either capacity is an in-built imperative of corporate responsibility and governance.

Finally, beyond the conventional legal sense in which a corporation might also be a forum in which important questions of human rights arise and sometimes become litigated, corporations are also important institutions of society, sites of human flourishing, members of multi-stakeholder networks, and corporate systems within wider systems of governance, regulation and responsibility – all of which have important links to human right concerns. One important question for the future concerns the extent to which international and national legal systems can develop suitable doctrines that mediate between public interests, business needs and human rights protection.

NORMATIVE AND CONCEPTUAL DIMENSIONS OF HUMAN RIGHTS

> The issue of whether companies (and, by extension, multinationals) can be subject to direct obligations under international law has generated a huge amount of literature of late. The general view is that such obligations not only are a theoretical possibility, but are justified by the enormous economic and political influence of multinationals, and their clear capacity to affect the enjoyment of human rights. For the time being, though, there is little in the way of jurisprudence on the *substance* of those rights, and a lack of proper enforcement mechanisms.
>
> – Dr Jennifer Zerk, *Multinationals and Corporate Social Responsibility*[8]

In terms of what 21st century society values, 'a human rights approach to CSR provides us with a rich discourse for the articulation of moral priorities in contemporary societal contexts that has clear relevance to emerging social expectations that corporations make a more proactive contribution to the solution of grave social problems', according to Professor Campbell.[9] Internationally, much ink has been spilt in extrapolating strands of business responsibility from the self-stated imposition by the Universal Declaration of Human Rights (UDHR) of responsibility for human rights awareness and advancement upon 'every organ of society', which arguably includes corporations implicitly in its reach. As Professor Louis Henkin from Columbia University famously remarked, this fundamental statement of responsibility for universal human rights 'excludes no one, no company, no market, no cyberspace [and] applies to them all'.[10] Similarly, the preamble to the UN Norms acknowledges the primacy of state responsibility for human rights, but adds that 'transnational corporations and other business enterprises, as organs of society, are also responsible for promoting and securing the human rights set forth in the Universal Declaration of Human Rights'. The UN Millennium Goals include explicit references to the role of 'the private sector' in some actions, for example, and implicitly contemplate corporate involvement in other actions toward these goals.

Although still in the embryonic stage, steps are being taken towards an emerging international law of corporate responsibility, together with the theory-building necessarily underlying and justifying the development of this body of law. Various theoretical tools are available for conceptually marrying and developing the necessary intersections between international law, corporate law and human rights law.[11] 'If states and international organizations can accept rights and duties of corporations in some areas, there is no theoretical bar to recognizing duties more broadly, including duties in the human rights area', argues University of Texas law professor, Steven Ratner, suggesting that 'even corporations themselves, while generally disdaining the idea of increased international regulation, have come to accept the idea of duties to protect human rights'.[12] The leading companies constituting the Business Leaders Initiative on Human Rights (BLIHR), for example, believe that 'the interests of both business and society would be best served by greater international clarity concerning the responsibilities of business for respecting, protecting, promoting and, in certain cases, fulfilling human rights'.[13]

Conceptually, as Professor Ratner argues, making corporate legal responsibilities in the area of human rights a function of corporate capacity to harm the core of human dignity upon which those rights are founded means, in operational terms, that 'corporate responsibility will depend upon the enterprise's proximity to the violation as determined by its relationship to the government, its nexus to the affected populations, the individual right at issue, and principles of attribution that connect those committing the violations to the company'.[14] Similarly, human rights lawyers David Kinley and Junko Tadaki suggest that a conceptual framework for human rights duties of corporations needs 'appropriate conceptual architecture' that meets international human rights law's central objective of protecting human rights by preventing human rights abuses, providing measures of human rights compliance, and promoting the awareness and application of human rights standards in a way that is responsive to a corporation's own conduct as a duty bearer as well as its influence or control over third parties with whom corporations have dealings that affect human rights.[15]

If the societal values and purposes underlying free enterprise and human rights share a common foundation or connection, their mutual recognition and support are an important part of the systemic and regulatory architecture of 21st century society. One strand of thinking points to the central value of individual liberty and autonomy underlying free enterprise and human rights alike.[16] Although the economic freedom and liberty essential for the system of private property ownership and freedom of contract underpinning the modern business corporation leads to arguments on one level that 'the ideas of free enterprise and human rights share a common ground', corporate practice demonstrates on other levels that 'uninhibited free enterprise often is at odds with respect for individual integrity, a central tenet of international human rights'.[17]

At the same time, the extension of corporate responsibility to morally forceful and legally relevant human rights obligations of corporations remains fraught with multiple objections and counter-responses.[18] For example, the fact that corporations make profits rather than act as charities, moral arbiters or substitute governments does not negate the fact that changes in the geopolitical landscape are causing a rethink of the place of TNCs in meeting public expectations, securing public goods and sharing systems of global governance and regulation. Similarly, whatever differences exist in the respective responsibilities of state and non-state actors for human rights, corporations have a demonstrated capability to affect a wide range of human rights for a vast number of people.

LOCATING CORPORATIONS AND HUMAN RIGHTS IN THE LANDSCAPE OF RIGHTS-PROTECTION MEASURES

The International Domain

> The most glaring illogicality of Westphalian international law is that it applies only to states and not to the transnational corporations whose global activities generate more product and greater influence than many UN member states will ever possess . . . Given their actual and potential complicity in human rights violations and their capacity – so much greater than individuals – for paying reparations, how long can multinationals keep their heads below the parapet of international law?
>
>   – Author and human rights lawyer, Geoffrey Robertson QC[19]

The specific ways in which corporations might engage with human rights within their orbit of operations form part of a larger canvas of rights-protection measures across public, private and community sectors, on one hand, and national, transnational and international boundaries, on the other. 'The international community is still in the early stages of adapting the international human rights regime to the challenges posed by globalization', according to Professor Ruggie.[20] Considered from the perspective of international law and policy, important rights-protection measures include: (i) international laws, principles and norms concerning human rights; (ii) promotion and advancement of universal human rights through infusion of human rights elements in national laws; (iii) incorporation of human rights measures in transnational and international trade, investment and other agreements; (iv) facilitation and support of multi-stakeholder CSR standard-setting initiatives and networks focused upon human rights issues; (v) development of international agreements, instruments and protocols devoted specifically to human rights issues (e.g. UDHR, the European Convention on Human Rights and the International Covenant on Civil and Political Rights); and (vi) development of supranational and international institutions with human rights fostering, monitoring and enforcement responsibilities.

Countries can become subject to obligations under international law to implement national measures for protecting and enforcing human rights. Consistently with the orthodox position of nation-states as the main holders of obligations under international law, national governments are therefore the primary points for implementing domestic legal, regulatory and policy arrangements to give effect to international obligations affecting corporations. Matters of particular relevance here for CSR and human rights include domestic implementation of international human rights instruments applicable to corporate and non-corporate actors alike, domestic facilitation of investigation and prosecution of any corporate involvement in international crimes, creation of civil causes of action domestically for extra-territorial corporate breaches of relevant international standards, and judicial incorporation of international norms in domestic legal suits against corporations.

International and Transnational Contractualization of Rights-affecting Mechanisms

International trade, investment and aid agreements can make trade relations contingent upon a country's adherence to internationally recognized human rights. Still, what might be described as 'a growing imbalance in global rule-making' has emerged in the last few decades, in favour of market globalization elements such as enhanced transnational legal protection for intellectual property rights (e.g. TRIPS) and trade dispute resolution (e.g. WTO), with the development of effective regimes lagging significantly behind for 'equally valid social objectives' in the labour, human rights and environmental domains.[21] Investment and funding in developing countries are increasingly based upon the recipients meeting accepted benchmarks for good governance and responsible business behaviour. The World Bank Group's International Finance Corporation (IFC), for example, specialises in providing financial assistance to the private sector in developing countries (often in conjunction with states) for poverty-alleviating investment, development and infrastructure, with IFC financing being contingent upon a business complying with good social and environmental practices, which embrace human rights amongst other concerns.

Agreements between governmental and business parties can generate questions at the intersection between international law, public law, contract law and human rights law. In particular, governmental and business entities might enter into investment and development agreements, the terms of which may advance or alternatively hinder the cause of human rights. Especially in developing countries, stabilization clauses in contracts between host governments and project investors can affect the operational consequences of laws in those jurisdictions designed to advance the cause of human rights. They can do so, for example, by limiting the applicability of those laws to particular projects, compensating business parties for their additional costs, inhibiting governments from changing project-affecting laws after a project's commencement, and providing other disincentives for host governments to enforce any supervening human rights or humanitarian obligations in ways that might interfere with project needs.[22]

Accordingly, in model recommendations on investment agreements, the United Nations Commission on International Trade Law (UNCITRAL) and the OECD both recommend limited rather than expanded use of stabilization clauses. Under such authoritative guidelines, blanket compensation rights and unspecified damages for supervening laws affecting investments are unacceptable, while the range of legal changes capable of triggering such remedies is confined to 'specific legislative changes that target the particular project, a class of similar projects or privately financed infrastructure projects in general', or changes in financial or economic conditions that are reasonably unforeseeable at the point of signing agreements.[23] 'All business organizations, in the private and public sectors alike, are subject to changes in law and generally have to deal with the consequences that such changes may have for business . . . as an ordinary business risk', notes UNCITRAL.[24] The human rights impact of stabilization clauses and other features of the interaction between foreign investment and human rights (e.g. human rights issues in resolving investor–state disputes) are an ongoing subject of major study in the field of corporations and human rights, including the post-UN Norms work agenda for the UNSRSG.[25]

Transnational Corporate Liability for Human Rights

It's only a matter of time before some company becomes the Enron of human rights abuse. If we're not careful, it could be ours. A growing wave of lawsuits in the United States allege that companies like ours contribute to human rights abuses through their global operations. Human rights cases before US courts have challenged corporate practices in supply chain management, lending, labor management, product testing, and marketing . . . We need to act now to assess our risks and implement programs to reduce them.

– Former Senior Vice President for Global Affairs at the Gap, Elliot Schrage, writing a hypothetical internal memo from the Corporate Counsel to the CEO of a typical multinational corporation[26]

The 'risk environment' for corporations in the international human rights arena is progressively expanding, despite the limited way in which international law presently regulates the civil and criminal liability of corporations.[27] In the absence of a comprehensive international framework and correlative enforcement mechanisms for corporate responsibility and liability, litigation against parent companies or group enterprises in North America, the UK and elsewhere seeks to hold them 'legally accountable in developed country courts for negative environmental, health and safety, labour or human rights impacts associated with the operations of members of their corporate family in developing countries . . . by testing the boundaries of existing legal principles, rather than by calling for new regulation'.[28]

Human rights litigation involving corporations is only part of 'the broad civil society agenda on globalization and corporate responsibility', in which 'foreign direct liability claims are one way of pursuing corporate responsibility among many, including social and environmental auditing, stock exchange listing and disclosure requirements, minority shareholder resolutions by concerned individuals or organizations, or pressure on investment funds to withdraw support for recalcitrant companies'.[29] In this way, transnational legal liability for corporate irresponsibility also joins the comparative body of CSR-related law and regulation highlighted in Chapter 5. Similarly, 'transnational litigation should be only one of a number of strategies aimed at lessening the instances of TNC human rights abuses, or promoting good TNC behaviour', as part of a wider menu of strategies including 'domestic litigation, NGO and consumer pressure, the promotion of socially responsible investment, and self-regulation'.[30] Considered from these perspectives, human rights litigation can form part of a multi-pronged strategy by transnational civil society groups in targeting particular TNCs. It also forms part of a wider system of state and non-state CSR regulation.

One chief avenue of foreign direct liability for companies looks at corporate liability under national law for breaches of international norms. This avenue's paradigm manifestation in the USA lies in the jurisdiction for courts to hear claims of corporate harm 'in violation of the law of nations or a treaty of the United States', under the Alien Tort Claims Act (ATCA). In its landmark exposition of the contemporary capacity of the ATCA to embrace private causes of action for breaches of international law, the US Supreme Court's decision in *Sosa v Alvarez-Machain*[31] contemplates that, in the absence of contravening legislation, the door is left open for courts to entertain a fairly narrow set of claims grounded in international norms of widespread international acceptance and sufficient specificity for judicial recognition.

International human rights advocate and lawyer, Geoffrey Robertson QC, argues that *Sosa*'s careful judicial line-drawing still permits 'claims against corporations which can plausibly be said to have aided and abetted genocide, breaches of the Geneva Conventions, widespread and systematic torture, [and] forced labour and war crimes', and hence leaves open the possibility of claims against business enterprises involved with governments whose state police, security or military forces commit human rights breaches that benefit their business operations.[32] Still, the narrow range of actions under international law to which ATCA attaches is therefore likely to cover only a small part of human rights abuses involving corporations. Of course, that might not be much comfort to TNCs involved in ATCA litigation, where a disparity remains between the relative lack of substantive success of unsettled human rights claims, on one hand, and the litigation, reputational, and other costs for corporations fighting these claims, on the other.

Another avenue of liability seeks to locate liability under the ordinary laws of their home jurisdiction for parent companies and others within multinational corporate group enterprises for the actions of subsidiary or group companies within host countries of business activity.[33] This kind of litigation raises a multitude of legal obstacles concerning control of companies, separate legal entities, limited liability for shareholders, corporate veil-piercing issues (e.g. enterprise liability), choice of forum and applicable law, corporate complicity in the actions of others, foreign sovereign immunity (where state actions are also involved), contractual indemnities and assignments of liability, individual and joint liability for negligence and other tortious wrongs, and a variety of other legal issues.[34] The state of the law in North American and Anglo-Commonwealth jurisdictions is neither uniform nor completely settled. 'The intersection between company law principles, which dictate corporate/shareholder separation even in the context of multinational groups, contract principles (regarding separation and allocation of responsibilities within multinational economic networks), and tort principles, which dictate that people should take reasonable care that others are not damaged by actions over which they have control, has yet to be clarified', concludes Dr Sarah Joseph from the Castan Centre for Human Rights Law.[35]

Human rights litigants seeking redress for corporate abuses of human rights undoubtedly face hurdles because of informational and resourcing disparities relative to companies, as well as from laws advantaging business in human rights litigation (e.g. laws favouring limited liability, preventing group enterprise liability and foreign direct liability, and regulating choice of forum and governing law).[36] At the same time, other human rights advocates are engaged in social coalitions and multi-stakeholder initiatives on human rights in partnerships with business. They face the real difficulties of working with companies to find common ground on guidelines for human rights matters. Together with business, they must confront the tensions inherent, for example, in pushing for more transparent disclosure and reporting of corporate information on human rights of the kind sought by advocates of CSR, given the wariness of business to make public anything that will encourage additional complaints or official investigations or even be used in litigation against them.[37] Conversely, business has to consider its willingness to trade off its general dislike of extra business regulation and its reluctance to see corporations directly accountable under international law against better guidance for business on human rights implementation and possibly improvements for business, not only in risk management of human rights compliance but also in the rules and procedures of human rights litigation worldwide.

What further possibilities lie ahead for human rights lawsuits against companies? 'Numerous other potential tactics have been described in academic journals but may be on their way to court registration offices' in claims filed by human rights victims, public advocacy groups, and plaintiff lawyers, according to Dr Joseph.[38] These innovative legal possibilities include claims of unjust enrichment of businesses at the expense of dispossessed indigenous groups and other communities, dissolution of companies that breach international human rights laws or otherwise breach the public trust in ways that justify revocation of their corporate charters, accommodation of human rights and environmental concerns in the fulfilment of directors' duties owed to a company, and claims of unfair competition by businesses that secure unconscientious advantage over competitors through breaches of human, consumer and other rights.[39]

Other possibilities include extending corporate fiduciary obligations to vulnerable groups affected by business operations, recasting other conventional legal duties and doctrines in rights-focused terms, expanding corporate sustainability obligations to embrace human rights dimensions of business chains and partnerships, directing standard business laws (such as competition and investment laws) towards testing human rights compliance claims and refashioning contract law doctrines to accommodate human rights and public interest concerns, such as doctrines surrounding public policy grounds for avoiding contractual liability or even terminating an agreement. For example, entry points for ventilating unjustified claims of human rights compliance, as well as ethical production and investment practices, arise under laws regulating non-constitutionally protected commercial speech in the USA, false representations about products under competition and investment laws in Australia, and possibly even European Union directives on the sale and marketing of goods.[40]

In the era of climate change, greenhouse gas reduction and emission trading regimes, tentative links are being made between the adverse effects of climate change and the resultant consequences from a human rights perspective for vulnerable communities, not least in terms of threats to life, health and property, if the worst scenarios of climate change are realized. Climate change litigation in the future is likely to touch not only liability under international environmental and human rights laws for corporate and state actions that exacerbate the damage of greenhouse gases and other climate change risks for mass populations,[41] but also domestic laws regulating climate change risk and liability for major product manufacturers, resource developers and energy users. In the context of review by courts of the lawfulness of decisions by public officials in granting licences and other approvals for business and development projects, ongoing litigation across a number of jurisdictions focuses upon the extent to which public officials need to take account of the potential impact of mining operations and other project activities upon greenhouse gas emissions.[42]

Other areas of potential legal liability for corporations at the intersections of climate change and human rights include general civil and criminal liability (e.g. under the law of public and private nuisances, product liability and tort), and liability for company directors and managers for breach of corporate duties. In addition, there is the prospect of corporate liability for flawed reporting of climate risk assessment and management in a variety of business and investment reporting contexts, regulatory investigation and prosecution for non-disclosure and non-compliance under relevant environmental protection laws, and shareholder-initiated corporate governance initiatives (e.g. shareholder proposals concerning climate change).[43] In short, innovative legal claims against business for human rights transgressions generally and climate change complications for human rights in particular are far from being fully tested or exhausted. They are a growth area of business litigation in the 21st century.

Sovereign States and Human Rights

Bills of rights and corporations
Contemporary models for bills of rights have a variety of direct and indirect implications for corporations, human rights and CSR in ways that also promote human rights due diligence by corporations – a matter that is of increasing importance in light of the emphasis placed upon business human rights due diligence by the UNSRSG. National and sub-national jurisdictions with legislative bills of rights can foster human rights protection in corporate contexts in a variety of ways. Bills of rights can engage political, business and community actors in legislative scrutiny, advocacy or reform at various levels of legal, moral and political debate that concern the regulation of business and its social responsibility.

Even in jurisdictions where companies are not completely precluded from claiming the protection of human rights, there are often limits on the nature and extent of rights that might be claimed by corporations.[44] If human rights are rights that belong to human beings because of intrinsic human dignity, autonomy, and freedom, their extension to artificial legal entities such as corporations is problematical, which is why some bills of rights allow only individuals to claim the benefit of human rights against the state. Moreover, any extension of human rights to corporations must overcome the hurdle of inconsistency with other aspects of corporate and commercial law.[45]

In both the UK and a couple of Australian jurisdictions with legislative bills of rights, corporations that undertake functions of a public kind, especially through public outsourcing and contracting arrangements for essential public services and venues, can find themselves subject to similar obligations as governmental entities in accommodating relevant human rights considerations.[46] Indeed, the gap in the scope of protection for human rights in outsourcing essential service delivery is a key area of controversy surrounding human rights implications at the point of intersection between the public and private sectors.[47] Other mechanisms for business engagement with human rights at the interface of the public and private sectors under bills of rights include opt-in mechanisms for non-state organizations to adopt human rights obligations.[48]

Where a bill of rights requires governmental officials and agencies in their exercise of public responsibilities to decide and act in ways that are rights-compliant, this can have a variety of flow-on effects for business. A business seeking a lease, licence or other formal approval from a governmental decision-maker might need to ensure that the subject matter of their proposal is also rights-compliant, particularly if the public official or agency is lawfully required to consider the impact of their decision upon human rights protected under a bill of rights. Here, for example, a human rights impact assessment (HRIA) might form part of preparatory due diligence for a business in securing the necessary governmental approval. In particular circumstances, governmental officials might even be required to take human rights consequences into account as relevant considerations in exercising statutory discretions and other forms of statutory decision-making authority. Indeed, a failure to take human rights considerations into account adequately or at all might generate other legal consequences and remedies for third parties seeking to overturn any governmental approval or otherwise obstruct a business project. For example, a public official's failure to take proper account of relevant human rights considerations might constitute grounds for judicial review or other claims of unlawfulness.[49]

In addition, a commercial entity the business of which relies upon governmental procurement and outsourcing might find that human rights compliance is explicitly or implicitly built into performance conditions for their contracts with government, given that the contracting public authority might be bound to honour human rights protected under a bill of rights. Indeed, where there are concerns within a legislating jurisdiction about any possible gaps in available protection for human rights in the context of governmental procurement, outsourcing and other contracting arrangements with the private sector, public policy reasons might justify reference to standard contractual provisions governing human rights in all such arrangements, with flow-on implications for human rights standards in the private and not-for-profit sectors.[50]

In particular, this introduces related issues of standard-selection, risk allocation and contractual performance requirements for businesses securing governmental work, in terms of ensuring that their supply and distribution chains also meet these human rights standards. Where these primary and secondary contractual provisions reflect requirements of national or sub-national bills of rights that themselves implement or otherwise draw upon a country's international human right obligations, they form part of a global system of rights-protection that transcends a country's politico-legal borders. In these ways and more, bills of rights that ostensibly belong to the realm of government, public law and even international law can also have CSR-related implications.[51]

In terms of policy and regulatory design, it is important to determine whether or not an applicable bill of rights applies to all levels of government and across the public, private, and not-for-profit sectors. The direct or indirect application of bills of rights to business also forms part of national responses to the mandate and reports of the UNSRSG. In 21st century Australian debate about a possible national charter of rights, for example, material produced for the National Human Rights Consultation Committee, suggests that the Terms of Reference for the National Human Rights Consultation permit new rights-protection options involving business that include both state measures (such as a national statutory human rights charter affecting business as well as government) and non-state measures (such as enhanced human rights education and training for professionals who advise or work in business). In particular, the National Human Rights Consultation Background Paper outlines existing and new mechanisms that potentially open up enhanced business engagement in rights-protection on multiple levels:[52]

(1)   business interaction with 'a strong human rights non-government organisation sector';
(2)   business participation in 'bilateral human rights dialogue' on the world stage;
(3)   business engagement in lobbying and influencing rights-based parliamentary scrutiny of laws;
(4)   business consequences of enhanced rights-based incorporation in decisions by governmental departments and agencies on matters affecting business;
(5)   direct application of a charter to business;
(6)   business involvement in a new National Human Rights Action Plan;
(7)   business adoption, use, and advocacy of a non-binding 'community charter of people's rights and responsibilities';
(8)   business consequences and uses of 'greater community participation in policy and legislative development'; and
(9)   'human rights training and education [in] specific professions'.

If CSR means anything at all, it points to at least a socio-ethical responsibility (and sometimes even a responsibility that is regulated in more direct ways) to advance the cause of human rights in business organizations. Bills of rights can be expected to foster a national human rights culture of which that forms part, regardless of the formal reach of any bill of rights across sectoral boundaries. As argued in public submissions to the National Human Rights Consultation Committee, a holistic cost-benefit analysis of the 'compliance costs' measured against business benefits suggests that business can gain overall advantages through enhanced governmental rights-protection, as follows:[53]

(1)   offering business and market advantages of 'minimising human rights breaches and maximising economic participation';
(2)   'improving the overall regulatory framework', especially in advance scrutiny of proposed laws for human rights implications, with a view to reducing the need for subsequent changes in the laws affecting business;
(3)   giving businesses the opportunity 'to show their corporate social responsibility credentials', with flow-on multiple benefits for business, in generating goodwill and credibility with governments in contributing to their social, economic, and environmental justice agendas, as well as in achieving competitive advantages and market differentiation;
(4)   optimizing the financial performance of business, given the link between sustainable business profitability and human rights as an aspect of corporate social responsibility; and
(5)   enhancing the capacity of business to address human rights risks within an integrated approach to financial and legal risk management.

Other legislative mechanisms

In addition to an overarching bill of rights, a legislating jurisdiction might also introduce rights-specific laws (e.g. anti-discrimination laws), which become part of standard legal compliance for corporations. Specific rights-based components of general laws at national and sub-national levels might oblige corporations and other actors to respect designated categories of human rights (e.g. employment rights, privacy rights and environmental rights), whether or not those rights are otherwise formally recognized under international law or applicable bills of rights.

Embedding human rights within ordinary corporate governance, decision-making and reporting activities is an important part of mainstreaming human rights within corporate responsibility and governance. In terms of directors' duties under UK law, for example, human rights concerns are most relevant to 'the interests of the company's employees' and 'the impact of the company's operations on the community and the environment', as well as 'the desirability of the company maintaining a reputation for high standards of business conduct', which are all mandatory considerations for directors in meeting their duty to promote the company's success for the benefit of its members.[54] Human rights information is also relevant to designated categories of information for inclusion in the UK business review, including matters relating to 'the impact of the company's business on the environment', 'the company's employees' and 'social and community issues', at least 'to the extent necessary for an understanding of the development, performance or position of the company's business'.[55]

Legislative rules and other requirements for pre-enactment scrutiny of legislation by legislatures can also incorporate reference to the impact of proposed laws upon human rights, both generally and in contexts that concern corporations in particular. Where proposed laws and amendments must also be rights-compliant, the human rights dimensions must be factored into law reform advocacy by companies seeking to influence the direction of governmental policy-making and lawmaking, as well as other submissions and commentary surrounding exposure drafts of legislation for public comment.

Executive and judicial branches of government

More broadly, as the democratic state acts through executive decision-making and judicial adjudication as well as through legislative action, obligations upon the state to take adequate account of human rights considerations potentially affects all arms of government, in ways that impact upon how the state addresses human rights concerns that arise in matters concerning the legal rights and obligations of others, including business. Considered from the perspective of the executive arm of democratic government, a range of institutions, bodies and public officials might have human rights responsibilities conferred upon them. Governments can establish rights-protection agencies (e.g. anti-discrimination bodies), rights-orientated public roles (e.g. human rights ombuds- and spokespersons), rights-focused departmental units (e.g. UK Human Rights Unit), rights-focused legislative committees (e.g. legislative scrutiny committees), rights-based protocols for policy-making, and rights-focused administrative review mechanisms. Governments that adopt CSR as a policy priority invariably include human rights as a basic prong of a whole-of-government approach to CSR policy and regulatory reform.

In terms of the judicial arm of democratic government, judges are engaged in questions of developing laws (in the case of judge-made law) as well as interpreting and applying laws (in the case of constitutions and legislation) that might directly or indirectly concern human rights, including contexts in which human rights matter for business under the law. Where courts have an obligation under a bill of rights to interpret legislation in a way that is consistent with human rights, laws that might be of general application to business and others must be interpreted and applied in ways that are sensitive to this human rights dimension. Human rights litigation can affect companies directly (as when companies are legally held to account directly for breaches of human rights laws) as well as indirectly (as when conventional legal causes of action are conditioned or even recast in rights-based terms, such as reconceptualizing 'duty of care' issues in human rights terms, to address corporate failures to provide harassment-free and non-discriminatory workplaces). In short, intersections between human rights and business arise in many different ways in the work of constitutional interpretation, legislative law-making, executive government and judicial adjudication.

Organizational Dimensions of Human Rights

> Existing corporate social responsibility initiatives, many of which have emerged in response to specific controversies, typically cover only a limited set of rights and apply selectively to individual companies or particular country contexts, such as conflict areas. There are no widely agreed overarching standards for all businesses, but instead many different standards that address select human rights, select companies or industries, or select countries or situations. The result is a messy and inconsistent patchwork of voluntary pledges that have limited application, generally do not fully align with international human rights norms, and in any case are frequently disregarded in practice.
>
> – Human Rights Watch, *On the Margins of Profit: Rights at Risk in the Global Economy*[56]

Considered from an organizational perspective, human rights and business concerns may be integrated within organizational strategizing, decision-making and reporting systems. Corporate boards might adopt an organizational CSR policy that includes business-related human rights concerns, allocate particular rights-related responsibilities to designated directors and other corporate actors, and develop human rights management plans along with other standard corporate plans. Here, NGOs and companies might work together in developing and implementing CSR and human rights management plans (as in Amnesty International Australia's *Just Business: a Human Rights Framework for Australian Companies*).

As part of a whole-of-organization CSR approach, a corporation might do a number of things. It might include reference to human rights standards in contractual arrangements for the company's supply and distribution chain. It might also include human rights reporting within standard internal and external reporting practices. It might even initiate HRIAs along with socio-economic impact studies and environmental impact assessments (EISs) for all major new business projects and developments, and commit publicly to a range of rights-related and CSR-orientated standards (e.g. the UN Global Compact and the GRI).

Beyond organizational CSR policies, the human rights of corporate stakeholders harmed by corporate abuses of power might be the subject of corporate and directors' obligations, as when corporate boards can or must consider the impact of their decisions upon various corporate stakeholders. Where corporate governance regulatory requirements embrace notions of accountability to stakeholders, human rights issues might factor into corporate governance arrangements. Corporate risk assessment and management requirements might require corporations and their boards to account to investors and other reporting audiences for material business risks, which might include human rights risks and ways of addressing them, including HRIAs and other aspects of corporate human rights due diligence explored later in this chapter. To the extent that institutional investors and other bodies investing in corporations have a legal responsibility to consider and disclose how their investment decision-making is informed by socioethical, environmental, labour, and human rights considerations, a company's external business environment exerts pressure upon corporate activity in ways that are responsive to human rights concerns.

Voluntary industry and corporate codes of conduct sometimes avoid incorporating organizational sensitivity to internationally accepted human rights standards that are not already enshrined in law, under the mistaken belief that this automatically increases potential litigation risk or actual organizational liability, or is properly left aside as a governmental responsibility beyond business compliance with applicable human right laws.[57] However, as Professor Campbell shows, this misses the opportunity of perceiving human rights elements of codes of conduct through 'a discourse in which legal voluntariness is not to be equated with moral optionality so that self-regulation (when involving human rights) need not be weak regulation', allowing businesses and industries with rights-sensitive codes of conduct 'to develop rule-based concretisations of human rights that have direct relevance to the operations of MNCs . . . and are primarily directed at voluntary rather than coercive implementation'.[58]

The future of human rights policy and practice as applied to corporate codes of conduct, at least in the European Union, is articulated in the European Commission's 2001 Green Paper on a European framework for CSR in these terms:[59]

> With respect to human rights, there is a need for ongoing verification where the implementation and compliance with codes is concerned. The verification should be developed and performed following carefully defined standards and rules that should apply to organizations and individuals undertaking the so-called 'social auditing'. Monitoring, which should involve stakeholders such as public authorities, trade unions and NGOs, is important to secure the credibility of codes of conduct. A balance between internal and external verification schemes could improve their cost-effectiveness, in particular for SMEs. As a result, there is a need to ensure greater transparency and improved reporting mechanisms in codes of conduct.

Codes of conduct concerning human rights also serve to illustrate the variety and levels of regulation that characterize the 21st century global business environment. Commentators highlight the many norm-shaping and other regulatory interactions now in play for business and human rights, under a meta-regulatory system in which state regulation is a necessary but not sufficient baseline of CSR and human rights regulation:[60]

(T)he articulation of norms about CSR or human rights by disparate participants in the transnational public sphere . . . can also be understood as a type of quasi-regulation that can foster future changes in companies' social behavior, particularly if consumers, investors, or NGOs incorporate the norm as their expectation of responsible behavior, thereby punishing companies that fail to meet the norm-based expectation, just as they punish companies that fail to meet the expectations created by law.

Similarly, for meta-regulatory theorists, this expansive view of regulation 'involves a shift of emphasis from internal to external forces and processes by looking to the contribution of civil society, through public opinion, NGO activity, consumer response and shareholder input' as a vital form of 'external accountability to civil society', with an equally important 'back-up framework of legal support to enable these bodies to fulfill their monitoring and critical functions effectively'.[61] In other words, business organizations are subject to a series of interactive 'hard' and 'soft' regulatory norms, each of which has different but nevertheless real force from an organizational standpoint.

THE DRAFT UN NORMS ON HUMAN RIGHTS RESPONSIBILITIES OF COMPANIES

The Structure and Elements of the UN Norms

The UN Norms represent a ground-breaking attempt by the UN Sub-Commission on the Promotion and Protection of Human Rights to promulgate a comprehensive statement of international human rights obligations for TNCs. They originated through a special working group of the UN Sub-Commission on the Protection and Promotion of Human Rights that straddled the late 20th and early 21st centuries. Notwithstanding their lack of official legal status under international law, the controversy surrounding them and their fate in the processes and reports associated with the UNSRSG, nevertheless the UN Norms are likely to remain important markers for academic, regulatory and business debate about the international human rights responsibilities of TNCs for some time to come.

The UN Norms emphasize the 'primary responsibility' of nation-states in 'ensuring that transnational corporations and other business enterprises respect human rights'.[62] Drawing upon the UN Global Compact's idea of a corporation's responsibility within its 'sphere of influence', the UN Norms directly (and controversially) impose upon transnational corporations and businesses 'the obligation to promote, secure the fulfillment of, respect, ensure respect of and protect human rights recognized in international as well as national law', and to do so '(w)ithin their respective spheres of activity and influence'.[63] The provisions of the UN Norms fall into five main categories:[64]

(1)   conventional civil and political rights (e.g. rights of equal treatment, non-discrimination, and personal liberty and security);
(2)   traditional economic, social and cultural rights (e.g. rights to safe and healthy workplaces, and adequate wages and living standards);
(3)   'third generation' group and collective rights (e.g. rights relating to indigenous communities, vulnerable social groups and environmentally sustainable development);

(4)   realization and infringement of rights in corporate operations (e.g. corporate secu-
      rity arrangements and corporate engagement with state military and law enforce-
      ment authorities); and
(5)   extension of human rights machinery to broader CSR concerns (e.g. corporate fair
      trading and consumer concerns).

The UN Norms also contemplate a number of steps for transnational corporations
and businesses in implementing their human rights obligations. The first step requires
them to 'adopt, disseminate and implement internal rules of operation in compliance
with the Norms'.[65] Secondly, they must take other measures to implement the UN Norms
and report this implementation periodically.[66] Thirdly, the Norms are to be applied and
incorporated in contractual and non-contractual interactions with others in a company's
supply and distribution chain. Fourthly, beyond what transnational corporations and
businesses might do in their own right in implementing and periodically evaluating
their compliance with the UN Norms, conventional UN monitoring and other governmental mechanisms would apply to corporate treatment of the UN Norms, including
input from NGOs and other stakeholders about their implementation and violation.[67]
Fifthly, nation-states are to provide 'the necessary legal and administrative framework'
for ensuring implementation of the UN Norms by transnational corporations and businesses.[68] Finally, these transnational organizations are made liable for compensation
and other remedies for non-compliance with the UN Norms, through legal mechanisms
under national and international law.[69] None of this is intended to limit the obligations
of nation-states for human rights under domestic and international law, or to limit the
obligations and responsibilities of transnational corporations and businesses beyond the
field of human rights.[70]

In some ways, the UN Norms were ahead of their time, not least in their positioning
at the intersection of continuing controversies about international law, corporate responsibility and human rights. They reflect underlying notions about corporate responsibility under international law that arguably are further advanced than the present state of
international law on corporate responsibility. They use key notions of corporate 'spheres
of influence' and 'complicity' that need more clarification and development in legal definition, regulatory guidance and business practice. As others argue, they highlight what
a common framework of accepted categories of human rights and minimum universal
human rights standards for business might look like, without conclusively settling debate
about the need for such a framework generally, and one of that kind in particular. Their
design, structure and content do not lend themselves to easy or complete implementation, even by businesses favourably disposed towards them.[71] They provoke hostile reactions from influential states, business lobby groups and others, fuelled by concerns about
a 'top down' imposition of corporate responsibility for human rights directly under
international law, in advance of the development of a 'bottom up' consensus from governments, businesses and NGOs about this outcome.

Criticisms of the UN Norms

Collected together in the first major international document to bring together comprehensively the concerns of CSR, human rights and international law, the UN Norms were

> In our view, any further push to have the Norms adopted in their current form is a lost cause – whatever the merits of such an argument. That said, . . . it is hard to see past the existing core substantive provisions of the Norms. If one was indeed to start all over again, then the list of rights relevant to corporate enterprise one would almost certainly draw up, the emphasis on the direct but not exclusive legal responsibility being borne by states, and the attendant directions given to states as to how and what policies and procedures they should implement domestically to enforce those standards, would look not unlike what the Norms provide today . . . (F)ar from being a failure, the Norms have been a beneficial and fruitful initiative, reinvigorating debate on the issue of business and human rights, raising new and important concepts regarding regulation of [transnational corporations] and enforcement of human rights obligations, and articulating a core set of standards for going forward.
>
> – Human rights lawyers David Kinley, Justine Nolan, and Natalie Zerial[72]

always bound to be contentious. As experienced human rights scholars note, such controversy is an occupational hazard for any initiative that transforms 'soft' law into 'hard' law, imposes obligations directly upon corporations and otherwise moves beyond solely state-based responsibility for human rights.[73] Criticisms of the UN Norms for including a catalogue of rights beyond a strict conception of human rights, and for going beyond the accepted position on corporate responsibility under international law, must be viewed in that light. This is especially the case given that 'the Norms were an attempt to remedy this piecemeal approach to CSR by uniting these obligations in one document . . . to conjoin the national and international levels of CSR', by articulating and locating universal standards of corporate responsibility for human rights within an effective international legal framework for CSR, 'amalgamating states' responsibilities with direct regulation of corporate action'.[74]

The UN Norms have also been criticized for failing to distinguish properly between the variety of international legal norms and their different consequences, especially in terms of the different consequences of customary international legal obligations, 'soft law' and 'hard law' standards, treaty-based regimes and the multiple enforcement mechanisms applicable under different international laws and other instruments.[75] Undoubtedly, imposing any responsibility directly upon corporations for human rights under international law, in parallel with the conventional responsibility of states in this area under international law, but with unclear demarcation between respective state and corporate responsibilities, moves the international agenda on business and human rights beyond the largely voluntary and self-regulating initiatives of 'soft' international law norms. Perhaps understandably, the result is characterized by leading commentators in terms of 'unorthodox' and even 'polarizing' effects of the UN Norms, dooming them in their original form as 'a lost cause'.[76]

The controversy surrounding the UN Norms resulted in the parent UN Commission on Human Rights pointing to their unofficial standing and referring them for further consideration, within a wider brief on human rights and business, leading to the 2005 appointment of Professor Ruggie as the UNSRSG, with a mandate to undertake the following tasks:

(a)   To identify and clarify standards of corporate responsibility and accountability for transnational corporations and other business enterprises with regard to human rights;

(b)   To elaborate on the role of States in effectively regulating and adjudicating the role of transnational corporations and other business enterprises with regard to human rights, including through international cooperation;

(c)   To research and clarify the implications for transnational corporations and other business enterprises of concepts such as 'complicity' and 'sphere of influence';

(d)   To develop materials and methodologies for undertaking human rights impact assessments of the activities of transnational corporations and other business enterprises;

(e)   To compile a compendium of best practices of states and transnational corporations and other business enterprises. [77]

Given the UNSRSG's admission that Ruggie's appointment stemmed, in part, from the need for a circuit-breaker in the stalemate between extensive business opposition to the UN Norms and widespread support for them amongst human rights NGOs,[78] in retrospect it would have been surprising if his reports had simply continued the previous trajectory of the UN Norms. The UNSRSG accepted the usefulness of the UN Norms in cataloguing human rights affected by business, collating important source documents for international human rights standards, and identifying pertinent voluntary initiatives in rights-protection.[79] Nevertheless, despite their acknowledged benefit as a human rights inventory, he heavily criticized the development of the UN Norms as an exercise which 'became engulfed by its own doctrinal excesses', made 'exaggerated legal claims', contained 'conceptual ambiguities' and 'highly contentious' proposals, and created considerable 'confusion and doubt' amongst multiple human rights audiences.[80]

In the end, two insurmountable obstacles in the UNSRSG's eyes stood in the way of accepting the UN Norms in their original form.[81] The applicability of the UN Norms directly to corporations and other business enterprises as a complete and binding code lacked an authoritative basis in 'hard' as well as 'soft' international law. Their over-inclusiveness of rights yet to be accepted as corporate responsibilities under international law could not be remedied by limiting their coverage of rights to those generating a threshold consensus, without diluting the universality of human rights.[82]

In addition, the UN Norms imprecisely allocated human rights responsibilities amongst nation-states and corporations without evidence of a coherent underlying principle for assigning responsibilities according to the respective societal roles of states and corporations. The identified weakness lies in asking concepts like corporate 'spheres of influence', for example, to do more work than they can reasonably bear conceptually, legally and operationally, at least at this stage of their development. According to the UNSRSG, 'attributing the same range of duties to corporations that currently apply to states, differentiated only in degree within undefined corporate "spheres of influence", would generate endless strategic gaming and legal wrangling on the part of governments and companies alike'.[83]

The UNSRSG's position therefore soundly rejects the purported use of the 'sphere of influence' formula under the UN Norms and looks instead to an alternative basis – one grounded heavily in business human rights due diligence as the principal means of satisfying 'the corporate responsibility to respect human rights':[84]

The concept of a corporate 'sphere of influence' is widely used in corporate social responsibility discourse. In response to his mandate requirement to research and clarify the concept, . . . he reached the conclusion that [the] sphere of influence concept combines too many different dimensions to serve as the basis for defining the scope of due diligence, and that influence by itself is an inappropriate basis for assigning corporate responsibility.

On these bases, the UNSRSG concluded not only that 'the flaws of the Norms make that effort a distraction from rather than a basis for moving the Special Representative's mandate forward', but also that 'the divisive debate over the Norms obscures rather than illuminates promising areas of consensus and cooperation among business, civil society, governments and international institutions with respect to human rights'.[85] All of this points to the need for further legal, policy and regulatory development, directed towards delineating any residual use for notions of corporate 'spheres of influence', articulating differences in the conditions under which enforceable human rights obligations can attach to nation-states and corporations, harmonizing the application of international corporate obligations in different countries, and complementing enhancement of corporate responsibility for human rights under international law with other forms of human rights regulation for business too.[86]

In light of reactions to the UN Norms by the UNSRSG and others, the position concerning the UN Norms is not so much one of going back to the drawing board afresh, but rather one of restarting dialogue about corporate responsibility for human rights from a standpoint in which the UN Norms can no longer operate as a fully agreed and developed roadmap for corporate and regulatory action. Still, they remain an important ongoing reference point, because of the undoubted contributions that the UN Norms make to an understanding of the kinds of human rights implicated in corporate activity, the interactive role of national and international legal regimes in regulating both state and corporate responsibility for human rights, and the kinds of governmental and non-governmental mechanisms that might be contemplated in implementing human rights within business contexts.[87]

So, although in hindsight the UN Norms set a common framework for corporate responsibility for human rights that arguably was premature in terms of garnering consensus about enforceable corporate obligations under international law, that framework still has other roles to play in ongoing dialogue about corporations and human rights.[88] In addition, prominent businesses are already on record in using the UN Norms in practice, whatever future directions that application might take.[89] Decades from now, the present state of official disfavour for the UN Norms may yet prove to be a case of losing one battle on the way to winning the war on achieving a universal framework for corporate human rights responsibility under international and domestic law.

Beyond the UN Norms

Multi-stakeholder initiatives on business and human rights
The future global agenda on business and human rights occupies a spectrum between enhancing nation-state and intergovernmental responsibility for holding business accountable on human rights grounds, on one hand, and improving business self-regulation and cooperative initiatives on human rights and business, on the other.[90] Between those points on the spectrum lies a series of international standards and practices covering business

and human rights according to the UNSRSG, including the obligations of countries to prevent and punish corporate human rights abuses, corporate liability and accountability for involvement in international crimes, other forms of corporate responsibility for human rights under international law, and corporate leadership and participation in multi-stakeholder human rights standard-setting initiatives.[91]

In light of failed attempts at this stage to transform the UN Norms into 'hard' law, achieving a premium balance between 'hard' and 'soft' law initiatives in the international human rights arena remains the key strategy, especially given the success of alliances on various levels between governmental, business and community organizations 'to establish voluntary regulatory systems in specific operational contexts', as well as innovative 'self-regulation by business through company codes and collective initiatives, often undertaken in collaboration with civil society'.[92] Reflecting on the available menu of options for enhancing human rights, and the success that is only now achievable through interaction between politico-regulatory, market and social mechanisms, the UNSRSG signals what is needed in the near future in the international human rights arena, but in words that have wider resonance for other areas of CSR too:[93]

> All of these approaches show some potential, despite obvious weaknesses. The biggest challenge is bringing such efforts to a scale where they become truly systemic interventions. For that to occur, States need to more proactively structure business incentives and disincentives, while accountability practices must be more deeply embedded within market mechanisms themselves . . . (N)o single bullet can resolve the business and human rights challenge. A broad array of measures is required, by all relevant actors.

As the influential Business Leaders Initiative on Human Rights (BLIHR) notes in its groundbreaking 'road test' of the UN Norms, societal expectations of business worldwide are heading more in the direction of some business responsibility for human rights than in the opposite direction, some of business' most effective contributions to human rights do not come through official regulation, and some competitive advantage flows to businesses that go beyond the legal minimum on human rights.[94] The overwhelming consensus of the leading businesses in the BLIHR is 'a shared view that businesses, particularly those operating in multiple countries around the world, would benefit from the development of a common framework made up of principles and standards that would clearly articulate the nature and extent of business responsibilities concerning human rights', according to the BLIHR's honorary chair, Mary Robinson.[95]

Indeed, all stakeholders from government, business and civil society worldwide potentially benefit from an overarching common framework for business and human rights from a range of policy, regulatory and practical perspectives. Responsible businesses have multiple interests that a common framework might address, such as: (i) standardized reporting requirements on business-related human rights matters; (ii) business support for human rights and accountability for serial corporate human rights abusers; (iii) business guidance in implementing and reporting human rights practices; (iv) business involvement in multi-stakeholder human rights initiatives and standard-setting; (v) business benefits from improvements in the certainty and consistency of laws and litigation procedures governing corporate liability for human rights breaches across different countries of operation for TNCs; (vi) guidelines for risk management and assessment in the insurance and investment communities; and (vii) bolstered governmental infrastructure support for business and human rights.[96]

The emerging needs of global and national systems of trans-modal governance, multi-order regulation and inter-related responsibility provide new impetus for shared responsibility on human rights between governmental, business and community organizations. International 'soft' law developments promoting greater corporate responsibility for human rights are evident in standard-setting by supra-national bodies (e.g. ILO), accountability mechanisms for intergovernmental initiatives (e.g. International Finance Corporation (IFC) performance standards and OECD National Contact Points (NCPs)), and multi-stakeholder regulation-setting to enhance human rights protection (e.g. Voluntary Principles on Security and Rights for the extractive sector).[97] In the eyes of the UNSRSG, these 'soft' law developments reflect 'increased State and corporate acknowledgement of evolving social expectations and recognition of the need to exercise shared responsibility' for human rights.[98]

Towards new frameworks for business and human rights

The need for 'a common conceptual and policy framework' as a new platform for global discussion and action on business and human rights is recognized on all sides of the CSR and human rights debates.[99] 'Every stakeholder group, despite their other differences, has expressed the urgent need for a common framework of understanding, a foundation on which thinking and action can build in a cumulative fashion', according to the UNSRSG.[100] In his 2008 report for the UN Human Rights Council, the UNSRSG suggests a three-pronged framework based upon the organizing principles of 'protect, respect and remedy', again reinforcing and illustrating the importance of principle-based frameworks in the CSR domain:[101]

> The framework rests on differentiated but complementary responsibilities. It comprises three core principles: the State duty to protect against human rights abuses by third parties, including business; the corporate responsibility to respect human rights; and the need for more effective access to remedies. Each principle is an essential component of the framework: the State duty to protect because it lies at the very core of the international human rights regime; the corporate responsibility to respect because it is the basic expectation society has of business; and access to remedy, because even the most concerted efforts cannot prevent all abuse, while access to judicial redress is often problematic, and non-judicial means are limited in number, scope and effectiveness. The three principles form a complementary whole in that each supports the others in achieving sustainable progress.

Immediate signs of the willingness of the international business community to work within this framework appeared in the joint endorsement of the UNSRSG's proposed framework by the International Organisation of Employers (IOE), the International Chamber of Commerce (ICC) and the Business and Advisory Committee to the OECD (BIAC):[102]

> The IOE, ICC and BIAC believe that the proposed framework – the state responsibility to protect human rights, the corporate responsibility to respect human rights and access to remedies – is an appropriate and focused way of summarising the current state of business and human rights discussions. It will also provide an effective way to further the debate surrounding these issues.

> In particular, the proposed framework recognises four key elements that have been missing or under-emphasised in the past. Firstly, the root causes of most human rights abuses are based

in governance gaps, specifically the failure or inability of governments to protect human rights within their own jurisdictions. Secondly, most human rights abuses occur in countries with weak governance, limited political or civil freedoms, high levels of corruption or in actual conflict; any serious effort to address human rights abuses must address these dynamics. Thirdly, governments and businesses have distinct and very different responsibilities in relation to human rights, and confusing these responsibilities would not serve to protect human rights. And lastly, these issues apply to all companies, including state-owned and private, small and medium-sized, national and multinational companies.

The key strength of such a framework is five-fold. It potentially unblocks the gridlock of polarized debate surrounding the UN Norms. It provides a coherent, overarching and 'multi-tiered' platform for approaching the work of human rights and business that might yet become a 'functional authoritative focal point' for all CSR actors.[103] It represents a baseline of concerns about human rights and business with which many people in government, business and civil society can agree, whatever disagreement exists between them about the elements and priorities of a global human rights platform. It therefore offers a consensus starting point for working through, at more detailed levels, how the respective interests and responsibilities of governments, business and civil society fit together in advancing human rights worldwide, at the same time as it directs attention towards three distinct avenues of that implementation. More broadly, it offers lessons for handling other transnational governance challenges, and reinforces the new realities of shared global governance and regulation between state and non-state institutions.[104]

Conversely, the UNSRSG's framework also has its limitations. It is light on what many NGOs would regard as the minimum legal infrastructure needed to hold corporations accountable worldwide for corporate irresponsibility. Structurally, the three-pronged framework differentiates functional responsibilities to protect and respect human rights for state and non-state actors respectively, in ways that do more to reinforce rather than revisit conventional distinctions between mandatory and voluntary obligations, on one level, and between governmental and non-governmental responsibilities, on another level, despite the complex regulatory interactions and normative justifications in play.

In defining the critical element of corporate responsibility to respect human rights as a responsibility that exists separately from state responsibilities for human rights, for example, the UNSRSG frames it as a basic socio-ethical obligation. Some of its features are normatively controversial in corporate theory (e.g. a business 'licence to operate' from society), lie beyond the current state of international human rights law and national corporate laws, and derive their force from a richer notion of regulation than the orthodox mandatory–voluntary dichotomy can offer:[105]

> (T)he baseline responsibility of companies is to respect human rights. Failure to meet this responsibility can subject companies to the courts of public opinion – comprising employees, communities, consumers, civil society, as well as investors – and occasionally to charges in actual courts. Whereas governments define the scope of legal compliance, the broader scope of the responsibility to respect is defined by social expectations – as part of what is sometimes called a company's social licence to operate.

The key challenge of such a framework lies in creating universal consensus for its core focus, especially in the face of NGO pressure to 'complement' the framework by targeting corporate human rights abuses more fully.[106] Rejecting the call by NGOs for the UN

Human Rights Council 'to broaden the focus beyond the elaboration of the "protect, respect and remedy" framework . . . and to include an explicit capacity to examine situations of corporate abuse', Sir Geoffrey Chandler (the inaugural chair of the Amnesty International UK Business Group) called instead in 2008 for acceptance of this framework as the foundation for business and human rights, 'since a clear articulation of human rights principles for all companies is the essential precondition of an ultimate regulatory framework'.[107] At the same time, talk of such frameworks again reinforces the point that long-lasting global CSR solutions must transcend conventional boundaries between international and national domains, mandatory and non-mandatory regulation, public and private concerns, and hence governmental and non-governmental responsibilities.

In mid-2008, the UN Human Rights Council welcomed Professor Ruggie's reports as UNSRSG, and recognized the need to advance the operationalization of the threefold 'protect, respect, and remedy' framework.[108] To further this work, his mandate was extended for another three years, after which time Professor Ruggie proposed to make further 'recommendations for states and specific guidelines for companies', especially in terms of human rights due diligence by companies across organizational, sectoral and geographical boundaries.[109] At the time of writing, the UNSRSG's framework was starting to become a reference point in national legislative resolutions,[110] UN-supported national reviews of corporate law's treatment of human rights, and national legislative inquiries into business and human rights.[111]

OTHER HUMAN RIGHTS FOUNDATIONS FOR BUSINESS

While it is important not to confuse CSR and human rights, it is likely that any *direct* obligations for multinationals will emerge primarily from human rights law. However, much more work is needed on the standards that companies must observe, and the allocation of legal responsibilities, not only between multinationals and states, but between the various components of the multinationals themselves.

– Dr Jennifer Zerk, *Multinationals and Corporate Social Responsibility*[112]

Mapping the Human Rights Policies and Practices of the FG500

Based on the survey of the *Fortune* Global 500 (FG500) corporations by the UNSRSG, a number of common features figure strongly in the human rights policies and practices of major TNCs. These reported results can serve as a useful reference point for other corporations on human rights practices for business. The starting point is a stated set of principles or practices relating the human rights dimensions of the operations of the business to the overall organization and its management, either as part of a wider policy on CSR or else as a stand-alone human rights policy.[113] The range of human rights covered might vary somewhat according to industry sector and geographical region, although some rights (e.g. non-discrimination, workplace health and safety, and labour rights) figure universally or at least more prominently than others.[114] In identifying those corporate stakeholders embraced by a company's human rights policy, the company is effectively delineating its own 'sphere of influence'.[115]

Given the regime of international human rights law, the next plank in a rights-related CSR policy covers the international human rights instruments and other laws referenced in the policy, together with their national cognates and enforcement mechanisms.[116] At this stage in the evolution of global standards, core sources commonly cited and used by FG500 corporations include ILO declarations and conventions, the UDHR, the Global Compact and the OECD Guidelines for Multinational Enterprises.[117] Consultation with external stakeholders is another common step in the formulation of corporate human rights policies, with relevant NGOs and industry representative bodies topping the list of external stakeholders consulted by FG500 firms.[118]

Internal monitoring and reporting systems for overseeing corporate human rights performance are another key plank in corporate human rights policies and management plans, with a majority of FG500 firms having such systems in place.[119] Increasingly, as the law of directors' duties and business judgments becomes more focused upon how well corporate executives manage risks by putting in place appropriate oversight systems and controls,[120] the existence and quality of such internal monitoring and reporting mechanisms across organizational levels and their interaction with boardroom oversight become part of standard corporate machinery for human rights risk-avoidance as much as for other aspects of corporate risk-avoidance too.

The extent to which generic CSR and sustainability reporting specifically include human rights criteria and elements remains variable amongst FG500 firms and other business organizations worldwide.[121] Notwithstanding the interdependence between a company's social and financial performance, 'only a handful of companies combine social and financial reporting, despite the fact that the former has sustainability implications for the latter'.[122] Voluntary self-regulation does not necessarily identify or meaningfully address all important human rights affected by a business, and different companies have different catalogues, interpretations and applications of rights for their various business contexts, some of which are 'so elastic that the standards lose meaning, making it difficult for the company itself, let alone the public, to assess performance against commitments'.[123] Even the much-lauded GRI, with its 'standardised protocols to improve the quality and comparability of company reporting', and both its coalition-building with other collective initiatives (e.g. the Global Compact) and its tentative endorsement in some recent governmental reports on CSR,[124] still has some way to go in penetrating common business usage in reporting.

Some of the major weaknesses of voluntariness in CSR, at least from systemic and global perspectives, are exposed by the variances in coverage, accountability and assurance mechanisms for reported human rights management and compliance adopted by FG500 firms and other bodies.[125] Outside auditing, verification or other assurance of a company's sustainability reporting by professional services or consulting firms is not yet a standard feature incorporated within business responsibility and sustainability reports, despite the growing critical mass of independent ratings agencies, mainstream share analysts, institutional investors, SRI funds, and others increasingly interested in such assurance, as well as the emergence of global assurance standards such as

International Auditing and Assurance Standards Board ISAE3000 and AccountAbility AA1000AS.[126]

This further highlights the gaps between mandatory and voluntary regulation, and between companies in developed and developing economies, as well as the need for both generic standardization and firm-specific customization once standard-setting and coalition-building initiatives reach a critical mass and scale. Tools for large TNCs in developed economies do not necessarily suit businesses of different sizes in those economies or even large businesses in emerging economies, and voluntary initiatives always risk leaving well-intentioned late movers or ill-intentioned corporate harm-causers out of the loop of scrutiny. These frame-setting features and their accountability mechanisms are also affected by the pragmatic realities of what is necessary to bring the designated corporate actors and other bodies on board for any multi-stakeholder standard-setting initiatives on human rights, of the kinds explored in Chapter 2.

In the end, the final mapping of corporate human rights policies and management plans by the UNSRSG confirms that 'many, if not most of the world's major firms are aware that they have human rights responsibilities, have adopted some form of human rights policies and practices, think systematically about them and have instituted at least rudimentary internal and external reporting systems as well'.[127] Tracking these commonalities in the practical operationalization of business-related human rights engagement is another important step on the path towards developing a post-UN Norms framework for business and human rights.

Business-initiated Human Rights Operational Guides

What other developments inform either the path towards a global framework for business and human rights, or at least organizationally based frameworks that companies might adopt in meeting human rights obligations? As part of its contribution to the development of business frameworks concerning human rights, the influential BLIHR suggests that 'a common framework on business and human rights . . . would ideally be made up of three components':[128] '1. Concepts to clarify the role of business in the area of human rights'; '2. The range of relevant standards drawn from international human rights law'; and '3. Processes for applying the concepts and standards in a business context'. The joint initiative of the BLIHR, the Office of the UN High Commissioner for Human Rights and the UN Global Compact in developing *A Guide for Integrating Human Rights Into Business Management* outlines a range of step-by-step processes for integrating human rights considerations within standard business strategic and operational elements, categorising human rights actions successively associated with 'strategy', 'policies', 'processes and procedures', 'communications', 'training', 'measuring impact and auditing' and 'reporting'.[129]

Under this framework, human rights steps relating to strategy include: identifying human rights risks, opportunities and priorities; developing human rights business strategies; and developing and enforcing human rights elements within job descriptions for management and staff responsibilities. Here, embedding human rights in corporate processes and procedures involves the establishment of systems and procedures for identifying and managing 'human rights-related risks and opportunities'. Building human rights elements into corporate performance assessment and auditing involves selecting 'relevant performance indicators for measuring human rights impact across the different functions of your business', undertaking human rights audits and using results of those audits 'to inform the strategic development of your business', thus reinforcing another aspect of synchronization between a company's business model, human rights and CSR. This also serves as an internal organizational exercise in human rights due diligence. Finally, including human rights dimensions in corporate reporting means identifying and prioritizing relevant human rights impacts for a company, selecting appropriate reporting audiences, developing appropriate reporting templates and guidelines, disclosing relevant information and analysis within an appropriate form of corporate reporting, and including reference to relevant external standards (e.g. Global Compact, GRI, etc.).

Building and expanding upon a rich body of literature and experience on human rights guidance for companies, the Business Impact Task Force of UK-based Business in the Community (BITC) identifies the following operational steps in moving from first-time adoption to a position of business leadership in becoming a socially responsible business in the area of human rights.[130] Level 1 steps for first-time adopters of socially responsible human rights practices in business are:

- Conduct an initial review of:
  - legislation
  - human rights in mainstream company decision-making
  - human rights issues for the company within its sphere of operations
- Establish confidential grievance procedures for workers to raise concerns about working conditions
- Ensure a senior manager is charged with taking responsibility for driving progress in this area

Level 2 steps for businesses looking to consolidate and become more sophisticated in their business approach to human rights are:

- Draw up a human rights policy, incorporating an explicit commitment to support the UDHR and core ILO standards in the company's business principles and/or code of conduct. The commitment should apply to all the company's core operations and to its relations with business partners.
- Draw up a human rights policy and implementation plan, including the setting of relevant objectives and targets
- Communicate the policy and plan widely within the business and to partners, e.g. suppliers, sub-contractors
- Conduct training for staff to raise awareness of human rights

Level 3 steps for businesses with more critical or public exposure to human rights issues in their business, or seeking to position themselves as business leaders and standard-setters in the area of human rights practices for business, are:

- Set benchmarks relating to the human rights strategy against which the company in general, and managers and employees in particular, can be measured
- Measure and report against stated objectives and performance indicators. Use credible third-party auditors.
- Build human rights criteria into social impact assessments from the pre-investment risk analysis phase onwards
- Review human rights practices of business partners and be prepared to terminate contracts where necessary

- Engage in effective two-way consultation and dialogue with interested parties including critics
- Be prepared to enter into dialogue with government to raise human rights concerns either unilaterally or collectively with other companies who share similar concerns

Some of these steps mirror authoritative guidance elsewhere, especially on business impact assessment, verification and reporting in the human rights domain. Some of them dovetail with recent innovations in legislated corporate responsibility, such as the requirement under UK-style business reviews to assess business chain compliance with social and environmental standards. Some of them evidence the emerging trend of strategically relating CSR-related concerns, including treatment of human rights, to a company-specific business model, in ways that align human rights responsibilities throughout the organization. Many of them dovetail with corporate legal and regulatory obligations, and hence inform holistic organizational approaches to business compliance and due diligence from a whole-of-organization perspective, with business-related human rights matters forming part of a wider whole. This can also be done in ways that relate particular organizational systems and procedures to particular human rights.[131] All of them again reinforce the company-specific way in which wider societal concerns such as human rights are addressed in business contexts, in ways that transcend mere mandated compliance with human rights law.

In sum, whatever happens from here in the enhancement of international legal responsibility of corporations for human rights, the present state of voluntary corporate self-regulation on human rights also needs significant improvement. This is particularly vital in the areas of standard-development, company-specific application of standards, use of HRIAs and other human rights due diligence measures, and a variety of 'check and balance' accountability mechanisms, all within an overall systemic framework of different layers and forms of regulation impacting upon one another. As the UNSRSG concludes in his critical assessment of the present state of corporate self-regulation on human rights:[132]

> In formulating their human rights policies, companies typically draw on international instruments or initiatives. But the language of standards is rarely identical, and in some instances it is so elastic that the standards lose meaning, making it difficult for the company itself, let alone the public, to assess performance against commitments . . . The Achilles heel of self-regulatory arrangements to date is their underdeveloped accountability mechanisms. Company initiatives increasingly include rudimentary forms of internal and external reporting, as well as some form of supply chain monitoring. But no universally – or even widely – accepted standards yet exist for these practices . . . Relatively few companies that engage in large footprint projects seem ever to have conducted a fully-fledged human rights impact assessment, although a larger number includes selected human rights criteria in broader social/environmental assessments. And only a few such projects provide for community complaints procedures or remedies.

Human Rights 'Due Diligence' Contexts

In the aftermath of global debate about the UN Norms, human rights due diligence constitutes one of the key priorities for the UNSRSG in his mandate beyond the UN Norms. Due diligence on human rights is a crucial part of what he framed for the UN Human Rights Council in 2008 as 'the corporate responsibility to respect human

Corporations are subject to a range of domestic human rights law obligations in Australia that necessarily entail a corporate duty to respect human rights in certain circumstances. There is, however, no generally applicable legal duty to respect international human rights laws that applies to Australian corporations, and the extent to which the State's international human rights obligations have been incorporated into domestic law so as to create direct human rights obligations for corporations is limited.

There are, though, due diligence processes that a corporation must undertake to meet its general legal obligations that either accommodate or are at least amenable to consideration of human rights laws or standards. This may be the case regardless of whether the legal obligations to which these due diligence processes attach mandate corporate compliance with human rights . . . As such, these due diligence processes may provide a means of incorporating consideration of human rights standards into operational and legal compliance processes. This, in turn, may allow a corporation to decide, on an informed basis, how to meet a duty to respect human rights, if such a duty is incorporated into Australian domestic law.

– Report by law firm Allens Arthur Robinson for the UN Special Representative of the Secretary General for Business and Human Rights[133]

rights'.[134] Due diligence has more than one meaning in legal and business contexts. Professor Ruggie explains the concept of due diligence in the human rights context as 'the steps a company must take to become aware of, prevent and address adverse human rights impacts'.[135] In the human rights context more broadly, due diligence embraces compliance due diligence, project due diligence, investment due diligence, contract due diligence, takeover due diligence, public sector due diligence, and other forms of human rights due diligence too. As with other ways in which CSR-related elements are folded into standard business matters, due diligence in the context of human rights is a growth area of research, regulation and practice in the 21st century.

Importantly, human rights due diligence is already incorporated in, or at least facilitated by, what many companies already do in meeting their general legal obligations, even in the absence of an overriding legal obligation under international or national law for companies to respect internationally recognized human rights. 'Comparable processes are typically already embedded in companies because in many countries they are legally required to have information and control systems in place to assess and manage financial and related risks', as the UNSRSG explains.[136] Business elements of human rights due diligence include a company's rights-compliant standard business contracts, rights-compliant supply and distribution chain, contingent liabilities from current or prospective human rights litigation, and prospective litigation and reputational risk assessment from a human rights perspective. At the same time, some key ways of placing rights-related elements on the corporate radar (e.g. socio-ethical risk assessments) involve mindsets and skills that are still non-conventional in many boardrooms, with implications for the mix of skills and expertise in recruiting, training, and assessing corporate executives.

According to Professor Ruggie, due diligence by business on human rights has the following critical elements.[137] A company should have a human rights policy. Ideally, it must be backed with high-level boardroom and management commitment, outlined with sufficient operational guidance to give it meaning, and integrated throughout the company. Viewed from a global perspective, the corporate obligation to respect rights covers the rights recognized in the international bill of rights and ILO conventions as a minimum baseline, whatever the extent to which those rights are actually recognized and enforced in any place where the company does business. As a corporate obligation to respect rights also includes avoiding undue harm to human rights, human rights impact assessments must become a standard feature of corporate planning and operations. This extends beyond conventional risk assessments, social impact studies and environmental impact studies. Finally, a holistic approach to monitoring, auditing and reporting a company's progress on human rights will contribute to a wider system of multi-stakeholder dialogue and standard-setting, as well as lead to continuous improvement in that company's human rights performance.

US law firm Wachtell, Lipton, Rosen and Katz describes the level of organizational detail and integration this involves in their outline of the UNSRSG's proposal for HRIAs:[138]

> According to [the UNSRSG], a human rights impact assessment would include the following components:
> i. A description of the proposed business activity;
> ii. A catalogue of the legal, regulatory and administrative frameworks to which the activity is subject, as well as the international human rights frameworks that apply to the area in which the business will operate;
> iii. A description of the human rights conditions in the area surrounding the business activity before significant activity begins;
> iv. A statement of what is likely to change because of the business activity, which may include identifying multiple scenarios or predicting outcomes based in varying levels of intervention. Relevant factors include country-specific human rights challenges as well as the potential human rights impact of the company's activities and of the relationships associated with those activities;
> v. A prioritization of the human rights challenges for the company;
> vi. A management plan that includes both recommendations to address human rights challenges and provisions for the monitoring of baseline indicators.

In practical terms, the UNSRSG suggests a three-pronged framework of principles for corporate activation of human rights due diligence.[139] First, companies must relate human rights issues to their various places of business operation, as part of assessing the national contexts in which their business occurs, and hence the human rights challenges they face. This includes learning from governmental, NGO and related reports about human rights and business in particular national contexts, as well as taking account of the totality of national and international laws bearing upon human rights in each country as well as the 'potential gaps between international standards and national law and practice'. Secondly, companies must assess the human rights impact of their activities in those contexts, including an identification and adjustment of those corporate policies and practices that harm human rights, drawing from a set of activities defined by corporate capacities 'as producers, service providers, employers, and neighbours' that includes 'the production process itself; the products or services the company provides; its labour and employment practices; the provision of security for personnel and assets; and the company's lobbying or other political activities'. Finally, companies must avoid potential complicity in human rights abuses, 'through the relationships connected to their activities, such as with business partners, suppliers, State agencies, and other non-State actors'. This includes preventative monitoring of core business activities (e.g. providing goods and services) and non-core business activities (e.g. providing vehicles, equipment or other support to third parties), vigilant scrutiny of the human rights track records of others with whom companies deal, and active avoidance of companies' own potential involvement in human rights abuses committed by others.

Both now and into the future, a series of human rights 'due diligence' contexts arise for business. Despite other differences, the common element in all of these contexts is a need for some reason to know and perhaps disclose how an organization meets relevant human rights standards. Such organizational knowledge and disclosure presuppose the existence of a suitable human rights due diligence programme, as part of an otherwise comprehensive organizational due diligence programme. Risk management systems required under corporate law and regulation can encompass human rights risks as one form of material business risks, as part of an overall system of corporate compliance and risk management. An aspect of 'approaching the risk-management side of CSR', for example, involves 'proper systems for monitoring risk across the supply chain'.[140]

Business due diligence on human rights is also an essential precursor to any public claims by businesses who seek reputational or other competitive advantages from their human rights performance. Otherwise, even in the absence of binding international or national human rights obligations for corporations, the public statements and compliance record of corporations concerning human rights can lead to legally actionable claims under public and private law, including failure to satisfy preconditions for governmental approvals and licences, loss of governmental certification or other standard-setting qualifications, breach of contract performance conditions, failure to meet legal standards of reasonable care and due diligence, misrepresentation and misleading conduct, and wrongful corporate disclosure and reporting.[141] Even in the absence of a comprehensive international framework for corporate human rights responsibility, TNCs 'may have little choice but to address human rights concerns as part of their business management strategy, particularly where they invest in conflict zones, politically corrupt states or less developed countries'.[142]

Accordingly, due diligence processes needed to meet general legal obligations might require or permit attention to human rights aspects of the following kinds:[143]

(1) corporate compliance with laws with specific human rights elements (e.g. anti-discrimination, employment, and privacy laws);
(2) business impact assessments for project and infrastructure development (e.g. socio-economic impact studies, EISs and HRIAs);
(3) rights-related preconditions for granting governmental approvals and licences for business infrastructure and development proposals;
(4) compliance with directors' duties and defences (e.g. adequate consideration of the relation between rights-related stakeholder interests and long-term corporate success);
(5) corporate responses to shareholder action including litigation (e.g. shareholder proposals, institutional investor dialogue and climate change litigation);

(6) satisfaction of ESG and SRI concerns of institutional investors;
(7) conformance with investment decision-making requirements (e.g. ethical, labour, environmental and human rights considerations in choosing or realizing investments);
(8) corporate governance requirements for corporate responsibility and sustainability reporting (e.g. reportable human rights risks and business success drivers as 'material business risks'); and
(9) integrated risk management for corporations and their business chains of rights-based business risks.

In each context for human rights diligence, it is necessary to distinguish between 'hard' and 'soft' law requirements, mandatory and permitted actions under existing law, and current and emerging (or potential) practice. For example, a company might introduce a due diligence procedure to ensure that its treatment of human rights concerns in business operations meets its voluntary commitment to a designated business code (e.g. 'soft' law). Similarly, a company might need a due diligence procedure to ensure that relevant human rights concerns are adequately covered in boardroom decision-making and corporate reporting frameworks in those jurisdictions (e.g. the UK) where considering relevant non-stakeholder matters and reporting on supply and distribution chain arrangements are mandatory under the law. Finally, even if human rights concerns have not figured hugely in due diligence practice in merger, acquisition and takeover contexts, clearly they are now on the forward-looking corporate radar (e.g. rights-based litigation risk assessments).

Responsible investment and sustainable development generate their own due diligence needs covering human rights. 'Beyond the basics, prudent companies include a CSR perspective when considering new projects [as] part of systematic due diligence for new investments', notes *The Economist* in its 2008 CSR report.[144] In the finance and investment community, there is growing appreciation among some analysts that 'looking at the quality of a company's CSR policy may be a useful pointer to the quality of its management more generally', adds *The Economist*.[145] 'Hard' and 'soft' law standards on investment decision-making can lead to due diligence to ensure that relevant human rights matters are considered as preconditions for financial and security arrangements in project-based corporate lending, and disclosed in investment decision-making as part of an assessment of socio-ethical, environmental and other considerations affecting responsible investment, at least where they fit within the overarching notion of 'labour standards or environmental, social or ethical considerations [that] are taken into account in the selection, retention or realisation of the investment', for example.[146] Project infrastructure development needs due diligence procedures to meet conditions of sustainable development, especially in satisfying public approval and licencing requirements through socio-economic impact studies, HRIAs and other necessary evidence of rights-sensitivity as an aspect of business–community relations, sustainable development, and now climate risk too.

Human rights due diligence also arises in a variety of public sector contexts. At the level of policy-making and regulation, governments might have due diligence procedures in place to check compliance with 'human rights criteria in their export credit and investment promotion policies, or in bilateral trade and investment treaties', which are 'points at which government policies and global business operations most closely intersect'.[147] Nation-states also need a means of demonstrating to the international community that they are meeting their international legal obligations in holding corporations to account for any human rights breaches, as part of state obligations to protect human rights under 'hard' international law, as well as in standard-setting and monitoring mechanisms under 'soft' international law.[148] Public officials making rulings on business project applications or objections might need to satisfy themselves that all relevant human rights aspects are in order, especially in jurisdictions with an overarching bill of rights, as must business enterprises that are subject to such requirements in performing or managing public activities. Finally, governments that seek to become models of human rights practice, in requiring all business and community suppliers of advice and services to government to meet applicable human rights standards, need effective monitoring and compliance checks as another form of rights-related due diligence.[149]

THE FUTURE OF BUSINESS AND HUMAN RIGHTS

The world needs new rules of engagement for business and human rights in the 21st century. Elements of a 21st century framework are slowly emerging in the post-UN Norms era from the UNSRSG's work on human rights and business, rights-focused multi-stakeholder initiatives, and scholarship at the intersection of international, public, private (especially corporate) and human rights law. Some US commentators are already claiming that 'directors' fiduciary duties now include a duty to be aware of human rights risks and potential violations within a company's global operations and to develop policies and management procedures to reduce the risks of such violations', with human rights violations being framed specifically as 'part of the liability risks that directors need to consider, at least to the extent of ensuring that the company has established appropriate information and reporting systems to assess risks of human rights violations, as well as policies to address conditions that may give rise to such risks'.[150] Enhanced business due diligence on human rights advances this agenda too.

The last word on the forward-looking agenda for human rights and business under international law belongs to the UNSRSG.[151] The international legal regime must further elucidate the obligations of nation-states, both individually and together as the international community of nations, to hold corporations accountable on human rights grounds, in ways that support rather than undermine the governance roles and capacities of nations. In turn, nation-states need to improve how they use multiple regulatory mechanisms to build human rights incentives, sanctions and accountabilities into market dynamics and their regulation of markets, especially in the post-GFC world. The legal focus on making corporations accountable for their human rights wrongdoing must be accompanied by attention to shared responsibilities, reformed institutional practices and improved systemic processes in deepening the socio-political infrastructure for human rights, in recognition that 'an individual liability model alone cannot fix larger systemic imbalances in the global system of governance'.

Hence, future solutions on business and human rights require a multi-pronged approach and new rules of engagement between the major players, with all of government, business and civil society having roles in the shared governance and regulation of business and human rights worldwide. In the end, the regulatory path ahead for business and human rights remains at least a mix of state-based responsibility for developing universal agreements on CSR and human rights, non-state regulation of business and human rights from transnational corporate and civil society initiatives, development of national and international dispute and remedial measures concerning human rights claims against corporations, extension of nation-state and extra-territorial responsibility for rights-affecting corporate activity, and expansion of correlative legal and regulatory mechanisms.[152] In turn, this generates a need for innovation in cross-disciplinary and transnational theory-building, exploration of interactions and reformulations of doctrines across different legal areas and jurisdictions, translation of legal and regulatory measures for different kinds of business enterprises (e.g. TNCs, SMEs, and social and not-for-profit enterprises), changes in official approaches to regulatory design and implementation, reformation of business mindsets and practices, and generation of 'greenfield' research about all of these things and their impact upon the relation between business and human rights. This is the future of the interface between business and human rights in the 21st century.

NOTES

1. Bottomley, 2002: 47.
2. Campbell, 2006: 263.
3. A/HRC/4/35, [20].
4. Ruggie, 2007a: 21.
5. ECDGESA, 2001: 14.
6. On some of these roles see Bottomley, 2002.
7. Bottomley, 2002: 47.
8. Zerk, 2006: 304; original emphasis.
9. Campbell, 2007: 557.
10. Henkin, 1999; 25.
11. Ratner, 2001: 449.
12. Ibid.: 488.
13. BLIHR, 2006: 5.
14. Ratner, 2001: 524.
15. Kinley and Tadaki, 2004: 962–963.
16. Emberland, 2006; 2.
17. Ibid.
18. On the following objections and counter-responses see Muchlinski, 2007: 432–433, 436–438.
19. Robertson, 2006: 186–187.
20. Ruggie, 2008c: 3.
21. Ruggie, 2002: 4–5.
22. Baue, 2007.
23. UNCITRAL, 2001: 140–142; and UNCITRAL, 2004: model provisions 38–40.
24. UNCITRAL, 2001: 141. On these and other points concerning stabilization clauses see Hildyard and Muttit, 2006.
25. See, for example, the joint study by the World Bank Group's International Financial Corporation (IFC) and the UN Secretary-General's Special Representative on Business and Human Rights, on investment agreements and human rights. The author discloses that, through his consultancy work for Allens Arthur Robinson, he has assisted in research undertaken for the International Bar Association and the SRSG on due diligence, fiduciary duties and human rights.
26. Schrage, 2003: 16.
27. A/HRC/4/35, [27].
28. Ward, 2001: 1.
29. Ibid.: 4.

30. Joseph, 2004: 153.
31. 542 US 692 (2004).
32. Robertson, 2006: 189.
33. Ward, 2001: 2–3.
34. Ibid.; and Joseph, 2004.
35. Joseph, 2004: 143. The author is also a member of this research centre in his university role.
36. Ward, 2001.
37. Ibid.
38. Joseph, 2004: 152.
39. Ibid.: 152–153.
40. Joseph, 2004: 105–107.
41. Leavitt, 2004.
42. E.g. the legal proceedings involving the Overseas Private Investment Bank (OPIC), various NGOs and some US cities concerning the extent to which the National Environmental Policy Act applies to decisions concerning the impact of greenhouse gases from projects worldwide upon 'the quality of the human environment' (in the USA); and *Minister for the Environment and Heritage v Queensland Conservation Council* [2004] FCAFC 190; *Wildlife Preservation Society of Queensland Prosepine/Whitsunday Branch v Minister for the Environment and Heritage* [2006] FCA 736; *Gray v Minister for Planning* [2006] NSWLEC 720; *Queensland Conservation Council v Xstrata Coal Queensland Pty Ltd* [2007] QCA 338; and *Gippsland Coastal Board v South Gippsland SC* [2008] VCAT 1545 (in Australia).
43. On the legal implications of climate change for companies see Healy and Tapick, 2004.
44. Walker, 2007: 3; and *R v Broadcasting Standards Commission ex parte BBC* [2001] QB 885.
45. ALRC, 2008: [7.58]-[7.60].
46. E.g. Human Rights Act 1998 (UK), s.6 (3); and Charter of Human Rights and Responsibilities Act 2006 (Vic), s.4 (1).
47. E.g. UK JCHR, 2007; and *L v Birmingham City Council* [2007] UKHL 27.
48. Human Rights Act 2004 (ACT), s 40D.
49. E.g. Human Rights Act 1998 (UK), ss 6, 7 and 8; and Charter of Human Rights and Responsibilities Act 2006 (Vic), ss 38–39.
50. UK JCHR, 2007: 16–23 and 38–39; and EU Directive on Public Sector Procurement HL Paper 77, HC 410, as implemented in the UK in the Public Contracts Regulations 2006, SI 2006/5.
51. On some of these implications see O'Donahoo and Howie, 2006.
52. Australian Government, 2008: 10, and 12–14.
53. Santow and Johnson, 2009a; and Santow and Johnson, 2009b.
54. Companies Act 2006 (UK), s.172.
55. Ibid., s. 417(5).
56. Misol, 2008.
57. Campbell, 2006: 256.
58. Ibid.: 256–257.
59. ECDGESA, 2001: 15.
60. Williams and Conley, 2005b: 101.
61. Campbell, 2006: 264.
62. UN Norms, Art 1.
63. Ibid., Art 1.
64. Muchlinski, 2007: 443–447.
65. UN Norms, Art 15.
66. Ibid:, Art 15.
67. Ibid., Art 16.
68. Ibid., Art 17.
69. Ibid., Art 18.
70. Ibid., Art 19.
71. BLIHR, 2006: 19.
72. Kinley et al, 2007: 31 and 42.
73. Ibid.: 33.
74. Ibid.
75. E.g. Zerk, 2006: 277.
76. Kinley et al, 2007; 36, 32.
77. Commission on Human Rights, *Promotion and Protection of Human Rights*, Communication to the United Nations Economic and Social Council (UN Doc. E/CN.4/2005/L.87, 2).
78. E/CN.4/2006/97, [55].
79. E/CN.4/2006/97, [57]–[58].

80. E/CN.4/2006/97, [59].
81. E/CN.4/2006/97, [59]–[69].
82. Ruggie, 2007a: 9.
83. Ibid.: 10–12; original emphasis.
84. Ruggie, 2007c: [2]–[3], [5]–[6] and [10].
85. E/CN.4/2006/97, [69].
86. Ruggie, 2007a.
87. Kinley et al, 2007; 34, 42.
88. Ibid.: 41–42.
89. BLIHR, 2006.
90. Ruggie, 2007a: 13.
91. Ibid.: 13.
92. A/HRC/4/35, [85]–[87].
93. Ibid., [85].
94. BLIHR, 2006: 6.
95. Ibid.: 1.
96. Ward, 2001. On mapping governmental initiatives for CSR and human rights see Ch 4.
97. A/HRC/4/35, [45]–[62].
98. Ibid., [62].
99. A/HRC/8/5, [8].
100. Ruggie, 2008b: 4.
101. A/HRC/8/5, [9].
102. Joint statement dated May 2008 by the IOE, ICC and BIAC, submitted for the Eighth Session of the UN Human Rights Council on the third report of the Special Representative of the UN Secretary-General on Business and Human Rights.
103. Ochoa, 2008.
104. Ibid.
105. A/HRC/8/5, [54].
106. Statement dated 20 May 2008 by Action Aid, Amnesty International, EarthRights International, Friends of the Earth International, International Federation for Human Rights, International Network for Economic, Social and Cultural Rights, Human Rights Watch, International Commission of Jurists, Oxfam International, Rights & Accountability in Development, and Women's Environment and Development Organization, submitted for the Eighth Session of the UN Human Rights Council on the third report of the Special Representative of the UN Secretary-General on Business and Human Rights.
107. Sir Geoffrey Chandler, 'Comment on the Joint NGO Statement on a Follow-On Mandate for Professor Ruggie', 28 May 2008.
108. A/HRC/8/L.8.
109. Ruggie, 2008c: 2.
110. See Ch 4.
111. E.g. 2009 inquiry into business and human rights by the UK Joint Committee on Human Rights.
112. Zerk, 2006: 310; original emphasis.
113. E/CN.4/2006/97, [33].
114. A/HRC/4/35, [67].
115. E/CN.4/2006/97, [36]; and A/HRC/4/35, [68].
116. E/CN.4/2006/97, [34]; and A/HRC/4/35, [69].
117. E/CN.4/2006/97, [34]; and A/HRC/4/35, [69].
118. A/HRC/4/35, [69].
119. E/CN.4/2006/97, [37]; and A/HRC/4/35, [72].
120. Dine, 2005.
121. E/CN.4/2006/97, [35]; and A/HRC/4/35, [72].
122. Ibid., [78].
123. Ibid., [74].
124. PJCCFS, 2006; CAMAC, 2006.
125. On the following summary and discussion of features of voluntarism see E/CN.4/2006/97, [53]; and A/HRC/4/35, [74]–[85].
126. HRC/4/35, [79].
127. E/CN.4/2006/97, [38]; and A/HRC/4/35, [72]–[74].
128. BLIHR, 2006: 3.
129. As referred to in ibid.: 16.
130. BITF, 2000: 11, 13.

131.   Castan Centre et al, 2008.
132.   Ruggie, 2007a: 24–26.
133.   AAR, 2008: 1. The author was involved as a consultant in the preparation of this report.
134.   A/HRC/8/5, [9].
135.   Ibid., [56].
136.   Ibid., [56].
137.   Ruggie, 2008a: [59]–[64]
138.   Wachtell, 2008: 2.
139.   Ruggie, 2008c: [19]–[22].
140.   *The Economist*, 2008: 12.
141.   Muchlinski, 2007: 456–457.
142.   Ibid.: 448.
143.   Some of these aspects appear in AAR, 2008, in which the author was involved.
144.   *The Economist*, 2008: 12.
145.   Ibid.: 22.
146.   E.g. Corporations Act 2001 (Cth), s.1013D(1)(l).
147.   Ruggie, 2007a: 16.
148.   Ibid.: 13.
149.   The author acknowledges the benefit of discussions on such aspects of human rights due diligence with his Allens Arthur Robinson colleagues, Rachel Nicholson, Craig Phillips and David Robb.
150.   Williams and Conley, 2005b: 87–88.
151.   On the following future improvements and quoted comments see Ruggie, 2007a: 26–30.
152.   Kinley et al, 2007b: 474–475.

10. Advancing the 21st century corporate social responsibility agenda

A GRAND GLOBAL CORPORATE SOCIAL RESPONSIBILITY PROJECT

> The defining challenge of the twenty-first century will be to face the reality that humanity shares a *common fate on a crowded planet*. That common fate will require new forms of global cooperation, a fundamental point of blinding simplicity that many world leaders have yet to understand or embrace . . . There are no solutions to the problems of poverty, population, and environment without the active engagement of the private sector, and especially the large multinational companies. Yet the main objective of such companies is to earn profits rather than to meet social needs. The two are definitely not incompatible, but they are not the same. It will take hard work to bring together the leaders of business, government, and nongovernmental organizations to ensure that private-sector incentives and societal needs are harmonized [so] that the self-organizing forces of a market economy [are] guided by overarching principles of social justice and environmental stewardship . . .
>
> – Professor Jeffrey Sachs, Director of Columbia University's Earth Institute, and author of *The End of Poverty* and *Common Wealth: Economics for a Crowded Planet*[1]

21st Century Geopolitical Convergence Towards Corporate Social Responsibility

CSR is now everybody's business, whether you are for it, against it or ambivalent about it. All citizens of the world have a stake in global CSR that goes beyond being passive objects of stakeholder consultation, marginal participants in corporate governance, bystanders in corporate law and disempowered victims of corporate irresponsibility.

A grand CSR project is unfolding worldwide, building momentum towards a new era of corporate responsiveness to trans-modal governance, multi-order regulation and inter-connected responsibility. This grand global CSR project remains a 21st century work-in-progress. Constructing tools for this grand CSR project at its highest levels of philosophical abstraction (e.g. theorizing about corporate legitimacy) and collective effort (e.g. undertaking CSR-sensitive law reform across jurisdictions) is as important as discovering what works on the ground to embed CSR within individual companies and industry sectors (e.g. integrating CSR within standard business models).

Even without a universal master controller, this organic CSR project is developing on a number of different fronts all at once. It incorporates stages of CSR awareness-raising, justification-testing, consensus-building, cooperation-fostering, standard-setting, system-modelling, regulation-shaping and practice-embedding. For example, exemplary CSR 'soft' norms such as the OECD Guidelines for Multinational Enterprises, the ILO Tripartite Declaration and significant UN-sponsored initiatives (especially the UN Global Compact, UN Principles for Responsible Investment, Millennium Goals and the UNSRSG's mandate on business and human rights), in combination with other land-mark CSR initiatives such as the GRI, play important roles in mass awareness-raising international consensus-building, cross-jurisdictional standard-developing and main-streaming of CSR in global business practice.

The digital age of the 21st century offers unparalleled scope for new forms of corporate democratization, networking, and monitoring. This technological age of the internet is cited by CSR commentators and democratic theorists alike as one of this century's most powerful tools of corporate communication and accountability.[2] Referring to the 'historically unprecedented degree of technology-driven transparency, scrutiny and account-ability' of the 21st century business environment as 'perhaps the most important and enduring of all the CSR drivers we have encountered', the authors of one transnational legal analysis of CSR view this key driver as one that 'makes this new global iteration of CSR different in kind and degree from the old 19th and 20th century "shareholder versus stakeholder" debates, and different as well from previous CSR phases', such as those con-cerned with CSR as 'corporate philanthropy', 'corporate statesmanship', 'strategic CSR', 'opportunity creation', and even 'a system perspective [on] sustainable development'.[3]

The fact that CSR has become a recurring theme at recent meetings of world leaders – both before and after the global financial system's crisis of 2008–2009 – suggests that CSR has achieved a new level of importance in the 21st century global order. At a G8 meeting in 2009, world leaders emphasized the elements of a post-GFC approach to international financial responsibility and regulation that relates at least some CSR concerns to reform of corporate and financial regulatory systems on a global scale. Calling for 'an enhanced global framework for financial regulation and supervision' and 'an international level playing field' to address 'flaws in international economic and financial systems', the G8 leaders not only targeted reforms in 'the areas of corporate governance, market integrity [and] financial regulation and supervision' (amongst others).[4] They also expressed their collective commitment 'to tackling the social dimension of the crisis', given that '(t)he impact of the economic crisis on labour markets can undermine social stability', as well as ensuring that '(t)he emergency response to the economic crisis should not overlook the opportunity to facilitate a global green recovery putting our economies on a path towards more sustainable and resilient growth'.[5]

CSR is squarely in the spotlight of these concerns, as conceded by the G8 leaders, but in terms that still cling to voluntariness as a foundation for business commitment to CSR, in defiance of the more nuanced systemic relations between mandatory, voluntary, and other forms of regulation in the 21st century:[6]

> Conscious of the complementary role played by governments and the private sector in reaching a sustainable growth, we call for enhanced efforts to avoid wider consequences of the financial crisis and to promote responsible business practices. To this end we promote the dissemination of internationally-recognised *voluntary* Corporate Social Responsibility (CSR) standards to

raise awareness among our governments, citizens, companies and other stakeholders. We will further promote and foster Corporate Social Responsibility through encouragement of adherence to the existing relevant international instruments, in accordance with our Heiligendamm commitments. We also welcome the work of relevant international institutions (ILO, OECD, UN Global Compact) to incorporate CSR into business practices and encourage them to work together in a coherent way in order to achieve synergy effects with existing CSR instruments.

In these ways and others, the world is clearly in the process of reconstructing CSR as a force which is integral rather than marginal to 21st century concerns of global governance, public policy and civil society. CSR is now the product of a new interplay between the governmental, business and community sectors, in shaping CSR into something suited for 21st century conditions of globalizing societies and economies, with the character of 'an emerging model of corporate social responsibility (CSR)-oriented societal governance' that transcends traditional forms of societal governance associated with the ideals of a liberal market economy, on one hand, and the welfare state, on the other.[7] Indeed, the world is reaching a turning point at which the inevitability of CSR overtakes the remaining opposition to it. CSR is quickly becoming established in the 21st century as a governmental and intergovernmental policy priority for the G8/G20, EU and other leading institutions. Its connection to important 21st century politico-regulatory and socio-economic issues such as climate change, sustainable development, responsible investment, human rights and developing markets solidifies its new place as a geopolitical priority in its own right and as a means to those ends. Having attracted policy attention at governmental levels within the EU, UK, USA and other Western democratic systems, CSR shows early signs of attracting governmental policy attention in China and other emerging powerhouse economies too.[8]

In short, the world has reached a critical point already this century in the maturation of CSR as a mainstream preoccupation for multiple governmental, business and community actors. This result is evidenced collectively by a mushrooming and multi-pronged CSR movement worldwide, an emerging body of transnational and international CSR-related law and regulation, a growing appreciation of the importance of strategic approaches to business–society relations, a marked shift towards integrating CSR-related elements within standard elements of corporate governance and responsibility, and an increased capacity for CSR's methodology to fulfil its promise. Fuelled by all of these developments and more, the haphazard and highly selective ways in which CSR has been pursued in much pre-millennium business activity, as shaped by prevailing corporate law and regulation, is giving way to a 21st century appreciation of the need for business–society relations to be aligned more fully from a series of governmental, business and societal perspectives.

'The economic and political power that corporations have gained, in particular, compared with many individual states, appear to be supported by liberal corporate law systems and definitions of CSR that accept a relaxed response to corporate activity, largely leaving the solution to be constructed by the companies themselves', argues Professor Charlotte Villiers.[9] In her eyes, at least part of the solution lies in mechanisms which 'recognize a collective power and responsibility to ensure corporate accountability', thus reinforcing the reality of mutual yet differentiated ownership of today's challenges of governance, regulation and responsibility for multiple CSR actors.[10] Moreover, 'a corporate social responsibility agenda should not permit the denial of an internationally shared power and responsibility to eradicate the global structural inequalities that currently allow companies to commit abuses', she adds.[11] Here, the grand global CSR project meets systems of trans-modal governance, multi-order regulation and inter-related responsibility.

The responsibility, governance, and sustainability of 21st century global corporations turns in part on how well they meet new challenges from within and beyond their corporate regulatory systems. The multiple sources of these challenges stem from a new global systemic order of governance, regulation, and responsibility in a post-GFC world. The various politico-regulatory, socio-economic, eco-ethical, and other dimensions of that global order are still unfolding in their focus and impact upon corporations, in ways illustrated throughout this book. Much remains to be done in transforming corporations to deal with a world of governance beyond government, regulation beyond law, and responsibility beyond state sanctions and market norms. In this 21st century world, the GFC is only one landmark event in the refashioning of the terms of engagement between politics, markets, and society, on the path towards what the presenter of the 2009 Reith Lectures describes as 'revitalising our public discourse in democratic life'.[12] Professor Michael Sandel goes on to foresee 'market-mimicking governance', 'market triumphalism', and the resultant 'impoverished public discourse' potentially giving way to a deeper appreciation of 'the moral limits of markets' and the promise of 'a new citizenship' and 'a new kind of politics – a politics of the common good'.[13]

This unfolding world is itself responsive to the grand global CSR project outlined in this chapter. Under its influence, our notions of territorial and institutional sovereignty can be recast to embrace what some regulatory theorists describe as a global 'sovereignty of citizens', to challenge 'the sovereignty of big business over globalizing regulation' and 'to protect the community from the abuse of corporate power',[14] through enhanced institutions and mechanisms of business regulation worldwide, which themselves are responsive to new visions of the regulatory state and 'new governance' ideas.[15] Corporate democracy's different planes need to engage with democracy's present evolution towards deliberative democracy and other manifestations of 'monitory democracy', which is characterized 'by the growth of many different power-scrutinising mechanisms and their spreading influence within the fields of government and civil society, both at home and abroad, in cross-border settings that were once dominated by empires, states and business organisations'.[16]

Accordingly, CSR now forms part of a 21st century response to the reality that governments, businesses and communities share some problems and challenges in common for which CSR offers at least part of the answer, with each of those groups having some ownership of that overall need and various individual and cross-cutting roles to play in meeting that responsibility. This means that new rules of engagement are needed for CSR, given the fragmented ownership and control of CSR to this point within and across regions and sectors. CSR cannot be left to any of international institutional initiatives, national mandatory regulation, corporate self-regulation or community and NGO influences alone. Accordingly, new governance and regulatory mechanisms are needed, in which all players have a part to play within the overall system, no single player or sector dominates alone, and all parts of an overall system of CSR architecture are synchronized with one another, in setting the rules of engagement as well as the standards expected for CSR.

Towards a Global Meta-framework for Corporate Social Responsibility

So, in light of everything so far, what needs targeting in the legal and regulatory architecture surrounding CSR? What are the possibilities of a blueprint for reform? What are the critical avenues for future research? These key questions are the remaining ones for this book.

The global CSR project outlined here must lead to coordinated action by CSR actors across all of the domains of government, business and civil society. In the light of CSR's relationship to G8-nominated geopolitical concerns such as climate risk, sustainable development and socio-economic prosperity, the world must take advantage of the present global momentum towards CSR to embed suitable transnational and international architecture for its next phase of development. At the levels of policy, law and regulation, this requires a new holistic and systemic focus upon corporate responsibility, governance and sustainability. At the very least, a framework of CSR-focused international agreements is necessary, building upon existing moves towards an international law of corporate responsibility and governance. Recognition of the regional success of 'the European Union's multi-layered approach to CSR' in regulating corporations, for example, can still sit side by side with recognition that 'a formalized, international framework is preferable'.[17]

'This century's global cooperation won't be led by any single country [and] will be based on global agreements and international law', predicts special adviser to the UN Secretary-General on the Millennium Development Goals, Professor Sachs.[18] 'The next step is a global agreement for real action rather than a mere framework for recognizing the problem', urges Professor Sachs, given the 'interlocking roles in global problem solving [of] the public sector, private sector, and not-for-profit sector'.[19] Focusing specifically on the Millennium Promises, he argues that '(e)ach company needs to be part of the solution and needs to stretch its activities beyond normal market activities'.[20] Accordingly, at some point in the first quarter of the 21st century, a foundational international agreement on CSR is needed to set the framework of international governance and regulatory architecture for CSR.

The critical question is whether that overarching initiative can happen at the outset or only as the culmination of a series of more discrete international agreements, starting with specific aspects of multinational corporate responsibility and liability. Existing international agreements affecting corporations in the areas of foreign corruption, environmental pollution and intellectual property are milestones on the way to a more complete international law of corporate responsibility and liability. International agreements on CSR will be informed by 'hard' and 'soft' international legal norms governing corporate responsibility and governance, the emerging body of comparative CSR law and regulation across major corporate regulatory systems, transnational and regional standard-setting and multi-stakeholder mechanisms orientated around business–government–society relations, and corporate and boardroom systems for the integration of CSR. The fate of the rights-focused UN Norms raises questions about the extent to which some aspects of international agreement on multinational corporate responsibility and liability are achievable in isolation, especially without an overarching international framework for multinational corporate responsibility and governance. 'Given the complexity of international corporate groups, and the range of possible national approaches, a *general* treaty on liability for corporate abuses is an unlikely prospect at present', suggests Dr Jennifer Zerk.[21]

A global meta-framework for CSR must also accommodate existing whole-of-government policy and regulatory approaches to CSR in a number of countries and regions. This helps in fostering an environment in which good corporate governance, responsibility and sustainability become a race to the top instead of a race to the bottom. For example, the CSR policy frameworks in the EU and UK not only establish legitimacy and structures for CSR policy and regulatory initiatives within government, but also stimulate CSR-focused interactions between governmental, business and community bodies, leading to multi-stakeholder CSR initiatives and other CSR-enhancing mechanisms. The menu of reform options collectively offered by Australia's most recent official CSR inquiries offers a different kind of common framework, in the form of an agenda for governmental, business and community involvement in enhancing CSR, removed from the traditional fixation upon socialization of directors' duties and corporate reporting as the paradigm manifestations of CSR-related policy and law reform.

Of course, any such meta-framework on the global stage must establish itself in the face of scepticism about the possibility of arriving at anything meaningful for CSR in the absence of truly universal values and policy goals in a world of endemic moral and political disagreement. Still, there remains a level on which corporate responsiveness to trans-modal governance, multi-order regulation and inter-related responsibility can both shape and use such a meta-framework in moving towards systemic corporate governance, responsibility and sustainability outcomes. This overarching enterprise is supported by justificatory rationales as diverse as the pragmatic realities of transnational trends in corporate democratization and shared global interests in sustainable governance and development, on one hand, and overarching theories as diverse as international social concession theory,[22] integrative social contracts theory (ISCT), CSR meta-regulatory theory,[23] corporate constitutionalism[24] and global popular sovereignty,[25] on the other.

Recasting Sovereignty and Corporate Social Responsibility

The topic of CSR brings together some interwoven strands of political, social and economic justice, which also touch upon deeper issues of sovereignty, democracy, governance, citizenship and morality, amongst others.[26] Even if the supposedly dominant Anglo-American and Anglo-Commonwealth single-theory perspective of shareholder primacy prevails to this point, it still faces major questions now about its frames of reference and its limits, at the same time as it refashions itself from within and responds to conditioning influences and pressures from without. In particular, it must respond one way or another to the many developments worldwide which converge in their promotion of the world's peoples as the ultimate governors, regulators and beneficiaries of systems of market capitalism. In short, this points to the people, and not governments or even TNCs, as the ultimate sources and beneficiaries of all forms of institutional power, especially state and corporate power.

Viewed through the prism of conditions underpinning the exercise of institutional power over others, all theorizing here converges on a common destination. The legitimacy of power to affect others rests upon those people affected by exercises of power and who suffer its consequences having proper avenues of consideration, influence and accountability for their legitimate interests. At its most basic level, the rationale lies in 'recognizing the need to justify the use of political power to all those who are substantially subject to its dominion'.[27] Although even more deliberative forms of dialogue and control between shareholders and corporations can never fully encapsulate the common good, '(t)he argument for extending deliberation to corporations, whose decisions significantly affect people's basic liberties and opportunities in the society' is reflected in the shareholder-focused call of corporate democracy that 'spans the realms of government and civil society by insisting on more public deliberation in both legislatures and corporate boardrooms about the governance, environmental performance, workplace conditions, and investments of large companies', according to deliberative democracy advocates Amy Gutmann and Dennis Thompson.[28]

Moreover, at least some of the values of deliberative democracy (e.g. reciprocity, respect, liberty, opportunity and fairness) and some of its mechanisms (e.g. meaningful democratic engagement and accountability between the rulers and those ruled, mutual reason-giving between institutional power-wielders and citizens, and communication-enabled contestation and deliberation about a plurality of interests) arguably apply beyond the public domain to the corporate and civic domains too, not least in furthering 'the aims of deliberative democracy for society as a whole'.[29] In short, the conditions for the legitimacy of institutional forms of power-wielding are a product of the relation between those who wield power and those who are affected by power, as a complex relation that does not treat the people simply as the passive objects of corporate power as a form of institutional power-wielding. Rather, the people in a variety of individual and collective forms are active subjects in the conferment and use of power. The people are the donees of power to governments who make laws about corporations. The people are influencers of governmental regulation of corporations. The people are participants in broader forms of regulation affecting corporations. The people in the form of shareholders fulfil a societal role as exercisers of corporate discipline and accountability. The people in the form of non-shareholders fulfil a societal role as members of regulatory communities and participants in corporate governance arrangements in particular jurisdictions. And so on.

This grand theme of making people the masters and not the servants of institutional power-wielding permeates exercises of public and corporate power alike, although its implications have both commonalities and differences in each domain. In the governmental domain, for example, we might think that 'the best way to understand government both within nations and globally is through the lens of service', so that government is best theorized as a relationship of service to the people under conditions of interdependence between those ruling and ruled.[30] In the cross-over between the governmental and corporate domains as different societal domains in which different forms of institutional power are exercised over others, we might theorize a social contract between all societal institutions and actors, for example, and hence a correlative social 'licence to operate' for business, or some other justificatory account of corporate democracy and justice. Alternatively, we might view states and companies alike as institutions in which important values of due deliberation, contestation and consideration of interests are engaged – a standpoint shared by deliberative democracy and corporate constitutionalism alike.

The big questions of capitalism, democracy and justice therefore intersect at the point where corporations and markets wield power over citizens' lives for better or for worse, on one hand, and where citizens and their governments wield power over corporations and markets in promoting corporate responsibility and curbing corporate irresponsibility, on the other. The fact that sovereignty of the people has its own controversies, different shades of meaning, and competition with rival conceptions of sovereignty does not detract from the central point of grounding legitimacy for the lawful exercise of state and non-state power over people in preconditions for democratic governance accepted by the people.[31] These themes of sovereignty and power are evident in the vivid depiction of the 21st century corporation by corporate watchdog Ralph Nader, whatever reactions Nader's views might otherwise provoke:[32]

> The corporate supremacists of early-twenty-first-century America are at the pinnacle of their domination over our political economy, our culture, our educational institutions, our choice of technologies, and our foreign and military policies . . . Their concentrated power over all levels of government, their centralized control of the mass media, and their penetration of the minds of youngsters, with daily brain-shredding entertainment by violence and addiction, has made them both the financiers and practitioners of oligarchy and plutocracy.

> Yet, the residual stamina of our weakened democracy still contains the seeds of its own regeneration. Like nature abused by polluters until a tipping point is crossed at which time it turns against its abusers with a ferocity known as the collapse of ecosystems, the citizenry can take and take and take only so much of the humiliating abuses of their work, their dignity. Eventually there must come a point when they will reassert their own sovereignty against the soulless control of those artificial entities that our state governments charter without responsibility or accountability – large corporations.

As a politico-legal concept, sovereignty is now being conceptualized in terms of a triangulation between the conditions that justify international recognition of state-based sovereignty, the conditions for the proper exercise of that sovereignty, and the conditions of mass popular consent underlying it.[33] This reconceptualization of sovereignty finds expression in a variety of forms. It accounts for the limits of nation-state sovereignty that are exposed not only in stripping away sovereignty's conventional dogmas of exclusive vesting, territorial control and indivisible power, but also in contemporary moves towards cross-national integration and supranational jurisdiction (e.g. the EU), authorized international military intervention in state-based human rights violations (e.g. in Kosovo), and international legal debates about the correlation between responsibilities and obligations concerning human rights, for state and non-state actors alike.[34] It underscores points of distinction between what are termed '*opaque* sovereignty' (which treats what happens within a nation-state's borders as exclusively an internal matter of concern), '*translucent* sovereignty' (which permits limited external penetration of national sovereignty, based upon the international community's assessment of the legality of what nation-states do) and '*transparent* sovereignty' (which locates sovereignty's legitimacy dually in a sovereign state's compact with its people as well as with the international community).[35]

Recasting sovereignty is also apparent in the rationales for different manifestations of sovereignty over time, especially modern republican sovereignty.[36] This higher-order enterprise underpins relations between national sovereignty (e.g. the authority of the state), democratic sovereignty (e.g. the law-making sovereignty of elected legislatures) and popular sovereignty (e.g. the people as the ultimate source of all political and legal authority). It is a theme in the reconfiguration of governance and regulation in the global political order to find a place for transnational civil society organizations, amongst others, in international relations, global public policy and transnational business regulation.[37] It underlies the legitimization, democratization, constitutionalization, socialization and even humanitarianization of exercises of both politico-legal and corporate power.[38] It takes legal form in the invocation of 'the people', whether universally in the conditions of human dignity and common morality that support human rights, collectively in the doctrines of common good and public interest underpinning public law and policy, or individually in private law's invigorated concern for individual autonomy, freedom and vulnerability.[39]

It locates ultimate normative force for societal governance and regulation of business in such sources, for example, as the consent of the politically governed, the empowerment of business stakeholders as citizen-regulators, the community's 'licence to operate' for business, and the social contract between members and institutions of communities and whole societies, translated to the international stage in such ideas as ISCT and international concession theory.[40] Refusing to limit society's economic choices to an 'an oppressive, government-run economy and a chaotic and unforgiving capitalism', US President Barack Obama called in his pre-election manifesto for an updated 'social compact to meet the needs of a new century', grounded like the Roosevelt-era New Deal in 'a bargain between government, business, and workers', as well as Roosevelt's understanding that 'capitalism in a democracy required the consent of the people', with correlative implications for the role of government and the people's stake in facilitating and sometimes correcting free-market forces.[41] Here, new relations are fashioned between contemporary forms of capitalism, democracy, and sovereignty. Accordingly, sovereignty's nature and justification must be rethought on a number of levels in the 21st century, not least to take account of shared and collective challenges to orthodox state-based sovereignty from planetary climate change, globalized economies, international terrorism, universalization of human rights, transnational business impact upon humanity, and other challenges of worldwide governance, responsibility and regulation.

Whatever arguments can be made on all sides about free-market globalization, deregulation and privatization in the era of corporate capitalism, the central problem remains one of ensuring that global democratic society gains the advantages of markets without suffering the disadvantages (and limits) of market forces and the capture of governments and populations alike by big business, without the existence of any central world authority charged with this oversight responsibility.[42] 'The mechanisms of national policy and intergovernmental cooperation are poorly suited to governing multinationals in a way that matches the reality of transnationally coordinated economic networks', especially since countries and their leaders 'are tied to domestic policy constituents and constrained by the need not to impinge on other countries' sovereignty', as Halina Ward explains.[43] This connection between the limits of national sovereignty, the gaps and excesses of market forces, and the facilitation of corporate irresponsibility through unbridled and narrowly conceived corporate self-interest underlies many CSR-based criticisms of corporate capitalism, resulting in searches for new regulatory and normative constraints upon corporate use and abuse of power.

According to Princeton University philosopher, Professor Peter Singer, national sovereignty has no intrinsic moral worth, but rather derives its value from 'the role that an international principle requiring respect for national sovereignty plays, in normal circumstances, in promoting peaceful relationships between states' as a 'secondary principle'.[44] Considered from the perspective of the governance, regulatory and responsibility needs of a global community, sovereignty itself can be reoriented away from its traditional emphasis upon respecting the control of nation-states over what happens within their own borders, to embrace a shared responsibility to protect and possibly other responsibilities too, so that '(t)he limits of the state's ability and willingness to protect its people are also the limits of sovereignty'.[45] Analogous arguments might be made that the limits of a corporation's willingness to play its part as an organ of societal governance, regulation and responsibility are the limits of legitimacy for its claim to operate in the interests of its corporate constituency, however that constituency might be defined.

In proposing their programme for sovereignty over global business regulation, international regulatory scholars Professors John Braithwaite and Peter Drahos canvas developments in sovereignty from the Treaty of Westphalia of 1648 onwards, concluding that '(n)ational sovereignty and parliamentary sovereignty were purchased at the price of republican sovereignty of the people, which became progressively more subservient to finance capital', creating conditions that lead to 'the progressive destruction of the sovereignty of citizens by the securitization and corporatization of the world . . . and by its contractualization'.[46] In reconceiving national sovereignty and legislative sovereignty as sovereignties that are 'subordinate' to republican sovereignty of the people, they use republican sovereignty's belief that all organized power must be subject to the sovereignty of the people to aim for 'the republican aspiration of a set of institutional arrangements that provides improved assurance against domination of citizens by concentrations of power, combined with the best feasible mechanisms to give all citizens channels through which they can participate in deliberations over the shape of those arrangements'.[47] Their particular concern lies in the direction of new democratic global decision-making mechanisms, including the possibility of an additional, citizen-elected UN Assembly or even a re-drafted UN Charter by a convention of delegates elected by citizens of the world. The function of such an international body extends beyond mere checks and balances upon other global decision-making institutions, and also forms part of 'a plural web of dialogic influences', in which the organized power of states and corporations interacts with 'a network of assertive and competent social movements – a women's movement, an environment movement, a human rights movement and so on'.[48]

At this point, reconfigured notions of sovereignty interact with global developments related to CSR, such as the rise of cross-sectoral social alliances, governmental and multistakeholder standard-setting, wider meta-regulating influences upon business–society relations, and corporate cooperation in pursuing 'a larger conception of the global public interest'.[49] Indeed, Braithwaite and Drahos emphasize what it means for a citizen-focused account of global business regulation to retake at least some control of that agenda from entrenched state and corporate interests, as follows:[50]

> Our view is therefore that because of capture or corruption of states by business, sometimes reinforced by races-to-the-bottom in the world system motivated by the desire to lower regulatory costs, regulatory standards are very often lower than required for the sovereignty of citizens to secure maximum freedom. We are therefore interested to use our data to illuminate how NGOs might activate webs of global influence to transform races-to-the-bottom to global ratcheting-up of standards. This is not a utopian agenda: our data show that, at least with respect to regulation of the environment, safety and financial security, racheting-up of stand-

ards from a low base is a more dominant dynamic of the late twentieth century than driving them further down . . .

By now it should be clear that there are two major conceptual planks to the consumer movement's global campaigning. One is to ratchet-up regulatory standards where concentrated corporate power has kept those standards lower than undominated analysis and dialogue among citizens reveals to be warranted. The second is to lower prices and increase economic efficiency by championing competition, dismantling monopoly sustained by concentrated corporate power. Together, they offer a regulatory thrust and a deregulatory thrust grounded in *a common republican philosophy of the sovereignty of citizens over domination by corporate and state power.*

Our normative judgment, grounded in a republican concern for freedom as the non-domination of a sovereign people, is that when NGOs campaign to ratchet-up global regulatory standards, they are very often acting in the public interest defined in this republican way.

Of course, doubts can always be raised about the extent to which groups such as NGOs and other 'transnational civil society' (TCS) actors truly represent the public interest, the common good, and civil society.[51] At the same time, '(t)he criticism that civil society activists are unrepresentative deflects hard questions away from the legitimacy of existing political institutions as if they are unquestionably representative, when it is the very unresponsiveness of such institutions that creates the conditions for TCS activism in the first place'.[52] However, at the very least, notions of popular sovereignty parallel on some levels some contemporary conceptions of democracy, which locate its expression not simply in majoritarian democracy, but in the shared enterprise of the three institutional branches of democratic government and a democratically governed people, together honouring the full preconditions for democracy through the interactions of majoritarian rule, parliamentary oversight, electoral democracy, judicial decision-making and citizen engagement and participation.[53]

Conceptual insights and tools already exist in the democratic constitutional foundations of some countries to reconceptualize sovereignty of the people, both collectively (as the ultimate source of national constitutional authority and equal participants with institutional power-wielders in their own governance) and individually (in terms of the foundations of individual human dignity reflected in basic human rights and a country's various legal doctrines, including laws regulating business concern for others).[54] Whatever the limits in extending such ideas from the national stage to a global one, one of the key challenges for 21st century CSR is to relate these questions of sovereignty to the political, regulatory and societal landscapes within which corporations are responsive to transmodal governance, multi-order regulation and inter-related responsibility.

GLOBAL LEGAL AND REGULATORY ARCHITECTURE FOR CORPORATE SOCIAL RESPONSIBILITY

Conceptual Challenges in Recasting and Reforming Corporate Law and Regulation

In the end, a large part of corporate responsibility and governance still remains fundamentally shaped by corporate law and regulation. No major 'reorientation of corporate ends' is possible without reconceptualization and even reconfiguration of the purpose and content of corporate law and regulation.[55] Accordingly, CSR cannot be fully understood or implemented without attention to its legal and regulatory dimensions, given the actual changes and reformatory potential of major CSR-related legal and regulatory initiatives already this century.

The 21st century witnesses closer connections than ever before between conventional corporate responsibility, corporate governance, and CSR, with implications for corporate law and regulation too. Both nationally and internationally, corporate law and governance reform must transcend abstract debates about constituency-based accounts of corporations (e.g. shareholder primacy and stakeholder pluralism), to recast corporate law and governance in terms of the relations between the corporate enterprise, its constituencies, and the surrounding societal and global contexts. As the authors of a 21st century transnational legal account of CSR conclude, '(t)he seven principles [of 'integrated, sustainable decision-making', 'stakeholder engagement', 'transparency', 'consistent best practices', 'the precautionary principle', 'accountability', and 'community investment'] are in fact part of a converging corporate law *lex mercatoria* that, far from erecting shareholder primacy as a standalone concept, situates corporate responsibilities to shareholders within the broader social context in which corporations operate'.[56] For countries in the Anglo-American and Anglo-Commonwealth tradition, this turns debates about corporate and shareholder value towards accounts of corporations that situate them as one system within a variety of systems of interests, norms, and impacts. Only then can corporate law and governance begin to engage fully and transjurisdictionally with increasingly interconnected systems of governance (e.g. global public policy development), regulation (e.g. state and non-state standard-setting), and responsibility (e.g. interdependent responsibility of corporations, markets, and socio-economic systems for sustainable development).

Such a reform impetus can be viewed through the prism of both internal and external pressures upon corporate law and regulation, such as the internal challenge to conventional shareholder-based corporate models in Anglo-American and Anglo-Commonwealth systems by contrarian, progressive, corporate constitutionalist, and other schools of corporate legal and regulatory thinking, as well as the external challenges to corporate democracy by deliberative democracy,[57] monitored democracy,[58] and other evolutions in democratic governance. Either way, corporate law and regulation has no other option other than to engage with the politics of values – a timeless enterprise in which the roles, limits, and relations of governments, markets, and civil society are recast in the wake of each generation's challenges and circumstances. The question is whether or not the global business environment of the 21st century in the aftermath of the GFC offers reasons 'to rethink the role of markets in achieving the public good', especially if there is now a demonstrable risk that '(d)emocratic governance is radically devalued if reduced to the role of handmaiden to the market economy' as Harvard's Professor Sandel argues in the 2009 Reith Lectures.[59]

Orthodox corporate law in the Anglo-American and Anglo-Commonwealth worlds therefore must meet new challenges to its shareholder-centric and market-orientated focus from the different quarters of new corporate legal theory, post-GFC regulatory thinking, and recasted relations between market economies and democratic governance. In addition, it must accommodate new forms of regulation which stem from state and non-state sources and also reflect a broader base of societal values than the norms captured in corporate law alone. Indeed, if the global post-GFC exploration of disconnections between markets and the common good also highlights connections between enduring business profitability and sustainable societies, some rethinking of the place of corporate law and regulation in that landscape is necessary too. Whatever the resultant changes to corporate law on national or international fronts, wider aspects of the external business environment also have a transformative effect upon business, markets, and corporate regulatory systems from within, as exemplified in the literature on corporations as social enterprises, reflexive systems, and 'learning' organizations.[60]

The post-millennial receptivity of corporate law to CSR is starting to differ in important ways from the pre-millennial position. Corporate law and governance are evolving to embrace CSR. For example, human rights concerns present challenges to conventional framing of corporate law largely around the private wealth-generating interests of shareholders, and hence inform much of the contemporary shareholder–stakeholder debate. 'Housing corporate responsibility in corporate law provides an opportunity to mainstream human rights issues into the corporate arena', supported by corporate regulation that requires companies 'to include reference to material non-financial issues, which might include human rights compliance', notes international human rights lawyer, Justine Nolan.[61]

In particular, corporate governance's conventional concern with matters such as shareholder discipline over corporate management, corporate compliance and financially focused risk management and reporting is being joined by corporate governance's emerging concern with wider issues of corporate responsibility and sustainability. To varying degrees, CSR-sensitive elements are working their way into the law and regulation affecting corporations internationally and nationally. Corporate law across multiple jurisdictions is grappling in different ways with the relations between different corporate constituencies, corporate success and the needs of wider society, especially through the infusion of CSR-sensitive elements into the core areas of boardroom and investment decision-making, corporate risk management and business reporting. Business practice worldwide is becoming more sophisticated in its engagement with different manifestations of CSR, self-regulation of CSR, standard-setting on CSR, and use of CSR in strategic management of business–society relations for competitive advantage.

Accordingly, meaningful reform of corporate law and regulation to make companies and their managements more orientated towards CSR can no longer focus simply upon directors' obligations and corporate reporting as the traditional objects of attempts to socialize corporate law. In the absence of proper alignment between a number of systemic elements – namely, public policy and regulation that makes CSR a government priority, a framework of law and regulation that mainstreams CSR in a balance of directive and supportive measures, a range of business–society standard-setting influences, and full business engagement with all of these things – any corporate decision-making, compliance and reporting processes that ostensibly look CSR-sensitive risk falling prey to CSR 'greenwashing'. In that event, these processes pay lip service to CSR and are not productive of meaningful organizational CSR outcomes and CSR public policy goals, thus fuelling anti-CSR criticism of CSR's costs and failures.

At the same time, the design and ideology of corporate law in Anglo-American and Anglo-Commonwealth systems already allows significant scope for CSR-orientated actions by directors, even under the existing law of directors' duties and defences. This result is exemplified in this exchange between the moderator and a senior barrister (Neil Young QC) at a corporate governance forum hosted by the Australian Securities and

Investments Commission in 2008, in the context of a panel discussion about climate change and CSR:[62]

> Moderator: Do directors that take the view that they should take into account corporate social responsibility issues need to be prepared to defend taking that view?
>
> Young: No, I don't think so. I think the law is fairly clear that that kind of judgment would be beyond attack or approach in terms of directors' duties. Directors aren't obliged to take that long-term view but if they do so I don't think they could be attacked on the basis that they're acting otherwise than *bona fide* or in the best interests of the corporation . . . It will be left to the courts but the basic duties at the moment are broadly cast. It's a duty to act *bona fide* in the interest of the corporation and this'll accommodate a board that determines that the best interests of the corporation are to act as a good corporate citizen and adopt 21st century practices in many areas.

Reflecting on the lessons of American and European CSR debates, Lord Wedderburn identifies the democratic imperatives operating upon corporate law and governance as follows:[63]

> The problems of the national and of the multinational corporation are here brought into the same focus. The need is for mechanisms, both internal to and external to the enterprise, through which wider social responsibility can emerge, procedures which will inevitably modify the objective of maximising profit without attempting to replace it at a stroke by some other substantive formula. To this quest both the American and the European debates on corporate social responsibility have contributed . . . Such procedures, though, cannot in a democracy be determined wholly by or within the corporation itself. External processes of rule-making are involved. It is a public, not a private issue of responsibility within society . . . (I)f the law can, or should, no longer assume that profit-maximisation is the only touchstone of corporate responsibility, it is obliged to give to private capital some new guidance, nationally and internationally, on the price which it demands today for that very special privilege.

The pre-millennial debate about corporate law being compartmentalized away from CSR is shifting to a debate about recasting corporate law itself to engage with CSR. For example, the focus of CSR debate related to corporate law is no longer confined mainly to the immunization or penetration of corporate law by CSR considerations, but now also includes the CSR-related interplay between the 'hard' rules of corporate law and the 'soft' norms of other corporate regulation, especially in light of the explosion of significant multi-stakeholder standard-setting initiatives now in play in the CSR arena worldwide. As Professor Stephen Bottomley and Dr Anthony Forsyth conclude in their contribution to one of a wave of 21st century books on CSR from legal and regulatory perspectives, 'much of the action regarding corporate social responsibility therefore occurs outside the parameters of the statutes, and it is in this sense that we can talk about a "new corporate law": a system of corporate regulation that depends as much (if not more) on non-statutory mechanisms and methods, which in many cases can have a more immediate impact on corporate operations'.[64] In short, the 21st century is witnessing a shifting of the regulatory landscape for corporations, from within corporate law and governance as well as from its surrounding environment. As a result, the orientation and content of 21st century corporate law and regulation must move beyond the frames of reference set in classic 20th century corporate debates, says Professor Janet Dine:[65]

> The company becomes very much more complex than a shareholder-driven profit maximisation machine. The resultant company looks very different. What is clear is that, while this under-

standing of companies is nearer the 'real picture' than the stylized vision that we are given by theorists, company law and discussions of corporate governance have not changed to embrace the new reality and remain stuck in the 1930s, debating the consequences of the Berle and Means understanding of separation and control by 'aligning' managers' interests with shareholder interests, rather than addressing the reality of the complex webs of systems of control which make up company decision-making.

The specific public policy goals for good corporate governance, responsibility and sustainability that are developed under whole-of-government policy and regulatory approaches to CSR provide another level on which public interest notions and standards relate back to corporate law and regulation. The law provides existing or potential opportunities for public interest notions to infuse and reform corporate legal doctrines in other ways too. This potential for 21st century CSR-orientated legal reform, at least across Anglo-American, Anglo-European and Anglo-Commonwealth jurisdictions, is evident in a select sample of 21st century corporate law reform suggestions of particular relevance for the CSR themes in this book, as canvassed below.

Bakan's *The Corporation* and Corporate Law Reform

Mass awareness-raising of multinational corporate irresponsibility received a stimulus in the early 21st century through the popular documentary, *The Corporation*, based upon Professor Joel Bakan's best-selling book of the same name. In Professor Bakan's view of the dominant model of Anglo-American corporate law, the corporation is an entity that is structurally designed to pursue shareholder profits above all else.[66] On Bakan's characterization, the prevailing corporate model in the USA and major industrialized nations 'compels executives to prioritise the interests of their companies and shareholders above all others and forbids them from being socially responsible – at least genuinely so'.[67] Accordingly, 'the corporation's fundamental institutional nature' is 'its unblinking commitment to its own self-interest', so that corporate directors and managers 'must always put their corporation's best interests first and not act out of concern for anyone or anything else (unless the expression of such concern can somehow be justified as advancing the corporation's own interest)'.[68] 'Corporations and the culture they create do more than just stifle good deeds – they nurture, and often demand, bad ones', Bakan concludes.[69]

In short, the corporation 'is deliberately programmed, indeed legally compelled, to externalize costs without regard for the harm it may cause to people, communities, and the natural environment', and '(e)very cost it can unload onto someone else is a benefit to itself, a direct route to profit'.[70] Bakan thus depicts the modern corporation as an amoral, profiteering, self-serving, harm-causing organization:[71]

As a psychopathic creature, the corporation can neither recognize nor act upon moral reasons to refrain from harming others. Nothing in its legal make-up limits what it can do to others in pursuit of its selfish ends, and it is compelled to cause harm when the benefits of doing so outweigh the costs. Only pragmatic concern for its own interests and the laws of the land constrain the corporation's predatory instincts, and often that is not enough to stop it from destroying lives, damaging communities, and endangering the planet as a whole . . . All the bad things that happen to people and the environment as a result of corporations' relentless and legally compelled pursuit of self-interest are thus neatly categorized by economists as externalities – literally, other people's problems.

In Bakan's eyes, this structurally produced corporate irresponsibility needs to be reigned in by new forms of governance and regulatory controls upon corporations. His radical reform suggestions all stem from his stance that root and branch reform of the structural design of corporations and the corporate regulatory regimes surrounding them is the only way forward, especially in light of the deep problems stemming from 'the corporation's legal mandate to pursue, without exception, its own self-interest'.[72] In short, his suggested regulatory reforms are to: (i) reinvigorate government regulation as the principal tool for making corporations serve the public interest; (ii) toughen policy and regulatory consequences for socially irresponsible corporations and their directors; (iii) infuse environmental and other laws with the precautionary principle of non-harm; (iv) prevent capture of official regulators by business; (v) improve local community involvement in corporate regulation; and (vi) enhance protective and monitoring capacities for third parties and representative groups affected by corporations.[73]

To strengthen political democracy, for example, he urges electoral reform to re-engage citizens in democratic politics, together with eradication of the ways in which he thinks corporations exert undue influence on politics, beyond a reasonable role in expressing business concerns and cooperating in public policy initiatives, through their governmental lobbying, political donations, campaign financing, interchange of personnel and public–private partnerships.[74] In the community sphere, he calls for removal of corporate sponsorship with the capacity to exploit for corporate purposes organizations that he thinks should be protected by public regimes, such as schools and universities, public and cultural institutions, and essential community services.[75] In the international domain, he recommends that nations work together to transform what he sees as the neoliberal politico-economic ideological agenda and practices of supranational institutions (e.g. the WTO, IMF and World Bank) 'away from market fundamentalism and its facilitation of deregulation and privatisation'.[76]

Bakan is not alone in urging radical reform of the status quo in corporate law and practice. Others who see no alternative to design-level surgery for orthodox corporate law recognize the importance of building a platform for CSR upon a baseline of fundamental change in corporate law itself:[77]

> Externally, corporations must move from being the private domain of shareholders to being responsible to the democratic order . . . In the long run, it won't be enough to rely on voluntary initiatives, toothless codes of conduct, enlightened leadership, or reforms that proceed company by company. We must ultimately change the fundamental governing framework for all corporations in law . . . The belief seems to be that if we put managers through ethics courses, write voluntary codes, teach environmental stewardship, and encourage stakeholder management, we can somehow counteract the overwhelming legal and structural power of shareholders. But we can't . . . When a problem is supported by or caused by law, the solution must be in the law. Today, shareholder primacy is in our law . . . And legal mechanisms can only be counteracted by other legal mechanisms.

Stiglitz and Global Multinational Regulatory Reform

Nobel Prize-winning economist and globalization scholar, Joseph Stiglitz, includes CSR reform as one prong of his five-pronged reform agenda for improving the alignment between the 'private incentives' driving multinational corporations and their 'social costs and benefits'.[78] First, given the inherent limits on what the CSR movement can achieve on its own, he recommends raising standards of socially responsible business behaviour through enhanced regulation, to stop 'a race to the bottom' by those businesses whose irresponsibility or treatment of CSR as a PR problem appears to secure them some short-term competitive advantage.[79] Secondly, in terms of limiting the abuse of multinational corporate power, especially in developing economies, he urges a supra-national solution (in place of piecemeal national solutions) to the problem of global cartels, monopolies and other anti-competitive behaviour, with 'a global competition law and a global competition authority to enforce it'.[80]

Thirdly, he recommends expanding corporate governance law and regulation to enhance the accountability of companies and corporate executives to stakeholders, in ways that responsibly walk the fine line between corporate wealth-generating accountability to shareholders and due accommodation of the interests of others adversely (although lawfully) affected by corporate activity.[81] Importantly, this includes better mechanisms for remedying and compensating in a company's home country the victims of corporate irresponsibility in its host sites of operation, especially in developing countries. The limited success of the US Alien Tort Claims Act in producing court decisions in favour of claims by victims of actionable corporate irresponsibility abroad underscores this gap in transnational corporate accountability. 'Of course, corporations would like to restrict such suits, but, if we are to make globalization work, there is a need to establish such provisions worldwide', argues Stiglitz.[82] Similarly, the complementary measure of making companies choose between allowing adverse judgments of courts in their host countries of operations to be enforceable in their home jurisdictions, or else submitting to judgment afresh according to the standards of their home jurisdictions, is characterized here as 'simply one of the prices that one has to, and should, pay if one wants to do business in a country – including, in particular, extracting that country's natural resources'.[83]

In other words, the shared interest of responsible TNCs, governments and global citizens in harnessing the benefits of globalization while limiting its costs means that the architecture of successful globalization is likely to include some institutional features of benefit to TNCs (e.g. safeguards for market competition) as well as some institutional features which they might regard as increasing the costs and risks of business (e.g. increased avenues of liability). As with many business reactions to the UN Norms, business acceptance of enhanced regulatory accountability is likely to be predicated upon an overall package of institutional measures with perceived correlative benefits for business too. Such an overall package of measures forms part of the global CSR meta-framework outlined earlier in this chapter.

His fourth major prong of TNC-focused reform is 'the creation of international legal frameworks and international courts – as necessary for the smooth functioning of the global economy as federal courts and national laws are for national economies'.[84] This reform includes correlative innovations such as global class actions in international or national courts, as well as a system of internationally subsidized legal aid and assistance for claims based upon corporate activity in developing countries.[85]

Finally, as a twin set of safeguards against corporate misbehaviour, he recommends a comprehensive global net of legal prohibitions against foreign corruption and bribery of officials, together with reducing the capacity for hiding ill-gotten gains of corporate misdeeds by broadening the rules against bank secrecy internationally beyond the inroads already established for the investigation and prosecution of terrorism.[86]

All of these reforms are responsive to the central undercurrent of Stiglitz's argument: '(t)he lesson here . . . is simple: incentives matter, and governments and the international community must work harder to ensure that the incentives facing corporations are better aligned with those they touch, especially the less powerful in the developing world'.[87] This reinforces the wider systemic point that successful CSR reform ultimately rests upon a well-aligned and balanced package of institutional measures of corporate responsibility, governance and regulation both nationally and internationally, the transparent costs and benefits of which for businesses, the interests they serve and the communities in which they operate are readily apparent to all.

Villiers' Approach to Integrating National and International Legal Reform

Despite the normative case for CSR, its progress is hindered not only by the orthodox structure of corporate law, but also by problems of definition, its presumed voluntariness, the multiplication of standards, the lack of adequate checks and balances in the externally regulated business environment, and transnational corporate power's constraining influence upon state regulation of corporate use and abuse of power.[88] To address such concerns through integrated national and international legal reform, building especially upon UN human rights reform proposals, Professor Charlotte Villiers suggests a range of measures in curbing transnational corporate irresponsibility.[89]

On her view, these measures include: (i) the harmonization and rationalization of the multiplicity of CSR standards globally; (ii) the provision of 'extraterritorial and universal jurisdiction where corporate abuses occur outside the home state or by subsidiaries of a parent company'; (iii) the alignment of national regimes of civil and criminal law with international standards of redress for infliction of corporate harm; and (iv) the expansion of actionable corporate harm to embrace corporate complicity and wrongdoing by companies and those associated with them (e.g. state partners, corporate subsidiaries and supply/distribution chain members). They also include (v) the integration of 'hard' and 'soft' law measures within tightened enforcement regimes; (vi) the exceptional penetration of the corporate veil where justified (e.g. long-term liability to mass victims of corporate negligence); (vii) the 'proceduralization' of mechanisms of dialogue, consideration, representation and participation for corporate stakeholders; and (viii) the structural reinforcement of this internal 'proceduralization' by externally set CSR outcomes and sanctions for corporate failures to achieve them (e.g. 'the threat of closure for companies who are identified as failing to act within the CSR boundaries').

Such measures reflect a view of both the real risks and incidences of corporate irresponsibility and the relation between sovereign states, markets, and democratic accountability that travels beyond the legal status quo for corporate governance and responsibility. As with other reforms canvassed in this chapter, the legitimacy and necessity for such remedial measures ultimately rest upon socio-ethical justifications and evidence which are inherently contestable. Underpinning this view is a 21st century transnational business environment in which national corporate law and regulation must connect more fully than in the past with public policy, democratic accountability, and multi-faceted regulatory oversight concerning corporations across the globe. Putting these suggested measures into practice will be easier within an internationally accepted CSR meta-framework which does not focus unevenly on one aspect (e.g. corporate liability) at the expense of others (e.g. corporate advantage).

Transnational Legal Reform Progress According to Kerr, Janda, and Pitts

According to the transnational legal assessment of CSR commentators Michael Kerr, Richard Janda, and Chip Pitts, a significant gap still remains between shareholder primacy's dominant grip upon national corporate regulatory systems across the globe and the reforms urged in the CSR-related legal literature. In particular, this gap between CSR aspirations and business reality is reflected to one degree or another in reforms which are grounded in socialization of directors' duties and boardroom governance, enhancement of corporate transparency and disclosure, imposition of extra-territorial and networked liability for transnational corporate irresponsibility, sensitization of business to public policy goals, incorporation of CSR concerns within trade and investment regimes, and development of more sophisticated CSR standard-setting and architecture on the international legal stage.[90]

Still, in line with the growing body of transnational CSR-related law and regulation canvassed in Chapters 5 and 6 and available for regulatory modelling across corporate regulatory systems, some narrowing of the gap between theory and practice is occurring. In their tracking of such developments, these CSR commentators point to significant evolutions in corporate thinking, regulation, and practice across many corporate regulatory systems, for example, towards stakeholder-sensitive corporate obligations and governance, mandated CSR-related corporate reporting, national regulation of multinational corporate responsibility for environmental and human rights abuses, heightened regulatory attention to the nexus between sustainable societies and sustainable profits and markets, and development of regulatory CSR tools and standards such as socio-environmental and human rights assessments, business supply and distribution chain requirements, and market indexes and corporate rating systems.[91]

In terms of global legal architecture for CSR, these CSR commentators foresee further progress on the twin fronts of 'continued rationalisation and evolution of soft law global instruments and multi-stakeholder "voluntary" initiatives' and a strengthened global legal framework largely of 'a meta-regulatory form whereby governments set or endorse the relevant standards but allow for different paths to implementing those standards'.[92] Although the world still lacks the collective political will and mass popular consensus at this early stage of the 21st century for a series of CSR-related international agreements, they view the progress made by the UNSRSG towards a global human rights framework for business and the CSR standard-setting by major world institutions such as the UN as together providing the stimulus for national CSR law and regulation and the groundwork for international CSR agreements to come.[93] Here again, CSR's national and global legal architecture is heavily dependent upon CSR meta-regulation in its design and implementation, thereby transcending the division between mandatory and voluntary corporate regulation and also bridging the gap between corporate regulatory theory and practice.[94]

Greenfield's Contrarian and Progressive Approach to Corporate Law Reform

Contrarian corporate law scholars such as Professor Kent Greenfield claim that 'most of us in the United States, as well as many people throughout the world, would be better off if corporate law were different'.[95] In addition to making the provocative claim that the terrorist attacks of September 11 emerged from a context shaped by flaws in the orthodox system of corporate law and governance, as well as from failures in the market for air travel in producing what society now needs in safeguarding passengers on flights, Greenfield highlights the societal and global significance of corporate law in these terms:[96]

> Corporate law is a big deal . . . Why should anyone care who does not teach or work in the area? The answer is that corporate law determines the rules governing the organization, purposes, and limitations of some of the largest and most powerful institutions in the world. The largest corporations in the world have the economic power of nations. By establishing the obligations and priorities of companies and their management, corporate law affects everything from employees' wage rates (whether in Silicon Valley or Bangladesh), to whether companies will try to skirt environmental laws, to whether they will tend to look the other way when doing business with governments that violate human rights.

'What is crucial is the question of how we construct a legal framework for corporations that maximizes the probability that businesses will serve the interests of society as a whole', urges Greenfield, in proposing new principles and policies as the underlying basis for corporate law.[97] In many ways, the transformation of 21st century corporate law is one of the most important arenas for transforming corporate responsiveness to systems of governance, regulation and responsibility. Our conceptions of the good society provide an overriding justification for our conceptions of good corporate responsibility and governance in society. The values and interests of a good society do and should underlie corporate law as much as they underlie other areas of law. 'Only after we recognize the place of corporate law as one small element of a larger political landscape can we then craft a bundle of legal rules and regulatory programs that are likely to move us toward our collective goals', advises Greenfield, adding that 'corporate law, just like every other area of common and statutory law, is predicated upon our collective political decisions about what we want our society to look like'.[98] In terms that harken back to the deep debate over the appropriateness for 21st century conditions of a basic corporate model developed centuries ago, Greenfield argues that corporate law's mandate for directors 'to reduce all decisions to a solitary standard: the financial return to the shareholders in terms of dollars . . . is no more rational in the boardroom of a twenty-first century corporation than in the factories of a nineteenth-century English milltown [whereas] (a) more sophisticated model of decision making, on the other hand, would recognize both the humanity of the decision makers and the humanity of stakeholders by asking corporate directors to do more than simply reduce every decision to a financial one'.[99]

Greenfield recommends a number of corporate law reforms to enhance good corporate responsibility and governance. Doctrines relating to corporate capacity and power could be used to constrain corporations from engaging in illegal and unlawful behaviour at home and abroad, in ways that go to the heart of the use and abuse of corporate power in society-damaging ways as a central concern of corporate law itself, and not simply as a topic of concern in how the company treats different groups of shareholders, for example, or for remedying outside corporate law in criminal, tort and other regulatory laws.[100] In terms of an emerging international law of corporate responsibility, for example, this could mean 'that corporations have the duty, as a matter of domestic *corporate* law, to act lawfully even in foreign nations', as questions of legality would go to the heart of the proper use of corporate power as a matter of domestic corporate law, bolstered by foreign corporate liability regimes, international legal norms applicable to individuals and corporations as well as nation-states, and correlative enhancement of shareholder-based discipline over companies for their activities at home and abroad.[101] These reforms would have correlative implications for the grounds for breaching a director's duty of care, the preconditions for shareholder remedies, the basis for actions by the company against relevant corporate actors, and the foundations for state intervention in corporate affairs.[102]

Corporate governance is framed by Greenfield in terms of 'methods of decision making that offer procedural fairness among the various stakeholders', within a reconceptualized vision of corporate law committed to the sustainable creation and fair distribution of corporate wealth.[103] As sustaining the profitable existence of a company over time is not an end in itself, and worthy of societal support within corporate law and elsewhere only if sustaining the corporation also sustains society, corporate law must accommodate a full and transparent account of all costs and benefits of corporate activity, from both corporate and societal perspectives, as 'the key to sustainability is for those who contribute to the firm to receive the benefits (or suffer the costs) of the firm in rough proportion to their contributions'.[104] In turn, this requires a reconfiguration of corporate law so that 'directors need to be held to a fiduciary obligation to all the firm's stakeholders that varies according to the nature of the contributions of the stakeholders to the success of the firm', in ways that are amenable to some pre-existing conceptualizations of directors' duties as duties owed to the company and not to any particular corporate constituency, but with bolstered participatory, deliberative and enforcement mechanisms for relevant stakeholding groups and not just shareholders.[105]

Going hand in hand with reconceptualized corporate fiduciary duties would be the reconfiguration of the largely process-based grounds for reviewing corporate decisions, consistently with much pre-existing law (with its notions of due consideration, expert advice, and so on), but reoriented towards a fuller recognition of 'the contributions of all the firm's stakeholders' and of the corresponding interests costs and benefits, together with correlative stakeholder enforcement mechanisms.[106] Taking into account the social costs of corporate activity in business models and regulation also promotes the regulatory value of transparency. Once again, this is not simply an academic argument, as influential members of the investment community also point to the importance of making transparent the connections between the true costs, benefits and impacts of corporate activity:[107]

> As a long-term diversified investor, we oppose companies behaving in a way which knowingly passes costs on to other companies or to the taxpayer, and as such is socially or environmentally unacceptable, or unethical. It makes no sense if business success is achieved by creating other costs ('externalising costs') which the beneficial owners of companies will ultimately pay for.

> In summary, a company's primary consideration should be the generation of long-term shareholder value, and this should be based on appropriate financial disciplines, competitive advantage, and within a framework which is economically, ethically and socially responsible and sustainable.

None of this could happen overnight. Measures designed to promote truthful and accurate corporate disclosure to investors and corporate regulators in the marketplace could also provide the impetus and perhaps even models for enhancing full and truthful disclosure to employees and other corporate stakeholders, not least as part of a wider corporate law project of increasing the quality of corporate deliberation, communication, and empowerment.[108] 'The contours of these procedural characteristics would have to be developed over time by common law courts just as the procedural requirements under traditional doctrines have been spelled out over time by common law courts', notes Greenfield.[109] Similarly, any increase in the complexity or costs of enhanced stakeholder involvement for boards or shareholders would need to be assessed from the overall systemic perspective of 'whether the increase of monitoring costs to shareholders would be offset by the decrease in monitoring costs to other stakeholders'.[110] In short, Greenfield argues that most of his reform suggestions 'would require only minor changes in current law' and 'are readily achievable: relaxing the profit maximization norm; ending Delaware's dominance; creating an antifraud law for workers; requiring directors to owe a fiduciary duty to workers; enforcing corporations' duty to obey the law'.[111]

Mitchell's Solutions for 'Corporate Irresponsibility'

Similarly, George Washington University's Professor Lawrence Mitchell advocates reforms that mainly work within the existing corporate regulatory system, or else tinker with it largely at its margins, notwithstanding his acceptance that 'the unconstrained corporate ability to profit any way you can leads to immoral and irresponsible behaviour'.[112] The problem he diagnoses is one of short-term maximization of stock prices as the pervasive motivator and measure of the corporate enterprise's success. In his eyes, the basic cause of that problem lies in the existing corporate legal structure's encouragement of management-orientated short-termism and the externalization of corporate costs and other corporate harms it produces for society. In short, the tunnel vision of short-term profits for shareholder gain threatens the welfare of important corporate stakeholders (notably employees and consumers) and even companies themselves.[113]

His solution lies mainly in the justification of normative changes to business behaviour, bolstered by some legal reforms that all promote a more long-term view of corporations for those who manage and invest in them. On this account, part of the solution lies in giving boards the freedom to act and decide responsibly, uninhibited by the constraints of short-termism and excessive shareholder control. 'A long-term focus, which includes not only investing for the future but caring that profits are made responsibly and morally, is good not only for society, but also for business', he argues.[114] This primarily requires reforms that enable both boards and investors to focus on 'long-term sustainability' instead of 'short-term stock price maximization', by freeing boards from stockholder control (including the option of creating self-perpetuating boards), creating taxation incentives for stockholders and corporate executives alike to retain stock ownership over the long term, and changing financial reporting standards and practices to reflect long-term rather than short-term performance analysis and data.[115]

In this way, Mitchell seeks to reorientate the corporate structure towards the long term, while retaining the efficiency of centralised management, but with a newly structured focus and accountability for the means that management chooses in the pursuit of profit.[116] 'The basic idea . . . is to let managers manage; trust them to run their corporations in responsible and accountable ways, taking into account the moral and social propriety of their behaviour as well as the profitability of their actions', he concludes.[117] In addition, unless society successfully frees corporate executives 'from the need to be slaves to the market, to be chained to the bottom line', through the legal and normative changes he suggests, the only other possible futures in Mitchell's eyes 'are our eventual self-destruction or extensive regulation of business by government'.[118]

The Report of the Citizen Works Corporate Reform Commission

In The Report of the Citizen Works Corporate Reform Commission, Lee Drutman and Charlie Cray crystallize 'two possible approaches to changing corporate governance to make corporations more socially responsible'.[119] One approach involves working with the mechanisms of shareholder primacy and control to make corporations and those who manage them more socially and environmentally responsible, while the alternative approach strikes at the heart of shareholder primacy itself in its reformatory impact upon systems of corporate governance. Drutman and Cray offer the following reforms to mitigate shareholder primacy's downside in terms of the social and environmental costs of corporate responsibility:[120]

> As we see it, there are a few different approaches to addressing the problem of shareholder primacy, each of which has both promise and shortcomings. One is to change the laws that define the duties and responsibilities of the corporation, its directors, and its officers. Another is to institutionalize various stakeholders who represent noninvestor concerns in the corporate governance structure, possibly through broader stakeholder ownership. A third is to develop and promulgate new legal theories of corporate governance that take into account a more expansive purpose of the corporation. A fourth is to change the attitudes and expectations of investors so that there is less external pressure on corporations to maximize profit. The final approach we offer is to simply require corporations to disclose all their activities publicly instead of just disclosing their finances, essentially forcing them to evaluate their performance based on a number of nonfinancial indicators, and thus giving concerned shareholders a greater ability to measure a broader set of corporate behaviors.

Describing these reforms as 'mutually reinforcing', Drutman and Cray also acknowledge that even 'rewiring the corporation to make it more accountable is ultimately a poor substitute for establishing meaningful citizen control over corporations through democratically created laws'.[121] As with all of the reform suggestions canvassed in this chapter, the deeper justification of each reform is integrally connected to the underlying account of corporate responsibility, governance and sustainability from which it proceeds. By conceptualizing 'the people's business' as a reinvigorated form of 'citizen sovereignty' which remakes corporations as the people's 'servants' instead of their 'masters', Drutman and Cray outline a foundational rationale that 'the most effective way to control corporations will be to restore citizen democracy and to reclaim the once widely accepted principle that corporations are but creatures of the state, chartered under the premise that they will serve the public good, and entitled to only those rights and privileges granted by citizen-controlled governments', as a means to the end of ensuring 'the just and sustainable economy that we seek, an economy driven by the values of human life and community and democracy instead of the current suicide economy driven only by the relentless pursuit of financial profit at any cost'.[122] This approach resonates with earlier discussions of corporate democracy and popular sovereignty.

Corporate Constitutionalism's Recasting and Reform of Corporate Decision-making

The perspectives of CSR meta-regulation, corporate constitutionalism and other theories converge at the point of highlighting how and why public values and private self-interest are both implicated in the corporate enterprise and the legal architecture surrounding corporate governance (e.g. compliance systems, sustainability reporting requirements and stakeholder-sensitive directors' duties).[123] As discussed previously, Professor Bottomley's account of corporate constitutionalism reconceives shareholders in terms of their roles and interests as corporate members, and not simply as providers of financial capital, with consequential implications for the 'accountability', 'deliberation' and 'contestability' of corporate decisions. Here, the focus is upon the implications for CSR-related reform.

If, consistently with the model of shareholder primacy, a broader conception of corporate responsibility and governance is achievable that better accords with the values truly underlying that model, says Bottomley, corporate laws and practices can and must adapt accordingly. Bottomley advances the possibility of extending the catalogue of people covered by directors' duties to include more than just shareholders, which he concedes goes into the deeper territory of stakeholder theories and CSR.[124] However, this expansion is a controlled rather than an open-ended one. On this account, it does not open the way to multi-fiduciary substantive duties and obligations to multiple stakeholders. It simply acknowledges what is now enshrined in UK corporate law and US corporate constituency laws, as well as widely accepted in Australian corporate law – namely, that the orthodox corporate regulatory model permits rather than prohibits due consideration of non-shareholder interests – and that more attention needs to be given to *voluntary* means of encouraging corporate responsibility to be responsive to the requirements of corporate constitutionalism.[125] Put that way, the viability of CSR rests upon a foundation of shareholder-engaging reinvigoration of corporate responsibility and governance, in a form that corporate executives can embrace despite its difference from the prevailing legal and economic model of corporations, but still in synchronicity with its underlying motivations.[126]

Indeed, with direct reference to CSR in mind, Bottomley expresses a related challenge for 21st century corporate law, regulation and practice in these terms:[127]

> (A)s important as issues of corporate social responsibility are, they must be built upon a robust and searching examination of the ways in which the role of shareholders can be revitalised . . . By giving greater attention to the role of shareholders as members of (as opposed to their role as investors in) a corporation, by encouraging and then taking seriously their input through processes of deliberation, by investigating the use of corporate interest groups, it is quite feasible that shareholders – of all types – can be a means whereby the concerns and interests of corporate employees, of tort victims, of consumers and others can be factored into corporate decisions. Corporate law should encourage shareholders to be active as members, to consider and make use of the options offered by deliberation and contestation rather than those offered by passivity and exit. In this way shareholders can act as conduits to introduce other ideas and interests into corporate deliberations.

In this context, one option which garners support from the different perspectives of corporate constitutionalism,[128] business meta-regulation[129] and corporate democratization involves the formalization of meaningful accommodation of interplays between shareholder and non-shareholder interests through the device of 'corporate interest groups' (CIGs). Mirroring existing manifestations of 'intermediary activity' in corporate affairs, such as shareholder-initiated meeting proposals and intra-company alliances of shareholders and employees on corporate issues, these CIGs can act as both 'information intermediaries' and 'deliberative intermediaries' in corporate affairs, informing the consideration and contestability of collective corporate interests through the active involvement of shareholders as corporate members, but with enhanced mechanisms of representation, support and engagement in corporate meetings, proxy voting and other aspects of corporate governance.[130] Again, this resonates with deeper issues of the legitimization, democratization, constitutionalization and socialization of corporate power, as reflected in the thematic underpinnings of corporate constitutionalism itself.

Dine's Reformation of 21st Century Corporate Governance and Boardroom Oversight

A limited conception of corporate responsibility and governance, which focuses upon 'mechanisms for aligning the governance of the company with shareholders' interest in profit maximisation', conflicts with the broader vision of corporate responsibility and governance offered by Professor Janet Dine, under which a broader notion of regulation ensures that 'companies have proper systems in place to ensure their compliance with the requirements of society generally'.[131] One of the constant themes of this book is that part of this corporate complexity can usefully be captured through the prism of corporate responsiveness to wider systems of governance, regulation and responsibility within which companies operate.

Professor Dine crystallizes both the present implications and the possible law reform opportunities that flow from these developments, as follows. Corporate cultures are changing in response to new forms of regulation, producing a 'new culture of risk assessment and required response by setting up implementation systems'.[132] In turn, this means that 'directors' duties are being reformulated to cover devising and supervising systems of risk control, requiring them to assess the risk to the company of failing systems'.[133] Instead of viewing business regulation of both old and new kinds simply as an unwanted but unavoidable cost of doing business, producing the lowest common denominator response of the minimum compliance required by law, many corporations increasingly see the interests behind such regulation as 'an integrated part of the corporate objective' in a way that inserts those stakeholding interests into the corporation's strategizing, deliberations and actions from this enhanced perspective of 'risk assessment and required response', so that 'it is those risks that are to be weighed, not the moral or social claims of interest groups'.[134] Where the risks to companies and those affected by them are significant and coincide, policy reform questions arise about the appropriate means of enforcing this duty of directors to implement proper systems of risk control or alternatively for compensating those harmed by this failure of duty.[135]

Other innovations in corporate liability and remedies might also be necessary, on this risk-based account of corporate and boardroom responsibility. As a counter-balance to conventional regulatory and corporate power blocs, public interest groups (such as environmental agencies concerned about effectively regulated environmental protection and employees concerned about effectively regulated workplace health and safety) might compete to be given officially sanctioned regulatory responsibility to seek enforcement of proper controls upon the human rights, environmental and social responsibilities of corporations, at least in cases of clear breakdown, regulatory capture or corruption.[136] Conventional grounds for removing unfit directors might be recast to include, within the relevant notion of unfitness, elements that focus upon '(p)utting the company at risk from failure to create other systems protective of groups other than shareholders', with flow-on implications for compensatory legal remedies too.[137] Similarly, corporate law's rules preventing conduct of a corporation's affairs in ways that are unfairly prejudicial to members could be widened to include other groups as well.[138] In other words, viewing boardroom responsibility from this overarching risk-focused perspective opens the way to recasting other aspects of corporate law and regulation too.

Hence, corporate responsibility and governance are reconditioned through the interplay of these internal risk controls and new forms of external stakeholder involvement in regulating corporations, as described by Dine in these terms:[139]

> The point is to create a company law right to force companies, via their managers, to take on board the responsibilities inherent in the power that a company's property rights bestow on it . . . Company responsibility for systems would extend to responsibility for suppliers, subsidiaries and all over whom the property right gives significant dominion, whether at home or abroad . . . In this way, it is suggested, the vision of companies can be changed and broadened . . . However, the possibility of extending enforcement measures to groups other than shareholders would mean that the narrow objectives of service to shareholders would be changed and a more inclusive culture would understand that the objectives of society and the objectives of companies must be made to work in some degree of harmony.

Accordingly, we might anticipate the eventual development of 'a risk assessment framework which [opens] up the discourse to value rather than price on the basis of an understanding of the multiple consequences of differing actions and inactions, including the type of society which is implicit in the choices made' – a move that itself reopens debates about economic, distributive and social justice amidst 'the complexity of the interrelations between the world trade system and ecological concerns'.[140] This reflects the corporate reality that the shift to corporate responsibility and sustainability 'will be unlikely to be effective unless mechanisms to achieve sustainable development can become part of the internal governance systems of companies rather than outside encouragement', which can be given impetus only if 'the underlying social understanding of the purpose companies serve changes fundamentally'.[141]

In describing what a revitalized and global form of 'concession' theory might offer to the regulation and practice of TNCs, Professor Dine urges a forward-looking policy and regulatory approach. Under this approach, the exercise of state power over corporations reflects the substance of societal expectations, those expectations inform a developing CSR jurisprudence that transforms itself from vague and aspirational CSR goals into more concrete outcomes, and those outcomes then infuse 'the decision-making machinery of a company', in ways which go beyond mere corporate PR:[142]

> The first step is to identify the source of the 'concession' under which TNCs operate in a global market. It is then necessary to attempt to identify agreed norms which should be applied, and finally to identify an enforcement mechanism which might effectively deliver compliance . . . Much work remains to be done to identify a sound basis for responsibility, to identify the values that should be espoused by an international concession theory and to feed them into systems of corporate governance.

This suggestion fits a meta-regulatory framework for CSR and TNCs. It walks the fine line between a completely state-mandated and law-driven approach to TNCs, and an approach that exposes TNCs in uncontrolled fashion to societal expectations, governance needs and other influences, especially of the kind feared by critics of the new global order of governance and regulation involving civil society.[143] The relevant control here comes through the way in which those influences are related to TNCs, matched by the control that TNCs exert in shaping and responding to these influences.

At a broader level, the enterprise of devising new accounts of corporate responsibility, governance and sustainability that meet the global realities of TNCs is an enterprise in which internationally based 'concession' theories are joined also by other 'justice theories that have an appropriate application to corporate globalization and capitalism as it exists worldwide', whether those justice theories are framed in terms of Rawlsian principles of justice,[144] just conditions for human flourishing,[145] 'prudential justice' or some other fundamental account of justice.[146] Indeed, we might even transcend conventional accounts of social contracts between business and others in society to embrace a new global vision of societal compacts in the 21st century era of interdependent systems of governance, regulation and responsibility, addressing shared concerns of climate change, sustainable development, universalization of human rights, poverty eradication, and their ilk.

Common Themes in the Reform of Corporate Law and Regulation to Improve Corporate Social Responsibility

The corporate legal and regulatory reforms canvassed above work with the presumed status quo under the shareholder primacy norm, incrementally develop or modify it, radically reshape it, or call for its replacement by largely untested alternatives (as is the nature of much reform). Perhaps surprisingly, quite a significant number of reform suggestions can be achieved within the frameworks of existing legal doctrines and business practices, through recasting, new applications or minor modifications (e.g. Greenfield, Villiers, Mitchell, Bottomley, and Drutman and Cray). At a wider level, many of these reform suggestions reflect dissatisfaction with the corporate status quo's capacity to capture fully the needs of corporate responsiveness to systems of trans-modal governance, multi-order regulation and inter-related responsibility in meeting the unfolding societal and global challenges of this century which CSR addresses.

Some common themes emerge from this sample and related reforms in earlier chapters. First and foremost, one strong undercurrent is that individual reform suggestions must be positioned within an overall justificatory account of corporate responsibility and governance, as well as a balanced package of measures which reflects a holistic view of the business impact of enhancing CSR through a combination of governmental, business and community means. Aspects of this theme are reflected in suggestions to combine enhanced business regulation with correlative business and market incentives promoting those regulatory ends, such as streamlining the overall business reporting burden while strengthening CSR-related disclosure in particular. Aspects of it are also glimpsed in the recognition by official 21st century CSR inquiries that the traditional law-based focus on debates about socializing directors' duties and corporate reporting obligations must be extended to embrace other governmental, business and community avenues of pursuing CSR too.[147]

Holistic approaches are evident in the overall balance between mandated reform of corporate decision-making mechanisms for CSR ends and otherwise sensitizing corporate decision-making mechanisms to the moderating regulatory influence of interest group involvement of various kinds (e.g. Parkinson, Parker, Bottomley, Dine, Kerr et al, Drutman and Cray, and Villiers). As many of these reform suggestions also mean increases of one kind or another in national and international business regulation (e.g. Bakan, Stiglitz, Greenfield, Kerr et al, Zerk, and Villiers), there is a need to locate such regulatory enhancements in an overall system of regulatory improvements that is sensitive to both business costs (e.g. increased business liability and risk) and business benefits (e.g. enhanced safeguarding of free trade and open competition), both individually and as corporate members of wider systems.

Secondly, at the level of international business regulation, various reform suggestions cover enhanced international and transnational architecture for regulating legal gaps in business accountability across both home and host countries of business operations (e.g. Bakan, Stiglitz, Greenfield, Zerk, and Villiers), improving international and intergovernmental institutional support (e.g. Bakan, Kerr et al, Stiglitz, and Villiers), and tightening international protection for fair trade, open competition and other foundations of efficient and effective business for social ends (e.g. Bakan, and Stiglitz). Inevitably, part of this enterprise also looks to an emerging international law of corporate responsibility, with elements that extend beyond the current state of international law in offering both incentives for corporate responsibility and disincentives for corporate irresponsibility. This dovetails with ongoing developments in international law and governance at the interface of business and human rights.[148]

Thirdly, at the level of national corporate regulatory regimes, many of these reform suggestions concentrate upon modifying corporate law's structures and doctrines in removing the evils of short-termism (e.g. Mitchell, and Deakin), recasting and opening up corporate law to other influences and their flow-on implications for ancillary corporate law doctrines (e.g. Parkinson, Greenfield, Dine, and Zerk), and making corporations amenable to a broader panorama of legal and regulatory influences beyond state-based rule-making and standard-setting (e.g. Parker, Bottomley, Dine, Kerr et al, Zerk, and Villiers). Some reconceptualization of the basis of directors' duties is involved, so that the performance of directors' duties to corporations becomes more attuned than currently to a broader range of societal influences (e.g. Parkinson, Greenfield, Dine, Zerk, Kerr et al, and Drutman and Cray), without degenerating into the traps of infinite stakeholder obligations, irreconcilable conflict over multi-stakeholder goals and unworkable boardroom decision-making frameworks. Very little reform can happen in practice without some responsibility for change being sheeted home to corporate directors and managers, especially in terms of aligning societal regulatory influences more closely with the management, accountability and other organizational structures within which they work.

Fourthly, there is a recurring theme of opening up corporate decision-making structures and processes to a broader range of informational bases, interest group dynamics, corporate governance and accountability mechanisms, and regulatory influences other than those conventionally associated with shareholder-based orthodoxy, within a reconceived understanding of corporate success in society. Put another way, what happens inside corporations is responsive in new ways to new forms of external influence, many of which enhance a richer set of both business and societal values in the long term (whatever their short-term costs) than those associated with corporate orthodoxy.

Aspects of this theme are reflected, for example, in Parkinson's ideas about CSR as 'a process concept' involving procedural duties of consultation, consideration and disclosure. They are seen in Dine's recasting of corporate law's traditional concern for aligning management and shareholder interests, so that corporate law also works towards closer harmonization of corporate and societal relations, through mechanisms that are truly inclusive of the multiple regulatory agents and influences prevailing upon 21st century corporations. They are evident in Bottomley's conception of shareholders taking active responsibility as corporate members for ventilating all aspects of a company's internal and external relations, through mechanisms that work through shareholders while also engaging multiple webs of regulatory influence. They are present in Villiers' 'proceduralization' mechanisms for corporate stakeholders, and their correlation with external regulatory mechanisms too. Similarly, they are displayed in Parker's meta-regulatory exhortation to align self-regulating corporate responsibility and governance processes with corporate responsibility and governance outcomes that accord with public policy goals directed towards improving CSR, through regulatory influences that include (but are not limited to) state-based regulation.

Other accountability mechanisms involving non-shareholding stakeholders include employee and other stakeholder representative groups for decision-making purposes (e.g. Parkinson), enhanced corporate monitoring roles for stakeholder groups (e.g. Bakan) and public interest groups (e.g. Dine), and corporate interest groups to enhance the deliberative, contestable and democratic characteristics of corporate decision-making (e.g. Bottomley). At the same time, some suggested mechanisms for improving corporate responsibility and governance in CSR-supportive ways concentrate upon meaningful shareholder participation and influence (e.g. Greenfield, and Bottomley), while others seek to remove directors from the overbearing influence of shareholder short-termism (e.g. Mitchell).

Fifthly, in terms of improved corporate disclosure and accountability, a number of reform options have the common theme of opening up the internal and external audiences and purposes for corporate communication, dialogue and reporting. This includes informational, disclosure and reporting mechanisms designed to broaden the decision-making basis for corporate decision-making organs and the societal ends thereby served (e.g. Bottomley, Parker, Kerr et al, Dine and Villiers), to improve the capacity of corporate decision-making to identify and factor societal costs of corporate activity into the business equation (e.g. Greenfield, and Drutman and Cray), to enhance the capacity for outside parties to participate in corporate governance, monitoring and accountability (e.g. Parkinson, Bakan, Parker, and Dine) and to increase corporate transparency and disclosure of social, environmental and human rights impacts in the interest of the public 'right to know' (e.g. Zerk). More broadly, enhanced corporate disclosure and reporting can facilitate better alignment between corporate success and the full scope of what society values in market and non-market terms (e.g. Dine, and Villiers), through mechanisms that still work with market-orientated and industry-based norms and benchmarks (e.g. Dunfee).

Finally, these reform suggestions canvass a variety of business integrity mechanisms to promote socio-ethical business behaviour in dealings with governments, communities and other businesses. These mechanisms cover various forms of official and other regulation designed to minimize corporate irresponsibility of various kinds (e.g. Bakan, Mitchell, and Zerk), prevent regulatory capture by business (e.g. Bakan, and Reich), reduce undue business influence over government policy and regulation (e.g. Bakan, and Reich), outlaw official corruption and bribery (e.g. Stiglitz, and Dine), and enhance corporate disclosure of the social and environmental consequences of onshore and offshore business operations (e.g. Zerk). These regulatory mechanisms are also intended by those suggesting them to optimize both governmental framework-setting and business choice-making in designing and implementing CSR standards (e.g. Kerr et al), eradicate corporate profit-eering from corporate and social harms (e.g. Stiglitz), prevent corporate capture of community activities (e.g. Bakan), create counterweights to corporate power blocs (e.g. Dine) and improve alignment of good corporate responsibility practices and social ends served by those practices (e.g. Parker, Bottomley, and Villiers).

This also reflects a broader consensus (e.g. Bakan, Greenfield, and Reich) that the corollary of shareholder primacy's presumed dominance under major corporate regulatory regimes, which places inevitable limits on what corporations pursuing profit-making for shareholder wealth-generation can do for the rest of society, is a greater role for governmental regulation in making corporations more responsive to social ends, whatever the extent to which they improve their own self-regulation towards those ends under other regulatory influences. In the end, however, all of these various suggestions for reforming corporate law and regulation in favour of enhanced corporate responsibility, governance and sustainability stand or fall on their underlying normative foundations.

CORPORATE SOCIAL RESPONSIBILITY'S FUTURE RESEARCH AGENDA

The future research agenda for CSR contains key areas of cross-disciplinary, theoretical and empirical research. The global importance of CSR achieving mass normative acceptance and being properly regulated points to the special role of scholarship and law respectively in this enterprise. 'CSR can only benefit from fuller engagement with the academic and legal community on the difficult issues that arise in attempts at regulation', according to leading human rights lawyers.[149] An important building block of this global CSR research project must be the development of a genuine cross-disciplinary explanation and justification of corporate governance, responsibility and sustainability from transnational and global perspectives at a primary level of analysis. This foundational work will facilitate the development of an international law of corporate responsibility, governance and sustainability, but with sufficient flexibility at secondary levels of analysis to accommodate the important differences in politics, history and culture that have informed the ongoing convergence and divergence of corporate models and systems of regulation worldwide.[150]

A second area of ongoing research draws upon cross-disciplinary and cross-jurisdictional sources in pursuing a 21st century agenda for reconciling the needs of corporate capitalism, market economies, civil society and the forces of globalization prevailing upon each. Having recast our understanding of corporate success in terms of good corporate governance, responsibility and sustainability, much work remains to be done in relating that understanding to wider aspects of societal and global governance, regulation and responsibility. In particular, adequate 'theoretical lenses' and documented evidence are both needed on the 21st century relations between nation-states, transnational civil society and TNCs in contesting 'global public goods' in the 'global public domain'.[151]

This avenue for research embraces topics as diverse as the involvement of transnational civil society organizations in global governance and regulation affecting corporations, the inculcation of 'public' accountability mechanisms in the structures and behaviours of 'private authority' and 'private governance' of corporations, the empirical investigation of opportunities and case studies in the strategic manipulation of the CSR agenda by a variety of CSR actors, the place of university teaching and learning in the discourse and enculturation of transnational civil society activism, and other aspects of a research agenda in which empirical research and normative theory on global public affairs unite in reconfiguring our world-view on CSR.[152]

National governmental reports on the implications of CSR for the global economy highlight the 21st century need for CSR education and training in universities and workplaces, together with the need for new research on business tools for exercising CSR and measures of the socio-economic impacts of business, as well as new research on the connection between CSR and global governance, security, and human rights challenges.[153] Most significantly, the CSR research community must address the present imbalance between CSR research and knowledge in the global public commons and that which is not publicly shared, as described by one national governmental report on CSR in these terms:[154]

> CSR is a relatively small field of research, both nationally and internationally, so the amount of research-based knowledge is limited. Much of the empirical knowledge in the field resides with private enterprises and consultancies. The research is often initiated and funded by various special interest groups (companies, other commercial actors, ministries and their administrative agencies and NGOs).

At the same time, sustainable global enterprises of the 21st century must innovate their own approach to investment in research and development (R&D), especially in a business investment in developing countries and regions. This requires multi-pronged attention to adapting technological innovations to local needs, re-evaluating the use of patents for start-up ventures, extrapolating business applications from local practices and developing major research facilities in emerging economies.[155]

As CSR progressively interacts with corporate governance, this intermingling produces a third necessary area of CSR-related research, located within a fourth field of research concerning corporate governance generally, from a range of comparative, conceptual and operational standpoints. 'Documenting and analysing different governance practices across countries and putting these practices in a particular historical and political context will be the basis of important future research', conclude three of Australia's leading corporate law and governance experts.[156]

More broadly, the distinct strands of old and new visions of corporate responsibility, corporate governance and CSR are being brought together in scholarship on corporate responsibility and sustainability, and related studies. The focus of this area of research extends beyond contemporary corporate governance's accommodation of both shareholder democracy and stakeholder engagement as major business drivers.[157] It also embraces the translation of social objectives of corporate governance, organizational systems of corporate governance and discrete aspects of corporate governance.

Successfully governing sustainable global enterprises in the 21st century, for example, requires new approaches to the relationship between a company's commitment to sustainability and its approach to the company's human and intellectual capital. Cornell University's Stuart Hart highlights this connection as follows:[158]

Much could be accomplished if the message contained in the corporate sustainability vision statement were actually integrated into corporate recruiting, leadership development, and performance evaluation . . . (I)gnoring students' commitment to social responsibility, ethics, and sustainability in the recruiting process may be a missed opportunity for firms committed to such aims . . . When it comes to training and development, few MNCs have yet reached the point that they consider global sustainability a significant enough issue to make it an integral part of the leadership development process. Fewer still have made sustainability performance an integral part of the performance evaluation and promotion process. The time is now for corporations to close the loop on their own rhetoric by recruiting, developing, and rewarding people who display capability and imagination in moving the company and the world toward sustainability.

The 21st century relationship between nation-states, societal and global governance and CSR forms an important fifth area of future research. This research area has multiple strands. The different models of public policies and rationales for CSR must be explored further in their connection to changing conceptions and models of governance drawn from the welfare state and market capitalism, including the tension between different national and regional approaches to CSR from the different standpoints of economic globalization and national competitiveness, environmental protection and sustainable development, and social justice and civil society.[159]

A sixth area of necessary CSR-related research covers the specific legal and regulatory reform issues targeted by national and supranational governmental bodies, often from geopolitical, intergovernmental and national policy perspectives. For example, the European Commission identifies 'a need for more interdisciplinary research on CSR, in particular on: links at the macro-and-meso-levels between CSR, competitiveness and sustainable development; the effectiveness of CSR in reaching social and environmental objectives; and issues such as innovation, corporate governance, industrial relations, and the supply chain', with 'CSR as practiced by SMEs [being] an important research topic in its own right'.[160] Australian calls for further research on how SMEs relate to CSR reflect the global need for more research in this area too.[161] Indeed, SMEs are driven to CSR in their own right and as members of multinational business services chains. Grant Thornton's 2008 international business report assesses the impact of CSR upon 'privately held businesses' as follows:[162]

(P)rivately held businesses appear more likely to adopt ethical business practices for practical commercial reasons than any other. Although unsurprising, it offers an insight into ways in which organisations and governments can improve global corporate social responsibility . . . While saving the planet is a concern, by far and away the main drivers for action on corporate social responsibility are recruitment and retention issues followed closely by cost management . . . Another factor is the demand of the large corporates. CSR frameworks are filtering down the supply chain, influencing the business practices of privately held businesses . . . Corporate social responsibility is no longer the domain of the large corporate and is now a necessity rather than a choice.

Responding to the Commission's communication, the European Parliament's 2007 CSR resolution urges 'that future CSR research go beyond the simple "business case"' for CSR. It calls for a designated proportion of 'social sciences and humanities research to be devoted to business in society' under designated EU research programmes, as well as the inclusion 'in future cooperation agreements with developing countries chapters on research, monitoring and help to remediate social, human and environmental problems in operations and supply chains of EU-based companies in third world countries'. It also focuses the attention of the European Alliance for Corporate Social Responsibility upon 'a substantial increase in the uptake of CSR practices amongst EU companies, the development of new models of best practices by genuine leaders among companies and trade union bodies regarding different aspects of CSR, the identification and promotion of specific EU action and regulation to support CSR, and the assessment of the impacts of such initiatives on the environment and on human and social rights', with flow-on implications for research about such 'core benchmarks of success'.[163]

Similarly, the CSR policy framework set by the UK Government includes a number of research-related initiatives, including sectoral reporting guidelines for corporate impact upon poverty alleviation, CSR pathways to governmental development goals and exploration of connections between market competitiveness, corporate responsibility and other policy areas.[164] In addition to promoting 'Responsibility Deals' as a new form of compact between governmental, business and community actors, as a means of steering business towards market mechanisms that embody public policy goals on corporate responsibility and sustainability, the alternative UK Government (but in power from 2010) supports research targeting global business chain issues, including labour standards and abuses, private voluntary initiatives (PVIs) to enhance business responsibility, and governmental incentives for PVIs. The UK Conservative Party Working Group on Responsible Business (CPWGRB) also recommends financial support for 'research on the impact of improved voluntary standards on company competitiveness, for example by academic institutions'.[165] In addition, the CPWGRB cites the need for development of measurement criteria for 'Responsibility Deals', with politico-regulatory actors working with 'other bodies, notably NGO specialists and academics'.[166]

The Australian Government's Corporations and Markets Advisory Committee (CAMAC) is more cautious in its 21st century review of CSR law and regulatory reform, nevertheless offering at least contingent support for aspects of a CSR-related research agenda. 'There may be some scope for government to assist companies, investors and other interested parties to understand better the range of issues relating to corporate responsibility through collating and disseminating information and, if necessary, commissioning relevant research or other material', concludes CAMAC.[167] The Australian Parliamentary Joint Committee on Corporations and Financial Services (PJCCFS) is more specific and focused in its research-related recommendations in its 21st century CSR report. 'The committee recommends that the Australian Government, in consultation with relevant sections of the business community, undertake research into quantifying the benefits of corporate responsibility and sustainability reporting', recommends the PJCCFS.[168]

Improvement in the conceptual and operational treatment of the relations between business and human rights on national and global fronts constitutes a seventh future research direction. This includes further conceptual, comparative and applied research on harmonization of CSR standards, CSR-sensitive business models for aligning business–society relations, business frameworks for CSR policy implementation and integration of CSR concerns in business management and reporting. Professor Dine identifies a collection of future research areas related to companies, international trade and human rights, including exploratory research on the benefits for the global market of freedom of movement for workers between developing and developed states, revision of the functions and purposes of nation-states and notions of sovereignty, and improvements to international financial and investment architecture.[169] More fundamentally, a truly global cross-disciplinary approach is needed to address the normative foundations and limits of CSR as a morally desirable and legally necessary foundation for business, especially in connection with human rights and the dynamics of political, economic and legal power in play.[170]

The work of the UNSRSG on business and human rights since the promulgation of the draft UN Norms identifies necessary policy, regulatory and empirical research on the interplay between business and human rights. This includes further research on human rights due diligence in a variety of regulatory contexts, potential applications of human rights impact assessments (HRIAs), interactions between investment and human rights, and the rights-inhibiting consequences of particular contractual conditions (e.g. stabilization clauses) in state–business project agreements.[171] Building upon the research emerging from the work of the UNSRSG, other experts highlight the need for more research on various aspects of the investor–state process, including model investment agreement clauses and other mechanisms for making the international investment agreement regime more conducive to state and business protection of human rights.[172] Documented evidence and case studies of corporate human rights abuses and complicity in state human rights violations are needed in tandem with further scholarship and policy development on international corporate responsibility for human rights.[173] The policy and legal reform implications of implementing the UNSRSG's three-pronged 'protect, respect, and remedy' framework worldwide also demand further research.

An eighth future research direction concerns transnational civil society organizations, and their modes of operation and interaction with business, government and communities. In particular, more empirical research from multi-disciplinary perspectives is needed on the range of ways in which NGOs and others contribute to CSR law-building and regulation-setting, and their effectiveness in doing so under different political, geographical and other conditions.[174] The heavy emphasis within CSR literature on the development and advocacy of normative bases for CSR needs to be matched by more research using social science methods that explore the actual impact of phenomena such as regulation upon CSR and the multiple societal sectors and actors engaged with it.[175]

For example, this includes 'a need for systematic research on the practice of including civil society actors in government negotiation delegations', as part of a wider empirical examination of how transnational civil society actors influence geopolitical outcomes, which itself forms part of the grand CSR project's focus upon 'a reconfiguring of state-society relations [that] can simultaneously empower the state in some respects while empowering civil society in others'.[176] Of course, even the emerging body of research on transnational civil society activism must be positioned with a wider body of cross-disciplinary knowledge that focuses not only upon the roles of different agents in world politics, but also upon the different normative bases for assessing those roles, from perspectives grounded in different theoretical standpoints in history, politics, sociology and international relations, as much as in economics, business and law.[177] Such case studies must inevitably engage with theory too, so that their interpretation takes account of alternative theoretical perspectives that might explain the dynamics informing their results and their applicability to different situations.[178]

A ninth future research direction covers evidence-based assessment of CSR change management within corporations. Research is needed on designing and implementing corporate frameworks for 21st century risk management, decision-making and reporting, together with correlative investment decision-making frameworks. Research on how these frameworks are structured and used is a vital part of keeping track of the CSR-influenced shifting ground on fiduciary duties, business management systems, corporate disclosure and reporting, institutional investment engagement and other corporate governance arrangements. The UN Principles for Responsible Investment, for example, specifically encourage research on embedding ESG considerations in institutional investment analysis and decision-making.

Finally, given the gulf between how many boardrooms operate in practice under existing corporate regulatory regimes and how corporate constitutionalist, meta-regulatory and other late 20th and early 21st century counter-responses to shareholder primacy envisage the internal and external regulatory influences in play in corporate decision-making, much theoretical and empirical work still remains to be done on the inner workings of boardroom decision-making, specifically from a CSR perspective. In particular, more research is needed on the design and testing of boardroom decision-making frameworks that integrate CSR, not least in evaluation of business risks, drivers and opportunities from politico-regulatory, socio-economic, eco-environmental and other essential business perspectives. The inner workings of what is sometimes called 'the black box' of the boardroom still remain a mystery to many audiences who are affected by it, regulate it or study it.[179]

CONCLUDING REMARKS

Ultimately, none of the research or activity concerning CSR matters unless CSR makes a demonstrable and considerable difference to the lives of people and the state of the communities in which they live across the globe, and extensive research into even this most basic connection is still lacking.[180] 'For many years I have preached that social responsibility and profitability converge over the long term . . . (b)ut I've never been able to prove this proposition nor find a study that confirms it', notes *Supercapitalism*'s author, Professor Robert Reich.[181]

In too many cases, embarking on regulatory and corporate paths of meaningful engagement with CSR is derailed by fears of diluting core business models, eroding corporate and market efficiency, overcomplicating corporate decision-making and adding unnecessary extra business regulation without correlative business benefits. All of these concerns are corporate and regulatory reefs to be navigated, but none of them properly prevents engagement with CSR in its 21st century guises.

The state of CSR's evolving trajectory and manifestations in the early 21st century is already exerting pressure to recast debate about corporate responsibility, governance and sustainability on a number of fronts all at once. All rhetoric aside, the expanding discussion of 'enlightened shareholder value', 'responsibility deals',[182] 'compassionate capitalism',[183] 'citizen investors',[184] 'corporate sustainability', 'corporate citizenship', 'Third Way' corporate 'relegitimization',[185] 'enlightened globalization',[186] 'social business'[187] and 'co-creation'[188] between governmental, business and community entities in developing economies leads in at least one direction. It highlights the potential for recasting corporate governance, responsibility and sustainability in terms of accommodating corporate responsiveness to the systems of trans-modal governance, multi-order regulation and inter-related responsibility that characterize the globalizing 21st century business environment in the ways canvassed in this book.

The world is still in the process of settling its 21st century terms of engagement with CSR. The old ethics of corporate governance, responsibility and regulation kept the concerns of corporate law separate from the concerns of other areas of law. The new ethics revisit the integration of societal values and public policies that all areas of law and other forms of regulation serve. The old ethics kept that multi-pronged corporate focus largely disengaged from related concerns of societal governance, regulation and responsibility. The new ethics explore the points of relation, intersection and mutual reinforcement between these dimensions of governance, regulation and responsibility. The old ethics viewed corporate law and corporate governance chiefly in terms of interactions between corporations, management and shareholders. The new ethics locate those interactions in a more complex crucible of business, societal and global interests. The old ethics saw CSR as a marginal and voluntary business add-on. The new ethics view CSR as an essential and integrated part of core business models and competitive strategies for corporate success.

The old ethics left CSR's implementation largely to organizational discretion. The new ethics encourage a more balanced assessment of CSR's advantages and expenses from both organizational and societal standpoints, with mechanisms that at least recast and possibly even reform the relations between corporations, their constituencies and the world at large. The old ethics saw governmental regulation, corporate self-regulation, business and investment industry regulatory initiatives, and other community regulatory influences in a zero-sum competition for the right to set the CSR regulatory agenda. The new ethics see them cooperatively engaged in shared and mutually interactive CSR regulation.

The old ethics relegated social well-being to either a primary responsibility of the state or a by-product of unregulated market forces. The new ethics look to market dynamics and the state working together in ways that reset rules of engagement for corporate regulation and practice in CSR-enhancing ways. The old ethics asked 'why' about CSR. The new ethics ask 'how'.[189] CSR is a 21st century force to be reckoned with, an idea the time for which has definitely come, and a precondition of both corporate viability and planetary survivability for the generations that follow.

NOTES

1.   Sachs, 2008: 3–4, 52; original emphasis.
2.   E.g. Keane, 2008; and Kerr et al, 2009.
3.   Kerr et al, 2009: 532–534.
4.   G8, 2009: [25] and [27].
5.   G8, 2009: [36] and [39].
6.   G8, 2009: [53]; emphasis added.
7.   Midttun, 2005: 159–160, 165.
8.   E.g. SASAC, 2008.
9.   Villiers, 2008: 103.
10. Ibid.: 105.
11. Ibid.: 108.
12. Sandel, 2009: Lecture 2, p 10.
13. Sandel, 2009: Lecture 1, p 4; Lecture 2, p 4; Lecture 4, pp 8 and 9.
14. Braithwaite and Drahos, 2000: 628–629.

15. E.g. Nourse and Shaffer, 2009.
16. Keane, 2008: 2.
17. MacLeod, 2005: 541.
18. Sachs, 2008: 51.
19. Ibid.: 291–292, 294.
20. Ibid.: 321, 323.
21. Zerk, 2007: 31. The UNSRSG has not recommended a new international treaty binding MNCs on human rights.
22. E.g. Dine, 2005.
23. E.g. Parker, 2007.
24. E.g. Donaldson, 1989.
25. On different notions of sovereignty relevant in this context see Braithwaite and Drahos, 2000.
26. Corcoran, 1997: 55–60.
27. Ibid.: 62.
28. Ibid.: 34.
29. Ibid.: 33–34.
30. Mulgan, 2007: 7.
31. Allan, 2001: 221.
32. Nader, 2004: vii.
33. On the legitimising conditions for state-based sovereignty see Bobbitt, 2008: 452–487; and Singer, 2002: 163–164.
34. Bobbitt, 2008: 464–472.
35. Ibid.: 453, 468, and 469–470; original emphasis.
36. On republican sovereignty see Braithwaite and Drahos, 2000.
37. On the role of transnational civil society organizations in global governance and regulation see Price, 2003; Ruggie, 2004; and Slaughter, 2004.
38. On democratization and constitutionalization of corporate power see Bottomley, 2007.
39. On collective and individual manifestations of 'the people' in Anglo-Commonwealth law see Finn, 1995.
40. On ISCT and international concession theory see respectively Donaldson and Dunfee, 1999; and Dine, 2005.
41. Obama, 2006: 152, 154, 158, 176, 180.
42. Mitchell, 2001: 13.
43. Ward, 2001: 1.
44. Singer, 2002: 163–164.
45. Ibid.: 164.
46. Braithwaite and Drahos, 2001: 603–604.
47. Ibid.: 604.
48. Ibid.: 607–609.
49. Slaughter, 2004: 240.
50. Braithwaite and Drahos, 2001: 610–611; emphasis added.
51. E.g. Anderson, 2005; Henderson, 2001a; and Henderson, 2001b; cf Price, 2003.
52. Price, 2003: 591.
53. Dworkin, 1996.
54. E.g. Finn, 1995; 6; and Breyer, 2005: 3.
55. Parkinson, 1993: viii.
56. Kerr et al, 2009: 535, 541.
57. E.g. Gutmann and Thompson, 2004.
58. E.g. Munck, 2006.
59. Sandel, 2009: Lecture 1, p 4; and Lecture 4, p 7.
60. E.g. Parker, 2002; and Parker, 2007.
61. Nolan, 2007.
62. ASIC, 2008: 47, 49.
63. Wedderburn, 1985: 44.
64. Bottomley and Forsyth, 2006: 3.
65. Dine, 2005: 269.
66. Bakan, 2004: 37.
67. Ibid.: 35.
68. Ibid.: 50.
69. Ibid.: 53.
70. Ibid.: 72–73.

71. Ibid.: 60–61.
72. Ibid.: 160.
73. Ibid.: 161–162.
74. Ibid.: 162–163.
75. Ibid.: 163.
76. Ibid.: 164.
77. Kelly, 2001: 146–148.
78. Stiglitz, 2006: 198.
79. Ibid.: 198–199.
80. Ibid.: 202–203.
81. Ibid.: 203–205.
82. Ibid.: 205.
83. Ibid.: 206.
84. Ibid.: 207.
85. Ibid.: 208.
86. Ibid., 208–209.
87. Ibid.: 210.
88. Villiers, 2008: 90–91, 108.
89. Ibid.: 106–108.
90. Kerr et al, 2009: 592–607.
91. Ibid.: 593–601.
92. Ibid.: 603.
93. Ibid.: 605–606.
94. Ibid.: 606–607.
95. Greenfield, 2006: 5.
96. Ibid.: 4–5.
97. Ibid.: 130.
98. Ibid.: 37.
99. Ibid.: 234–235.
100. Ibid.: 73–94 and 102–105.
101. Ibid.: 104–105.
102. Ibid.: 94–98.
103. Ibid.: 147.
104. Ibid.: 130 and 136–137 and 144.
105. Ibid.: 148–149.
106. Ibid.: 238–239.
107. Hermes, 2006: 4.
108. Greenfield, 2006: 187–216.
109. Ibid.: 239.
110. Ibid.: 239–240.
111. Ibid.: 242.
112. Mitchell, 2001: 277. On the following summary of Mitchell's diagnosis of the problem of corporate irresponsibility and his suggested solutions see Mitchell, 2001: 3–4 and 277–278.
113. Keay, 2007c: Part 2.1.C.
114. Mitchell, 2001: 3.
115. Ibid.: 3–4, 112–115, 119 and 183–186.
116. Ibid.: 184, 278.
117. Ibid.: 185.
118. Ibid.: 278.
119. Drutman and Cray, 2004: 129.
120. Ibid.: 118–119.
121. Ibid.: 119.
122. Ibid.: 280.
123. Bottomley, 2007: and Parker, 2007.
124. Bottomley, 2007: 178.
125. Ibid.
126. Ibid.
127. Bottomley, 2007: 175, 178.
128. Ibid.: 139–141.
129. Ayres and Braithwaite, 1992: 56, cited in Bottomley, 2007: 139.
130. Bottomley, 2007: 138–139.

131. Dine, 2005: 268.
132. Ibid.: 276.
133. Ibid.: 277.
134. Ibid.: 276.
135. Ibid.: 277.
136. Ibid.: 278.
137. Ibid.: 279.
138. Ibid.: 278.
139. Ibid.: 277–279.
140. Ibid.: 247–248.
141. Ibid.: 237.
142. Ibid.: 233–234, 249.
143. E.g. Henderson, 2007a; and Henderson, 2001b.
144. Rawls, 2001: 10–12.
145. Finnis, 1980.
146. Madsen, 2008: 845–846.
147. E.g. PJCCFS, 2006; and CAMAC, 2006.
148. See Chs 4 and 8.
149. Kinley et al, 2007b: 471–472.
150. E.g. Orts, 2009. The author acknowledges the benefit of discussions with Eric Orts on these points.
151. Ruggie, 2004: 499–500.
152. Price, 2003; and Ruggie, 2004.
153. Norwegian Ministry of Foreign Affairs, 2009: 102–103.
154. Ibid.: 102.
155. Hart, 2007; 233–234.
156. Austin et al, 2005: 47.
157. Garratt, 2003: 243, 245.
158. Hart, 2007: 231–232.
159. Albareda et al, 2007: 405.
160. COM(2006)136: 7.
161. Allen Consulting Group, 2008.
162. Grant Thornton, 2008: 14–15.
163. European Parliament resolution of 13 March 2007 on Corporate Social Responsibility.
164. UK Government, 2004: 13.
165. CPWGRB, 2008: 17.
166. Ibid.: 12.
167. CAMAC, 2006: 169–170.
168. PJCCFS, 2006: xxiv.
169. Dine, 2005: 290–292.
170. Campbell, 2007: 529, 542–543, 551–553.
171. E.g. Shemberg, 2008.
172. Mann, 2008.
173. Muchlinski, 2007: 439.
174. See generally Price, 2003; and Ruggie, 2004.
175. Scott, 2008: 172.
176. Price, 2003: 588, 591–592.
177. Ibid.: 598–605.
178. Ibid.: 600.
179. The author acknowledges the benefit of discussions with his ARC Linkage Grant Project colleagues on this aspect in both public and private sector contests; see also Leblanc and Gillies, 2005.
180. I am grateful to the discussions and insights of the Zicklin Centre for Business Ethics' Professor Bill Laufer on this important research need.
181. Reich, 2008: 7.
182. CPWGRB, 2007.
183. Benioff and Southwick, 2004.
184. Davis et al, 2006.
185. Wheeler, 2002: 170.
186. Sachs, 2005: 358.
187. Yunus, 2007.
188. Brugmann and Prahalad, 2007.
189. *The Economist*, 2008: 8.

Bibliography

Accounting Standards Board (ASB) (2006), *Reporting Statement: Operating and Financial Review*, UK.

Ackerman, R. and R. Bauer (1976), *Corporate Social Responsiveness: The Modern Dilemma*, Virginia: Reston.

Albareda, L., J.M. Lozano and T. Ysa (2007), 'Public Policies on Corporate Social Responsibility: the Role of Governments in Europe', 74 *Journal of Business Ethics* 391.

Albrechtsen, J. (2006), 'This Business of Moral Coercion is Just a Hoax', *The Australian*, 29 March: 12.

Allan, T.R.S. (2001), *Constitutional Justice: A Liberal Theory of the Rule of Law*, Oxford: Oxford University Press.

Allen Consulting Group (2008), *Small and Medium-Sized Enterprises and Responsible Business Practices: An Initial Investigation*, Report to St James Ethics Centre, Sydney.

Allen, G. (2007), 'The Mutual Benefits of Giving', *The Australian Financial Review*, 14 June.

Allen, W. (1992), 'Our Schizophrenic Conception of the Business Corporation', 14 *Cardozo Law Review* 261.

Allens Arthur Robinson (AAR) (2008), *Corporate Duty and Human Rights Under Australian Law*, Report on behalf of the International Bar Association for the United Nations Special Representative of the Secretary General for Business and Human Rights (UNSRSG).

American Law Institute (ALI) (2005), *Principles of Corporate Governance: Analysis and Recommendations*.

Amnesty International Australia (2005), 'Are Human Rights Everyone's Business?' Submission to the Joint Committee on Corporations and Financial Services, Canberra: Amnesty International Australia, available at http://www.aph.gov.au/Senate/committee/corporations_ctte/completed_inquiries/2004-07/corporate_responsibility/submissions/sub90.pdf.

Anderson, H. and I. Landau (2006), 'Corporate Social Responsibility in Australia: a Review', Working Paper No 4 of 2006, Monash University Corporate Law and Accountability Research Group.

Anderson, K. (2005), 'Book Review: Squaring the Circle? Reconciling Sovereignty and Global Governance Through Global Government Networks: A New World Order', 118 *Harvard Law Review* 1255.

Anderson, S. and J. Cavanagh (1996), *The Top 200: The Rise of Global Corporate Power*, Washington, DC: Institute for Policy Studies.

Annan, K. (1999), UN Secretary-General's Address to the World Economic Forum, Davos (Switzerland), 31 January.

Arbour, L. (2008), 'Interview Transcript: Louise Arbour', *Financial Times*, 8 January.

Arden, Lady Justice M. (2007), 'Companies Act 2006 (UK): A New Approach to Directors' Duties', 81 *Australian Law Journal* 162.

Armour, J., S. Deakin and S. Konzelmann (2003), 'Shareholder Primacy and the Trajectory of UK Corporate Governance', 41 *British Journal of Industrial Relations* 531.

ASX Corporate Governance Council (2006a), *Principles of Good Corporate Governance and Good Practice Recommendations*, Exposure Draft of Changes, November, Sydney.

ASX Corporate Governance Council (2006b), *Review of the Principles of Good Corporate Governance and Best Practice Recommendations*, Explanatory Paper and Consultation Paper, November, Sydney.

Attenborough, D. (2007), 'Recent Developments in Australian Corporate Law and their Implications for Director's Duties: Lessons to be Learned from the UK Perspective', 18 (9) *International Company and Commercial Law Review* 312.

Austin, Justice R. (ed.) (2007a), *Company Directors and Corporate Social Responsibility: UK and Australian Perspectives*, Sydney: Ross Parsons Centre of Commercial, Corporate and Taxation Law Monograph Series.

Austin, Justice R. (2007b), 'Introduction', in Robert Austin (ed.), *Company Directors and Corporate Social Responsibility: UK and Australian Perspectives*, Sydney: Ross Parsons Centre of Commercial, Corporate and Taxation Law Monograph Series, pp. 1–2.

Austin, Justice R. (2007c), 'Commentary by Justice R P Austin: Australian Company Law Reform and the UK Companies Bill', in Robert Austin (ed.), *Company Directors and Corporate Social Responsibility: UK and Australian Perspectives*, Sydney: Ross Parsons Centre of Commercial, Corporate and Taxation Law Monograph Series, pp. 3–18.

Austin, R., H. Ford and I. Ramsay (2005), *Company Directors: Principles of Law and Corporate Governance*, Australia: LexisNexis Butterworths.

Australian Financial Review (AFR) (2006), 'Ethics Pays Off for Boards', 19 June.

Australian Government (Attorney-General's Department) (2008), *National Human Rights Consultation Background Paper*, Canberra, available at http://www.humanrights consultation.gov.au/.

Australian Institute of Company Directors (AICD) (2003), *A Guide to Sustainability in Your Company*: Directors' Checklist Series, Sydney.

Australian Labor Party (ALP) (2007), *National Platform and Constitution*, Australia, available at http://www.alp.org.au/platform.index.php.

Australian Law Reform Commission (ALRC) (2008), *For Your Information: Australian Privacy Law and Practice*, Final Report, Vol. 1, Report 108.

Australian Securities and Investments Commission (2003), *Section 1013DA disclosure guidelines (ASIC guidelines to product issuers for disclosure about labour standards or environmental, social and ethical considerations in product disclosure statements (PDS)*, available at http://www.asic.gov.au/asic/pdflib.nsf/lookupbyfilename/s1013da_final-guidelines.pgf/$file/s1013da_finalguidelines.pdf.

Australian Securities and Investments Commission (2008), *Climate Change – A New Challenge for Directors? (Panel Discussion)*, ASIC Summer School, available at http://www.watchdog.asic.gov.au/asic/pdflib.nsf/LookupByFileName/Corporate_governance_and_directors_duties.pdf/$file/Corporate_governance_and_directors_duties.pdf.

Australian Securities Exchange Corporate Governance Council (ASX CGC) (2003), *Principles of Good Corporate Governance and Best Practice Recommendations*, Australian Securities Exchange (ASX), available at http://www.saiglobal.com/Shop/Script/Details.asp?DocN=AS871065609029.

Australian Securities Exchange Corporate Governance Council (ASX CGC) (2007a), *Corporate Governance Principles and Recommendations*, Australian Securities Exchange, available at http://www.asx.ice4.interactiveinvestor.com.au/ASX0701/Corporate%20Governance%20Principles/EN/body.aspx?z=1&uid=.

Australian Securities Exchange Corporate Governance Council (ASX CGC) (2007b), *Supplementary Guidance on Principle 7: Recognise and Manage Risk*, 2007, Australian Securities Exchange, available at http://www.asx.com.au/about/pdf/principle7_additionalguidance.pdf.

Australian Securities Exchange Corporate Governance Council (ASX CGC) (2007c), *Media Release: Revised Corporate Governance Principles Released*, 2007, Australian Securities Exchange, available at http://www.asx.com.au/about/pdf/Mr2007082_revised_corporate_governance_principles.pdf.

Australian Treasury (2007), *Review of Sanctions in Corporate Law*, Australian Government.

Ayres, I. and J. Braithwaite (1992), *Responsive Regulation*, Oxford: Oxford University Press.

Backman, M. (1999), *Asian Eclipse – Exposing the Dark Side of Business in Asia*, Singapore: John Wiley & Sons (Asia) Pty Ltd.

Bainbridge, S. (2005), 'The Siren Song of Corporate Social Responsibility', online comment, *Tech Central Station*, 14 November, available at www2.techcentralstation.com.

Bakan, J. (2004), *The Corporation: The Pathological Pursuit of Profit and Power*, New York: Free Press.

Banerjee, S. (2005), 'The Problem with Corporate Social Responsibility', Working Paper, University of South Australia: International Graduate School of Management, available at http://www.unisa.edu.au/igsb/docs/WP-Banerjee.pdf.

Banerjee, S. (2007), *Corporate Social Responsibility: The Good, the Bad and the Ugly*, Cheltenham: Edward Elgar Publishing Limited.

Bantekas, I. (2004), 'Corporate Social Responsibility in International Law', 22 *Boston University International Law Journal* 309.

Baram, M. (2005), 'Foreword', in S. Tully (ed.), *Research Handbook on Corporate Legal Responsibility*, Cheltenham: Edward Elgar Publishing Limited.

Barker, G. (2007), 'The Left's Intellectual Vacuums', *The Australian Financial Review*, 4 May, 96.

Baue, B. (2007), 'Contracting Human Rights? Ruggie Teams with IFC on Study', online article, *SocialFunds website*, 26 October, available at www.socialfunds.com.

Baxt, B. (2004), 'Corporations Law A Fragile Structure', *The Australian Financial Review*, 19 November, 55.

Baxt, R. (2002), 'Directors' Duty of Care and the New Business Judgment Rule in the Twenty-First Century Environment', in Ian Ramsay (ed.), *Key Developments in Corporate Law and Trusts Law: Essays in Honour of Professor Harold Ford*, Australia: LexisNexis Butterworths, pp. 151–77.

Bebchuk, L. (2005), 'The Case for Increasing Shareholder Power', 118 *Harvard Law Review* 833.

Bebchuk, L. (2007), 'The Myth of the Shareholder Franchise', 93 (3) *Virginia Law Review* 675.

Bebchuk, L. and M. Roe (2004), 'A Theory of Path Dependence in Corporate Ownership and Governance', in Jeffrey Gordon and Mark Roe (eds), *Convergence and Persistence in Corporate Governance*, Cambridge: Cambridge University Press, pp. 69–113.

Beerworth, B. (2005), 'Directors Duties and Corporate Social Responsibility', *Seminar Paper*, CAMAC and Centre for Corporate Law and Securities Regulation Seminar, July.

Beerworth, B. (2007a), 'Should the Corporations Act Require Directors to Consider Non-Shareholder "Stakeholders"?', in Robert Austin (ed.), *Company Directors and Corporate Social Responsibility: UK and Australian Perspectives*, Sydney: Ross Parsons Centre of Commercial, Corporate and Taxation Law Monograph Series, pp. 39–43.

Beerworth, B. (2007b), 'Corporate Social Responsibility: Emerging Trends', Macquarie Graduate School of Management (MGSM) Presentation, Executive Breakfast Seminar Series.

Benioff, M., and K. Southwick (2004), *Compassionate Capitalism: How Corporations Can Make Doing Good an Integral Part of Doing Well*, Franklin Lakes, NJ: Career Press.

Berle, A. (1931), 'Corporate Powers as Powers in Trust', 44 *Harvard Law Review* 1049.

Berle, A. (1932), 'For Whom Corporate Managers Are Trustees: A Note', 45 *Harvard Law Review* 1365.

Berle, A. (1954), *The 20th Century Capitalist Revolution*, New York: Harcourt Brace.

Berle, A. (1960), 'The Corporation in a Democratic Society', in M. Anshen and G. Bach (eds), *Management and Corporations 1985*, New York: McGraw-Hill, pp. 63–98.

Berle, A. (1966), 'Foreword', in E. Mason (ed.), *The Corporation in Modern Society*, Cambridge, MA: Harvard University Press.

Berle, A. and G. Means (1968), *The Modern Corporation and Private Property* (revised edition), New York: Harcourt, Brace & World inc.

Bernstein, S. and B. Cashore (2007), 'Can Non-State Global Governance Be Legitimate?: An Analytical Framework', 1 *Regulation and Governance* 347.

Bessler W., F. Kaen and H. Sherman (1997), *Going Public, A Corporate Governance Perspective*, Working Paper Series, available at SSRN: http://ssrn.com/abstract=10488.

Bielak, D., S. Bonini and J. Oppenheim (2007), 'CEOs on Strategy and Social Issues', *The McKinsey Quarterly*, October, available at http://www.mckinseyquarterly.com/CEOs_on_strategy_and_social_issues_2056.

Black, A. (2006), 'Mechanims for Shareholder Activism under the Corporations Act', 13th AMPLA Annual Conference, Melbourne.

Black, J. (1997), *Rules and Regulators*, Oxford: Clarendon Press.

Black, J. (2001), 'Decentring Regulation: Understanding the Role of Regulation and Self-regulation in a "Post-regulatory" World', 54 *Current Legal Problems* 103.

Black, J. (2002), 'Critical Reflections on Regulation', 27 *Australian Journal of Legal Philosophy* 1.

Black, J. (2004), 'Law and Regulation: The Case of Finance', in Christine Parker, Colin

Scott, Nicola Lacey and John Braithwaite (eds), *Regulating Law*, Oxford: Oxford University Press, pp. 33–59.

Black, J. (2005), 'The Emergence of Risk Based Regulation and the New Public Management in the UK' [2005] *Public Law* 512.

Black, L. (2007), 'The Effect of Private Equity Takeovers on Corporate Social Responsibility', Australian Centre for Corporate Social Responsibility seminar paper, available at http://www.accsr.com.au/pdf/pet_speech_Leeora_Black_Opening.pdf.

Blair, M. ([1995] 2004), 'Ownership and Control: Rethinking Corporate Governance for the 21st Century', in Thomas Clarke (ed.), *Theories of Corporate Governance: The Philosophical Foundations of Corporate Governance*, London: Routledge, pp. 174–88.

Blair, M. (2003), 'Directors' Duties in a Post-Enron World: Why Language Matters', 38 *Wake Forest Law Review* 885.

Blair, M. and L. Stout (1999), 'A Team Production Theory of Corporate Law', 24 *Journal of Corporation Law* 751.

Blair, M. and L. Stout (2001), 'Director Accountability and the Mediating Role of the Corporate Board', 79 *Washington University Law Quarterly* 403.

Blair, M. and L. Stout (2006), 'Specific Investment: Explaining Anomalies in Corporate Law', 31 *Journal of Corporation Law* 719.

Bobbitt, P. (2008), *Terror and Consent: The Wars for the Twenty-first Century*, Melbourne: Allen Lane.

Boeger, N., R. Murray and C. Villiers (eds) (2008), *Perspectives on Corporate Social Responsibility*, Cheltenham: Edward Elgar Publishing Limited.

Bonini, S., J. Greeney and L. Mendonca (2008), 'Assessing the Impact of Societal Issues: A McKinsey Global Survey', *The McKinsey Quarterly*, available at http://www.mckinseyquarterly.com/Strategy/Strategic_Thinking/Assessing_the_impact_of_societal_issues_A_McKinsey_Global_Survey_2077.

Bonini, S., L. Mendonca and J. Oppenheim (2006), 'When Social Issues Become Strategic', *The McKinsey Quarterly*, Number 2, 20.

Bosch, H. (1995), *The Director At Risk: Accountability in the Boardroom*, Melbourne: Pitman Publishing.

Bosch, H. (2002), 'The Changing Face of Corporate Governance', 25 *University of New South Wales Law Journal* 270.

Bosch, H. (2006), 'Corporate Social Responsibility', Submission to the Corporations and Markets Advisory Committee, available at http://www.camac.gov.au/camac.nsf/by/Headline/PDFSubmissions_2/$file/HBosch_CSR.pdf.

Bottomley, S. (1997), 'From Contractualism to Constitutionalism: A Framework for Corporate Governance', 19 *Sydney Law Review* 277.

Bottomley, S. (1999), 'The Birds, the Beasts, and the Bat: Developing a Constitutionalist Theory of Corporate Regulation', 27 *Federal Law Review* 243.

Bottomley, S. (2002), 'Corporations and Human Rights', in Stephen Bottomley and David Kinley (eds), *Commercial Law and Human Rights*, Aldershot: Ashgate Dartmouth, pp. 47–68.

Bottomley, S. (2007), *The Constitutional Corporation: Rethinking Corporate Governance*, Aldershot: Ashgate.

Bottomley, S. and A. Forsyth (2007), 'The New Corporate Law: Corporate Social Responsibility and Employees' Interests', in D. McBarnett, A. Voiculescu and T.

Campbell (eds), *The New Corporate Accountability: Corporate Social Responsibility and the Law*, Cambridge: Cambridge University Press, pp. 307–35.

Bowman, S. (1996), *The Modern Corporation and American Political Thought: Law, Power, and Ideology*, University Park, Penn: Pennsylvania State University Press.

Bradley, M., C. Schipani, A. Sundaram and J. Walsh (1999a), 'The Purposes and Accountability of the Corporation in Contemporary Society: Corporate Governance at a Crossroads', 62 *Law and Contemporary Problems* 9.

Bradley, M., C. Schipani, A. Sundaram and J. Walsh (1999b), 'Foreword', 62 *Law and Contemporary Problems* 1.

Braithwaite, J. (2002), 'Rules and Principles: A Theory of Legal Certainty', (2002) 27 *Australian Journal of Legal Philosophy* 47.

Braithwaite, J. and P. Drahos (2000), *Global Business Regulation*, Cambridge: Cambridge University Press.

Branson, R. (2007), *Let's Not Screw It, Let's Just Do It: New Lessons for the Future*, Sydney: Random House.

Bratton, W. and M. Wachter (2007), 'Shareholder Primacy's Corporatist Origins: Adolf Berle and "The Modern Corporation"', University of Pennsylvania Institute for Law and Economics Research Paper No 07-24, Georgetown Law and Economics Research Paper No 1021273, available at http://ssrn.com/abstract=1021273.

Breyer, S. (2005), *Active Liberty: Interpreting Our Democratic Constitution*, New York: Alfred A. Knopf.

Brotherhood of St Laurence (BSL) (2007), Submission to the ASX Corporate Governance Council in Response to the Review of the Principles of Good Corporate Governance and Best Practice recommendations, February, available at http://www.bsl.org.au/pdfs/BSL_Subm_principles_Corp_gov_feb07.Pdf.

Bruch, H. and F. Walter (2005), 'The Keys to Rethinking Corporate Philanthropy', *MIT Sloan Management Review*, 1 September, pp. 49–55.

Brudney. V. (1982), 'The Independent Director – Heavenly City or Potemkin Village?', 95 *Harvard Law Review* 597.

Brugmann, J. and C.K. Prahalad (2007), 'Co-Creating Business's New Social Compact', *Harvard Business Review* (February), 80.

Burke, T. and J. Hill (1990), *Ethics, Environment and the Company: A Guide to Effective Action*, London: Institute of Business Ethics.

Burris, S., P. Drahos and C. Shearing (2005), 'Nodal Governance', 30 *Australian Journal of Legal Philosophy* 30.

Business Impact Task Force (BITF) (2000), *Winning with Integrity: Executive Summary*, London: Business in the Community (BITC).

Business Leaders Initiative on Human Rights (BLIHR) (2006), *Report 3: Towards a 'Common Framework' on Business and Human Rights: Identifying Components*, London, available at http://www.blihr.org/Reports/BLIHR3Report.pdf.

Business Roundtable (1997), *Statement on Corporate Governance*, Washington, DC: Business Roundtable.

Business Roundtable (2005), *Principles of Corporate Governance*, Washington, DC: Business Roundtable.

Cadbury, A. (2002), *Corporate Governance and Chairmanship: A Personal View*, Oxford: Oxford University Press.

Cadbury, A. (2003), 'The Challenge of Corporate Social Responsibility', CIPD Conference (Business in the Community (BITC)).

Campbell, T. (2006), 'A Human Rights Approach to Developing Voluntary Codes of Conduct for Multinational Corporations', 16(2) *Business Ethics Quarterly* 255.

Campbell, T. (2007), 'The Normative Grounding of Corporate Social Responsibility: A Human Rights Approach', in Doreen McBarnet, Aurora Voiculescu and Tom Campbell (eds), *The New Corporate Accountability: Corporate Social Responsibility and the Law*, Cambridge: Cambridge University Press, pp. 529–64.

Canadian Democracy and Corporate Accountability Commission (CDCAC) (2002), *The New Balance Sheet: Corporate Profits and Responsibility in the 21st Century*, Final Report of the CDCAC, Toronto, available at http://www.globelinx.ca/downloads/leboutiller(1).pdf.

Cane, P. (2003), *Responsibility in Law and Morality*, Oxford: Hart Publishing.

Carrigan, F. (2002), 'The Role of Capital in Regulating the Duty of Care and Business Judgment Rule', 14 *Australian Journal of Corporate Law* 215.

Castan Centre for Human Rights Law, International Business Leaders Forum, and Office of the UN High Commissioner for Human Rights (2008), *Human Rights Translated: A Business Reference Guide*, Melbourne: Castan Centre for Human Rights (Monash University).

Cata Backer, L. (2005), 'Multinational Corporations, Transnational Law: The United Nation's Norms on the Responsibilities of Transnational Corporations as Harbinger of Corporate Responsibility in International Law', Research Paper, SSRN, 2005; (2005) 37 *Columbia Human Rights Law Review* 101.

Caulkin, S. (2009), 'Social Concerns are Crunched Off the Agenda', *The Observer*, 5 April 2009.

CCPA and BCA (2007), *Corporate Community Investment in Australia*, Melbourne: CCPA.

Chatterji, A. and S. Listokin (2007), 'Corporate Social Irresponsibility', *Democracy: A Journal of Ideas*, Issue 3, Winter.

Cheffins, B. (2002), 'Comparative Corporate Governance and the Australian Experience', in Ian Ramsay (ed.), *Key Developments in Corporate Law and Trusts Law*, Sydney: Lexis-Nexis, pp. 13–38.

Cheney, G., J. Roper and S. May (2007), 'Overview', in Steve May, George Cheney and Juliet Roper (eds), *The Debate Over Corporate Social Responsibility*, Oxford: Oxford University Press, pp. 3–14.

Chinese Academy of International Trade and Economic Cooperation (CAITEC) (2008), 'Draft Guidelines on Corporate Social Responsibility Compliance by Foreign Invested Enterprises'.

Chiu, I. (2006a), 'The Paradigms of Mandatory Non-Financial Disclosure: A Conceptual Analysis: Part 1', 27 (9) *Company Lawyer* 259.

Chiu, I. (2006b), 'The Paradigms of Mandatory Non-Financial Disclosure: A Conceptual Analysis: Part 2', 27 (10) *Company Lawyer* 291.

Clarke, T. (ed.) (2004), *Theories of Corporate Governance: The Philosophical Foundations of Corporate Governance*, London: Routledge.

Clarke, T. (2005), Submission to the Inquiry into Corporate Responsibility by the Australian Parliamentary Joint Committee on Corporations and Financial Services.

Coffee, J. (2006), *Gatekeepers: The Professions and Corporate Governance*, Oxford: Oxford University Press.

Coglianese, C., T. Healey, E. Keating and M. Michael (2004), 'The Role of Government in Corporate Governance', Regulatory Policy Programme Report RPT-08, Cambridge, MA: Center for Business and Government, John F Kennedy School of Government, Harvard University.

Commission of the European Communities (2002), *Corporate Social Responsibility: A Business Contribution to Sustainable Development* (COM (2002) 347).

Commission of the European Communities (2006), *Implementing the Partnership for Growth and Jobs: Making Europe a Pole of Excellence on Corporate Social Responsibility*, Communication from the Commission to the European Parliament, the Council and the European Economic and Social Committee (COM(2006)136).

Commission on Human Rights (2005), *Promotion and Protection of Human Rights*, Communication to the United Nations Economic and Social Council (E/CN.4/2005/L.87), available at: http://www.humanrights.ch/home/upload/pdf/061129_E_CN4_2005_L87.pdf.

Company Law Review (1998), *Modern Company Law for a Competitive Economy*, London: Department of Trade and Industry.

Company Law Review Steering Group (CLRSG) (1999), *Modernising Company Law for a Competitive Economy: The Strategic Framework*, London: Department of Trade and Industry.

Company Law Review Steering Group (CLRSG) (2001), *Modern Company Law*, Final Report, London: Department of Trade and Industry.

Conger, J., E. Lawler and D. Finegold (2001), *Corporate Boards: New Strategies for Adding Value at the Top*, San Francisco, CA: Jossey-Bass Inc.

Conley, J. and C. Williams (2005–2006), 'Engage, Embed, and Embellish: Theory Versus Practice in the Corporate Social Responsibility Movement', 31 *Journal of Corporation Law* 1.

Conrad, C. and J. Abbott (2007), 'Corporate Social Responsibility and Public Policy Making', in S. May, G. Cheney and J. Roper (eds), *The Debate Over Corporate Social Responsibility*, Oxford: Oxford University Press, pp. 417–37.

Conservative Party Working Group on Responsible Business (CPWGRB) (2007), Consultation Paper, London, available at http://www.conservatives.com/pdf/responsible business.pdf.

Conservative Party Working Group on Responsible Business (CPWGRB) (2008), *A Light But Effective Touch*, London, available at http://www.concervatives.com/~/media/Files/Downloadable%20Files/A%20light%20but%20effective%20touch.ashx?dl=true.

Cooper, S. (2004), *Corporate Social Performance: A Stakeholder Approach*, Aldershot: Ashgate.

Corbett, A. and S. Bottomley (2004), 'Regulating Corporate Governance', in C. Parker, C. Scott, N. Lacey and J. Braithwaite (eds), *Regulating Law*, Melbourne: Oxford University Press, pp. 60–81.

Corcoran, S. (1997), 'The Corporation as Citizen and as Government: Social Responsibility and Corporate Morality', 2 *Flinders Journal of Law Reform* 53.

Corporate Responsibility (CORE) Coalition and Trade Justice Movement (2006),

'Companies Bill: Making Corporate Irresponsibility History?', Media Briefing, 10 October 2006, London: CORE Coalition.

Corporations and Markets Advisory Committee (CAMAC) (2005), *Corporate Social Responsibility*, Discussion Paper, Australian Government, available at http://www.camac.gov.au/camac/camac.nsf/byHeadline/PDFDiscussion+Papers/$file/CSR_DP.pdf.

Corporations and Markets Advisory Committee (CAMAC) (2006), *The Social Responsibility of Corporations*, Final Report, Australian Government, available at http://www.camac.gov.au/camac/camac.nsf/byHeadline.PDFFinal+Reports+2006/$file/CSR_DP.pdf.

Cox, E. (1995), *A Truly Civil Society*, Sydney: ABC Books.

Cox, J. and T. Hazen (2003), *Corporations*, 2nd edn, New York: Aspen Publishers.

Cradden, C. (2005), *Repoliticizing Management: A Theory of Corporate Legitimacy*, Aldershot: Ashgate.

Crane, A., A. McWilliams, D. Matten, J. Moon and D. Siegel (eds) (2008), *The Oxford Handbook of Corporate Social Responsibility*, Oxford: Oxford University Press.

Crowther, D. and L. Rayman-Bacchus (2004), *Perspectives on Corporate Social Responsibility*, Aldershot: Ashgate.

Dahl, R. (1972), 'A Prelude to Corporate Reform', *Business and Society Review* 17.

Dahl, R. (2000), *On Democracy*, New Haven, CN: Yale Nota Bene, Yale University Press.

Daianu, D. and R. Vranceanu (2005), *Ethical Boundaries of Capitalism*, Aldershot: Ashgate.

Daly, H. and J. Cobb Jr. (1989), *For the Common Good: Redirecting the Economy Toward Community, the Environment, and a Sustainable Future*, Boston, MA: Beacon Press.

Davies, P. (1997), *Gower's Principles of Modern Company Law*, 6th edn, London: Sweet & Maxwell.

Davies, P. (2005), 'Enlightened Shareholder Value and the New Responsibilities of Directors', Inaugural W.E. Hearn Lecture, University of Melbourne Law School, October.

Davis, I. (2005), 'The Biggest Contract', *The Economist*, 26 May, available at www.economist.com.

Davis, S., J. Lukomnik and D. Pitt-Watson (2006), *The New Capitalists: How Citizen Investors are Reshaping the Corporate Agenda*, Boston, MA: Harvard Business School Press.

Deakin, S. (2005), 'The Coming Transformation of Shareholder Value: An International Review', 13 (1) *Corporate Governance* 11.

Deloitte, Tusche Tohmatsu (2007), *In the Dark II: What Many Boards and Executives Still Don't Know about the Health of Their Businesses*, available at http://www.deloitte.com/dtt/article/o,1002,cid=146837,00.html.

den Hond, F., G.A. de Bakker and P. Neergaard (2007), *Managing Corporate Social Responsibility in Action: Talking, Doing and Measuring*, Aldershot: Ashgate.

Dent, G. (2007), 'Academics in Wonderland: The Team Production and Director Primacy Models of Corporate Governance', Working Paper 07–21, Case Research Paper Series in Legal Studies, Case Western Reserve University.

Department of Trade and Industry (DTI) (2007), *Companies Act 2006: Duties of Company Directors: Ministerial Statements*, London: Department of Trade and Industry.

Deva, S. (2004), 'Corporate Code of Conduct Bill 2000: Overcoming Hurdles in Enforcing Human Rights Obligations Against Overseas Corporate Hands of Local Corporations', 8 (1) *Newcastle Law Review*, 87.

Dhir, A. (2006), 'Realigning the Corporate Building Blocks: Shareholder Proposals as a Vehicle for Achieving Corporate Social and Human Rights Accountability', 43 *American Business Law Journal* 365.

Dine, J. (2000), *The Governance of Corporate Groups*, Cambridge: Cambridge University Press.

Dine, J. (2005), *Companies, International Trade and Human Rights*, Cambridge: Cambridge University Press.

Dodd, E.M. (1932), 'For Whom Are Corporate Managers Trustees?', 45 *Harvard Law Review* 1145.

Donald, M.S. and N. Taylor (2008), 'Does "Sustainable" Investing Compromise the Obligations Owed by Superannuation Trustees?', 36 *Australian Business Law Review* 47.

Donaldson, T. (1989), *The Ethics of International Business*, New York: Oxford University Press.

Donaldson, T. (2005), 'Defining the Value of Doing Good Business', *Financial Times: Mastering Corporate Governance*, 2 June, available at http://www.ft.com/pp.mcg.

Donaldson, T. and T. Dunfee (1999), *Ties that Bind: A Social Contracts Approach to Business Ethics*, Boston, MA: Harvard Business School Press.

Donaldson, T. and L. Preston (1995), 'The Stakeholder Theory of the Corporation: Concepts, Evidence, and Implications', 20 *The Academy of Management Review* 65.

Drutman, L. and C. Cray (2004), *The Peoples Business: Controlling Corporations and Restoring Democracy*, The Report of the Citizen Works Corporate Reform Commission, San Francisco, CA: Berrett-Koehler Publishers, Inc.

Dunfee, T. (1999), 'Corporate Governance in a Market With Morality', 62 *Law and Contemporary Problems* 129.

Dunfee, T. (2006), 'Do Firms with Unique Competencies for Rescuing Victims of Human Catastrophes Have Special Obligations?: Corporate Responsibility and the AIDS Catastrophe in Sub-Saharan Africa', 16 *Business Ethics Quarterly* 185.

Dunfee, T. and T. Fort (2003), 'Corporate Hypergoals, Sustainable Peace, and the Adapted Firm', 36 *Vanderbilt Journal of Transnational Law* 563.

Dunlop, I. (2008), 'Global Warming Negates Conventional Wisdom', *The Australian Financial Review*, 2 January, 55.

du Plessis, J., J. McConvill and M. Bagaric (2005), *Principles of Contemporary Corporate Governance*, Cambridge, New York: Cambridge University Press.

Dworkin, R. (1996), *Freedom's Law: The Moral Reading of the American Constitution*, Cambridge, MA: Harvard University Press.

Dworkin, R. (2000), *Sovereign Virtue: The Theory and Practice of Equality*, Cambridge, MA: Harvard University Press.

Dworkin, R. (2006), *Justice in Robes*, Cambridge, MA: The Belknap Press of Harvard University Press.

Easterbrook, F. and D. Fischel (1991), *The Economic Structure of Corporate Law*, Cambridge, MA: Harvard University Press.

Edwards, J. (2008), 'Capitalism: What Now?', *The Deal, The Australian* Business Magazine, November 2008 (Vol 1, No 2).

Eells, R. (1962), *The Government of Corporations*, New York: Free Press.

Eisenberg, M. (1998), 'Corporate Conduct that Does Not Maximize Shareholder Gain: Legal Conduct, Ethical Conduct, the Penumbra Effect, Reciprocity, the Prisoner's Dilemma, Sheep's Clothing, Social Conduct, and Disclosure', 28 *Stetson Law Review* 1.

Elhauge, E. (2005), 'Sacrificing Corporate Profits in the Public Interest', 80 *New York University Law Review* 733.

Elkington, J. ([1999] 2002), *Cannibals with Forks: The Triple Bottom Line of 21st Century Business*, reprinted (ed.), Oxford: Capstone Publishing.

Emberland, M. (2006), *The Human Rights of Companies: Exploring the Structure of ECHR Protection*, Oxford: Oxford University Press.

Engel, D. (1979), 'An Approach to Corporate Social Responsibility', 32 *Stanford Law Review* 1.

European Commission Directorate-General for Employment and Social Affairs (ECDGESA) (2001), *Promoting a European Framework for Corporate Social Responsibility* (Green Paper), Luxembourg: Office for Official Publications of the European Communities (http://ec.europa.eu/employment_social/publications/booklets/industrial_relations/pdf/ke3701590_en.pdf).

European Parliament (2007), Resolution of 13 March on *Corporate Social Responsibility: A New Partnership*, available at http://www.europarl.europa.eu/sides/getDoc.do?pubRef=-//EP//TEXT+TA+P6-TA-2007-0062+0+DOC+XML+V0//EN.

Farrar, J. (2005), *Corporate Governance: Theories, Principles, and Practice*, 2nd edn, Melbourne: Oxford University Press.

Farrar, J. (2008), *Corporate Governance: Theories, Principles and Practice*, 3rd edn, Melbourne: Oxford University Press.

Feldman D. and S. Altschuller (2007), 'The Bottom Line', *Democracy: A Journal of Ideas*, Issue 4, Spring.

Financial Services Authority (2007), *Principles-Based Regulation: Focusing on the Outcomes That Matter*, London: Financial Services Authority.

Finn, P. (1995), 'A Sovereign People, a Public Trust', in Paul Finn (ed.), *Essays On Law and Government (volume 1)*, North Ryde, Sydney: Law Book Company Ltd, pp. 1–32.

Finnis, J. (1980), *Natural Law and Natural Rights*, Oxford: Oxford University Press.

Finnis, J. (2003), 'Law and What I Truly Should Decide', 48 *The American Journal of Jurisprudence* 107.

Flannery, T. (2005), *The Weather Makers: The History and Future Impact of Climate Change*, Melbourne: Text Publishing Company.

Flannery T. (2008), 'Now or Never: A Sustainable Future for Australia?', *Quarterly Essay*, Issue 31, Melbourne: Black Inc.

FORGE Group (2002), 'Corporate Social Responsibility: Guidance for the Financial Services Sector', UK, available at http://www.bba.org.uk/pdf/forgeflyer.pdf.

Forstater, M., S. Zadek, D. Evans, A. Knight, M. Sillanpaa, C. Tuppen and A-M. Warris (2006), 'The Materiality Report: Aligning Strategy, Performance and Reporting',

London: jointly produced by AccountAbility, BP Group, and Lloyds Register Quality Assurance (LRQA).

Fox T., H. Ward and B. Howard (2002), *Public Sector Roles in Strengthening Corporate Social Responsibility: A Baseline Study*, Prepared for the Corporate Social Responsibility Practice Private Sector Advisory Services Department, The World Bank, Washington DC: The World Bank.

Frances, N. (2008), *The End of Charity: Time for Social Enterprise*, Crows Nest, N.S.W.: Allen & Unwin.

Franklin, D. (2008), 'Just Good Business', in *Just Good Business: A Special Report on Corporate Social Responsibility*, *The Economist*, 19 January.

Fried Frank (2007), 'Trends in the Use of Corporate Law and Shareholder Activism to Increase Corporate Responsibility and Accountability for Human Rights', Memorandum of Advice Prepared for the UN Special Representative on Business and Human Rights, available at http://www.business-humanrights.org/Documents/Fried-Frank-Memo-Dec-2007.pdf.

Friedman, M. ([1962] 2002), *Capitalism and Freedom*, Chicago, IL: University of Chicago Press (40th anniversary edition).

Friedman, M. (1970), 'The Social Responsibility of Business is to Increase its Profits', *New York Times Magazine*, 13 September.

Friedman, M. (2005), 'Making Philanthropy Out of Obscenity', 37 (5) *Reason* ('Rethinking the Social Responsibility of Business' Debate), 32.

G8 Summit (2007), *Growth and Responsibility in the World Economy*, G8 Summit Declaration, Heiligendamn, available at http://www.unglobalcompact.org/docs/about _the_gc/government_support/G8_summit_2007_Heiligendamn_Declaration.pdf.

G8 Summit (2008), *World Economy*, G8 Summit Declaration, Hokkaido, available at http://www.mofa.go.jp/policy/economy/submit/statement0810.html.

G8 Summit (2009), *Responsible Leadership for a Sustainable Future*, G8 Summit Declaration, L'Aquila, available at http://www.g8italia2009.it/static/G8_Allegato/G8_ Declaration_08_07_09_final,0.pdf.

G20 Leaders Statement (2009), *The Global Plan for Recovery and Reform*, London, available at http://www.g20.org/Documents/final-communique.pdf.

Galbraith, J.K. (1996), *The Good Society: The Humane Agenda*, New York: Houghton Mifflin.

Gare, A. (2006), 'The Neo-Liberal Assault on Australian Universities and the Future of Democracy: The Philosophical Failure of a Nation', 7 *Concrescence* 20.

Garratt, B. (2003), *The Fish Rots From The Head: The Crisis in our Boardrooms: Developing the Crucial Skills of the Competent Director*, London: Profile Books.

Gettler, L. (2006), 'New Climate is Cloudy for Top 100', *The Age*, 20 October, available at www.theage.com.au.

Global Reporting Initiative (GRI) (2002), *Sustainability Reporting Guidelines*, Boston, available at http://www.celb.org/ImageCache/CELB/content/travel_2dleisure/gri_ sf2002_2epdf/v1/gri_5f2002.pdf.

Global Reporting Initiative (GRI) (2005), *Sector Supplement for Public Agencies*, Pilot Version 1.0, Amsterdam, available at http://www.globalreporting.org/ ReportingFramework/SectorSupplements/PublicAgency/.

Global Reporting Initiative (GRI) (2006), *Sustainability Reporting Guidelines* G3,

Amsterdam, available at http://www.globalreporting.org/NR/rdonlyres/ED9E9B36-AB54-4DE1-BFF2-5F735235CA44/0/G3_GuidelinesENU.pdfGordon.

Gomez, P. and H. Korine (2005), 'Democracy and the Evolution of Corporate Governance', 13 (6) *Corporate Governance and International Review* 739.

Goodyear, C. (2006), 'Social Responsibility Has a Dollar Value', *The Age*, 27 July.

Gordon, J. (2004), 'The International Relations Wedge in the Corporate Governance Debate', in Jeffrey Gordon and Mark Roe (eds), *Convergence and Persistence in Corporate Governance*, Cambridge: Cambridge University Press, pp. 161–209.

Gordon, J. and M. Roe (eds) (2004a), *Convergence and Persistence in Corporate Governance*, Cambridge: Cambridge University Press.

Gordon, J. and M. Roe (2004b), 'Introduction', in Jeffrey Gordon and Mark Roe (eds), *Convergence and Persistence in Corporate Governance*, Cambridge: Cambridge University Press, pp. 1–32.

Gore, A. (2007), *The Assault on Reason*, London: Bloomsbury.

Grant Thornton (2008), 'Corporate Social Responsibility: A Necessity Not a Choice' (International Business Report 2008), UK.

Grayson, D. and A. Hodges (2004), *Corporate Social Opportunity!: Seven Steps to Make Corporate Social Responsibility Work for Your Business*, Sheffield: Greenleaf Publishing.

Green, J. (2007), 'Should the Corporations Act Require Directors to Consider Non-Shareholder "Stakeholders"?', in Robert Austin (ed.), *Company Directors and Corporate Social Responsibility: UK and Australian Perspectives*, Sydney: Ross Parsons Centre of Commercial, Corporate and Taxation Law Monograph Series, pp. 44–50.

Greenfield, K. (2006), *The Failure of Corporate Law: Fundamental Flaws and Progressive Possibilities*, Chicago, IL: University of Chicago Press.

Group of 100 Incorporated (2003), *Guide to the Review of Operations and Financial Condition*, Australia, available at http://www.group100.com.au/publications/g100_Review_Operations2003.pdf.

Group of 100 (G100) and KPMG (2008), *Sustainability Reporting: A Guide*, Australia, available at http://www.group100.com.au/publications/G100_guide-tbl-reporting2003.pdf.

Guarini, E. and E. Nidasio (2003), 'CSR Role in Public–Private Partnerships: Models of Governance', 2nd Annual Colloquium of the European Academy of Business in Society, Copenhagen.

Gutmann, A. and D. Thompson (2004), *Why Deliberative Democracy?*, Princeton, NJ: Princeton University Press.

Guy, R. (2008), 'Why Bail-Outs are Not Working', *The Australian Financial Review*, 11 October.

Hanks, J. (1991), 'Playing with Fire: Non-Shareholder Constituency Statutes in the 1990s', 21 *Stetson Law Review* 97.

Hansmann, H. (2005), 'How Close is the End of History?', 31 *Journal of Corporate Law* 745.

Hansmann, H. and R. Kraakman (2004a), 'The End of History for Corporate Law', in Jeffrey Gordon and Mark Roe (eds), *Convergence and Persistence in Corporate Governance*, Cambridge: Cambridge University Press, pp. 33–68.

Hansmann, H. and R. Kraakman (2004b), 'The Basic Governance Structure', in Reinier Kraakman, Paul Davies, Henry Hansmann, Gerard Hertig, Klaus Hopt, Hideki Kanda and Edward Rock, *The Anatomy of Corporate Law: A Comparative and Functional Approach*, Oxford: Oxford University Press, pp. 33–69.

Hansmann, H. and R. Kraakman (2004c), 'What is Corporate Law?', in Reinier Kraakman, Paul Davies, Henry Hansmann, Gerard Hertig, Klaus Hopt, Hideki Kanda and Edward Rock, *The Anatomy of Corporate Law: A Comparative and Functional Approach*, Oxford: Oxford University Press, pp. 1–20.

Hansmann, H. and R. Kraakman (2004d), 'Agency Problems and Legal Strategies', in Reinier Kraakman, Paul Davies, Henry Hansmann, Gerard Hertig, Klaus Hopt, Hideki Kanda and Edward Rock, *The Anatomy of Corporate Law: A Comparative and Functional Approach*, Oxford: Oxford University Press, pp. 21–32.

Hansmann, H., R. Kraakman and R. Squire (2006), 'Law and the Rise of the Firm', ECGI – Law Working Paper No 57/2006 (SSRN), available at http://papers.ssrn.com/sol3/papers.cfm?abstract_id=873507.

Hart, S. (2007), *Capitalism at the Crossroads: Aligning Business, Earth, and Humanity*, 2nd edn, Upper Saddle River: Wharton School Publishing.

Hayek, F. (1960), 'The Corporation in a Democratic Society: In Whose Interest Ought It and Will It Be Run?', in M. Anshen and G. Bach (eds), *Management and Corporations 1985*, New York: McGraw-Hill, pp. 99–117.

Healy, K. and M. Tapick (2004), 'Climate Change, It's Not Just a Policy Issue For Corporate Counsel – it's a Legal Problem', 29 *Columbia Journal of Environmental Law* 89.

Hellicar, M. (2005), 'Managing Corporate Social Responsibility', Monash University Governance Research Unit Workshop on the Social Responsibility of Company Directors, Melbourne.

Henderson, D. (2001a), *Misguided Virtue: False Notions of Corporate Social Responsibility*, London: Institute of Economic Affairs and Wellington: New Zealand Business Roundtable.

Henderson, D. (2001b), 'The Case Against "Corporate Social Responsibility"', 17 (2) *Policy* 28.

Henkin, L. (1999), 'The Universal Declaration at 50 and the Challenge of Global Markets', 25 *Brooklyn Journal of International Law* 17.

Henry, K. (2008), *Keynote Address to ASIC Summer School*, Melbourne: ASIC, available at http://www.treasury.gov.au/documents/1346/HTML/docshell.asp?URL=Ministers_Speech_to_ASIC_Summer_School.htm.

Hermes Pensions Management Limited (2006), *The Hermes Principles*, available at http://www.hermes.co.uk/pdf/corporate_governace/hermes_principles.pdf.

Hertig, G. and H. Kanda (2004), 'Creditor Protection', in R. Kraakman, P. Davies, H. Hansmann, G. Hertig, K. Hopt, H. Kanda and E. Rock, *The Anatomy of Corporate Law: A Comparative and Functional Approach*, Oxford: Oxford University Press, pp. 71–99.

Hertig, G., R. Kraakman and E. Rock (2004), 'Issues and Investor Protection', in Reinier Kraakman, Paul Davies, Henry Hansmann, Gerard Hertig, Klaus Hopt, Hideki Kanda and Edward Rock, *The Anatomy of Corporate Law: A Comparative and Functional Approach*, Oxford: Oxford University Press, pp. 193–210.

Hewson, J. (2008), 'Time for Lateral Thinking', *The Australian Financial Review*, 10 October, 66.

Heydon, D. (1987), 'Directors' Duties and the Company's Interests', in Paul Finn (ed.), *Equity and Commercial Relationships*, Sydney: Law Book Co, pp. 120–40.

Higgins W. (2006), 'Globalisation and Neo-Liberal Rule', 57 *Journal of Australian Political Economy* 5.

Hildyard, N. and G. Muttit (2006), 'Turbo-Charging Investor Sovereignty: Investment Agreements and Corporate Colonialism', *Destroy and Profit: Wars, Disasters and Corporations*, Thailand, Phillipines and India: Focus on the Global South, available at http://www.focusweb.org/pdf/Reconstruction-Dossier.pdf.

Hill, J. (2007), 'Evolving "Rules of the Game" in Corporate Governance Reform', University of Sydney Law School Legal Studies Research Paper No 07/47, Vanderbilt University Law and Economics Research Paper No 07-19, available at http://ssrn.com/abstract =1000085.

Hinkley, R. (2000), 'Developing Corporate Conscience', in S. Rees and S. Wright (eds), *Human Rights, Corporate Responsibility: A Dialogue*, Annandale: Pluto Press, pp. 287–95.

Hinkley, R. (2002), '28 Words to Redefine Corporate Duties: The Proposal for a Code for Corporate Citizenship (Corporate Reform After Enron)', *Multinational Monitor*, 1 July, 18.

Hinkley, R. (2005), *Submission to the Inquiry into Corporate Responsibility* by the Australian Parliamentary Joint Committee on Corporations and Financial Services, available at http://www.aph.gov.au/senate/committee/corporations-ctte/completed_ inquiries/2004–07/corporate_responsibility/submissions/sub06.pdf.

Hinkley, R. (2007), 'Do No Harm: A Corporate Hippocratic Oath', *The Australian Financial Review*, 31 July, 63.

Hohnen, P. (2007a), 'By Invitation: The G8 and Responsible Business: Wading into CSR Waters', *Ethical Corporation*, 12 June.

Hohnen, P. (2007b), 'Governmental "Soft Power" Options: How Governments Can Use the "Soft Power" Art of Encouragement and Persuasion to Advance Corporate Engagement on Social and Environmental Issues', Discussion paper for the Global Compact Office for the 2007 Leaders Summit, Geneva: Global Compact.

Hopkins, M. (2004), 'Corporate Social Responsibility: An Issues Paper', Working Paper No. 27, Policy Integration Department, World Commission on the Social Dimension of Globalization, International Labor Office, Geneva.

Horrigan, B. (2002), 'Fault Lines in the Intersection between Corporate Governance and Social Responsibility', 25 *University of New South Wales Law Journal* 515.

Horrigan, B. (2003), *Adventures in Law and Justice*, Sydney: UNSW Press.

Horrigan, B. (2005a), 'Cleaning Up Their Act?: Current Government Inquiries', 70 *Precedent* 10.

Horrigan B. (2005b), 'Comparative Corporate Governance Developments – Key Ongoing Challenges from Anglo-American Perspectives', in S. Tully (ed.), *Research Handbook on Corporate Legal Responsibility*, Cheltenham: Edward Elgar Publishing, pp. 20–53.

Horrigan, B. (2005c), 'The Expansion of Fairness-Based Business Regulation – Unconscionability, Good Faith and the Law's Informed Conscience', 32 *Australian Business Law Review* 153.

Hughes, V. (2005), 'Values and Principles: Where Do We Go from Here?', Centre for Policy Development (4 August 2005), available at http://cpd.org.au/article/values-%2526amp%3B-principles%3A-where-do-we-go-here%3F.

Institute of Chartered Accountants in Australia (ICAA) (2008), *Broad Based Business Reporting: The Complete Reporting Tool – The New Benchmark in Business Reporting*, Sydney, available at http://www.charteredaccountants.com.au/Files/documents/BBBR_2008.pdf.

Institute of Chartered Accountants in England and Wales (ICAEW) (2007), Response to Conservative Party Working Group on Responsible Business' Interim Report, London, available at http://www.icaew.com/index.cfm/route/147855/icaew_ga/pdf.

Institutional Shareholders' Committee (ISC) (2002), *The Responsibilities of Institutional Shareholders and Agents – Statement of Principles*, available at http://www.ecgi.org/codes/document/isc_statement_of_principles.pdf.

International Chamber of Commerce (2008), *Joint Initial Views of the International Organisation of Employers, The International Chamber of Commerce and the Business and Industry Advisory Committee to the OECD to the Eighth Session of the Human Rights Council on the Third Report of the Special Representative of the UN Secretary General on Business and Human* Rights, available at http://www.biac.org/statements/investment/08-05_IOE-ICC-BIAC_letter_on_Human_Rights.pdf.

International Council on Mining and Metals (ICMM) (2007), Third Submission to the Special Representative of the UN Secretary General on Human Rights and Business, London, available at http://www.icmm.com/documents/215.

International Organisation of Employers, International Chamber of Commerce and the Business and Industry Advisory Committee to the OECD (2008), *Joint initial views of the International Organisation of Employers (IOE), the International Chamber of Commerce (ICC) and the Business and Industry Advisory Committee to the OECD (BIAC) to the Eighth Session of the Human Rights Council on the Third Report of the Special Representative of the UN Secretary-General on Business and Human Rights*, available at http://www.biac.org/statements/investment/08-05_IOE-ICC BIAC_letter_on_Human_Rights.pdf.

Jeffery, M. (2007), 'Legal Risks for Business in Climate Change Era', Presentation to MGSM-Law Forum, Sydney.

Johns, G. (2005), 'Deconstructing Corporate Social Responsibility', Speech to *CSR in Focus*, Melbourne.

Joseph, S. (2004), *Corporations and Transnational Human Rights Litigation*, Oxford and Portland, OR: Hart Publishing.

Kaplan, R. and D. Norton (2006), *Alignment: Using the Balanced Scorecard to Create Corporate Synergies*, Boston, MA: Harvard Business School Press.

Kay, A. (2006), 'United Kingdom', Comment, IFLR Supplement, available at www.iflr.com.

Keane, J. (2008), 'Monitory Democracy?: The Secret History of Democracy Since 1945', Public Lecture at the School of Journalism, Shanghai: Fudan University.

Keay, A. (2007a), 'Section 172(1) of the Companies Act 2006: An Interpretation and Assessment', 28 (4) *Company Lawyer* 106.

Keay, A. (2007b), 'Company Directors Behaving Poorly: Disciplinary Options for Shareholders', *Journal of Business Law* September, 656.

Keay, A. (2007c), 'Tackling the Issue of the Corporate Objective: An Analysis of the United Kingdom's "Enlightened Shareholder Value Approach"', 29 *Sydney Law Review* 577.

Kelly, M. (2001), *The Divine Right of Capital: Dethroning the Corporate Aristocracy*, San Francisco, CA: Berrett-Koehler Publishers.

Kernot, C. (2009), 'A Quiet Revolution', *Griffith Review 24: Participation Society*, Brisbane: Griffith University (in conjunction with ABC Books).

Kerr, M., R. Janda and C. Pitts (2009), *Corporate Social Responsibility – A Legal Analysis*, Canada: LexisNexis Canada.

Kinley, D., J. Nolan and N. Zerial (2007a), '"The Norms are Dead! Long Live the Norms!": The Politics Behind the UN Human Rights Norms for Corporations', in D. McBarnet, A. Voiculescu and T. Campbell (eds), *The New Corporate Accountability: Corporate Social Responsibility and the Law*, Cambridge: Cambridge University Press, pp. 459–76.

Kinley, D., J. Nolan and N. Zerial (2007b), 'The Politics of Corporate Social Responsibility; Reflections of the United Nations Human Rights Norms for Corporations', 25 *Companies and Securities Law Journal* 30.

Kinley, D. and J. Tadaki (2004), 'From Talk to Walk: The Emergence of Human Rights Responsibilities for Corporations at International Law', 44 *Virginia Journal of International Law* 931.

Kitney, D. and F. Buffini (2006), 'Ethics Pays off for Socially Aware Boards', *The Australian Financial Review*, 19 June 2006, 61.

Korten, D. (2001), *When Corporations Rule the World*, 2nd edn, Bloomfield, CN and San Francisco, CA: Kumarian Press and Berrett-Koehler Publishers.

KPMG (2005), International Survey of Corporate Responsibility Reporting, University of Amsterdam and KPMG Global Sustainability Services.

Kraakman, R., P. Davies, H. Hansmann, G. Hertig, K. Hopt, H. Kanda and E. Rock (2004), *The Anatomy of Corporate Law: A Comparative and Functional Approach*, Oxford: Oxford University Press.

Krause, D. (1985), 'Corporate Social Responsibility: Interests and Goals', in Klaus Hopt and Gunther Teubner (eds), *Corporate Governance and Directors' Liabilities: Legal, Economic, and Sociological Analyses on Corporate Social Responsibility*, Berlin and New York: Walter de Gruyter, pp. 95–121.

Kytle, B. and J. Ruggie (2005), 'Corporate Social Responsibility as Mismanagement; a Model for Multinationals', Corporate Social Responsibility initiative working paper number 10, 2005, John F Kennedy School of Government, Cambridge, MA: Harvard University.

Lahey, K. (2007), 'Understanding the CSR Landscape: A View from Corporate Australia', Address to the Australian Centre for Corporate Social Responsibility (ACCSR) Turning Point Conference, Sydney.

Langton, R. and L. Trotman (1999), 'Defining "the Best Interests of the Corporation": Some Australian Reform Proposals', 3 *Flinders Journal of Law Reform* 163.

Laufer, W. (2006), *Corporate Bodies and Guilty Minds*, Chicago, IL: University of Chicago Press.

Leavitt, N. (2004), 'When Nations' Decisions Cause or Intensify Environmental Damage in Ways that Hurt Humans, Is There an International Remedy?, From Global Warming in the North, to Tsunamis in South Asia', *Findlaw* website, 3 January, available at www.findlaw.com.

Leblanc, L. and J. Gillies (2005), *Inside the Boardroom: How Boards Really Work and the Coming Revolution in Corporate Governance*, Mississauga: John Wiley & Sons Canada.

Lee, I. (2005), 'Is There a Cure for Corporate "Psychopathy"?', 42 *American Business Law Journal* 65.

Lee, I. (2006), 'Efficiency and Ethics in the Debate about Shareholder Primacy', 31 *Delaware Journal of Corporate Law* 533.

Legge, J. (2008), 'Making Corporations Responsible', 27 *Dissent* 31.

Legislative Comment (2007), 'Companies Bill 2006 Receives Royal Assent', 28 (2) *Company Lawyer* 46.

Lepoutre, J., N. Dentchev and A. Heene (2004), 'On the Role of the Government in the Corporate Social Responsibility Debate', Annual Colloquium of the European Academy of Business in Society, Ghent.

Lepoutre, J., N. Dentchev and A. Heene (2007), 'Dealing With Uncertainties When Governing CSR Policies', 73 *Journal of Business Ethics* 391.

Line, M. (2004), 'Why Don't Sustainability Reports Talk About Sustainability', CSRnetwork, available at www.csrnetwork.com.

Lumsden, A. and S. Fridman (2007), 'Corporate Social Responsibility: The Case for a Soft Regulatory Model', 25 *Company and Securities Law Journal* 147.

Lydenberg, S. and K. Grace (2008), *Innovations in Social and Environmental Disclosure Outside the United States*, New York: Domini Social Investments and Social Investment Forum.

Mackay, H. (2006), 'Moral Maze: Telstra Part of a Bigger Problem', *Sun-Herald*, 8 October, 57.

Mackey, J. (2005), 'Putting Customers Ahead of Investors', ('Rethinking the Social Responsibility of Business' Debate), October, 37 (5) *Reason* 29.

MacLeod, S. (2005), 'Corporate Social Responsibility within the European Union Framework', 23 *Wisconsin International Law Journal* 541.

Madsen, P. (2008), 'Professionals, Business Practitioners, and Prudential Justice', 39 *McGeorge Law Review* 835.

Magnan, I. and D. Ralston (2002), 'Corporate Social Responsibility in Europe and the US: Insights from Businesses' Self-Presentations', 33 (3) *Journal of International Business Studies* 497.

Mallesons Stephen Jacques (2005), Submission to the Inquiry into Corporate Responsibility by the Australian Parliamentary Joint Committee on Corporations and Financial Services, available at http://www.aph.gov.au/senate/committee/corporations_ctte/completed_inquiries/2004–07/corporate_responsibility/submissions/sub99.pdf.

Mann, H. (2008), *International Investment Agreements, Business and Human Rights: Key Issues and Opportunities*, Canada: International Institute for Sustainable Development.

Marshall, S., R. Mitchell and I. Ramsay (eds) (2008), *Varieties of Capitalism, Corporate Governance and Employees*, Carlton (Victoria): Melbourne University Press.

May, S., G. Cheney and J. Roper (eds) (2007), *The Debate Over Corporate Social Responsibility*, Oxford: Oxford University Press.

McAuley, I. (2001), 'In Defence of Economics: Why Public Policy Doesn't Need the Triple Bottom Line', Paper presented at the National Institute for Governance Triple Bottom Line Seminar, Canberra.

McBarnet, D., A. Voiculescu and T. Campbell (eds) (2007), *The New Corporate Accountability: Corporate Social Responsibility and the Law*, Cambridge: Cambridge University Press.

McBeth, A. (2004), 'A Look at Corporate Code of Conduct Legislation', 33 (3) *Common Law World Review* 222.

McConvill, J. (2005), 'Directors' Duties to Stakeholders: A Reform Proposal Based on Three False Assumptions', 18 (1) *Australian Journal of Corporate Law* 88.

McConvill, J. and M. Joy (2003), 'The Interaction of Directors' Duties and Sustainable Development in Australia: Setting Off on the Uncharted Road', *Melbourne University Law Review* 4.

McCorquodale, R. (2001), 'Feeling the Heat of Human Rights Branding: Bringing Transnational Corporations within the International Human Rights Fence', 1 (4) *Human Rights and Human Welfare* 21.

McFarlane, J. (2005), 'Challenging the Role of Corporations in Society', Speech at University of Melbourne's 2005 Town and Gown, Melbourne.

McIntosh, M., R. Thomas, D. Leipziger and G. Coleman (2003), *Living Corporate Citizenship: Strategic Routes to Socially Responsible Business*, London: FT Prentice Hall.

Mendonca, L. and J. Oppenheim (2007), 'Investing in Sustainability: an Interview with Al Gore and David Blood', *The McKinsey Quarterly*, May.

Mickelthwait, J. and A. Wooldridge (2005), *The Company*, New York: The Modern Library.

Midttun, A. (2005), 'Policy Making and the Role of Government: Realigning Business, Government and Civil Society: Emerging Embedded Relational Governance Beyond the (Neo) Liberal and Welfare State Models', 5 (3) *Corporate Governance* 159.

Millon, D. (2000), 'New Game Plan or Business as Usual?: A Critique of the Team Production Model of Corporate Law', 86 *Virginia Law Review* 1001.

Millon, D. (2001), 'The Ambiguous Significance of Corporate Personhood', *Washington & Lee Public Law and Legal Theory Research Paper Series*, Working Paper No 01-6.

Mintzberg, T., R. Simons and K. Basu (2002), 'Beyond Selfishness', 44 (1) *MIT Sloan Management Review* 67.

Misol, L. (2008), *On the Margins of Profit: Rights at Risk in the Global Economy*, Human Rights Watch and the Center for Human Rights and Global Justice at New York University School of Law, available at http://www.hrw.org/en/reports/2008/02/18/margins-profit.

Mitchell, L. (2001), *Corporate Irresponsibility: America's Newest Export*, New Haven, CN: Yale University Press.

Mitchell, L. (2007), 'The Board as a Path Towards Corporate Social Responsibility', in D. McBarnet, A. Voiculescu and T. Campbell (eds), *The New Corporate Accountability: Corporate Social Responsibility and the Law*, Cambridge: Cambridge University Press, pp. 279–306.

Mitchell, R., A. O'Donnell and I. Ramsay (2005), 'Shareholder Value and Employee Interests: Intersections Between Corporate Governance, Corporate Law and Labour Law', Research Report, Centre for Corporate Law and Securities Regulation and Centre for Employment and Labour Relations Law, University of Melbourne.

Mongoven, B. (2007), 'A Potential Tool for Protecting Human Rights in the Third World', Stratfor (Strategic Forecasting Inc).

Monks, R. and N. Minow (1991), *Power and Accountability*, New York: Harper-Collins.

Monks, R. and N. Minow (2004), *Corporate Governance*, 3rd edn, Oxford: Blackwell.

Muchlinski, P. (2007), 'Corporate Social Responsibility and International Law: The Case of Human Rights and Multinational Enterprises', in D. McBarnet, A. Voiculescu and T. Campbell (eds), *The New Corporate Accountability: Corporate Social Responsibility and the Law*, Cambridge: Cambridge University Press, pp. 431–58.

Muhammad, Y. (2008), *Creating a World Without Poverty: Social Business and the Future of Capitalism*, New York: PublicAffairs Books.

Mulgan, G. (2007), *Good and Bad Power: The Ideals and Betrayals of Government*, London: Penguin Books.

Munck, G.L. (2006), 'Monitoring Democracy: Deepening an Emerging Consensus', Annual Conference of the Society for Latin American Studies, Nottingham, UK, 31 March–2 April.

Nader, R. (2004), 'Foreword', in L. Drutman and C. Cray, *The People's Business: Controlling Corporations and Restoring Democracy* (The Report of the Citizen Works Corporate Reform Commission), San Francisco, CA: Berrett-Koehler Publishers, Inc, pp. vii–x.

New Zealand Securities Commission (NZSC) (2004), *Corporate Governance in New Zealand: Principles and Guidelines – A Handbook for Directors, Executives, and Advisers*, available at http://www.seccom.govt.nz/publications/documents/governance_principles/index.shtml.

Nolan, J. (2007), 'Corporate Responsibility in Australia: Rhetoric or Reality?', *University of New South Wales Faculty of Law Research Series 47*.

Nonet, P. and P. Selznick (1978), *Law and Society in Transition: Toward Responsive Law*, New York: Harper & Row.

Norwegian Ministry of Foreign Affairs (2009), *Corporate Social Responsibility in a Global Economy*, Report No 10 (2008–2009) to the Storting, Norway.

Nourse, V. and G. Shaffer (2009), 'Varieties of New Legal Realism: Can a New World Order Prompt a New Legal Theory?', Research Paper No 09-17, Legal Studies Research Paper Series, Minneapolis: University of Minnesota Law School.

Obama, B. (2006), *The Audacity of Hope: Thoughts on Reclaiming the American Dream*, Melbourne: The Text Publishing Company.

Ochoa, C. (2008), 'The 2008 Ruggie Report: A Framework for Business and Human Rights', 12 (12) *ASIL Insight*, The American Society of International Law.

O'Donahoo, P. and E. Howie (2006), 'Victorian Charter of Human Rights' (Focus: Corporate Responsibility), Allens Arthur Robinson (AAR), available at http://www.aar.com.au/pubs/ldr/focroct06.htm.

Organisation for Economic Co-operation and Development (OECD) (2000), *OECD Guidelines for Multinational Enterprises Revision 2000*, Paris: OECD Publications Service.

Organisation for Economic Co-operation and Development (OECD) (2004), *OECD Principles of Corporate Governance*, Paris: OECD Publications Service.

Orlitzky, M., E.L. Schmidt and S.L. Rynes (2003), 'Corporate Social and Financial Performance: A Meta-analysis', 24 *Organizational Studies* 403.

Orts, E. (1992), 'Beyond Shareholders: Interpreting Corporate Constituency Statutes', 61 *George Washington Law Review* 14.

Orts, E. (1993), 'The Complexity and Legitimacy of Corporate Law', 50(4) *Washington and Lee Law Review* 1565.

Orts, E. (2002), 'Corporate Governance, Stakeholder Accountability, and Sustainable Peace', 35(2) *Vanderbilt Journal of Transnational Law* 549.

Orts, E. (2009), *Rethinking the Firm: Theories of the Business Enterprise*, New York: Oxford University Press.

Parker, C. (2002), *The Open Corporation: Effective Self-Regulation and Democracy*, Cambridge: Cambridge University Press.

Parker, C. (2007), 'Meta-regulation: Legal Accountability for Corporate Social Responsibility', in Doreen McBarnet, Aurora Voiculescu and Tom Campbell (eds), *The New Corporate Accountability: Corporate Social Responsibility and the Law*, Cambridge: Cambridge University Press, p. 207.

Parker, C., C. Scott, N. Lacey and J. Braithwaite (2004), *Regulating Law*, Oxford: Oxford University Press.

Parkinson, J. (1993), *Corporate Power and Responsibility: Issues in the Theory of Company Law*, Oxford: Clarendon Press.

Parliament of the Commonwealth of Australia, *Journals of the Senate No.18–23*, June 2008, available at http://parlinfo.aph.gov.au/parlInfo/download/chamber/journals/2008-06-23/toc_pdf/jnlf_018.pdf;fileType=application%2Fpdf#search=%22(%20senate)%2042%20journals%22.

Parliamentary Joint Committee on Corporations and Financial Services (PJCCFS) (2006), *Corporate Responsibility: Managing Risk and Creating Value*, Canberra, Australian Government.

Perrini, F., S. Pogutz and A. Tencati (2006), *Developing Corporate Social Responsibility: A European Perspective*, Cheltenham: Edward Elgar Publishing Limited.

Porritt, J. (2007), *Capitalism: As If The World Matters*, Sterling VA: Earthscan.

Porritt, J. (2009), 'The Death of CSR?', *Forum for the Future*, 10 October 2008, available at http://www.forumforthefuture.org.uk.

Porter, M. (1990), *The Competitive Advantage of Nations*, New York: The Free Press.

Porter, M. and M. Kramer (2002), 'The Competitive Advantage of Corporate Philanthropy', *Harvard Business Review*, December.

Porter, M. and M. Kramer (2006), 'Strategy and Society: The Link between Competitive Advantage and Corporate Social Responsibility', 84 *Harvard Business Review* 78.

Porter, M. and M. Kramer (2008), 'Strategy and Society: The Link between Competitive Advantage and Corporate Social Responsibility', in M. Porter, ed., *On Competition, Updated and Expanded Edition*, United States: Harvard Business School Publishing.

Prahalad, C. K. (2005), *The Fortune at the Bottom of the Pyramid: Eradicating Poverty Through Profits*, Upper Saddle River, NJ: Wharton School Publishing.

Price, R. (2003), 'Transnational Civil Society and Advocacy in World Politics', 55 *World Politics* 579.

Ramsay, I. (2005a), 'Reform Rush Would Be Unwise' (10 February 2005), *The Australian Financial Review* 63.

Ramsay, I. (2005b), 'Pushing the Limits for Directors' (5 April 2005), *The Australian Financial Review* 63.

Ramsay, I. (2005c), 'Directors' Duties and Stakeholder Interests', 21 (4) *Company Director* 21.

Ramsay, I. (2005d), 'Public Show and Tell is the Way to Incentivise Directors and Their Companies to Behave Nicely', *The Age*, 21 July 2005.

Ramsay, I., G. Stapledon and J. Vernon (2001), *Political Donations by Australian Companies*, Research Report, Melbourne: Centre for Corporate Law and Securities Regulation, Faculty of Law, University of Melbourne.

Ratner, S. (2001), 'Corporations and Human Rights: A Theory of Legal Responsibility', 111 *Yale Law Journal* 443.

Rawls, J. (2001), *Justice as Fairness: A Restatement*, Cambridge, MA: Belknap Press.

Rees, S. and S. Wright (eds) (2000), *Human Rights, Corporate Responsibility: A Dialogue*, Sydney: Pluto Press.

Reich, R. (2007), *Supercapitalism: The Transformation of Business, Democracy, and Everyday Life*, New York: Alfred A. Knopf.

Reich, R. (2008), 'The Case Against Corporate Social Responsibility', Goldman School of Public Policy Working Paper No GSPP08-003, available at http://ssrn.com/abstract=1213129.

Ribstein, L. (2005), 'Sarbanes-Oxley after Three Years', *New Zealand Law Review* 365.

Ridehalgh, N. and A. Petersen (2007), 'Climate for Change Has Arrived', *The Australian Financial Review*, 24 May, 63.

Robertson, G. (2006), *Crimes Against Humanity: The Struggle for Global Justice*, 3rd edn, Camberwell: Penguin Books.

Roe, M. (2004), 'Modern Politics and Ownership Separation', in Jeffrey Gordon and Mark Roe (eds), *Convergence and Persistence in Corporate Governance*, Cambridge: Cambridge University Press, pp. 252–92.

Ross, C., E. Mills and S. Hecht (2007), 'Limiting Liability in the Greenhouse: Insurance Risk-Management Strategies in the Context of Global Climate Change', 26A *Stanford Environmental Law Journal* 251.

Roy, W. (1997), *Socializing Capital: The Rise of the Large Industrial Corporation in America*, Princeton, NJ: Princeton University Press.

Rudd, K. (2006), 'A Faith Short of Compassion When it Sacrifices Social Justice', *The Sydney Morning Herald*, 9 November.

Rudd, K. (2008a), 'The Children of Gordon Gekko', *The Australian*, 6 October 2008, 8.

Rudd, K. (2008b), 'Leadership for Long Term Sustainability: The Roles of Government, Business and the International Community', Speech to the National Business Leaders Forum on Sustainable Development', Canberra.

Ruggie, J. (2002), 'Taking Embedded Liberalism Global: The Corporate Connection', Working Paper on International Relations, Politics Research Group, John F. Kennedy School of Government, Harvard University.

Ruggie, J. (2004), 'Reconstituting the Global Public Domain – Issues, Actors, and Practices', 10(4) *European Journal of International Relations* 499.

Ruggie, J. (2006), *Promotion and Protection of Human Rights*, Interim Report of the Special Representative of the Secretary-General on the Issue of Human Rights and Transnational Corporations and Other Business Enterprises, E/CN.4/2006/97.

Ruggie, J. (2007a), *Business and Human Rights: Mapping International Standards of Responsibility and Accountability for Corporate Acts*, Report of the Special Representative of the Secretary-General on the Issue of Human Rights and Transnational Corporations and Other Business Enterprises, A/HRC/4/35.

Ruggie, J. (2007b), 'Business and Human Rights: The Evolving International Agenda', Corporate Social Responsibility Initiative, Working Paper No. 31, John F. Kennedy School of Government, Harvard University.

Ruggie, J. (2007c), *Clarifying the Concepts of 'Sphere of Influence' and 'Complicity'*, Report of the Special Representative of the Secretary-General on the Issue of Human Rights and Transnational Corporations and other Business Enterprises (A/HRC/8/16), available at http://198.170.85.29/Ruggie-companion-report-15-May-2008.pdf.

Ruggie, J. (2008a), *Protect, Respect and Remedy: A Framework for Business and Human Rights*, Report of the Special Representative of the Secretary-General on the Issue of Human Rights and Transnational Corporations and Other Business Enterprises, A/HRC/8/5.

Ruggie, J. (2008b), 'Next Steps in Business and Human Rights', Remarks by Professor John R. Ruggie, UN Special Representative for Business and Human Rights, Royal Institute of International Affairs, Chatham House, London.

Ruggie, J. (2008c), 'Statement to United Nations Human Rights Council Mandate Review', Geneva.

Ruggie, J. (2009), *Business and Human Rights: Towards Operationalizing the 'Protect, Respect and Remedy' Framework*, Report of the Special Representative of the Secretary-General on the Issue of Human Rights and Transnational Corporations and Other Business Enterprises for the UN Human Rights Council, UN (A/HRC/11/13).

Sachs, J. (2005), *The End of Poverty: How We Can Make It Happen In Our Lifetime*, London: Penguin Books.

Sachs, J. (2008), *Common Wealth: Economics for a Crowded Planet*, Camberwell: Penguin Group.

Sampford, C. and V. Berry (2004), 'Shareholder Values, Not Shareholder Value: The Role of "Ethical Funds" and "Ethical Entrepreneurs" in Connecting Shareholders' Values with Their Investments', 13 (1) *Griffith Law Review* 115.

Sandel, M. (2009), *A New Citizenship*, Annual Reith Lectures, UK: BBC, transcript available on BBC Radio 4 at http://www.bbc.co.uk/programmes/b00kt7rg.

Sands, P. (2005), *Lawless World: America and the Making and Breaking of Global Rules*, Australia: Penguin Books.

Santow, E. and F. Johnson (2009a), 'Would an Australian Charter of Rights be Good for Business?', Position paper for the National Human Rights Consultation, UNSW Gilbert + Tobin Centre of Public Law.

Santow, E. and F. Johnson (2009b), 'All Need to Protect Rights', *The Australian Financial Review*, 3 April 2009, at p. 42.

Saul, J. Ralston (1995), *The Doubters Companion: A Dictionary of Aggressive Common Sense*, Ringwood Victoria: Penguin Books.

Savitz, A. and K. Weber (2006), *The Triple Bottom Line: How Today's Best Run*

Companies are Achieving Economic, Social, and Environmental Success – and How You Can Too, San Francisco, CA: Jossey-Bass.

Schmidt, R. and G. Spindler (2004), 'Path Dependence and Complementarity in Corporate Governance', in Jeffrey Gordon and Mark Roe (eds), *Convergence and Persistence in Corporate Governance*, Cambridge: Cambridge University Press, pp. 114–27.

Schrage, E. (2003), 'Memorandum – Emerging Threat: Human Rights Claims', (August) *Harvard Business Review* 16.

Schwab, K. (2008), 'Global Corporate Citizenship: Working with Governments and Civil Society', 87(1) *Foreign Affairs*, Council on Foreign Relations.

Scott, C. (2008), 'Reflexive Governance, Meta-Regulation and Corporate Social Responsibility: the "Heineken Effect"', in N. Boeger, R. Murray and C. Villiers (eds), *Perspectives on Corporate Social Responsibility*, Cheltenham: Edward Elgar Publishing Limited, pp. 170–85.

Sealy, L. (1987), 'Directors' "Wider" Responsibilities – Problems Conceptual, Practical and Procedural', 13 *Monash University Law Review* 164.

Selznick, P. (2002), *The Communitarian Persuasion*, Washington, DC: Woodrow Wilson Center Press.

Sen, A. (2000), *Development as Freedom*, New York: Anchor Books.

Senate Standing Committee on Legal and Constitutional Affairs (SSCLCA) (1989), *Company Directors' Duties: Report on the Social and Fiduciary Duties and Obligations of Company Directors*, Australian Senate, Canberra.

Sheehy, T. (2006), 'We Don't Need a Big Stick', *The Australian Financial Review*, 06.04.06, 62.

Shell, R. G. (2004), *Make the Rules or Your Rivals Will*, New York: Crown Business.

Shemberg, A. (2008), 'Stabilization Clauses and Human Rights', International Finance Corporation (IFC) and United Nations Special Representative to the Secretary General on Business and Human Rights, available at http://www.business-humanrights.org/Links/Repository/111788/jump.

Shergold, P. (2009), 'Global Financial Crisis and Economic Downturn: Implications for Corporate Responsibility', Issues Paper No 1, Sydney: Centre for Social Impact.

Sherry, N. (2008), 'Speech to Committee for Economic Development of Australia', Sydney, available at http://www.treasurer.govau/DisplayDocs.aspx?doc=speeches/2008/030.htm&pageID=005&min=njs&year=&DocType=.

Sherry, N. (2009a), 'Closing Keynote Address to Australian Centre for Corporate Social Responsibility 3rd Annual Conference', Canberra: Australian Treasury.

Sherry, N. (2009b), 'Corporate Responsibility – Alive and Well', Keynote Address to Property Council of Australia, Canberra: Australian Treasury.

Simons, R., H. Mintzberg and K. Basu (2002), 'Memo to: CEOs', *FastCompany*, June, Issue 59, 117.

Singer, P. (1993), *How Are We to Live?: Ethics in an Age of Self-Interest*, Melbourne: The Text Publishing Company.

Singer, P. (2002), *One World: The Ethics of Globalization*, New Haven, CN: Yale University Press.

Singer, P. (2007), 'Hey Buddy, You Can Spare a Few Billion', *The Sydney Morning Herald*, 6–7 January, 15.

Skinner, M. and J. Pearce (2007), 'United States Supreme Court Hands Down Important

Climate Change Decision', *Focus: Climate Change Litigation – April 2007*, Allens Arthur Robinson.

Slaughter, A.M. (2004), *A New World Order*, Princeton, NJ: Princeton University Press.

Smith, S. (2004), *Contract Theory*, Clarendon Law Series, Oxford: Oxford University Press.

Social Accountability International (2001), *Social Accountability 8000* (SA8000), New York: Social Accountability International.

Special Representative of the UN Secretary General (SRSG) on Business and Human Rights (2007), 'Business and Human Rights: Mapping International Standards of Responsibility and Accountability for Corporate Acts', A/HRC/4/035.

Sperling, G. (2005), *The Pro-Growth Progressive: An Economic Strategy for Shared Prosperity*, New York: Simon and Schuster.

Standards Australia (2003), *Corporate Social Responsibility*, Australian Standard (AS 8003), Sydney.

Statement of the European Corporate Governance Forum on the Comply-Or-Explain Principle (2006), available at http://europa.eu/rapid/pressReleasesAction.do?reference =IP/06/269&format=HTML&aged=0&language=EN&Language=en.

State-Owned Assets Supervision and Administration Commission of State Council (SASAC) (2008), *Instructing Opinions About State-Owned Enterprises (SOEs) Fulfilling Social Responsibility*, PRC.

Stiglitz, J. (2006), *Making Globalisation Work: The Next Steps to Global Justice*, Camberwell: Allen Lane (Penguin Books).

Stiglitz, J. (2007), 'Multinational Corporations: Balancing Rights with Responsibilities', Grotius Lecture, 10th annual meeting of the American Society of International Law, Washington, DC.

Stout, L. (2002), 'Bad and Not-So-Bad Arguments for Shareholder Primacy', 75 *Southern California Law Review* 1189.

Stout, L. (2004), 'On the Nature of Corporations', *Deakin Law Review* 33.

Stout, L. (2007), 'The Mythical Benefits of Shareholder Control', 93 *Virginia Law Review* 789.

Strandberg, C. (2008), *The Role of the Board of Directors in Corporate Social Responsibility*, Canada: The Conference Board of Canada.

Sunstein, C. (1996), *Legal Reasoning and Political Conflict*, New York: Oxford University Press.

Susskind, A. (2008), 'Enlightened Self-Interest at the Heart of CSR', 46 (5) *Law Society Journal*, (NSW) 20.

Tate, A. (2007), 'The Effect of Private Equity Takeovers on Corporate Social Responsibility', Australian Centre for Corporate Social Responsibility seminar paper, available at http://www.accsr.com.au/pdf/pet_speech_Alison_Tate.pdf.

Teubner, G. (1985), 'Corporate Fiduciary Duties and Their Beneficiaries: A Functional Approach to the Legal Institutionalisation of Corporate Responsibility', in K. Hopt and G. Teubner (eds), *Corporate Governance and Directors' Liabilities*, Berlin: Walter de Gruter, pp. 149–77.

The Economist (2005), 'The Good Company: A Survey of Corporate Social Responsibility', 22 January.

The Economist (2007), 'In Search of the Good Company', 8–14 September.

The Economist (2008), 'Just Good Business: A Special Report on Corporate Social Responsibility', 19 January.

The Law Society's Company Law Committee, the Company Law Sub-Committee of the City of London Law Society, and the Law Reform Committee of the General Council of the Bar (2005), *Company Law Reform White Paper: The Response of the Law Society's Company Law Committee, the Company Law Sub-Committee of the City of London Law Society, and the Law Reform Committee of the General Council of the Bar*, London, available at http://www.lawsociety.org.uk/documents/downloads/dynamic/complawreformwhitepaperlawscoresresponse.pdf.

Tonuri, D. (2007), 'The Effect of Private Equity Takeovers on Corporate Social Responsibility', available at http://www.accsr.com.au/pdf/pet_speech_David_Tonuri.pdf.

Twining, W. (2000), *Globalisation and Legal Theory*, London: Butterworths.

Uhrig, J. (2003), *Review of the Corporate Governance of Statutory Authorities and Office Holders*, Canberra: Commonwealth of Australia.

United Kingdom Government (2004), *Corporate Social Responsibility: a Government Update*, London, available at via www.csr.gov.uk.

UK Joint Committee on Human Rights (2007), *The Meaning of Public Authority Under the Human Rights Act*, Ninth Report of Session 2006-07, London: Stationery Office Limited.

United Nations Commission on International Trade Law (UNCITRAL) (2001), *UNCITRAL Legislative Guide on Privately Financed Infrastructure Projects*, New York: United Nations.

United Nations Commission on International Trade Law (UNCITRAL) (2004), *UNCITRAL Model Legislative Provisions on Privately Financed Infrastructure Projects*, New York: United Nations.

United Nations Environment Programme Finance Initiative (UNEP FI) Asset Management Working Group (AMWG) (2005), *A Legal Framework for the Integration of Environmental, Social and Governance Issues into Institutional Investment*, London, available at http://www.unepfi.org/fileadmin/documents/freshfields_legal_rep_20051123.pdf.

United Nations Global Compact (UN GC) and Dahlberg Global Development Advisors (2007), *Business Guide to Partnering with NGOs and the United Nations*, Report 2007/2008.

United States Climate Action Partnership (USCAP) (2007), *A Call for Action*, Consensus Principles and Recommendations from the US Climate Action Partnership: A Business and NGO Partnership.

US Government Accountability Office (GAO) (2005), *Globalization: Numerous Federal Activities Complement U.S. Business's Global Corporate Social Responsibility Efforts*, GAO Report to Congressional Requesters, August.

US Securities and Exchange Commission (SEC) (2002), *Commission Statement About Management's Discussion and Analysis of Financial Condition and Results of Operations*, Washington, DC, available at http://www.sec.gov/rules/other/33-8056.htm.

Villiers, C. (2006), *Corporate Reporting and Company Law*, Cambridge: Cambridge University Press.

Villiers, C. (2008), 'Corporate Law, Corporate Power and Corporate Social Responsibility', in N. Boeger, R. Murray and C. Villiers (eds), *Perspectives on Corporate Social Responsibility*, Cheltenham: Edward Elgar Publishing Limited, pp. 85–112.

Visentini, G. (1998), 'Compatibility and Competition Between European and American Corporate Governance: Which Model of Capitalism?', 23 *Brooklyn Journal of International Law* 833.

Wachtell, Lipton, Rosen, and Katz (2008), 'A United Nations Proposal Defining Corporate Social Responsibility for Human Rights', May.

Waddock, S. (2006), 'Building the Institutional Infrastructure for Corporate Social Responsibility', Corporate Social Responsibility Initiative, Working Paper No. 32, John F. Kennedy School of Government, Cambridge, MA: Harvard University.

Walker, R. Lord (2007), 'What Difference Can a Human Rights Charter Make?', Joint Seminar of the Human Rights Law Resource Centre and the Victorian Equal Opportunity and Human Rights Commission, available at http://www.hrlc.org.au/files/RV1EGTE462.Walker%20%What%20Difference%20Can%20a%20Charter%20Make.pdf.

Wallman, S. (1991), 'The Proper Interpretation of Corporate Constituency Statutes and Formulation of Director Duties', 21 *Stetson Law Review* 163.

Ward, H. (2001), 'Governing Multinationals: The Role of Foreign Direct Liability', Briefing Paper New Series No 18, London: Royal Institute of International Affairs.

Ward, H. (2003), 'Legal Issues in Corporate Citizenship', Swedish Partnership for Global Responsibility, available at http://www.regeringen.se/content/1/c6/02/18/54/46e90176.pdf.

Ward, H. (2004), *Public Sector Roles in Strengthening Corporate Social Responsibility: Taking Stock*, Washington, DC: World Bank and International Finance Corporation.

Ward, H. (2008), 'Corporate Social Responsibility in Law and Policy', in N. Boeger, R. Murray and C. Villiers (eds), *Perspectives on Corporate Social Responsibility*, Cheltenham: Edward Elgar Publishing Limited, pp. 8–38.

Ward, H., E. Wilson, L. Zarsky and T. Fox (2007), 'CSR and Developing Countries: What Scope for Government Action?', United Nations Sustainable Development Innovation Briefs, Issue 1.

Wedderburn, Lord (1965), *Company Law Reform*, London: Fabian Society.

Wedderburn, Lord (1985), 'The Legal Development of Corporate Responsibility: For Whom Will Corporate Managers be Trustees?', in Klaus Hopt and Gunther Teubner (eds), *Corporate Governance and Directors' Liabilities: Legal, Economic, and Sociological Analyses on Corporate Social Responsibility*, Berlin and New York: Walter de Gruyter, pp. 3–54.

Weil, Gotshal & Manges LLP (2008), 'Corporate Social Responsibility for Human Rights: Comments on the UN Special Representative's Report Entitled "Protect, Respect and Remedy: A Framework for Business and Human Rights"', Memorandum of Advice, 22 May.

Welsh, B. (2007), 'The Effect of Private Equity Takeovers on Corporate Social Responsibility', Paper at joint seminar for ANZ and The Australian Centre for Corporate Social Responsibility, Victoria.

Wheeler, S. (2002), *Corporations and The Third Way*, Portland, OR: Hart Publishing.

Whitman, M., M. Zald and G. Davis (2008), 'The Responsibility Paradox!', 6 (1) *Stanford Social Innovation Review* 31.

Williams, C. and J. Conley (2005a), 'An Emerging Third Way?: The Erosion of the Anglo-American Shareholder Value Construct', 38 *Cornell International Law Journal* 493.

Williams, C. and J. Conley (2005b), 'Is there an Emerging Fiduciary Duty to Consider Human Rights?', 74 *University of Cincinnati Law Review* 75.

Wilson, T. (2005), 'The Pursuit of Profit at all Costs: Corporate Law as a Barrier to Corporate Social Responsibility', 30 (6) *Alternative Law Journal* 278.

Wood, D. (2002), 'Whom Should Business Serve?', 14 *Australian Journal of Corporate Law* 266.

World Business Council for Sustainable Development (WBCSD) (2000), *Corporate Social Responsibility: Making Good Business Sense*, January.

World Commission on Environment and Development (Brundtland Commission) (1990), *Our Common Future* (Australian edition), Melbourne: Oxford University Press.

World Economic Forum (WEF) (2007), 'Global Risks 2007: A Global Risk Network Report', available at http://www.weforum.org/pdf/CSI/Global_Risks_2007.pdf.

Yunus, M. (2007), *Creating a World without Poverty: Social Business and the Future of Capitalism*, New York: Public Affairs.

Zadek, S. (2001a), *Third Generation Corporate Citizenship: Public Policy and Business in Society*, London: The Foreign Policy Centre and AccountAbility.

Zadek, S. (2001b), *The Civil Corporation: The New Economy of Corporate Citizenship*, London: Earthscan.

Zappala, G. (2003), 'Corporate Citizenship and the Role of Government: the Public Policy Case', Research Paper No 4 2003–2004 (December), Australian Parliamentary Library Research Paper Series, Canberra.

Zerk, J. (2006), *Multinationals and Corporate Social Responsibility: Limitations and Opportunities in International Law*, Cambridge: Cambridge University Press.

Zerk, J. (2007), *Corporate Abuse in 2007: A Discussion Paper on What Changes in the Law Need to Happen*, The Corporate Responsibility (CORE) Coalition, available at http://www.corporate_responsibility.org/module_images/corporateabuse_discussionpaper.pdf.

Zoellick, R. (2009), 'Poor Must Not be Forgotten in Fixing Global Crisis', *The Australian Financial Review*, 7 January, 47.

Index